Examining the Roles of IT and Social Media in Democratic Development and Social Change

Vikas Kumar
Chaudhary Bansi Lal University, India

Geetika Malhotra
Chaudhary Bansi Lal University, India

A volume in the Advances in Electronic Government, Digital Divide, and Regional Development (AEGDDRD) Book Series

IGI Global
DISSEMINATOR OF KNOWLEDGE

Published in the United States of America by
IGI Global
Information Science Reference (an imprint of IGI Global)
701 E. Chocolate Avenue
Hershey PA, USA 17033
Tel: 717-533-8845
Fax: 717-533-8661
E-mail: cust@igi-global.com
Web site: http://www.igi-global.com

Copyright © 2020 by IGI Global. All rights reserved. No part of this publication may be reproduced, stored or distributed in any form or by any means, electronic or mechanical, including photocopying, without written permission from the publisher.
Product or company names used in this set are for identification purposes only. Inclusion of the names of the products or companies does not indicate a claim of ownership by IGI Global of the trademark or registered trademark.

Library of Congress Cataloging-in-Publication Data

Names: Kumar, Vikas, 1979- editor. | Malhotra, Geetika, 1989- editor.
Title: Examining the roles of IT and social media in democratic development and social change / Vikas Kumar and, Geetika Malhotra, editors.
Description: Hershey, PA : Information Science Reference, 2020. | Includes bibliographical references and index. | Summary: "This book explores the methods and applications of social media within community development and democracy"-- Provided by publisher.
Identifiers: LCCN 2019034088 | ISBN 9781799817918 (hardcover) | ISBN 9781799817925 (paperback) | ISBN 9781799817932 (ebook)
Subjects: LCSH: Internet--Political aspects. | Social media--Political aspects. | Information society--Political aspects. | Democratization. | Social change.
Classification: LCC HM851 .E954 2020 | DDC 303.48/33--dc23
LC record available at https://lccn.loc.gov/2019034088

This book is published in the IGI Global book series Advances in Electronic Government, Digital Divide, and Regional Development (AEGDDRD) (ISSN: 2326-9103; eISSN: 2326-9111)

British Cataloguing in Publication Data
A Cataloguing in Publication record for this book is available from the British Library.

All work contributed to this book is new, previously-unpublished material.
The views expressed in this book are those of the authors, but not necessarily of the publisher.

For electronic access to this publication, please contact: eresources@igi-global.com.

Advances in Electronic Government, Digital Divide, and Regional Development (AEGDDRD) Book Series

ISSN:2326-9103
EISSN:2326-9111

Editor-in-Chief: Zaigham Mahmood, University of Derby, UK & North West University, South Africa

MISSION

The successful use of digital technologies (including social media and mobile technologies) to provide public services and foster economic development has become an objective for governments around the world. The development towards electronic government (or e-government) not only affects the efficiency and effectiveness of public services, but also has the potential to transform the nature of government interactions with its citizens. Current research and practice on the adoption of electronic/digital government and the implementation in organizations around the world aims to emphasize the extensiveness of this growing field.

The Advances in Electronic Government, Digital Divide & Regional Development (AEGDDRD) book series aims to publish authored, edited and case books encompassing the current and innovative research and practice discussing all aspects of electronic government development, implementation and adoption as well the effective use of the emerging technologies (including social media and mobile technologies) for a more effective electronic governance (or e-governance).

COVERAGE

- Public Information Management, Regional Planning, Rural Development
- Knowledge Divide, Digital Divide
- Social Media, Web 2.0, and Mobile Technologies in E-Government
- Adoption of Innovation with Respect to E-Government
- E-Government in Developing Countries and Technology Adoption
- Online Government, E-Government, M-Government
- Citizens Participation and Adoption of E-Government Provision
- Issues and Challenges in E-Government Adoption
- Frameworks and Methodologies for E-Government Development
- Case Studies and Practical Approaches to E-Government and E-Governance

IGI Global is currently accepting manuscripts for publication within this series. To submit a proposal for a volume in this series, please contact our Acquisition Editors at Acquisitions@igi-global.com or visit: http://www.igi-global.com/publish/.

The Advances in Electronic Government, Digital Divide, and Regional Development (AEGDDRD) Book Series (ISSN 2326-9103) is published by IGI Global, 701 E. Chocolate Avenue, Hershey, PA 17033-1240, USA, www.igi-global.com. This series is composed of titles available for purchase individually; each title is edited to be contextually exclusive from any other title within the series. For pricing and ordering information please visit http://www.igi-global.com/book-series/advances-electronic-government-digital-divide/37153. Postmaster: Send all address changes to above address. Copyright © 2020 IGI Global. All rights, including translation in other languages reserved by the publisher. No part of this series may be reproduced or used in any form or by any means – graphics, electronic, or mechanical, including photocopying, recording, taping, or information and retrieval systems – without written permission from the publisher, except for non commercial, educational use, including classroom teaching purposes. The views expressed in this series are those of the authors, but not necessarily of IGI Global.

Titles in this Series

For a list of additional titles in this series, please visit:
https://www.igi-global.com/book-series/advances-electronic-government-digital-divide/37153

Employing Recent Technologies for Improved Digital Governance
Vasaki Ponnusamy (Universiti Tunku Abdul Rahman, Malaysia) Khalid Rafique (Azad Jammu and Kashmir Information Technology Board, Pakistan) and Noor Zaman (Taylor's University, alaysia)
Information Science Reference • © 2020 • 383pp • H/C (ISBN: 9781799818519) • US $195.00

Political Decision-Making and Security Intelligence Recent Techniques and Technological Developments
Luisa Dall'Acqua (University of Bologna & LS TCO, Italy) and Irene M. Gironacci (University of Swinburne, Australia)
Information Science Reference • © 2020 • 170pp • H/C (ISBN: 9781799815624) • US $195.00

Tools, Strategies, and Practices for Modern and Accountable Public Sector Management
Graça Azevedo (University of Aveiro, Portugal) Jonas Oliveira (Instituto Universitário de Lisboa (ISCTE-IUL), Portugal) Rui Pedro Marques (University of Aveiro, Portugal) and Augusta Ferreira (University of Aveiro, Portugal)
Information Science Reference • © 2020 • 372pp • H/C (ISBN: 9781799813859) • US $215.00

Leveraging Digital Innovation for Governance, Public Administration, and Citizen Services Emerging Research and Opportunities
Nidhi Vij Mali (University of Mississippi, USA)
Information Science Reference • © 2020 • 194pp • H/C (ISBN: 9781522554127) • US $195.00

Learning Cities, Town Planning, and the Creation of Livelihoods
Idowu Biao (University of Botswana, Botswana)
Information Science Reference • © 2019 • 312pp • H/C (ISBN: 9781522581345) • US $215.00

For an entire list of titles in this series, please visit:
https://www.igi-global.com/book-series/advances-electronic-government-digital-divide/37153

IGI Global
DISSEMINATOR OF KNOWLEDGE

701 East Chocolate Avenue, Hershey, PA 17033, USA
Tel: 717-533-8845 x100 • Fax: 717-533-8661
E-Mail: cust@igi-global.com • www.igi-global.com

Editorial Advisory Board

Sri Aliami, *Nusantara PGRI University, Indonesia*
Ron Berger, *College of Law and Business, Israel*
Ioseb Berikashvili, *Caucasus University, Georgia*
Marco Briziarelli, *University of New Mexico, USA*
Biplab Loho Choudhury, *Visva-Bharati University, India*
K. S. L. Das, *Gokte Institute of Technology, India*
Rasika Dayarathna, *University of Colombo, India*
Tankeshwar Kumar, *Guru Jambhewshwar University of Science and Technology, India*
Prabin K. Panigrahi, *Indian Institute of Management, Indore, India*
Daniel J. Power, *University of Northern Iowa, USA*
Ambika Sharma, *Indian Institute of Technology, India*
Dev Vrat Singh, *Central University of Jharkhand, India*
Dejene Tessema, *Wolkite University, Ethiopia*

Table of Contents

Detailed Table of Contents

With the current development of information and communication technology, it must be a good time for democracy. Democracy depends on deliberation and good information. Most people of modern society are ubiquitously connected to the Internet through their smartphones, they can anytime engage in public discourse, express their views without the help of any representative, or search information to make a good decision. The technology is supposed to make people more connected with each other and more knowledgeable than their predecessors. However, rather than raising the quality of democracy, the same technology is now considered to have threatened democracy. The technology makes it easy for irresponsible people to spread disinformation and hate speech. And the technology also makes people unable to deal with the abundant irresponsible information. To mitigate the problem, it is necessary for social media platform to be able to trace the true identities of its users, just like what has already been done in ecommerce or "sharing economy" platforms.

This chapter explores a fundamental tension of social media by considering their socially reproductive and (potentially) transformative function. The claim is that while media and communication technologies have historically fueled both aspiration and fear of social change, their ability to shape societies are contingent on the specific

Parliamentarians were expected to be angry and upset with political opponents in front of their party comrades. Hence the mass media logic of conflict is transferred online and also with network media logic, favouring attention-maximising, witty one-liners. This foregrounds polarisation and dissent at the expense of discussion and debate.

Social media has emerged as a dominant digital medium platform in contemporary society. The quick development of social media has instigated changes concerning the way publics to interact with a group of people with similar ideologies, the quality of information they share, or the opportunity to acquire and share ideas. Social media use has a major influence on public relations, marketing, and political communication. Therefore, politicians are formulating their strategies to reach increasingly networked individuals. The chapter defines political engagement concept, focuses on excessive use of social media to understand how the emergence of digital citizenship is changing political engagement. In addition to this, the chapter also examines whether the use of social media exercise any effect on 2014 and 2019. General elections outcome or not and discuss the proposed conceptual framework for future empirical testing. The chapter highlights the various concerns needed to be taken care of while using social media as a marketing tool for promoting political participation and engagement.

The utilisation of social media in Egypt has irrevocably changed the nature of the traditional Egyptian public sphere. One can see the Egyptian online society as a multiplicity of networks. These networks have developed, transformed, and expanded over time, operating across all areas of life. Audiences started to utilise social media platforms providing detailed descriptions of Egyptian street politics, generating public interest and reinforcing citizen democracy. This trend changed the way audiences consumed news, with media organisations starting to expand their presence online so that, as well as providing news content, they also provided audience a 'space' to interact. This chapter establishes understanding on the role

Preface

Information technology has given rise to many digital platforms in the new global society and Social Media is one the most important platform in them. It has emerged as the essential part of communication and reached into every part of the world. The rapid development of social media and information technology has created a system similar to that of the nervous system in humans and also caused changes in how audiences interact within each other: the ideologies the share, the availability of information, the opportunity to acquire and share ideas; all have been affected. Social media has rooted in our society and everyone - young, old, rich, poor have come-up to use this new media of communication. Everyone is always in a frenzy, when it comes to socializing online. Even the corporate world has taken the bandwagon and businesses have become very active online, posting updates and answering questions. Most importantly, Social Media plays an important role in raising awareness, communicating authority, proving authenticity and encouraging participation in the Society. It is about all these developments, the present volume speaks.

Technology is changing the society by changing the environment we adapt to, from Open Diary to My spaces, Twitter and Facebook. In turn, the word "social networks" has become a synonym for the human society as par as the communication is concerned. Blogs, content communities, social networking sites, and virtual games have created an impactful virtual social world. In the last decade or so, many changes have been witnessed in the society, mainly from the perspective of higher education, medical care, personal safety, security and transportation. Each one of them is however has got a lot of contribution from Information Technology and Social Media. Not only the quality of life has improved, but it has also ventured into areas, where better management of technology, processes and information has been important. Social networks have also facilitated the academic research by several ways in terms of data collection, ready-to-use tools, proactive respondents and quick results: these factors contributed significantly to the authenticity and timeliness of the data. Well planned and used, the social media offers many lines of thoughts to the human beings. As we move forward in 2020, many innovations or emerging trends in information technology will impact the society through remarkable offerings.

The growing diversity of social networks and their various applications in different areas of human life and society have also raised many questions. Some of them talk about the positive side, whereas a number of them raise the negative aspects of these. Researchers around the world are working to answer these questions, as well as to delineate the most important challenges and opportunities. This book offers an in-depth look at some of these questions related to social networks and information technology with their specific applications to democratic development and social change. On one hand, we have been witnessing the increased access to social media and information technology has resulted in an array of new uses; innovativeness in processes, empowerment of the marginalised segments of society, benefits to the research community, improvement in citizen centric services, improved transparency and reduced corruption have added a number of success stories to the democracies. On the other hand, we are still groping in the confusions when it comes to understanding the place of the social media and information technology in the shifting landscapes of democracy, government practices and social welfare around the Globe.

The studies show that it is the irony of current technological development that information technologies are not only used to inform, but increasingly to misinform. It has been shown that social networks increase interactions between people. But instead of strengthening social cohesion, it makes society more divided. Interactions do not always reflect the strength of social ties, but also the hostility of different social or political groups. Having easy access to information, many people do not become wise, but they feel overwhelmed by harmful information. Modern democracy seems to go in the opposite direction to a more informed and participatory citizenship. People are now not only overwhelmed by an indigestible amount of information, but also prone to take decisions on the basis of same. Irresponsible people seem to be easily fool others or at least spread erroneous information that makes it difficult to differentiate between the true or false information. The popularity of the notions, such as erroneous information and post-truth, reflects a serious information challenges faced by the democracy.

Today, the digital divide is less worrying for people, because smartphones are no longer a luxury and people are generously using them to access the Internet, and especially the social networks. Communication between them and the exchange of information has never been as easy and economical as today. That is why, many people are permanently connected to the Internet. People live their virtual lives at the same time as their physical lives, even though the two lives can be separated or intertwined. In social networks, users are not just passive audience: they interact, participate and even become self-created celebrities. By having access to social networks, people can become target of prejudice mobilization and they can also participate in the mobilization of prejudices. With a simple click, without writing anything, users of social networks can possibly turn opinions into campaigns.

In traditional media, the reports and opinions can be reconciled separated to some extent by involving experts and the public in discussions on a variety of views. Various points of view can lead the public to understand the complexity of the problems. However, either for management purposes or to guide the debate in a particular direction or interest, the media imposes restrictions and guidance. In social networks, such restrictions are non-existent. Everyone can participate, but in the long run, the reconciliation of views may not be achieved. The problems may not be resolved, but only forgotten or ignored, as there are other emerging problems. Media does not need to be selected by journalists to express the opinions and people can simply learn by interacting, discussing or following the arguments of others. However, it can also fall into the trap of echo chambers, where it engages in a social environment that only reinforces its prejudices.

The present book volume argues that Internet and social networks have allowed people to exercise their citizenship. It is easy for anyone to express their opinions to the public. It is also easy for someone to share and disseminate information that is considered important. The quality of democracy is also partially influenced by the quality of information and knowledge. The Internet gives us access to all the information to allow us to be better informed. However, today, the Internet, and especially social networks are populated by misinformation created by a number of users or groups. This mass dissemination of erroneous information has two origins. First, it is our growing dependence on prejudice. Prejudice is our cognitive energy to simplify the world, hence being overwhelmed by the abundance of information confuses us. Not knowing is uncomfortable and that is why we are looking for a way to know or feel about knowing. Prejudices provide us with a categorization system to simplify and control the information in our environment. Second, our willpower is stronger than our willingness to know. Not only are we less willing to meet other people with different points of view than we are, but we also do not want others to know. Often, we want others to misunderstand something if this misunderstanding benefits us. Hence, we run away from our responsibility.

The chapters in this volume provide examples of more positive as well as more negative discourses on the roles of social media and information technology for promoting democracy and social change. We as editors have not wanted to put our foot down in this debate; we leave it to the reader to evaluate the benefits and constraints of social media and information technology in the contexts within which these chapters are written. As such, this volume will serve very well as material for discussion and further discourse. Indeed, the picture is often more complicated than fervent positive and negative sides claim. The very different contexts within which social media and information technology are used and appropriated today make it difficult to generalize on an overall positive or negative "effect" of a communication platform and a technological practice.

The first chapter, "Democracy, Technology, and Human Irresponsibility," by Ikbal Maulana, focuses on current developments of information and communication technology and the expected responsible behaviour from the users. The article argues that it must be a high time for the democratic practices in society due to the availability of strong ICT tools and practices. However, Democracy has a strong dependence on the deliberation and good information. Most people of modern society are ubiquitously connected to the Internet through their smartphones and they can anytime engage in public discourse, express their views without the help of any representative, or search information in order to make a good decision. The technology is supposed to make people more connected with each other and more knowledgeable than their predecessors. However, rather than raising the quality of democracy, the same technology is now considered to have threatened democracy. Technology makes it easy for irresponsible people to spread wrong information and hate speech. The problem is further complicated with the availability of huge amount of information and people find it difficult to deal with the abundant irresponsible information. To mitigate the problem, it is necessary for social media platform to be able to trace the true identities of its users. This chapter explores the causes of the current informational problems, such as massive spread of fake news. The phenomenon of people easily becoming irresponsible in virtual network has been discussed to identify the social and technological issues surrounding the new media.

In the second chapter, Joseph L. Flores explores a fundamental tension of social media by considering its socially reproductive and (potentially) transformative function. The claim is that while media and communication technologies have historically fuelled aspiration and fear of social change, their ability to shape societies are contingent on the specific social relations in which they operate. By investigating social media's economic practices, the reproductive relations that influence platform's capabilities to reproduce and transform existing social contexts are examined. To illustrate this, political discourse via social media platforms have been used to argue that social media's current capitalist mode of production exemplifies an antagonism between exploitative/emancipatory tendencies and reproductive/transformative aspects, which are further articulated by a liberal ideology. Author has come with strong arguments and a lot of examples have been presented to support them. The chapter is well versed with the existing theories in the domain.

Chapter 3, "ICT and Transmedia Storytelling for Democratic Development in the Russian Political Landscape," discusses the role of information and communication technology (ICT) in Alexey Navalny's political campaign during the 2013 mayor elections in Moscow. The aim is to analyse that how the use of ICT across multiple media platforms contributed to the development of democratic practices in the Russian political landscape. Navalny's westernized, bottom-up political campaign was innovative in the country, because it involved the novel manners of engaging the public via online fundraising, door-to-door canvassing, engagement of volunteers, digital projects, and meetings with voters, which were not common practices at that time in Russia. Although Navalny lost the election, his candidacy represented advancement in terms of the use of ICT and transmedia storytelling to promote democratic development in the midst of autocratic Russia.

Moving ahead of Russia, Chapter 4 presents an interesting study on the 2014 Swedish elections. Jakob Svensson attends to the interactions between campaigning politicians (Members of Parliament (MPs)) and traditional news media in an online space of social networking, namely Twitter during the 2014 elections. This extensive study has presented a type of media authority through traditional news media and their online presences in the 2014 Swedish elections. The study revealed that the interactions were often charged with emotions and could be understood as a way to negotiate status and group (party) belonging, something that is particularly important for campaigning politicians in a party-based democracy. By studying the interactions between Parliamentarians and traditional news media, the study concludes that Parliamentarians were expected to be angry and upset with political opponents in front of their party comrades. Hence the mass media logic of conflict is transferred online and also with network media logic, favouring the attention maximising witty one-liners.

The fifth chapter, "Social Media Use and Young Citizens Political Engagement in India: How Political Parties Use Social Media to Engage Voters," is another interesting study on the largest democracy of the world. Authors discuss the novel concept of political engagement and propose a conceptual model inculcating precursors and outcomes of political engagement in Social Media settings. The impact of social media on political engagement has been discussed with specific reference to the general elections in India in 2014 and 2019. Determinants and drivers of the political engagement have been presented using both the theoretical and practical perspectives. Social media research prospects have been presented from the perspective of political parties to have a better engagement between the contesting candidates and the voters. Authors have also suggested a number of possible uses of social media to utilise this political engagement for strengthening the society.

Ahmed El Gody in the chapter "Social Networks, Media, and the Egyptian Revolution: Building Democratic Front" presents that how the utilisation of social media in Egypt has irrevocably changed the nature of the traditional Egyptian public sphere. One can see the Egyptian online society as a multiplicity of networks. These networks have developed, transformed and expanded over time, operating across all areas of life. Audience started to utilise social media platforms providing detailed descriptions of Egyptian street politics, generating public interest and reinforcing citizen democracy. This trend changed the way audiences consumed news, with media organisations started to expand their presence online so that, as well as providing news content, they also provided audience a 'space' to interact. This chapter has been able to establish the understanding on the role of social media in developing an Egyptian networked public sphere. It very well elaborated the role played by social media in post 2011 revolution democratisation process.

In Chapter 7, Yang and Kang have employed a case study approach to examine the law protests in Hong Kong during the regime of President Xi. The protests in Hong Kong have been covered by the electronic media and the authors have taken a very specific example of the Microblogs. The study becomes very much important as it presents an interesting example of the Social Media control by Chinese Govt. Authors have presented the interrelations among social media, surveillance technologies, civil society, state power, economic development, political process, and democratization in China as demonstrated in Hong-Kong's Anti-Extradition Law Protests. Both the legal and technical aspects have been covered with a lot of support from literature. The chapter has very well covered the contribution of *Weibo* platform in formation of a public sphere and the emergence of Chinese civil society.

Chapter 8, "Direct Benefit Transfer Using Aadhaar: Improving Transparency and Reducing Corruption," by Bhardwaj and Cyphert, details the success stories of Direct Benefit Transfer in removing corruption and implementing transparency in India. The chapter provides a very good overview of the integration of information technology for the implementation of citizen centric services in India. The study is very much important as the enrolment number is very much higher for "Aadhaar", hence it provides a good picture of implantation to the citizens, including less IT literate. A number of schemes including the Pradhan Mantri Matru Vandana Yojana (PMMVJ), State Health Society (Bihar), Aadhaar Enabled Payment System (AePS), Nutrition and Health Tracking System (NHTS), Aadhaar Enabled Public Distribution System (AePDS), and Adhaar Enabled Fertilizer Distribution System (AeFDS) have been presented by the authors. Along with these, the chapter illustrates how the processes have improved for purchasing a new SIM card for mobile or transfer of land to support the authentication and removing fake entries. The chapter addresses administrative, technology and legal challenges, which the initiative faced during its implementation.

Juan Du in Chapter 9 investigates China's internet regulatory mechanism through a systematic analysis of Internet law in China. The chapter argues that China has developed a hybrid Internet regulatory model, which values both external defense and internal control of in pursuit of the cyber security. This also combines the hierarchical regulation with horizontal monitoring to address the challenges brought by contemporary network society. Based on Michel Foucault's governmentality theory, the Internet panoptic-fortification model is developed to illuminate China's internet regulatory mechanism. The model features the centralized control, the establishment of Chinese sovereign cyberspace, the implementation of the network real-name system and the Internet-surfing record backup system, and the tight ideological control. This chapter suggests that China's Internet law has become a state instrument to promote the social discipline in the sovereign cyberspace, and the Internet regulatory mechanism serves for the national security and social stability in a broader context.

Osée Kamga in Chapter 10, "Social Media as Disruptive Technologies in an Era of Fake News: Examining the Efficacy of Social Media in the Shaping of the Political Landscape in Africa," focuses specifically on Sub-Saharan Africa, it borrows Christensen's concept of "disruptive technologies" and uses it as a framework to analyse the processes of social media appropriation in the political field in that part of the continent. The chapter articulates ways in which social media are transforming the political landscape in the region and wonders about the outcome of these processes in the backdrop of the emerging and spreading of fake news.

In Chapter 11, "Role of Social Media in Environmental Democracy," Manju Lata and Anu Gupta focus on environmental democracy, which involves three mutually reinforcing rights that, while independently important, operate best in combination: the ability for people to freely access information on environmental quality and problems, to participate meaningfully in decision-making, and to seek enforcement of environmental laws or compensation for damages. There are three fundamental rights: Access to Information, Citizen Participation and Access to Justice. Social media can certainly play a vital role in all the three fundamental rights. The present chapter attempts to identify the role of social media in these three fundamental rights with reference to environmental democracy. The chapter starts with an introduction to environmental democracy and associated challenges. It then builds a model based on social media to lead to the successful environmental democracy campaigns.

Anuradha Tiwari and Tarakeshwar Gupta explore the various dimensions of change that have happened due to information technology and social media in a democratic setup. The aim of the chapter "Role of IT and Social Media in Democratic Change: Paraphernalia Around Information Technology and Social Media" is to highlight how social change has occurred due to innovation in information technology and social media. Authors have very well demonstrated that how information technology and social media have improved the social well-being and quality of life. Education, healthcare, personal security and, transport have been considered as the prime drivers of social change and authors have presented very good examples to demonstrate the change.

This volume targets everyone who is interested in IT, social media, and their role in promoting democratic development and social change. Thus, it creates interest to the researchers, practitioners, policy makers, civil society organizations, students as well a general public. Given that we have not gone with a specific bias on the positive or negative side of social media and IT, reader has enough examples and claims to delve into specific debates on this. The rich contextual data covered in the chapters is very well suited for further discussions about the roles of IT and social media in democratic development and social change.

We sincerely hope that this edited volume shall provide insight to different aspects and perspectives of ICT, democracy and social change to researchers, students, practitioners, policy makers and other interested in this field. We hope that the chapters will serve as material for discussing, criticizing and thus developing our understandings of the relationships between ICTs, democracy and social change. The book will serve as a wonderful academic reference for the researchers and academicians and at the same time, it will serve as a resource guide for the practitioners.

Vikas Kumar
Chaudhary Bansi Lal University, India

Geetika Malhotra
Chaudhary Bansi Lal University, India

Acknowledgment

A real piece of academic reference can never be created without the contribution of many intellectuals. We would like to express our heartfelt gratitude to all individuals and groups, who have contributed to this book and supported us in one or the other manner.

Our sincere thanks to Prof R. K. Mittal (Vice Chancellor, Chaudhary Bansi Lal University, Bhiwani) and Prof. Jitender Bhardwaj (Registrar, Ch. Bansi Lal University, Bhiwani) for their continued support and guidance towards the completion of this project. We are indebted to Late Prof. Anil Kumar Pundir (Guru Jambhewshwar University, Hisar), who has always been a divine force behind all our endeavours. Prof. Mukesh Chaturvedi (Sharda University, Greater Noida) has always supported us through his inspiring words and advice. Thanks are also due to all the Editorial Advisory Board Members for their valuable inputs and critical remarks on different aspects of the book.

We should not fail to mention the name of IGI Global, their administrative and editorial staff for providing us this wonderful opportunity to serve as editors and working towards this academic project. Special thanks to Lindsay Wertman for her continuous support by providing us valuable inputs and keep us updated. We are indebted to all the authors and contributors for reposing their confidence in us, sending their original contributions and working as per the tight deadlines. We are thankful to the reviewers from academia and industry, who worked very hard to make this work a novel piece.

We would like to pen down the support and help from our colleagues Dr. Pawan Gupta, Dr. Satvir Singh, Dr. Sunit Bharatwal, Mr. Jitender Kumar, Mr. Mool Raj and Ms. Priyanka from Chaudhary Bansi Lal University, Dr. G. K. Sethi (from M L N College, Yamunanagar) Dr. Surender Kumar (from Jaipuria Institute of Management, Noida, India), Dr. Saurabh Mittal (from G L Bajaj Institute of Management & Research, Greater Noida, India), and other peers from academia, who have motivated and helped us a lot in this project. Our special thanks to Mr. Deepak Aggarwal and

Ms. Manju Sharma (from the Chaudhary Bansi Lal University) for helping with a lot of documentation and editorial work for the book.

Finally, a lovely mention goes to our parents, family members and friends for the time stolen out of their share and support in completing this project.

Vikas Kumar
Chaudhary Bansi Lal University, India

Geetika Malhotra
Chaudhary Bansi Lal University, India

Chapter 1
Democracy, Technology, and Human Irresponsibility

Ikbal Maulana
https://orcid.org/0000-0002-3727-3809
Indonesian Institute of Sciences (LIPI), Indonesia

ABSTRACT

With the current development of information and communication technology, it must be a good time for democracy. Democracy depends on deliberation and good information. Most people of modern society are ubiquitously connected to the Internet through their smartphones, they can anytime engage in public discourse, express their views without the help of any representative, or search information to make a good decision. The technology is supposed to make people more connected with each other and more knowledgeable than their predecessors. However, rather than raising the quality of democracy, the same technology is now considered to have threatened democracy. The technology makes it easy for irresponsible people to spread disinformation and hate speech. And the technology also makes people unable to deal with the abundant irresponsible information. To mitigate the problem, it is necessary for social media platform to be able to trace the true identities of its users, just like what has already been done in ecommerce or "sharing economy" platforms.

INTRODUCTION

Irony of current technological development is that information technology is used not only to inform, but increasingly to misinform. Internet allows people to find and know each other, and social media allows them to easily connect with each other

DOI: 10.4018/978-1-7998-1791-8.ch001

Copyright © 2020, IGI Global. Copying or distributing in print or electronic forms without written permission of IGI Global is prohibited.

(Kumar & Nanda, 2019a). But, as politicians make social media as the battleground for spreading their political ideas and agenda, its users begin to lose their innocence. They become active political citizens and are no longer remain the passive observers, who are waiting for the voting day to take influential action. But, in many cases, rather than being critical toward elites, forcing the latter to serve them better, most social media users let themselves being led by political actors who exploit their sentiment and prejudices. Consequently, they adopt hostile attitudes toward social groups having opposing views. Particularly during political contestation, having access to any information does not make them wiser. They let themselves be overwhelmed by prejudiced information (Maulana, 2018a).

Most often social media becomes an "echo chamber" where social groups of like-minded people get together and strengthen their prejudices against other social groups, thus increases polarization (Tufekci, 2017). Political polarization is easily recognizable on social media and it has threatened democracies all around the world, not only in new democratic countries but also in long established ones (Carothers & O'Donohue, 2019). Social media has been suspected to drive the polarization. "Social media, it seems, amp up moral and emotional messages while organizing people into digital communities based on tribal conflicts" (De-Wit et al., 2019). But, the impact, as shown by some studies may be subtler than people might think. Social media is suspected to cause polarization because it puts users in "echo chambers" that expose them only to the ideas they already agree with. However, a study in the US on self-identified Republicans and Democrats shows that exposing people to opposing views on social media can increase polarization as well (Bail et al., 2018). Social media is also suspected to make "Indonesians perceive that polarisation is potentially greater than it really is—and politicians are encouraging that perception" (Tapsell, 2019). Social media may distort their sense of reality that it is worse than it really is.

Democracy on the other hand is supposed to be qualitatively improved, if the public have better access to political information and opportunities to give feedback. The Internet gives them almost any information they need to know. With the information searching and communication opportunities enabled by the information and communication technology (ICT), public decision making should be more participative, inclusive and argumentative. Despite the many discouraging news about the spread of hate speeches and fake news through social media, successful utilizations of ICT for the improvement of democracy have been made in some parts of the world. For example, in Taiwan, a platform called vTaiwan was established to facilitate the conflicting parties to deliberate contentious issues and draft statements about how matter should be solved. Using this platform, they have been successful in solving the conflict between the ride-hailing service and traditional taxi industry by finding consensus that are accepted by all parties (Miller, 2019). Some platforms that facilitate participative decision making have been made. One of them is Pol.is, which is used for vTaiwan.

However, these democratic innovations are still too few and almost invisible to many people. What is more visible is that technology seems to lead democracy to the brink of its demise. Ironically, it is not because people cannot express their voices, on the contrary, they can flood public discourses with any kind of opinion, frame or take on politics, including any disinformation. People are now not only overwhelmed by indigestible amount of information, but also polluted by disinformation. Many people seem to be vulnerable to certain types of informational manipulation. Irresponsible people, politicians or businesses, develop the craft of manipulating others through information spread on social media. Social media has been massively used in political and electoral campaigns, including the E.U. referendum in the U.K. and the U.S. presidential election, the outcome of which have shocked the world (DiFranzo & Gloria-Garcia, 2017). Donald Trump has been suspected to use fake news to help him win the US presidential election (Parkinson, 2016). Political polarization was also experienced by Indonesian people during the 2019 presidential election despite that the two presidential candidates were not too distinct. The active engagement of the proponents of both candidates on social media had transformed the presidential contestation into a divisive identity politics (Tapsell, 2019). The popularity of notions, such as fake news, misinformation, disinformation, and post-truth, reflects the severity of the informational challenges faced by our democracy.

THE CONSTITUTION OF RESPONSIBLE MEMBERS OF SOCIETY

From the philosophical perspective, anyone can only be held responsible, if one has freedom to choose one's actions (Sen, 2009). Having responsibility enables one to be praised or blamed. If one cannot choose one's action, then one is not praiseworthy or blameworthy for one's actions. Responsibility is the consequence of one's freedom. One becomes moral agent only because one has agency, freedom to choose. But, society requires order that is having certain level of predictability (Giddens, 1984). If social life is totally unpredictable, having no pattern across time and spaces, life will be unbearable. It is as if society has to be restarted every time, having no continuity, which also implies that it is not a society, just a random encounter of individuals. Social order is established by imposing constraints on freedom, not eliminating it. Society even develops through the establishment of institutions, which "reduce uncertainty by providing a structure to everyday life" (North, 1990, p. 3). Society cannot allow its individual members to go their own way, only valuing their self-interest but ignoring their collective interests.

Society needs to discipline its members to be responsible of their duties. Fortunately, the opportunity to discipline them is there. They cannot escape to be disciplined because they have bodies that make them bound to their society. Their bodies make them visible to other people. They cannot just pop up and disappear from their social environment. According to Foucault (1995), "It is the fact of being constantly seen, of being able always to be seen, that maintains the disciplined individual in his subjection" (p. 187).

The responses of other people toward us, their comments or gaze or body language, make life like stage performance in front of audiences (Goffman, 1959). Different social environments are different stages that require individuals to follow different scripts. Such a script is not neccesarily to be seen as an obligation that forces a person to behave in a certain way, it "may strike the obligated person either as a desired thing or as an onerous one, in short, as a pleasant or unpleasant duty" (Goffman, 1967, p. 50). Besides that, having obligation is not generally perceived as being trimmed of one's freedom. A healthy society needs responsible members, who not only can fight for their own interests, but also exert and regulate themselves either for themselves as well as the common good of their society. The interest of society and that of oneself is not necessarily contradictory, because "The moral responsibilities of one's acts and choices are also an important basis for creating the unity and continuity of the self... The self is a capacity for making choices, taking responsibility, and exerting self-control" (Baumeister, 1997, p. 193).

That people act in accordance to 'social script' is not because they want to conceal their thoughts and please others, but, according to Merleau-Ponty (2005), "because we are literally what others think of us and what our world is" (p. 122). Other people's responses are mirrors through which one sees oneself. Since anyone gets different responses from different social groups, one may develop multiple social selves (James, 1927), which allow one to switch from one role to another, and try on "multiple roles, tries on different hats, different lives, forging selves whose unity is at best tentative and provisional, selves waiting to be dissolved into new combinations or even discarded for brand new editions when life changes and new challenges arise" (McAdams, 1997, p. 48).

One's body is not only something that binds one into particular time and space where others are co-present, the body is also a medium through which thoughts and feeling manifests. Baumeister (1997) writes "Understanding of selfhood begins with awareness of one's body, and the body continues to be an important basis of selfhood throughout life" (p. 192). The self begins with the body, but, sometimes the body seems to go its own way, escaping from one's control. Sometimes the body even betrays what one want to present oneself (Maulana, 2018b). When one wants to look and sound confident, one's body does not cooperate. Unfortunately, other people seem to believe more in one's body than in one's intention. Lie detector was invented because people believe more in one's body rather than what one says.

Generally one's body as it appears to others is perceived by others as oneself. "On the other hand, man has a body. That is, man experiences himself as an entity that is not identical with his body, but that, on the contrary, has that body at its disposal. In other words, man's experience of himself always hovers in a balance between being and having a body, a balance that must be redressed again and again" (Berger & Luckmann, 1966, p.68). In direct interaction people know each other partly from what is shown by each other's body. That is why they need to control their self-presentation by manipulating the presentation of their bodies. How one wants to be seen and one's position in society determine bodily presentation one makes in front of other people.

Living in a society, having relations with other members of society, individuals position themselves in a 'social space' of symbolic categories and ties. This social space is structured by particular rules specifying "rights and obligations relevant to persons having a particular social identity, or belonging in a particular social category" (Giddens, 1984, p. 89). These rules create order, by giving constraints as well as incentives to members of society. They can be explicit or tacit, formal or informal. As people grow up within these rules, they will get used to them, no longer see them as imposing rules, even accept them as their identities. The rules do not only manifest as regulative processes, but also as normative and even cognitive processes that guides the way they think of their actions (Scott, 2014).

Society, including that under authoritarian government, cannot leave its members with no choice whatsoever. Leach (1962) postulates, "In all viable systems there must be an area where the individual is free to make choices so as to manipulate the system to his own advantage" (Leach, 1962, p.133). One may willingly comply with social norms, but "norms figure as 'factual' boundaries of social life, to which a variety of manipulative attitudes are possible" (Giddens, 1984, p. 4). Indeed, norms, just as many other forms of institutions" are evolving and, therefore, are continually altering the choices available to us" (North, 1990, p. 6).

By forming a society, people seek to balance between sacrifying part of individual freedom and establishing the predictability of social life, that is by imposing responsibility on themselves. Hence, various institutions are established. Norms alone are insufficient to regulate social relations, any society also needs regulative rules, which are legally sanctioned and enforced. That modern industrial society can develop into a complex system is partly due to the support of contractual relations. Anyone has freedom to choose or not to choose a contractual relation. But, once one has chosen to engage in a contractual relation, one cannot do anything but comply it. The contractual relations "face the individual with a set of circumstances which limit available options of action" (Giddens, 1984, p. 177). Power, bureaucratic hierarchy, and money allow members of society to expect from each other without having to develop mutual understanding or consensus over and over again (Habermas, 1984). In capitalist society money can replace personal interactions to satisfy the interests of two interacting parties. Yet, we cannot avoid of needing others. And our need of others burden us with certain responsibilities. We have to be worthy for others to have right to take advantage from therm. Unfortunately, the impersonality of our dependence lead us to think that we do not need other people, we do not need to develop mutual understanding and commitment with one another. It may not give any problem in one condition, but when the mode of interacting changes, the lack of understanding can threaten our social bondages.

RELEASING FROM SOCIAL BONDAGE

Anyone's personal self is very much embedded in social context that one, especially in the early phase of one's life, cannot choose. Anyone has been helplessly thrown into a world in particular society and history, including social class and gender (Heidegger, 1962). One just has to accept one's social surrounding, if one wants to stay there. But, anyone cannot live on one's own. Society does not only impose obligations on its members, but also provides many things they cannot get if they live isolated from one another.

Even though facing the same social environment, individuals generally make different responses, which indicate that they do have choices. Human being is not a passive entity who just waits to be shaped by its surrounding. Human being is an active agent actively existing in the world. From the perspective of symbolic interactionists, "the self was primarily a social construction, crafted through linguistic exchanges with others" (Harter, 1997, p. 81). In any society, there is power that emerges from previous collective interactions that influence present actors' options of actions, but the power emerges from the interactions among various autonomous agents, hence "Power within social systems which enjoy some continuity over time and space presumes regularized relations of autonomy and dependence between actors or collectivities in contexts of social interaction. But all forms of dependence offer some resources whereby those who are subordinate can influence the activities of their superiors" (Giddens, 1984, p. 16). Power cannot be escaped, because it is pervasive social phenomena. But, it is not only negative and repressive but can also be productive and enabling (Foucault, 1978), allowing individuals to grow and flourish if they can take advantages of it properly. Social forces can take the forms of either constraints or demands that affect individuals and can be felt directly by them within the immediate situation of action or have affected their process of reasoning and motives over a long period of upbringing and growth to adulthood (Giddens, 1984).

Generally, people do not mind to sacrifice part of their freedom in return for social supports and advantages. They can control themselves not to demand more from others, not to express more of their opinions, or even to hide part of their true selves. However, a society may also exert burdensome pressure on individuals by expecting them to develop particular self-characteristics, such as self-determined, unique and fulfilled. This demands individuals to make active efforts, making considerable and sustained exertion. Therefore, "When something happens to cast the self in a less desirable light, the person may experience a crisis" (Baumeister, 1997, p.208).

Indeed, if one does not have to risk anything, socially or physically, one prefer to express rather than hide one's true self. Hence, one seeks to develop a close circle of friends who allow one not to conceal too much of one's true self. In real life one can only choose a small number of close friends, but usually one cannot choose one's neighbors or colleagues. Living among other people one has to constantly restrain oneself. Since one needs to develop relationships with various people, one has to take their demand and approval into account, which "may alternatively lead to the suppression of authentic opinions or behaviors and the display of what others need to observe or want to hear" (Harter, 1997, p. 82). It does not mean that the true self is developed by ignoring other people's influences. On the contrary, the true self is the result of a long interaction and self-reflection, that is, the interaction between one and others, and between one and oneself. One cannot ignore others, because one can only learn to know oneself through the mirror of other people's responses.

A healthy balance between autonomy and dependence is necessary for social integration (Giddens, 1984). This is also what one has to learn through life. Too much dependent on significant others, if they are irresponsible, may lead one to construct "a false self that does not mirror one's authentic experiences. Thus, one may incorporate opinions of others toward the self that do not correspond to events as experienced" (Harter, 1997, p.81-82). Even though "democracy has traditionally been regarded as having to do with the concern to satisfy the desires, needs, and interests of the populace and also giving regard to its numerous opinions" (Barnhart, 1969, p. 281), that is only formally true. Sociey cannot accommodate full freedom of its members. Different social groups in democratic society have different constraints and demands to which members of the group should conform. If you do not want to, you can find another group that suits you. However, it is often impractical to find new group just because you cannot conform to some of their values. Many people are aware that they cannot get everything they want. Therefore, some degree of adaptation will be tolerated. You also have to accept the norms as a package, you cannot just select some of them and ignore others.

REPRESENTATION AND THE LOST OF CITIZENS' POWER

Democracy is based on the ideal that everyone's life is equally morally important (Wall, 2007), hence, everyone has the right to participate in the self-determination of society. Democratic system is established for continually finding the balance and reciprocity between collective self-determination and the individual self-determination of citizens. To make "citizens experience their government as their own, as representing them, they must experience the state as in some way responsive to their own values and ideas" (Post, 2005, p. 145). According to theories of participatory democracy, "democracy functions better when larger numbers of people participate in policy making more frequently by promoting accountability and legitimacy" (Jaramillo & Wright, 2015, p. 284). In a democratic system, citizens have either the responsibility or opportunity to engage in public decision making, either by making decision on their own or by choosing representatives to do (Post, 2005). Therefore, modern democracy is facing two evolving issues: the political equality of citizens and the problem of representativeness.

Any democratic government, according to common view, must have a commitment to political equality. This commitment will translate the ideal of equality into political institutions that distribute political standing equally to all citizens (Wall, 2007). The common practice in many self-proclaimed democratic countries around the world is that political equality is given in the form of equal votes. They can claim that they are already democratic if they have free elections in which every adult citizens can vote. But it is not uncommon that a country may experience political unrest even though they have already had the so the called free election. From Egypt to Indonesia, they had election with high level of participatory, but then they had political turmoil that caused the fall of their dictators. In such cases, voting is experienced just as a mechanism for decision making, not as a self-determination process (Post, 2005). Political institutions can be designed to allow voting, but remain oppresive.

Besides that, defining equal political power is problematic. Anyone cannot just be made equal to everyone else. Social and economic inequalities can be caused by different social origins, the realized natural endowment, and even chance opportunities and accidents. Such inequalities are not only inevitable but can also be advantageous in maintaining social cooperation (Rawls, 2005), because individuals can complement each other's advantageous and compensate each other's weaknesses.

Differences may cause political problems as well. Social and economic differences, which are regarded as inevitable, may also lead the different capacity to exercise power. For example, "Citizens with more money or greater access to public forums can exercise greater control over political outcomes than those with less money or less access to such forums" (Wall, 2007, p. 420). The complexity and historical development of political life of society may lead to the development of a particular form of democratic participation, which in turn require a particular definition of democratic equality, and also "Equality in the context of voting will be different than equality in the context of communication within public discourse" (Post, 2005, p.147).

Defining political equality merely as equal vote is far from from sufficient. It needs to be understood more as equal opportunity to exercise political power. However, since people are not homogeneous, differences in capacity and commitment to involve in public affair is natural. Rather than giving them equal political power, it is more appropriate to give them a fair opportunity to influence the outcome of political decision or to hold public office (Wall, 2007).

Democracy is not only about ensuring individual freedom, but also about managing collective life. Living together requires individuals to coordinate their lives together, because they may have conflicting interests. "Political freedom implies the freedom of people who determine and realize themselves both as individual subjects and as members of a community" (Dibos, 2002, p. 12). In order to reach the integration of members of society, either they have to work together to reconcile their competing interests, or let the forces of random combinations of deliberate actions to produce certain order (Habermas, 1984).

Society is anything but homogeneous. Since every citizen may have her/his own interests and aspirations and even stubbornness to compromise with others, society can be unmanageable if each individual citizen demands to be heard and accommodated. The population of citizens as a whole, if they are too many to meet in one place, are implausible to engage in public decision making. Hence, in most cases, the representative democratic system is the most viable solution to manage the distribution and rotation of power while keeping the effectiveness of decision making. "Citizens hire the president, senators, representatives, judges, bureaucrats, and soldiers to serve the public as employees, as public servants. At the local level, the citizens hire police, firemen, teachers, and other public employees to serve their immediate local needs. Whom the citizens hire is determined by elections and other agreed-upon procedures" (Parker, 2014, p. 78). And to finance all public services and those being hired to serve, citizens are willing to be taxed.

Implementing representative democracy, while at the same time preserving political power of individual citizens, is not easy. Barber (2003) reminds us about the possible detachment of the representatives from their constituents, which can cause that "Citizens become subject to laws they did not truly participate in making; they become the passive constituents of representatives who, far from reconstituting the citizens' aims and interests, usurp their civic functions and deflect their civic energies" (Barber, 2003, p. 147).

In an ideal representative democracy the interests and opinions of the people "would be accurately and effectively represented in the processes of making and critically evaluating public policies and programs, while some form of governmental device would be set up as a means of checking and guaranteeing the accuracy and effectiveness" (Barnhart, 1969, p. 281). However, due to the complex dynamics of politics, the ideal often remains a goal that continuously needs to be pursued. Emerging issues often have made politicians have opinions different from their constituencies. The interactions among politicians in parliaments often make them reach consensus different from their previous views. Political development can separate the representatives from the represented, while the former still claim to represent the latter. Hence, citizens can lose their political power in complex political processes.

TECHNOLOGICAL EMPOWERMENT OF CITIZENS

Today digital access divide is no longer an issue. As smartphones are no longer luxury, many people can easily access to the Internet. According to *Our World in Data*, today, at least 3.5 billion from 7.7 billion people in the world are online. The larger part of them are social media users, with Facebook having 2.4 billion users, and YouTube and Whatsapp having more than one billion users each (Ortiz-Ospina, 2019). Connecting with each other and sharing information have never been easier and cheaper than it is right now. People experience their daily life both online and offline, which can be either separated or intertwined. Even at the same time anyone can live multiple virtual lives. Social media does not just expand users' social network, connecting them to a larger number of known and unknown people, but also allow them to be constantly engaged with public life. Any time they can experience both private and public lives. Some, if not all parts of their identities are hidden from others, and some selected parts are deliberately shown to public. Social media allows users to experience the lives which in the past could only be enjoyed by celebrities. Even today there are many self-made celebrities on social media, people who can make themselves stars on Instagram or YouTube. On social media users are not just passive audiences, they can interact, participate and even become the self-made celebrities.

Having access to social media, people are no longer the passive target of the mobilization of bias. They can participate in the mobilization of bias themselves. The simplicity of using social media eases anyone to exercise one's citizenship. Anyone can express political view to one's social network with ease. Even one can support a political view with just a single click, without having to write anything. Therefore, politics after social media has radically changed. Citizens can any time interact with one another or even with politicians, responding and criticizing them. They do not need to wait until the next election to give feedback to the political system and it is no longer expensive to mobilize public opinions, even though it is not guaranteed that anyone will them.

Current information and communication technology opens the opportunity to transform current representative democracy to be more engaging and participative. Social media has become public sphere that anyone can easily access and participate. Social media is no longer a complement to conventional media. To many users, it has become the ultimate media, even their world itself. And conventional media more frequently report what happens on social media just like they report events in the real world. Politicians and government can no longer ignore its importance. Increasingly more policy makers using social media, especially Twitter, to promote their policy. Pioneered by Trump, some world leaders use Twitter to attack both foreign leaders and adversaries at home, replacing dignified political communications (Laine, 2019).

For a long time conventional media have played important role in both providing information to public and organizing public opinions. The media help audiences to understand the socio-political development of their world, and their understanding of the world indirectly shapes the world and themselves. While conventional media play the role as the intermediary between viewers and the world they want to observe, social media allows people to directly involve in the world itself. Social media users can observe the sociopolitical development directly and be active parts of that development, not just the passive target of mobilization bias by elites (Maulana, 2016). On social media everyone can participate in public affair without needing to be selected by journalists who come to interview. There is no constraint of distance or social class in exercising the citizenship on social media. However, it will be constrained by cognitive bias and processing limit. The inability to deal with information overload may lead people to fall into the trap of prejudices (Maulana, 2018a) or of echo chambers, where you are engaged in social environment that only strengthen your prejudices (Harris & Harrigan, 2015). However, the ethical use of social media is certainly a big challenge and must be taken into account for democratic communication (Kumar & Nanada, 2019b)

POLITICAL CHALLENGES OF SOCIAL MEDIA

The Internet opens the opportunities to access any information or correct any misinformation. If people are willing to take advantages of such opportunities, it would improve not only democracy and public decision making, but also social cohesion. With possible connection to anyone and access to search engine, suspicious information can be verified and corrected, and, hence, unfounded prejudices can be overcome.

Socio-political life has always been quite complex for most people. Social media increases this complexity by increasing the number of relationships and the size of social network. And the Internet excessively multiplies information about this world, making it much more complex. The Internet, including social media, make people overwhelmed by information and faced with problems many of which are incomprehensible. Feeling not-knowing is uncomfortable, and not knowing about something of great concern to us can even be unbearable. Anyone will feel relieved in one can come out of the feeling of not knowing, and move into the position that one feels understand what one is facing with (Taylor, 2004). Emotionally, we feel more comfortable to have the illusion of knowing rather than admitting of our not knowing. And the main source for creating the illusion of knowing is our prejudices, because prejudices consist of sets of information that are internally semi-coherent. Prejudice is human's subconscious strategy to overcome the feeling of not-knowing. On social media or the Internet users cannot verify any incoming information, so, to save their cognitive energy, they filter information using their prejudices. The information that does not fit with their prejudices will be immediately ignored. If many other peole share the prejudices, then they will feel that these are confirmed justified. This is the reason why people prefer to be in their echo chambers.

As social media has become its own world, it also grows political. People do not just connect with each other, they also draw boundary creating social groups that include some people and excluding others. The groups, if they are purely virtual, are more characterized by ideas, because geographical proximity does not play any role. Prejudices have been develop not only to deal with the the complexity of information, but also with the complexity of conflicting interests. These are strategies to cognitively simplify the world and politically draw boundary between our group (in-group) and other groups (out-groups) (Allport, 1979). These provide categories that can be used as simplifying and ordering devices and can "help us to discriminate clearly between those who belong and those who do not" (Brown, 2010, p. 36).

Prejudiced people tend to be biased against outgroups (Allport, 1979). They can easily redistribute information that is in accord with their prejudices, which is often at the cost of other people's interests. They will not take time to check that information. Therefore they are vulnerable to be influenced by fake news. Fake news is more persuasive than the truth because it is created to fit particular prejudices.

On the Internet there is true information as well as false information. Since the volume of information is too large, it is difficult to verify the truth of every incoming information, to distinguish every true information from the false one. To publish information on conventional media, people have to pass through editorial filters. On social media there is no such filter, there is no control over quality of information. The information freedom on social media is only constrained by users' consciences and social considerations. While this freedom allows anyone to participate in public discourses, it also makes socio-political life discursively more chaotic.

The irresponsible informational freedom and people's vulnerability to prejudices have contributed to the massive spread of fake news, which severely affects public choices. During EU referendum in UK, the US presidential election, and Indonesian presidential election, just few examples, social media has been intensively used to influence public choice, which have also caused political polarization in the nations (DiFranzo & Gloria-Garcia, 2017; Parkinson, 2016; Tapsell, 2019). The problem with social media is that it allows many-to-many communication and each user is a source of information. The sources of distortion of information are too many to handle.

For some people, the will to power might is stronger than the will to be true. If political victory matters more than the truth, then misinformation or disinformation does not matter as long as it is shared and believed by a large number of people. Widely believed false information, for example false accusation, can be devastating, can be a strong weapon to weaken political rivals. When people are not held responsible for spreading lies and disinformation, then democracy is in danger.

Digital communication is an impoverished communication. People do not present themselves fully in front of each other. The impoverished communication weakens individuals' sensitivity that they interact with fellow human beings who have their own feelings. During political contestation, social media users who do not personally know and do not intend to know each other can be in hostile confrontation with each other. This hostility is also conditioned by the fact that they cannot identify each other in actual life. Besides that, this technology also allows us to respond instantly that makes us to be reactive without careful thinking.

THE DISAPPEARANCE OF BODY, SOCIAL CONSTRAINTS AND RESPONSIBILITIES

Social media affects behavior of its users through different mechanism from that of conventional media. Conventional media affects its consumers' behaviors through its content, which influences the belief and then attitude of its consumers, which in turn determines their behaviors (Slater, 2007). Even though social media content will affect just as does the content of conventional media, but it is the media itself, not its content, that has major impact on its users. It is the way social media changes communication among users that changes users' behavior.

Social media is the platform for social network on which users can interact with each other or which allows users to observe each other without having to interact. The user of social media is far more like a citizen of a country rather than a user of a hammer. In actual life, an individual and society influence each other, even though the latter has stronger influence over the former. However, society is much more than just a collection of its present members. Society has institutions that regulate the actions and interactions of its members, and the institutions have been developed throughout its history (Berger & Luckmann, 1966). Institutions can be enforced on members of society because the latter have bodies that bind them to their society. The phenomena of virtual society cannot be explained by social theories that implicitly assume that social interactions are carried out only by actors who have bodies. In such theories, body cannot be eliminated from social system, "All social systems, no matter how grand or far-flung, both express and are expressed in the routines of daily social life, mediating the physical and sensory properties of the human body" (Giddens, 1984, p. 36).

That body binds anyone to society is not only in the sense that one cannot instantly appear and disappear from one's social environment, but anyone's body is also social. When a body is present among other bodies, it has to adjust its presentations and actions to the others. People communicate with one another through their bodies, and "The body communicates not only by means of words but also via paralinguistic means, nonverbal language (facial expressions, body relaxation, etc.), and gestures and movement (kinaesthetics), as well as spatial position and posture (prozemics), the entity of the body itself (height, weight, and so on), clothing, information, consumption, advertising, and so on" (Fortunati, 2005, p. 53). Hence, people have rich information exchanges in body-to-body communication. They can better evaluate the trustworthiness of one another when they meet in person because when someone is untrustworthy, one's words, facial expression and gestures tend not to match (Kumar & Pradhan, 2015).

Social world is constructed through the interactions and coordination of individuals whose intentions are hidden from each other. Even though individuals' minds are hidden form one another, they are able to coordinate themselves and develop mutual understanding through the mutual adjustment of one another, "an adjustment made possible by means of a communication which takes the form of a conversation of gestures in the earlier evolutionary stages of that process, and of language in its later stages" (Mead, p. 77). Despite the hiddenness of mental states from the eyes of everyone, people believe they know when when they reach mutual understanding, because "mental tuning (the congruence of mental states) is reflected in the congruence of physical behavior between interactants" (Contarello, 2003, p. 125).

On social media, the body disappears, and so do the richness and trustworthiness of body-to-body communication. Everything presented on virtual world is merely information. The photograph of one's body is an information that can be manipulated or improved to one's liking. Even if the photograph is not digitally manipulated, it has already passed through the filter of selection, which makes it the best picture representing one's body. The utilization of social media allows people to move from body-to-body communication to avatar-to-avatar communication. What a social media user presents to her social network as herself is an avatar, a digital information that represents her. It can be manipulated, and even can also take another person's picture totally different from hers. On social media one can make up any identity one likes and conceals one's true identity. With the virtual identity that is detached from the actual, one can live virtual life separated from one's actual life. Technically using fake and true identity is the same, no one is more difficult than the other. And with fake identity one can spread any information without any risk, because one's actual self cannot be persecuted unless one left the trace of one's true identity.

Social media has not only become world of its own, it has also increasingly affected our physical world, socially and politically. Abundant information is being produced and exchanged every moment. However, it is not the information that necessarily makes us knowledgeable and wise. The disappearance of the body from virtual communication makes us difficult to evaluate the trustworthiness of information sources.

PROTECTING DEMOCRACY

Democracy has rarely been eliminated by foreign armed forces or alien ideologies. More often it is weakened by the decay caused by internal factors, such as "by complacency in the guise of privatism, by arrogance in the guise of empire, by irresponsibility in the guise of individualism, by selfishness in the guise of obsessive rights, by passivity in the guise of deference to experts, by greed in the guise of productivity" (Barber, 2003, p. xxix). In a democratic system, people are not only being given the right of free speech, to have any view, but also supposed to pay attention to many, if not every important, views. Democracy relies on critical citizens, who can judge and select views or representatives having particular views. Therefore, the greatest threat to democracy, which includes freedom, is not foreign military aggression, but the laziness of its people. Therefore, according to Louis Brandeis, one of America's greatest Supreme Court justices, public discussion is not only a right, but also a duty (Sunstein, 2007).

To sustain democracy, giving people the right of free speech is not enough, "it must ensure that people are exposed to competing perspectives. The idea of free speech has an affirmative side. It imposes constraints on what government may do, but it requires a certain kind of culture as well" (Sunstein, 2007, p. xi). The culture imposes particular norms, which in turn demand responsibility of the people, that is the responsibility of being active citizens.

The Internet and social media ease users to exercise their citizenship. Democracy requires people to be citizens, that is, those who choose with deliberation and act with responsibility (Barber, 2003), and these technologies can help them to do so. They can express their views on any issue and easily participate in public discourses. But these technologies can indirectly threaten democracy in two ways. First, these technologies help irresponsible people to easily spread disinformation. Second, these technologies expose people, who are cognitively limited, to so many interactions and so much information. The incapability to digest the abundant information will make them vulnerable to prejudices. And social media easily facilitate users to form echo chambers to inter-subjectively confirm their prejudices.

Having so many contacts, switching from one interaction to another interaction, and even simultaneously having multiple interactions weaken people's ability to pay sufficient attention on anything. In order to minimize their cognitive energy, when facing political issues, they tend to follow what their social groups think about them. And in order to be less confusing or to minimize their confusion, they tend to network with like-minded people. Under this condition, people can easily get confirmation from the others. They live in an echo chamber that strengthen their prejudices. In this condition, the Internet that allows them to search for any information, to understand different views, has been wasted.

Having access to technology that enables them to conceal their true identity, irresponsible people can easily spread fake news and hate speeches, which in turn can damage democracy. Democracy should not only respect other people's right but also knowledge and facts. Through democracy, people seek to reach consensus or select decisions which may not be agreed by all but will affect all members of society. It will be difficult to achieve that before we can agree in the most basic thing in collective decision making that is, accepting facts. If everybody can make up their own fact, social life will be chaotic. This kind of irresponsibility can threaten the continuity of democracy.

Democracy cannot be preserved without shared agreement in facts. If anyone can make up one's own facts, it would be difficult to reach consensus in society. And one of the reasons that people tend to be irresponsible on social media is because their virtual identities are detached from their actual identities. So, it is now increasingly necessary to develop virtual system in which the true identity is required to be its user. Using this system, we can take advantage of the easiness of virtual interactions and force each other to be responsible of anything being said. It is technically possible. The development of ecommerce and the so called "sharing economy", such as Uber and Airbnb, indicates that to certain extent trustworthiness among strangers can be enforced. The technological system makes one feel secure, for example, to buy goods from a shopper that one has never seen, or go in a car with a total stranger. It is because any account of the ecommerce is traceable to one's true identity and a certain level of trust can be established between the identities (Pradhan & Kumar, 2016). Technically it is also possible to make any social media account traceable to the true identity of a particular user (Kumar & Bhardwaj, 2018). So, when the user acts irresponsibly, such as spreading disinformation, a court can demand the social media platform to show the real identity of the user.

CONCLUSION

Individuals need freedom and also predictability of social life. Predictability requires order, and order constrains choices. These conflicting needs of freedom and of order are reconciled by establishing the notion of responsibility. Only a free person can have responsibility. But, to achieve societal order, society cannot wait for all its members to recognize their responsibility to establish it. Democracy has been established to manage collective interests and to deal with different, and sometimes conflicting, interests of free citizens. Having a large number of citizens who are unable to meet in one place, a country will have no choice but to establish a representative democratic system. But, this system allows the possibility that the representatives are separated from those being represented. Social media and the Internet empower people to actively exercise their citizenship from the convenience of their private places. But, these technologies do not only facilitate responsible citizens, but also irresponsible people. The latter can easily use them to spread disinformation and hate speech. Even though the former can counter irresponsible information with the correct and constructive information, the effect is weakened because there most people are overwhelmed by abundant information that makes them unable to distinguish the truth from the false. And this inability makes many people rush to use prejudices. With the success of ecommerce and the so-called sharing economy, it can be shown that to some extent the trustworthiness of users can be enforced. Even though more complicated, similar technique to enforce trustworthiness of social media users should be enforced as well, that is, by making any account traceable to true identity. Most importantly, the responsible behavior of the citizens is at the top to effective use the media freedom.

REFERENCES

Allport, G. W. (1979). *The Nature of Prejudice (25th Anniv)*. Reading, MA: Addison-Wesley.

Bail, C. A., Argyle, L. P., Brown, T. W., Bumpus, J. P., Chen, H., Hunzaker, M. B. F., ... Volfovsky, A. (2018). Exposure to opposing views on social media can increase political polarization. *Proceedings of the National Academy of Sciences of the United States of America*, *115*(37), 9216–9221. doi:10.1073/pnas.1804840115 PMID:30154168

Barber, B. R. (2003). *Strong Democracy: Participatory Politics fora New Age (Twentieth)*. Berkeley, CA: University of California Press.

Barnhart, J. E. (1969). Democracy as Responsibility. *The Journal of Value Inquiry*, *3*(4), 281–290. doi:10.1007/BF00139978

Baumeister, R. F. (1997). The Self and Society: Changes, Problems, and Opportunities. In *Self and Identity: Fundamental Issues* (pp. 191–217). Oxford, UK: Oxford University Press.

Berger, P. L., & Luckmann, T. (1966). *The Social Construction of Reality*. London, UK: Penguin Books.

Brown, R. (2010). *Prejudice: Its Social Psychology (Second)*. West Sussex, UK: Wiley-Blackwell.

Carothers, T., & O'Donohue, A. (2019, October 1). How to Understand the Global Spread of Political Polarization. Retrieved from https://carnegieendowment.org/2019/10/01/how-to-understand-global-spread-of-political-polarization-pub-79893

Contarello, A. (2003). Body to Body: Copresence in Communication. In L. Fortunati, K. Katz, & R. Riccini (Eds.), *Mediating the Human Body. Technology, Communication, and Fashion*. Mahwah, NJ: Lawrence Erlbaum Associates.

De-Wit, L., Brick, C., & van der Linden, S. (2019, January 16). Are Social Media Driving Political Polarization? Retrieved from https://greatergood.berkeley.edu/article/item/is_social_media_driving_political_polarization

Dibos, A. (2002). Democracy as Responsibility, Meaning, and Hope: Introductory Reflections on a Democratic Project in Education. *Journal of Thought*, *37*(1), 11–24.

DiFranzo, D., & Gloria-Garcia, K. (2017). Filter bubbles and fake news. *XRDS: Crossroads. The ACM Magazine for Students*, *23*(3), 32–35. doi:10.1145/3055153

Fortunati, L. (2005). Is Body-to-Body Communication Still the Prototype? *The Information Society*, *21*(1), 53–61. doi:10.1080/01972240590895919

Foucault, M. (1978). The History of Sexuality: Vol. I. *An Introduction*. New York, NY: Pantheon Books.

Foucault, M. (1995). *Discipline and Punish*. New York, NY: Vintage Books.

Giddens, A. (1984). *The Constitution of Society - Outline of the Theory of Structuration*. Cambridge, UK: Polity Press.

Goffman, E. (1959). *The Presentation of Self in Everyday Life*. New York, NY: Doubleday.

Goffman, E. (1967). *Interaction Ritual*. New York, NY: Anchor Books.

Habermas, J. (1984). Theory of Communicative Action: Vol. 1. *Reason and the Rationalization of Society*. Boston, MA: Beacon Press.

Harris, L., & Harrigan, P. (2015). Social Media in Politics: The Ultimate Voter Engagement Tool or Simply an Echo Chamber? *Journal of Political Marketing*, *14*(3), 251–283. doi:10.1080/15377857.2012.693059

Harter, S. (1997). The Personal Self in Social Context: Barriers to Authenticity. In R. D. Ashmore, & L. Jussim (Eds.), *Self and Identity: Fundamental Issues* (pp. 81–105). Oxford, UK: Oxford University Press.

Heidegger, M. (1962). *Being and Time*. Oxford, UK: Blackwell.

James, W. (1927). *The principles of psychology*. New York, NY: Dover.

Jaramillo, M., & Wright, G. D. (2015). Participatory Democracy and Effective Policy: Is There a Link? Evidence from Rural Peru. *World Development*, *66*, 280–292. doi:10.1016/j.worlddev.2014.08.011

Kumar, V., & Bhardwaj, A. (2018). Identity Management Systems: A Comparative Analysis. *International Journal of Strategic Decision Sciences*, *9*(1), 63–78. doi:10.4018/IJSDS.2018010105

Kumar, V., & Nanda, P. (2019a). Social Media in Higher Education: A Framework for Continuous Engagement. [IJICTE]. *International Journal of Information and Communication Technology Education*, *15*(1), 109–120. doi:10.4018/IJICTE.2019010107

Kumar, V., & Nanda, P. (2019 b). Social Media to Social Media Analytics: Ethical Challenges. [IJT]. *International Journal of Technoethics*, *10*(2), 57–70. doi:10.4018/IJT.2019070104

Kumar, V., & Pradhan, P. (2015). Trust Management Issues in Social-Media Marketing [IJOM]. *International Journal of Online Marketing*, *5*(3), 47–64. doi:10.4018/IJOM.2015070104

Laine, T. (2019, November 1). Thumb-Boat Diplomacy Could Undo U.S. Foreign Policy. Retrieved from https://foreignpolicy.com/2019/11/01/trump-policymakers-twitter-promote-policy-condemn-adversaries/

Maulana, I. (2016). Social Media as Public Political Instrument. In M. Adria, & Y. Mao (Eds.), *Handbook of Research on Citizen Engagement and Public Participation in the Era of New Media*. Hershey, PA: IGI Global; doi:10.4018/978-1-5225-1081-9.ch013

Maulana, I. (2018a). Mutual Understanding in the Age of Vulnerable Truth. In B. L. Cook (Ed.), *Handbook of Research on Examining Global Peacemaking in the Digital Age*. Hershey, PA: IGI Global. doi:10.4018/978-1-5225-3032-9.ch005

Maulana, I. (2018b). Spontaneous Taking and Posting Selfie: Reclaiming the Lost Trust. In S. Hai-Jew (Ed.), *Selfies as a Mode of Social Media and Work Space Research* (pp. 28–50). Hershey, PA: IGI Global; doi:10.4018/978-1-5225-3373-3.ch002

McAdams, D. P. (1997). The Case for Unity in the (Post)Modern Self: A Modest Proposal. In *Self and Identity: Fundamental Issues* (pp. 46–78). Oxford, UK: Oxford University Press.

Merleau-Ponty, M. (2005). *Phenomenology of Perception*. London, UK: Routledge Classics.

Miller, C. (2019, October 26). Crossing Divides: How a social network could save democracy from deadlock. Retrieved from https://www.bbc.com/news/technology-50127713

North, D. (1990). *Institutions, Institutional Change and Economic Performance*. Cambridge, MA: Cambridge University Press. doi:10.1017/CBO9780511808678

Ortiz-Ospina, E. (2019, September 18). The rise of social media. Retrieved from https://ourworldindata.org/rise-of-social-media

Parker, R. B. (2014). Two Visions of Democracy. In A. E. Cudd, & S. J. Scholz (Eds.), *Philosophical Perspectives on Democracy in the 21st Century* (pp. 75–86). Heidelberg, Germany: Springer. doi:10.1007/978-3-319-02312-0_6

Parkinson, H. J. (2016, November 14). Click and elect: how fake news helped Donald Trump win a real election. Retrieved from https://www.theguardian.com/commentisfree/2016/nov/14/fake-news-donald-trump-election-alt-right-social-media-tech-companies

Post, R. (2005). Democracy and Equality. *Law, Culture, and the Humanities*, *1*(2), 142–153. doi:10.1191/1743872105lw013oa

Pradhan, P., & Kumar, V. (2016). Trust Management Models for Digital Identities. [IJVCSN]. *International Journal of Virtual Communities and Social Networking*, *8*(4), 1–24. doi:10.4018/IJVCSN.2016100101

Pradhan, P., & Kumar, V. (2016). Trust Management Models for Digital Identities. [IJVCSN]. *International Journal of Virtual Communities and Social Networking*, *8*(4), 1–24. doi:10.4018/IJVCSN.2016100101

Rawls, J. (2005). *Political Liberalism, Expanded Edition*. New York, NY: Columbia University Press.

Scott, W. R. (2014). *Institutions and Organizations: Ideas, Interests, and Identities* (4th ed.). Thousand Oaks, CA: Sage.

Sen, A. (2009). *The Idea of Justice*. Cambridge, MA: Harvard University Press. doi:10.2307/j.ctvjnrv7n

Slater, M. D. (2007). Reinforcing Spirals: The Mutual Influence of Media Selectivity and Media Effects and Their Impact on Individual Behavior and Social Identity. *Communication Theory*, *17*(3), 281–303. doi:10.1111/j.1468-2885.2007.00296.x

Sunstein, C. R. (2007). *Republic.com 2.0*. Princeton, NJ: Princeton University Press.

Tapsell, R. (2019, March 22). The polarisation paradox in Indonesia's 2019 elections. Retrieved from https://www.newmandala.org/the-polarisation-paradox-in-indonesias-2019-elections/

Taylor, D. (2004). Beyond learning theory. In E. Hargreaves, & A. Varchevker (Eds.), *In Pursuit of Psychic Change: The Betty Joseph Workshop* (pp. 136–149). New York, NY: Brunner-Routledge.

Tufekci, Z. (2017). *Twitter and Tear Gas: The Power and Fragility of Networked Protest*. New Haven: Yale University Press.

Wall, S. (2007). Democracy and Equality. *The Philosophical Quarterly*, *57*(228), 416–428. doi:10.1111/j.1467-9213.2007.495.x

Chapter 2
The Politics of Social Media: Mediating Ambivalences in the Era of Political Populism

Joseph L. Flores
University of New Mexico, USA

ABSTRACT

This chapter explores a fundamental tension of social media by considering their socially reproductive and (potentially) transformative function. The claim is that while media and communication technologies have historically fueled both aspiration and fear of social change, their ability to shape societies are contingent on the specific social relations in which they operate. By investigating social media's economic practices, primarily platform capitalism, the reproductive relations that support user-generated content that influence platform's capabilities to reproduce and transform existing social contexts are examined. To illustrate this, political discourse via social media platforms have been used to argue that social media's current capitalist mode of production exemplifies an antagonism between exploitative/emancipatory tendencies and reproductive/transformative aspects, which are further articulated by a liberal ideology.

INTRODUCTION

In the political economic study of mass media, illustrated and exemplified through the understanding that the flow of information and communication is linear and one-way, the distribution of content stems from a small number of producers to a large number of recipients (Bechmann, 2012; Wittel, 2016). Professionally created

DOI: 10.4018/978-1-7998-1791-8.ch002

Copyright © 2020, IGI Global. Copying or distributing in print or electronic forms without written permission of IGI Global is prohibited.

content is the key element in the business model of legacy media companies and is coupled with subscriptions, advertising, and/or licensing fees (Bechmann, 2012). Hallin and Mancini (2004) suggest that legacy news organizations in the United States are examples of the North Atlantic or liberal model of media which exists as a system that emphasizes profit, professionalism, and individualized representation (Benson, Blach-Orsten, Powers, Willig, & Zambrano, 2012). Epitomized by the we write, you read model of production (Deuze, 2003), content is a mass-produced product made daily and disseminated professionally.

The current age of media is historically significant, and considerably different, primarily due to social media platforms. Fundamentally, this difference lies in social media platforms operating as a key element and a main constituent of contemporary economies (Fuchs, 2015; Briziarelli & Karikari, 2016; Fuchs & Mosco, 2016). Since the media industry is considered to be profitable due to its potential for future-oriented growth, the integration of telecommunications, the computer industry at large, and the Internet into capitalism was the prerequisite for the expansion of the movement of capital (Knoche, 2015). In the political economic, social, and capitalist context of today, one dominated by social media platforms and their owners, a new class of individuals, corporations and entities capitalize on the information they collect and own through a vast infrastructure to sense, record and analyze data (Srnicek, 2017). As such, data serves crucial capitalist functions. In short, data educate and give advantage to algorithms; enable the coordination and outsourcing of workers; allow for the optimization and flexibility of productive processes; make possible the transformation of low-margin goods into high-margin services; and the analysis of data itself becomes a generative form of data (Srnicek, 2017).

As social media endures its rapid and influential integration into the logic of capitalism, and as capitalism continues to evolve through an informational character, the relationship between the two maintains development under and through deep-rooted tensions (Fuchs, 2016; Fuchs & Mosco, 2016; Briziarelli & Karikari, 2016). Moreover, the antagonism between our understanding of the normative role of media technologies and its place in society is long-lasting and forever changing. For instance, the history of mass media indicates that each new emerging technology is inevitably accompanied by a prediction of the total collapse of the previous technologies (Mosco, 2005; Tay & Turner, 2010). However, as Joyce (2018) notes, though new technology enables more active audiences, it does not mean that media corporations abandon their practices. Instead, it is important to contextualize that actions which change the innerworkings of the media ecosystem trigger multifaceted chains of reactions that inevitably seek new forms of balance.

The arrival of new media technologies can initiate major shifts in what is technically possible while being accompanied by utopic and/or dystopic sentiments. For example, in a more utopic inclination, social media are the supposed champions of the resurrection of both the general public sphere (Habermas, 1981) and the subaltern public sphere that can present opportunities for minority and oppressed groups to organize and participate in politics (Fraser, 1990; Lee, So, Lee, Leung, & Chan, 2018). Alternatively, and more perniciously, they have been theorized to: expand the depths of commodification, particularly in uncolonized spheres of social life (boyd, 2010), including the commodification (and mediatization) of political identities (Turner, 2019); hamper and obstruct democratic possibilities (Dean, 2009); and, in more bleak theorizations, represent capital's totalizing aspiration to not just know reality, but to own and make reality (Zuboff, 2015). Nonetheless, they are responsible for creating new levels of sociability and are fundamental as a site for the reproduction of the social (Thorburn, 2016).

Perhaps most representative of social media's utopic and dystopic idealizations lie in their political use. As such, social media platforms have been theorized as both a positive and a detriment to political activities. Positively, they have been viewed from the vantage point of supplementing activism and existing as activism in a digital form. For example, some activists have focused specifically on determining how algorithms work in different environments (Varis & Hou, 2019) while some scholars argue that activist practices need to be understood as socio-technical assemblages (Chadwich, 2017). Further, social media platforms can be seen as sites of assemblages of actions, discourse, and tools "associated with digital technologies, which have come to be recognized by specific groups of people as ways of attaining particular goals" (Jones, Chik, & Haffner, 2015, p. 3). In a more damaging way, however, social media platforms have long been positioned as contributing to the echo chamber effect that may destroy the public sphere (Andrejevic, 2013) and are even considered to be "Architectures of Serendipity" because they provide users with an ecosystem of content that already aligns with their pre-existing views (Sunstein, 2018). Ultimately, there is a contradiction between viewing the technology, and its political use, as both emancipating and/or coercive.

Particularly pertinent in current research, given the rise of fascist and right-winged political actors around the globe, is the investigation of the political effects of social media with respect to right-wing and fascist groups (Caiani & Kröll, 2015; Caiani & Parenti, 2013; Froio & Gattinara, 2015). Whereas social media platforms and all of their democratic possibilities are revered when used to oppose oppressive contexts (Etling, Faris, & Palfrey, 2010; Laer & Aelst, 2010), the same features appear to be more detrimental when it comes to right-wing mobilization. Therefore, it is not surprising to see that scholars have increasingly invested efforts to understand these phenomena in relation to its social and political implications (e.g., Barberá, Jost, Nagler, Tucker, & Bonneau, 2015; Giglietto & Selva, 2014). Nonetheless, it has been argued that social and digital media have become the site of a metapolitical battle – where movements have learned to exploit the logics of new media and old media to draw attention of a broad audience to its message (Maly, 2019).

As a representative of the far-right, ultra-nationalist, anti-globalization ascent of political actors, Donald Trump's 2016 presidential run, in many ways, provides a prime instance in which a metapolitical battle can be explored. In discerning the difference between exploitative "labor" and emancipatory "work" (Fuchs & Sevignani, 2013), and in a consideration of how social media platforms exist in a landscape of distributed media composed of digital things (Wittel, 2016), the argument is that Trump's Twitter use exacerbates and intensifies the ideological underpinnings of social media platforms which, in short, include notions of freedom of speech and freedom of the press. Ultimately, social media platforms, and the political participation on behalf of a presidential candidate like Donald Trump, aggravates the capability of platforms to mediate multiple messages.

In using Donald Trump's political discourse via his Twitter profile, the argument unfolds by demonstrating how social media is capable of generating social transformation and social reproduction in particular ways (Bloch, 1986; Thorburn, 2016). After reviewing the role of media in social formations, this paper is structured into three main sections: first, the link between media and the utopian/dystopian societal dispositions is laid out while showing how consistent aspirations and fears of social change are triggered by (new) media technologies; second, in order to illustrate a perspective that teases out the utopic/dystopic tensions, it is crucial to situate media as an ideological process that links the dialectic between working and laboring and that is exacerbated by a landscape of distributed media made up of digital things; and finally, the political discourse of Donald Trump is used to exemplify the fusion between the working/utopic/transformative and the laboring/dystopic/reproductive features of social media.

MEDIA AND ITS HISTORICAL RELEVANCE

How societies come to organize themselves through time – its social formation – and the process of social mediation, i.e. how different elements/subjects of society come to interact, communicate and exchange information, are intricately and intimately intertwined. As both processes are based on the production and reproduction of social relations, media could not exist without a social field and a sense of sociability and, at the same time, a social community could not be constructed without an adequate means of social coordination. In other words, the means of communication are key components because they operate as the site wherein the material and symbolic means of social reproduction emerge (Fuchs, 2012; Thorburn, 2016).

From an economic standpoint, the means of communication play an important role in the reproduction of the social experience because they "permit the acceleration in the circuits of capital" and it cements the reproduction of labor power to "the exclusion of other elements of human life" (Thorburn, 2016, p. 384). Manzerolle and Kjosen (2015) argue that the means of communication are key components to circulate capital because they are the means by which capital communicates itself in and through society. In the age of networked communication, subsuming social reproduction into capital creates overarching cultures of surveillance, commodification, and consumption (Dean, 2009; Zuboff, 2015; Thorburn, 2016).

This seems to be a possible explanation as to why there are constant ambivalent sentiments associated with mediated communication that favor media as part of a feared or welcomed social change. As such, media and media technologies can be seen as guiding technological utopia and dystopia. For Gendron (1977), technological utopia is a particular contemporary ideology that assumes that the advancement of science and technology will eventually fulfill an ideal society in which scarcity, sufferance, and mortality will be overcome. Conversely, technological dystopia is associated with devastating changes containing images of technology mediating most aspects of human life that it contaminates humanity and forecloses genuine social intercourse (Gendron, 1977). Therefore, media have been celebrated in its ability to overcome physical and temporal distances between human beings while also at the same time being accused of creating distances in otherwise intimate social relations (Jacobs, 1992).

The cultural circumstances in which media operate have significantly changed but nonetheless remain consistent with the ideology of a technologically driven history. Gendron (1977) notes that in post-industrial capitalism, the mode of economic development which shifts the main goal of capital from industrial production to consumption, serves as a possible foundation for a utopic situation through a technological revolution that generates development, improvement, and the eradication of any societal issues. Theorizations of this post-industrial economy collided with media studies by way of attempting to account for user labor online as part of the emphasis of the service-based economy through immaterial labor (Lazzarato, 1996).

Though part of a broader argument concerning labor in the often criticized dichotomous framework of Fordist/post-Fordist capitalism, Lazzarato (1996) contends that immaterial labor - comprised of two aspects: the information content of the commodity (or computer work) and the cultural content of the commodity (objects such as fashions, tastes, and public opinion) – does not replace material labor but only extends it. Moreover, immaterial labor is also an attempt to characterize the way the Internet and technology influence labor in how the structuring of the Internet affects capital and the strive for control with an emphasis on the technological structure and an ever-growing dependency on it for labor (Galloway, 2004).

The reliance on digital technologies and networked communications for capital expansion has created an era with the relentless production of communication both at work and home due to digital devices dominating work and home life. As Huws (2014) puts it, the "electronically mediated conversation" has become favored over direct voice or glance both of necessity at work and choice at home (p. 14). Labor and leisure converge, and the convenience of the technology obscure the actual amount of work they demand (Gregg, 2011). More maliciously, Haraway (1991) makes the argument that the interaction between human and machine has created a certain type of cyborg and Lazzarato (2006) goes as far to call it machinic enslavement. Since social media platforms have created a structure that affords them the ability to capitalize on networked communication, social interactions become reduced to a series of user-generated interactions with the platforms, i.e. status updates, likes, posts, favorites, and retweets, and which are all commodifiable (Dean, 2009; Dean, 2014; Thorburn, 2016).

MEDIATION AND MEDIA IN SOCIAL REPRODUCTION

For Hjarvard (2008), mediation represents a quasi-ontological account of the complexity of social life as a whole but does not do enough to describe media as a historic force. For some scholars, understanding the prominent role of media as a historic driver has been conceptualized through the concept of mediatization. Mediatization, as a research endeavor, has been prevalent enough to be called media theory's word of the decade (Corner, 2018) and has become "one of the most vibrant fields of international media and communication research" (Adolph, 2017, p. 11). In general, mediatization is an attempt to make sense of the long term structural and cultural effects of media (Couldry & Hepp, 2013) while expressing a meta-process, a force, that, together with globalization, individualization and commercialization, have fashioned modernity. According to Peters (2009), most media pass through five stages: the technical invention, cultural invention, legal regulation, economic distribution, and social mainstream, and which carry significant consequences for mediation, and mediating, social relations.

For Krotz (2008) mediatization means "the historical developments that took and take place as a result of change in (communication) media and the consequences of those changes" (p. 23). Further, Adolph characterizes mediatization as a process:

usually tied to the genealogy of media-technological innovation and the institutionalization of a media system (expansion, commercialization, etc.), thus native to a modern social formations and often used diagnostically to make sense of accelerated social change (a media-centered perspective on the media as drivers of social processes) (p. 24).

More broadly, mediation is understood as the loss of contact with nature (Peters, 1999), as an alienating new model of society and rational apparatus, which imprisons people in Kafka bureaucratic labyrinths (Marx, 1867), as a simulation of reality (Baudrillard, 1989), or, on a mass level, operate as a way to produce stereotypes (Lang & Lang, 2009). For Horkheimer & Adorno (1973), mediation is a metaphor that belongs to a conceptualization of modernity understood in its contradictory nature and for Singer (1973), mediation performs a disruptive function by offering minority groups transformative possibilities through acts of protest.

While the mediatization literature provides an important historical account of media, the investigative lens tends to be so wide that it overlooks the materially (re) productive effects of media, thus favoring a broad notion of media effects instead of media being understood as a means of material production. For example, Aouragh (2012) notes that the forces and organizations of labor are the economic structures of society from which emerge a certain polity and politics, and these in turn merge in different ways, "depending on the historical situation in which it occurs" (p. 520). Citing Marx and Engels, Aouragh argues that class, which is simultaneously the ruling material force of a society and its intellectual force, represent the interrelation of business and the production of ideas. As such, mediation suggests the presence of normative representations of social relations, contingent on what form of mediation is at stake and whether each technological transformation is a continuation and a unique transformation manifested in ways depending on a particular development.

To summarize, mediated communication represents an historical evolution of modernity, wherein a promise of human emancipation and the constant danger of humanity's imprisonment are constantly present. Both represent dichotomous aspects of a general acknowledgement about the power of media to shape our society. Next is a discussion in how distributed media and implementation of digital things furthers these anxieties.

DIGITAL TECHNOLOGY, DISTRIBUTED MEDIA AND POLITICS

Particularly prevalent in current political communication research is the notion of how social media has changed the practices of information distribution. Entman and Usher (2018) argue that due to social media's maturation, scholars must, "re-evaluate the processes through which news is produced, distributed, assimilated, and acted upon" (p. 298). For them, this need to reevaluate stems from a consideration of the imbalances in discourse between the left and right, the rise of hegemonic tech companies, and the political possibilities for civic participation in late-capitalist democracy. Ultimately, Entman and Usher argue that the 21st century's hope of more efficient communicative practices involving political communication has not produced a more accountable government but has instead stiffened the hierarchy of control. Part of their argument rests on the assessment of what they term "digital pump-values," how the flow of political information is influenced by platforms, analytics (data about audience behavior), algorithms, ideological media, and rogue actors (hackers, bots).

The pump-value metaphor, which for them is intentionally mechanistic, reflects how these new digital and digitized features both enhance (pump) and diminish (value) communication flows (Entman & Usher, 2018). More broadly, they directly confront the role of digital technology, data, and the Internet. Things which encompass and create the possibility of distributed media are inherently comprised of digital things. In order to give a political economic perspective to social media platforms in this current media context, Wittel (2016) argues that in the age of digital technologies, there should be a fundamentally different political economic approach to a different media landscape.

In the age of mass media, the means of production were expensive. Most people could not afford the ownership of all the necessary assets to contribute to the production of print media or broadcast media. Of course, this meant that only a limited number of media organizations produced and disseminated media content to a large number of consumers. Thus, the appropriation of Marxist theory in the age of mass media results from a very specific historic reality, from historically unique concerns that were generated by mass media technologies (Wittel, 2016).

Contemporarily, however, digital technologies have brought about a fundamentally different media landscape where mass media is not the only source of content production and dissemination. Whereas mass media are hierarchical, linear, with a control center and one-way flow of media content from few producers to many recipients, distributed media functions via a networked, non-linear, multi-directional and reciprocal flows of content from (potentially) many producers to (potentially) many consumers. As such, distributed media is a conceptualization of the social organization of media while the term digital media is used to refer to the technology (Wittel, 2016). The distinction between distributed media and digital technologies is important in that the logic of distributed media is profoundly shaped by the qualities and capabilities of digital technologies. Digital technologies can re-mediate older forms of media such as text, sound, images, and moving images as digital code; they can integrate communication and information or communication media; digital objects can endlessly be reproduced at minimum costs; they do not carry any weight, thus they can be distributed at the speed of light.

More crucially, however, the phenomenological qualities of digital technologies carry profound implications for the social. Primarily, the number of media producers increases dramatically in the digital age. Secondly, digital technologies enable new social forms of media production and media distribution. Third, as the number of media producers increases media themselves become ubiquitous in that all aspects of the social world and our lives become mediated, from the global and public to the most intimate aspects of our existence (Livingstone, 2009). Fourth, digital technologies are not just media technologies, they are built into all productive processes (Castells, 2008). As such, the digital economy now is not just the ICT economy anymore, it is simply the economy (Briziarelli & Karikari, 2016).

In the relationship between media and politics, the shift from mass media to social media impacts the approaches to understanding the influence of media and media technologies in political situations. Armbrust (2007) and Ulrich (2009) remind researchers of the need to historicize technological developments due to the common tension between historical continuity and change. Eagleton (1976) argues that historicizing is not merely tracing the technical forces in themselves but also contextualizing the place they occupy within a whole mode of production. For example, Deibert (1997) notes that in replacing the time-consuming technique of parchment with papyrus, there were implications and consequences for European Protestantism and for the upcoming bourgeoisie and other social classes, as well.

Though social media's impact in the 2016 United States presidential election may seem novel, it is a descendant of previous tactics used by politicians to skirt legacy and traditional media. Beginning in the 1980s, the rise of entertainment platforms like talk radio and television talk shows was coupled with more prominent political roles, eventually giving rise to the infotainment genre (Moy, Xenos, & Hess, 2009; Owen, 2018). Politicians turned to these avenues of new media to circumvent mainstream, legacy media in order to insert more voice over the news agenda. Moy et. al. (2009) argue that the infotainment emphasis of new media at this early stage offered political leaders and candidates a friendlier venue for presenting themselves to the public. The fusion of politics and entertainment attracted audiences that typically had been disinterested in public affairs (Williams & Delli Carpini, 2011). Of course, the affordances of these new media channels, coupled with the rise of celebrity politicians and social media platforms, created space for "spectacle of excess" and "reality TV presidents," where the tools of language and props are used to ignite and maintain audience attention (Owen, 2018; Blankenship, 2019).

Across both the legacy and social media political economic approaches, however, is the tension between understanding media's need for capital to survive and their (apparent) public service. Since media has been historically situated as both a private good, i.e. commodity, and a public good because it (at least to some degree) constitutes itself as the public sphere, media institutions have a social, cultural, and political function while always being driven by economic interests. Wittel (2016) argues that it is this dual nature that which allows media companies to make the argument that they are an independent force who supposedly safeguard democracy. Since the contemporary media ecosystem is profoundly different, media content is now not only produced by employees working in and for companies, it is also created by the labor of those who engage in the dissemination of content, in the usage of social media platforms, and in the interaction with the platform themselves and all which carry implications for the political possibilities stemming from the platforms.

WORK VS LABOR: IDEOLOGICAL (RE) PRODUCTION VIA SOCIAL MEDIA PLATORMS

According to Briziarelli & Karikari (2016), one of ideology's interventions in the social media environment is its ability to combine the objective element of producing actual media content and the subjective element of consciousness. Due to social media's ability to combine the production of value with the subjective motivations that leads users to produce and reproduce content for free and enjoy doing it, users are led to willingly produce content. Marx and Engels (2001) argue that the production of consciousness and the production of ideology are linked to concrete human activity:

the production of ideas, concepts and consciousness is first of all directly interwoven with the material intercourse of man, the language of real life. Conceiving, thinking, the spiritual intercourse of men, appear here as the direct efflux of men's material behavior [...] Consciousness does not determine life: life determines consciousness (Marx & Engels, 2001, p. 35-36).

For scholars like Rey (2012), there is a question as to whether or not social media users can be considered alienated and/or exploited since the labor that they provide is contingent on their own happiness. Rey argues that users are ultimately not disconnected from the content that they produce on the site and are free to create what they choose. Juxtaposed to the traditional factory where workers are coerced into accepting exploitative conditions, social media platforms are unable to exploit users because the content users provide is not a result of overt coercion. The point in considering the distinction between work and labor is not to determine whether or not happiness is contingent on producing content for social media platforms, but to acknowledge the role of ideological work on behalf of users participating within the platform logic(s). Here, the desire of sociability must not only push back against an idealist approach to ideology that prefers reducing ideology as a concept related to representation or how media texts signify, but of the ideological significance in the platform itself (Briziarrelli, 2014).

On the one hand, scholars note that not all media are social because only those that support communication enable social actions and sociality. Contingent on a definition of communication that conceives of communication as a reciprocal process between at least two humans, the exchange of symbols creates a sense of meaning to the communicative acts and to the platforms that host them. As a kind of screen essentialism (Berry, 2014), this understanding of social activity fronts communication and symbolic interaction and notes that media only become social in the interactions between individuals that can evolve to create social community. Though it is true that this definition of social media centers the ability to communicate and construct community through communicative interactions in order to be considered social, it essentializes the construction of the screens and platforms where interactions take place while disregarding the material necessities (and social relations) required to assemble the technological products.

On the other hand, other authors like Fuchs (2017) argue that all media are social. For these scholars, media are always part of society because aspects of society are always present in the technological artifacts that are used. For example, Fuchs argues that the building of a computer does not happen in a vacuum outside of social relations, therefore the ideas, thoughts, and writings that happen on a computer must be considered as part of society. Moreover, software programs that computer applications are built on, and the hardware components that process them, are also the result of social relations and are therefore social products (Berry, 2014). Importantly, then, this broad understanding of sociality implies that social media sites like Facebook, Twitter, and YouTube are not only social in that they host social interactions between individuals and groups, but that they are social because they are ultimately products of social relations like the television, radio, posters, books, wall paintings and "all other forms of information" before them (Fuchs, 2017, p. 10).

In the age of computing and social media platforms, all computing systems, and all web applications, should be considered social because they store and transmit human knowledge that originate in the social relations of society (Fuchs, 2017). Web 2.0's Internet capabilities, including but not limited to coding, software and hardware production, and algorithm production and performativity are all historically specific and socially embedded in broader networks of social relations and institutional ensembles (Berry, 2014). Crucially, however, the audience's consciousness and their adoption of specific worldviews do not passively reflect so-called real life but instead interacts with it and cannot be reduced to an instrumentalized epiphenomenon of productive logics. The process of production of ideology and consciousness generating through the prod-users activity does not happen in a vacuum and is emerged in a pre-existing ensemble of ideas and practices. Precisely, the production of ideology interacts with previous existing worldviews that contribute to give meaning to both media and their usages, primarily through the constitutive use of language.

Social networking sites like Facebook, YouTube and Twitter are distinct because they are integrated platforms that combine an amalgamation of media, information, and communication technologies. This amalgamation of information enables the convergence of cognition, communication and cooperation and not only integrate a level of sociality but encourage the display of integrated roles (Fuchs, 2017). With data on social media platforms existing as text, videos, images, Likes, shares, posts, the use of emoticons, and commenting, these platforms inherently depend on user-based interactions (Cohen, 2008; Lee, 2011) and the commodification of user labor on social media requires sophisticated techniques of collecting, analyzing and manipulating these kinds of data (Beer, 2009; Kang & McAllister, 2011; McStay, 2011). Fundamentally, the function of social media and its impacts on political communication lie in their ability to capitalize on community, communication, and cognition, all which are the result of user labor (Fuchs, 2017).

One way to conceive the use of social media platforms is prod-using, prosumption, or a combination of simultaneous producing and consuming. Prosumption involves the interrelationship between production and consumption (Ritzer, 2015) and is a crucial component in theorizing how users actively participate in an ecology of sharing, liking, and content creation. For Ritzer, not only are consumption and production always interrelated and intertwined, but prosumption is a "hybrid that always involves a mix of production and consumption" (p. 414). As such, data, understood as raw material, is then commodified by media corporations, and is always dependent on the work of social media users. Moreover, some scholars argue that value derives from the ability to exploit communication practices as labor-time where, ultimately, time spent on social media platforms is paramount in the process of prosumer commodification transformed into economic capital (Fuchs, 2012).

Fuchs and Sevignani (2013) lay out the dialectical aspects of producing this content with an investigation into how Marx conceives of, and differentiates between, labor and work. Basing their distinction on Marx's statement that "labor which creates use-values and is qualitatively determined is called 'work' as opposed to 'labor'; labor which creates value and is only measured quantitatively is called 'labor', as opposed to 'work'" (p.138), Fuchs and Sevignani argue that the two concepts are different because:

"Labor is a necessarily alienated form of work, in which humans do not control and own the means and results of production. Work in contrast is a much more general concept common to all societies. It is a process in which humans in social relations make use of technologies in order to transform nature, culture and society in such a way that goods and services are created that satisfy human needs" (p. 240).

Consequently, the two moments oppose each other when it comes to human emancipation because freedom only begins when labor ends. Through work, human intentions become bound to the product, and in such a product, people are able to see and recognize themselves. Conversely, labor causes multiple kinds of alienation to the workers and it disrupts the moment of genuine creative activity fundamental in the experience of working. On social media platforms, the distinction between work and labor is in trying to understand an economy that meshes together production and entertainment (Lund, 2014). Specifically, Lund points out the parallel conceptual distance between 'work' and 'labor' and 'play' and 'game' as well as parallel affinities between 'work'/'play' and 'labor/game.' In the field of knowledge working, the valorization of labor is heavily contingent on the imaginative, creative activity of people (Lazzarato, 1996). In the existing social relation that encompass social media, working and laboring are fused: on the one hand, the social media user is unpaid, alienated from their own product and from the work process, and ultimately, becomes a commodity sold to advertising industries; on the other hand, the user is a worker constructing their own identity through generating the social environment around them and is propelled by a sense of social and political engagement. In essence, the social media user is alienated by their own unpaid laboring but could feel emancipated in the construction of sociability.

As promoted by Fuchs and Mosco (2016), a theory of communication should center and demonstrate how communication and culture are material practices. Importantly, they maintain that this must also fore front how labor and language are mutually constituted, and how communication and information are dialectical instances of the same social activity – the social construction of meaning. McGuigan (2014) argues that means of communication, as entire social projects that serve social needs, are themselves means of productions that include forms of language and advanced forms of communication technology that are always socially and materially reproduced. With platforms that existentially need users to interact with them in order to beget more capital, the social construction of meaning, and the communicative technological infrastructures through which this meaning circulates, distributes ideology with a political motive and as part of domination and exploitation fundamentally and always through the use of language.

In line with the Marxian notion of productive consumption (Nixon, 2011; Ritzer, 2015), the audience is then active in producing consciousness and articulating its ideas by consuming commodified culture. What is stimulating about social media is the practical productive activity of the audience that leads to problematize, or at least sophisticate the idea, that the audience is the recipient of the ideological process. Most recognizably, the interest of ideology, or in the result of ideology, media studies tend to be fixated on the communication process that channels ideology rather than ideology itself. Consequently, ideology is almost never linked to labor and material production but is instead reduced to a "result" in the powerful tradition of mass communication effects (Briziarelli & Karikari, 2016).

SOCIAL MEDIA AND POLITICS: THE LIBERAL IDEOLOGY

According to Bell (2014), liberalism is a specter, an apparition, that continuously haunts Western political thought and practice. For some, Bell notes, liberalism is a site of the modern, "an object of desire," even a telos of history (p. 683). For others, liberalism is representative of a logic of capitalism, a descent into moral relativism, or exists as a mark of ambivalence, an "ideological prerequisite for living a reasonably comfortable life in affluent democratic states" (Bell, 2014, p. 683). In 1644, *Aeropagitica's* demand for a "free open encounter" (p. 50) between ideas and trade implied that the liberalization of the market and the public sphere where tightly connected (Rosenblatt, 2011). When it comes to the relationship between media and politics, liberalism (and a liberal media), is commonly believed to be a necessity in order to have a functioning government. Drastically, they are thought to serve as the "eyes, the ears, and the conscience of the public…[T]hey can promote justice or cause injustice" (Oswald, 2009, p. 389).

With the onset of social media platforms, both the resurgence of a liberal public sphere ideology that tries to colonize all social experiences (Negt & Kluge, 1993) and the assertion of a technological utopianism that equates hi-tech progress with social progress, manifests with the introduction of a novel means of communication (Mosco, 2005). It is crucial to recognize that the digital culture of sharing is premised on a fundamental contradiction: Web 2.0 programs and platforms have increased venues and participatory possibilities for public expression, interpersonal communication and social engagement yet they simultaneously exploit digital sharing to fuel the web's exchange economy (Stadler & Sützl, 2011; Banning, 2016). Stadler and Sützl (2011) urge researchers to be critical of the contradiction between the culture of sharing amongst users and the commercial ambitions of the platforms in which the sharing takes place. In fact, Banning argues more directly that due to this contradiction, online sharing is best illuminated through a neologism called "info-liberalism" which is described as an umbrella term for critiques of the close alignment between neoliberal capitalism and digital communication.

Albeit somewhat idealistic, it nonetheless remains an important point to note that media serve several essential roles in a democratic society. Primarily, they are to inform the public in order to provide citizens with the information needed to make decisions about leadership and policy. Media act as checks on government actions, sets the agenda for public discussions, provides a forum for political expression, and facilitates community building in various ways (Owen, 2018; Anderson, 2006).

Optimistically, social media can satisfy the same function as legacy media and media's liberalist ideals. They provide unprecedented access to information and can reach audience members through personalized, interpersonal interactions. Social media platforms allow users and average citizens to participate in political protests and can foster community building that transcend physical boundaries through extensive networking capabilities. And, overall, social media platforms continue the trend of liberal media by seeking to directly engage the public in political activities, such as encouraging others to get out and vote, contacting public officials, volunteering and taking part in protest movement (Owen, 2018).

Arguably, social media platforms intensify the notion of liberal media in the West and are characterized by multi-dimensional systems which incorporates broadcast logics, economies, and are a site where media and cultural practices converge (Jenkins, Ford, & Green, 2013). For example, they are contingent on the U.S. American liberal fantasy of protecting free speech and the press; the rely on the free-market disposition not to regulate forms of expression and channels of political communication; they exist due to the platform's capacities, and frankly, their existential need, to harvest personal data, facilitate sharing, and micro-targeting advertising; and, when used in by political candidates, they heighten the U.S. American tendency to spectacularize a political election with horse-race headlines tactics and click-bait practices that serve to generate revenue for journalistic outlets of all types (Jamieson, 2018). By making it possible for users to not only consume but to also create, share, and comment on content with those in their networked community, platforms revolutionized communication long ago and have had particularly drastic effects on political communication.

SOCIAL REPRODUCTION THROUGH SOCIAL MEDIA

Broadly, social reproduction refers to the processes through which populations reproduce themselves and the material bases of the economy. Importantly, social reproduction is understood as the intergenerational maintenance and reproduction of life and designates the ways in which physical, emotional, and mental labor is necessary for the production of human populations is socially organized (Thorburn, 2017; Bezanson & Luxton, 2006; Federici, 2012). Social reproduction is a site wherein human beings and capital complete the reproduction of living bodies, and in contemporary times, struggles over social reproduction are increasingly channeled through digital networks just as much as they are channeled through embodied, physical practices (Thorburn, 2016; Thorburn, 2017). In the long neoliberal period, Dyer-Witheford (2015) notes that the working-class power and its capacities for resistance have significantly been destabilized. Consequently, human beings have been made more vulnerable to the shifts and swings of the market economy where the capitalist relations of the global South are making a previously stable global North unstable (Dyer-Witheford, 2015; Thorburn, 2017).

Generally defined and described as an on-going relational struggle between waged workers and capitalist owners, capital is a system of social relations engaged in a perpetual process of expansion through formal and real subumption (Thorburn, 2016; Thorburn, 2017). In the process of social reproduction, how this system and its participants are reproduced on a daily and intergenerational basis is an important frame through which to consider processes of accumulation. In analyzing the reproduction of the capitalist system, Marx (1978) notes that capital endeavors simultaneously to reproduce human labor-power alongside the conditions of capitalist social relations. The range of writings on social reproduction is broad but in general theories of social reproduction signify three levels: the reproduction of individual labor power; the reproduction of the total workforce of a given capitalist social formation; the reproduction of the capitalist system itself (Thorburn, 2017).

When it comes to the role social media platforms play in social reproduction, platforms like Facebook, first, outsource and crowdsource the labor of media production through the producer-consumer, a practice of cost reducing that coincides with layoffs in media industries (Deuze, 2007). Along with the aforementioned notion that digital media and social media platforms capitalize on community, communication and cognition (Fuchs, 2017), Terranova (2004) argues that digital media environments function with the same dynamics as contemporary capitalism in which value can be traced to the affective energies of workers and consumers, to the valorization of symbol manipulation and communication in knowledge work.

Huws (2003) notes that the exploitative aspect of unpaid labor in social media derives from the tendency of capital to offload labor costs onto consumers which "burden the consumers of unpaid labor" (p. 69). Smythe's (1981) political economic perspective of television media led to a perspective of drawing consideration to the role of communication into the broader system of social reproduction of capital. In recontextualizing Smythe, Fuchs (2012) argues Facebook represents a means of production, which converts audience labor of lending attention to actually providing information/content to media owners as commodities to be sold to the advertising industry. Since Smythe's analysis concerned media such as TV and radio, the question to ponder now is how the context of online social platforms, characterized by extraordinary levels of participation, through user-generated content, and the ability to create varied channels of communication, allows for the application of audience labor.

In the same vein, Scholz (2011) argues that Facebook yields value through the audience by providing instrumental material and information for advertisers. Fuchs (2012) further argues that the principal source of Facebook's value is communication and sociability, originating from their ability to have access to information, to hoard it, process it, analyze it, and finally, distribute it to its customers. Since the informational content consists of a variety of data: specific demographics, personal information regarding tastes, habits, status; information about the kind of communicative channels users utilize to socialize; performative information about the specific way users socialize (Briziarelli & Karikari, 2016), Facebook provides extraordinary detailed profiles of individuals, localized and networked communities, consequently offering important clues on consumers habits and consumer affective relations (Scholz, 2011).

Secondly, social media platforms valorize audience labor in having the audience provide unpaid services and volunteer work. Scholz (2011) indicates that many Facebook users deliver, voluntarily, their time and energy for usage. Social media platforms at large, however, emphasize the role of the user's digital labor with a focus on ideology. Language, and the affective use of the tools of language, are a central component to the reproduction of social relations that engendered and continuously support the functions of social media platforms and digital capitalism.

For Fuchs (2010), the focus on labor and new media is on what media extract from audiences rather than what media put into messages. Observed from this viewpoint, value from the audience relates to the valorization of user engagement, including, but not limited to communication, in general, on platforms, the construction of community, the production of messages, and content production where "just as industrial capitalism relied on appropriating physical labor, digital communicative or surveillance capitalism thrives on appropriating users' digital labor" (Charitsis, Yngfalk, & Skålén, p. 822).

Precisely, capital accumulation is created by users creating content, establishing and maintaining relations with others, updating their profiles and all of the accumulated time spent on the platforms. Significantly, work time, i.e. actual time that users are on social media platforms, results in a prosumer commodity that is bought and sold to advertisers and is always based on demographic data and interests (Fuchs, 2012). In centering Bourdieu's social, cultural, and symbolic capital, Fuchs argues that the economic value production is connected to digital media use where users employ social media to accumulate social relations (social capital), accumulation of qualification, education and knowledge (cultural capital) and an accumulation of reputation (symbolic capital). This is the kind of informational economy based on affective relations (Arvidsson & Colleoni, 2012), also described by terms such as "Thank you economy," "Social Economy," or the "Gift economy" (Vaynerchuck, 2011).

Another way in which social media platforms reproduce existing social relations is by alienating its workers/users, distancing them from an imaginable awareness of their actual position inside the procedures of valorization. According to Fuchs and Sevignani (2013), users are alienated from themselves because they are coerced to use the platforms by way of peer pressure and a lack of viable alternatives; users are estranged from "the instruments of labor" because they do not own the communication platform itself and because their "brains, hands, mouths, ears and speech, the Internet and platforms" are instrumentalized "for advertising" (p.257 - 258). Furthermore, users are alienated from the "objects of labor"—which the authors identify as shared representations of experiences "through a legally binding agreement" (p. 259). Finally, users are alienated from the product of labor due to the peculiar divide between use-value and exchange-value of symbolic produce online: the "use-values that Facebook users create are at the same time commodities that Facebook offers for sale on a market" (p. 259).

Fuchs and Sevignani (2013) also describe an inverse type of fetishism which portrays how users deny the reifying features in their relationship with Facebook by emphasizing the social gratifications they gain from using the service. In the realm of digital labor, the fetish character of the commodity takes on an inverted form. Consequently, the commodity character of Facebook data is hidden behind the social use-value of Facebook, i.e. the social relations and functions enabled by platform use (Briziarelli & Karikari, 2016). The inverse fetish of Facebook is typically expressed in statements like "Facebook does not exploit me because I benefit from it by connecting to other users." (Briziarelli & Karikari, 2016, p.261).

In sum, social media platforms function as an authoritative re-producer of the essential social relations (i.e. audience's unpaid labor, link to the advertising industry), and more broadly, the necessary ideological and cultural logic of capitalism. As previously mentioned, however, ideology does not simply serve instrumental goals but also link those to more utopic aspirations. Thus, in the next section, the value of affective networks on social media, including the notion of individual freedom and its political value in possible transformation is discussed.

SOCIAL TRANSFORMATION THROUGH POLITICAL TWITTER: THE VALUE OF AFFECTIVE NETWORKS

In its political transformative possibilities, it is important to situate the potential transformative features of social media in their capability to create the very community, communication and cognition that which they capitalize on. Since platforms are seemingly open, users have the ability to create content, organize community, and take advantage of a reality that has not yet been apprehended. In this anticipatory consciousness of the platforms, users are able to perceive the unrealized emancipatory potential in the social media platforms. On the one hand, social media platforms need to be considered an occurrence that additionally justifies, colonizes and commodifies more realms of our lives. On the other, any understanding of a private sphere becomes a commodity that is sold. Consequently, the unpaid and exploited labor of making, producing and creating content establishes an environment that is made to feel like more positive working.

Situated in this work, however, is another potentially transformative feature of the platforms. In their capability to create connectivity, they are able to facilitate the mobilization of people in specific circumstances. Primarily, one of the bases of their political economy is founded on affective relations that allow for exploitation and political utilization.

In the case of Donald Trump during the 2016 election, Trump's use of social media, particularly Twitter, exacerbated the evolution of politicians skirting legacy media to reach potential voters. Though, again, not new, Trump's use of Twitter is particularly striking. For example, Trump performed better in areas the lacked traditional, legacy news outlet (Musgrave & Nussbaum, 2018). In their review of subscription data and election results, Musgrave and Nussbaum show that Trump outperformed the 2012 Republican presidential nominee Mitt Romney in counties with the lowest numbers of new subscribers but did not do particularly well in areas with heavier circulation. By attracting voters in so-called "news deserts" - places with minimal newspaper subscriptions, print or online – Trump hit higher-than-expected numbers. For Trump, the use of his Twitter may not only be "the only way to fight a VERY dishonest and unfair 'press'" (realDonaldTrump, 2017, Dec. 30) but it is an effective tool to promote a compelling and provocative campaign strategy, i.e. – utilizing the affective capabilities within the formation of the networks.

Borrowing from Hardt and Negri (2004), affective media production agrees with the notion that affective and immaterial forms of labor are increasingly a part of the hegemonic sphere of production. While Hardt and Negri speak of the general condition of capital to harness "networks based on communication, collaboration and affective relationships" (2004, p. 66), authors like Jutel (2018) focus on media production. Since Twitter gives Trump the ability to (presumably) construct his own messages, the emergence of mobile devices as the terrain for market expansion transforms traditional content and practice to reflect the affective character of social media from audiences and users. This affective solicitation is not just a strategy to keep up with new media practices but instead represents the perfection of the media's model of audience commodification.

The notion of affective labor, as conceived by both autonomist Marxists and libertarian cyber-utopians, has primarily sought to identify new emancipatory modes of politics emerging through affective media labor. In the affective media theory, networked communication needs to be deemed rhizomatic "upending the ideological divide between individualism and collectivism" (Coleman, 2014, p. 49-50). The rhizome metaphor, taken from Deleuze and Guattari (1987), is where politics is dispersed with no central locus as a flow between bodies with "no beginning or end" (p. 27) and for affective networks to function, there must be creative autonomy from the "mechanism of control [that] contradict the productivity of biopolitcal power" (Hardt & Negri, 2009, p. 144). In many ways, this is a worthy explanation of Donald Trump's ascent to the presidency. Based on the strategies of affective media, his campaign lacked the discipline and the national infrastructure of conventional politics but was instead fueled, and continues to be fueled by, the energy of social media users whose labor overcame a 4-to-1 advertising spending shortfall against Hilary Clinton (Murray, 2016).

Additionally, Dean's (2010) notes that the reading of new subjectivities of neoliberal individualization is one of community without community and whatever critical potential exists, affective media produces a notion of social transformation corresponding to its own logic (Jutel, 2018). And in the case of Donald Trump, one of the more perplexing political potential in affective media is in channeling drive and affect in complex circuits of capital and in creating antagonistic division, which are preconditions for the political. As Dean (2010) notes, affective encounters bind users in circuits of capital and drive to "extend affective networks without encouraging – and indeed, by displacing their consolidation into organized political networks" (p. 42).

Since social media sites offer a promise of de-alienation (Fisher, 2012), social media grant users control of the process of communication, thus self-expression, including crucial identity building aspects. Fisher notes that the paradox of social media like Facebook lie in the fact that the more socially reproductive the higher the potential for de-alienation. Further, there is "an analysis of media as a dynamic site of struggle between audience (labor) and media providers (capital), a struggle that revolves on time (Fisher, 2012, p. 172). Social media platforms reproduce the ambivalences of a productive activity that, in the 21st century capitalism, involves a "complex reality in which extraction of labor value and a degree of self-realization" are combined in a complex, intricate, and expansive network all buttressed by a liberal ideology.

Since Donald Trump's political possibilities were heavily reliant on the use of social media, social media in this instance mediate not only the ideals of liberal media and liberal ideology, but simultaneously function to reproduce existing social structures and transform the political landscape. In other words, Trump's political positionality as a far-right conservative, anti-globalist not only contradicts the notions of a utopia undergirded by a technological structure but fundamentally rely upon the contradictions which social media rely upon: the notions of a public sphere being resurrected in order to skirt "legacy and traditional media" while functioning to serve the interests of capital, specifically, digital capitalism. The progressive notion of using technology in order to bring about social change, as noted above, has already been questioned and scrutinized. Understanding the complicated relationship that social media has with commodification and its political potential has long been a driving force behind research. In the particular instance of Donald Trump, and in his strategic use of data and data specific advertising, the combination of user labor, distributed media, digital technologies, and the role of media continue to manifest in multifaceted and complex ways.

CONCLUSION

Following the 2016 election, social media has (again) taken center stage in the debate about its use and implications in the political process. As argued above, every (new) communication technology brings with it a dual nature of optimism and pessimism that pushes the possibilities of both commodification and in the potential political reach and influence in social and political organization.

Through the approach of this paper that forefronts a materialist perspective, social media's capability of producing social change is both enabled through the (apparent) possibilities of the platforms and constrained through the social relations in which the platforms operate. Thus, the possibilities brought on by social media are heavily shaped by political and economic interests and also by the persistence in the cultural and social life of powerful utopic/dystopic accounts. In the powerful narratives of utopic and dystopic potentialities, it is important to recognize that human agency must be accounted for. Not only are social relations exclusively produced by people partaking in everyday life activities, but the relationship between social media and (platform) capitalism will continue to crystallize in institutions such as the market, the law, the state and notions of liberal ideology and democracy will all be affected by the affective media industries.

The consideration of language and communication technology as part of the means of production in the social construction of meaning is significant because it relies on recognizing that language and communication technology are intrinsic to all forms of labor and social organizational patterns that constitute essential elements of the productive force, and the social relations of production. Crucially, this outlook underscores the historical significance of language and its relationship with communication technology and media, especially in its evolutionary forms. In an era of digital and communicative capitalism, this relationship is emphasized in its importance.

Further, with the current age of media operating as a key element and main constituent of contemporary economies, digital technologies, and digital media, have had, and continue to have, profound impacts on the possibilities of political communication. Donald Trump's use of Twitter during the 2016 presidential election in the United States exacerbates and intensifies the ideological underpinnings that propel the ability to mediate multiple messages in the social media landscape. Within this digital media environment, social media platforms utilize the affective energy of users and the valorization of symbol manipulation and communication to greatly intensify capitalism's ability to colonize new spheres of life via the ability to capitalize on a variety of data and data collection practices.

In conclusion, social media platforms function as an authoritative reproducer of the essential social relations through necessary ideological and cultural logics of capitalism. In a political communicative context, such as the one evaluated here, the ability to capitalize on affective media production speaks to condition of capital to harness the networks of computer networks and the (social) networks of user networks.

REFERENCES

Adolph, M. (2017). The identity of mediatization: Theorizing a dynamic field. In O. Driessens, G. Bolin, A. Hepp, & S. Hjarvard (Eds.), *Dynamics of mediatization: Institutional change and everyday transformations in a digital age* (pp. 11–33). London, UK: Palgrave. doi:10.1007/978-3-319-62983-4_2

Anderson, B. (2006). *Imagined Communities*. London, UK: Verso.

Andrejevic, M. (2013). Whither-ing critique. *Communication and Critical/Cultural Studies*, *10*(2-3), 222–228. doi:10.1080/14791420.2013.812592

Aouragh, M. (2012). Social Media, Mediation and the Arab Revolutions. *TripleC*, *10*(2), 518–536. doi:10.31269/triplec.v10i2.416

Armbrust, W. (2007). New Media and Old Agendas: The Internet in the Middle East and Middle Eastern Studies. *International Journal of Middle East Studies*, *39*(4), 531–533. doi:10.1017/S0020743807071048

Arvidsson, A., & Colleoni, E. (2012). Value in informational capitalism and on the internet. *The Information Society: An International Journal*, *28*(3), 135–150. doi: 10.1080/01972243.2012.669449

Banning, M. E. (2016). Shared entanglements – Web 2.0, info-liberalism & digital sharing. *Information Communication and Society*, *19*(4), 489–503. doi:10.1080/1369118X.2015.1061573

Barberá, P., Jost, J. T., Nagler, J., Tucker, J. A., & Bonneau, R. (2015). Tweeting from left to right is online political communication more than an echo chamber? *Psychological Science*, *26*(10), 531–1542. doi:10.1177/0956797615594620 PMID:26297377

Baudrillard, J. (1988). *Jean Baudrillard, Selected Writings*. Stanford, CA: Stanford University Press.

Bechmann, A. (2012). Towards Cross-Platform Value Creation. *Information Communication and Society*, *15*(6), 888–908. doi:10.1080/1369118X.2012.680483

Beer, D. (2009). Power through the algorithm? Participatory web cultures and the technological unconscious. *New Media & Society*, *11*(6), 985–1002. doi:10.1177/1461444809336551

Bell, D. (2014). What Is Liberalism? *Political Theory*, *42*(6), 682–715. doi:10.1177/0090591714535103

Benson, R., Blach-Orsten, M., Powers, M., Willig, I., & Zambrano, S. V. (2012). Media systems online and off: Comparing the form of news in the United States, Denmark, and France. *Journal of Communication*, *62*(1), 21–38. doi:10.1111/j.1460-2466.2011.01625.x

Berardi, F. (2009). The Soul at Work: From Alienation to Autonomy. Translated by F. Cadel and G. Mecchia, with preface by J. E. Smith. Los Angeles, CA: Semiotext(e).

Berry, D. (2014). *Critical Theory and the Digital*. New York, NY: Bloomsbury Academic.

Bezanson, K., & Luxton, M. (2006). *Social Reproduction: Feminist Political Economy Challenges Neoliberalism*. Montreal, Canada: McGill Queen's University Press.

Blankenship, C. (2019). President, Wrestler, Spectacle: An Examination of Donald Trump's Firing Tweets and The Celebrity Appresident as Response to Trump's Media Landscape. *The Journal of Communication Inquiry*. doi:10.1177/0196859919833785

Bloch, E. (1986). *The principle of hope*. Cambridge, MA: The MIT Press.

Boyd, D. (2010). "Social network sites as networked publics: Affordances, dynamics, and implications." In N. Papacharissi (Ed.), *Networked Self: Identity, Community, and Culture on Social Network Sites* (pp. 39-58). New York, NY: Routledge.

Briggs, A., & Burke, P. (2005). *A Social History of Media From Gutenberg to the Internet*. Cambridge, MA: Polity Press.

Briziarelli, M. (2014). The Ideological Reproduction: (Social) Working and Laboring in Digital Landscapes. *TripleC, 12*(2), 1–21. doi:10.31269/triplec.v12i2.537

Briziarelli, M., & Karikari, E. (2016). Mediating Social Media's Ambivalences in the Context of Informational Capitalism. *International Journal of Civic Engagement and Social Change, 3*(1), 1–22. doi:10.4018/IJCESC.2016010101

Caiani, M., & Kröll, P. (2015). The transnationalization of the extreme right and the use of the Internet. *International Journal of Comparative and Applied Criminal Justice, 39*(4), 331–351. doi:10.1080/01924036.2014.973050

Caiani, M., & Parenti, L. (2013). *European and American extreme right groups and the Internet*. London, UK: Routledge.

Castells, M. (2008). The New Public Sphere: Global Civil Society, Communication Networks, and Global Governance. *The Annals of the American Academy of Political and Social Science, 616*(1), 78–93. doi:10.1177/0002716207311877

Chadwick, A. (2017). *The hybrid media system: Politics and power*. Oxford, UK: Oxford University Press. doi:10.1093/oso/9780190696726.001.0001

Charitsis, V., Yngfalk, A. F., & Skålén, P. (2018). "Made to Run": Biopolitical Marketing and the Making of the Self-Quantified Runner. *Marketing Theory*. Published online. Accessed September 24, 2018. doi:10.1177/1470593118799794

Cohen, N. (2008). The valorization of surveillance: Towards a political economy of Facebook. *Democratic Communiqué, 22*(1), 5–22.

Corner, J. (2018). *'Mediatization': Media theory's word of the decade. Media Theory*, May 21. Available at http://mediatheoryjournal.org/john-corner-mediatization/

Couldry, N., & Hepp, A. (2013). Conceptualizing Mediatization: Contexts, Traditions, Arguments. *Communication Theory, 23*(3), 191–202. doi:10.1111/comt.12019

de Saint Simon, H. (1964). *Social organization, the science of man and other writings*. New York, NY: Harper & Row.

Dean, J. (2009). *Democracy and other neoliberal fantasies: Communicative capitalism and left politics*. Durham, NC: Duke University Press. doi:10.1215/9780822390923

Dean, J. (2010). Affective networks. *Media Tropes, 2*(2), 19–44.

Dean, J. (2014). Communicative Capitalism: This Is What Democracy Looks like. In J. S. Hanan, & M. Hayward (Eds.), *Communication and the Economy: History, Value, and Agency* (pp. 147–164). New York, NY: Peter Lang.

Deibert, R. (1997). *Parchment, Printing, and Hypermedia: Communication in World Order Transformation*. New York, NY: Columbia University Press.

Deleuze, G., & Guattari, F. (1987). *A Thousand Plateaus* (B. Masummi, Trans.). Minneapolis, MN: Minnesota University Press.

Deuze, M. (2003). The web and its journalisms: Considering the consequences of different types of news media online. *New Media & Society*, *5*(2), 203–230. doi:10.1177/1461444803005002004

Deuze, M. (2007). Toward an ethics of the sociable web: A conversation between Trebor Scholz and Mark Deuze. Retrieved from http://mailman.thing.net/pipermail/idc/2007-July/002652.html

Dyer-Witheford, N. (2015). *Cyber-Proletariat: Global Labour in the Digital Vortex*. London, UK: Pluto Press. doi:10.2307/j.ctt183p1zg

Eagleton, T. (1976). *Marxism and Literary Criticism*. Berkeley, CA: University of California Press.

Eagleton, T. (2007). *Ideology: An Introduction* (2nd ed.). New York, NY: Verso.

Entman, R., & Usher, N. (2018). Framing in a Fractured Democracy: Impacts of Digital Technology on Ideology, Power and Cascading Network Activation. *Journal of Communication*, *68*(2), 298–308. doi:10.1093/joc/jqx019

Etling, B., Faris, R., & Palfrey, J. (2010). Political change in the digital age: The fragility and promise of online organizing. *SAIS Review (Paul H. Nitze School of Advanced International Studies)*, *30*(2), 37–49.

Federici, S. (2012). *Revolution at Point Zero: Housework, Reproduction, and Feminist Struggle*. Oakland, CA: PM Press.

Fisher, E. (2012). How less alienation creates more exploitation? Audience labor on social network sites. *TripleC*, *10*(2), 171–183. doi:10.31269/triplec.v10i2.392

Fourier, C. (1971). *Design for Utopia: Selected Writings. Studies in the Libertarian and Utopian Tradition*. New York, NY: Schocken.

Fraser, N. (1990). Rethinking the public sphere: A contribution to the critique of actually existing democracy. *Social Text*, *25*(26), 56–80. doi:10.2307/466240

Froio, C., & Gattinara, P. C. (2015). Neo-fascist mobilization in contemporary Italy. Ideology and repertoire of action of CasaPound Italia. *Journal of Deradicalization*, *15*(2), 86–118.

Fuchs, C. (2010). Labor in Informational Capitalism and on the Internet. *The Information Society: An International Journal*, *26*(3), 179–196. doi:10.1080/01972241003712215

Fuchs, C. (2012). With or without Marx? With or without Capitalism? A rejoinder to Adam Arvidsson and Eleanor Colleoni. *TripleC*, *10*(2), 1–12. doi:10.31269/triplec.v10i2.434

Fuchs, C. (2015). *Culture and Economy in the Age of Social Media*. Abingdon, UK: Routledge Publishing. doi:10.4324/9781315733517

Fuchs, C. (2016). Critical Theory of Communication: New Readings of Lukács, Adorno, Marcuse, Honneth and Habermas in the Age of the Internet. London, UK: University of Westminster Press

Fuchs, C. (2017). *Social Media: A Critical Introduction* (2nd ed.). Thousand Oaks, CA: Sage.

Fuchs, C. (2018). Propaganda 2.0: Herman and Chomsky's Propaganda Model in the Age of the Internet, Big Data and Social Media. In J. Pedro-Carañana, D. Broudy, & J. Klaehn (Eds.), *The Propaganda Model Today: Filtering Perception and Awareness* (pp. 71–92). London, UK: University of Westminster Press. doi:10.16997/book27.f

Fuchs, C. (2018b). *Digital Demagogue: Authoritarian Capitalism in the Age of Trump and Twitter*. London, UK: Pluto. doi:10.2307/j.ctt21215dw

Fuchs, C., & Mosco, V. (Eds.). (2016). *Marx in the Age of Digital Capitalism*. Leiden, The Netherlands: Brill Publishers. doi:10.1163/9789004291393

Fuchs, C., & Sevignani, S. (2013). What is digital labor? What is digital work? What's their difference? And why do these questions matter for understanding social media? *TripleC*, *11*(2), 237–293. doi:10.31269/triplec.v11i2.461

Galloway, A. (2004). *Protocol: How Control Exists After Decentralization*. Cambridge, MA: The MIT Press. doi:10.7551/mitpress/5658.001.0001

Gendron, B. (1977). *Technology and the human condition*. New York, NY: St. Martin's Press.

Giglietto, F., & Selva, D. (2014). Second screen and participation: A content analysis on a full season dataset of Tweets. *Journal of Communication*, *64*(2), 260–277. doi:10.1111/jcom.12085

Gregg, M. (2011). *Work's Intimacy*. Cambridge, MA: Polity Press.

Guess, A., Lyons, B., Montgomery, J. M., Nyham, B., & Reifler, J. (2019). *Fake news, Facebook ads, and misperceptions: Assessing information quality in the 2018 U.S. midterm election campaign*. Retrieved from http://www.dartmouth.edu/~nyhan/fake-news-2018.pdf

Guess, A., Nyhan, B., & Reifler, J. (2018). *Selective Exposure to Misinformation: Evidence from the consumption of fake news during the 2016 U.S. presidential campaign*. Retrieved from http://www.dartmouth.edu/~nyhan/fake-news-2016.pdf

Habermas, J. (1991). *The structural transformation of the public sphere: An inquiry into category of bourgeois society*. Cambridge, MA: The MIT Press.

Hallin, D., & Manchini, P. (2004). *Comparing Media Systems*. Cambridge, MA: Cambridge University Press. doi:10.1017/CBO9780511790867

Haraway, D. (1991). A Cyborg Manifesto: Science, Technology, and Socialist-Feminism in the Late Twentieth Century. In *Simians, Cyborgs and Women: The Reinvention of Nature* (pp. 149–181). New York, NY: Routledge.

Hardt, M., & Negri, A. (2000). *Empire*. Cambridge, MA: Harvard.

Hardt, M., & Negri, A. (2004). *Multitude: War and Democracy in the Age of Empire*. London, UK: Penguin Books.

Hardt, M., & Negri, A. (2009). *Commonwealth*. Cambridge, MA: Harvard. doi:10.2307/j.ctvjsf48h

Hjarvard, S. (2008). The Mediatization of Religion: A Theory of the Media as Agents of Religious Change. In *Northern Lights 2008, Yearbook of Film & Media Studies* (p. 7). Bristol: Intellect Press. doi:10.1386/nl.6.1.9_1

Horkheimer, M., & Adorno, T. (1974). *The Dialectics of enlightenment*. London, UK: Verso.

Huws, U. (2003). *The making of a cybertariat: Virtual work in a real world*. New York, NY: Monthly Review Press.

Huws, U. (2014). *Labor in the Global Digital Economy*. New York, NY: Monthly Review Press.

Jacobs, N. (1992). *Mass media in modern society*. New Brunswick, NJ: Transaction Publishers.

Jamieson, K. H. (2018). *Cyberwar: How Russian Hackers and Trolls Helped Elect a President – What We Don't, Can't, and Do Know*. New York, NY: Oxford University Press.

Jenkins, H., Ford, S., & Green, J. (2013). *Spreadable media: Creating value and meaning in networked culture*. New York, NY: NYU Press.

Jones, R. H., Chik, A., & Hafner, C. A. (Eds.). (2015). *Discourse and digital practices: Doing discourse in the digital age*. London, UK: Routledge. doi:10.4324/9781315726465

Joyce, S. (2018). *Transmedia Storytelling and the Apocalypse*. Basingstoke, UK: Palgrave MacMillan. doi:10.1007/978-3-319-93952-0

Jutel, O. (2018). American populism, Glenn Beck and affective media production. *International Journal of Cultural Studies*, *21*(4), 375–392. doi:10.1177/1367877916688273

Kang, H., & McAllister, M. (2011). Selling you and your clicks: Examining the audience commodification of Google. *TripleC*, *9*(2), 141–153. doi:10.31269/triplec.v9i2.255

Kleiner, D. (2010). *The Telekommunist Manifesto*. Amsterdam, The Netherlands: Institute of Network Cultures.

Knoche, M. (2015). The Media Industry's Structural Transformation in Capitalism and the Role of the State: Media Economics in the Age of Digital Communications. *TripleC*, *14*(1), 18–47. doi:10.31269/triplec.v14i1.730

Krotz, F. (2008). Media Connectivity: Concepts, Conditions, and Consequences. In A. Hepp, F. Krotz, & S. Moores (Eds.), *Connectivity, Networks and Flows: Conceptualizing Contemporary*. New York, NY: Hampton Press.

Laer, J. V., & Aelst, P. V. (2010). Internet and social movement action repertoires. *Information Communication and Society*, *13*(8), 1146–1171. doi:10.1080/13691181003628307

Lang, K., & Lang, G. E. (2009). Mass Society, Mass Culture, and Mass Communication: The Meanings of Mass. *International Journal of Communication*, *3*(20), 998–1024.

Lazzarato, M. (1996). *Immaterial labor. In radical thought in Italy: A potential politics*. Minneapolis, MN: University of Minnesota Press.

Lazzarato, M. (2006). *The Machine*. European Institute for Progressive Cultural Politics. October. Retrieved from http://eipcp.net/transversal/1106/lazzarato/en

Lazzarato, M. (2009). Neoliberalism in Action: Inequality. *Insecurity and the Reconstruction of the Social*, *26*(6), 109–133. doi:10.1177/0263276409350283

Lee, M. (2011). Google ads and the blindspot debate. *Media Culture & Society, 33*(3), 433–447. doi:10.1177/0163443710394902

Lee, P. S. N., So, C. Y. K., Lee, F., Leung, L., & Chan, M. (2018). Social media and political partisanship – A subaltern public sphere's role in democracy. *Telematics and Informatics, 35*(7), 1949–1975. doi:10.1016/j.tele.2018.06.007

Livingstone, S. (2009). On the mediation of everything. ICA Presidential address 2008. *Journal of Communication, 59*(1), 1–18. doi:10.1111/j.1460-2466.2008.01401.x

Lund, A. (2014). Playing, Gaming, Working and laboring: Framing the concepts and relations. *TripleC, 12*(2), 735–801. doi:10.31269/triplec.v12i2.536

Maly, I. (2019). New Right Metapolitics and the Algorithmic Activism of Schild & Vrienden. *Social Media + Society,* 1-15. doi/ doi:10.1177/2056305119856700

Manzerolle, V., & Kjosen, A. (2015). Digital Media and Capital's Logic of Acceleration. In C. Fuchs, & V. Mosco (Eds.), Marx in the Age of Digital Capitalism (151-179). Boston, MA: Brill.

Marx, K. (1867). Capital: A critique of political economy.: Vol. 1. *(B. Fowkes, Trans.)* London, UK: Penguin Classics.

Marx, K. (1978). Capital: Volume Two. (D. Fernbach, Trans.) London, UK: Penguin Books, Harmondsworth, in association with New Left Review.

Marx, K., & Engels, F. (2001). *The German ideology Part One*. New York, NY: International.

McGuigan, J. (2014). *Raymond Williams on Culture & Society: Essential Writings*. Thousand Oaks, CA: Sage. doi:10.4135/9781473914766

McStay, A. (2011). Profiling phorm: An autopoietic approach to the audience-as-commodity. *Surveillance & Society, 8*(3), 310–322. doi:10.24908s.v8i3.4166

Mosco, V. (2005). *The digital sublime - myth, power, and cyberspace*. Cambridge, MA: The MIT Press.

Moy, P., Xenos, M. A., & Hess, V. K. (2005). Communication and Citizenship: Mapping the Political Effects of Infotainment. *Mass Communication & Society, 8*(2), 111–131. doi:10.120715327825mcs0802_3

Murray, M. (2016). *Clinton maintains ad spending advantage over Trump*. NBC, October 4. Available at http://www.nbcnews.com/politics/2016-election/clinton-maintains-ad-spending-advantage-over-trump-n659331?cid=smtw

Musgrave, S., & Nussbaum, M. (2018, April 4). *Trump thrives in areas that lack traditional news outlets Relentless use of social media and partisan outlets helped him swamp Clinton and exceed Romney's performance in places lacking trusted local news media*. Retrieved from https://www.politico.com/story/2018/04/08/news-subscriptions-decline-donald-trump-voters-505605

Negt, O., & Kluge, A. (1993). *Bourgeois and proletarian public sphere*. Minneapolis, MN: University of Minnesota Press.

Nixon, B. (2011). Dialectical method and the critical political economy of culture. *TripleC*, *10*(2), 439–456. doi:10.31269/triplec.v10i2.371

Oswald, K. (2009). Mass Media and the Transformation of American Politics. *Marquette Law Review*, *77*(2), 385–414.

Owen, D. (2018). The New Media's Role in Politics, In BBVA Open Mind, *The Age of Perplexity: Rethinking the World We Knew.*

Owen, R. (1995). *A new view of society and other writings*. New York, NY: Penguin.

Pedro-Carañana, J., Broudy, D., & Klaehn, J. (2018). *The Propaganda Model Today: Filtering Perception and Awareness*. London, UK: University of Westminster Press. doi:10.16997/book27

Peters, B. (2009). And lead us not into thinking the new is new: A bibliographic case for new media history. *New Media & Society*, *11*(1&2), 13–30. doi:10.1177/1461444808099572

Peters, J. (1999). *Speaking into the air: A history of the idea of communication*. Chicago, IL: University of Chicago Press. doi:10.7208/chicago/9780226922638.001.0001

Rey, P. J. (2012). Alienation, exploitation, and social media. *The American Behavioral Scientist*, *56*(4), 399–420. doi:10.1177/0002764211429367

Ritzer, G. (2015). Prosumer Capitalism. *The Sociological Quarterly*, *56*(3), 413–445. doi:10.1111/tsq.12105

Rosenblatt, J. P. (2011). *Milton's selected poetry and prose: authoritative texts, biblical sources, criticism*. New York, NY: W.W. Norton & Co.

Scholz, T. (2011). Facebook as Playground and Factory. In D. E. Wittkower (Ed.), Facebook and Philosophy, 241–252. Chicago, IL: Open Court.

Singer, B. D. (1973). Mass society, mass media and the transformation of minority identity. *The British Journal of Sociology*, *24*(2), 140–150. doi:10.2307/588374

Smythe, D. (1981). *Dependency road: Communication, Capitalism, Consciousness, and Canada*. Santa Barbara, CA: Praegar Publishing.

Srnicek, N. (2017). *Platform Capitalism*. Cambridge, UK: Polity Publishing.

Stalder, F., & Sützl, W. (2011). Ethics of sharing. *International Review of Information Ethics, 15*, 2–3. Retrieved from http://www.i-r-i-e.net/inhalt/015/015_full.pdf

Sunstein, C. (2018). *Republic: Divided Democracy in the Age of Social Media*. Princeton, NJ: Princeton University Press.

Tay, J., & Turner, G. (2010). Not the Apocalypse: Television Futures in the Digital Age. *International Journal of Digital Television, 1*(1), 31–50. doi:10.1386/jdtv.1.1.31/1

Terranova, T. (2004). *Network culture: Politics for the information age*. London, UK: Pluto Press.

Thorburn, E. D. (2016). Networked Social Reproduction: Crises in the Integrated Circuit. *TripleC, 14*(2), 380–396. doi:10.31269/triplec.v14i2.708

Thorburn, E. D. (2017). Social Reproduction in the Live Stream. *TripleC, 15*(2), 423–440. doi:10.31269/triplec.v15i2.774

Turner, J. (2019). Death By A Thousand Hyperlinks: The Commodification of Communication and Mediated Ideologies. In C. Battista, & M. Sande (Eds.), *Critical Theory and the Humanities in the Age of the Alt-Right* (pp. 173–192). London, UK: Palgrave Macmillan. doi:10.1007/978-3-030-18753-8_10

Ulrich, B. (2009). Historicizing Arab Blogs: Reflections on the Transmission of Ideas and Information in Middle Eastern History. *Arab Media & Society*, 8. Retrieved from http://www.arabmediasociety.com/?article=711

Varis, P., & Hou, M. (2019). Digital approaches in linguistic ethnography. In K. Tusting (Ed.), *The Routledge handbook of linguistic ethnography*. Abingdon, UK: Routledge. doi:10.4324/9781315675824-17

Vaynerchuck, G. (2011). *The Thank You Economy*. New York, NY: HarperBusiness.

Williams, B. A., & Delli Carpini, M. X. (2011). *After Broadcast News*. New York, NY: Cambridge University Press. doi:10.1017/CBO9780511846366

Wittel, A. (2016). Digital Marx: Toward a Political Economy of Distributed Media. In C. Fuchs, & V. Mosco (Eds.), *Marx in the Age of Digital Capitalism* (pp. 68–105). Leiden, The Netherlands: Brill Publishers. doi:10.1163/9789004291393_004

Zuboff, S. (2015). Big Other: Surveillance Capitalism and the Prospects of an Information Civilization. *Journal of Information Technology*, *30*(1), 75–89. doi:10.1057/jit.2015.5

KEY TERMS AND DEFINITIONS

Audience Labor: A political economic perspective that deliberates and contemplates audience as a fundamental productive feature in the media business model.

Digital Things: The technological, material, components of distributed media, i.e. cell phones, computers, hardware components.

Distributed Media: Contrary to mass media, distributed media is a way to conceptualize the social organization of media content production.

Ideology: An outlook/worldview (such as liberal/fascist ideology) that performs as a mediating and reproductive strength of a certain set of social relations.

Labor: A historically specific kind of work stemming from an extremely advanced social organization of production, producing specific kinds of social relations. It is coercive and exploitative.

Mediation: Simultaneously a concrete and conceptual way to talk about mediated communication.

Political Economy of Media: The study of the social relations, particularly the power relations, which mutually constitute the production, distribution, and consumption of resources, including communication resources.

Prod-User: The user operating in the web 2.0 environment and blurs the margins between the production and consumption of media material.

Social Media: Web-based multimedia production and distribution tools incorporating text audio, photo, and video, capabilities, which are characterized by allowing users to create and share content or to partake in social networking.

Social Reproduction: A process that tends to meaningfully reproduce a given set of social relations.

Social Transformation: A process that tends to meaningfully change a specified set of social relations.

Technological Utopia: The particular modern ideology assuming that the progress of science and technology will ultimately accomplish an ideal society in which human scarcity, sufferance and mortality are overcome.

Work: A basic anthropological requirement; leads human beings to act upon nature to produce and make material products necessary for survival. Also, it is a practical and creative activity that permits people to express themselves through objects.

Chapter 3
ICT and Transmedia Storytelling for Democratic Development in the Russian Political Landscape

Renira Rampazzo Gambarato
https://orcid.org/0000-0001-7631-6608
Jönköping University, Sweden

Sergey Medvedev
Technological University Dublin, Ireland

ABSTRACT

This chapter discusses the implementation of information and communication technology (ICT) and transmedia storytelling in Alexey Navalny's political campaign during the 2013 Moscow mayoral election in Russia. The aim is to analyze how the use of ICT across multiple media platforms contributed to the development of democratic practices in the Russian political landscape. Navalny's westernized, bottom-up political campaign was innovative in the country because it involved novel manners of engaging the public via online fundraising, door-to-door canvassing, engagement of volunteers, digital projects, and meetings with voters, for instance, which were not common practices at the time in Russia. Although Navalny lost the election, his candidacy represented advancement in terms of the use of ICT and transmedia storytelling to promote democratic development in the midst of autocratic Russia. If the democratic progress in the country will be maintained, it remains to be seen. The methodological approach is based on the transmedia analytical model developed by Gambarato (2013).

DOI: 10.4018/978-1-7998-1791-8.ch003

Copyright © 2020, IGI Global. Copying or distributing in print or electronic forms without written permission of IGI Global is prohibited.

INTRODUCTION

For several years, the mayoral elections in Moscow were deliberately cancelled, and the mayor was directly appointed by the Kremlin (Indina, 2014). However, the 2013 Moscow mayoral election was shaken by the opposition candidate Alexey Navalny and his westernized, grassroots political campaign. Navalny is a lawyer, whistle-blower, and staunch activist fighting against endemic corruption in Russia. In 2010, his anti-corruption blog posts (Navalny, n.d.) and website (RosPil, 2014) became digital phenomena. Since then, he has become a protagonist in Russian politics. His 2013 campaign was replete with innovations in the Russian context, such as online fundraising, door-to-door canvassing, engagement of volunteers, digital projects, and meetings with voters, for instance. Although he lost the election, his candidacy represented advancement in terms of both the use of new media and the promotion of democratic practices in the midst of autocratic Russia. Considering that Navalny almost succeeded in challenging the Kremlin candidate, the campaign destroyed the myth that the current government would always win, even in a fair election. The chapter's goal is to analyze the transmedia strategies (Gambarato & Alzamora, 2018) of Navalny's campaign in order to highlight how the use of information and communication technology (ICT) concretely contributed to the democratic development in Russia (Gambarato & Lapina-Kratasyuk, 2016; Gambarato, 2018).

The 2013 Moscow mayoral election was the very first social media election in Russia, and its roots can be traced to the 2011–2012 opposition movement. Navalny's campaign was an extension and consequence of this movement, which involved fundraising for rallies and the creation of Facebook groups aiming at gathering people offline during the opposition protests, among others. In the summer of 2013, Navalny started campaigning using techniques that were new and even unknown in Russia, including ICT solutions such as online fundraising. Online tools were primarily created to pave an easier path for Navalny's supporters to become volunteers and spread the word about his political proposals, democratizing access to information. As the opposition candidate, he had limited access to mainstream media, especially television; therefore, the online campaign and its consequent expansion into offline activities were the alternative channel to reach the public in a legitimate, democratic manner.

In the context of the 2013 Moscow mayoral election, Russian political landscape played a leading role. Thus, this chapter first briefly introduces the Russian electoral system and explains the rise of Navalny. The theoretical framework explores the conceptualization of transmedia storytelling (Freeman & Gambarato, 2018) in the context of participatory politics and the methodological approach, based on the transmedia analytical model by Gambarato (2013), is presented and applied to Navalny's grassroots campaign, demonstrating how it incorporates ICT solutions in a transmedial way. Later the chapter discusses the westernized political campaign and its implications for democratic development in Russia. In conclusion, the findings of the research indicate that: 1) the campaign concretely employed transmedia strategies; and 2) transmedia tools, together with the innovative digital technologies incorporated by Navalny's campaign, contributed to engage audiences, democratize information, democratize access to capital, and amplify freedom of expression, especially throughout participation. Participatory culture and politics lead to the possibility of individuals to exert their voice and democratically influence on the society.

CONSIDERATIONS ON RUSSIAN POLITICAL LANDSCAPE

Russian Federation Electoral System

According to the Constitution of the Russian Federation (Chapter 1, Article 3), citizens shall be the bearers of sovereignty and the only source of power in the country: "The supreme direct expression of the power of the people shall be referenda and free elections" (Government of the Russian Federation, 1993). Since the Russian Federation had been formed from the ruins of the Soviet Union in 1991, citizens could elect the president of the country, bicameral parliament members, governors of provinces, and mayors of cities.

Nevertheless, during the mandates of Vladimir Putin as president (2000–2008), the number of elective offices started to be systematically reduced. In 2000, the direct elections for the Federation Council, the upper house of the Russian parliament, were repealed. Instead, Federation Council members were appointed by governors; in 2004, the gubernatorial direct elections were repealed as well. In 2005, the mixed-member proportional representation for the State Duma, the lower house of the Russian parliament, was replaced by proportional representation, which means that only the representatives of registered political parties were allowed to claim the seats in the lower house. Electoral districts were abolished. Thus, independent local representatives were expelled from both houses of the parliament. Although mayors are still elected by universal suffrage in the majority of Russian cities, since May 2014 city councils are authorized to revoke direct mayoral elections.

Chapter 3, Article 65 of the constitution states that Moscow and St. Petersburg are the "cities of federal importance" and have the status of provinces (Government of the Russian Federation, 1993). It means that the head of Moscow, who is still called mayor, is a governor in legal contemplation. Since the direct gubernatorial elections were repealed in Russia in 2004, Moscow and St. Petersburg became the only Russian cities where people could not elect mayors.

During the 2011 State Duma elections, multiple electoral violations were detected by independent observers. Consequently, Russia was shaken by waves of anti-government protests throughout the country. Around 100,000 Muscovites marched on the Moscow streets ("First We Take Sakharov Avenue," 2011). The unexpected rise of the opposition movement forced the Kremlin to search for ways of compromising with the society. As a result, in 2012, President Dmitri Medvedev, Putin's one-term heir, reinstated the direct gubernatorial elections (Roth, 2012). It was the first time in eight years that Moscow acquired the right to elect its head.

At that time, Sergei Sobyanin had been the assigned mayor of Moscow. On June 7, 2013, he announced his willingness to hold a snap mayoral election in the city. Although he technically vacated the seat to file his candidacy, he continued performing his mayoral duties until the day of the election on September 8, 2013 (Weaver & Clover, 2013). As Sobyanin publicly declared, his decision to hold the snap election was motivated by public demand ("Otstavka Sobyanina," 2013). However, as Russian political expert Dmitry Oreshkin noted, the Kremlin's willingness to reassign Sobyanin as the mayor of Moscow as soon as possible might have been provoked by the government's anticipation of the further decline of its popularity in the rebelling city (Krutov, 2013). Julian G. Waller interprets this as an attempt to 'tap into legitimacy as the new basis for political agency and self-promotion' (2013, p.6)'. Moreover, a substantial segment of Moscow citizens, especially the public sector workers, was still expected to vote for the current government as usual. Thus, Sobyanin was extremely confident that he would win the snap election in the first round. However, his certitude was challenged by the anti-corruption activist Alexey Navalny, who decided to run in the 2013 Moscow mayoral election as the opposition candidate. Analyst Denis Volkov commented that "authorities allowed Navalny to run against Putin-backed incumbent Sergei Sobyanin because he was not seen as a threat at the time" and "the authorities were not ready for him to be so effective" (Kovalyova & Smith, 2013, para. 7).

2011–2012 Opposition Movement in Russia and the Rise of Alexey Navalny

Born in 1976, Alexey Navalny is also the founder of The Anti-Corruption Foundation. In 2010, he launched the anti-corruption website *RosPil* (2014) and became prominent as an opposition blogger. On the pages of his *LiveJournal* blog (Navalny, n.d.), websites (Navalny, 2014), and social media profiles, Navalny exposes corruption in the Russian government, parliament, and state-controlled corporations (Yale World Fellows, n.d.). His foundation investigates parliament members' ownership of undeclared properties and assets in the US, as well as the illegal enrichment of President Putin's Ozero (Lake) cooperative friends. Navalny's incriminations were taken with great interest and supported by his Internet audience. Within a few months, Navalny's meme referring to the "party of crooks and thieves" became a common description of Putin's United Russia party. Nevertheless, it took some time before the popular blogger turned into a well-known Russian politician. Navalny took his first confident steps toward this status on the Moscow streets during the 2011–2012 anti-government protests.

The 2011–2012 protest movement began as a response to vote rigging during the 2011 Russian legislative election. The day after the election, on December 5, 2011, thousands of demonstrators, angry over ballot stuffing and falsifications, stood on Chistye Prudy Boulevard in protest against electoral fraud (Zotova & Feldman, 2011). Never before during Putin's era had thousands of people participated in anti-government demonstrations. Inspired by the success of the Chistye Prudy rally, people started self-organizing in social media networks, in which tens of thousands then demonstrated their willingness to attend the planned protest on December 10, 2011. Over 50,000 people participated in the rally, as claimed by the opposition on the day of the event. The rally targeted Prime Minister Vladimir Putin and his United Russia ruling party. During the demonstration, the crowd was chanting "Putin is a thief!", "No to police state!", "Russia without Putin!", "Freedom to political prisoners!", and "This is our city!" An even larger crowd of approximately 100,000 attended the For Fair Elections rally on December 24, 2011 ("First We Take Sakharov Avenue," 2011).

After the very first remarkable protest that occurred on Chistye Prudy Boulevard, Navalny was detained while he tried to walk along Moscow streets toward the Kremlin together with hundreds of protesters. Released on December 24, 2011, the blogger spoke on Sakharov Avenue, this time as a Protest Committee member and leader of the movement.

In order to legitimize the protest movement leaders, in June 2012, the Protest Committee decided to hold e-elections for the so-called Russian Opposition Coordination Council. The Central Electoral Committee of the Russian opposition was created specifically for that purpose. First, the protest movement supporters had to register on the website of the Central Electoral Committee (2012) to vote online. Then they were supposed to verify their identity with a small e-payment or passport number. Next, identification numbers were sent to the phones of the verified voters. Those who could not vote online had an opportunity to cast their votes at one of several locations (Gessen, 2012). The elections were held on October 20–22, 2012, after weeks of campaigning and multiple rounds of live debates on the Dozhd Internet TV channel. Alexey Navalny received the highest number of votes and became a legitimate leader of the Russian opposition. Leonid Volkov, head of the Central Electoral Committee and creator of its online voting system, was invited by Navalny to lead his Moscow mayoral campaign.

New ICT platforms had been actively introduced by the Russian opposition and its leaders since the beginning of the 2011–2012 rallies. Similar to the Arab Spring protests (Bodrunova, 2013), the self-organization of Russian protesters occurred mostly on Facebook. Bodrunova (2013) highlights that "social networks in their national making on the whole, like *Facebook* in Russia where a phenomenon of 'exodus from *Livejournal*' blog platform took place approximately a year before the outbreak of protests, making *Facebook* a new virtual milieu for 'Runet intelligentsia'" (p. 15). Nevertheless, VKontakte, the Russian equivalent of Facebook, also played a major role in this context: "While the Moscow protests that took place during the winter and spring of 2011/2012 were mostly organized via Facebook, it was VKontakte that served as a virtual meeting point for rallies outside the capital" (Kvasha, 2013, para. 6).

For the first time, crowdfunding and online payment tools had been applied in Russia to stage anti-government actions. The Protest Committee raised around 4 million rubles (US$ 114,000) to organize the rally on Sakharov Avenue (Smirnova & Surnacheva, 2012). It was also possible to watch the live streaming of the committee sessions, in which the dates, places, and programs of upcoming rallies were discussed.

Despite the Russian society being unprecedentedly active during 2011–2012, its non-violent resistance did not necessarily result in significant changes of Kremlin policies. On May 6, 2012, the day before Putin's presidential inauguration, the rally on Bolotnaya Square ended in carnage and mass detentions. On August 17, 2012, the three members of the Pussy Riot punk band were sentenced to two years in prison for their anti-Putin performance inside Moscow's Cathedral of Christ the Savior.

Moreover, in 2012, the Parliament passed several bills to suppress the enthusiasm of the Russian society. On June 8, 2012, administrative fines for violating protest regulations were increased to one million rubles (US$ 28,500) from the previous 1,000 rubles (US$ 28.50). The law prohibited protesters from covering their faces at demonstrations as well ("Federalny Zakon Rossiyskoy Federatsii," 2012). Since 2013, the Kremlin-controlled Parliament has: 1) labeled Russian, internationally financed nonprofit organizations as foreign agents; 2) authorized the government to block websites dedicated to extremism; 3) approved the anti-blasphemy law allowing jail sentences; 4) introduced fines for those who speak publicly about social equivalency for homosexual and heterosexual relations; and 5) banned the adoption of Russian orphans by US citizens (Barry, 2013).

The rise of conservative, isolationist, and authoritarian tendencies in Russia, along with the ineffectiveness of the nonviolent resistance, caused frustration in the society. As a result, the protest movement dissipated by 2013. Nevertheless, the 2011–2012 protests strengthened political participation at different levels. For instance, the Internet-active opposition supporters revealed new leaders in their midst, primarily Alexey Navalny, and learned how online technologies could be applied to offline civic engagement and the consequent democratic development. Navalny's 2013 Moscow mayoral election campaign reflected this experience, with its extensive use of ICT.

In May 2011, criminal proceedings were held against Navalny and his friend Ofitserov. Navalny and Ofitserov were accused of fraud and embezzlement of the corporate property of Kirov Forests, a state-owned timber company. In the trial, Russia's Investigative Committee stated that in 2009, Ofitserov established the Vyatskaya Lesnaya Kompaniya, which bought timber from Kirov Forests at a discounted price and sold it to private companies. According to the committee, Navalny, when serving as an advisor of Nikita Belykh, the governor of Kirov Oblast, had organized the scheme, which resulted in losses of US$ 500,000 to the regional budget. Navalny denied the accusations, claiming that the prosecution was politically motivated (Barry, 2012).

On April 10, 2012, the charge was dismissed when the prosecutor failed to offer evidence proving any criminal elements. However, on May 29, 2012, the charge was reinstated upon the personal decision of the head of Russia's Investigative Committee, who was earlier charged with corruption due to one of Navalny's investigations ("Bastrykin Vzyalsya za Navalnogo," 2012).

On July 18, 2013, when the snap mayoral election in Moscow had already been announced and Navalny's campaign had started, Navalny and Ofitserov were sentenced to five years in prison (Clover & Weaver, 2013). The conviction resulted in a public outcry and triggered a mass unauthorized rally in Moscow. Thousands protested in front of the Russian State Duma building near the Kremlin. The protesters placed Navalny's campaign stickers on the windows of the building and scrawled anti-Putin graffiti on its walls. The very next day, Navalny was released on bail and could then resume his campaign. Notwithstanding his release, Navalny's ordeal continued with new charges emerging, such as the libel conviction in April 2014 over his Twitter post calling a member of the ruling Russia Unity party a drug addict (Cassin, 2014). While the anti-corruption crusader was under house arrest and barred from communicating on social media, he was involved in one more trial, this time with his brother, accused of defrauding the Russian branch of the French cosmetic company Yves Rocher, although the company had withdrawn the charges ("Yves Rocher Withdraws Accusations," 2014). Navalny was sentenced to five-year probation in this case known as the Kirov Forest trial. The sentence came in December 2017, when he was already campaigning to the 2018 presidential election (Hincks, 2018). Consequently, he was officially barred from contesting the election — which was won by Putin — and called on his supporters to boycott it in the so-called Voters Strike. Despite all the accusations against Navalny, he was not excluded from the political scenario yet. Initiatives from his Anti-Corruption Foundation such as the 2017 documentary "Don't call him Dimon" (Navalny, 2017) on alleged ties between prime minister Dmitry Medvedev and Russian oligarchs continuously cause a stir in Russia. For instance, this documentary (viewed over 30,815,000 million times on YouTube as per June 2019) trigged marches across 100 cities attended mostly by very young people (The Moscow Times, 2017). In the online sphere, the documentary was an effective promotion for Navalny's Youtube channel so that in April 2018 he was awarded with the so-called Gold Play Button from YouTube for reaching 1 million subscribers (2,7 million subscribers as per June 2019) on the video aggregation platform. Moreover, "The role of online platforms in spreading independent reporting came to the fore after a wave of anti-corruption protests in major Russian cities in March [2017]. Word of the upcoming protests spread through private chats on WhatsApp and Telegram" (Sopova, 2017, para. 41), corroborating the relevance of ICT tools for freedom of speech and participatory politics.

TRANSMEDIA ANALYSIS OF NAVALNY'S GRASSROOTS CAMPAIGN

Methodology

This chapter's theoretical background relies on the concept of transmedia storytelling (TS), a term coined by Jenkins (2003, 2006) that refers to the integrated media experiences that occur in a variety of media platforms and are able to attract audience engagement. Although Jenkins conceptualized TS in the early 2000s, the phenomenon of telling stories across different media is not new and even the word transmedia has been around at least for decades. In the 1970s, for instance, the journalist Bernard Levin already named *Transmedia and the Message* one chapter of his book *The Pendulum Years: Britain in the Sixties* (1970). Jansson (2013) considered transmedia narratives as "increasingly inter-connected and open-ended circulation of media content between various platforms, where the subjects previously known as 'the audience' are increasingly involved in the production of flows" (p. 287). The essence of TS is "not about offering the same content in different media platforms, but it is the world building experience, unfolding content and generating the possibilities for the story to evolve with new and pertinent content" (Gambarato, 2013, p. 82). Installments of the narrative are distributed across multiple platforms in order to engage the audience and offer a more meaningful experience. Therefore, besides its inherent characteristic of incorporating multiple media platforms, TS involves audience engagement. Engagement implies two dimensions: first, the aspect of attracting interest or attention and second, the moment of getting involved or participating in something. Interaction and participation are core aspects of TS in terms of both fictional and nonfictional stories (Gambarato, 2012).

With its potential to attract interest in order to generate involvement, audience engagement has not been restricted to the entertainment domain, but it is also applied to social and political initiatives. Some well-known examples of transmedia strategies applied in the political sphere are Barack Obama's 2008 and 2012 presidential campaigns. Jenkins (2008, para. 2) presents his reflections on Obama's first campaign: "Obama has been the man for all platforms — a campaign which was as comfortable on YouTube or Second Life as it was on network television (…) and more importantly, understood the political process through a lens of media convergence, seeing old and new media, grassroots and corporate media working hand in hand to shape his public image and the campaign messages."

The opportunities for political engagement throughout new media and participatory culture are particularly pertinent for youth, who commonly are not primary players in formal institutions (Cohen et al., 2012, p. 4). Participatory politics could be defined as "interactive, peer-based acts through which individuals and groups seek to exert both voice and influence on issues of public concern" (Cohen et al., 2012, p. vi). This kind of participation in conjunction with ICTs includes being part of political groups/communities online and posting and sharing political content on social media networks. Participatory political acts can reach large audiences and mobilize networks, contribute to shaping the political agenda and providing feedback to political leaders, and enable the circulation of political information and the production of original user-generated content (UGC) (Cohen et al., 2012). Couldry (2010) argues that although the investment in so-called voice (of the producer, consumer, or *prosumer*) is crucial in the midst of participatory culture, it is often imbued with individualism, emphasizing the individual representation in detriment of the collectiveness. Therefore, the practices of listening in the social media context, could improve the awareness of political participation (Crawford, 2009).

Despite the fact that the theoretical and analytical implications of TS remain open, the analytical model developed by Gambarato (2013) is the method chosen to verify to which extend Navalny's grassroots campaign is transmediatic and how the campaign's ICT initiatives can lead to democratic improvement. The aim is to outline the campaign's essential features with regard to multiplatform media usage, audience participation, and transmedial strategies for democratic development. The relevance of the application of transmedia features in political campaigns refers to the potential that TS has to engage and motivate public participation and consequently to stimulate democratic practices. The analytical perspective is tailored for both fictional and nonfictional experiences. The model includes 10 distinctive topics guided by a series of questions. The work of Jenkins (2010), Long (2007), and

Strickler (2012) are directly implicated in the analytical model. A brief description of it is provided in Table 1.

Transmedia Strategies in Navalny's Campaign

In the summer of 2013, Navalny started campaigning using innovative techniques, especially involving digital projects. The ICT solutions were utilized in two ways: 1) to promote the candidate among Internet users directly by means of advertisements, official websites, social media communities, etc. and 2) to endorse the candidate among non-Internet users indirectly by attracting actual supporters and directing them to offline activities, such as meetings with voters, metro and traffic campaigning, among others. Even without the victory, Navalny's campaign represented a step forward in the direction of democratic development in the country, giving voice to the citizens, offering them the opportunity to experience participatory politics and transparency in the political sphere. The campaign itself was more important than the results; the following transmedia analysis sheds light on how his achievements were designed.

Premise and Purpose

To win in the Moscow mayoral election, a candidate must garner over 50% of the votes. If no one attains an absolute majority in the first round of voting, the top two candidates advance to the second one. In this situation, a relative majority of the votes cast is enough to win. The ultimate purpose of any election campaign is to win the race, but in this particular case, the fact that Navalny almost reached the second round was already a victory that would shake the stability of the United Russia ruling party in Moscow and challenge the balance of power in the country's political scenario. Moreover, the number of votes cast for Navalny could also be a factor influencing the possibility of his imprisonment, which remains to be seen to this day.

To be successful in achieving its purpose, the campaign had to find an effective method of communicating with voters. Television was (and is still) the leading source of information for the majority of Russians (Khvostunova, 2013), with nearly 100% of households in the country owning television sets (Dragomir & Thompson, 2011, p. 13). However, since major Russian news channels were (and remain) controlled by the government and enforced so-called stop-lists for opposition leaders, Navalny's team had to develop and implement an alternative communication strategy.

Certainly, Leonid Volkov was not a surprise choice to head Navalny's campaign. A technology entrepreneur himself, Volkov concretely influenced the decision to develop ICT solutions for campaigning. Under the circumstances, he planned the campaign

Table 1. Concise description of the transmedia project design analytical model

Topic	Practicable questions
1. Premise and purpose State clearly what the project is about and why it exists.	What is the project about? Is it a fiction, nonfiction, or mixed project? What is its fundamental purpose? Is it to entertain, to teach, or to inform? Is it to market a product?
2. Narrative It is the structure that storyworlds evoke in the transmedia milieu.	What are the narrative elements of the project? What is the summary of its storyline? What is the time frame of the story? What are the strategies for expanding the narrative? Are negative capability and migratory cues included? Is it possible to identify intermedial texts in the story?
3. World building A storyworld or story universe should be robust enough to support expansions, going beyond a single story.	When does the story occur? Which is the central world where the project is set? Is it a fictional world, the real world, or a mixture of both? How is it presented geographically? Is the storyworld large enough to support expansions?
4. Characters The features of the characters and how they appear across all the platforms should be consistent.	Who are the primary and secondary characters of the story? Does the project have any spinoffs? Can the storyworld be considered a primary character on its own? Can the audience be considered a character as well?
5. Extensions Transmedia storytelling involves multiple media in which the storyworld will unfold and be experienced.	How many extensions does the project have? Are the extensions adaptations or expansions of the narrative through various media? Is each extension canonical? Does it enrich the story? Are the extensions able to spread the content and provide the possibility to explore the narrative in-depth?
6. Media platforms and genres A transmedia project necessarily involves more than one medium and can also embrace more than one genre (science fiction, action, comedy, etc.).	What kind of media platforms (film, book, comics, games, etc.) are involved in the project? Which devices (computer, game console, tablet, mobile phone, etc.) are required by the project? How does each platform participate and contribute to the whole project? What are their functions in the project? Is each medium really relevant to the project? What is the rollout strategy to release the platforms? Which genres (action, adventure, detective, science fiction, fantasy, etc.) are present in the project?
7. Audience and market Scoping the audience is fundamental for a more appropriate delivery of the transmedia experience. The TS involves some level of audience engagement.	Who is the target audience of the project? What kind of "viewers" (real-time, reflective, and navigational) does the project attract? Do similar projects exist? Do they succeed in achieving their purpose? What is the project's business model? Was the project successful revenue-wise? Why?
8. Engagement All the dimensions of a transmedia project, at a lower or higher level, are drawn into the experience of people when engaging with the story.	Through what point of view (PoV) does the audience experience this world: first person, second person, third person, or a mixture of them? What role does the audience play in this project? What are the mechanisms of interaction in this project? Is there any participation involved in the project? Does the project work as a cultural attractor/activator? Is there UGC related to the story (parodies, recaps, mash-ups, fan communities, etc.)? Does the project offer the audience the possibility of immersion into the storyworld? Does the project offer the audience the possibility to take elements of the story and incorporate them into everyday life? Is there a system of rewards and penalties?
9. Structure The organization of a transmedia project, the arrangement of its constituent elements, and how they interrelate can offer concrete elements for analysis.	When did the transmediation begin? Is it a proactive or retroactive project? Is this project closer to a transmedia franchise, a portmanteau transmedia story, or a complex transmedia experience? Can each extension work as an independent entry point to the story? What are/were possible endpoints of the project? How is the project structured?
10. Aesthetics The visual and audio elements of a transmedia project should also contribute to the overall atmosphere and enhance the experience spread throughout multiple media platforms.	What kinds of visuals are used (animation, video, graphics, a mix) in the project? Is the overall appearance realistic or a fantasy environment? Is it possible to identify specific design styles in the project? How does audio work in this project? Are there ambient sounds (rain, wind, traffic noises, etc.), sound effects, music, and so forth?

Source: **Gambarato, 2014**

strategy toward building an army of online and offline volunteers. Therefore, various online tools were specially created to intensify the wave of civil activism. "At the beginning our main objective was to turn supporters into volunteers," Navalny said in his post-campaign report (2013, p. 43). The intention was for volunteers to form a connecting link between the candidate and those voters who could not be reached online. The ICT initiatives imply that the candidate's platform and criticism toward the ruling party can reach a greater number of citizens both directly by means of online solutions and indirectly by the volunteers' offline work.

Narrative

On June 4, 2013, a snap Moscow mayoral election was announced. Less than two weeks later, by June 16, Navalny's campaign team was already formed and started implementing its strategy. The campaign had less than three months to raise the candidate's rating for the election that would be held on September 8, 2013.

From the beginning, the campaign applied a set of online and offline extensions to inform the audience about the candidate's platform and to tell his story. However, extensions such as distribution of newspapers, traffic campaigning, distribution of political advertisement materials in the metro, etc., needed volunteers to be involved in the process of promoting the candidate. Consequently, several online extensions were created specifically to recruit volunteers and direct them to both offline and online activities. For instance, the campaign website mosvpiska.navalny.ru functioned as a kind of *couch surfing*—an online service that connects travelers to find a place to stay or share their homes while traveling. This initiative offered people outside Moscow the opportunity to find places to stay in the city, in case they were willing to be campaign volunteers. According to Navalny (2013, p. 41), the service attracted 3,100 users, including foreigners. Extensions such as this one worked as migratory cues for those who wanted to support Navalny with volunteering, e-payments, and so forth. Thus, the campaign created a system that would grow organically, generating new actors internally, which configures a transmedial core feature. The more actors it would involve, the more effective the results would be. Soon the campaign turned into an extensive system, endorsing Navalny with tens of websites and thousands of volunteers. Those who were not involved in volunteering activities were reached by the campaign through newspapers, protest materials, radio, online outlets, among others, and could also participate in Navalny's daily election rallies across Moscow.

In terms of content, the narrative of the opposition candidate's campaign was built primarily around five major issues: healthcare, housing and communal services, migration, transport, and cost of living ("The Platform of Alexey Navalny," n.d.). These themes were chosen as probably the most relevant issues for the majority of the Moscow population. Concomitantly, Navalny's slogan "Change Russia, Start from Moscow" was actively circulated. The slogan appealed to politically engaged citizens and opposition supporters and implicitly directed the campaign beyond practical city issues.

The narrative incorporated gaming elements such as a progress bar on team.navalny.ru (for a graphic display of the volunteers' personal contributions to the campaign) and an online quest on popilili.com. The popilili.com online game was jointly designed by Navalny's team and the White & Fluffy agency. In Russian, *popilili* means "they have stolen (a budget)." In the game, players had to find out which government spending led to misappropriation of the Moscow funds. While playing, users learned more about Navalny's platform regarding the city's major issues.

Intermediality was highly present in the whole project, since it referred to the 2011–2012 Russian opposition movement and the US grassroots campaigns. Navalny's Western-style politicking was inspired by Obama's 2008 presidential campaign and meetings with American politicians when he was a fellow at Yale University in 2010; Navalny even mentioned the American TV series *The Wire*, *Homeland*, and *House of Cards* as other inspirations (Bershidsky, 2013). The characteristics of the narrative involving installments of the story spread across different media platforms, gaming elements, and intermediality, reinforce the transmedial nature of the campaign and help its content appeal to broader audiences.

World Building

The campaign took place in Moscow, the capital of the Russian Federation, in the summer of 2013. The cradle of contemporary Russian opposition, Moscow has been stirring the country with mass opposition rallies since 2011. The city is the wealthiest in Russia and differs from the rest of the country, with a relatively high number of people working in the private sector of the economy, who are financially independent from the government and prosperous enough to claim civil rights, particularly freedom. Internet penetration is at the highest level in Moscow (73%), compared to other Russian cities. The country's overall Internet penetration was 52% in 2013 (Yandex, 2013, p. 4). All these factors made it possible for the Russian opposition to operate a grassroots campaign in the Moscow mayoral election.

The project was planned to have a friendly expansion. Several of its online extensions did not produce any content by themselves. Instead, users utilized them to arrange their offline and online volunteering activities and thus expand the boundaries of the campaign and engage the public. For instance, the number of places for distribution of political advertisements or homes to be involved in the so-called *Navalny to every house* online project depended entirely on the initiative of Navalny enthusiasts, characterizing a transmedia strategy to engage audiences.

Theoretically, the campaign spread over the whole city, yet the geographic boundaries of Navalny's campaign were set with every single action of its volunteers.

One of these actions was performed on July 18, 2013. The day Navalny and Ofitserov were sentenced to prison, a rally broke out in front of the State Duma building. The rally was unauthorized, spontaneous, and prepared solely by Navalny's supporters via Facebook. The action must be regarded as part of the campaign; after the protests, the oppositionist was released and could proceed with his election race.

The Navalny campaign rallies occurred mainly at the periphery of Moscow, where he was not particularly strong (Navalny, 2013, p. 14). The population in the outskirts of Moscow is not as friendly to the opposition as the residents in the prosperous areas around the city center. The former represents the older segment of Moscow citizens, who usually do not access the Internet as actively as the younger, white-collar workers downtown. Never before had the Russian opposition attempted to grab this older group's attention or really included them in its campaign actions. As a result, on the day of the election, almost equal numbers of votes cast for Navalny came from the Moscow periphery and the city center ("Kak Moskva Vibirala Mera," 2013).

TS is not about a character-centered world, but about a story universe robust enough to be expanded across multiple media platforms. Navalny's campaign managed to develop above and beyond the candidate's personal story, creating a storyworld worth participating. This aspect contributed to participatory politics and democratization of information.

Characters

The story has Alexey Navalny as the protagonist and his main election opponent Sergei Sobyanin as the antagonist. As an anti-corruption activist, Navalny was nominally proposed as a Moscow mayoralty candidate by the Republican Party of Russia–People's Freedom Party (RPR–Parnas), a liberal opposition party that represented the entire opposition movement. Throughout the campaign, Navalny held meetings with more than 40,000 citizens in total; he was the only candidate to do so (Navalny, 2013, p. 13). Since the Russian political scenario does not have a tradition of election rallies, they aroused much interest among the citizens and received extensive media coverage.

Despite being his political opponent, Sobyanin facilitated Navalny's participation in the election. In order to legitimize his position as the mayor of all Muscovites, Sobyanin supplied Navalny with the signatures of the United Russia municipal deputies, which were essential for Navalny's registration as a candidate. Some experts, such as Stanislav Belkovsky, stated that it was Sobyanin who succeeded in persuading the Russian authorities to set Navalny free, when the Kremlin had to decide whether or not the oppositionist should be sentenced to prison (in the Kirov

Forests case) (Vasilyeva & Isachenkov, 2013). "Sobyanin needs Navalny to make the mayoral elections look legitimate," Belkovsky argued. "He suffers from a provincial complex, and he wants to prove to Moscow's residents that his election victory is honest" (Vasilyeva & Isachenkov, 2013, para. 17). Illegal interference in Navalny's campaign process was minimal, compared with the usual Russian election practices. Sobyanin also significantly reduced the vote rigging on the day of the election. If he could easily win even in a relatively fair election, Sobyanin would probably prove himself to Vladimir Putin as a safe person to be the Kremlin's candidate for president of the Russian Federation in the 2018 election.

In the elections, Sobyanin adhered to the campaigning style commonly practiced in contemporary Russia. In contrast to Navalny's participatory-oriented campaign, Sobynin's presence in online and offline activities was rather limited. His headquarters focused on promoting the candidate through traditional media, primarily television and newspapers. Altogether, the television reach of Sobyanin's campaign had exceeded 250 million contacts, while all the other candidates combined had managed to gain just as few as 1.5 million contacts ("Analiz Reklamnykh Kampaniy," 2013).

On August 7, 2013, more than 200 ICT entrepreneurs expressed their support for Navalny as a candidate in exchange for his willingness to fight against inappropriate government business regulations, corruption in the city, and so forth. It was the first time in Russian political history that businesspeople signed a social contract with a candidate. The action provided the signatories with the status of campaign actors, since the social contract was not an act of charity, as it usually happens with the obligation of Russian businesses to finance the United Russia ruling party. In this case, it was a win-win deal and a democratic improvement.

Moreover, the volunteers were also primary characters in Navalny's campaign. The structure of the campaign strongly relied on single volunteers' actions, which implied that they played a crucial role in influencing voters' decisions to cast their votes for Navalny. Although the number of volunteers could seem not necessarily impressive and the impact of each single volunteer must be limited, as a group they significantly affected the campaign's momentum. The audience could also be considered a character of Navalny's campaign for two main reasons: they had every opportunity to be involved and to participate in the candidate's campaign, and they determined the election results. The power of the grassroots campaign favored political and social awareness.

Extensions

In terms of content, it is meaningful to extract single extensions from the whole transmedia project to classify multiple content types spread across its platforms. The campaign had 32 extensions overall: 1) Navalny's 89 meetings with 40,000 voters

(Navalny, 2013, p. 13); 2) 2,756 so-called cubes (square tents with Navalny's image and campaign goals printed on the sides) on Moscow streets (Navalny, 2013, p. 21); 3) visual campaign advertising, using slogan stickers, banners on citizens' balconies, labeled T-shirts, and badges; 4) 15.95 million free campaign newspapers (Navalny, 2013, p. 33); 5) 3 million after-meeting, free campaign newspapers (Navalny, 2013, p. 34); 6) 4 million campaign leaflets (Navalny, 2013, p. 35); 7) 24 online videos and teasers; 8) navalny.ru website with the candidate's platform and campaign news; 9) pd4.navalny.ru campaign fundraising online service; 10) cube.navalny.ru with the information on Navalny's cubes; 11) mosvpiska.navalny.ru with the *couch surfing* service for volunteers; 12) passport.navalny.ru website to aggregate information about the users of all of the campaign's online platforms and their activities; 13) v.navalny.ru campaign personal calendar-planner; 14) entrepreneurs.navalny.ru with Navalny's social contract to be signed; 15) dom.navalny.ru geo-targeted social network for campaign volunteers; 16) moskva.navalny.ru volunteers' online service for campaigning on social networks; 17) team.navalny.ru website to arrange for personal involvement in the campaign; 18) five.navalny.ru website with five key campaign issues; 19) popilili.com online game; 20) za.navalny.ru with speeches of famous personalities in support of Navalny; 21) vote.navalny.ru get-out-the-vote platform with five reasons to vote in the Moscow mayoral election and simple directions on how to find the local polling station; 22) Navalny's personal blog, navalny.livejournal.com; 23) communities on Facebook, VKontakte, Twitter, Odnoklassniki, and Instagram; 24) campaign e-mailing; 25) online commercials; 26) radio commercials; 27) political advertisements in newspapers; 28) political advertisements on route taxis; 29) mass rallies in Sokolniki Park and on Sakharov Avenue and the post-election rally on Bolotnaya Square; 30) online application for election observers; 31) *Navalny to every house* online interactive map in which people could register themselves by typing their e-mail and physical addresses; and 32) a detailed campaign report.

The process of campaigning in the metro and traffic areas consisted of distributing free campaign newspapers and thus functioned as the method of delivering the newspaper extension. In transmedia projects, the boundaries of single extensions may not replicate those of single platforms; they may extend beyond single platforms and simultaneously utilize the capabilities of several others. For instance, Navalny's cubes were not exclusively based on offline square tents, but also online on cube.navalny.ru and mosvpiska.navalny.ru.

All the extensions were canonical, which is a core principle of TS, and provided voters with a variety of consistent messages about the candidate's platform. Some extensions were created to inform, while others involved the audience in cooperating and volunteering activities, such as street and online protests, crowdfunding, and observing the election. Since political campaigns are based on promoting a candidate, the extensions of Navalny's campaign actively utilized the power of sharing, contributing to the democratization of information and participatory politics. Online extensions encouraged the dissemination of content on social networks and informed users, especially the young audience, on how they could help endorse the candidate offline.

Media Platforms and Genres

Navalny's campaign was opportunely planned to unfold both online and offline in order to embrace young and senior audiences, the city center and periphery, and digital natives and media illiterates. "A turn to new media is not a turn away from offline activity" (Cohen et al., 2012, p. xi). The integration between digital media platforms such as the Internet and mobile phones, traditional media such as radio and print media, and offline activities such as metro and traffic campaigning, perfectly characterized Navalny's strategy during the electoral process.

For instance, besides the numerous websites and social media networks involved in the campaign, its YouTube channel released more than 20 videos per month. A one-minute video released on September 1, 2013 went viral with over 2.8 million views ("Vremya Prishlo!," 2013). The video featured a guerrilla marketing campaign launched by Navalny's team at the end of August 2013. In the campaign, military shipping boxes were distributed on the streets with parachutes attached and "The time has come! Take up arms!" slogan written on them. When passers-by opened the boxes, they turned out to be filled with Navalny's campaign-branded pens, imprinted with the slogan "Your vote is your arms" ("Vremya Prishlo!," 2013).

As a novelty in the Russian political scenario, the online game popilili.com registered 43,300 users during the campaign (Navalny, 2013, p. 42). The use of the Internet as a platform to spark awareness and aggregate involvement was successfully implemented by Navalny's team, denoting both a transmedial feature and a democratic practice. The print media was extensively used as well, for instance, with a massive distribution of newspapers with the candidate's program for the city and stickers with slogans such as "Change Russia. Start with Moscow.", "Only Navalny. Only Hard Work.", and "Navalny my Mayor." This approach, especially with the distribution of newspapers in Moscow's metro stations, was very effective because people could read them during the ride. Volunteers went 3,662 times to share the newspapers in various metro stations; a total of 581,010 copies were delivered to the public (Navalny, 2013, p. 24). Navalny (2013, p. 22) was the only candidate who did it. Overall, the number of newspapers distributed during the campaign reached 15.95 million (Navalny, 2013, p. 33). According to the 2010 Census, Moscow's population is over 11 million (Russian Federal State Statistics Service, 2011). Printed materials, including leaflets, were also given to drivers during a two-week period in the so-called traffic campaign. However, this effort did not last longer due to insufficient funds (Navalny, 2013, p. 25). The stickers were displayed on doors/cars/windows and functioned as an alternative to the lack of opportunity to use TV and major radio broadcasts. The stickers were abundantly spread throughout the city.

Regarding the technological devices involved in the campaign, computers, mobile phones, and radios were required to gain full access to its contents. Since Navalny had restricted access to television, TV sets were less relevant to his campaign. Tablets were also used by Navalny's team, specifically to conduct opinion polls.

The documentary could be considered as the main media genre employed by the campaign, in the sense of depicting real-life situations, events, and characters. It could be argued that the action genre was also used by Navalny's team to portray an extremely dynamic candidate and his army of active volunteers. Action includes movement but more so, excitement. The campaign period was brief; therefore, the rollout strategy basically involved simultaneous actions because both online and offline extensions would not have much time to be experienced. Nevertheless, his team noticeably focused primarily on building the campaign's infrastructure in the beginning (June–July 2013) and on boosting both online and offline campaign activities toward the end of the electoral process in August–September 2013 (Navalny, 2013, pp. 5–6). Navalny's campaign used several media platforms to distribute the content in a transmedial manner, focusing on engaging ICT users and nonusers as well. This initiative contributed to promote social equality.

Audience and Market

The demographic segment of the campaign's target audience ranged from 18-year-old citizens to older ones, encompassing the voting-age population in Moscow. From youngsters to seniors, from students to professionals, from wealthy Muscovites to less fortunate ones—Navalny's campaign was designed to reach them all: "While Navalny's reliance on the Internet for his anti-corruption activities has earned him a loyal following of young people, his online initiatives have also appealed to older people who are fed up with corruption" (Kravtsova, 2013, para. 33). Besides all the digital initiatives, his team focused also on fostering the candidate's direct contact with voters by means of meetings. These meetings were held throughout the city, covering central and peripheral areas, and differentiated Navalny from other mayoral contenders, who preferred to interact with the population less directly. The opposition candidate held three meetings a day, and the ones near metro stations attracted larger audiences (Navalny, 2013, p. 16).

As Navalny's campaign chief Leonid Volkov explained, the campaign is absolutely new in terms of fundraising amounts, number of volunteers and digital projects, but the meetings with the public are what really make it innovative. The main aim of the election campaign, he said, was to reach those people who have not yet decided which candidate to vote for (Kravtsova, 2013, para. 12).

Navalny was interested in the support from society and therefore promoted meetings specifically with businesspeople, intellectuals, artists, poets, and musicians, congregating the financial and cultural sectors, that is, a more affluent crowd. Navalny's campaign gained momentum; toward the end of the electoral period, the number of visitors on his websites increased significantly (Navalny, 2013, p. 39). Navalny's report (2013) showed that the audience mainly accessed his major website when coming from social media, which demonstrated the power of social networks in redirecting the audience: 1) 53% of visitors came from Twitter, 2) 31% from VKontakte, 3) 14% from Facebook, and 4) 2% from Odnoklassniki (p. 44).

Because Navalny could not count on television to reach the majority of Moscow population, the campaign invested in the Internet and radio advertising, taking advantage of the lower costs and huge penetration. The major system of Internet advertisement used by the campaign was Google AdWords. This online advertising service places advertisements at the top, the bottom, or beside the list of results Google displays after a specific search query. In fact, 70% of people who were not interested in politics clicked more on Navalny's Internet advertisements than others did. The campaign report suggested that the probable reason was that they did not know about the candidate and were interested to obtain more information (Navalny, 2013, p. 46). It seemed that the campaign was able to congregate different kinds of users, who could be involved at varying levels. To paraphrase Murray (1997, p. 257), the campaign embraced real-time, reflective long-term, and navigational viewers, who eventually accessed the content, followed the whole campaign development, and explored all the connections among different parts of the campaign.

Navalny's team claimed that only 55% of the adults in Moscow listened to the radio. For instance, Auto Radio 90.3 FM, which had the highest reach among Moscow's radio stations during the election period ("Dannye po Auditorii," 2013), refused to broadcast Navalny's advertisements for fear of punishment by the government. Most of the radio spots were aired on Echo of Moscow, which is recognized as "the last bastion of free media in Russia" and is "the most popular independent station" in Russia (Panibratov, 2012, p. 49). On the radio, the advertisements targeted audiences of different ages and income levels, reaching 5.457 million people, according to the campaign's report (Navalny, 2013, pp. 49–50).

A few days prior to the election, *The New Yorker* mentioned remarkable achievements performed by Navalny's campaign. Among them, the highlights were: 1) the fact that Navalny was able to run at all, considering all his criticisms of the government and the allegedly false and politically motivated criminal charges against him; 2) the unprecedented campaign techniques, which managed to congregate over 15,000 volunteers; and 3) despite Russia's pervasive political cynicism, the campaign's drawing on private fundraising (Lipman, 2013).

Although in Western countries, political fundraising is common, Navalny's was exceptional in terms of being a novelty in Russia and the amount of money raised. The total fundraising amount collected during the campaign exceeded 103.4 million rubles (nearly US$ 3 million). Such a huge amount of money raised from small donations of ordinary people had never happened before, according to Navalny (2013, p. 71). Crowdfunding, a grassroots initiative, characterizes TS and democratizes access to capital. However, in May 2014, the Moscow City Elections Commission investigated the offices of the Internet company Yandex and the homes of opposition members suspected of "pocketing funds designated for opposition leader Alexei Navalny's mayoral campaign last year" (Brennan, 2014a, para. 1). Moreover, his campaign had been accused of using Yandex's payment service *Yandex.Money* "to receive illegal funds from abroad" (Brennan, 2014a, para. 5). No irregularities were proven. Navalny claimed once more that these searches constituted an attempt by authorities to limit the opposition's ability to raise money through the Internet and to discredit opposition members who are (at the time of this writing) candidates for the 2014 Moscow City Duma (Brennan, 2014a).

In an effort at public transparency about the administration and spending of the campaign funds, Navalny's report presented the following numbers: 1) 40% of the money was spent in campaign production; 2) 27% in advertisement (Internet, radio, and newspapers); 3) 26% in street campaigning (cubes, traffic, metro, etc.); and 4) 7% in other expenses (office supplies, office rent, surveys, etc.) (Navalny, 2013, p. 75).

Engagement

Engaging the audience in Navalny's campaign did not simply focus on drawing people's attention to the candidate and urging them to vote for him. The goal was to raise awareness about Navalny himself and his program for the city, as well as to involve the audience as volunteers who could spark enthusiasm for the candidate, aggregate more people, and then vote for him. In this context, the campaign functioned both as a cultural attractor (connecting a community around common interests) and a cultural activator (giving them something to do), improving democratic practices.

Navalny (2013) said: "We destroyed the stereotype that for a politician it is useless to have volunteers" (p. 4). Common community participation was the campaign's strategic move toward real results at the polls. However, it was not simple to achieve in Moscow. Difficulties were encountered in obtaining permission for the meetings, for instance. To bypass the government regulations and restrictions imposed on public political events, such as marches, demonstrations, and rallies, Navalny's team decided to use the law of elections and follow the procedures designed for the campaign process. The meetings were scheduled at 4:00, 6:00, and 8:00 p.m. to accommodate different audiences. The structure of the meetings involved cubes, a stage, chairs for elderly people, umbrellas as protection from either the sun or the rain, and the sound system. After the meetings, newspapers were published, incorporating the information discussed. Overall, during the campaign, 32 editors produced 68 newspapers, which reached a circulation of 3 million copies (Navalny, 2013, pp. 15–16). Navalny's team invited people to participate by means of letters and posters placed in the residential buildings' mailboxes. Generally, from one to several hundred people attended the ordinary daily meetings with the candidate. The election attracted 2.3 million voters, the total number of the turnout in Moscow (33.23%) ("Pri Luzhkove Takogo Ne Bylo," 2013).

Besides the meetings with voters, Navalny also held meetings with volunteers, aimed to create horizontal connections. For offline activities, volunteers could distribute printed materials such as newspapers, leaflets, and stickers; participate in the campaign cubes by talking to the public about the candidate's ideas; or simply wear t-shirts and support Navalny, among other tasks. Regarding online activities, they could spread the word about the campaign on social networks; through a special service (ICT solution), they could send up to 20 emails a day to random users of VKontakte who were Moscow residents, or they could place over their avatar the virtual "white Navalny on red circle" (Suleymanov, 2013, para. 3).

On the one hand, offline activities characterized the possibility for the audience to (physically) be immersed in the campaign. On the other hand, the arsenal of campaign memorabilia (pens, stickers, bags, t-shirts, banners, bracelets, flags, balloons, among others) represented opportunities for the audience to extract elements that were part of the campaign universe and to incorporate these into their daily lives. Both immersion and extractability are core principles of TS.

Navalny's supporters were also poll watchers during the election, which was another method of engagement and a crucial way to improve democratic development in the country. In his *LiveJournal* blog (Navalny, n.d.), the candidate encouraged his supporters to participate in the process of monitoring the election. The campaign actively collaborated with Russian independent, nonprofit organizations (e.g., Golos Association) specialized in training election observers. Consequently, around 80% of voting places were monitored by independent observers, including those assigned by Navalny's team. Half of the polling stations had at least two independent watchers monitoring the process (Navalny, 2013, p. 70).

Concerning different viewpoints, the campaign could be experienced from all the perspectives. For example, the volunteers' activities were experienced in the first person, the meetings and oral communication could involve a second-person perspective, and significant aspects of the extensions were experienced in the third person.

UGC, such as memes, parodies, and mash-ups were vastly available during the campaign process. Among the most popular were memes such as "Keep calm and vote for Navalny," "Yes we cat" (in reference to Obama's slogan "Yes we can"), and parodies featuring Navalny, Sobyanin, and Putin.

As discussed earlier in the chapter, interaction and above all, participation contributed to the transmedial development of the campaign and directly influenced the election results and arguably, the democratic processes in Russia.

Structure

The Navalny campaign's transmedial approach was planned from the beginning, which characterized a proactive transmedia project. "The two [Navalny and Volkov] set up a headquarters and a bank account and started accepting donations and signing up volunteers. By early August, according to Volkov and Navalny, the campaign had more than $1 million and 14,000 volunteers" (Bershidsky, 2013, para. 4). Due to Volkov participation, the organization of the campaign resembled an ICT company. The campaign started with eight people; at the end, there were 300 (60 of them coordinating the campaign) (Navalny, 2013, pp. 7–8).

The series of extensions incorporated in the process functioned as independent entry points to Navalny's story universe, corresponding to the way a transmedia franchise operates. Within this structure, each extension, spread across multiple media platforms, could work as a door opened for the audience to be acquainted with the candidate and be inspired to engage in the campaign.

The organization of the campaign comprised the following areas: 1) street campaigning; 2) ICT and the Internet; 3) financial security; 4) sociology; 5) creation of materials; 6) law; 7) support for street campaigning; 8) office support; 9) press services; and 10) poll watchers (Navalny, 2013, p. 9). Navalny's transmedia franchise offered alternatives, especially the ICT ones, to attract the audience engagement, amplifying the access to information.

Aesthetics

The design of Navalny's campaign was remarkably simple yet efficient. It incorporated various graphic elements, videos, photographs, light projections, printed materials, and so forth. Both the websites and the offline materials presented clean, clear, subtle, minimalist, and sophisticated designs. The overall aesthetics, characterized by the predominance of white and light blue colors, as well as by elegant fonts and clean layouts, corroborates the message conveyed by the candidate: young and fresh change for Russia to the detriment of the current populist and autocratic government.

The Progress Party, Navalny's center-right political party, propagated a platform that stood for conservative economic measures and a liberal social approach, as opposed to that of President Putin and his United Russia party. While Putin's party logo highlighted the Russian flag and its three colors (white, blue, and red), the colors of Navalny's party logo were turquoise and white. In a country profoundly marked by the red hues of the Communist era, turquoise and white played a more neutral role in the Russian political spectrum. These colors figured predominantly in Navalny's campaign, from the websites to the cubes, from the printed materials to the campaign's report. Moreover, the prevalent use of white can be traced back to the 2011–2012 opposition movement. During those protests, white stripes were actively utilized and became the symbol of the opposition. Describing the rally in Moscow on December 9, 2011, an anonymous participant stated: "Some came with signs, flags, white flowers. Many had white stripes - symbol of the opposition" (Russialize, 2011, para. 6). White could also be interpreted as an allusion to snow (a constant presence in Russian winters) and a symbolism of virtue, purity, and peace. The color white was so massively used that Putin was asked whether the white stripes-wave during the protests could become the symbol of a color revolution. He answered,

Talking about color revolutions... It is a practiced scheme. We know well how it worked in Ukraine. Now this scheme is being imposed on Russia. When I saw people with these white stripes on their chests I thought they had hanged some contraceptives on themselves ("Putin says Opposition White Stripes," 2011, para. 2).

Although red is the color that provokes the most response among humans (DeLong & Martinson, 2012), it was hardly seen in Navalny's campaign. Its distance from the Communist past and the urge for change are probably two of the underlying motivations. Overall, the campaign portrayed a realistic environment and only in a few occasions opted for a more playful design, as could be found in the popilili.com online game, which presented a cartoonish look. The visual elements of the transmedia campaign enhanced the overall experience spread throughout multiple media platforms and collaborated to unify the campaign.

DISCUSSION

Grassroots Political Campaign and Democratic Development in Russia

In the snap Moscow mayoral election in 2013, officially, Sergei Sobyanin won in the first round, with 51.37% of the votes, while Alexey Navalny garnered 27.24%. The oppositionist did not acknowledge the election results. He claimed the results from the second-round ballot, insisting that his opponent received only 49% by an independent vote count. In any case, the outcome was considered a huge victory, since Navalny's ratings managed to increase from 4–6% in the first official survey in the beginning of the electoral process to more than 27% at the polls. The elections demonstrated the usefulness of grassroots transmedia campaign strategies in overcoming the state propaganda machine, improving democratic practices and strengthening the opposition movement (Gambarato & Lapina-Kratasyuk, 2016). From the beginning, it was a crucial challenge to involve enough people who were ready to volunteer. Russian society is relatively inert and basically does not have a tradition of peaceful mass actions. However, Navalny's team successfully developed a political campaign with the core elements that characterize TS: multiple media platforms, expansion of content, and audience engagement. The campaign took advantage of gaming elements, UGC, and ICT solutions, such as online interactive communications and networking, to generate interest from the Internet audience and to spark political and social equality. From the perspective of verbal communication, the campaign found a common language with volunteers, especially the youth, offering opportunities for participatory politics to grow. Since the younger generation constituted the vast majority of volunteers, the campaign addressed them in an informal style, including jokes in operational recommendations for the distribution of political advertisements. The campaign conveyed the impression of volunteering as a responsibility that could eventually be fun and amusing as well. With regular trainings and celebrations held in the campaign headquarters, a team of associates was ultimately consolidated.

Navalny's team supplied users with comprehensive information on campaign activities, so everyone could find an appropriate format for personal involvement, raising the democratization of information and offering concrete steps toward political participation. Depending on their individual capabilities, Muscovites could distribute campaign advertisement materials at their own homes or anywhere in the city, display a campaign poster from a balcony, or donate money to the campaign, among other types of support. For those who preferred volunteering from home, the campaign designed 'Navalny to every house' online interactive map on dom.navalny.ru which essentially was a geo-targeted social network. First, people registered themselves on the website with an email and address. Consequently the address appeared on the online map of the website as a check mark, so that the other users could see they have a lot of like-minded folks in their neighbourhood and beyond it, they are part of a movement. From a practical perspective, the website assigned simple tasks to the registered users such as to report if the campaign newsletters were delivered to their residential building, for instance. With the help of volunteers, free campaign newspapers had been delivered to almost every mailbox in Moscow, and political advertisements were disseminated in the most crowded city places, such as metro stations and surrounding areas, shopping malls, and crossroads. Transmedia strategies within Navalny's campaign embraced a variety of online and offline media platforms and played a relevant role in the development of participatory culture and politics in the country.

This election campaign demonstrated that enough people in Russia were ready to invest their money in political changes. Citizens from all the 82 regions in Russia donated money to Navalny's race. Male donors comprised the majority (85%), with an average donation amount of approximately 1,000 rubles (US$ 28.50) overall in Russia and 2,000 rubles (US$ 57) in Moscow. The donors' average age was 36 years old (Navalny, 2013, p. 72); 16,694 payments were transferred during the campaign, and this was the first time that a candidate undertook this initiative in Russia (Navalny, 2013, p. 3). The number of donations increased each time Navalny posted on his blog, calling for support (Navalny, 2013, p. 73). This fact illustrates the power of blogging and sharing across social media networks and demonstrates the effectiveness of ICT solutions in democratic practices. According to Navalny (2013), the crowdfunding strategy resulted in approximately 97.3 million rubles (US$ 2.78 million) received from private donors (ordinary citizens), accounting for 94% of the campaign's total budget and making this a record for crowdfunding in the country (p.72). Navalny (2013) released a post-campaign report with a breakdown of all the expenditures. $3,100,000 that Navalny managed to raise was just under the budget of the rival Sobyanin campaign. The incumbent Mayor spent $3,240,000. To translate it into votes, Navalny spent $4.9 per vote (632,697 votes all together), and Sobyanin spent much less, only $2.7 per vote (1,193,178 votes in total). These numbers seem to be not in favour of Navalny. But to look at this from a different perspective, Navalny entered the race in July 2013 polling well below 10 points according to all the pollsters. Over the course of his campaign, he managed to increase that number to 27 per cent when the votes were counted on September 9. On the other hand, about 45-50 per cent were ready to vote for Sobyanin at the dawn of the campaign and he won the election with only 51.5 per cent. That makes the Navalny campaign significantly more effective in transforming investments into new supporters.

As mentioned, 200 entrepreneurs signed a social contract with Navalny during the campaign. Despite the possibility of reprisal, these entrepreneurs expressed their position openly and thus shook the Russian political system. If a citizen disagrees with the government's official position, in contemporary Russia, such an individual is considered a traitor by the Kremlin. Expressions such as "fifth column" and "national traitors" have entered the current political discourse of the country (Yoffa, 2014). With their signatures, the entrepreneurs declared that society still had the right to an independent view on Russian politics, favoring the freedom of expression.

Nevertheless, in February 2014, Navalny was accused of bail violation and placed under house arrest. "The fact that Navalny was not taken into custody during the investigation is unusual in terms of Russian judicial practice, and experts theorize that this move is part of a campaign to discredit him" (Rozanov, 2014, para. 11). He was prohibited from using the Internet. Once, when the oppositionist tried to update his blog through his wife's and colleagues' access, one of the posts was called extremist by the state prosecutor, and the blog was then blocked. Other relevant accusations followed, including his last conviction in 2017 in the Kirov Forest trial, which Navalny claims are all politically motivated. He is not alone: "In October [2018], Europe's top human rights court ruled that a 2014 fraud conviction Russia levied against Navalny was 'arbitrary and manifestly unreasonable'" (Hincks, 2018, para. 19). The effort to discredit Navalny does not imply that his campaign did not succeed in contributing to improve democracy in the country. On the contrary, it is exactly because he managed to involve the public in his campaign that the government seems to invest in injuring his reputation. Moreover, Navalny continued to take advantage of transmedia strategies to reach the audience outside the state controlled mainstream media, such as in the case of "Don't call him Dimon." TS features and ICT initiatives collaborated together to raise awareness of the importance of public transparency, freedom of speech, and participatory politics.

The ICT initiatives of Navalny during the 2013 mayoral elections paved a way for a more data-driven approach to campaigning in the future. In 2015 and 2018, the ICT department of Alexey Navalny's foundation introduced new applications for better harvesting called Zhnets (Harvester) and Zhnets-2018 (Harvester 2018) respectively. The former was designed to help volunteers work in the field. For instance, the app broke down the city of Novosibirsk with a population of over 1,5 million into 250 routes for efficient canvassing, guided volunteers from door to door, counted all the collected data and ranged it by specific parameters (Navalny, 2015). Zhnets-2018 was even more technologically sophisticated as it was able to automatically verify scanned documents, was programmed to send SMS (short message service) and email notifications to voters, and served as a pipeline that provided the campaign and its regional managers with relevant data on voters for advanced analytics (Zhyzhylkin, 2018). Along with the online sphere, the opposition kept on looking for new opportunities for using public spaces in their struggle for reaching out to the citizens. During the 2017 election campaign, local authorities consistently denied Navalny the right to get locations for his rallies across the country. The solution was found in using private territories which are not regulated by the state acts on public gatherings. In Irkutsk, for instance, Navalny held a rally on the territory of a furniture factory provided by a local businessman. Later in the same city people voted to offer Navalny the surroundings of their apartment building for a rally. In Tombov, a rally was organized on the car parking at a shopping mall.

'The Hand of the West'

Alexey Navalny is primarily a blogger. In contrast to politically oriented bloggers in the US, who usually have clear positions and place themselves on one side or the other of the ideological divide, the majority of Russian bloggers probably write from a more independent perspective (Etling et al., 2010, p. 19). In Navalny's case, the anti-corruption crusade seems to be his side in the Russian political spectrum. Consequently, it seems that his political adversaries try to destabilize him precisely with corruption allegations.

Despite the different realities and contexts between Russia and the West, Navalny evidently followed the Western-style campaigning. Navalny openly stated that many of his ideas were copied from the American television drama *The Wire*, such as installing street podiums for meetings with voters, with chairs and umbrellas (in case of rain or intense sunlight) for elderly people. He considered this kind of meetings as the best way to increase participation in elections, based on foreign experience, and believed that this action distinguished his campaign (Navalny, 2013, p. 14). "A charismatic 37-year-old lawyer in jeans and a white shirt with rolled-up sleeves, Mr Navalny acts like an American politician. In a country where politics takes place behind the high Kremlin walls, this is new" ("Inspired by 'The Wire'," 2013, para. 3).

Nevertheless, the westernized approach was not restricted to the opposition candidate. Sobyanin, in 2013, also favored subtle details to gain the middle-class respect "by creating perks and promoting the illusion that Moscow is a typical European city. Ranks of shiny red city bicycles sprang up, parking meters were put in place, city parks and playgrounds revamped" ("Inspired by 'The Wire,'" 2013, para. 8). Navalny's speech was marked by an intimate tone conveying the message: "I know what you need, because I need the same things" (Kravtsova, 2013, para. 17). His opponents recognized the similarities between his campaign and that of Obama in 2008, especially in the change-oriented slogans, an allusion to Obama's "Change we can believe in" and "Yes we can," and the poses in official photographs with head and arm raised. Other similitudes between Navalny and the West that reflected novelties in Russia included fundraising, which was so new in the country that the campaign just used the English word for lack of an equivalent Russian term, transmedia strategies, ICT initiatives, and the distribution of stickers bearing the candidate's slogans, as Bershidsky pointed out: "Moscow is full of cars with Navalny bumper stickers, hardly ever used in previous Russian campaigns" (2013, para. 5).

Navalny incorporated traditional American campaign techniques, such as canvassing for votes and fundraising dinners, which may have changed the political scenario in Russia even without the victory. However, the opposition movement that he represents has been suffering from drawbacks since the end of the 2013 elections. "'The opposition is not doing so well right now,' says Boris Nemtsov, one of the liberal (…) leaders. 'A lot of our comrades are behind bars, some people are wanted by the authorities, and some have emigrated'" (Rozanov, 2014, para. 20). Boris Nemtsov himself was assassinated on the Bolshoy Moskvoretsky Bridge near the Kremlin on February 27, 2015.

The Russian Opposition Coordination Council, established in 2012, fell apart already in 2013. According to sociologist Lev Gudkov:

The ideas put forth by the opposition – honest elections, anti-corruption, and electoral reforms – were supported by about half the population at first. The numbers dropped off as the Kremlin launched a propaganda rhetoric campaign that stressed concepts such as 'the hand of the West' and 'foreign agents' [non-profit organizations receiving funding from abroad were required to register as foreign agents] (Rozanov, 2014, para. 23).

The Kremlin propaganda seemed to have influenced the population, although in Moscow, the situation is slightly different. For instance, on "March 15, 2014, an anti-war rally against Russian military intervention in Ukraine drew 50,000 people, according to the organizers" (Rozanov, 2014, para. 26). Indeed, the annexation of Crimea can be considered another factor in the decline of public support for opposition groups. The Russian population (in general) strongly supports the government's attitude toward Ukraine, and Putin's popularity significantly increased because of it (Taylor, 2014).

The Levada Center, an independent research organization, found that a record high 85 percent of Russians would likely not take part in political protests. The poll, which was based on the opinions of a representative sample of 1,602 adults across 45 Russian regions, also revealed that 95 percent of Russians had not participated in protests in the past year (Tétrault-Farber, 2014, para. 2).

Additionally, the Russian policy on Ukraine seems to play a major role in distracting domestic eyes and minds. The State Duma's opposition deputy Dmitry Gudkov stated, "The population's reluctance to protest does not mean that it is necessarily happier or more satisfied. Citizens are just being distracted from domestic problems by state authorities' insistence on the presence of foreign enemies in Ukraine and the West" (Tétrault-Farber, 2014, para. 6). In contrast to Dmitry Gudkov's positive prediction that "there will come a time when authorities will no longer be able to distract Russians from the problems at home" (Tétrault-Farber, 2014, para. 8), the sociologist Lev Gudkov declared that "by winter of this year [2014], willingness to support or participate in protests had sunk to an all-time low since the collapse of the Soviet Union" (Rozanov, 2014, para. 2).

Moreover, concrete factors involving the recent Russian legislation could have contributed to the decline in the protest sentiment, such as the imposition of "criminal sanctions on repeat offenders of Russia's laws against unsanctioned public gatherings" (Tétrault-Farber, 2014, para. 10) and the so-called blogger law that is regarded as Putin's attempt to silence opponents. The law imposes tighter control on Russian blogs and websites that attract more than 3,000 daily visits. "The new rules will require popular bloggers to register by name with Russia's communications oversight agency and conform to regulations on the mass media" (Prentice, 2014, para. 8).

As a consequence of all government measures, laws, and policies, and especially the accusations against Navalny, his popularity dropped, according to a poll conducted in April 2014. "Once the darling of Russia's opposition movement, Alexei Navalny has seen his reputation fall in recent months as he has made more headlines for the criminal cases launched against him than for his political activities" (Brennan, 2014b, para. 1). Similarly, amid the anti-corruption protests following the release of the "Don't call him Dimon" documentary in 2017, Navalny popularity did not increase. "Attitudes toward the politician are also unchanged. In June, 30 percent of those polled said Navalny is acting in the interests of the West when he publishes his anti-corruption reports, compared to 28 percent who held this view in March" (The Moscow Times, 2017, para. 5). However, it is relevant to highlight that "Lavada Center began conducting polls on Navalny in 2011 when his recognition was just 6 percent. The numbers spiked in mid-2013 and have remained around 50 percent since" (The Moscow Times, 2017, para. 6). As demonstrated by the analysis, the implementation of ICT in Navalny's campaign concretely influenced participatory practices in Russia. Nevertheless, it is too soon to evaluate the permanence of democratic exercise in the country.

CONCLUSION

Post-Soviet Russia has consistently suppressed political freedom over the past decades. The need for change urged by the oppositionists was the primary incentive for Navalny's supporters. He surprisingly had good numbers in the 2013 Moscow mayoral election. The opposition movement in the city's central Bolotnaya Square reached its peak in 2011–2012 and culminated in the unprecedented, westernized transmedia campaign developed by Navalny's team. Navalny's campaign set the example for the other regions of the country. His techniques, "seem surreal in contrast with the top-down, financially murky way Russia has conducted its political business until now" (Trudolyubov, 2013, para. 3). Indeed, his transmedia strategies can be replicated by everyone in Russia, as observed in Murmansk (Navalny, 2013, p. 4) and in the 2014 Moscow City Duma elections with the presence of cubes, for instance. However, the number of citizens who are prepared for radical political action is rather limited. The most relevant criticisms hurled at Navalny relate to his style of nationalism, abundance of finding fault with authorities, and lack of elaborate plans on how to improve the current situation.

TS strategies directly contribute to attract interest and attention, and to get people involved in something by means of interaction and participation. Participation leads to the possibility of individuals to exert their voice and influence on the results of the transmedial experience. Moreover, participatory politics constitute a vital strategy in leading the population to increase their levels of voice and control and change the political landscape (Cohen et al., 2012, p. x). The findings of the research indicate that "Navalny's novel tactics have encouraged Russians in the street to speak candidly with his campaign workers, giving the feel of a genuine democratic contest" (Trudolyubov, 2013, para. 3). In a recent series of blog posts entitled "Participatory politics in the age of crisis," Jenkins (2019) reminds us about the distinction made by de Huszar (1945) between "talk-democracy" and "do-democracy," arguing that "democracy had become a thing of words rather than actions" (Jenkins, 2019, para. 3). For de Huszar, "Democracy is something you do; not something you talk about. It is more than a form of government, or an attitude or opinion. It is participation" (1945, xiii) and it is in this context that TS and ICT have the concrete potential to set the political action in motion. Navalny's transmedia campaign attracted and activated democratic development. Indeed, the commotion generated by the campaign was extended beyond Navalny's profile and turned into a hint of hope for democratic development in Russia. To reiterate, the campaign itself was far more important than the results. Russian society gained in strength. If this strength will be maintained, it remains to be seen.

REFERENCES

Analiz reklamnykh kampaniy kandidatov v mery Moskvy v razlichnykh media [The analysis of advertising campaigns of Moscow's mayoral candidates in different media] (2013, September 23). *Advertology*. Retrieved from http://www.advertology.ru/article117613.htm

Barry, E. (2012, July 31). Russia charges anticorruption activist in plan to steal timber. *The New York Times*. Retrieved from http://www.nytimes.com/2012/08/01/world/europe/aleksei-navalny-charged-with-embezzlement.html?_r=0

Barry, E. (2013, January 12). Russian lawmakers aim at foreign cars, films and schooling in patriotic purge. *The New York Times*. Retrieved from http://www.nytimes.com/2013/01/13/world/europe/ russian-lawmakers-move-to-purge-foreign-influences.html? pagewanted=all

Bastrykin Vzyalsya za Navalnogo i Belykh [Bastrykin gets down to Navalny and Belykh] (2012, July 7). [Video file]. Retrieved from http://www.youtube.com/watch?v=H3u7BKl6oKU

Bershidsky, L. (2013, August 26). What Alexei Navalny learned from Obama. *Bloomberg View*. Retrieved from http://www.bloombergview.com/articles/2013-08-26/what-alexei-navalny-learned-from-obama

Bodrunova, S. S. (2013). Fragmentation and polarization of the public sphere in the 2000s: Evidence from Italy and Russia. Global Media Journal German Edition, 3(1), 1–35.

Brennan, C. (2014a, May 23). Yandex offices searched during investigation into Navalny backers. *The Moscow Times*. Retrieved from http://www.themoscowtimes.com/article/500749.html

Brennan, C. (2014b, May 26). Navalny's popularity takes a dive, poll says. *The Moscow Times*. Retrieved from http://www.themoscowtimes.com/news/article/navalnys-popularity-takes-a-dive-poll-says/500899.html

Cassin, R. (2014, April 22). Navalny convicted of Twitter libel, could be jailed [Web log post]. Retrieved from http://www.fcpablog.com/blog/2014/4/22/navalny-convicted-of-twitter-libel-could-be-jailed.html# Central Electoral Committee (2012). *Elections*. Retrieved from http://cvk2012.org/

Clover, C., & Weaver, C. (2013, July 18). Russian opposition leader Alexei Navalny jailed for five years. *The Financial Times*. Retrieved from http://www.ft.com/intl/cms/s/0/ 82cc107e-ef71-11e2-8229-00144feabdc0.html#slide0

Cohen, C., Kahne, J., Bowyer, B., Middaugh, E., & Rogowski, J. (2012). *Participatory politics: New media and youth political action*. Oakland, CA: Mills College School of Education.

Couldry, N. (2010). *Why voice matters: Culture and politics after neoliberalism*. London, UK: Sage.

Crawford, K. (2009). Following you: Disciplines of listening in social media. *Continuum, 23*(4), 525–535. doi:10.1080/10304310903003270

Dannye po Auditori [Audience data] (2013). *TNS-Global*. Retrieved from http://www.tns-global.ru/services/media/ media-audience/radio/radio-index/information/

De Huszar, G. B. (1945). *Practical application of democracy*. New York, NY: Harper. doi:10.2307/2263272

DeLong, M., & Martinson, B. (2012). *Color and design*. London, UK: Berg.

Dragomir, M., & Thompson, M. (Eds.). (2011). *Mapping digital media: Russia*. London, UK: Open Society Foundation.

Etling, B., Alexanyan, K., Kelly, J., Faris, R., Palfrey, J., & Gasser, U. (2010). *Public discourse in the Russian blogosphere: Mapping RuNet politics and mobilization*. Cambridge, MA: Berkman Center for Internet & Society, Harvard University.

Federalny Zakon Rossiyskoy Federatsii ot 8 Iunya 2012 g. N 65-FZ g. Moskva [Federal law of Russian Federation, 2012, June 8, N 65-FZ, Moscow] (2012, June 9). *Rossiyskaya Gazeta*. Retrieved from http://www.rg.ru/2012/06/09/mitingi-dok.html

First we take Sakharov Avenue. The capital sees its biggest demonstration yet against the Kremlin. (2011, December 31). *The Economist*. Retrieved from http://www.economist.com /node/21542205

Freeman, M., & Gambarato, R. R. (Eds.). (2018). *The Routledge companion to transmedia studies*. New York, NY: Routledge. doi:10.4324/9781351054904

Gambarato, R. R. (2012). Signs, systems and complexity of transmedia storytelling. *Estudos em Comunicação, 12*, 69–83.

Gambarato, R. R. (2013). Transmedia project design: Theoretical and analytical considerations. *Baltic Screen Media Review, 1*(1), 80–100. doi:10.1515/bsmr-2015-0006

Gambarato, R. R. (2014). Transmedia storytelling in analysis: The case of final punishment. *Journal of Print and Media Technology Research, 3*(2), 95–106.

Gambarato, R. R. (2018). Russia: Interactive documentary, slow journalism and the transmediality of Grozny: Nine Cities. In M. Freeman, & W. Proctor (Eds.), *Global convergence cultures: Transmedia earth* (pp. 206–226). New York, NY: Routledge. doi:10.4324/9781315188478-13

Gambarato, R. R., & Alzamora, G. (Eds.). (2018). *Exploring transmedia journalism in the digital age*. Hershey, PA: IGI Global. doi:10.4018/978-1-5225-3781-6

Gambarato, R. R., & Lapina-Kratasyuk, E. (2016). Transmedia storytelling panorama in the Russian media landscape. *Russian Journal of Communication*, *8*(1), 1–16. doi:10.1080/19409419.2015.1121789

Gessen, M. (2012, October 22). For fair elections. *The New York Times*. Retrieved from http://latitude.blogs.nytimes.com/2012/10/22/russian-opposition-stages-alternative-election/?_php=true&_type=blogs&_r=0

Government of the Russian Federation. (1993). The constitution of the Russian Federation. Retrieved from http://www.constitution.ru/en/10003000-01.htm

Hincks, J. (2018, March 13). Your complete guide to Russia's presidential election. *Time*. Retrieved from https://time.com/5196905/russia-presidential-election-2018-candidates/

Indina, T. (2014). Moscow mayoral elections & another Navalny effect. Retrieved from http://www.newmediacenter.ru/2014/01/22/moscow-mayor-elections-another-navalny-effect/

Inspired by "The Wire" (2013, September 7). *The Economist*. Retrieved from http://www.economist.com/news/europe/21585043-charismatic-dissident-runs-american-style-campaign-inspired-wire

Jansson, A. (2013). Mediatization and social space: Reconstructing mediatization for the transmedia age. *Communication Theory*, *23*(3), 279–296. doi:10.1111/comt.12015

Jenkins, H. (2003, January 15). Transmedia storytelling. *Technology Review*. Retrieved from http://www.technologyreview.com/news/401760/transmedia-storytelling/

Jenkins, H. (2006). *Convergence culture. Where old and new media collide*. New York, NY: New York University Press.

Jenkins, H. (2008, November 13). Obama: The candidate for all platforms [Web log post]. Retrieved from http://henryjenkins.org/2008/11/whew_i_am_still_trying.html

Jenkins, H. (2010, April 27). Hollywood goes "transmedia" [Web log post]. Retrieved from http://henryjenkins.org/2010/04/hollywood_goes_transmedia.html

Jenkins, H. (2019, May 30). Participatory politics in the age of crisis: Henry Jenkins & Nico Carpentier (part I) [Web log post]. Retrieved from http://henryjenkins.org/blog/2019/5/30/participatory-politics-in-an-age-of-crisis-henry-jenkins-amp-nico-carpentier-part-i

Kak Moskva vibirala mera [How Moscow chose the mayor] (2013, September 9). *Vedomosti*. Retrieved from http://www.vedomosti.ru/special/map/moscow-map-2013?utm_source= vedomosti&utm_medium= widget&utm_campaign=vedomosti&utm_content=link

Khvostunova, O. (2013, December 6). A brief history of Russian media. *The Interpreter*. Retrieved from http://www.interpretermag.com/a-brief-history-of-the-russian-media/

Kovalyova, A., & Smith, A. (2013, September 6). Protests ahead of Moscow vote as Putin critic Navalny surges in polls. *NBC News*. Retrieved from http://www.nbcnews.com/news/other/protests-ahead-moscow-vote-putin-critic-navalny-surges-polls-f8C11089526

Kravtsova, Y. (2013, August 22). Navalny's campaign relies on innovation. *The Moscow Times*. Retrieved from http://www.themoscowtimes.com/news/article/navalnys-campaign-relies-on-innovation/484899.html

Krutov, M. (2013, June 4). Politolog Dmitry Oreshkin: Sobyanin poka populyaren [Political expert Dmitry Oreshkin: Sobyanin is popular yet]. *Radio Svoboda*. Retrieved from http://www.svoboda.org/content/article/25006532.html

Kvasha, S. (2013, April 4). Eastern Europe's largest social network VKontakte refuses to pay for copyrighted music. *Russia Beyond the Headlines*. Retrieved from http://rbth.asia/society/2013 /04/04/eastern_ europes_largest_social_network_vkontakte_refuses_to_pay_for_c_45849.html

Levin, B. (1970). *The pendulum years: Britain in the Sixties*. London, UK: Jonathan Cape.

Lipman, M. (2013, September 6). Alexey Navalny's miraculous, doomed campaign. *The New Yorker*. Retrieved from http://www.newyorker.com/online/blogs/newsdesk/2013/09/aleksey-navalnys-miraculous-doomed-campaign.html

Long, G. (2007). *Transmedia storytelling: Business, aesthetics and production at the Jim Henson Company*. (Unpublished master's thesis), Massachusetts Institute of Technology, Cambridge, MA.

Murray, J. (1997). *Hamlet on the Holodeck: The future of narrative in cyberspace*. Cambridge, MA: MIT Press.

Navalny, A. (2013). Alexey Navalny: Kandidat v mery Moskvy 2013: Otchet o predvybornoy kampanii [Alexey Navalny: Candidate for Moscow mayor 2013]. Campaign Report.

Navalny, A. (2014). Navalny. Retrieved from https://navalny.com/

Navalny, A. (2015). Chto takoe sistema Zhnets i pochemu ona prekrasna [What Zhnets system is and why it is beautiful]. Retrieved from https://navalny.com/p/4343/

Navalny, A. [Alexey Navalny] (2017, March 2). Don't call him "Dimon." [Video file]. Retrieved from https://www.youtube.com/watch?v=qrwlk7_GF9g

Navalny, A. (n.d.). Navalny [Web log]. Retrieved from http://navalny.livejournal.com/

Otstavka Sobyanina i dosrochnie vibory mera: prichiny i posledstviya [Sobyanin's resignation and snap elections: causes and consequences] (2013, June 6). *RIA Novosti*. Retrieved from http://web-balancer-main.rian.ru/politics/20130604/941316905.html

Panibratov, A. (2012). *Russian multinationals: From regional supremacy to global lead*. London, UK: Routledge.

Prentice, A. (2014, April 29). Putin foes fear Internet crackdown as 'blogger law' sails through. *Reuters*. Retrieved from http://www.reuters.com/article/2014/04/29/us-russia-internet-idUSBREA3S0QF20140429

Pri Luzhkove takogo ne bylo: moskvichi pokazali rekordno nizkuyu yavku ["With Luzhkov was not like this" Muscovites showed a record low turnout] (2013, September 9). *RBC*. Retrieved from http://top.rbc.ru/politics/09/09/2013/875417.shtml

Putin says opposition white stripes look like condoms (2011, December 15). *Gazeta.ru*. Retrieved from http://en.gazeta.ru/bears/2011/12/15/f_3928598.shtml

RosPil. (2014). Retrieved from http://rospil.info/

Roth, A. (2012, April 30). Russia's regional governors to be directly elected. *The Telegraph*. Retrieved from http://www.telegraph.co.uk/sponsored/rbth/politics/9236729/Russia-regional-governors.html

Rozanov, D. (2014, May 12). Winds of change leave Russia's opposition out in the cold. *Russia Beyond the Headlines*. Retrieved from http://m.rbth.com/politics/2014/05/12/winds_of_change _leave_russias_opposition_out_in_the_cold_36525.html

Russialize. (2011, December 10). Bolotnaya Square protest: Today we saw a civil society that is capable of great things [Web log post]. Retrieved from http://russialize.tumblr.com/post/ 14014318702/bolotnaya

Russian Federal State Statistics Service. (2011). Vserossiyskaya perepis naseleniya 2010 [2010 National Population Census]. Retrieved from http://www.gks.ru/free_doc/new_site/perepis2010/ croc/perepis_itogi1612.htm

Smirnova, E., & Surnacheva, E. (2012, February 2). Na chto potrachen «Koshelyok Romanovoy» – dengi 24 dekabrya [What «Romanova's Wallet» was spent for – the money of December 24th]. *Slon*. Retrieved from http://slon.ru/russia/ kuda_potrachen_ koshelek_ romanovoy_dengi_24_ dekabrya-736878.xhtml

Sopova, A. (2017, November 3). How independent Russian newsrooms keep reporting. *Nieman Report*. Retrieved from https://niemanreports.org/articles/how-independent-russian-newsrooms-keep-reporting/

StricklerE. (2012). *10 questions*. Retrieved from http://transmediadesign.wordpress.com/assigments/ 10-questions/

Suleymanov, S. (2013, August 28). How the Moscow mayoral candidates are winning the Internet. *The Interpreter*. Retrieved from http://www.interpretermag.com/how-the-moscow-mayoral-candidates-are-winning-the-internet/

Taylor, A. (2014, March 13). We treat him like he's mad, but Vladimir Putin's popularity has just hit a 3-year high. *The Washington Post*. Retrieved from http://www.washingtonpost.com/blogs/ worldviews/wp/2014/03/13/we-treat-him-like-hes-mad-but-vladimir-putins-popularity-has-just-hit-a-3-year-high/

Tétrault-Farber, G. (2014, May 13). Public's desire to protest hits record low. *The Moscow Times*. Retrieved from http://www.themoscowtimes.com/news/article/publics-desire-to-protest-hits-record-low/500066.html

The Moscow Times. (2017, July 17). Anti-corruption protests didn't make Navalny more popular – Poll. Retrieved from https://www.themoscowtimes.com/2017/07/17/navalny-protests-didnt-make-him-popular-poll-a58404

The platform of Alexey Navalny. (n.d.). Retrieved from http://five.navalny.ru/medicine.html

Trudolyubov, M. (2013, September 6). An election in Russia (well, almost). *The New York Times*. Retrieved from http://www.nytimes.com/2013/09/07/opinion/an-election-in-russia-well-almost.html?_r=2&

Vasilyeva, N., & Isachenkov, V. (2013, July 19). Russian opposition leader freed in surprise move. *Associated Press*. Retrieved from http://bigstory.ap.org/article/prosecutors-ask-free-russian-opposition-leader

Vremya Prishlo! Vooruzhaysya! [The time has come! Take up arms!] (2013, September 1). [Video file]. Retrieved from http://www.youtube.com/watch?v=DM6xm5JB_dQ

Weaver, C., & Clover, C. (2013, June 4). Moscow mayor surprises Russian opposition by calling election. *The Financial Times*. Retrieved from http://www.ft.com/cms/s/0/000a3534-cd2b-11e2-90e8-00144feab7de.html#axzz2xTcSGsmo

Yale World Fellows. (n.d.). *Alexey Navalny: Biography*. Retrieved from http://worldfellows.yale.edu/alexey-navalny

Yandex. (2013). *Development of the Internet in Russia's regions*. Retrieved from http://download.yandex.ru/company/ya_russian_regions_report_2013.pdf

Yoffa, J. (2014, March 28). Putin's new war on "traitors". *The New Yorker*. Retrieved from http://www.newyorker.com/online/blogs/newsdesk/2014/03/putin-new-hunt-for-internal-enemies.html

Yves Rocher withdraws accusations against Navalny on eve of hearing (2014, April 22). *The Moscow Times*. Retrieved from http://www.themoscowtimes.com/news/article/yves-rocher-withdraws-accusations-against-navalny-on-eve-of-hearing/498738.html

Zhyzhylkin, G. (2018). IT infrastruktura shtabov Navalnogo i sbor podpisey: Zhnets-2018 [IT infrastructure of Navalny's campaign offices and the signature collection: Zhnets-2018]. *Habr*. Retrieved from https://habr.com/ru/company/fbk/blog/347320/

Zotova, N., & Feldman, E. (2011, December 16). December 5 and 6, Moscow. *Novaya Gazeta*. Retrieved from http://en.novayagazeta.ru/politics/50111.html

KEY TERMS AND DEFINITIONS

Grassroots: Pertaining to ordinary people, especially contrasted with an elite.

Migratory Cues: Story bridges, signals that can motivate the audience to migrate from one medium to another within the same story universe.

Oblast: A type of administrative division such as a province or region.

Poll Watcher: A representative appointed by a candidate, a political party, or an institution to observe the election day and look for any violations of the law.

State Duma: The legislative lower house of the Federal Assembly of Russia.

The Wire: HBO television series (2002–2008) about the city of Baltimore in Maryland, USA, with deep discussions of social and political themes.

Transmedia Franchise: A series of independent media outlets, which function as entry points to a common story universe.

Chapter 4
A Study of Politicians in a Hybrid Media Setting During the 2014 Swedish Elections:
A Logic Polarisation and Dissent

Jakob Svensson
Malmö University, Sweden

ABSTRACT

This chapter attends to the interactions between campaigning politicians and traditional news media in an online space of social networking. Studying campaigning Parliamentarians on Twitter during the 2014 Swedish election, traditional news media and their online presences represented a form of authority. The interactions were often charged with emotions and could be understood as a way to negotiate status and group (party) belonging, something that is particularly important for campaigning politicians in a party-based democracy like Sweden. By studying the interactions between Parliamentarians and traditional news media, the study concludes that Parliamentarians were expected to be angry and upset with political opponents in front of their party comrades. Hence the mass media logic of conflict is transferred online and also with network media logic, favouring attention-maximising, witty one-liners. This foregrounds polarisation and dissent at the expense of discussion and debate.

DOI: 10.4018/978-1-7998-1791-8.ch004

Copyright © 2020, IGI Global. Copying or distributing in print or electronic forms without written permission of IGI Global is prohibited.

INTRODUCTION

This chapter attends to interactions between MPs (Members of Parliament) and traditional news media on Twitter during the 2014 Swedish election campaign. The research question the chapter attends to is how campaigning politicians interacted with journalists and traditional news media on Twitter during the 2014 elections. In particular the chapter attends to how mass media and network media logics intersected in this context of campaigning MPs interacting with traditional news media.

Today a great deal of the social and political dynamics of public life takes place online and we therefore need to pay attention to issues related to the use of social media platforms in relation to news and politics. We live in a hybrid media system, in which the online and the offline intersect, actors and agency are shaped by older as well as newer logics (Chadwick, 2013). One way such hybridity is manifested is in political actors' interaction with traditional news media and journalists online. In my previous studies of online participation, traditional news media (and their online presences) have represented a form of authority (Svensson, 2015; Svensson & Larsson, 2016). If your position on a political issue could be verified by a link to a traditional news media outlet, it would strengthen the validity of that position. Hence, to link to traditional news media in online discussions becomes a 'link of verification' (Svensson, 2015); displaying a 'privileged access to the truth' (Carpentier, 2014). Traditional news media and their representatives – as long as they confirm users' standpoints – indeed seems to represent valuable sources of information.

I became aware of this practice when studying participation in a so-called online cultural public sphere (Hermes, 2006), a LGBTQ dating site and political discussions there (Svensson, 2015). Debaters linked to traditional news – mostly tabloid newspapers – to prove their point, that they were right and their opponents wrong. This practice reappeared in a data set of Swedish MPs on Twitter during the 2014 elections. When MPs attacked political opponents on Twitter, or retweeted party/alliance comrades, journalists and links to traditional news texts were often used to justify their stances (Svensson & Larsson, 2016). Through such practices, political actors strategically negotiated status and group (i.e. party belonging), something that is particularly important for politicians campaigning in a party-based democracy like Sweden (Arter, 1999). To make a political career in a party-based democracy, it is within the party you need to position yourself as it is mainly your party comrades that hold the keys to political positions. In this chapter, campaigning Swedish MPs online interactions are therefore understood as reflexive and strategic, (here two sides of the same coin). Reflexively negotiating group/ party belonging and strategically seeking advantages campaign-wise – as well as strategically positioning one-self within the party hierarchy – are not seen as in a dichotomous relationship to each other here.

In order to study campaigning politicians' interaction with traditional news media online, I will revisit the 2014 data set of tweeting politicians. The aim is to discuss the logics and intersections of logics behind MPs interactions in this hybrid media setting. The question the chapter seeks to answer is to discern the hybrid media logic in this particular context of campaigning Swedish MPs. Before attending media logics and hybridity, I will first attend to the rise of social media in late modernity and the role of traditional news in online political communication.

Setting: The Rise of Social Media and Reflexive Communication in Late Modernity

Social media (Fuchs, 2014, pp. 32-33) is connected to the rise of so-called Web 2.0., the architecture of online user participation that enable many-to-many publication (Bakir, 2010, pp. 2-3). O'Reilly argued in 2005 that if a website is going to be defined as *social*, the user must be able to contribute to the content on that site, have the possibility to control his or her information, and the design is supposed to be interactive and useable (O'Reilly, 2005). Ellison and boyd's 2007 definition of Social Networking Sites (SNSs) elaborates on this definition further. They discuss SNS as different by allowing the user to articulate their social network and making it visible to other users. SNSs are thus defined as web-based services allowing users to create (semi)public profiles, connecting this profile to other users (often self-selected), whose contacts in turn will be made accessible by the service (Ellison & boyd, 2007, p. 2). boyd (2011) highlights four characteristics of SNS; profiles, friend lists, public commenting tools and stream-based updates. Larsson (2017) similarly underlines as common characteristics for social media platforms possibilities for users 1) to post content, 2) to redistribute content (through sharing, retweeting or reposting content), c) to interact through chats, comments, mentions and @replies, and d) to acknowledge other users through favouring content (through so-called likes). Hence, social media platforms are at the same time loci for spreading information, socialising as well as site for explicit and calculated self-presentations (boyd, 2011, p. 43).

The rise of social media has indeed been remarkable. The most visited internet sites were social media platforms already in 2009 (Bakir, 2010,). As much as 1 billion participate in net-based communities on a regular basis (depending on how you count, Kosinetz, 2011). With networks allowing for high-speed broadband to mobile phones, social media platforms have been established as the main locus for mediated communication and socialisation (at least among the young crowd as a Swedish study as early as 2010 has indicated (Medierådet, 2010)). Today internet penetration in Sweden is at 96% ("Internet World Stats", 2019). The level of social media use is also high with 71% of the population logging into a social media platform daily during 2018 (Nordicom, 2019). Hence, there is no doubt that the media and communication landscape is changing with the rise of social media. This leads to structural, architectural and social developments with its own significance beyond the technical aspects of digitalisation (Dahlgren, 2009, pp. 39-40). At the same time, we should not overestimate the transformative power of social media. Early celebratory discourses (see for example Benkler, 2006; Shirky, 2009) have been challenged by more pessimistic claims (see for example Morozov, 2011; Fuchs, 2014). Studies of politicians on social media platforms also show that they tend to under-exploit these platforms' interactive potential (Larsson & Svensson, 2014). It is also important to remember here that social media platforms corporate and governed by a capitalist logic of making a profit. Social media evolve in tandem with society and culture and thus reflect power relations in society at large.

This study is based on the platform Twitter. Twitter emerged in 2006 and is an internet-based service in which users have a public profile where they broadcast short messages/updates that then become publicly aggregated together across users, and users can decide whose messages/updates they wish to receive, but not who can receive their messages/updates (Fuchs, 2014, pp. 179-180). Tweets are publicly available and thus easy for researchers to access. Twitter had about 500 million registered users in 2014 (the year of data collection) out of which half logged in at least once a month. The # (hashtag) RT (retweet) and @message buttons were introduced in 2008 and 2009 (van Dijck, 2013, p. 71). The hashtag enables users to group posts together by topic, the RT enables users to resend someone else's tweet and the @message to direct a tweet to a specific other user (van Dijck, 2013, pp. 71-72). Hence, Twitter allows a study of connections/ relationships between users, and who interacts with whom. In Sweden in 2015 (a year after the data collection) 18% of internet users visited Twitter sometimes (a decrease from 2014 with 4%), and 6% daily ("Twitter", 2019). While not as popular as Facebook and YouTube, Twitter is commonly known as an 'elite' medium as the platform is particularly popular among politicians and journalists.

I have made the argument elsewhere that online interactions often are reflexive (Svensson, 2011). Indeed, reflexivity is a central theme in our time (which is sometimes referred to as reflexive modernity, see Beck, 1995). Social media have made it easier for people to communicate and reflect upon themselves and their communication within larger and self-made peer networks. Digital technology thus works in tandem with socio-cultural processes of individualisation and reflexivity in late modernity (Svensson, 2011). A continuous emphasis of the self as something that can be managed, bears upon the individual to such a degree that the self becomes a *reflexive* project (Giddens, 1991, p. 32). And for this, social media platforms offer a plethora of possibilities to expand on who we are (Gergen, 2002, p. 234). It thus seems that the late modern self, trying to confirm who she really is, uses social media to both monitor her identity as well as test it in front of selected others and peers (Svensson, 2011). In general, social media users wish that their online postings will be recognised by likes, links and thumbs up from their selected peers (i.e. online friends). Such recognition can in turn be used to negotiate group belonging and reaffirm status within the group. In other words, users invite peers to 'supervise' them in order to secure a place on the social arena, increase status and popularity (Livingstone, 2008). Likewise, politicians also have a peer group to relate to; the party. In a previous study of a campaigning politician I found how the party was central in that she amplified messages and performances of party comrades (not seldom emanating from offline news media) by spreading them on her social media platforms, and she virtually patted the backs of party comrades by praising them in her social media channels (Svensson, 2014a). The party peer group is especially important in a party-based democracy like Sweden (Arter, 1999) where the party is of utmost importance for an individual MP seeking to make a political career.

Let us then turn to the Swedish political party landscape. At the time of data collection, Sweden was governed by a conservative alliance of the *Conservative* (Moderaterna), the *Christian Democrats*, the *Liberals* and the *Centre Party*. They faced an opposition of mainly *Social Democrats* and the *Green Party*. Both parties had expressed their interest of ruling together and this attempt was supported by the *Left Party*. These three parties formed the so-called red-green alliance. The polls up to Election Day predicted a majority for the red-green alliance and a possible parliamentary entry of the left-leaning *Feminist Initiative*.

What do we know about Swedish parties' tweeting practices during the 2014 election campaign? The underdog and newcomer *Feminist Initiative* was by far the most active party on Twitter with 1610 tweets the month running up the elections (Larsson, 2017). This can be compared to the *Social Democrats* with their 1062 tweets, and *Sweden Democrats* with only 83 tweets. Number of tweets and election results did not correlate though. On Election Day, the *Feminist Initiative* did not reach the threshold level of four percent to get into parliament. The red-green alliance while receiving more votes than the conservatives was not able to secure the majority in the Chamber. Besides, the nationalistic immigration hostile party, the *Sweden Democrats*, more than doubled their support.

Traditional News Media in Political Communication on Social Media

Social media is not in a dichotomous relationship to traditional offline media. This has been underlined in accounts of hybridity. In Chadwick's (2013) award winning work, he describes the emergence of a diverse, fragmented and polycentric media environment facilitated by digital communication. In particular he argues that so-called *new* media does not displace the so-called *old* media, but rather facilitates the emergence of a hybridised media system, that there is a degree of interdependence between traditional offline media and digital media. The relationship between journalistic institutions and social media platforms is being intensified where it seems the former are becoming increasingly dependent on the latter as more and more traffic to the traditional news sites are routed through Facebook and Twitter (see for example Barberá, Vaccari & Valeriani, 2017).

The aspects of contemporary hybridity that I wish to zoom in on here, is that of the presence of traditional news media and their representatives in an online space of political communication. Studying political discussions in an online LGBTQ community, links to traditional news media, mostly to tabloids and daily broadsheets were abundant (Svensson, 2014b). These links were often used to confirm the standpoint of the user participating in the discussion. As discussed earlier, with a link to traditional news media, it seemed the argument became solidified and justified, a kind if verification that indeed the claim in the posting was true. Similarly, in a study of tweeting MPs during the 2014 elections we found that traditional news media actors were important interaction partners (Svensson & Larsson, 2016). Going into some of these tweets in which traditional news media were linked to, it became apparent that traditional news media were considered as convincing and important sources of information, and hence good to use for justifying MPs opinions.

In this chapter we return to the data set of tweeting MPs from the 2014 Swedish elections. Originally, we set out to study with whom Swedish MPs interacted (Svensson & Larsson, 2016). Twitter provides a relatively straight-forward manner to study this. We found that MPs most often retweeted their party comrades and alliance colleagues (so called *virtual back-patting*, Svensson, 2014a) but @messaged their political opponents. Let's zoom on these interactions here in this chapter.

In the (RTs) retweets we find many traditional news journalists and editorial writers. *Niklas Svensson*, political reporter at tabloid newspaper *Expressen* was retweeted 97 times by a variety of MPs and *Expressen*'s own account was retweeted 87 times. Channel 4 news' twitter account (*nyheterna*) was retweeted 59 times and editorial writer at right-wing daily *Svenska Dagbladet Tove Lifvendahl* was retweeted 50 times. Public service broadcaster *SVT*s news' account (*svtnyheter*) was retweeted 31 times and editorial writer at social democratic tabloid *Aftonbladet Anders Lindberg* 30 times and so on. If we found an account with retweets across the political alliances then we could be almost certain a journalist was behind the account. MPs indeed considered it important to align themselves and their campaign to traditional news media actors and mass media texts.

Much like for RTs, traditional news media and their journalists were also present among the most @replied. The most @replied account belonged to *Aftonbladet* editorial writer *Anders Lindberg*. Receiving 64 @replies, he was more popular than

Table 1. 10 most retweeted traditional news media accounts

Niklas Svensson	@niklassvensson	Journalist at Expressen (97 RTs)
Expressen	@Expressen	Tabloid Newspaper (87 RTs)
TV4 Nyheterna	@Nyheterna	Channel 4 news (59 RTs)
Tove Lifvendahl	@ToveLifvendahl	Political editor at SvD (50 RTs)
SVT Nyheter	@svtnyheter	Public Service TV news (31 RTs)
Anders Lindberg	@anderslindberg	Editorial writer at Aftonbladet (30 RTs)
SVT din röst	@svtdinrost	SVT requesting citizen to make their voices heard (27)
Helle Klein	@HelleKlein	Editor in chief at Dagens Arbete (25 RTs)
Svenska Dagdladet	@SvD	Broadsheet Newspaper (24 RTs)
Daniel Swedin	@danielswedin	Editorial Writer at Aftonbladet (24 RTs)

tabloid competitor *Niklas Svensson*, political reporter at the more liberal-conservative tabloid *Expressen* (who received 21 @replies). Political reporter *Owe Nilsson* at the press agency TT received 20 @replies, and liberal daily *Dagens Nyheter* chronicle writer *Emmanuel Karlsten* and left-leaning (and at the time) freelance journalist *Helle Klein* were @replied 18 times each. We also found journalists from more rural news media in the sample such as the news director at the local daily *Gefle Dagblad* (*Magnus Lundquist*) who received 25 @replies. As with the RTs the journalists in the sample were addressed by a variety of different MPs across the political alliances. A guess here is that MPs sought attention from traditional news media actors by @messaging them.

Hence, we know that traditional news media were present in the interaction of MPs on Twitter during the 2014 election campaign. But the question this article seeks to answer is how mass media and network media logics intersected in this context of campaigning MPs interacting with traditional news media? This leads me to the next section which attends to the theoretical framework of media logics.

Table 2. 10 most @messaged traditional news media accounts

Anders Lindberg	@anderslindberg	Editorial writer at Aftonbladet (64 @s)
Magnus Lundqvist	@GDmagnus	News director at local Gefle Dagblad (25 @s)
Niklas Svensson	@niklassvensson	Journalist at Expressen (21 @s)
Owe Nilsson	@owenil	Journalist at the news agency TT (20 @s)
Emmanuel	@emanuelkarlsten	Journalist at daily Dagens Nyheter (18 @s)
Helle Klein	@HelleKlein	Editor in chief at Dagens Arbete (18 @s)
Sakine Madon	@Sakine	Editor at Vestmanlands Läns Tidning (14@s)
Viktor Barth-Kron	@viktorbk	Journalist at daily Dagens Nyheter (13 @s)
Tomas Ramberg	@TomasRamberg	Commentator at public service radio (11 @s)
Amanda Björkman	@AmandaLBjorkman	Editorial writer at Dagens Nyheter (11 @s)

Media Logics

Logics has come to imply thought and reason and has thus been connected to the study of forms of arguments. Logics are understood as sense-making/ meaning-generating frameworks for practices and experiences (Thornton, Ocasio & Lounsbury, 2012, p. 12; Lowrey, 2017, p. 380). Logics thus organize work (Dahlgren, 1996, p. 63) and provide stability to social behaviour (Asp, 2014, p. 259).

Within media and communication studies, Altheide and Snow's 1979 book of media logics is a classic. They sought to understand the role of media as constituting and recognising social reality. According to them, "media logic functions as a form through which events and ideas are interpreted and acted upon" (p. 240). They particularly emphasise that media logics are interactive and based on various participants (such as audience/user interpretation as well as media content and organisation), rather than on one-way relationships in which media dictate the definitions of reality (Altheide & Snow, 1979, p. 236).

What did Altheide and Snow mean with logic? They talk about *formats* as ways to select and organise material, the style of presentation, the focus, emphasis and the *grammar* of media (Altheide & Snow, 1979, p. 10). Indeed, the medium impacts the communication as it *formats* the content (Lundby, 2014, p. 7). According to Strömbäck and Esser (2014, p. 381), logics should be understood as appropriate behaviour that is consistent and reasonable within the rules and norms of the institutional context. Indeed, many scholars understand logics as *specific rules* that govern a domain, for example how news are selected, interpreted and constructed in journalism valuing conflict over conformity (Lundby, 2014, p. 28). These rules then impact other domains, such as politics.

Within politics, the theory of media logics is largely based on politicians' quest for mass media coverage. Asp (1986) showed early how politicians were influenced by, and adjusted themselves to the demands of mass media, how they geared their statements towards conflict in order to have a better chance of mass media coverage. Today, as politicians and parties are migrating to social media platforms, it has been argued that politicians express themselves in short "twitterable" phrases. Researchers have thus attempted to apply the theory of media logics to digital media. Van Dijck and Poell (2013) were early in outlining what they label *social media logic*. Klinger and Svensson (2015 and 2016) have in their turn outlined what they label *network media logics*. Their argument is that social media platforms are characterised by different, though overlapping, logics from mass media, with regard to media production, distribution and usage (Klinger & Svensson, 2015). This is further delineated by connecting it to three aspects of mass media's logic: professional ideals, commercial imperatives and technological affordances (Klinger & Svensson, 2016). Network media logics are, in short, based on ideals of sharing reflexive and personal information among peers and like-minded, principles of connectivity and popularity, ideals of viral spread and attention-maximization, favoring witty one-liners over long analyses, affording updating in peer and interest-based networks.

Media logics are also central to the concept of hybrid media systems. Chadwick (2013) argues that "political and media actors shape and are shaped by older and newer media logics" (p. 22). However, understanding media systems as hybrid does not dissolve the different logics between traditional mass media and social media platforms. For example, traditional mass media are often found online, and video platforms such as YouTube have become more TV-like with *channels* that users can *subscribe* to. In increasingly hybrid media systems, mass media and network media logic tend to overlap and intertwine. Mass media logic and network media logic should thus not be understood as dichotomous concepts that are mutually exclusive.

The hybrid media system is based upon conflict and competition between older and newer media logics but it also features important pockets of interdependence among these logics. (Chadwick, 2013, p. 207).

In fact, the idea of hybridity relies on at least two definable components that either converge into a hybrid form. The question is what does this media logic look like in a setting of campaigning Swedish MPs? What happen when mass media and network media logics collide in a hybrid media setting of campaigning Swedish MPs interacting with traditional news media actors on Twitter? This is what this study is about.

Method and Data Collection

In order to get to the specific rules that formatted the content (i.e. logics) on Twitter when campaigning Swedish MPs interacted with traditional news actor during the 2014 elections, focus will be on emotions expressed in these interactions. Rules, norms and values are particularly visible in emotions. Elias (1939/1998) for example argued that emotions carry with them information and clues about accepted and preferred behaviours of a given society in a given situation. When we reflect on what we ought to feel, and when we observe how our peers assess our interactions, we are consciously, or unconsciously, adhering to the norms and rules (i.e. logics) in the given situation (Elias, 1939/1998). Through emotions expressed in interactions between campaigning MPs and traditional news on Twitter it will be possible to study logics at play in this hybrid media setting. How do mass media and network media logic intersect in this context of campaigning MPs interactions with traditional news media on Twitter?

In this article, an earlier data set of interacting campaigning MPs is revisited. The sample consists of all tweeting MPs tweets two weeks up to the elections. At the time of data-gathering, it was easy to access all Swedish MPs Twitter accounts through the site Twixdagen (www.twixdagen.se, accessed May 2014, no longer working). The Swedish Parliament has 349 members, 169 of those had a Twitter account in May 2014. These 169 accounts were our empirical entry points. The focus of the data gathering has been on the so-called hot phase of campaigning, i.e. the two last weeks from September 1st to Election Day on September 14th. During this period, the 169 MPs tweeted 23,825 times (see Svensson & Larsson, 2016 for more details on the data collection).

In the first study, the focus was on with whom MPs interacted (see Svensson & Larsson, 2016). To study this, we singled out retweets (RTs) and @messages in the collected sample. It can be argued though that the practice of retweeting is a kind of broadcasting, a re-distribution of tweets penned by others. However, by making this other user visible, still indicates some kind of interconnectedness, that you acknowledge and follow this other user and want to interact with what this user's tweets (by agreeing, contesting or questioning the content in the tweet). In other words, we argue that retweeting can be conceived of as a form of interaction. Compared to retweeting, @Messaging is a more direct way of addressing a particular other user. Signalling a clear conversational tendency, @messages are used to contact, react to or in other ways engage with another Twitter user (Twitter, 2014). Almost half of the tweets (11,467) were RTs (48 percent). Moreover, 5,685 tweets in the material were identified as @messages (24 percent of the collected material). Hence, in approximately one fourth of the tweets, MPs were directly addressing someone else.

In this material of RTs and @messages traditional news media accounts were manually identified (by going through all retweeted and @messaged accounts). By traditional news media is meant a news outlet that uses print, radio or TV as their principal platform of dissemination. About 9% of this material (1488 out of 17152 tweets) was retweeting or @messaging a traditional news media account. Not having the resources to study all of these tweets in detail, the ten most retweeted and the ten most @messages traditional news media accounts were selected for an in-depth qualitative reading (see tables 1 and 2 above). 669 RTs and @messages were studied (representing about 45% RTs and @messages to traditional news media accounts in the total sample).

For the in-depth and qualitative reading of these tweets I first studied them at face value. The tweets were read manually one by one to identify emotions expressed in this sample of RTs and @messages. In the data collection I have limited the range of emotion studied to negative and positive emotions since there established practices on how to identify such emotions in written texts to rely upon. So how where positive and negative emotions identified? Expressions of anger, dissatisfaction, disappointment, disapproval, frustration, criticisms, lack of faith and fear for the future were identified as expressions of negative emotions (see Boote, 1998; Wirtz & Mattila, 2004; Russmann, 2017). Positive emotions were identified when something or someone were optimistically highlighted or applauded such as focusing on qualifications and accomplishments, in a celebratory fashion (see Djupe & Peterson, 2002; Lau & Pomper, 2001). Also, expressions of pleasant surprises were identified as positive. In other words, rather than a positive or negative tone, the sample consists of expressions of emotions within the sampled RTs and @ messages. In a majority of the collected tweets (69% of the tweets, 462 out of 669 tweets), positive or negative emotions were expressed. About two thirds of these were expressions of negative emotions. I have also studied the Twitter context in which the tweets were composed and the interaction they sparked.

RESULTS

Expressions of positive and negative emotions were visible in MPs @messages to, and RTs of, traditional news media. By retweeting traditional news media, MPs adhered to the mass media logic of conflict and dissent (Asp, 1986). Transferred to an online environment, this meant that polarising – but also witty and catchy – tweets from the traditional news media actors, were likely to be retweeted by MPs. @Messages were, perhaps not surprisingly, more conversational. @Messages with emotions with traditional news media journalists mostly commented mass news texts, praising certain articles but also expressing dissatisfaction about unfavourable coverage or what MPs sometimes considered errors in their texts. This was about trying to understand each other and reaching a mutual agreement, rather than merely attacking each other and attaching unfavourable labels to political opponents. Below I will attend to these results in more detail.

Retweeting Traditional News Media

The study of MPs displaying emotions by retweeting traditional news media confirms previous studies in the field. Traditional news media are treated as particularly valuable if confirming the MP and his/her standpoint and party line; i.e. a link of verification, showing that your opinion is true and that of your opponent is false (Svensson, 2015). For example, political editor in chief Tove Lifvendahl (@ToveLifvendahl) at conservative daily SvD (Svenska Dagbladet) was retweeted by conservative MP Lena Asplund (@lenaasplund) when she criticised Social Democratic foreign minister candidate Margot Wallström. Another example is Anki Johansson (@ ankijohansson, Social Democrat) retweeting Helle Klein (@HelleKlein, Editor in chief at labour union newspaper Dagens Arbete) criticising at the time conservative Prime Minister Fredrik Reinfeldt. The retweets thus functioned to justify MPs political opinions and seems to have been directed towards the in-group of party comrades, expressing and confirming political opinions in front of the party peer group rather than discussing them.

Most emotions expressed in the tweets were negative, and by retweeting them the MPs in a sense attacked their political opponents. Retweeting a traditional news media actor thus functioned as a justification that you and your political comrades were right (and that your opponents are wrong) rather than as an invitation for deliberation. For example, Morgan Johansson (@johanssonmorgan, Social Democrat) retweeted Anders Lindberg (@anderslindberg, editorial writer at social democratic tabloid Aftonbladet), when he in a tweet criticised conservative MPs' surprise over Social Democratic party leader Stefan Löfven. In general emotions in the RTs underlined a general expression of frustration about the political opponent. Another example is liberal-conservative tabloid Expressen (@Expressen) tweets attacking Stefan Lövfen. They were retweeted by Center Party MP Anders Åkesson (@andersaakesson) and conservative MP Lars Beckman (@beckmansasikter). By recirculating such tweets, right-wing MPs contributed to portraying left-wing opponents in an unflattering manner in front of their followers (mostly party comrades). This confirms emotions displays as both reflexive and strategic at the same time.

It is relatively easy to connect the political colour of the editorial page of the newspapers retweeted with the party colour of the MP retweeting it. For example, of the 50 times conservative editorial writer Tove Lifvendahl was retweeted, 49 of them came from the conservative alliance parties' MPs. Of the 30 times social-democratic editorial writer Anders Lindberg was retweeted only 8 came from conservative alliance parties. This can be compared to the account *svtdinröst* (svtyourvoice), a traditional news media account without a political colour (arguably) since it belonged to the national public service broadcaster (SVT). This account was retweeted a lot, but these RTs did not contain as many emotions as the retweeted newspapers and their editorial writers.

At the centre of negative RTs was the immigration hostile, islamophobic and nationalistic party the Sweden Democrats. For example, the only time conservative editorial writer Tove Lifvendahl was retweeted by an MP from a red-green alliance party (Left Party MP Lars Ohly, @OhlyLars), it was when she implicitly compared Sweden Democrats youth organisation behaviour to Nazi practices. Another example is conservative MP Lars Beckman retweeting Anders Lindberg's attack on the Sweden Democrats in a tweet in which he labelled the party as "disgusting". The Sweden Democrats seemed particularly gratifying to attack. Important to mention here is the Swedish political context. The potential (and in opinion polls predicted) growth of the Sweden Democrats would rock the party-political establishment with two clear blocs (left and right) that have dominated Swedish political landscape since the beginning of representative democracy. Hence, they were particularly threatening to the political establishment.

The few positive emotions displayed in the RTs were mostly in relation to retweeting for the MP favourable opinion polls broadcasted in news media. One example is Lars Beckman (conservative, @beckmansasikter) retweeting public service broadcaster SVT news' (@svtnyheter) tweet that the conservative alliance was closing in on the red-greens in the latest opinion polls with and added expression of hapiness. The daily broadsheet Svenska Dagbladet's (@SvD) tweet concerning the conservative alliance approaching the red-greens in the opinion polls was retweeted four times by conservative alliance MPs et cetera.

Another example of positive emotions in the RTs is when a traditional news media actor declared that the retweeting MPs party leader had won a debate. Editorial writer Helle Klein (@HelleKlein) for example proclaimed that Left Party leader Jonas Sjöstedt has won a debate, and this was then retweeted by Left Party MP Wiwi-Anne Johansson (@wiwiannejoh). As with the more negative RTs it is possible that also positive RTs were directed towards the peer-group of party comrades. However, these had a more mobilising tone than the negative ones.

Emotions in the RTs were to a vast majority those expressed in the retweeted tweets composed by the traditional news media organisation or by the journalist. The exception is when the retweeting MP added an exclamation to underline something in the tweet. For example, when Ali Esbati (@aliesbati, Left Party) retweeted Daniel Swedin's (@danielswedin, editorial writer at Aftonbladet) tweet about a "left wind" among young voters, and adding to the tweet that this made him happy. But most often, RTs were about recirculating emotional displays in the original tweets.

Sometimes the emotions re-circulated originated offline from the party leaders televised debates. For example, when the tabloid Expressen live-tweeted from public service broadcaster SVTs debate, emotion displays in the actual debate were picked up in Expressen's tweets and then re-circulated by the MPs. Stefan Lövfen (Social Democrat) for example laughed at Jan Björklund (Liberal). This was picked up by Expressen and then retweeted by Tina Acketoft (@TinaAcketoft, Liberal). Twitter, with its affordance of re-circulation of information thus seems to increase the buzz rather than contributing with new information.

The fascination for party leaders' emotion displays can be traced back to the logic of mass media favouring conflict and personalisation (Asp, 1986). For visibility in the news, emotion displays becomes an obvious part in an election campaign. Hence the vast amount of emotions found in this material can be linked to traditional news media tendency to favour polarisation and conflict over consent and agreement. In this sense, the mass media logic and the polarised atmosphere of an election campaign intersected towards a climate of emotionally displayed dissent and conflict. By retweeting traditional news media tweets, the logic of mass media was thus transferred online.

However, it is not as simple as the logic of mass media being transferred integrally to the online. Rather the logic of mass media becomes intertwined with aspects of network media logics, favouring attention maximising content in peer networks of like-minded. As such tweets should be witty to be retweeted. Some attacks were definitely more retweetable than others. For example, editorial writer Tove Lifvendahl tweeted about how "four shades of red" (alluding to the four opposition parties and also the popular Swedish movie "Four Shades of Brown") represented an unappealing image of the future. This was retweeted by five conservative MPs. Another example is Expressen's live tweets of Liberal party leader Björklund's one-liner attacks on Gustav Fridolin (Green Party), that he had "talked for 40 minutes and promised away 40 million". This was retweeted by Andreas Norlen (@ andreasostgote, conservative) and Anna Steel (@AnnaSteele, liberals). Especially Expressen's live tweeting during the party leaders' debate offered possibilities for other MPs to retweet polarising and catchy one-liners expressed to the network of followers. Expressing surprise in tweets also worked well for being retweeted. An example is when left leaning editorial writer Helle Klein to her surprise cheered for Björklund (Liberals) when he debated Åkesson (party leader of the Sweden democrats). This tweet was retweeted four times by conservative alliance party MPs (but not by anyone from the red-green parties).

The hybridity between social media and traditional news media becomes especially apparent in MPs RTs of tabloid Expressen's live coverage from the public service broadcaster debate. There are even some examples of angry criticism directed towards SVT, expressed by retweeting newspaper journalists' accounts. For example, Aftonbladets Anders Lindberg criticised that a former mentor of the Sweden Democratic party leader was invited to comment a debate on national public service broadcaster SVT. This critique was then retweeted by Social Democratic MP Tomas Eneroth (@TomasEneroth). Another example is Lindberg criticising daily Dagens Nyheter "sucking up to the conservative alliance government", retweeted by Lars Ohly (@OhlyLars, Left Party) and so on.

Studying RTs of traditional news media in which emotions were displayed, it seems that traditional news media was used as a mouthpiece, a vehicle through which own opinions could be expressed, a political persona could be negotiated. traditional news media appears to be particularly valuable for campaigning MPs as an authority, a valuable source useful for confirming ones' opinions and political identity. Emotions, campaigns and mass media logic of conflict thus converged on Twitter towards a heightened environment of polarisation and dissent.

@Messages

The @messages between campaigning MPs and traditional news media were more conversational and interrogative than the circulation of news media texts in the RTs. Through the @message function, Twitter allowed MPs to enter into discussion about the content of news media texts that MPs sometimes thought were untruthful or that issues and persons were incorrectly framed by the traditional news media actors. One typical example is the exchange between Social Democrat MP Elin Lundgren (@ElinLudis) and journalist at liberal broadsheet Gefle Dagblad Magnus Lundqvist (@GDMagnus). Lundgren being angry for incorrect party names in the newspaper. Another example is Hanif Bali (@hanifbali, conservatives) @messaging with daily DNs journalist Viktor Barth-Kron (@viktorbk) trying to influence the journalist about a story on the Green Party.

This is about MPs entering into discussions about details in reported stories, often contesting them. Another example is Maria Ferm (@MariaFerm, Green Party) @ messaging with tabloid Aftonbladet Anders Lindberg concerning a news story on pupils protesting the presence of a Sweden Democratic politician at their school. The exchange concerned the framing of whether the students had the right to protest against the presence of the anti-immigration party at their school, or whether it was correct to call the police (that apparently the school management had done) to stop this manifestation against democratically elected politicians.

It also seems that what was considered unfair criticism, raised emotions among the MPs. The @messages and the presence of traditional news media on Twitter allowed MPs to directly engage with the journalists and also attempt to nuance their news stories. One example is Abir Alsahlani (@AbirAlsahlani, Center Party) @ messaging with Amanda Björkman (@AmandaLBjorkman, editorial writer at liberal broadsheet Dagens Nyheter) in order to dissociate herself from opinions attributed to her and the Center Party in Björkman's editorial.

Other traditional news media actors could also be used when arguing with a journalist. For example, liberal MP Roger Haddad (@RogerHaddadfp) @messaged with Anders Lindberg to direct him to public service broadcaster SVTs coverage of a public school in order to show that not only private schools performed poorly. This was a hot topic during the campaign, whether private schools were misbehaving and only in the business for the money. Anders Lindberg's text was critical of allowing private interests into core welfare services such as education. The right-wing argument was that the quality of education should be central, and then it does not matter whether it is a public or private actor that provides it.

Emotions were thus expressed differently in the @messages compared to in the RTs. In the RTs the vast majority of the emotions was those already displayed in the original tweets, expressed by the traditional news media actor. In the @messages the emotions displayed were expressed by the MPs themselves, i.e. their emotional reactions to coverage in traditional news. An example is Cecilia Dalman Eek (@ dalmaneek, Social Democrat) @messaging with journalist Emmanuel Karlsten (@ emanuelkarlsten). He tweeted a poll suggesting that first time voters would lean towards the left. Cecilia commented this as "fantastic and heart-warming". Another example is left-leaning editorial writer Helle Klein's (@HelleKlein) discussing whether Stefan Lövfén (party leader of the Social Democrats) forcefully shoved, or gently pushed away Center party leader Annie Lööf during a televised debate when she tried to hand over a report to him. Conservative MP Kent Persson (@kentpersson) @messaged with Helle Klein and said that she can "call it whatever ever she wants, it is still a completely unreasonable behaviour of a candidate for the post of prime minister". Hence, with the @messages the MPs tried to influence/ discuss with the journalists while the RTs were to a vast majority just re-circulated as they were. In both cases in becomes clear that traditional news media are considered as important tools during an election campaign, also online.

An interesting observation is the use of emoticons. They were virtually absent in the sample of RTs, but not in the @messages. In the RTs traditional news media tweets were used as a tool to display attacks against political opponents. In the @messages MPs and traditional news media journalists more often entered into discussion with each other, and in this more conversational context, emoticons were used to replace body language, mostly a smiley ☺ in order to underline that the MPs were stating something/ criticising in a friendly manner. For example, Mats Pertoft (@MatsPertoft, Green Party) @messaged with journalist at liberal-conservative tabloid Expressen Niklas Svensson (@niklasvensson) concerning the price of petrol in Sweden. He criticises Svensson and states that Sweden does not have the highest petrol prices in Europe, but ends his @message with a smiley.

All exchanges were not as conversational in nature. Some MPs used the @messages to simply make their disagreement with a journalist visible to their followers and also to other traditional news media actors. Twitter allows to @message several accounts in the same tweet. As such the @message also functioned to make others aware of one's opinions, or of a news media text the tweeting MPs favoured or wanted to contest. One example of this is Hanif Bali (@hanifbali, conservative) @messaging with Amanda Björkman at daily Dagens Nyheter to let her know that he disagreed with her. But he also let others know about this disagreement since in the same tweet he @messaged other editorial writers as well as party comrades. Attention maximising is indeed part of the network media logic, and in a hybrid media system in which traditional news media actors are available online they become important intermediaries for MPs wanting to be seen and get through the noise and potentially also into the traditional news themselves. For example, Green Part MP Maria Ferm (@MariaFerm) trying to get journalist Viktor Barth-Kron (@viktorbk) attention.

Viktor tweets about what appears to be poor results of the Green Party in Danderyd (a wealthy Stockholm suburb). Maria @messages the journalist to let him know that she will tweet about this later that night.

There are examples of MPs advising/ pushing journalists to attack opponents. Helen Pettersson (@hepe, Social Democrat) directed Aftonbladets Anders Lindberg to what he considered "an absurd statement" by the conservative alliance in the county of Västerbotten (northwest of Sweden). There are also examples of MPs praising journalists when they did report on an opponent in an unfavourable manner. One example is Lars Beckman (@beckmansasikter, conservatives) @messaging with journalist Magnus Lundqvist (@GDMagnus). He praises his newspaper for a "good scoop" when they revealed that a Social Democratic local politician had used taxpayers' money carelessly. At the same time, he makes this exchange visible through also @messaging social democratic politicians in the same tweet. This is an apparent example of how also @messages are used for polarisation and how newspaper journalists become vehicles for displaying attacks against political opponents.

It was not only MPs who were taking advantage of traditional news media actors' presence on Twitter for their campaigns and negotiations of group/ party belonging. The @messages also reveal how journalists sometimes conducted their research on Twitter. For example, Tomas Ramberg (@TomasRamberg, commentator at public service radio) @messaged with Staffan Danielsson (@staffand, Center Party). Tomas wanted to know whether Staffan had questioned the party leader. "Absolutely NOT" (in capital letters), he answered. Another example is Ramberg's exchange with Jens Holm (@holmjens, Left Party) on the red-green stance on the fur industry concerning a statement from Stefan Lövfén (Social Democratic prime minister candidate of the red-greens).

This underlines the tight connections between traditional news media actors and politicians. Former Left Party leader Lars Ohly (@OhlyLars) @messaged with Anders Lindberg in what seems to be a friendly jokey manner if he could get a job at Aftonbladet after the election (commenting on opinion polls not favourable for the Left Party). What does this do the democracy when the ties between MPs and the ones who are put to scrutinise them are this tight? The problem is if Twitter becomes an elite medium for those already powerful, yet another platform for the elite to interact and reinforce their ties and thus also their power. The advantage with Twitter is that the platform is open, semi-public in that everyone can follow accounts and thus also scrutinise power, whether it is political or journalistic power.

CONCLUSION

This study underlines the hybridity between social media and traditional news media in this setting of campaigning MPs. It shows clearly that the different functions of Twitter are used quite differently. RTs are very unidirectional while @messages are more conversational. Social media can thus not be studied as a coherent whole. There are vast differences even within a platform in how different functions are used. The study also suggests that in this hybrid media setting of social media platforms and traditional news media, traditional news media actors are still the authorities in that politicians use their tweets as valuable (re)sources in their political attacks and identity expressions, and that they @messaged with traditional news media in order to correct stories, or to get into the news themselves. In both RTs and @messages it became rather apparent that expressions of emotions were used strategically and reflexively in order to attack opponents in front of the peer group of party comrades

The aim of this article was to discuss and understand the logics at play, as well as intersections of logics, in this particular hybrid media setting of campaigning Swedish MPs interacting with traditional news media on Twitter through RTs and @messages. This was approached through a study of how campaigning politicians interacted with journalists and traditional news media on Twitter during the 2014 elections. So, what does this study tell us about the logics at play here? What took place on Twitter during the elections is clearly in line with the mass media logic of conflict. To be angry, upset and even outraged by political opponents was the expected behaviour by the MPs here. When the mass media logic of conflict is transferred online and intersects with the network media logic of short retweetable and catchy one-liners, polarisation is foregrounded at the expense of deliberation and debate. Hence, we can conclude that in this hybrid media setting, drawing from both mass media and network media logics, we end up with a hybrid media logic of polarisation and dissent.

We shall not forget either that some of these RTs and @messages were quite entertaining, catchy and fun. Still, who can defend him/ herself from an attack, and an unflattering etiquetting in 140 signs? Regardless if witty or not, these attacks are not about sparking a discussion. After all, a Twitter attack on the opponent says more about the one sending it than the opponent attacked. This is indeed about negotiating the party belonging, and not about an illuminating deliberation in front of voters trying to make an informed decision on whom to vote for. We can see thus see how in this campaign setting, the logics of mass and network media converged towards an environment underlining polarisation and conflict.

This is indeed a. rather gloomy conclusion, especially as the object of study here are what can be argued pillars in democracy, elected representatives and the journalists whose job it is to scrutinize these representatives. If you believe in deliberation and debate, something that indeed was a promise of web 2.0. during its first celebratory years (Bakir, 2010). However, it is important to understand the campaigning context here as well as the focus on emotion displays in the study. Indeed, generalizability is hard to claim and this hybrid media logic of polarisation and dissent needs to be studied in other contexts as well. Still, the results of this does resonate with recent discussions of filter bubbles, fake news and alternative facts in the wake of Donald Trump's presidency in the United States. But as always, we can conclude that more studies are needed.

REFERENCES

Altheide, D. L., & Snow, R. P. (1979). *Media Logic*. Beverly Hills, CA: Sage.

Arter, D. (1999). *Scandinavian politics today*. Manchester, UK: Manchester University Press.

Asp, K. (1986). *Mäktiga massmedier: Studier om politisk opinionsbildning (Powerful Mass Media: Studies of Political Opinion Shaping)*. Stockholm, Sweden: Akademilitteratur.

Asp, K. (2014). News media logic in a New Institutional Perspective. *Journalism Studies*, *15*(3), 256–270. doi:10.1080/1461670X.2014.889456

Bakir, V. (2010). *Sousveillance, Media and Strategic Political Communication. Iraq, USA, UK*. New York: Continuum.

Barberá, P., Vaccari, C., & Valeriani, A. (2017). Social Media, Personalisation of News Reporting, and Media Systems' Polarisation in Europe. In M. Barisione, & A. Michailidou (Eds.), *Social Media and European Politics. Rethinking Power and Legitimacy in the Digital Era* (pp. 25–52). London, UK: Palgrave MacMillan. doi:10.1057/978-1-137-59890-5_2

Beck, U. (1995). *Att uppfinna det politiska; Bidrag till en teori om reflexiv modernisering (To Invent Politics. Contribution to a Theory of Reflexive Modernization)*. Göteborg: Daidalos.

Benkler, Y. (2006). *The Wealth of Networks: How Social Production Transforms Markets and Freedom*. New Haven, CT: Yale University Press.

Boote, J. (1998). Towards a comprehensive taxonomy and model of consumer complaining behavior. *Journal of Consumer Satisfaction, Dissatisfaction & Complaining Behavior*, *11*, 140–151.

Boyd, D. (2011). Social Network Sites as Network Publics. Affordances, Dynamics and Implications. In Z. Papacharissi (Ed.), *A Networked Self* (pp. 39-59). New York: Routledge.

Carpentier, N. (2014). 'Fuck the clowns from Grease!!' Fantasies of participation and agency in YouTube comments on a Cypriot Problem documentary. *Information Communication and Society*, *17*(8), 1001–1016. doi:10.1080/1369118X.2013.875582

Chadwick, A. (2013). *The Hybrid Media System. Politics and Power*. Oxford, UK: Oxford University Press. doi:10.1093/acprof:oso/9780199759477.001.0001

Dahlgren, P. (1996). Media Logic in Cyberspace: Repositioning Journalism and its Publics. *Javnost - the Public, 3*(1996), 59-72.

Dahlgren, P. (2009). *Media and Political Engagement. Citizens, Communication, and Democracy*. New York: Cambridge University Press.

Djupe, P. A., & Peterson, D. (2002). The impact of negative campaigning: Evidence from the 1998 Senatorial primaries. *Political Research Quarterly*, *55*(4), 845–860. doi:10.1177/106591290205500406

Elias, N. (1998). The Social Constraint towards Self-Constraint. In S. Mennell, & J. Goudsblom (Eds.), *Norbert Elias. On Civilization, Power, and Knowledge*. Chicago, IL: The University of Chicago Press. (Original work published 1939)

Ellison, N., & Boyd, D. (2007). Social Network Sites: Definition, History and Scholarship. *Computer-Mediated Communication, 13*(1). Retrieved from http://onlinelibrary.wiley.com/doi/10.1111/j.1083-6101.2007.00393.x/full

Fuchs, C. (2014). *Social Media. A Critical Introduction*. London, UK: Sage. doi:10.4135/9781446270066

Gergen, K. J. (2002). The challenge of absent presence. In J. E. Katz, & M. Aakhus (Eds.), *Perpetual Contact. Mobile Communication, Private Talk, Public Performance* (pp. 227–241). Cambridge: Cambridge University Press. doi:10.1017/CBO9780511489471.018

Giddens, A. (1991). *Modernity and Self-Identity: Self and Society in the Late Modern Age*. Cambridge, UK: Polity Press.

Hermes, J. (2006). Hidden Debates: Rethinking the Relationship Between Popular Culture and The Public Sphere. *Javnost - The Public, 13*(4), 27-44.

Klinger, U., & Svensson, J. (2015). The Emergence of Network Media Logic in Political Communication. A Theoretical Approach. *New Media & Society*, *17*(8), 1241–1257. doi:10.1177/1461444814522952

Klinger, U., & Svensson, J. (2016). Network Media Logic. Some Conceptual Clarification. In A. Bruns, G. Enli, E. Skogerbö, A. Larsson, & C. Christensen (Eds.), *Routledge Companion to Social Media and Politics* (pp. 23–38). London, UK: Routledge.

Kosinetz, R. (2011). *Netnografi*. Lund: Studentlitteratur.

Larsson, A. O. (2017). Going viral? Comparing parties on social media during the 2014 Swedish election. *Convergence*, *23*(2), 117–131. doi:10.1177/1354856515577891

Larsson, A. O., & Svensson, J. (2014). Politicians online – Identifying current research opportunities. *First Monday*, *19*(4). doi:10.5210/fm.v19i4.4897

Lau, R. R., & Pomper, G. M. (2001). Negative campaigning by US Senate candidates. *Party Politics*, *7*(1), 69–87. doi:10.1177/1354068801007001004

Livingstone, S. (2008). Taking risky opportunities in youthful content creation: Teenagers use of social network sites for intimacy, privacy and self-expression. *New Media & Society*, *10*(3), 393–411. doi:10.1177/1461444808089415

Lowrey, W. (2017). The Emergence and Development of News Fact-Checking Sites. Institutional logics and population ecology. *Journalism Studies*, *18*(3), 376–394. doi:10.1080/1461670X.2015.1052537

Lundby, K. (2014). *Mediatization of politics: Transforming democracies and reshaping politics*. Berlin, Germany: De Gruyter Mounton.

Medierådet. (2010). *Unga & Medier 2010. Fakta om barns och ungas användning och upplevelser av medier* (Youth & Media 2010. Facts about children's and youths' use and perceptions of media). Stockholm, Sweden: Kulturdepartementet. http://www.medieradet.se/upload/Rapporter_pdf/Ungar%20och%20medier%202010.pdf

Morozov, E. (2011). *The Net Delusion: How Not to Liberate the World*. London, UK: Penguin Books.

Nordicom. (2019). *Mediebarometern 2018*. Göteborg: Nordicom.

O'Reilly, T. (2005). *What is Web 2.0*. Design Patterns and Business Models for the Next Generation of Software; Retrieved from oreilly.com/web2/archive/what-is-web-20.html

Russmann, U. (2017, May). *Going Negative on Facebook*: Paper presented at the 67th Annual Conference of the International Communication Association (ICA), San Diego, CA.

Shirky, C. (2009). *Here Comes Everybody. How Change Happen when People Come Together*. London, UK: Penguin Books.

Strömbäck, J., & Esser, F. (2014). Mediatization of politics: Transforming democracies and reshaping politics. In K. Lundby (Ed.), *Mediatization of Communication* (pp. 374–404). Berlin, Germany: De Gruyter Mounton.

Svensson, J. (2011). The Expressive Turn of Citizenship in Digital Late Modernity. *JeDEM eJournal of eDemocracy, 3*(1), 42-56.

Svensson, J. (2013). Power, Identity and Feelings in Digital Late Modernity. The Rationality of Reflexive Emption Displays Online. In T. Benski, & E. Fischer (Eds.), *Internet and Emotions* (pp. 17–32). London, UK: Routledge.

Svensson, J. (2014a). Amplification and Virtual Back-Patting. The Rationalities of Social Media Uses in the Nina Larsson Web-Campaign. In A. M. G. Solo (Ed.), *Political Campaigning in the Information Age* (pp. 59–65). Hershey, PA: IGI Global. doi:10.4018/978-1-4666-6062-5.ch003

Svensson, J. (2014b). Participation as a Pin. Political Discussions in an Online Swedish LGBT Community. In A. Ionas (Ed.), *Proceedings of the 14th European Conference on eGovernment ECEG 2014* (pp. 235-241). Reading: Academic Conferences and Publishing International Ltd.

Svensson, J. (2015). Participation as a Pastime Political Discussion in a Queer Community Online. *Javnost-The public, 22*(3), 283-297.

Svensson, J., & Larsson, A. O. (2016). Interacting with Whom? Swedish Parliamentarians on Twitter during the 2014 Elections. *International Journal of E-Politics*, *7*(1), 1–15. doi:10.4018/IJEP.2016010101

Thornton, P. H., Ocasio, W., & Lounsbury, M. (2012). *The Institutional Logics Perspective. A New Approach to Culture, Structure and Process*. Oxford, UK: Oxford University Press. doi:10.1093/acprof:oso/9780199601936.001.0001

Twitter. (2014). *What are @replies and mentions?*

Van Dijck, J. (2013). *The Culture of Connectivity. A Critical History of Social Media*. Oxford, UK: Oxford University Press. doi:10.1093/acprof:oso/9780199970773.001.0001

Van Dijck, J., & Poell, T. (2013). Understanding social media logic. *Media and Communication*, *1*(1), 2–14. doi:10.17645/mac.v1i1.70

Wirtz, J., & Mattila, A. S. (2004). Consumer responses to compensation, speed of recovery and apology after a service failure. *International Journal of Service Industry Management*, *15*(2), 150–166. doi:10.1108/09564230410532484

Chapter 5
Young Citizen's Political Engagement in India:
Social Media Use by Political Parties

Mandakini Paruthi
School of Management Studies, Chaitanya Bharathi Institute of Technology, India

Priyam Mendiratta
School of Business Studies, Sharda University, India

Gaurav Gupta
School of Business Studies, Sharda University, India

ABSTRACT

Social media has emerged as a dominant digital medium platform in contemporary society. The quick development of social media has instigated changes concerning the way publics to interact with a group of people with similar ideologies, the quality of information they share, or the opportunity to acquire and share ideas. Social media use has a major influence on public relations, marketing, and political communication. Therefore, politicians are formulating their strategies to reach increasingly networked individuals. The chapter defines political engagement concept, focuses on excessive use of social media to understand how the emergence of digital citizenship is changing political engagement. In addition to this, the chapter also examines whether the use of social media exercise any effect on 2014 and 2019. General elections outcome or not and discuss the proposed conceptual framework for future empirical testing. The chapter highlights the various concerns needed to be taken care of while using social media as a marketing tool for promoting political participation and engagement.

DOI: 10.4018/978-1-7998-1791-8.ch005

Copyright © 2020, IGI Global. Copying or distributing in print or electronic forms without written permission of IGI Global is prohibited.

INTRODUCTION

Social media has emerged as a dominant digital platform in the present-day digital society (Kumar & Nanda, 2019b). It has become an essential part of community discussions and communication. The quick development of social media has instigated changes concerning the way publics interact with group of people with similar ideologies, the quality of information they share or the opportunity to acquire and share ideas. Social media platforms are increasingly being accessed and used at all times and places, resulting in major impact on public relations, marketing, and political communication. Therefore, politicians are also utilizing the social media in formulating their strategies to reach increasingly networked individuals (Pradhan & Kumar, 2015). They are giving more preference to social media attention of the public in driving political engagement.

Due to this very fact, social media has become an integral part of political communication during the elections. Social media platforms make it possible for contenders to have a dialogue with their constituents and for citizens to interact with each other. Politicians use social media platforms like Facebook, Twitter, You Tube etc. for propagating their views, broadcasting the updated information and getting engaged in political discussions. As a result of this, citizens are well versed with the political and economic issues of the country. The development of social media has completely changed the political landscape of the country (Calderaro, 2018). Recent advancements in growth and popularity of social media has attracted the attention of political communication researchers. The main objective of the study is to investigate the political impact of social media as a new marketing tool that help the publics to obtain political information as well as interact with others on the Web.

The paucity of research examining political engagement directs the need for research in the area of political communication and social media. Last decade has witnessed a number of studies focusing on using web 2.0 technologies for democratic engagement (Jensen, 2016; Loader et al., 2015; Harris &Harrigan, 2015). Still, there exists lack of theoretical and empirical research on candidates' social media presence and the political engagement behaviour of the public. The present research examines the potential of the social media to stimulate political engagement, especially among younger citizens (Bakker & de Vreese,2011; Bennett, 2008; Dahlgreen,2011).There is a contradictory information concerning Web2.0's influence in creating new political participation in social media activities. Newness in social media campaigns help in mobilizing and reinforcing political participation.

The current research study is first of its kind in defining the concept of political engagement, proposing a framework and analysing the present trend of youth interactive participation and involvement through social media in 2014 and 2019 general elections in India.

Political Engagement

The concept of engagement is not new to the academic literature. It has been explored in various academic disciplines such as educational psychology, sociology, political science, and organizational behaviour from different perspectives (Paruthi and Kaur, 2017; Kumar and Nanda, 2019 a).Many eminent researchers and practitioners have endeavoured to define political engagement. A general review of previous studies reveals that engagement does not occur inside any medium; rather, it happens inside the individual (Mollen and Wilson 2010; Paruthi and Kaur, 2017). In short, engagement deals with users' emotions and feelings but social media platforms arouse this intrinsic feeling and mobilizes young citizens to cast their vote.

As political engagement concept can take on various forms such as participation in communities/forums, interactive participation in organizations and political actions. Consequently, there lacks a consensus on the conceptualization of political engagement construct. Adler and Goggin (2005) were of the view that political engagement embraces how an individual interactively participates in an online community to enhance the community and the conditions for others. But, having a thin line of distinction between political knowledge and engagement, the proposed definition does not offer clarity of ideas. Because, discussing political knowledge and political engagement in general can possibility lead to misunderstandings on how politically knowledgeable and engaged individuals are. Taking this into consideration, the current study endeavours to define the political engagement concept as "a psychological state of mind and internal feelings of the individuals / citizens. It is this intrinsic feeling of emotional connection, which provokes citizens to interact with the contesting political party or candidate and with other individuals on social media platform". This approach allows individuals to express themselves in several ways, and without giving attention of this viewpoint, a complete understanding of political engagement is not even imaginable.

Though, voting is identified as one of the forms of political engagement, but it should not be treated as only means of measuring it. Because, voting dismisses that chunk of individuals who are involved in other types engagement behaviours such as volunteering or protesting.

Framework and Political Participation on Social Media

A review of prior studies revealed that in the first decade of 21st century most of the research studies were engrossed either on political engagement or on social media (Koc-Michalska & Lilleker, 2016; Kahne & Bowyer, 2019). Many studies were carried out in western countries of the world especially in U.S (Kahne & Bowyer, 2018). While reviewing the existing literature, it was found that most of the studies related to political engagement have primarily focused on elections. But these studies have not examined discussions, likes, shares, comments on posts, discussion threads through social media. There exists a research gap that is needed to be addressed.

Wojcieszak (2009) defined the two types of political engagement. First type of political engagement deals with supporting and encouraging a political motion and, second, interactive participation in communities/ groups. The researchers were of the view that internet and web technologies has proved to be quite significant in engaging active citizens and has increased online political participation.

The present research study has employed uses and gratification theory (UGT) to propose the conceptual framework for the study. UGT theory views users as active and proficient in examining and evaluating various types of media to achieve their communication goals (Wang, Fink, & Cal, 2008). The basic premise of the theory is that individuals seek out media and particular content to attain definite gratifications (West & Turner, 2010). While advocating the use of internet in UGT, Papacharissi and Rubin (2000) found five main motives why people use the Internet, with information-seeking beingthe most prominent. Informed citizens who are aware of their needs find ways to actively seek out information to fulfil those latent needs. This approach has proved to be appropriate for studying political participation and engagement. Only a few studies have examined the relationship between social media users and their engagement in political process and in other political activities (Kenski & Stroud, 2006; Jennings & Zeitner, 2003;Shah, Kwak, & Holbert, 2001). It was found that enhanced access to political information on internet has increased the number of knowledgeable citizens who interactively participate in politics (Bimber, 1998). Based on UGT, the current research study proposes socializing, entertainment, social status and information seeking as four drivers or precursors of political engagement within social media settings. The present study proposes political interactive participation as the outcome of the model. Figure 1 illustrates conceptual framework of the study.

Socializing, entertainment seeking, social- status, and information seeking are identified as four possible drivers of political engagement. The terms are defined as

1. **Socializing:** Citizens are more interested in talking and meeting with others to achieve a sense of community and peer support on the particular topic of interest.
2. **Entertainment:** citizens are engaged with social media to amuse themselves.
3. **Social Status:** citizens sought out or maintained their personal status, as well as those of their friends, through the online participation.
4. **Information Seeking:** citizens use the media to receive information about related news update on political parties.

Figure 1. Proposed conceptual model

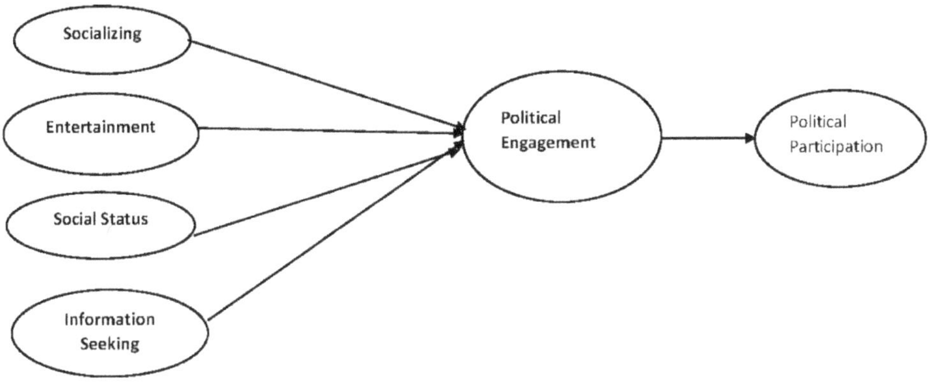

Political Engagement Outcome: Political Participation

It has been conceived that political participation has turned from exclusive behaviour of small elites, into one of public action. Verba and Nie (1972) in their germinal studies believed that pro institution behaviour in which citizens elect politicians, or make appeals to influence a decision- making process as political participation. On the contrary, Weiner (1971) included all volunteer actions to influence public policy, administration, and policy makers, which made political participation include behaviours outside of the current system. Suh (2013) defines political participation as "volunteer or mobilized actions which intend to exert their influence on decision makers whether or not these are legal". Political participation can be mainly divided into a vote and participation not related to a vote. At basic level, political participation is considered as voting in election campaign or opting out of this option. But in a broader sense, a political participation includes a vote, a political or non-political campaign, and a contact with politician for any kinds of influences, and cooperation with others.

Suh (2013) identified institutional and non-institutional as two types of political participation. Institutional political participation is directly linked with the election of an official through participation in vote, political rallies, and joining parties. Non-institutional participation indirectly influences political process encompassing signing petitions, boycotts, and demonstrations (Sarkar and Islam, 2017). With the advancement of internet, new forms of political participation have taken birth which are separate from traditional forms. The web technologies have made possible a variety of online political activities such as writing emails to politicians, visiting campaign websites, donating money online, and so forth (Gibson, Lusoli, & Ward, 2005).

Social Media and Youth Political Engagement

The youth of today is living in the era where the vast ocean of information is just a click away. This "born digital" generation, where the use of social media has become more of a necessity to stay abreast with the dynamics of their surroundings rather than a choice, is using social media at an ever-increasing pace. According to an article published in Social Media Today, it was observed that the teenagers, the torchbearers of our future, spent roughly nine hours in a single day on various social media platforms. Out of this total nine hours, sixty percent of the accessibility was through a mobile (Social Media Today, 2017). Therefore, in the world of tweets and re-tweets, it won't be wrong to state that the youth spends a greater proportion of its lifetime on social media, in contrast to the traditional media, like reading newspapers. This can be attributed to the fact that social media has a wider reach, better accessibility and real-time information update to its credit as compared to the traditional media. In terms of categorization based on Indian users, the following applications feature in the most used category [Figure 2].

Making the masses conscious of their roles and responsibilities in a contemporary society, social media can also be used as an effective and efficient tool for furthering the political objectives of a country. The earlier perception of individuals towards the youth of the society in terms of their disengagement in politics in a democratic

Figure 2.
(Source: Statcounter Globalstats, 2019)

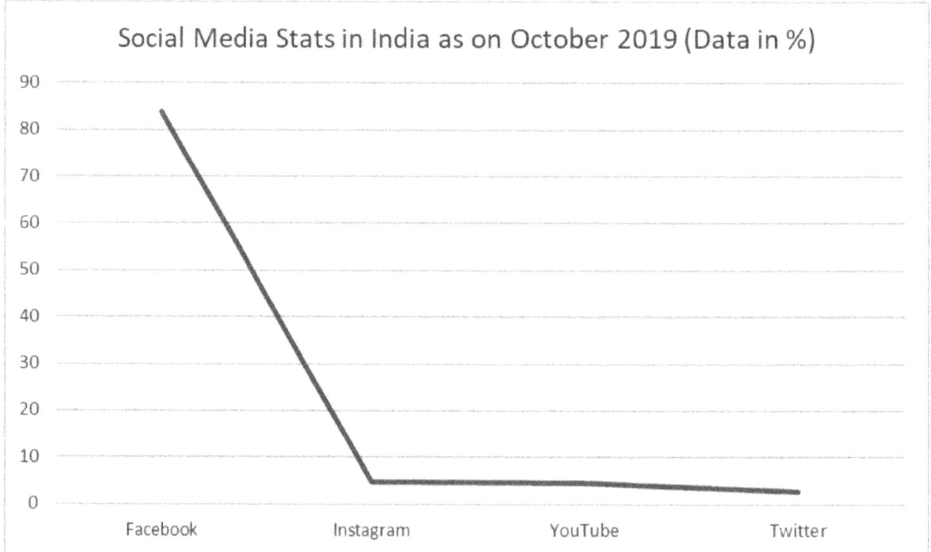

set up has been proved to be wrong by many academic researchers recently (Loader, B. D., Vromen, A., & Xenos, M. A., 2014). It has been observed that world over, the youth is becoming increasingly interested in politics (Freechild Institute- Advancing Youth Engagement Worldwide Since 2001). In democratic countries, where people are gifted with the right to speak and share their personal views, social media is emerging as a popular forum for political discussions and sensitization. It can be touted as a platform where there is an expression and exchange of opinions, fund-raising, pursuing, promoting a culture of casting votes as well as jointly work on deep-rooted issues in an economy (Kahne, J., Middaugh, E., & Allen, D., 2014). They have defined "participatory politics" or "political engagement" as an umbrella term with sub-sets of wide-ranging activities including "electoral activities, activism, civic activities and lifestyle politics." They have provided insights into this concept of participatory politics by stating some supporting examples. Say, simply listening to a speech on the television in your home would not be political engagement albeit, acting on that speech by posting it on social media, providing your views on that piece of information and making your contribution in spreading an awareness for the same among other individuals would amount to political engagement. Previous researches have coined a rather interesting term of "engaged sceptics." What does this mean? This stands for young people who are involved in the politics of the society they reside but are wary of the political leaders. This implies that the young generation believes in the foundation of politics but does not really connect with the traditional, old school thought of how these parties work (Milan, A., 2005).Political marketing is not restricted to traditional marketing, but its presence on digital media has also been marked. Social media is a type of digital media that creates a political marketplace where applicants, government officials and political parties can use social media to drive public opinion in the required direction. Today, social media has become a very strong instrument for expressing views, thoughts and opinions, and has become an important instrument for creating opinion. Web 2.0 technologies, according to Palmer and Koening-Lewis (2009), provide the buzz web experience that represents their commitment to sharing data. It is not limited to content readers prepared by site owners, but also active content generators to share their personal experiences, provide feedback, and express their feelings in positive, negative, or neutral ways (Luo & Zhang, 2013). Social Media is an online application platform which facilitates interaction, collaboration, and sharing of content. They are more concerned with the deep-rooted issues of the current society which is of an immediate concern for them and try to engage only in meaningful politics.

With a deep penetration of social media in people's everyday lives, especially the youth of a country, the political parties are increasingly using social media as a platform to seek their attention and to ignite a spark of "political activism" in them (European Parliamentary Research Service Blog, 2015). Sashi Tharoor (A former union minister) was only an Indian politician with a tweeter account and 6,000 supporters in the 2009 Indian general election (Robinson, Schulz, Cotten, Hale, & Williams, 2016). Roughly 150 million electors were on social media during India's 2009 general election, which was also called the' linked' generation. These voters were very simple to link so most political parties jumped in to join the platform for social networking to impact this voters section. Indian general elections in 2014 were active on social media, political parties ' operations and their discussion. Volume buzz, retweet figures and supporters were the main measuring tools to define trendy and popular politicians (Swamy, 2014). Twitter was the medium of choice for individuals to participate in and consume political material in the 2014 general election. There was on Tweeter user engagement with content, news breaks, and impact on political discourse or media setting ability. However, between 1 January and 12 May 2014, a total of 56 million election-related tweets were published (Chao, 2014).

Researchers are of the opinion that a deep penetration of social media in the everyday life of individuals has the power to attract new people into the political sphere who were disassociated earlier, attributing this to lower barriers of participation and communication (Michalska, K. K., Lilleker, D. G., & Vedel, T., 2016). Social media can serve as a two-way benefit for the political parties. On one hand social media can help the parties to get as close to the target audience as they can, without really relying on the traditional media, and on the other hand, they can receive a feedback from the audience through their participation in discussions groups, chat rooms, blogs and posts. Blogs were lately found to be a significant medium of political revelations. Blog readers were found to be increasingly involved in a wide range of engagement activities (Zuniga, H. G., Veenstra, A., Vraga, E., & Shah, D., 2010). It has been observed in the past that the existing traditional sources of information sharing like televisions and print media are no longer an effective. Instead, individuals are now moving to newer emerging platforms of mass information like blogs and websites of Government (Gurevitch, M., Coleman, S., & Blumler, J. G., 2009). This feedback can help the political parties formulate their policies in a manner which can help them to increase their potential voter base by customizing those policies to the needs and demands of the youth. Hence, social media has revolutionized the wheels of democracy. It has aided in thinning the line of difference between the politically enlightened and politically indifferent groups. In a study conducted in Britain amongst the college students, the most advantageous use of social media cited by the respondents was that such platforms lend them a voice which cannot be otherwise heard by the policymakers (Committee of Experts on Media Pluralism and Transparency of Media Ownership, 2017).

Focusing on the Indian landscape, it is a country dominated by young population. According to a report published by Government of India in the year 2017, it has been forecasted that the youth population in India will be 31.8% as a proportion of the total population by the year 2031. Therefore, one cannot argue that the political framework of the country can work without factoring in the youth of the country. In Harvard Political Review, 2013, it was found that higher engagements on the social media can be positively correlated to higher political engagements. Hence, extending the implications of this study, India being a country where a pool of young people resides, or on similar lines for any country having a high proportion of young population, political participation should be higher. According to Quartz India, 2019, more than three-fourths of the youth population in India elaborately researches for every political candidacy in their respective constituencies. Social media has helped the people to be aware of their rights and duties and the youth of the country is not shrugging this duty off their shoulders, apparently. The severity of the sensitization amongst the youth can be judged from the following data, covering around 2 lakh Indian youth in a survey by Inshorts Pulse [Table 1]

Social media can help the youth of a country in increasing their political engagement and participation by helping them to openly express their "political preferences", without having them to actually become a member of any political party. In a study conducted in Britain, it was found that "online political expression" amongst the youth was high, however, it varied due to socio-demographic background of the youth and their political inclinations (Keating, A., & Melis, G., 2017).

In a survey by Common Sense Media, it was stated that social media has become the most common source of getting information, especially for the age groups between 13 to 18, and the use of social media as a channel for achieving political objectives by various parties is nothing but to state the very obvious (Kahne, J., & Bowyer, B., 2019).

Social Media and its Effect on 2014 and 2019 General Elections

Rallies and crowd gatherings, touted as the traditional tools of reaching out to the masses, entail a huge cost and leave a huge dent in the party funds. In the millennial generation, internet usage is seen as an effective move to advertise election

Table 1. Awareness among the Indian youth towards political candidacy in their respective constituencies

What the Indian Youth Thinks	Data (in thousands)
Think voting should be a compulsion	85
Should cast their votes without any fail	63
Conduct elaborate research prior to voting	74

Source: Quartz India, 2019

propagandas, both in terms of cost and its deep penetration in the society. Prior research studies revealed that three social media platforms were primarily used in the 2014 Lok Sabha Elections, namely, Facebook, Twitter and Google (Kaur, M., & Rajesh, V., 2016), apart from the traditional channels. Political parties have used social media in the past for increasing their vote bank. To cite an example, in a very recent article published on June 2019 with the headline "How Modi's Twitter strategy of following his supporters worked in his favour", it was highlighted that Modi has a total number of 2,000 people whom he follows, and these people are majorly the ordinary residents of the country, having no one-to-one connections with him. These are mostly the citizens who can be termed as "die-hard" supporters of him and in strong opposition of primarily the Congress party (Quartz India, 2019). On the other hand, it was also found that the people followed by Rahul Gandhi are either big politicians or public figures. This is a perfect instance of how to use social media to show a politician's support back to his people. Hence, social media connectivity gives a sense of belongingness to the citizens to the party with which they idolize.

The article also brings to fore a very exciting fact. This strategy of following back his common supporters can be traced back to the year 2013, following which in the 2014 Lok Sabha elections, he secured a sweeping victory. Another major politician not very far behind was Barack Obama. Hence, both immensely popular leaders amongst the common people. Perhaps, this virtual bond made possible due to the social media is the reason of their mass popularity. To top it all, the 2014 Lok Sabha elections are being popularized by "#TwitterElection" due to the fact that it was one of the largest elections in the democratic history where a majority of the sensitization happened by the use of internet, as highlighted in a research by Stanford University. It was observed that in 2014 the NDA was much more aggressive on its social media usage in contrast to other opposition parties like UPA and AAP. Therefore, it was concluded that the primary reason of NDA's sweeping win was their recognition of the effective use of social media, in which other parties were left behind (Lu D., Shah A., & Kulshrestha, A., 2014). In another research conducted on the pattern of social media usage by the different political parties, it was underlined that two parties namely, BJP and AAP majorly used Twitter for their political manifestos in most creative ways, whereas on the other hand, INC mostly used social media for posting criticism. Talking about the youth of the country, primarily focusing on first-time voters, it was observed that "on an average for one percent increase in proportion of first-time voters was associated with 2.5 percent increase in BJP's vote share" (Ahmed S., Jaidka K., & Cho J., 2016).

Shifting our focus to the 2019 general elections, in a study by "Lokniti- Centre for Study of Developing Societies", two issues were analysed upon in context of their effect on users of social media, i.e., the airstrike in Balakot and the Nyay scheme launched by Congress. It was found that the people who use social media were 20 percentage points more sensitized with respect to the Balakot airstrikes as opposed to the people who were not using any social media platform. On the other hand, talking about the Nyay scheme, it was found that one voter out of the two voters simultaneously, could never have been aware of this scheme if they were not using any of the social media platforms (moneycontrol, 2019). This highlights the importance of social media in creating a voter base for the political parties. Some quick facts were brought to fore in an article showcasing the power of social media to help BJP win elections and conquer Congress. To cite a few, the total number of followers on Twitter for both Modi and other BJP handles were close to 142 million whereas, it was only 23 million for Congress and Rahul Gandhi. As compared to the year 2014, in the year 2019, social media usage had increased by 155% over a span of five years. Leveraging on this opportunity, spending close to Rupees 20 crore on social media, BJP outdid Congress by a big margin (Livemint, 2019). In the months starting from 20th of February to 26th of April, 2019, BJP had spent approximately Rupees 6 crore on Google in the form of political advertisements, which was almost ten times of the expenses incurred by Congress on the same platform. Talking about Facebook, BJP spent Rupees 1.32 crores over roughly three months beginning from February to end of April. Some other unofficial expenditures incurred through the party's Facebook pages were close to Rupees 4.50 crores over the same months. These expenditures were much higher in number as compared to the expenditures incurred by the other contesting political parties (The Wire, 2019).

Almost all the Indian political parties have their presence on social media. A statement coming from the BJP's Information Technology cell, "One can say that these elections would be WhatsApp elections", referring to the 2019 general elections, the use of social media cannot be belittled. Citing another example to elucidate the "multiplier effect" of social media, it was hypothetically assumed that if each of the 29 states have 15,000 groups on WhatsApp, a political party can cater to almost 110 million people. To compare the severity of this figure, it was contrasted with the figure of 170 million people who helped BJP win the Lok Sabha election in the year 2014 (The Economic Times, 2018).

Throwing some light on how the IT cells of the two major opposition parties work, i.e., BJP and Congress, the parties have dedicated man force to handle the social media campaigning, taking an example from the Karnataka Assembly Elections [Table 2]

With so much rigor on the use of social media for a state's assembly election, imagine the situation at a national level general election. In a survey conducted by Stanford University and later highlighted by The Hindustan Times in 2017, it was observed that ahead of general elections in the year 2014, NDA followers posted a whopping 2.5 million tweets, whereas only a million tweets were posted by the followers of both UPA and AAP parties, thus signalling a positive feedback on NDA's social media usage.

Table 2. Allocation of man force for social media campaigning by political parties

	BJP	Congress
Location	Malleshwaram	Cunningham Road
Size	30 people including tech professionals and volunteers	25 to 30 people including tech professionals and volunteers
Mandate	Handling of social media campaigns, disseminate and manage online content	Focusing on social media, developing campaigns, providing feedback for online and offline events

Source: The Economic Times, 2018

As per the Transparency Report on "Political advertising on Google", it is highlighted that since 19th of February 2019, BJP has spent an enormous sum of Rupees 123,909,750 whereas, INC has spent Rupees 30,447,500. Breaking down the expenditure, it can be seen that these expenses reached a high during the general election period in 2019 [Table 3]

Therefore, analysing the above data from the 2014 and 2019 Lok Sabha elections, the amount of spending on social media can be somewhat correlated to the fate of the political parties in the outcome of the results.

Table 3. Expenses incurred by BJP and INC on political advertising during general election period in 2019

Date of the respective Month	BJP (in rupees)	INC (in rupees)
February 17, 2019	1,115,750	Data not Available
February 24, 2019	5,811,750	Data not Available
March 3, 2019	2,091,000	Data not Available
March 10, 2019	2,732,750	Data not Available
March 17, 2019	637,750	Data not Available
March 24, 2019	2,948,000	54,000
March 31, 2019	193,500	977,500
April 7, 2019	16,166,500	2,395,500
April 14, 2019	18,398,250	2,429,750
April 21, 2019	30,319,750	15,111,500
April 28, 2019	21,867,500	2,026,000
May 5, 2019	9,826,000	4,111,250
May 12, 2019	11,801,250	3,341,750

(Source: Google Transparency Report, 2019)

FUTURE RESEARCH DIRECTIONS

Present study focuses only on social media and political engagement but, it does not discuss the impact of cultural factors on political engagement. Future researchers can use the cultural orientation and study its role in influencing political engagement. In addition to this, the study only proposes the conceptual framework. Future research could employ the quantitative research methods to test the proposed conceptual model. Also, the current study has only considered social media buzz in Indian context. The impact of social media on political engagement can be studied from the context of different countries and contexts.

CONCLUSION

From the forgoing exploration, it can be concluded that a country's political system's mainstay in the current times is the social media. The winning party in 2014 as well as 2019 general elections relied heavily on social media to connect with the masses. Therefore, this research can be of prime importance to the political parties to design their agendas and preferences for the next wave of general elections. A greater proportion of the total funding for the campaigns may be allocated to the advertisements through the use of social media. Moreover, such campaigns should be majorly targeted to the youth of a country, especially in the case of countries like India where the first-time voters can make or break a political party. The youth, due to a great exposure on a global basis via social media, is much more sensitive to the happenings around the world and knowingly choose their leader. The locus of attention is getting shifted from the traditional modes of campaigning to innovative ideas leveraging the internet connectivity penetrated in the deepest corners of the society. Parties are effectively designing their crusades to capture the attention of the youth of the country, the future of any nation. To aid the political parties in succeeding with this objective, social media is undoubtedly playing a significant role.

REFERENCES

Adler, R. P., & Goggin, J. (2005). What do we mean by "civic engagement"? *Journal of Transformative Education*, *3*(3), 236–253. doi:10.1177/1541344605276792

Ahmed, S., Jaidka, K., & Cho, J. (2016). The 2014 Indian elections on Twitter: A comparison of campaign strategies of political parties. *Telematics and Informatics*, *33*(4), 1071–1087. doi:10.1016/j.tele.2016.03.002

Bimber, B. (1998). The Internet and political mobilization: Research note on the 1996 election season. *Social Science Computer Review*, *16*(4), 391–401. doi:10.1177/089443939801600404

Calderaro, A. (2018). *Social media and politics*. Cardiff University. doi:10.4135/9781526416513.n46

Chao, R. (2014). How much influence did social media have on India's election? Retrieved August 25, 2019 http://techpresident.com/news/wegov/25062/India-election-social-media-influence

Council of Europe. (2019). *Study on the use* of *internet in electoral campaigns.* Retrieved from https://rm.coe.int/study-use-of-internet-in-electoral-campaigns/1680776163(accessed on 10th August, 2019)

Economic Times. (2019). *How the mobile phone is shaping to be BJPs most important weapon in elections.* Retrieved from https://economictimes.indiatimes.com/news/politics-and-nation/how-the-mobile-phone-is-shaping-to-be-bjps-most-important-weapon-in-elections/articleshow/65508743.cms

Economic Times. (2019). *Social Media Engineering- How Congress BJPs war room are trying to woo voters in Karnataka.* Retrieved from https://economictimes.indiatimes.com/news/politics-and-nation/social-media-engineering-how-congress-bjps-war-room-are-trying-to-woo-voters-in-karnataka/articleshow/63445558.cms

European Parliamentary Blog. (2019). *The role played by social media in political participation and electoral campaigns.* Retrieved from https://epthinktank.eu/2014/02/12/the-role-played-by-social-media-in-political-participation-and-electoral-campaigns/ (European Parliamentary Blog)

Freechild Organization. (2019). *Youth and Politics.* Retrieved from https://freechild.org/youth-and-politics/(accessed on 5th August, 2019)

Gil de Zúñiga, H., Veenstra, A., Vraga, E., & Shah, D. (2010). Digital democracy: Reimagining pathways to political participation. *Journal of Information Technology & Politics*, *7*(1), 36–51. doi:10.1080/19331680903316742

Globalstats, S. (2019) *Social Media Stats in India.* Retrieved from https://gs.statcounter.com/social-media-stats/all/india (accessed on 3rd November, 2019)

Gurevitch, M., Coleman, S., & Blumler, J. G. (2009). Political communication—Old and new media relationships. *The Annals of the American Academy of Political and Social Science*, *625*(1), 164–181. doi:10.1177/0002716209339345

Harris, L., & Harrigan, P. (2015). Social media in politics: The ultimate voter engagement tool or simply an echo chamber? *Journal of Political Marketing*, *14*(3), 251–283. doi:10.1080/15377857.2012.693059

Hindustan Times. (2019). *BJP way ahead of competition on social media in 2014, says Stanford University*. Retrieved from https://www.hindustantimes.com/india-news/bjp-way-ahead-of-competition-on-social-media-in-2014-says-stanford-university-study/story-6Uq81HOwstzCwgCmiSyMWI.html(accessed on 25th July, 2019)

Jensen, M. J. (2017). Social media and political campaigning: Changing terms of engagement? *The International Journal of Press/Politics*, *22*(1), 23–42. doi:10.1177/1940161216673196

Kahne, J., & Bowyer, B. (2019). Can media literacy education increase digital engagement in politics? *Learning, Media, and Technology*, *44*(2), 211–224. doi:10.1080/17439884.2019.1601108

Kahne, J., Middaugh, E., & Allen, D. (2015). Youth, new media, and the rise of participatory politics. *From voice to influence: Understanding citizenship in a digital age, 35*.

Kaur, M., & Verma, R. (2018). Social media: An emerging tool for political participation. In Media Influence: Breakthroughs in Research and Practice (pp. 1-8). IGI Global.

Keating, A., & Melis, G. (2017). Social media and youth political engagement: Preaching to the converted or providing a new voice for youth? *British Journal of Politics and International Relations*, *19*(4), 877–894. doi:10.1177/1369148117718461

Kenski, K., & Stroud, N. J. (2006). Connections between Internet use and political efficacy, knowledge, and participation. *Journal of Broadcasting & Electronic Media*, *50*(2), 173–192. doi:10.120715506878jobem5002_1

Kent Jennings, M., & Zeitner, V. (2003). Internet use and civic engagement: A longitudinal analysis. *Public Opinion Quarterly*, *67*(3), 311–334. doi:10.1086/376947

Koc-Michalska, K., Lilleker, D. G., & Vedel, T. (2016). Civic political engagement and social change in the new digital age.

Kumar, V., & Nanda, P. (2019). Social Media in Higher Education: A Framework for Continuous Engagement. [IJICTE]. *International Journal of Information and Communication Technology Education*, *15*(1), 109–120. doi:10.4018/IJICTE.2019010107

Kumar, V., & Nanda, P. (2019). Social Media to Social Media Analytics: Ethical Challenges. [IJT]. *International Journal of Technoethics*, *10*(2), 57–70. doi:10.4018/IJT.2019070104

Kumar, V., & Pradhan, P. (2015). Trust Management Issues in Social-Media Marketing [IJOM]. *International Journal of Online Marketing*, *5*(3), 47–64. doi:10.4018/IJOM.2015070104

Livemint. (2019) *How smart viral content helped BJP Trump Congress on social media.* Retrieved from https://www.livemint.com/politics/news/how-smart-viral-content-helped-bjp-trump-congress-on-social-media-1559663323348.html(accessed on 12th July, 2019)

Loader, B. D., Vromen, A., & Xenos, M. A. (2014). The networked young citizen: social media, political participation and civic engagement.

Luo, X., & Zhang, J. (2013). How do consumer buzz and traffic in social media marketing predict the value of the firm? *Journal of Management Information Systems*, *30*(2), 213–238. doi:10.2753/MIS0742-1222300208

Ministry of Statistics and Programme Implementation (MOSPI). (2019). *Youth in India.* Retrieved from http://mospi.nic.in/sites/default/files/publication_reports/Youth_in_India-2017.pdf(GOI Report)

Mollen, A., & Wilson, H. (2010). Engagement, telepresence and interactivity in online consumer experience: Reconciling scholastic and managerial perspectives. *Journal of Business Research*, *63*(9-10), 919–925. doi:10.1016/j.jbusres.2009.05.014

Moneycontrol.com. (2019) *Influence of social media during elections might have been exaggerated.* Retrieved from https://www.moneycontrol.com/news/politics/influence-of-social-media-during-elections-might-have-been-exaggerated-study-4090561.html(accessed on 25th July, 2019)

Palmer, A., & Koenig-Lewis, N. (2009). An experiential, social network-based approach to direct marketing. *Direct Marketing: An International Journal*, *3*(3), 162–176. doi:10.1108/17505930910985116

Papacharissi, Z., & Rubin, A. M. (2000). Predictors of Internet use. *Journal of Broadcasting & Electronic Media*, *44*(2), 175–196. doi:10.120715506878jobem4402_2

Paruthi, M., & Kaur, H. (2017). Scale development and validation for measuring online engagement. *Journal of Internet Commerce*, *16*(2), 127–147. doi:10.1080/15332861.2017.1299497

Politics, H. (2019). *Youth political engagement era social media.* Retrieved from http://harvardpolitics.com/hprgument-posts/youth-political-engagement-era-social-media/

Quartz. (2019). *How India's youth feel about elections 2019.* Retrieved from https://qz.com/india/1583361/how-indias-youth-feel-about-elections-2019/(accessed on 9th August, 2019)

Quartz. (2019). *Modi's Twitter strategy of following common Indians worked.* Retrieved from https://qz.com/india/1630274/modis-twitter-strategy-of-following-common-indians-worked/(accessed on 28th July, 2019)

Report, T. (2019). *Political Advertising for India.* Retrieved from https://transparencyreport.google.com/political-ads/region/IN?hl=en(accessed on 12th August, 2019)

Robinson, L., Schulz, J., Dunn, H. S. Aguiar, P., Artopoulos, A., Baldwin, J., ... & Straubhaar, J. D. (2016). Communication and Information Technologies Annual. Emerald.

Safiullah, M., Pathak, P., Singh, S., & Anshul, A. (2017). Social media as an upcoming tool for political marketing effectiveness. *Asia Pacific Management Review*, *22*(1), 10–15. doi:10.1016/j.apmrv.2016.10.007

Sarker, M. M., & Islam, M. S. (2017). Social Capital and Political Participation: A Case Study from Rural Bangladesh. *European Review Of Applied Sociology*, *10*(15), 54–64. doi:10.1515/eras-2017-0009

Shah, V., Nojin Kwak, R., & Lance Holbert, D. (2001). Connecting" and" disconnecting" with civic life: Patterns of Internet use and the production of social capital. *Political Communication*, *18*(2), 141–162. doi:10.1080/105846001750322952

Social Media Today. (2019) *How much time do people spend on social media.* Retrieved from https://www.socialmediatoday.com/marketing/how-much-time-do-people-spend-social-media-infographic(accessed on 6th August, 2019)

Stanford. (2019). *India's #TwitterElection 2014.* Retrieved from http://snap.stanford.edu/class/cs224w-2014/projects2014/cs224w-24-final.pdf

Suh, H., Yee, J., & Chang, D. (2013). Type of trust and political participation in five countries: Results of social quality survey.

Swamy, R. (2014). Did social media really impact the Indian elections? Retrieved August 25, 2019 http://gadgets.ndtv.com/social-networking/features/did-social-media-really-impact-the-indian-elections-527425

The Wire. (2019). *BJP Modi political funding money*. Retrieved from https://thewire.in/politics/bjp-modi-political-funding-money(accessed on 11th August, 2019)

Verba, S., & Nie, N. H. (1987). *Participation in America: Political democracy and social equality*. University of Chicago Press.

Wang, Q., Fink, E. L., & Cai, D. A. (2008). Loneliness, gender, and parasocial interaction: A uses and gratifications approach. *Communication Quarterly*, *56*(1), 87–109. doi:10.1080/01463370701839057

Weiner, M. (1971). Political participation: Crisis of the political process. Crises and Sequences in political development, 159-204.

Wojcieszak, M. (2009). "Carrying online participation offline"—Mobilization by radical online groups and politically dissimilar offline ties. *Journal of Communication*, *59*(3), 564–586. doi:10.1111/j.1460-2466.2009.01436.x

Chapter 6
Social Networks, Media, and the Egyptian Revolution:
Building Democratic Front?

Ahmed El Gody
https://orcid.org/0000-0002-1736-5976
Örebro University, Sweden

ABSTRACT

The utilisation of social media in Egypt has irrevocably changed the nature of the traditional Egyptian public sphere. One can see the Egyptian online society as a multiplicity of networks. These networks have developed, transformed, and expanded over time, operating across all areas of life. Audiences started to utilise social media platforms providing detailed descriptions of Egyptian street politics, generating public interest and reinforcing citizen democracy. This trend changed the way audiences consumed news, with media organisations starting to expand their presence online so that, as well as providing news content, they also provided audience a 'space' to interact. This chapter establishes understanding on the role of social media in developing an Egyptian networked public sphere. Further, the chapter discusses the role social media plays in post 2011 revolution democratisation process. This study employed qualitative ethnography (nethnography) and network analysis on 20 Egyptian news and social media newspapers and websites to monitor online deliberation.

DOI: 10.4018/978-1-7998-1791-8.ch006

Copyright © 2020, IGI Global. Copying or distributing in print or electronic forms without written permission of IGI Global is prohibited.

INTRODUCTION

The opening months of 2011, world witnessed a series of turmoil events in Egypt that soon lead to uprisings toppling President Mubarak 30-years regime. The Egyptian revolution was the most media exposed event in the Arab World, not only because of Egypt's position as a main political hub in the Middle East/ North Africa, but also for citizen using different forms of social media to voice Egyptian opposition to the world. Even with the Egyptian government shutting Internet lines, cutting off mobile communications, confiscating newspapers, imprisoning protesters, blocking media websites, and scrambling satellite signals to limit coverage of the events, Egyptian activists curbed government pressure to voice their cause online. This lead many label the Egyptian revolution as the 'Facebook' or the 'Twitter' revolution.

Internet service reached Egypt in 1993. The Introduction and utilisation of Information Communication Technologies (ICTs) has irrevocably changed the nature of communication and news consumption. One can see the Egyptian online society as a multiplicity of networks that expanded and developed over time operating across all areas of everyday life. Several Egyptians become active and indeed interactive online citizens (sometimes journalists), providing detailed descriptions of Egyptian street politics, posting multimedia material, generating public interest and reinforcing citizen power and democracy.

Internet services reached Egypt through The Egyptian Universities Network and the Supreme Council of Universities (Abdullah, 2005). Between 1993 and 1996, Internet penetration rate did not exceed 0.1 per cent of the population. Poor Economic conditions, limited infrastructure, high illiteracy rate and cultural beliefs contributed to the humble connectivity. Globalization pressure, however, forced the Egyptian government to recognize the power of ICTs as an important factor in achieving sustainable development (Dutta, 2006). To promote Internet connectivity and use, the Egyptian government decided to commercialize Internet use keeping control, however, over the Internet through effective monitoring and regulations (Kamel, 2002). Internet commercialization helped to increase Internet population. The partnership between the government and the private sector led to the establishment of several Internet nodes in rural areas that boosted the number of users, as well as helped in closing the internal digital divide.

Realizing how strong a communication and information technology sector could contribute to the economy, the Egyptian government in 1999 created a new Ministry of Communications and Information Technology (MCIT) (Ministry of Communication and Information Technology, 2011; Amin, 2003). Ahmed Nazif, who in July 2004 became the last prime minister of Egypt before the 2011 revolution, headed the new ministry. Nazif, led a technocrat/ businessmen government that believed that technology can be controlled and managed if steered by the right policies (Abdullah,

2005). Government investment paid off, Internet users increased from 460,000 in 1996 to nearly 1 million users by the turn of the century (El Gody, 2003).

While the Egyptian government saw the deterministic side of Information technologies, the Egyptian people saw the social reform side that could be utilized by various sectors of the society. Between 2000 and 2019 Internet users increased nine folds, reaching 50.5 million users with 40 per cent penetration and a 9 per cent annual digital growth (El Gody, 2012; Ministry of Communication and Information Technology, 2019). Almost all internet users are on social media. With Facebook, YouTube, and WhatsApp penetration range between 89-97 percent of Internet users in Egypt (Global webindex, 2019, Ministry of Communication and Information Technology, 2019). These sectors could be created, grouped and regrouped with a developmental agenda of their own (Murphy, 2010).

From the society's perspective, the Egyptian government underestimated the ability of online communication in creating avenues for alternative forms of media spaces to develop. The government never considered ICTs as a medium or a tool for social education that ultimately would lead to liberation, and incorrectly believed that it could control ICTs usage and agenda as they had successfully done for the past 60 years in other technical areas (Radsch, 2016). Online users saw in ICTs, especially the Internet, a tool that if properly utilized, could lead to greater freedoms, giving a voice to the marginalized groups/ political actors in a more global context (Radsch, 2008; 2016).

Social media- lead to a more horizontal (between audience) and less vertical (from government to the audience) communication model in Egypt, enabling the people to bypass traditional mass media controlled by the regime, and allowing the society to create a developmental agenda of their own (El, Gody, 2016; Ghareeb, 2000). Hudson (2006) and Radsch (2016) discussed how the rapid introduction and spread of new online technologies "Accelerated the erosion of the state's monopoly over the framing and ratification of identities and loyalties, and the public's perception of public issues" (Hudson, 2006, p. 1). Audience/ activists' utilization of social media did not only break the government's news coverage monopoly, but also the citizen's politics of silence (Hafez, 2006; Radsch, 2016). According to Hafez (2006) Internet websites compensated for feeble political parties facilitating new trends in politics, affecting the dynamics of democratization by reducing the isolation of movements for political change, and by circumventing obstructions created by those currently in power paving the road to the 2011 revolution.

The mushroom of Egyptian online population coincided with the flourish of online content surpassing 120 million pages mark between 2008-2018 (Information and Decision Support Centre, 2019). Examining Table one, of what Egyptians visit online, it is clear that social networks-online communities and news and media portals, top Egyptian online experience. Regionally, Egyptian news websites top the most visited websites in the Middle East, with almost 35 per cent of online news media content in the Arab world emerging from Egypt, and with nearly 30 per cent of Arab bloggers being Egyptians. Over 42 million Egyptians use Facebook (forming quarter of Arab users and nearly 2 per cent of Facebook users worldwide) and another 8 million using YouTube making Egyptians rank the 23rd country globally in terms of users (El Gody, 2016; medium.com, 2019).

After 2011, the utilisation of social media in Egypt has irrevocably changed the nature of the traditional Egyptian public sphere. One can see the Egyptian online society as a multiplicity of networks. These networks have developed, transformed and expanded over time, operating across all areas of life. Nonetheless, in essence they are socio-political in origin. Audiences started to provide detailed descriptions of Egyptian street politics, posting multimedia material, generating public interest, and reinforcing citizen power and democracy. This trend changed the way audiences consumed news, with traditional media -especially independent and opposition-started to access online information to develop their media content and to escape

Table 1. Top web sites Egyptians watch

Site Name	Type
Facebook	Social Network and online communities
Google.com.eg	Search Engine, Blog tool, News Service
YouTube	Arts and entertainment, TV movies, and streaming
Instagram	Social Network and online communities
Youm7.com	News and media Portal
Masrawy	News and media Portal
yallakoora	Sports news and media
Mawdoo3	News and Online Forum
Twitter	Social Network and online communities
Elbalad news	News and media Portal
Al Watan news	News and media Portal
Pinterest	Social Network and online communities
akoam	Social Network and online communities
almstaba	Arts and entertainment, TV movies, and streaming
russiatoday	News and media Portal
Al Masry AlYoum	News Portal
mytedata	Filesharing and hosting
soundcloud	Arts and entertainment, music streaming
Linkedin	Social Network and online communities
Shorouknews	News Portal

Sources: Internet Statistics, Alexa 2019, Similarweb 2019

Source: Internet Statics, Alexa 2019 and Similarweb 2019

government control. Several political and media organisations also started to expand their presence online so that, as well as providing information/news content to attract audiences, they also provided them with a 'space' to interact amongst themselves and with media organisations. This called for the introduction of a new type of journalism requiring a conscious sense of how to reach out to citizens and listen to them, and to have citizens listen and talk to each other.

This chapter aims to establish understanding on the role of social media in developing an Egyptian networked public sphere. Further, the chapter aims to discuss the utilization of social media in Egyptian media emphasizing the role it plays in post 2011 revolution democratization process.

METHODOLOGY

Surveying the development of Social media in Egypt, this study employed qualitative ethnography and semi structured interviews in four media newsrooms (*Al Ahram, Akhbar Al Youm, Al Masry Al Youm* and *Al Watan*) to study journalists' utilization on social media websites. The researcher spent two weeks in each of the newsrooms newsroom in 2011, 2013, 2015 and 2018 investigating journalists use of social media in their news. This study also used nethnography and network analysis on twenty Egyptian news and social media platforms (including: Egyptian youth for change, Kefaya, Shayfenkom, Egyptian organization for human rights, Egyptian constitution for change, We are all khaled Said, 6th April, Rasd, Misrdigital, Manalalaa, sandmonkey, Ten minutes news, Al Hakika, Freedom and Justice, Muslimbrotherhood, the youth of moslim brotherhood, Dogma, Al Dostor, Al Youm7, Al Shorouk interactive, Scaf) to monitor online deliberation between audiences. routine. This was followed by netnography for two weeks for two weeks to examine online deliberation.

DIFFUSION AND UTILIZATION OF SOCIAL MEDIA IN EGYPTIAN NEWS MEDIA.

The Egyptian media ecology has been shaped by loyalty to the regime during the past 60 years. One can use William Rugh's 1987 classification of Egyptian journalism as "Stagnant, centralized, monolithic, and apathetic to audience views" (Rugh, 1987, p. 83). Indeed, the Egyptian authoritative regime controls broadcast media through direct ownership and the print media by applying strict laws (El Gody, 2005). The media role is to follow main policies of the government, and their purpose is to promote its political and economic agenda. Governed by principles of obedience and respect for the political establishment, Egyptian journalists did not reach beyond the limits of a traditional system of relationship between the political class and the rest of the population (Amin, 2003).

Liberal hopes that accompanied the advent of satellite technologies in Egypt were broken by a strict centralized political system which believes that controlling media is important for dominating mass opinion and stabilizing the political system (Alterman, 1998). Arguments for a limited freedom of expression cluster around one reason: the preservation of the nation's unity and cultural coherence. Those factors, ultimately, led to the failure of the Egyptian traditional media to [adopt] newer forms of media (Schleifer, 2005).

Social media found a favourable stagnant public space for its rapid development in Egypt. Being more democratic and less restrictive for information flow, social media allowed audiences to create a stronger and more robust civic 'knowledge' society and offered a forum for new actors to start to develop. Citizens became publishers of information as opposed to being merely receivers; creating a more active public opinion and a marketplace for ideas (El Gody, 2013).

The basis of the information revolution centres around the utilization of technological advancements. At its forefront is the growth of ICTs and in particular social media offering itself as an interactive platform for development. New technologies provided alternative form(s) of media channels where audience became involved in debating current events, criticizing politics, public officials and sharing personal experiences regardless of time and space. Social media introduced new spaces, where people could bypass government-controlled media regime, creating parallel communication system(s) to produce a democratization agenda of their own. The more audience joining the online world, the more Egyptians cluster into networks, and the more active virtual participation occurs and more Egyptians are close in reaching their development goals (El Gody, 2013).

Turning to Egyptian media, the advent of ICTs offered news organizations the possibility of developing new types of journalism and communication, that are radically different from traditional system offering new challenges and possibilities for the industry for enriching the network society's agenda. Dar Al Tahrir daily newspaper *Al Gomhuria* was the first Egyptian newspaper to have a hybrid version of its daily newspaper in 1996. A decade later, 67 publications -including all major news organizations- have an online presence. Yet though this trend may suggest that newspapers are bypassing tight government control over means of information and are communicating and interacting with their audience; such a conclusion should be questioned. Available evidence rather indicate that what Egyptian media are doing is shovelling their static traditional version online (El Gody, 2007). Interviewing senior staff from the main three governmental newspapers *Al Ahram*, *Al Akhbar* and *Al Gomhuria* -which combined at that point of time dominated more than 90% of daily newspaper circulation in Egypt in 2005-, agreed that "too much is made about the power of the Internet." Adding that newsroom staff rarely used the ICTs to gather information since the news agencies and the government are faster, more focused, credible and more reliable (El Gody, 2005).

Gans (2003) and Singer et al (2008) suggested that newspapers were under attack losing grounds as they did not aim to serve, interact with or develop their citizens. The attacks further included the process of news making, which the audience considered the important issue, and the demanded shift from 'top-down, official-source-oriented news to focus on audience participation. Garrison (2008) added that it is the diffusion of ICTs in the making of news that could serve perhaps as the 'missing link' in today's journalism formula. Till 2008, Egyptian print media organizations and journalists did not yet understand the use ICTs. Organization online presence was seen as an extension to the traditional media. For news organizations, their online version is presumed to expand organization geographical foot in an attempt to increase its popularity hence circulation. Content, on the other hands, remained static. In an age of interactive media, Egyptian newspaper circulation, especially government media, are still losing ground to alternative and independent media reaching an 80% loss in circulation by 2018 (El Khazen, 2007; El Gody, 2018).

Creation of an Alternate Media

On the other hands, Egyptian online socio-political discussions -between 2000 and 2008- were at high, especially after 9/11 events. Activists saw in the Internet an opportunity to curb government pressure creating a 'space' in which individuals participate in discussions about matters of common concern, enabling people to bypass the controlled regimes and traditional mass media, allowing the society to create a developmental agenda of their own (El Gody, 2009; cf. Rheinglold, 1993).

The development of the Internet as an alternative media followed three stages according to Courtney Radsch (2008): the experimental stage, the activist stage and the diversification stage. In the Experimental stage, few media, individual bloggers and journalists discovered in the Internet a publishing platform, and started to publish news that challenge the mainstream media using picking online alternative tips and information as source of information. A study conducted by Stephen Quinn (2004) on new media's role during the third Gulf War showed that many Egyptians relied primarily on alternative media websites to get news about the war. The survey showed that the number of searches for 'Al Jazeera online' was three times more than any other searching terms. This shows how Internet technologies became an alternative source of information (Quinn, 2004).

This stage was followed by the Activist stage, during which online media started expanding towards the audience agenda aligning themselves with civil movements like Kifaya and Muslim Brotherhood. Activist movement in Egypt has been growing since 2004. Since then over 3000 online active political groups organized over 3000 demonstration to express their opposition to government reforms, policies, and corruption (El Gody, 2008, Radsch, 2008).

The final stage the Diversification and Fragmentation Stage witnessed an expansion in the number and magnitude of thousands of alternative media outlets pushing themselves in Egyptian public realm including activists, Leftists, Muslim Brotherhood, cultural and personal bloggers, Copts, Bahaaies, homosexuals, Salafis, social commentators and personal bloggers (Radsch, 2008; Hamdy, 2009) These groups utilized the technologies creating posts that became considered a weapon against the restricted flow of information enforced by the Egyptian government. This expresses a shift in the media's influence in society, as people now take information from alternative sources rather than traditional ones (Fahmi, 2009).

Ammar Bakkar (2008) defined the online active actors as individuals communicating in cyberspace. He studied how they and how they represent 'themselves' as well as bodies and organizations –networks- they are affiliated or sympathize with and how they perceive the 'other' in their online dialogue. Bakkar examined the discourse associated with audience online conversations in order to understand the nature of communication in Egypt and the Arab world. He identified ten actors in the Egyptian blogsphere: the Extremist, the Liberal, Official, Religious, Young, Women, Elite, and Civil e-societies, in addition to Egyptian Communities in the West and Business Organizations voices.

Bakkar (2008) further found out that some voices/conversations are "higher" than others… some of these voices are "larger in quantity. They use stronger expressions in terms of judging other voices, opinions, and ideas, control the platform, and are organized based on ideology or cultural beliefs. Voices start "screaming" when they put efforts to exclude other voices. They scream so no other voices are heard." (Bakkar, 2008) Bakkar analysis echoes Castells' discussion on actors' power inside a network where the network is alive only when there is active dialogue within the network as well as between different network nodes. Castells defines a power network when: the number of discussions within the network is available; second, the power of the network is measured by the number of discussions between different members associated to that network; third, that the power of actor network within the sphere differs according the topic of discussion; finally, the news value to the networks in one hand and the degree of member participation on the other (Bakkar, 2008; Castells, 2009).

Egyptian online users can further be classified in three different modes of activities: activism, political bridging, and public sphere engagement. *Activists* present when users directly involve themselves in social movements beyond the virtual world while using messages and writings to identify their stand, position themselves, spread information, coordinate action, and magnify the impact of contentious politics. For example, branding their motto "Islam is the answer" to Egypt problems, conservative Muslim Brotherhood activists use tens of local national websites ranging from news, discussion groups and bloggers through which they directly involve themselves with political, economic and social programs (El Gody, 2008; Radsch, 2008).

The *Political bridging* is the state when users primarily address issues that were voiced by minorities (voice of the voiceless) using messages to bridge information to the masses. Political bridgers view themselves as a venue for dialogue and intercultural exchange of ideas. Noted peaks of this type of avant-garde, users followed events such as 9/11, the London bombings and the Danish cartoon controversy, as advocators tried to alter western misperception of the East through constantly attempting to modify negative image of Islam and Arabs in the West (Bakkar, 2008; Radsch, 2008).

The *public-sphere engagement* is the state when users tend to deeply engage themselves with public arguments about domestic politics and the effect of global politics on daily life. They provide citizens with the most vibrant, argumentative and often most informative commentary available. Unlike activists, they are not organized or try to become agents of social change. An illustrative case is that of cyber-feminists, who by some accounts are more active than their male counterparts in using this medium to promote change (El Gody, 2008; Radsch, 2008; Hamdy, 2009).

Scholars have been elaborating on the role played by the new wave of 'neo journalists' in facilitating conversation cross nation state initiatives. Moore (2003) likened the role of the social software tools like blogs to a 'second superpower' capable of being used for 'nation motivation'. Similarly, Ito (2004) invested hope in the power of citizen journalists to facilitate an emergent democracy through its ability to support a network of local and global conversation and debate. This network created a power that exceeded traditional mass media forms through the network's ability to allow ideas and opinions to arise from the pooled collective wisdom of the network.

Convergence of Mainstream and Social Media

In Egypt's democratizing society, journalism function is expected to be more than a source for news, but a bridge between events on the streets and the Internet (Fahmi, 2009; Fahmy 2010). They needed to be seen as a body to enhance interaction among various groups and actors in order to influence public opinion and mobilize support. Journalists are needed to create a form of Agenda cutting on government mainstream media creating an alternative form of media including news from margins to the mainstream news media became available in networked information societies. Rutigliano (2008) argues that bloggers with small audiences can generate widespread attention for the ignored information and help creating a public sphere. In addition, the availability for everyone in society made it a vital way to communicate information and ideas. It can be used as a virtual space, where people can be informed and they can interact (Rutigliano, 2008; Fahmy 2010).

Social media redefined media role in democratizing societies from simply reporting about the political process to that of being "an active participant in shaping, influence upon, indeed an integral role of the political process (Blumer & Gurevitch, 1995). Among the institutions that contribute to the make-up of the public sphere in a network society, the media perhaps perform the most critical function playing the role of a mediator in the information transactions within the networked sphere. Although journalism main role continues to keep citizens engaged, promoting grassroot democracy by informing, educating and mobilizing the public activists started leading citizen on discussions of local issues providing them alternative point of view other than the state control (Radsch, 2008; Pitnak, 2010). The media are not a neutral participant or an impassioned chronicler. They are either a legitimizer of the status quo or an innovator of the existing social equilibrium.

One of the journalists' main tasks was to offer a forum for debate in order to create a networked sphere where different opinions are there and can be heard between the nodes and arrows (Dahlgren, 2006; Peterson, 2006; Kaplan, 2010). Pierandrei (2002) stated that the impact of ICTs on Egyptian newspapers lies in the shaking up of media organizations to think for the first time on the needs of the audience in order to survive. Convergence of ICTs into newsroom structure and practices grew to be the "core function" of the new journalists.

Creating 'network journalists' seemed to provide the missing link in the Egyptian traditional model of journalism and in realizing democracy through encouraging citizen engagement. The missing links in cyber-democracy are structure and facilitation. The power of journalists within the network nodes lies in their interactivity and tapping into audience interest by engaging themselves in constructing meaningful messages. This required the Egyptian journalists to act as gate watchers over the process of network communication instead of their traditional role as gate keepers, as the relative 'stability' and centralized 'control' of linear news flows was inevitably over. Therefore, government agenda "if you publish it they will come" could not work in today's 'converged network transitional society. (Ardic, 2012; El Gody, 2016)'

Development of Network Journalism

The development of online networks ultimately engendered a new form of journalism, social media journalism, consequently creating a conscious sense of how to reach to citizens and listen to them as well as enabling them to listen back and to each other (El Gody, 2012; Parks, 2005). Good Journalism has always been about networking. Deuze (2008) defines the journalist of the future as the professional who works as a node in the complex environment between technology and society between news and analysis between annotation and selection and between orientation and investigation between technology, different organizations, citizens and interest groups and the society. The utilization of Internet communication technologies in social media journalism practices have added a new dimension to the production and the consumption of news journalism in Egypt and have enabled the creation of new communication spaces where diverse voices engage in conversation about matters affecting daily lives. Egyptian mainstream journalism seems to be far away from that formula (Murphy, 2010).

In Egyptian experience as a transitional society moving towards democracy, political development is a central topic in which audience/journalists mediate. Indeed, journalists inform the audience and facilitate informed choices as 'gatewatchers', not as watchdog 'gatekeepers', in the power struggle between audience, media and politics. Adding, a lack of freedom in the traditional mainstream (whether offline or online) media has enabled the alternative independent online media to develop. News websites became the playground for political parties, activists, and groups from various ideologies creating 'online spaces of flows' to cater for the emerging needs of the readers. Political actors started to invest in creating news portals to attract communities and to enable these communities to interact with each other's ideas on the one hand and with the ideas of the news portals on the other (Hofheinz, 2005; El Gody, 2012).

NETWORK JOURNALISM: THE ROAD TO TAHRIR SQUARE

With Egyptian society moving into the digital age, more people are communicating in cyberspace not only to access information, but also to create a reality of their own. Even if it is only virtual, one day it proved it can cross boundaries to the real world. Egyptians started utilizing ICTs to debate current events, criticize the Government, public officials and political parties, share personal experiences, propose solutions to current socio-political problems, and construct various visions of the country's future (El Gody, 2012; Parks, 2005). Citizens quickly harnessed ICTs creating online news sites, blogs, video blogs, YouTube, podcasts, SMS text messages, mobile phone web publishing, and establishing accounts on social networks like Facebook and Twitter. This was mainly to produce and disseminate the people's journalism and advocacy at a faster pace than that of government control, regulations or censorship (Hamdy 2008).

During the past decade, over 180,000 'social news' websites evolved. Social media sites became the playground for activists, political parties, and groups from various entities to cater to the audience's emerging needs. Organisations started investing in ICTs infrastructure, and creating news portals to attract communities to interact and exchange their ideas among themselves, as well as with others (Hofheinz, 2005, El Gody, 2016; Radsch, 2018). Online news became more vibrant, more liquid, where content was customized, edited and re transmitted via various platforms (El Gody, 2012). Lawrence Pintak (2010) counted 13,500 active Egyptian citizen news journalism websites that provided "politically driven reportage on local events ...break[ing] numerous off-limits to the mainstream Egyptian media" (p. 299) by utilizing ICTs and thus clustering citizens around the idea of embracing democratic change.

Egyptian activists' online discussions were at a high between 2008 and 2010 as citizens began to cluster into groups, each with its own agenda, and to foster several scenarios for the democratization process. Egyptians saw in ICT sources a medium that was likely to have profound implications on their country's socio-political democratization. Activists and independent news organizations saw in the social media an opportunity to curb government censures, creating a common 'space' in which individuals and journalists participated in discussions about matters of common concern in an atmosphere free of coercion or dependencies, acquiescence or silence. Internet technology led to a more horizontal communication model in Egyptian society, enabling people to bypass the controlled regime and traditional mass media, allowing the society to create a developmental agenda of its own (El Gody, 2013).

Social networks, hence, fostered the flow of information, revealing news more quickly to their audience. Many scholars have been elaborating on the role played by the new wave of 'neo journalists' in facilitating information. One of the journalists' main tasks was to offer a forum for debate in order to create a networked sphere where different opinions are available and can be heard between the nodes and arrows (Kaplan, 2010). Pierandrei (2007) stated that the impact of ICTs on Egyptian newspapers lies in the 'shaking up' of media organisations, with the new paradigms forcing them to think about the needs of the audience. The utilisation of online activists and social media actor networks seemed to be the only way to survive. The convergence of ICTs including information networks into newsroom structure and practices grew to be the 'core function' of the new journalists. Pierandrei likened the role of social software tools such as blogs to a 'second superpower' capable of being used for 'nation motivation'.

Due to the tight control of the media in Egypt, several journalists started to operate websites to express their opinion freely. The early ring of citizen journalists included several members from *Al Shaab*, a banned pro-Muslim Brotherhood newspaper, which started publishing their stories online to curb government decision. New forms of convergence journalism, such as mixing text with audio-visual material, started to develop. Citizen journalists started to be a source of information for pan-Egyptian/Arab media, with notable citizen journalists including Wael Abbas, the author of the *Egyptian Awareness* blog, raising awareness of police brutality, when he posted a video depicting police violence and scooped a story about the harassment of women in Cairo.

Similarly, the Egyptian group of citizen journalists/bloggers, *Al-Mudawwenoon*, became a powerful tool of democratisation that inspired many citizens. Passive consumers of information become energetic participants or potential editors in a new kind of journalism where the mainstream media came under increasing pressure. Bloggers became a form of independent news agencies, giving the 'grass roots' up-to-the-minute news and other information. By 2010, the Egyptian blog ring included over 170,000 blogs, most of which are written by social reformers. Blogs are closely networked, following each other and influencing each other and creating a form of 'agenda cutting'. Social media, ICTs and web 2.0 applications brought opportunities to journalists and activists who wished to contribute to the news process. Traditional methods started to erode as citizens began to migrate to alternative media at the expense of traditional media. These alternative media successfully added to the widening spectrum of perspectives available, allowing for more representation of citizens and less attention to simply authoritative opinion. The Egyptian political blog rings, including the *Kefaya* (Enough!) movement, *Shayfenkom* (we are watching you), *Manalla*, and *Baheya*, are considered the best example of how Internet political activities can be taken from the virtual world to the real world, loosening a government's grip on the media. During the 2005 presidential elections, the online journalists ring opposed a fifth term for President Mubarak or the succession of his son Gamal, exposed the falsification of election results, and sought genuine democratic reforms in Egypt. Tens of thousands of citizens demonstrated in several protests which were organised through the Internet to support their cause. Similarly, during the 2010 Parliamentary elections, online activist organisations such as *Kefaya*, *U-shahid*, and *Shayfenkom* established monitoring committees and online teams during the elections, becoming the main authorities on frauds committed during the election process and gaining international recognition.

New forms of social activities, including Facebook, YouTube and Twitter journalism started to develop, among others, providing Egyptian citizen journalists with other platforms for socio-political activism, such as 'twittering' live demonstrations and strikes. In 2008, Esraa Abdel Fattah used Facebook to call for support for strikes by factory workers demanding higher wages, with over 100,000 respondents gathering in just a few days. The Egyptian Government, which started to feel the pressure caused by this Facebook group, detained Esraa in mid-April 2008 on charges of helping to organise the protest of April 6. However, Esraa was released on April 23 after a personal plea to President Mubarak. This Facebook group later became the April 6 Youth Movement, which is one of the main political movements.

During the several protests that lead to the January 2011 events, activists/journalists turned to Facebook, Twitter, blogs, and YouTube to voice their demands, exchange news, share thoughts and opinions, send updates and news about the uprising, and document incidents as they occurred (Poster, 2011). January events that escalated the revolution started when some individuals created a Facebook page called ''We are all Khaled Saed'' in response to the case of Khaled Saed, who police officers tortured to death. The page turned into the light of the revolution when its members called for a peaceful demonstration that was attended by thousands (Gvosdev, 2011). As the events progressed, Internet users, especially network journalists/activists employed Facebook, Twitter and other applications to disseminate information about the meeting places and the way the protestors were to reach Tahreer Square, where the ministries and parliament are located. Status updates and tweets played a very important role in providing information to the protestors about the police formations and plans. In addition, users provided information on how to protect protestors from the bombs that the police used. In an effort to suppress the uprising, the regime blocked more than 3500 Border Gateway Protocol routes operated by Egyptian service providers and shut down approximately 88% of the country's Internet access (Ackerman, 2011). Skilled users accessed Facebook and Twitter from proxy sites which allowed Internet surfing. Their online revolutionary spirit was infectious for those watching from afar. Foreign Policy magazine declared the Egyptian revolution the Twitter "news moment" of the year. The number of tweets posted about Egypt – many using #Jan25– jumped from 2,300 to 230,000 per day the week before Mubarak stepped down on the 11 February (Clarke and Kocak, 2019). In the words of one protester, Fawaz Rashed: "We use Facebook to schedule the protests, Twitter to coordinate, and YouTube to tell the world." (Singel, 2011).

In Egypt's January revolution, the convergence of social media into mainstream media perhaps performed the most critical function (see figure one), playing the role of a mediator in information transactions within the society. Traditional media, especially independent media, started to utilize social media as an alternative source for information and a platform to bridge between events on the streets and the Internet. This convergence has developed the role of the journalism in Egypt, altering it from simply reporting about the political process to instead being "an active participant in shaping, influencing the political process" The media's played a role to deeply engage with the public on arguments about politics and their effect on the audience's daily lives Given that social media tools can be leveraged to spread information, Social media have the potential to provoke and sustain political uprisings by amplifying particular news and information produced by media. Citizen and independent journalists utilization of social media created a new professional who works as a node in the complex environment between technology and society, news and analysis, annotation and selection, and orientation and investigation. As journalists cannot work in 'splinted isolation' anymore, particularly with the abundance of information and the facts that, first, the public are perfectly capable to access news and information for themselves, and second, the institutional players (profit, governmental, non-profit, activist) are increasingly geared towards addressing their constituencies directly instead of using the news media as a go-between.

Hunter (2011) stated that social media alone did not facilitate the Arab Revolution, but was a successful catalyst when combined with myriad methods of digital and traditional media'. The success of the revolution lied in journalists/ citizens utilisation of new technologies ability to integrate "journalism and technicians, writers and camera operators, news gatherers and news processors, and coordinate between print, radio, and television journalism and the audience". The rise of networking sites such as facebook, Youtube, Twitter, among others did encourage users to interact in ways that potentially disrupt existing and social structure. The rise of participatory culture indeed helped ordinary people to create their own content and distribute it via social networks creating a feeling of "Wow… I am not alone," as stated by Wael Ghoneim moderator of *We are All Khaled Said* page that sparked

Figure 1. Convergence of ICTs/ social media in the mainstream media

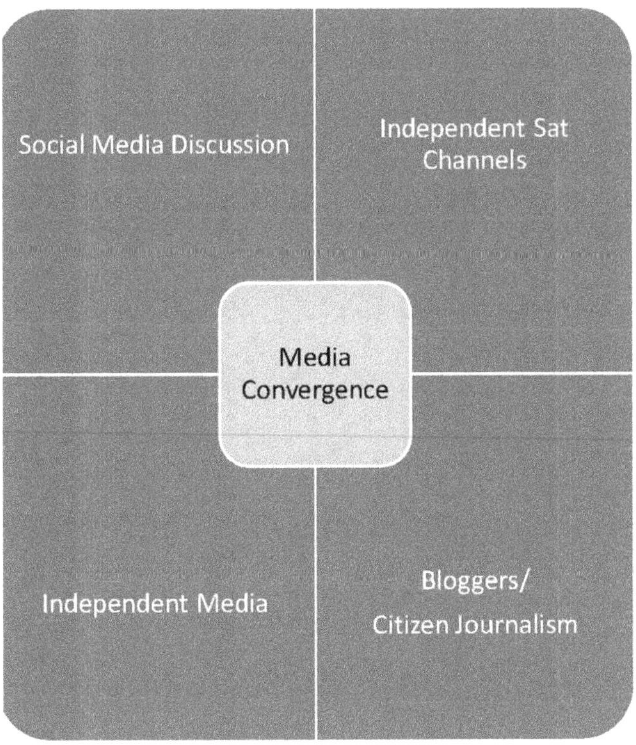

the idea of the revolution. These 'user-generated-content' enhanced traditional logic of political action among ordinary people showing that the "power of the people is stronger than the people in power".

Network Journalism Post January 25 Revolution: New Actors, New Agenda

Studying online deliberation in Egypt on twenty Egyptian social websites (including news, activists, blogs, and politicians platforms) and how they represent themselves and the bodies and organisations (networks as seen in figure two) they are affiliated or sympathise with. One can identify twelve online actors in the Egyptian cyber sphere: The Liberals, Former Officials, Military, Religious, Revolutionaries, Women, Extremists/Salafi's, Civil e-societies, in addition to Egyptian immigrant communities in the west and the voices of business organisations.

Three main groups benefited most from social media after the Egyptian revolution. The first group were political activists including networks from military, Liberals, revolutionaries, civil society and human rights groups that were deprived of their freedom of expression and coerced into silence for decades. The second group were the social groups that challenge social norms and traditions also found the Internet to be a medium where they could meet and create pressure groups to make their voices heard. Finally, the religious groups, especially Muslim Islamic Salafis who

Figure 2. Wordcloud of topics discussed on social media

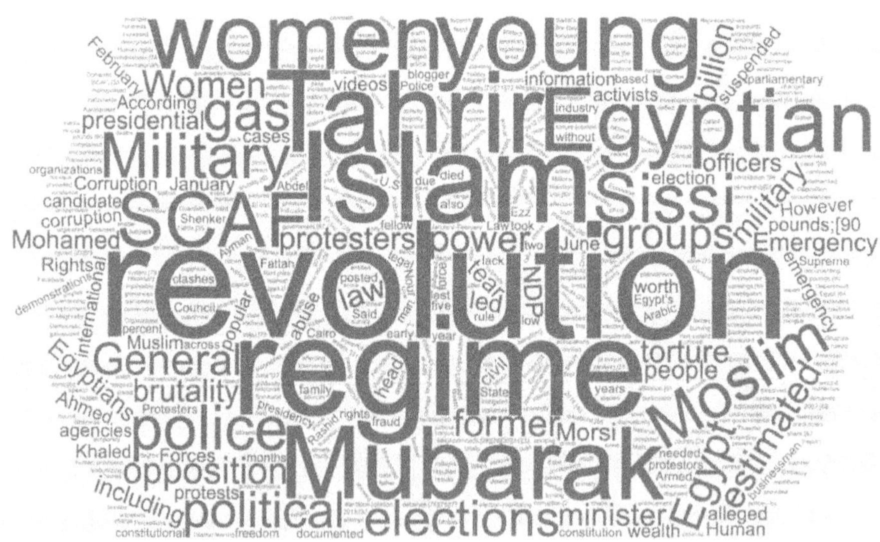

found in the social media avenue to express their ideologies and concerns and reach a wider audience.

Political Networks

Opposition parties and banned political groups and organisations such as the Muslim Brotherhood groups and revolutionary activists such as 6th April movement, who were deprived of their freedom of expression after 2013, used the Internet as a tool to engage users through newsgroups and chat rooms in discussions about political reform. "Gaining access to the Internet was a great triumph to voice our opinion and gain political ground," said Mahdi Akef, former Egyptian Muslim Brotherhood leader, in an interview with *Al Masry Al Youm* in response to the movement winning over 25 per cent of the 2005 Egyptian Parliamentary elections and 60 percent in the 2012 election. After 2013 revolution against the Muslim brotherhood regime, several of the Brotherhood social media avenues like *Ikhwan online* and *Freedom and Justice website* were banned however according to Fares (2016) the Muslim Brotherhood sympathisers created an online army whose purpose is to continue publish the brotherhood ideologies and opposition to the current system. Local and diaspora Social media accounts including *RASD*, *Mekameleen* among others further developed online forums and news portals that carry the brotherhood ideologies offering alternative news sources of information and analysis of the Egyptian current affairs (Faris, 2016). Other opposition groups, such as the Salfi opposition Al Noor (light) party, are using Internet technologies to send emails through specialised mailing lists and facebook groups, expressing their ideologies. Through the use of emails and social media they created intimacy with their audience and gained political support (El Sherif, 2015).

Social Change Networks

As more and more citizens –especially young- started joining the networked public sphere, many started to address the social rigidness in Egypt. After the revolution, their tone changed to become more active, they had heavily expanded their social networks and gained more confidence in their ability to change some pragmatic traditions. Thus, a parallel community of activists was created and strengthened by the fact that individuals who normally would not be involved in activism were now 'speaking out' and expressing themselves on the Internet. (Badran, 2011; Information and Decision Support Centre, 2019).

Religious Networks

Studying social media activities post 2011 revolution showed that between 35 and 65 per cent of the total number of Arabic websites were of religious nature. This estimate indicates the exceedingly large number of web pages with Islamic content that multiplied after the revolution, in response to the growing hate campaign against Islamic satellite channels during the Mubarak era.

Some of these websites, such as *Islam.net*, became internationally acknowledged in cultural dialogues. Prior to 25 January, Egyptian government was not tolerant towards many of the online religious content claiming that the majority were of extremist nature. This however did not hinder the development of online religious content. Examining online deliberation after 2011, it is noticeable that a growing number of religious groups. Several political actors started to create an Islamic front calling for a religious state, creating digital army to voice their cause. Some of them called for the adoption of the extremist interpretation of religion. Furthermore, there has also been a rise in cyber-terrorism sites and blogs promoting xenophobia and hate speech between and against Shiites, Sufis, and Christians.

Analysing social media deliberation revealed that eight years after the revolution, users are still interpreting the revolution using social media as an instrument to evaluate current events and prospects of rebuilding the state. This means that citizens are both expressing their opinions and views of the current political atmosphere and talking about the new institutions and how to build a new government.

In Egypt's democratisation initiative, the continuation of convergence and fusion of traditional media and social media perhaps can perform the most critical function by combining to play the role of a mediator in information transactions within the society. Media use social media as an alternative source of information and a platform to bridge events on the streets and the Internet. This convergence has developed the role of journalism in Egypt, altering it from simply reporting on the political process to actively shaping and influencing the political process. The media can play a role in deeply engaging with the public in regard to arguments about politics and their effect on the audience's daily lives. Given that social media tools can be leveraged to spread information, Shirkey (2009) argued that social media may have the potential to provoke and sustain political uprisings by amplifying particular news and information produced by independent media. Citizen and independent journalists' utilisation of social media has created a new professional who works as a node in the complex environment between technology and society, news and analysis, annotation and selection, and orientation and investigation. As journalists cannot work in 'isolation' anymore, particularly with the abundance of information and the facts that first, the public are perfectly capable of accessing news and information for themselves and, second, the institutional players (profit, governmental, non-profit, activist, etc.) are increasingly geared towards addressing their constituencies directly instead of using the news media as a go-between.

CONCLUSION

Eight years after the revolution, social media platforms still seem to be effective. Although the new government is pressuring freedom of the speech, passing laws to facilitate monitoring and censoring social media content; new generation of activists emerged innovating creative new ways to circumvent government anxiety. New social media platforms have emerged and existing ones have been redesigned. Messaging apps like WhatsApp and Telegram are used extensively to demonstrate government shortcomings. Similarly, Facebook live is used to real-time coverage of protests activities and to circumvent heavily biased state-controlled coverage (Clarke and Kocak, 2019).

Overall, social media seems to be as helpful for organizing protests today as it was in eight years ago. Most importantly, social media is seen as an educational content pool where people are learning how to implement 2011 goals from each other. Or as Clarke and Kocak (2019) stated that every year the 25 January anniversary brings an important reminder that social media, when put into the hands of activists, can still serve as a vital tool for seeking change, freedom and justice.

REFERENCES

Abdullah, R. (2005). Taking the E-train: The development of the Internet in Egypt. *Global Media and Communication*, *1*(2), 149–165. doi:10.1177/1742766505054630

Alexa. (2011) *Top Sites in Egypt.* Retrieved from http://www.alexa.com/topsites/countries; 2/EG

Alterman, J. (1998). *New media, new politics?: From satellite television to the Internet in the Arab world*. Washington: Washington Institute for Near East Policy.

Amin, H. (2003). *The Arabic Satellite TV Media: Accomplishments and challenges. Unpublished research carried by Pan Arab Research Centre (PARC) for the Egyptian Company for Satellites*. Cairo: Nilesat.

Anderson, J., & Eickelman, D. (2008) *New Media and New Publics in the Arab World.* Paper presented at *Nouveaux medias dans le monde arab: Colloque organisé par le GREMMO* (Groupe de recherches et d'études sur la Méditerranée et le Moyen-Orient). Université Lyon, France. Retrieved from http://faculty.cua.edu/anderson /photo.htm

Ardic, N. (2012). Understanding the "Arab Spring": Justice, Dignity, Religion, and International Politics in *Afro Eurasian Studies*, 1(1), 8-52.

Badran, M. (2011). Is ICT Empowering Women in Egypt? An empirical study. Retrieved from http://mak.ac.ug

Bakkar, A. (2008) Who Says What on the Arabic Internet? Notes About Content of Arabic Internet Messages, In the *Journal of Website Promotion*, (3)1-2, 2-13.

Bekheit, E. S. (2005). *Al Sahafa wal Internet* [Newspapers and the Internet]. Cairo, Egypt: Al Arabi.

Blumler, J., & Gurevitch, M. (1995). *The Crisis of Public Communication*. New York: Routledge.

Campbell, V. (2004). *Information Age Journalism. Journalism in an International Context*. New York: Arnold.

Clarke, K., & Kocak, K. (Forthcoming). Launching Revolution: Social and the Egyptian Uprising's First Movers. *British Journal of Political Science*.

Dahlgren, P. (2006). Doing citizenship: The cultural origins of civic agency in the public sphere. *European Journal of Cultural Studies*, *9*(3), 267–286. doi:10.1177/1367549406066073

Deuze, M. (2008). Understanding journalism as a network: How it changes, and how it remains the same. *Westminster Papers in Communication and Culture*, *5*(2), 4–23. doi:10.16997/wpcc.61

Dutton, W. (2008). The Fifth Estate Emerging Through the Network of Networks, *Prometheus*, (27), 1, 1-15. Retrieved from http://ssrn.com/abstract=1167502.

El Gody, A. (2000). *Egyptian based model for the uses and limitations of online journalism applications.* (Master's thesis), American University in Cairo.

El Gody, A. (2003). Egypt. In R. Stanbridge (Ed.), African Media and ICT4D: A Baseline Study on the State of Media Reporting on ICT and Information Society Issues in Africa. London, UK: Economic Commission for Africa.

El Gody, A. (2005). Arab media: Did it cover the same war. In S. A. Nohrstedt, & R. Ottosen (Eds.), *Journalism in Global Age*. Sweden: Nordicom.

El Gody, A. (2007). New Media New Censorship. In P. Seib (Ed.), *New Media and the New Middle East*. New York: Palgrave.

El Gody, A. (2008). *US Image in Arab Blogsphere. Paper submitted to the International Communication Association (ICA).* Conference Chicago.

El Gody, A. (2009). Development of Media Industry in Egypt, in The International Media Handbook (28th ed.), Hamburg, Germany: hans- bredow- Institut.

El Gody, A. (2012). *Journalism in a Network: Role of ICTs inside Egyptian newsrooms. Örebro.* Örebro University Press.

El Gody, A. (2016). Network Journalism and the Egyptian Revolution. In M. Ben Mousa, & A. Doui (Eds.), *Mediated Identities and New Journalism in the Arab World : Mapping the 'Arab Spring'*. London, UK: McMillan. doi:10.1057/978-1-137-58141-9_10

El Khazen, J. (2007). *Censorship and State Control in the Arab World*, Paper presented to the Arab Media Forum Dubai, United Arab Emirates

El Sherif, A. (2015). *Egypt's Salafists At A Crossroads*. Massachusetts: Carnegie Endowment for International Peace.

El Zalaky, I. (2008) *Egyptian Bloggers: Practices and Challenges*, Paper presented to the Conference on New Media and The Press Freedom Dimension. UNESCO Headquarters, Paris, February 15-16.

Fahmi, S. W. (2009). Blogger's Street Movement and the Right to the City. (Re) claiming Cairo's real and virtual "spaces of freedom". *Environment and Urbanization, 21*(1), 89–107. doi:10.1177/0956247809103006

Fahmy, N. (2010). *Revealing the "Agenda-Cutting" through Egyptian Blogs: An Empirical Study*. Paper presented to Online Journalism Symposium, Austin, TX.

Faris, D. (2015). *Dissent and Revolution in a Digital Age: Social Media, Blogging and Activism in Egypt*. New York: IB Tauris.

Freedomhouse. (2013). 'Egypt, Freedom in the World 2010' Retrieved from http://www.freedomhouse.org/template.cfm?page=251&year=2010

Gans, H. (2003). *Democracy and the news*. Oxford, UK: Oxford University Press.

Garrison, B. (2005). 'Online newspapers', in M. B. Salwen, B. Garrison, & P. D. Driscoll (Eds.), Online News and the Public, New Jersey: Lawrence Erlbaum Associates.

Ghareeb, E. (2000). 'New media and the information revolution in the Arab world: An assessment.' *Middle East Journal, 54*(3), 395-418. Retrieved from http://www.jstor.org /stable/ 4329508

Hafez, K. (2006). 'Arab Satellite Broadcasting: Democracy without Political Parties', *Transnational Broadcasting Studies* 15, 2006, Retrieved from www.tbsj ournal.com/Archives/Fall05/Hafez.html

Hamdy, N. (2009). Arab Citizen Journalism in Action: Challenging Main- stream Media, Authorities and Media Laws. *Westminster Paper in Communication and Culture*, *6*(1), 92–112. doi:10.16997/wpcc.110

Hamdy, N. (2010, Fall/Winter). Arab media adopt citizen journalism to change the dynamics of conflict coverage. *Global Media Journal Arabian Edition*, *1*(1), 3–15.

Hofheinz, A. (2005). The Internet in the Arab world: Playground for political liberalisation. *International Political Sociology*, *3*, 78–96.

Hudson, H. (2006). *From Rural Village to Global Village: Telecommunications for Development in the Information Age*. London, UK: Routledge.

Information and Decision Support Centre. (2010b). *Profiling Social Media in Egypt* (in Arabic) Retrieved from www.idsc.gov.eg

Ito, J. (2004). *Weblogs and emergent democracy*. Retrieved from http://joi.ito .com/static/emergentdemocracy.html

Kamel, S., & Hussein, M. (2002). The emergence of e-commerce in a developing nation Case of Egypt, *Benchmarking: An International- Journal, 9*(2).

Kaplan, A., & Haenlein, M. (2010). Users of the world, unite! The challenges and opportunities of Social Media. *Business Horizons*, *53*(1), 59–68. doi:10.1016/j.bushor.2009.09.003

Ministry of Communication and Information Technology. Egypt. (2013). Quarterly Statistics Retrieved from www.mcit.gov.eg

Ministry of Communication and Information Technology. Egypt. (2019). Quarterly Statistics Retrieved from www.mcit.gov.eg

Murphy, E. (2010). The Arab State and (Absent). *Civility in New Communicative Spaces Third World Quarterly*, *32*(5), 959–980. doi:10.1080/01436597.2011.578972

Pavlik, J. (2001). *Journalism and New Media*. New York: Columbia University Press. doi:10.7312/pavl11482

Pierandrei, E. (2007). 'Impact of covering New Media in Journalism: A New Tool to Foster Information in Egypt', (Master's thesis), The American University in Cairo.

Pintak, L. (2010). Arab media and Al Jazeera Effect. In *T. McPhail (Ed.), Global Communication: Theories, Stakeholders, and Trends*. Wiley-Blackwell.

Quinn, S., & Walters, T. (2004). Al-Jazeera: Ripples in a stagnant media pool. In R. Berenger (Ed.), *Global Media go to War*. Cairo, Egypt: American University in Cairo Press.

Radsch, C. (2008). 'The Evolution of Egypt's Blogosphere'. Paper presented at the annual meeting of the Middle East Studies Association MESA.

Radsch, C. (2016). *Cyberactivism and citizen journalism in Egypt: Digital dissidence and political change*. Washington, DC: Palgrave Macmillan. doi:10.1057/978-1-137-48069-9

Ragab. (2007). 'Egyptian Press: What do we Miss?' *Al Akhbar newspaper*, p. 8.

Rheingold, H. (1993). *The Virtual Community: Homesteading on the Electronic Frontier*. Reading, MA: Addison-Wesley.

Rugh, W. A. (1987). *The Arab Press: News Media and Political Process in the Arab World*. Syracuse, NY: Syracuse University Press.

Rutigliano, W. (2008). 'Covering the Unknown City: Citizen Journalism and Marginalized Communities', (Doctoral Dissertation), University of Texas, Austin.

Salama, S. (2009). *Al Sahafa Fauf Safeeh Sakhen* [Journalism over Hot Tin Roof]. Cairo, Egypt: Dar Al Ain.

Schliefer, A. (2005). 'The Impact of Arab Satellite Television on the Prospects for Democracy in the Arab World', *Transnational Broadcast Studies. Dar Al Kutub, 1*(2), 309–315.

Chapter 7
Will Microblogs Shape China's Civil Society Under President's Xi's Surveillance State?
The Case of Anti-Extradition Law Protests in Hong Kong

Kenneth C. C. Yang
https://orcid.org/0000-0002-4176-6219
The University of Texas at El Paso, USA

Yowei Kang
https://orcid.org/0000-0002-7060-194X
National Taiwan Ocean University, Taiwan

ABSTRACT

Western scholars have previously predicted Weibo and social media will provide Chinese netizens with an opportunity to foster its nascent civil society. However, the growing applications of surveillance technologies have challenged this rosy, yet deterministic prediction. This chapter argues that Jürgen Habermas's concept of public sphere is less likely to function properly, given the pervasive applications of surveillance technologies in China, which has fundamentally challenge its many assumptions. Using Habermas's analytical framework that is used to better comprehend the role of social media in Chinese politics, the authors argue that information technologies turn out to deteriorate the formation and maintenance of a public sphere for Chinese civil society. The authors employ a case study to examine the interrelations among social media, surveillance technologies, civil society, state power, economic development, political process, and democratization in China as demonstrated in Hong Kong's Anti-Extradition Law Protests.

DOI: 10.4018/978-1-7998-1791-8.ch007

Copyright © 2020, IGI Global. Copying or distributing in print or electronic forms without written permission of IGI Global is prohibited.

INTRODUCTION -

China is an emerging power with 1.35 billion people that are composed of over 50 different ethnicities (including the largest Han ethnic group, Hui, Manchu, Miao, Korean, Mongol etc.) (National Bureau of Statistics of China, 2013). Many political leaders around the world have acknowledged the rise of China in recent decades (Graham-Harrison, 2007; Shambaugh, 2013). China's rapid rise in the world politics has created widespread geo-political schisms in South China Sea (Center for Preventive Action, 2019) and other parts of the world. Former U.S. Secretary of State, Henry Kissinger, had argued that China's rise in politics and economics is irreversible, and advocated close collaborations between two superpowers to avoid potential conflicts and wars (Graham-Harrison, 2007).

Economic indices have undoubtedly already confirmed China's status as a global economic powerhouse after its GDP of $5.87 trillion surpassed Japan as the second-largest economy (Jacquez, 2012; Shambaugh, 2013). China's economic growth is expected to slow down between 2014 and 2019 to 6.8% (IBIS World, 2014) and recently published GDP figure in the 2nd Quarter of 2019 has shown its economic growth was hit hard by the trade war to slow down to 6.2% (He, 2019), the lowest figure in the past 27 years. Nevertheless, China remains to be one of the most robust economies in the world (Yao, 2014), given that the Chinese government still has a lot of incentive measures to promote its domestic growth, despite the current trade war with the U.S. (Chan, Kwan, & Thomsen, 2019). With its growing political and economic prominence (Graham-Harrison, 2007), China has been cultivating its soft power to expand its influence in international politics through its Confucius Institute and mass media out-reach as far as Africa (Lee & Melissen, 2011; Li, 2009; Shambaugh, 2013).

Nevertheless, increasing social unrest and rights defense movement have occurred across China (Biao, 2012; *The Economist*, 2012). These protests have grown more organized, according to a report by the Chinese Academy of Social Sciences (CASS) (*The Economist*, 2012). It is estimated in a report by J.P. Morgan and Chase that trade war continues with the U.S. will cost China 700,000 or more jobs (Bloomberg News, 2018). The worst case scenario means China will lose 5.5 million jobs and 1.3% of its GDP growth (Bloomberg News, 2018). The sudden rise of unemployment rate will cost the ruling Chinese Communist Party (henceforth CCP) regime its legitimacy (Richards, 2018). Losing "the Mandate of Heaven" can cause the CCP regime to collapse rapidly when social unrests occur and spread rapidly across China (Richards, 2018)

During this volatile phase of the modern Chinese history, information-communication technologies (ICTs) (such as *Weibo*) are likely to play an important role. Despite of the intentional aloofness of government media to create a façade of a harmonious society, angry protestors take advantage of the emergence of the Internet and social media (such as *Weibo*) in "enriching the modalities of activity in the rights defense movement, enhancing the mobilisation capacity of activists, and accelerating the systematisation of popular rights defence" (Biao, 2012, p. 29). Bondes and Schucher (2014) therefore envisioned such civil unrests are likely to increase the number of "online mass incidents" (p. 45) in China when Chinese citizens are mobilized to take part in political activities after decades of suppression. More and stronger social unrest has been predicted by analysts such as Harry Dent, on the basis of changing demographics and young migrants in China (Dent, 2018). These reports have shown that China, in spite of its economic success, is now faced with many urgent needs for social and political reforms to respond to these challenges from a nascent civil society. However, protests have now become a common tool for Chinese citizens to voice their discontent (Kelly-Meyrick, 2017). However, researchers have found that Chinese citizens often exercise what is called "hierarchical trust", defining as more trust for the central government, but less trust for the local government (Kelly-Meyrick, 2017). This distinction has been used to explain why increasing social unrests in China have less effect on the one-party regime (Kelly-Meyrick, 2017).

The authoritarian regime of President Xi Jing-Ping has further strengthened government control over the Internet to prevent any potential effect on the interests of the state or national security as stipulated in its 1997 law that criminalizes "problematic" online postings (Economy, 2018). The "seven baselines" were issued in August 2013 and has caused *Sina Weibo* to shut down more than 100,000 accounts to comply with this regulatory regime (Economy, 2018). In addition, China continues to use its well-known *the Great Firewall* to block foreign contents. In January 2015, China blocked citizens' access to VPNs that are used to circumvent the Great Firewall (Economy, 2018). *The Great Cannon* was implemented in Spring 2015 to adjust or replace Internet contents and forced several Internet operators to revise or remove contents deemed to be sensitive by Chinese government (Economy, 2018). The Chinese government also targeted the social media influencers to control their postings. A survey of 1.6 million Weibo users has confirmed that the number of Weibo posts dropped by 70% between 2011 and 2013 (Economy, 2018).

Xi's oppressive regime has to let to the pessimistic forecasts among many Western observers, culminating in the cover page story in *The Economist* (2018a, March 1, n.p.) which claims "*It bet that China would head towards democracy and the market economy. The gamble has failed.*" This chapter reexamines whether *Weibo* has created a public sphere to facilitate the formation and development of civil society in China. Using a case study of *Weibo* about Hong-Kong's *Anti-Extradition Protests* in 2019, the authors studied what this popular social media platform has accomplished to promote political engagement of Chinese citizens.

BACKGROUND

ICTs Development in China

ICTs broadly refer to the Internet, mobile/cellular phone, fixed and mobile broadband, and a variety of new media (ITU, 2014). ICTs are often claimed to be the driving force of new economy (Li & Meng, 2011). Same economic rationale has promoted China to actively develop these technologies through its incentive to attract talents, construct high-tech parks, and to deregulate policies and laws related to the ICT sectors (Hung, 2010; Meng & Li, 2011). ICTs are deemed as a priority in China's national development (Simon, 2011; Liu, 2013). Nevertheless, the Chinese government has shifted its rhetoric and shown its willingness to sacrifice economic growth to better control the Internet for national security reasons (Economy, 2018). For example, the banning of VPNs has shown China's attempt to impose stringent control of the Internet, even those the technology's popularity among academic community, multinational banks, and retailers (Economy, 2018).

One of the most influential ICTs in China is the Internet. According to the 41st Survey Report published by Chinese Internet Network Information Center (CNNIC) (2018, January), the total Internet users in China, as of December 31, 2017, have reached 772 million (55.8% of the total population of 1.3 billion), representing an increase of 40.74 million users (or 2.6%) compared with 2016 (CNNIC, 2018, January). Mobile Internet users have reached 753 million at the same period (about 97.5% of the total Internet population) (CNNIC, 2018, January). 28.2% of Chinese netizens has used television to access the Internet (CNNIC, 2018, January).

Weibo (Microblogs) in China

The growth of social media in China ranks number 1 (84.63 million or 10%) around the world, according to *The Global Digital Report 2018* (We are Social, 2018). In spite of relentless government crackdowns, microblogs have become one of the most popular among many social networking platforms in China (Chen, Zhang, Lin, & Lv, 2011; Economy, 2018; *The Economist*, 2014). Ironically, Chinese government has actively set up government microblogs to take advantage of the communicative functions of the social media platforms. According to CNNIC (2018, January), there are 134,827 government microblogs as of December 2017. *Weibo* can be considered as a Chinese version of Twitter (Sandoval, 2009; *The Economist*, 2012; Voice of America, 2012). However, *Weibo* is different from Twitter in terms of its country of origin, supported languages, the number of tweets per day, size of registered users, growth rate, and level of globalization (Chen et al., 2011). Overall, in spite of its rapid growth, *Weibo* only supports simplified and traditional Chinese characters and are mainly used by Internet users in the Greater China region (Chen et al., 2011). In general, it lacks the globalization potential of Twitter (Chen et al., 2011). Since *Weibo* was first launched in China in August 2009, *eMarketer.com* (2018) observes that around 25% of the Chinese population has adopted *Weibo* in 2018 and it is estimated that by 2021, over 400 million users (about 29.9%) will adopt *Weibo*.

In terms of total Chinese Internet users, *m*onthly active users of *Sina Weibo* have grown to 376 million (CNNIC, 2018). *Sina Weibo*, the most popular *Weibo* in China, is the most widely used platform in the first-tier cities –such as Beijing, Guangzhou, Shanghai, and Shenzhen (*China Internet Watch*, 2012/11/23). Several technological characteristics have made *Weibo* a particularly successful medium to create a less controlled space for many Chinese Internet users. Citing a BBC's report (May 12, 2008), Li and Rao (2010) observed that *Weibo* was widely reported to out-perform government-controlled mainstream media during the massive 2008 China earthquake, in terms of the releasing of the USGS tremor report. However, the effectiveness of *Weibo* as a communication platform depends on external political and social contexts unique to each mass incident (Tong & Zuo, 2014). In addition to the speed of information dissemination, Tong and Zuo (2014) observed that message characteristics, such as being short (about 140 Chinese words), have contributed to the success of *Weibo*. Furthermore, with the accumulative competition in the microblog market in China, commercial *Weibo* providers also introduced features such as privacy setting, controlled access, and cross-platform publications to enable users to disseminate information.

Despite the capabilities of *Weibo* to disseminate less censored news, Xi's new measures to control the Internet and many emerging media platforms though its new cybersecurity law have significantly reduced what these media can do to shape the public opinion, and sometimes alter government's policies (Kuo, 2018). For example, outcry from China's Internet users has led *Sina Weibo* to alter its anti-homosexuality measure to block gay-related contents because of "pornographic implications, promoting bloody violence, or related to homosexuality" (Kuo, 2018, n.p.). Internet users have used the hashtags *#iamgay* and *#iamgaynotapervert* to organize online protests to challenge the legality of *Sina Weibo*'s policy that is questioned to violate Article 38 of Chinese Constitution to protect individual personal dignity (Kuo, 2018).

Social media have been claimed to create China's civil society (Tu, 2016). Using *WeChat* as an example, Tu (2016) argued the closely-related interpersonal networks "provide a comfortable space for discussions and cultivate a series of alternative public spheres" to build association and solidarity (p. 343). Given this unique space, Tu (2016) further claimed that this social media platform encourages online debates and popular protests among Chinese Internet population. However, pessimists also present a drastically different perspective, claiming the ubiquitous presence of social media does not necessarily lead to a Western-style civil society, rather a "zombified civil society" (Gregory, 2018, n.p.) that is controlled by high-tech surveillance systems such as social credit system or artificial intelligence.

The suppression of any types of social protests, regardless of their causes, seems to support the pessimistic claim that social media is less likely to alter the current path of President Xi has taken. For example, the popular *#MeToo* (or *#Woyeshi* in Chinese) social protests of sexual harassment incidents has continued to be silenced by the government. Many feminists have bravely shared their personal stories and identified the molesters (one of them shared their experiences dated back 10 years ago as a college student at the prestigious Peking University), government censors have blocked public discussions to deter any traction to support this movement (Huang, 2018). "Agitators" of public order are often harassed by public security officers or put in prison (Huang, 2018).

OBJECTIVES OF THE CHAPTER

The emergence of civil society in the authoritarian China continues to be a topic worthy of investigation. Whether new ICTs are able to shape China's society is no doubt a topic that captures the attention of scholars, politicians, and businessmen. Furthermore, Internet policemen's rapid actions to delete "inappropriate" Weibo posts presents a major problem to collect data to study many social unrests in China (Huang, 2018). To address the data collection obstacle, the authors aim to use the recent *Anti-Extradition Law Protest* in Hongkong as a case study to analyze whether state power will face contestation to warrant subsequent re-distribution of power and possible political transformation in China. Thus, the main purposes of this chapter are to provide a detailed account of the role of social media, *Weibo*, in China and its special administrative region, Hong Kong, for this on-going social movement. Specifically, this chapter aims to show how *Weibo* contributes to the formation of a public sphere and the emergence of Chinese civil society to shape China's political future.

Microblogs and Chinese Nascent Civil Society

Popular Chinese microblog operators such as *Tencent* and *Sina* have offered *Wiexin* and *Weibo* applications, respectively (Mason, 2013). *Tencent* has claimed it has one billion daily active users (Iqbal, 2018). One of the main reasons for the past popularity of microblogs among activists in China has been attributed to the stringent government control and regulation over other media, which prompts isolated individuals to use these media platforms (Sullivan, 2012). The increasing influence of microblogs over political communication is also attributed to China's rapid urbanization, economic development, and ICT developments in recent years (Biao, 2012, Chan et al., 2012; Chen & She, 2012; Chen, 2014; Mou, Atkin, Fu, Lin, & Lau, 2013). State control over information in mass media is likely to be challenged among urban residents in China when access to the Internet is significantly improved. As a result, *Weibo* has become a major communication platform to bypass government's information control (Sullivan, 2014). Similarly, Zou (2013) observed that the emergence of *Weibo* has significantly impacted on past governments' control of public opinions by transforming the communication process from a top-down "dissemination to acceptance" (p. 54) to an interactive two-way reciprocal model.

Traditionally, the contestation between *Weibo* and state power can be best described in the case below to demonstrate how government policies can sometimes be altered to better respond to the public opinions. The detention of Sun Zhigang, a migrant worker, by the police in Guangzhou for missing his residence permit generated a heated discussion among Chinese Internet users (Hung, 2010). The Chinese government finally yielded to the public opinions and abolished a regulation that existed for over 20 years to repatriate migrants in China's big cities. Currently, the government has taken an active role in shaping public opinions online. For example, President Xi's tenure has drastically affected how the Internet and *Weibo* are regulated (Economy, 2013). Increasingly, the hired online commentators, also known as *50 Cent Party*, have been recruited from colleges and universities to create posts favorable to the government to guide or derail public discussions to comply with government's agendas (Economy, 2013; Waddell, 2017). An article published in the government-controlled *Global Times* has confirmed that the government does recruit the public commentators to guide public opinions on *Weibo* (Waddell, 2017).

Before Xi's regime, government surveillance, even though not as stringent as in Mao's Era, has slightly impacted on every aspect of Chinese people's lives (Alessi, 2012). Recent economic development, privatization, urbanization, and new technologies have further fostered a new generation of Chinese citizens that enjoy a state-run capitalistic society. The so-called "capitalism with Chinese characteristics" is a façade of "the Communist Party's capitalism", according to a Chinese scholar, Chen Xiaonong (2016). Overall, as of 2017, ownership of mobile phones has exceeded 101.97% penetration, mobile Internet penetration has also reached 1271.5 million users, and broadband subscribers of mobile Internet have also reached 348.5 million (National Bureau of Statistics of China, 2017). Young generations in China (often referred to as the *Post-80 and -90 Generation* in China to indicate the year they were born) have access to and rely heavily on new media since they were born (Wallis, 2011). For example, those who were born in the 1990s, i.e., *Post-90 Generation*, are influenced more by microblogs than traditional mass media (Kisselmann, 2014).

Identified as one of the three domains in modern governance, civil society is often defined as a non-profit organized community that "is guided by value-driven voluntarism and accommodates a wide range of organizational structures" (Leung, 2008, p. 7). In addition to political parties, informal grassroots that are involved in political activities are also part of civil society (Leung, 2008). Although the concept of civil society has been debated in terms of what it means in different historical, economic, and political contexts, it often refers to the "aggregate of non-governmental organizations and institutions that manifest interests and will of citizens" (http://dictionary.reference.com/browse/civil+society?r=66).

LITERATURE REVIEW AND ANALYTICAL FRAMEWORK

The emergence of ICTs has often been associated with their potential power to change society (Chen, 2014; Shirky, 2011). In the context of China, some observers have made audacious claims that "How Weibo is Changing China" as early as 2012 (Magistad, 2012). Magistad (2012) claims, "The microblog tool has opened a new battleground among Chinese authorities, internet companies and citizens – all testing the other's boundaries and resolve to criticize, censor and self-censor" (n.p.). The spatial metaphor that new ICTs are able to create for many Chinese netizens has prompted many scholars to use Jürgen Haberman's (1962) term, "public sphere," to describe the "space for discussion and agreement among politically engaged citizens, often before the state had fully democratized" (cited in Shirky, 2011, p. 6). This study appliesJürgen Habermas' concept of public sphere to examine the role of *Weibo* in creating a less censored place for public discussions among Chinese citizens to engage in civil society activities as demonstrated in the recent Anti-Extradition Law protests in Hong Kong.

Public Sphere and Social Media

Enabling citizens to take part in democratic deliberation is the main thesis of Habermas's theory of public sphere (1991). Through public discussions, free expression of opinions, and democratic decision-making, state power will be constrained (McGowan & Kaiser, 2014). Habermas (1989) applied the concept of public sphere to study the role of media in the institutional design of modern democracies. Habermas emphasizes three aspects of public sphere: being open to all, democratic, and enabling (i.e., allowing the public to command different resources) (cited in Fuchs, 2014). Other scholars (such as Benkler, 2006, Burgess & Green, 2009, Castells, 2009, Papacharissi, 2009) have touched upon various aspects of public sphere in the social media age, ranging from relationship exchange, communication protocol building, interaction with other cultures, etc. (Refer to Fuchs, 2014).

The metaphor of public sphere in *Weibo* is appropriate to understand its role in fostering the nascent civil society in China (Fuchs, 2014; Hassid, 2012; Hung, 2011; Tung, 2016). Both scholars have pointed out that the Chinese Internet users often feel less restricted in exchanging their viewpoints on a variety of issues (some issues are considered to be politically sensitive and censored when it comes to mainstream mass media). Although the Chinese government often frowns upon the unwelcome potential of mass mobilization through *Weibo* and takes aggressive measures to censor certain expressions that call for large-scale protests (King et al., 2013) to the extent of hiring 50 centers to derail public opinions online, Chinese Internet users often feel a sense of community beyond the constraints of time and geography when users exchange opinions in a variety of *Weibo* platforms.

Habermas (1962, 1984) defined the concept of public sphere as "a realm of our social life in which something approaching public opinion can be formed" (p. 49). His conceptualization of public sphere emphasizes the importance of access made available to all citizens to enable them to transform from private individuals into a public body. In the authoritarian China, tight control over its citizens' political activities often makes this process unimaginable and dangerous under Xi's hi-tech surveillance state. He pointed out that "citizens behave as a public body when they confer in an unrestricted fashion—that is, with the guarantee of freedom of assembly and association and the freedom to express and publish their opinions—about matters of general interest" (p. 49). In the process of forming a public body to create a civil society, communication media (such as the Internet, social media, magazines, newspapers, television, and radio) are viewed as "the media of public sphere" (p. 49). According to Fuchs (2012), for social media to become civil society media, they need to be run, owned, and controlled by citizens, and their contents need to address humans in their various social roles and for meaning making purposes.

As envisioned by Jürgen Habermas, the ideal role of social media should allow Chinese citizens to share, exchange, and disseminate information among those who converse in an Internet café, read newspapers and magazines, watch television, and listen to radio. These media are also easily accessible to interested Chinese citizens when compared with their opinions published in state-controlled mass media. With similarly effective agenda-setting functions of these social media, Chinese citizens are expected to be able to form a public body and civil society to take part in the democratic decision-making process, According to Habermas (2006), media and other ICTs are crucial to a democratic society, because "the *dynamics* of mass communication are driven by the power of the media to select, and shape the presentation of, messages and by the strategic use of political and social power to influence the agendas as well as the triggering and framing of public issues" (p.1). Several *Weibo*-prompted mass incidents that altered Chinese government's policies seem to attest to its potential to form a public sphere and to foster China's civil society. These examples support the claim that *Weibo* is able to create a public sphere to allow free expressions of public opinions before President Xi's era. However, the ruling Chinese Communist Party has taken active roles in censoring contents (Magistad, 2012). About 13% of *Weibo* contents have been deleted, according to King (cited in Magistad, 2012). In the past, government often took the approach to control *Weibo* communication by deleting social influencers' *Weibo* account or removing comments or posts critical of the government (Magistad, 2012). For example, popular blogger's account was deleted because these social influencers, such as Isaac Mao, in spite of his 30,000 followers, has been a vocal critics of China's space program as "a waste of money" (Magistad, 2012, n.p.).

The concept of public sphere has been applied to study the role of media in a democratic society (Harrison & Wessells, 2009; Mohd, 2009; Splichal, 2012; Yeung, 2008). In particular, the vital role of new ICTs to contribute to the development of civil society and the evolution of these societies into democracies have often been studied from Habermas's public sphere theory to study how citizens find a less restrictive space for a variety of functions in these media space. Scholars have tied the use of new ICTs with the democratization process. For example, Yeung (2008) used the term, "digital democracy", to describe the potential of these technologies to "expand the realm of civil society and revive political participation" (p. 8).

In the vein of discussing social media as liberating, empowering, and participatory technologies, characteristics of social media often center on their characteristics as 1) user participation, user-generated content, and crowdsourcing; 2) user-defined content; 3) network effects; 4) scalability; 5) perpetual beta; 6) reputation economy (Tuten & Solomon, 2013). Similarly, Yeung (2008) identifies several characteristics of these ICTs to contribute to democratic participation among civil society organizations; these characteristics include 1) levelling the playing field; 2) reaching out other organizations via alternate media; 3) staff empowerment, resource mobilization, and participatory media; 4) building virtual organizations through social networks; 5) regulatory constraints of these media. These characteristics clearly suggest the role of social media users in the process of creating public discourses, sharing and exchange opinions, participating in collective activities, and forming consensus within the community. The above-mentioned practices of democratic decision-making processes are instrumental to the development and maintenance of Chinese civil society in the end. The control of Internet and social media before President Xi seems to offer scholars a slight hope of civil society media in China because social media are able to support the formation of civil society and public sphere-- both conducive to democracy (Shirky, 2011). Furthermore, scholars have also argued that the power of social media like *Weibo* is not only to share information, but also to shape public opinions through discussions and opinion exchanges in the communication process (Tang & Sampson, 2012). Tang and Sampson (2012) found, through their study of three major incidents, that interactions between ICTs and traditional mass media were found to shape and direct news agendas in mainstream media.

Unlike his predecessors, President Xi has envisioned a China with its full government intervention in every aspect of its citizen's life. As such, his approaches to control the cyberspace is to "ensure that internet content more actively served the interests of the Communist party" (Economy, 2018, n.p.). Xi once said, "The internet has become the main battlefield for the public opinion struggle" (cited in Economy, 2018, n.p.). New technologies have been developed to ensure full control of the cyberspace, including the control of VPNs, the launch of *Great Cannon* to accompany its *Great Firewall*, and social credit system to penalize those who spread "fake news" (Economy, 2018). Stringent laws and regulations are also implemented to penalize *Weibo* users who spread rumors or lies that are seen by more than 5,000 individuals or shared more than 500 times will face defamation charges and 3 years in jail (Economy, 2018).

The changing political and social milieu in China bring up an important question about the roles of social media to foster China's nascent civil society or subsequent political reformation in President Xi's China. Specifically, the authors of this book chapter would explore the following two research questions:

Research Question 1: What are the roles of microblogs (such as *Weibo*) in fostering China's civil society in President Xi's China?
Research Question 2: How are microblog's attributes interacting with the changing political and social milieu in President Xi's China?

Using a Case Study Approach

To better understand the importance of public sphere and its relationship with the emerging civil society in China, the authors used one exemplar on-going mass incident in Hong Kong, SAR, China (*The Anit-Extradiction Law Protests*) as a focal point to analyze the role of microblogs in China's two territories and its contestation with the central CCP government, Hong Kong SAR government, civil society, and the publics in both Hong Kong and China. The authors followed the same case study approach adopted by past scholars in the literature (Bondes & Schucher, 2014; Sullivan, 2012; Tang & Sampson, 2012; Tong & Zhu, 2014; Tu, 2016). The case study method is appropriate to offer "an understanding of a complex issue or object and [can] extend experience or add strength to what is already known through previous research" (Jarreau et al., 2015; Soy, 1997; Yang et al., 2019). This research method can be combined with other quantitative and qualitative methods to offer more thorough analysis of a specific phenomenon (Jarreau et al., 2015). Furthermore, the case study approach allows researchers to focus on "detailed contextual analysis of a limited number of events or conditions and their relationships" (Soy, 1997; Yang et al., 2019).

Issues, Controversies, Problems

Anti-Extraction Law Protest in Hong Kong, SAR, China

After 156 years of British colonial rule, Hong Kong was officially handed over to China on June30/July1, 1997 (Levine, 1998). In 1984, both British and Chinese leaders signed the *Sino-British Joint Declaration on the Question of Hong Kong* which stipulates that China guarantees "One Country, Two Systems" that protects Hong Kong with a high degree of autonomy for its people and to ensure their lifestyle, social, economic systems will remain the same for 50 years after 1997 (Levine, 1998). Pessimists have concerns that "China would drastically curtail the rights and freedoms of Hong Kong residents" (Levin, 1998, n.p.), which unfortunately has become a reality as demonstrated in the rising number of civil protests during the past five years.

The large influx of Chinese immigrants to Hong Kong has made its residential property prices skyrocketed 242 times over the past 10 years (Peter, 2019). According to O'Neill (2017), a total of 1.5 million Chinese immigrants have moved to Hong-Kong through family union, investment, employment, or student visa schemes since 1997. A large number of immigrants also strains public housing, hospitals, schools, welfare systems, and jobs (O'Neill, 2017; Peter, 2019). There are also growing concerns among Hong-Kong residents that President Xi has meddled with the special administrative region's judicial, social, and political affairs to impact on The Basic Law, Hong Kong's mini-constitution (Blanchard, Holden, & Wu, 2017). The concerns are partially substantiated when a statement from Chinese Foreign Ministry announced unexpectedly the following (Blanchard et al., 2017, n.p.):

Now Hong Kong has returned to the motherland's embrace for 20 years, the Sino-British Joint Declaration, as a historical document, no longer has any practical significance, and it is not at all binding for the central government's management over Hong Kong. The UK has no sovereignty, no power to rule and no power to supervise Hong Kong after the handover.

Since the hand-over to China, several major social movements have occurred to protect the civil liberties of Hong Kong residents, when facing the relentless challenges from the Central Government in Beijing. For example, on July 1, 2003, a massive demonstration of 700,000 protestors had led to the withdrawal of Article 23 in *Hong Kong's Basic Law* and resignation of top government officials (CNN

World, 2003). Many of the protestors are from Hong Kong's traditionally a-political middle class and were forced to fight against the national security law that will infringe residents' freedom of speech (CNN World, 2003). From 2004 to 2013, several island-wide protests were organized to *Strive For Universal Suffrage in '07 & '08* and *Oppose Government Collusion, Striving for Universal Suffrage* to request the election of Hong Kong's chief executive (Bush, 2014), culminating in one of the island's largest demonstrations, *Occupy Central with Love and Peace* in 2013 and later *The Umbrella Movement* in 2014 (Iyengar, 2014). In spite of the severe prison terms for many participants and organizers of both *Occupy Central with Love and Peace* and *The Umbrella Movement* (Chan, 2019), Hong Kong residents continue to stage peaceful civil disobedience movements to protect their own freedoms as stipulated in the *Basic Law.*

A series of protests has been staged across various locations in Hong Kong over several weekends to fight against the controversial extradition law proposal (Pao, 2019). Lack of leadership of current Hong Kong Chief Executive, Carrie Lam Cheng Yuet-Ngor, excessive police violence, and what is worse, covert collaboration between the police and criminal Triad gang members to brutally beat up protestors, commuters, and bystanders at the Yuen Long MRT station have continued to deteriorate the situation (Channel News Asia, 2019). As of late July, *the Anti-Extradition Law Protest* has spiraled into a full-scale social movement to demand the implementation of full democracy in Hong Kong (Pao, 2019). Protestors now called for 1) the withdrawal of the extradition law, 2) universal suffrage to elect Hong Kong's chief executives and council men; 3) government's retraction of the official stance of the June 12 protest as a "riot"; 4) release of the detained anti-extradition protestors; 5) establishing an independent commission to investigate police brutality against protestors; 6) the resignation of Chief Executive Carrier Lam Cheng Yuet-Ngor (Pao, 2019).

SOLUTIONS AND RECOMMENDATIONS

This chapter employed Habermas's (1984, 1989) concept of public sphere to examine whether *Weibo* users (i.e., microbloggers) in Hong Kong and the Mainland China are making the most use of this social media platform as a tool to sharing and distribute information. Rather, their opinions about Hong Kong's Anti-Extradition Law protests have been influenced by the agenda setting of government's mass media and public opinion manipulation at *Weibo*. The authors examined the use of *Weibo* related to *The Anti-Extradition Law Protest* in Hong Kong. This study analyzed how *Weibo* has been used differently in two parts of China (i.e., the Mainland China and Hong Kong, SAR) to examine how their technological potentiality is limited to alert China's political realities.

Compared with the Mainland China, Hong Kong has an open and liberal social media landscape. *Facebook*, *Twitter*, *Instagram*, and their Chinese versions are available to its residents. While Chinese media and *Weibo* have portrayed Hong Kong's *Anti-Extradition Law Protest* as "a primarily violent, foreign-funded plot to destabilize the motherland, not a mass popular movement over Beijing's increased shadow over the semi-autonomous hub" (Coconuts Hong Kong & AFP, 2019, n.p.). The editorial of state-owned *Global Times* has also accused "the extreme opposition and demonstrators in Hong Kong have misunderstood the geopolitical factors and the current era. It is who completed miscalculated the situation" (*The Global Times*, 2019).

The authors examined how *Weibo* has discussed Anti-Extradition Law in Hong Kong (using the keywords phrases, "香港反送中"or *Anti-Extradition Law Protest*) to search *Sina Weibo* or Google.

Weibo as a Device to Bypass Existing Government Censorship in China

As seen in Figure 1, Hong Kong activists in this social movement has used *Twitter* to spread the information about the protest. Updates, videos, and action plans are documented and shared among interested readers. Several hashtags are set up for this movement: #antiELAB, #NoChinaExtradition, #HongKongProtests, or #HongKong:

Unlike what happened in China described by Zhao Jing, a Chinese media commentator, "In China we live in a society without freedom of speech, without a free press....... "There isn't any media outlet that can share 100% free press. With Twitter, for the first time you could freely explore your feelings without fear of your words being deleted by others" (Ramzy, 2011a, http://content.time.com/time/magazine/article/0,9171,2048171,00.html), Hong Kong residents have full access to a variety of Western and Chinese social media platforms. Unlike what happened in the Mainland China where government determined to halt the launch of microblogging services in China because of the 20th sensitive anniversary of *June 4 Tiananmen Square Massacre* and Uighur ethnic minority riot that killed nearly 200 people one month later (Ramzy, 2011a), there is no censorship in Hong Kong.

Weibo as a Mobilization Device

New information-communication technologies (ICTs) are often used to mobilize the public for a variety of social movement activities (Garrett, 2006). *Weibo* and other social media platforms often play significant roles in averting government's covering-up of major news events as significant as Hong Kong's *Anti Extradition Law Protest*. Online activism has significantly relied on social media to mobilize the

Figure 1.

society and recruit participants in Hong Kong. For example, posters are circulated via social media platforms to call for a full-scale strike on August 5, 2019 when the pro-Beijing mass media are less like to advertise the posters (Refer to Figure 2 below).

As such, the *Weibo* and other social media platforms have served as an alternative vehicle to mobilize resources to take part in the island-wide strike to pressure the SAR government to meet the demands of the protestors. As Habermas (2006) envisioned far before the popularity of social media, an ICT-enabled public sphere has been developed to liberate political engagement and participation of Chinese Internet users. The linkage between ICTs and democracy can be dated as early as

Figure 2.

Pool's (1983) proposition on the empowering capacity of new technologies in terms of social, economic, and political aspects. Some scholars have gone further to say that these ICTs can become a *liberation technology* (Diamond & Plattner, 2012, cited in Bondes & Schucher, 2014, p. 46) to encourage public engagement. Their prediction of what communication technologies can do to society as liberating or emancipatory can be observed in this example. The capability of social media to engage the public to take part in political activities is clearly demonstrated in the mobilization, congregation, and protest in the *Anti-Extradition Law*.

Because Hong Kong is adjacent to the Mainland China, protesters are fully aware of the censorship in China. To alter the public opinions in China and to mobilize their support, protestors stand at an overpass in Kowloon and have put up signs and shouts in both Cantonese and Mandarin to ask them to "Take a photo and put this on Weibo!" (Refer to Figure 3 below).

Bluetooth technology is also employed to send leaflets written in simplified Chinese to nearby smartphone by so-called digital word of mouth, hoping to spread what really happens about the protests among mainland visitors (Coconuts Hong Kong & AFP, 2019). As described, these types of technology-enabled public sphere has allowed for a transformation of the usual process by which mass public opinion is formed: "What does not exist in the media does not exist in the public mind, even if it could have a fragmented presence in individual minds" (Castells, 2007, p.241). The analyses presented here have demonstrated that social media can "produce a powerful vehicle for citizen mobilization" (Tang & Sampson, 2012, p. 468) through

Figure 3.

Coconuts Hong Kong
@CoconutsHK

At an overpass near the Silvercord shopping center in Kowloc
anti-extradition protesters hold up signs and shout in both Car
and Mandarin: "Take a photo and put this on Weibo!"
#HongKong #antiELAB #NoChinaExtradition
#HongKongProtests

rapid message dissemination and less stringent government control for the formation of public opinions – traditionally the domain of the mass media and influenced by ruling elites (Castells, 2007). Hsieh and Li (2014) elaborated that ICTs like *Weibo* function as an important tool for political discussion, opinion exchanges, political information seeking, and subsequent political participation.

On the other hand, discussions on *Sina Weibo* have been limited, likely due to the government censorship to remove "undesirable" posts. Only eleven posts were available after the key phrase search. The date ranges only July 26, 2019 to July 27, 2019. Among them, pro-Beijing posts dominate the discussions, criticizing the supporters of the protests as "garbage", "lost youth", "losers", and "traitors". Only one post among these 11 posts have presented a more objective view about this event in Hong Kong. The blogger, *B1ueError*, criticized the biased reporting in the Chinese and social media to describe some disorderly behaviours of the protests without focusing on what caused Hong Kong residents to protest. Other *Weibo* posts have taken the government stance and characterize the protests as "riots". Protestors are characterized as "anti-revolutionary" by one of the bloggers.

CONCLUSION

For the protestors in Hong Kong, *Weibo* has become a tool to create "an enabling environment" (Mathiason, 2013, p. 2). This bears much resemblance to Habermas's public sphere in explaining Internet users' behaviors. However, it is not to claim that emerging ICTs alone will be able to empower Internet users (Tang & Sampson, 2011). For example, Tang and Sampson (2012) studied the interactions between old and new media in the liberation process. However, for Chinese netizens, it is difficult to analyse, without the access to netizens' uncensored discussions, whether *Weibo* has functioned as a public sphere to allow them to freely discuss what *Anti-Extradition Law Protest* is about, what the demands of the protestors are, whether the SAR or CCP government have made any mistakes in pushing the law. As a result, it is difficult to speculate whether the Internet and other emerging ICTs have provided Chinese people with a more liberated channel to take part in the political process (Hung, 2010; Yang, 2003a). The stringent censorship measure described by King et al. (2013), has made it impossible to conclude *Weibo* will serve as a role to engage Chinese netizens for information-sharing, public discussions, and possible political participation--- essential experiences to foster China's nascent civil society. Internet mobs that sought out pro-Hong Kong/Taiwan independence celebrities often function as an ancillary censorship tool to bully people from speaking their minds through boycotts and commercial penalties (Zhou, 2019). The well-known Hong Kong actress, Charmaine Sheh Sze-man, has to retract her like of a video on #NoChinaExtradition and to issue a formal apologize to stress her patriotism (Zhou, 2019).

The emergence of public sphere in social media and its contribution to the formation and maintenance of a nascent civil society is clearly demonstrated in Hong Kong, a Chinese territory that is supposedly to enjoy 50 years of full autonomy after 1997. With its short-lived liberalization before President Xi's tenure, China has been thrown back to one man rule of Chairman Mao's era (Calamur, 2016; Frayer, 2019). Even though Chen (2014) has noted that the *Weibo* public sphere is an effective medium to cope with government's censorship and pervasive political control in China, Xi's China actually found that Weibo's role as a public sphere has continued to deteriorate by the jailing of famous bloggers (Economy, 2018), not just under house arrest in the past (Foster, 2011). As Shirky (2011) observed in the quote below: "Social media tools are not a replacement for real-world action but a way to coordinate it" (p. 6). It seems that external political factors may play a far more important role than social media's technological attributes in explaining the differences in how social media have helped foster a civil society for residents in two Chinese territories.

On the basis of the existing literature as to what *Weibo* can do to foster civil society in less democratic countries (Chen, 2014; Hsieh & Li, 2014; Hung, 2011; Shirky, 2011), this chapter demonstrates the role of *Weibo* in the case of Hong Kong's *Anti-Extradition Law Protest*. In conclusion, the metaphor of public sphere is often used to explain the relationship between public sphere and civil society. Deriving from Habermas (1996) to explain the process of forming civil society, Fuchs (2014) argued that "[t]he public sphere is both process and space" (p. 65). The emphasis on discursive process is particularly important in order to understand the role of social media in forming communities across geographical limits (Huang & Sun, 2014; Sullivan, 2012), mobilization, citizen engagement (Chen, 2014), etc.

REFERENCES

Alessi, C. (2012, March 12). Can China change? Interviewee: Minxin Pei, Director, Keck Center for International and Strategic Studies, Claremont McKenna College. Retrieved March 14, 2014 from http://www.cfr.org/china/can-china-change/p27688

Biao, T. (2012). Rights defence (*weiquan*), microblogs (Weibo), and the surrounding gaze (*weiguan*). *China Perspectives, 2012*(3), 29-41.

Blanchard, B., Holden, M., & Wu, V. (2017, June 30). China says Sino-British Joint Declaration on Hong Kong no longer has meaning.Retrieved on July 29, 2019 from Reuters.com.

Bloomberg News. (2018, September 11). Trade war with U.S. likely to cost China 700,000 jobs plus millions more if things get worse. *Bloomberg News*, Retrieved on July 27, 2019 from https://business.financialpost.com/news/economy/the-trade-war-will-likely-cost-china-700000-jobs-jpmorgan-says

Bondes, M., & Schucher, G. (2014). Derailed emotions: The transformation of claims and targets during the Wenzhou online incident. *Information Communication and Society*, *17*(1), 45–65. doi:10.1080/1369118X.2013.853819

Bush, R. (2014, September 2). *China's Decision on Universal Suffrage in Hong Kong*. Washington, DC: Brookings Institute.

Calamur, K. (2017, October 26). China's Xi Jinping Era. *The Atlantic*, Retrieved on July 29, 2019 from https://www.theatlantic.com/international/archive/2017/2010/china-xi/544035/

Castells, M. (2007). Communication, power and counter-power in the network society. *International Journal of Communication*, *1*, 238–266.

Castells, M. (2009). *Communication power*. Oxford, UK: Oxford University Press.

Center for Preventive Action. (2019, January 14). The top conflicts to watch in 2019: South China Sea. *Council on Foreign Relations*, Retrieved from https://www.cfr.org/blog/top-conflicts-watch-2019-south-china-sea

Chan, K., Kwan, W., & Thomsen, C. (2019). EM outlook: Look beyond trade tensions for sustainable growth trends. *Capital Ideas*, Retrieved on July 27, 2019 from https://www.thecapitalideas.com/articles/outlook/emerging-markets-outlook

Chan, L. (2019, April 24). Hong Kong's 'Occupy Central' activists handed prison terms. *Al Jazeera News*, Retrieved on July 29, 2019 from https://www.aljazeera.com/news/2019/2004/hong-kong-occupy-central-activists-handed-prison-sentences-190424013728788.html

Chan, M., Wu, X., Hao, Y., Xi, R., & Jin, T. (2012, July). Microblogging, online expression, and political efficacy among young Chinese citizens: The moderating role of information and entertainment needs in the use of Weibo. *Cyberpsychology, Behavior, and Social Networking*, *15*(7), 345–349. doi:10.1089/cyber.2012.0109 PMID:22780993

Channel News Asia. (2019, July 22). Masked men assault protesters, commuters in Hong Kong MTR station. *Channel News Asia*, Retrieved from https://www.channelnewsasia.com/news/asia/hong-kong-yuen-long-mtr-station-protesters-masked-men-white-11741840

Chen, J.-T., & She, J. (2012, June 18-21). *An analysis of verifications in microblogging social networks -- Sina Weibo*. Paper presented at 2012 32nd International Conference on the Distributed Computing Systems Workshops (ICDCSW), Macau, China.

Chen, S.-Y., Zhang, H.-M., Lin, M., & Lv, S.-H. (2011, December). *Comparison of microblogging service between Sina Weibo and Twitter.* Paper presented at the Computer Science and Network Technology (ICCSNT), Harbin, China.

Chen, W.-H. (2014). Taking stock, moving forward: The Internet, social networks and civic engagement in Chinese societies. *Information Communication and Society*, *17*(1), 1–6. doi:10.1080/1369118X.2013.857425

China Internet Network Information Center. (CINIC). (2012, December 31). *Basic data.* Retrieved September 17, 2014 from http://www1.cnnic.cn/IDR/BasicData/

China Internet Network Information Center. (CINIC) (2013, January). *Statistical report on Internet Development in China.* Retrieved May 1, 2014 from http://www1.cnnic.cn/IDR/ReportDownloads/201302/P020130221391269963814.pdf

China Internet Network Information Center. (CINIC). (2014, January). *Statistical report on Internet Development in China.* Retrieved on September 17, 2014 from http://www1.cnnic.cn/IDR/ReportDownloads/201404/U020140417607531610855.pdf

China Internet Watch. (2012, November 23). Penetration rate of Weibo and SNS in China. Retrieved December 8, 2012 from http://www.chinainternetwatch.com/1830/penetration-rate-of-weibo-and-sns-in-china/#ixzz2EZfmyDNn

Chinese Internet Network Information Center (CNNIC). (2018, January). *Statistical Report on Internet Development in China (The 41 Survey Report).* Beijing, China: Chinese Internet Network Information Center (CNNIC).

Coconuts Hong Kong & AFP. (2019, July 7). Tens of thousands rally as Hongkongers take anti-extradition protest to streets of Kowloon. *Coconuts Hong Kong*, Retrieved on July 29, 2019 from https://coconuts.co/hongkong/news/tens-of-thousands-rally-as-hongkongers-take-anti-extradition-protest-to-streets-of-kowloon/

Dent, H. (2018, June 4). Social unrest in China. *Economy & Markets*, Retrieved on July 28, 2019 from https://economyandmarkets.com/economy/demographic-trends/socialunrestinchina/

Economy, E. C. (2018, June 29). The Great Firewall of China: Xi Jinping's internet shutdown. *The Guardian*, Retrieved on July 28, 2019 from https://www.theguardian.com/news/2018/jun/2029/the-great-firewall-of-china-xi-jinpings-internet-shutdown

eMarketer.com. (2018, November 8). Weibo Now Used by Nearly 25% of Population in China. *eMarketer.com*, Retrieved on July 28, 2019 from https://content-na2011.emarketer.com/weibo-now-used-by-nearly-2025-of-population-in-china

Frayer, J. M. (2018, March 11). Analysis: Xi Jinping returns China to era of one-man rule. *CNBC News*, Retrieved on July 29, 2019 from https://www.nbcnews.com/news/world/analysis-xi-jinping-retuns-china-era-one-man-rule-n851531

Fuchs, C. (2014). Social media and the public sphere. *Triple C (Cognition, Communication, Co-Operation), 12*(1), 57-101.

Garrett, K. (2006, April). Protest in an information society: A Review of literature on social movements and new ICTs. *Information Communication and Society*, *9*(2), 202–224. doi:10.1080/13691180600630773

Graham-Harrison, E. (2007, April 3). China's inevitable rise risks conflict: Kissinger. *Reuters.com*, Retrieved on July 27, 2019 from https://www.reuters.com/article/us-china-kissinger-idUSPEK30303020070403

Gregory, E. J. (2018, August 20). Why China's zombified 'civil society' is a cautionary tale for the West. *National Interest*, Retrieved on July 28, 2019 from https://nationalinterest.org/feature/why-china%E2012%2080%2099s-zombified-civil-society-cautionary-tale-west-29312

Habermas, J. (1984). Theory of communicative action (T. McCarthy, Trans.). Boston, MA: Beacon Press.

Habermas, J. (1989). *The structural transformation of the public sphere: An inquiry into a category of bourgeois society*. Cambridge, MA: MIT Press.

Habermas, J. (1991). *The structural transformation of the public sphere: An inquiry into a category of bourgeois society* (T. Burger, Trans.). Cambridge, MA: The MIT Press.

Habermas, J. (2006, November 6). Political communication in media society: Does democracy still enjoy an epistemic dimension? The impact of normative theory on empirical research. *Communication Theory*, *16*(4), 411–426. doi:10.1111/j.1468-2885.2006.00280.x

Harrison, J., & Wessels, B. (2009). *Mediating Europe: New media, mass communications and the European public sphere*. New York: Berghahn Books.

Hassid, J. (2012). Safety valve or pressure cooker? Blogs in Chinese political life. *Journal of Communication*, *62*(2), 217–230. doi:10.1111/j.1460-2466.2012.01634.x

He, L. (2019, July 15). China's economic growth slumps to lowest in 27 years as the trade war hits. *CNN*, Retrieved on July 27, 2019 from https://www.cnn.com/2019/2007/2015/economy/china-gdp-growth/index.html

Heng, X.-N. (2016, July 14). Capitalism with Chinese Characteristics: From socialism to capitalism. *The Epoch Times*, Retrieved on July 28, 2019 from https://www.theatlantic.com/technology/archive/2017/2001/trolling-by-distraction/514589/

Hong Kong Free Press. (2019, June 13). Hong Kong's anti-extradition law protests were "riots", Beijing claims. *Hong Kong Free Press*, Retrieved on July 29, 2019 from https://www.hongkongfp.com/2019/2006/2013/hong-kongs-anti-extradition-law-protests-riots-beijing-claims/

Hsieh, Y.-L. P., & Li, M. H. (2014). Online political participation, civic talk, and media multiplexity: How Taiwanese citizens express political opinions on the Web. *Information Communication and Society*, *17*(1), 26–44. doi:10.1080/1369118X.2013.833278

Huang, E. (2018, July 27). China tried to crush #MeToo, but it's making a comeback. *QUARTZ*, Retrieved on July 28, 2019 from https://qz.com/1265510/china-tried-to-crush-metoo-but-its-making-a-comeback/

Huang, R.-G., & Sun, X.-Y. (2014, January). Weibo network, information diffusion and implications for collective action in China. *Information Communication and Society*, *17*(1), 86–104. doi:10.1080/1369118X.2013.853817

Hung, C.-F. (2010, October). The politics of China's *wei-quan* movement in the Internet Age. *International Journal of China Studies*, *1*(2), 331–349.

Iqbal, M. (2019, February 27). WeChat Revenue and Usage Statistics (2019). *Business of Apps*, Retrieved on July 28, 2019 from https://www.businessofapps.com/data/wechat-statistics/

Iyengar, R. (2014, September 3). 6 questions you might have about Hong Kong's Umbrella Revolution. *Time*, Retrieved on July 29, 2019 from https://time.com/3471366/hong-kong-umbrella-revolution-occupy-central-democracy-explainer-3471366-questions/

Kelly-Meyrick, R. (2017, July 10). Social unrest in China: A threat to regime legitimacy and the economy? *Global Risk Insights*, Retrieved on July 27, 2019 from https://globalriskinsights.com/2017/2007/social-unrest-china-threat-regime-legitimacy-economy/

Kim, J., Kim, J., & Kim, A. H. (2013, December 20). The communication adaptiveness and power dynamics of the state, the market, and civil society in the information age: The case of Korea. *Information Communication and Society*, *17*(8), 956–973. doi:10.1080/1369118X.2013.869241

King, G., Pan, J., & Roberts, M. E. (2013). How censorship in China allows government criticism but silences collective expression. *The American Political Science Review*, *107*(2), 326–343. doi:10.1017/S0003055413000014

Kuo, L. (2018, April 16). China's Weibo reverses ban on 'homosexual' content after outcry. *The Guardian*, Retrieved on July 28, 2019 from https://www.theguardian.com/world/2018/apr/2016/china-weibo-bans-homosexual-content-protest

Lee, K. Y. (2011, March 9). China's growing might and the consequences. *Forbes*, Retrieved September 15, 2014 from http://www.forbes.com/forbes/2011/0328/billionaires-11-current-events-lee-kuan-yew-china-consequences.html

Lee, S. J., & Melissen, J. (Eds.). (2011). *Public diplomacy and soft power in East Asia* (1st ed.). New York: Palgrave Macmillan. doi:10.1057/9780230118447

Levine, S. (1997, December 8). Hong Kong's return to China. *Encyclopædia Britannica*, Retrieved on July 29, 2019 from https://www.britannica.com/topic/reversion-to-Chinese-sovereignty-1020544

Li, J., & Rao, H. R. (2010). Twitter as a rapid response news service: An exploration in the context of the 2008 China earthquake. [EJISDC]. *The Electronic Journal on Information Systems in Developing Countries*, *42*(4), 1–22. doi:10.1002/j.1681-4835.2010.tb00300.x

Li, M. (Ed.). (2009). *Soft power: China's emerging strategy in international politics*. Lanham: Rowman & Littlefield Publishers.

Liu, R.-S. (2013, October). A survey of China's new media development in 3rd season 2013 (English). *China Media Report Overseas*, *9*(4), 95–99.

Magistad, M. K. (2012, August 9). How Weibo is changing China. *YaleGlobal Online*, Retrieved on July 28, 2019 from https://yaleglobal.yale.edu/content/how-weibo-changing-china

Mason, E. (2013, June). Shaking up the anaconda: The new face of censorship in China. *Index on Censorship*, *10*(2), 43–45. doi:10.1177/0306422013491869

Mathiason, J. (2013, June 20). *Information and communication technologies and e-participation for the empowerment of people and e-governance*. Paper presented at the Expert Group Meeting on E-Participation: Empowering People through Information Communication Technologies (ICTs), Geneva, The Switzerlands.

Meng, Q., & Li, M. (2001, September). *New economy and ICT development in China.* Helsinki, Finland: UNU World Institute for Development Economics Research. Retrieved September 15, 2014 from http://www.econstor.eu/bitstream/10419/53080/1/335220010.pdf

Mohd, A. (2009). *The public sphere and media politics in Malaysia.* Newcastle, UK: Cambridge Scholars.

Mou, Y., Atkin, D., Fu, H., Lin, C. A., & Lau, T. Y. (2013). The influence of online forum and SNS use on online political discussion in China: Assessing "Spirals of Trust." *Telematics and Informatics*, *30*(4), 359–369. doi:10.1016/j.tele.2013.04.002

Mou, Y., Fu, H., & Atkin, D. (2011). Predicting political discussion in a censored virtual environment. *Political Communication*, *28*(3), 341–356. doi:10.1080/10584609.2011.572466

O'Neill, M. (2017, June 17). 1.5 million Mainland migrants change Hong Kong. *ejinsights on the pulse*, Retrieved on July 29, 2019 from http://www.ejinsight.com/20170619-20170611-20170615-million-mainland-migrants-change-hong-kong/

Pao, J. (2019, July 14). Anti-extradition Hong Kong protesters march in Shatin. *Asia Times*, Retrieved on July 29, 2019 from https://www.asiatimes.com/2019/2007/article/anti-extradition-hong-kong-protesters-march-in-shatin/

Peter, T. (2019, July 22). Why Hong Kong's angry and disillusioned youth are making their voices heard. *South China Morning Post*, Retrieved on July 29, 2019 from https://www.scmp.com/magazines/post-magazine/long-reads/article/3019591/why-hong-kongs-angry-and-disillusioned-youth-are

Pool, I. D. S. (1983). Technologies of freedom. Cambridge, MA: Harvard University Press.

Ramzy, A. (2011a, February 17). Wired Up. *Time*, Retrieved March 1, 2014 from http://content.time.com/time/magazine/article/0,9171,2048171,00.html

Ramzy, A. (2011b, February 21). State stamps out small "Jasmine" Protests in China. *Time*, retrieved on March 1, 2014 from http://content.time.com/time/world/article/0,8599,2052860,00.html

Sandoval, G. (2009, March 24). China bans YouTube, Chinese officials confirm that they are blocking the Web's largest video site but haven't disclosed the reason. *The Wall Street Journal*, Retrieved April 30, 2014 from http://www.cnet.com/news/wsj-china-bans-youtube/

Shambaugh, D. L. (2013). *China goes global: The partial power*. Oxford, UK: Oxford University Press.

Shen, X. (2019, June 12). Chinese users are beating the censors to talk about Hong Kong. *Abacus*, Retrieved on August 20, 2019 from https://www.abacusnews.com/digital-life/chinese-users-are-beating-censors-talk-about-hong-kong/article/3014159

Shirky, C. (2011, January/February). The political power of social media: Technology, the public sphere, and political change. *Foreign Affairs*, 1–12.

Simon, J. P. (2011). *The ICT landscape in BRICS countries: Brazil, India, China*. Seville, Spain: European Commission Joint Research Centre, Institute for Prospective Technological Studies.

Soy, S. K. (1997). *The Case Study as a Research Method*. Retrieved on July 26, 2017 from https://www.ischool.utexas.edu/~ssoy/usesusers/l391d1b.htm

Splichal, S. (2012). *Transnationalization of the public sphere and the fate of the public* (1st ed.). New York: Hampton Press.

Sullivan, J. (2012, September). A tale of two microblogs in China. *Media Culture & Society*, *34*(6), 773–783. doi:10.1177/0163443712448951

Sullivan, J. (2014, February). China's Weibo: Is faster different? *New Media & Society*, *16*(1), 24–37. doi:10.1177/1461444812472966

Tang, L., & Sampson, H. (2012, July). The interaction between mass media and the internet in non-democratic states: The case of China. *Media Culture & Society*, *34*(5), 457–471. doi:10.1177/0163443711436358

The Economist. (2012, January 28). Unrest in China, A dangerous year, Economic conditions and social media are making protests more common in China—at a delicate time for the country's rulers. *The Economist*, Retrieved May 1, 2014 from http://www.economist.com/node/21543477

The Economist. (2014, January 18). From Weibo to WeChat. *The Economist*, Retrieved November 17, 2014 from http://www.economist.com/news/china/21594296-after-crackdown-microblogs-sensitive-online-discussion-has-shifted-weibo-wechat

The Economist. (2018a, March 1). How the West got China wrong. *The Economist*, Retrieved on July 28, 2019 from https://www.economist.com/leaders/2018/2003/2001/how-the-west-got-china-wrong

The Economist. (2018b, June 2). Perfected in China, a threat in the West. *The Economist*, p. 11.

Tong, J. G., & Zuo, L. D. (2014). Weibo communication and government legitimacy in China: A computer-assisted analysis of Weibo messages on two 'mass incidents.'. *Information Communication and Society*, *17*(1), 66–85. doi:10.1080/1369118X.2013.839730

Tuten, T. L., & Solomon, M. R. (2013). Social media marketing. Boston, MA: Pearson.

Waddell, K. (2017, January 27). 'Look, a Bird!' Trolling by Distraction. *The Atlantic*, Retrieved on July 28, 2019 from https://www.theatlantic.com/technology/archive/2017/2001/trolling-by-distraction/514589/

Wallis, C. (2011). New media practices in China: Youth patterns, processes, and politics. *International Journal of Communication*, *5*, 406–436.

We Are Social. (2018). Global Digital Report 2018. *We_Are_Social*, Retrieved on July 28, 2019 from https://digitalreport.wearesocial.com/download

Yang, G. (2003a). The Internet and civil society in China: A preliminary assessment. *Journal of Contemporary China*, *12*(36), 453–475. doi:10.1080/10670560305471

Yang, G. (2003b). The Internet and the rise of a transnational Chinese cultural sphere. *Media Culture & Society*, *25*(4), 469–490. doi:10.1177/01634437030254003

Yao, Y. (2014, November). *A new normal, but with robust growth: China's growth prospects in the next 10 years.* Paper presented at the Think Tank 20: Growth, Convergence and Income Distribution: The Road from the Brisbane G-20 Summit, Washington, DC.

Yeung, R. L. K. (2008, April). *Digital democracy: How the American and Hong Kong civil societies use new media to change politics.* Washington, DC: The Brookings Institution.

Zhou, V. (2019, June 14). An actress "liked" a video of Hong Kong protests, and regrets it. *inkstone*, Retrieved on July 29, 2019 from https://www.inkstonenews.com/politics/hong-kong-actress-charmaine-sheh-denies-supporting-anti-extradition-protests/article/3014491

Zhu, T., Phipps, D., Pridgen, A., Crandall, J. R., & Wallach, D. S. (2013). *The velocity of censorship: High fidelity detection of microblog post deletions*. Ithaca, NY: Cornell University Library.

Zou, L. (2013, October). The social effect system of Weibo public opinion (English). *China Media Report Overseas*, *9*(4), 53–57.

ADDITIONAL READING

Alqudsi-ghabra, T. (2012). Creative use of social media in the revolutions of Tunisia, Egypt, & Libya. *The International Journal of Interdisciplinary Social Sciences: Annual Review*, *6*(5), 147–158. doi:10.18848/1833-1882/CGP/v06i06/52097

Dahlberg, L. (1998). Cyberspace and the public sphere: Exploring the democratic of the net. *Convergence*, *4*(1), 70–84. doi:10.1177/135485659800400108

DeLong-Bas, N. J. (2011). *The New Social Media and the Arab Spring*. Oxford Islamic Institute Online.

Dowell, W. T. (2006, Summer). The Internet, censorship, and China. *Georgetown Journal of International Affairs*, *7*(2), 111–119.

Jacobson, T. (2008). Harmonious society, civil society and the media: A communicative action perspective. *China Media Research*, *4*(4), 31–38.

Kisselmann, O. (2014). China's post-90 generation is making its mark. Retrieved September 18, 2014 from http://www.digital-development-debates.org/issue-11-youth--lifestyle--chinas-post-90-generation.html

Yao, Y. (2014, November). *A new normal, but with robust growth: China's growth prospects in the next 10 years.* Paper presented at the Think Tank 20: Growth, Convergence and Income Distribution: The Road from the Brisbane G-20 Summit, Washington, DC.

Zheng, Y., & Wu, G. (2005). Information technology, public space, and collective action in China. *Comparative Political Studies*, *38*(5), 507–536. doi:10.1177/0010414004273505

KEY TERMS AND DEFINITIONS

Chinese Jasmine Revolution: The civil society movement is also known as *The 2011 Chinese Pro-democracy Protests*. Chinese Jasmine Revolution was a social movement organized and mobilized through China's popular social media, *Weibo*, to launch protests simultaneously in 13 major cities in China on the date of February 20, 2011. Despite national and international attention, the Chinese Jasmine Revolution did not lead to wide-spread protests in China. After the mass incident, a large number of dissidents had been arrested and detained by the Chinese Communist Party government.

Civil Society: The term, civil society, refers to a variety of not-for-profit and non-governmental organizations that enable the expression of the interests and values of the public as well as their members for cultural, ethical, political, philanthropic, scientific, and religious considerations.

Facial Recognition Technology: This term refers to a set of technology capable of identifying or verifying a person on the basis of his/her digital image or video. The technology has been advanced to recognize a person's posture to accurately identify an individual. The technology has been widely used by China for surveillance purposes of its citizens.

Public Sphere: Habermas (1962, 1984) defined the concept of public sphere as "a realm of our social life in which something approaching public opinion can be formed" (p. 49). Habermas's (1962, 1984) conceptualization of public sphere stresses the important of access to all citizens to enable them to transform from private individuals into a public body.

Social Credit System: A surveillance system that was implemented in China to standardize each citizen's social and economic reputation. A system that imitates the credit rating system in the advanced countries such as the U.S., each individual will be assigned a point on the basis of his/her past social, economic, and political behaviors. Individuals with lower ratings will be penalized for travel ban, difficulty in obtaining loan or mortgage, ostracism in society, etc.

Weibo **(Microblog):** The Chinese micro-blog and social networking website, equivalent to *Twitter* that is banned in China. *Weibo*, meaning microblog in Chinese, is a Chinese version of *Twitter. Weibo* services in China include Well-known *Weibo* companies include *Sina Weibo* and *Tencent Weibo* to offer retweeting, social sharing, and many social media functions.

Chapter 8
Direct Benefit Transfer Using Aadhaar:
Improving Transparency and Reducing Corruption

Aashish Bhardwaj
Guru Tegh Bahadur Institute of Technology, India

Dale Cyphert
University of Northern Iowa, USA

ABSTRACT

This chapter illustrates how Aadhaar, India's unique identity number, has been used to develop applications such as direct benefit transfer and micro payment solutions that improve existing governmental processes and lead to economic development. This chapter details the Aadhaar success stories of Direct Benefit Transfer in removing corruption and implementing transparency. Successful applications include Pradhan Mantri Matru Vandana Yojana (PMMVJ), State Health Society (Bihar), Aadhaar Enabled Payment System (AePS), Nutrition and Health Tracking System (NHTS), Aadhaar Enabled Public Distribution System (AePDS), and Adhaar Enabled Fertilizer Distribution System (AeFDS). Specific process improvement case studies illustrate purchasing new SIM cards and land transfer to support the authentication and removing fake entries. The chapter addresses administrative technology and legal challenges, which the initiative faced during its implementation.

DOI: 10.4018/978-1-7998-1791-8.ch008

Copyright © 2020, IGI Global. Copying or distributing in print or electronic forms without written permission of IGI Global is prohibited.

INTRODUCTION

Governmental priorities that have emerged in recent years include the need to strengthen individuals' social security and improve delivery mechanisms for poverty alleviation. These efforts ensure that vulnerable groups can withstand unforeseen shocks to income and continue to access basic goods and services at affordable prices. On the Indian subcontinent, the inability to verify individual identity has been one of biggest barriers to ensuring access to benefits and subsidies.

Over the years, the Indian government has initiated many systematic, large-scale plans or schemes for improving social welfare, but their effectiveness has been limited by corruption. In 1985, Prime Minister Rajiv Gandhi famously remarked that, "Of every rupee spent by the government, only 17 paise (17%) reached the intended beneficiary" ("Fund leakage," 2009). At that time, the problem was only vaguely understood as corruption, but an important mechanism for misappropriation was widely known to involve fake or duplicate beneficiaries. Traditional identity databases in India have been fraught with problems of fraud and duplicate or ghost beneficiaries. New methods to ensure individuals' access to social security benefits, environmental protections, and public health services are required to secure India's future.

With this objective, the Unique Identification Authority of India has started providing an Aadhaar (Unique Identification Number) to confirm the identity of every individual living in India. Aadhaar is designed to enroll residents into a database based on proper verification of their demographic and biometric information. This will ensure that public programs can rely on accurate participant data from their beginning. This allows country to strengthen its nine Digital India pillars deemed essential for effective governance (Ministry of Electronics, n.d. b).

In addition, Aadhaar provides a process to ensure access to financial products and services appropriate for helping weaker sections of the economy and low-income population groups to achieve financial inclusion. Financial inclusion has become one of the most critical aspects for India's national growth and development. For this purpose, the Reserve Bank of India has encouraged expansion of bank branches, especially in rural areas. Aadhaar attempts to remove ineligible beneficiaries from these Direct Benefit Transfer and Digital initiatives schemes.

This chapter begins with an overview of the Aadhaar implementation, then provides a detailed description of political challenges, technology challenges and legal challenges as they are addressed by the design of the database implementation. We conclude with the significant consequences of Aadhaar in terms of the financial inclusion of otherwise un-served Indian citizens.

System Overview

UIDAI has assigned Aadhaar to Indian citizens with 88.08% of the total population in India as of 29th August, 2019 (Unique Identification, 2019). A total of 1119 schemes from 74 Ministries have been implemented, with 452 Direct Benefit Transfer (DBT) applications from 56 Ministries. Other examples include transfer of subsidies for gas, scholarships and Public Distribution Systems (Direct Benefit Transfer, 2019a).

Figure 1 specifies the roles of different agencies in the overall framework for DBT implementation. The role of Ministries is to identify, verify and certify the beneficiaries for a scheme. Any ghost or duplicate entry is discarded at this point. The National Informatics Centre (NIC) role is to digitize the beneficiary database. This is a onetime process with entries inserted into the database. A primary role is played by the Unique Identification Authority of India (UIDAI) which helps residents to enroll for Aadhaar. Partnerships with the Reserve Bank of India (RBI), the National Payments Corporation of India (NPCI) and the Indian Bank Association (IBA) facilitate the transfer of funds directly into the accounts of beneficiaries. Banks play the role of beneficiaries' regular contact, opening bank accounts for recipients. These accounts might be Jan Dhan accounts, a financial inclusion program also facilitated with Aadhaar protocols that assist with a quick, hassle-free process. Residents may choose to link Aadhaar with a new account in any bank of their choice or to use a pre-existing account. Once beneficiaries have been identified and enrolled, NIC and UIDAI play no further role and government benefits will be deposited directly into their accounts. A full listing of Aadhaar related acronyms with definitions is included after the references.

This framework has been designed to prevent bogus and duplicate entries into the DBT database and thus prevent leakages in the government's welfare and subsidies distribution. Some success stories reported by the Direct Benefit Transfer (2019b) include the following.

- **Pradhan Mantra Matru Vandana Yojana (PMMVY):** The scheme is 100% DBT compliant with 99% of beneficiaries under the scheme enrolled using Aadhaar i.e. 4.75 millions. Issues resolved include beneficiaries receiving cash incentives on time. Discrepancy in amount of cash received by the State authorities and beneficiaries has been resolved. Pending funds since 2013-14 for many blocks have been released, and there have been no reports of stipulated amounts not being received or beneficiaries not aware of payments being made.
- **State Health Society (Bihar):** A pilot project digitized the health incentive payments to front line health workers like ASHAs, Anganwadi workers and beneficiaries. The objective is to increase transparency, timeliness and

Figure 1. Framework for direct benefits transfer

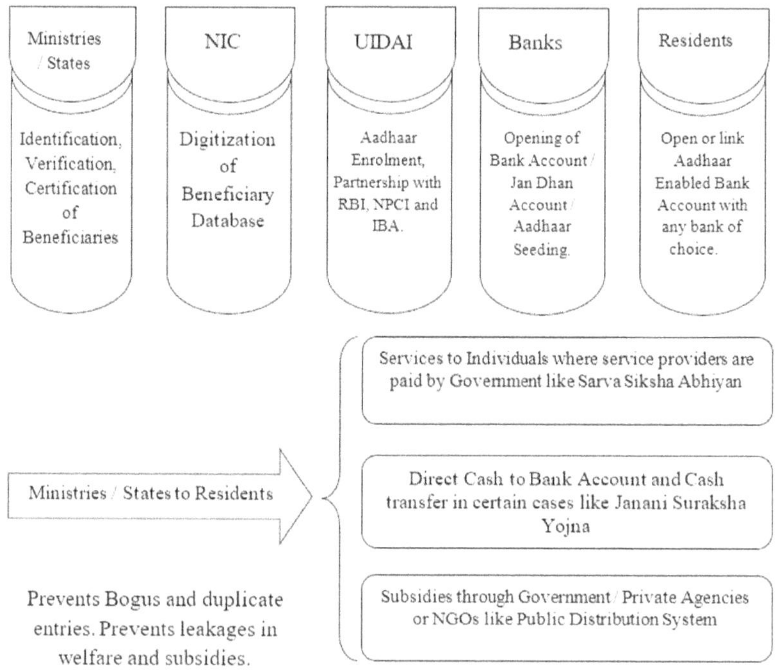

accuracy in the process. It is reported that about 75% of processing time is saved by health workers inquiring about payments which is utilized in field works now. Also delay in average time of receiving the payments has been reduced to 35%.

- **Chandigarh – Kerosene Free City:** Chandigarh has become the first State or Union Territory to be kerosene free since 1st April, 2016. With the help of UID, the Food and Supplies department has identified 35,000 families having LPG connections and still drawing subsidized kerosene oil. These names were removed, and a subsidized LPG connection was given to remaining households. This step made the city kerosene free with the help of newspapers, volunteers, pamphlets, and radio jingles.
- **Disbursement of Pensions:** The pilot project implemented in Krishna district of Andhra Pradesh. It got attraction from Government of India, Bill Gates Foundation, World Bank, Tanzanian Government and other States. The disbursement of pension at the beneficiary's door increases the habit of saving through use of a bank account. Technology used involved the JAM Trinity (Jan Dhan Yojana, Aadhaar, and Mobile number) with Micro ATMs.

- **AePS (Aadhaar Enabled Payment System):** The payment system for MGNREGS workers to improve transparency and efficient funds transfer has resulted in timely payments to genuine wage workers. It is using Aadhaar based authentication, so duplicate musters and other fraudulent practices are avoided. Mostly paperless procedures for bank accounts are opened through eKYC, and biometric attendance is recorded through finger printers and IRIS in the Aadhaar database.
- **NHTS (Nutrition and Health Tracking System):** Women and child health is prioritized by targeting pregnant and lactating women, children below 1 year of age, and malnourished children below 5 years. Information for these women was taken from Anganwadi Centre (AWC). A unique identifier was generated for each beneficiary with services required. The initiative is Aadhaar-based so benefits were directly transferred to concerned persons anywhere without any hindrance.
- **AePDS (Aadhaar Enabled Public Distribution System):** Aadhaar enabled Public Distribution System is an attempt to provide good quality food commodities to eligible beneficiaries. This system provides a monitoring option of commodities from warehouses to customers. Each shop is provided with an ePOS (Electronic Point of Sale) with biometric authentication of customers to prevent any corruption options. Cost of all these services is borne by government with zero investment from users.
- **AeFDS (Aadhaar Enabled Fertilizer Distribution System):** Aadhaar Enabled Fertilizer Distribution System (AeFDS) is an attempt to monitor the supply chain and provide correct fertilizers to farmers. This is authenticated by biometrics of farmers so that fertilizers reach the correct persons and at the correct time. It holds land records and soil analysis report which helps in supplying required fertilizers for the farmers. This helps in getting entitled fertilizers anytime and anywhere.
- **Project Biometric-Pur:** This project was first implemented for ensuring last mile connectivity for residents of Balrampur district, Chhatisgarh. This is a citizen centric project which prevents a lot of time and efforts of residents in getting benefits from Government. The project has altered the system of financial services distribution at multiple levels. Official's efforts are also saved in disabusing cheques and monitoring for payment to right beneficiaries.
- **SAMAGRA Portal:** A common integrated platform facilitates the population of Madhya Pradesh through a model of governance. It was started with SPR (Samagra Population Register) to create an online database for different types of beneficiaries with their requirements. This transformed the society to entitlement-based service delivery, single window; time bound

implementation, real time monitoring, efficient resource utilization and direct benefit transfer.

Specific financial savings have been documented in the financial press (Sahu, 2019). On the whole, key DBT schemes have brought savings of ₹35,457 crores in the first 11 months of fiscal 2019. Financial savings continue even after five years when the optimal performance had presumably been reached. The current savings were attributed to removal of fake beneficiaries in the PAHAL LPG subsidy program for new savings of ₹14,116 crores, another ₹10,000 crores reduced on the sale of subsidized fertilizer, and ₹4,168 crores from the rural employment MGNREGS Scheme.

Political Challenges: Digital India

The government of India initiated its Digital India flagship program on 3rd July, 2015 with a vision to make India a digitally empowered society, establish a knowledge economy, and provide services to all citizens electronically (Ministry of Electronics, n.d.a). This would be done by improving online infrastructure, internet connectivity and enabling the Indian population with technology tools. The initiative named 9 Pillars of Digital India, growth areas that would be critical for enhancing the life of every citizen (Figure 2).

The pillars represent a vision statement that weaves together initiatives undertaken by multiple Ministries and agencies across a vast nation with coordination from the Department of Electronics and Information Technology (DeitY).

- **Broadband Highways:** Both rural and urban access to the internet, along with a National Information Infrastructure (NII) to integrate network and cloud infrastructure. All village punchayats and urban buildings would include a communication infrastructure. NII will integrate current infrastructures, StateWide Area Network (SWAN), National Knowledge Network (NKN), National Optical Fibre Network (NOFN), Government User Network (GUN) and the MeghRaj Cloud for high speed access.
- **Information for All:** An open data platform will host ministry and department release of datasets, information and documents in an open format for use, re-use and redistribution for citizen use. To promote good governance, the government will pro-actively engage with citizens through web-based portals and social media, utilize online messaging, SMS and email.
- **Early Harvest Programmes:** A number of short timeline projects aim for immediate, high-impact gains. Projects include an IT platform for messages, government e-greetings, biometric attendance verification, Wi-Fi

for universities, secure inter-governmental email, standardized government email design, public Wi-Fi hotspots, educational conversion to eBooks, SMS based weather information with disaster alerts, and a national portal for lost and found children.

- **Electronics Manufacturing** Electronic manufacturing is seen as a key economic goal with a target of net zero imports by 2020.This will be achieved by promoting electronics manufacturing, coordinated actions on taxation, incentives, eliminating cost disadvantages, compulsory registration for safety standards, support for labs, incubators, clusters, MSME, research and development in electronics. Focus areas are on set top boxes, mobiles, VSAT, smart cards, micro-ATMs, smart energy meters, consumer and medical electronics.
- **Public Internet Access Programme:** All citizens would have local access to the internet through Post Offices and Common Services Centres (CSC). The target is one CSC in each gram panchayat for a total of 250,000 locations offering Aadhaar cards, e-Banking, utility bill payment, certificates, exam results, land records, MGNREGA job cards, and computer and language skill training. An additional 150,000 Post Offices will be converted into multiple services centre for providing CSC services.
- **Universal Access to Mobile Connectivity:** This initiative focuses on mobile network penetration in whole country targeting the 55,619 villages which are still lacking mobile connectivity. This will act as an encompassing force to change everything around citizens. This will help in booking train tickets, watching news, or withdrawing or depositing money in banks. The Department of Telecommunication is the nodal department for carrying out this task.
- **e-Kranti:** Government transformation began with the computerization of government departments but ultimately depends on digitized governance at every level of citizenship, government services, and transparency. This pillar takes a step forward for electronic delivery of services from previous initiatives like computerization in 1980, department/state specific initiatives of 1990, and the national e-governance plan in 2006. The key principles of e-Kranti are language localization, mobile first, electronic data preservation, mandatory standards, protocols, cloud by default, ICT infrastructure on demand, and integrated services and transformation.
- **e-Governance:** The vision for process re-engineering would make all government processes more efficient and is seen to be critical for all Ministries and Departments.

The guiding principles for achieving this are forms simplification, field reduction, user friendly, online applications with tracking options, online repositories, integration of services and platforms. All databases would be in electronic form, and departments and agencies should be automated for the analysis of data and resolving persistent problems.

- **IT for Jobs:** This pillar focuses on empowering youth through training on information technology for availing employment opportunities. The components under this are training for people from smaller towns and villages, training service delivery agents, training in North Eastern states, training on telecom and telecom related services, setting up of BPOs in every North Eastern states, and training people with skills needed for entrepreneurial delivery of IT services. The nodal department for this scheme is DietY.

With implementation of Aadhaar as a digital identity system, the vision of Digital India becomes easier to attain. Most initiatives have completion targets within a definitive timeframe, so any timesaving step becomes an advantage. More subtly, the Digital Pillars explicitly aim to pull many existing ministries, departments, and programs under one umbrella. With Aadhaar's single platform designed to digitize all databases and information related to an individual, all elements of the Indian government can tap its integrated services and platforms. The UIDAI tools, such as Electronic Data Interchange (EDI), Mobile Platform, and Payment Gateway, can be utilized by any government entity to reform service delivery to citizens and businesses in an integrated manner.

Figure 2. Pillars of digital India

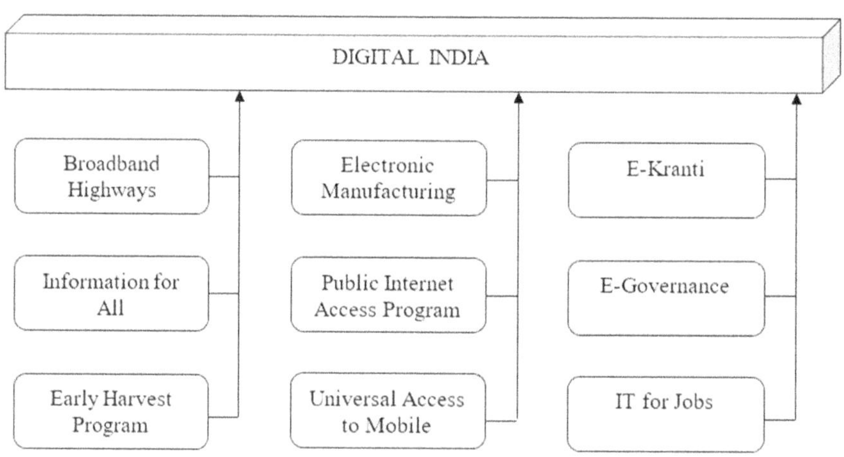

As a statement of political philosophy, the vision of Digital India promises digital infrastructure as a utility available to every citizen. One mechanism to achieve this involves Aadhaar, which ensures that every citizen is able to establish an exclusive, enduring, online and authenticable digital identity able to exercise the right to such a utility.

Initiatives already begun started by the Indian government include DigiLocker, Bharat Net, WiFi Hotspots, E-Hospitals, Skill India, E-Sign, Goods and Services Tax Netwrok (GSTN), Jeevan Praman, eTrade, and MyGov, with apps available such as Nirbhaya, Madad, Khoya Paya, and Himmat. Delivery of all these online public services requires electronic authentication of individual users which can be accomplished with a platform for establishing digital identity. Aadhaar serves as a proof of identity as well as a verification of address in an easily verifiable, cost-effective, online process. Aadhaar becomes even more efficient with its capacity for linkage with mobile numbers, bank accounts, ration cards, driving licenses, and other identity-dependent services.

As of the 2019-20 fiscal years, Aadhaar enables services delivered ₹408.08 crores through 35 separate services governed by 17 different ministries (shown below). The ubiquity of the service demonstrates its potential for fulfilling the Digital Pillar's main promise of integration across the vast range of government operations.

The services delivered through Aadhaar have the advantage of greatly reducing fraud, black-marketing, bribery and leakage of funds due to all manner of corruption. The added advantage of providing a transparent mechanism of Direct Cash Transfer to

Table 1. Aadhar Enabled Services

Department / Ministry	Aadhaar enabled Services
Animal Husbandry, Dairying and Fisheries	3
AYUSH	1
Coal	1
Economic Affairs	8
Electronics and Information Technology (MeitY)	1
Empowerment of Persons with Disabilities	1
Ex-Servicemen Welfare	6
External Affairs	1
Financial Services	4
Home Affairs	1
Labour and Employment	1
Land Resources	1
Posts	2
Revenue	1
Road Transport and Highways	1
School Education and Literacy	1
Telecommunications	1

beneficiaries provides evidence that the vision of transparent, effective, e-Governance can become an Indian reality.

The role of Aadhaar in Digital India is of very high importance as shown in Figure 3. Aadhaar will be used for different services like Ayushman Bharat for healthcare. E-Documents will be used to provide digital lockers for storing documents in secure and easy access manner. Other services include E-Signature, E-Governance, E-Payments through, Education, Social Security, Financial Inclusion, Food and Nutrition.

Technology Challenges: Process Improvement

Positively identifying an individual within any organization would be of utmost importance, and given the very large population of India, a robust method for identifying program participants and beneficiaries presents a significant challenge. Aadhaar has improved the process of identification, and further, the identification process provided has been easy for the programs to administer, with much less infrastructure and fewer manpower requirements than previous systems.

Technological challenges faced in implementation of an identification system include random number generation for the unique user identification number, end-to-end security issues, personal privacy protections, and effective encryption and decryption schemes for handling security issues (Chaudhuri & Konig, 2018; Mudliar et. al., 2018). These arise due to improperly designed architecture which leads to issues at the data capture stage, data managing stage or data reporting stage.

Data capture challenges are met by the Aadhaar database design which does not allow duplicate entries to get into system (Varma & Tyagi, 2017). This was achieved

Figure 3. Aadhaar in digital India

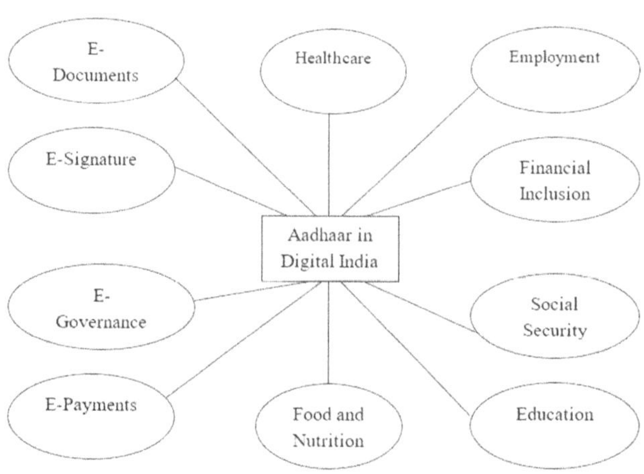

by UIDAI with a process that appointed independent vendors working on the data centres with separate networks guarded by firewalls and isolated (Economic Times, 2019, Aug 28).

Denial of service attacks represented the primary challenge in data management. The system was designed to allow approximately 100 trillion biometric matches each day in order to support and deliver one million Aadhaar numbers. In the process, duplication is avoided and data packets are archived, encrypted and stored on a separate system. The data is also divided into parts and stored in different databases to prevent single access to complete data. The data centers contain 15-20 peta bytes of Big Data for supporting infrastructure and benefits to public service delivery.

The key to success at the post-implementation reporting stage involves the entire ecosystem of Aadhaar based services (CDAC, n.d.). A system-wide ability to handle "Big Data" involves more than technical design, but also the capacity of the system to adopt the mindset of making decisions using data. Data integration across multiple sources, as well as among multiple vendors and partners is an issue that frequently takes a long time to address, but the multilevel design of the Aadhaar authentication model supports the widespread adoption necessary to realize the vision of Digital India.

Figure 4 shows the automated process using Aadhaar. In the identification, a person presents his or her 12-digit Aadhaar number to an Application Programming Interface (API) specifying the UIDAI identifier. Based on specific application requirements, the user provides an additional biometric input, such as an iris scan or fingerprint (Pati, Kumar & Jain, 2015). There can be an additional or replacement of biometric input with a One Time Password (OTP) sent from the registered mobile of a previously identified individual.

Authentication is then performed by the API by accessing the UIDAI database. The resulting authentication verifies identification details such as name, date of birth, gender, address, photograph, mobile number and email and can be used as a verified identity document within an electronic Know Your Customer (E-KYC) service (NSDL, 2016). At the same time effort of officials are also not wasted in tracking whether payment is received by the correct person or not. This has been possible with the implementation of direct balance transfer of subsidies into a person's account after one-time authentication done (Chaudhari & Koning, 2018). The paperless, onetime process removes the burdens of saving files physically and prevents degradation of paper files due to normal wear and tear. Most of the schemes engage in cashless transfer of funds which has removed the burden on currency notes and duplicate currency injections into the system. Authentication done through Aadhaar is purely in digital mode is in all ways easy, inexpensive and secure (Singh & Jackson, 2017).

Applications which are making use of this paperless and secure identification system include both government and business sectors offering such services as driving licenses, bank statement analyzers, permanent account number verifications, credit scores, goods and services tax (GST) verifications, voter verification, and transport authority registration certificate verifications. These entities can take various roles, serving as Authentication Service Agencies (ASA) that have secure (leased line) connectivity with UIDAI's data repository, Authentication User Agencies (AUA) that use the Aadhaar identification process on a contract basis through an ASA provider, and a sub AUA that accesses the Aadhaar authentication without any direct contractual relationship with UIDAI (DCAD, n.d.).

Process improvements can be expected to reduce transaction costs for government agencies, but the cost savings from secure identification alone have been impressive. The Direct Benefit Transfer (2019a) reported on 8 programs through March 2019 that reduced costs by a cumulative ₹141,675 crores. In all cases, savings accrued directly from the ability of the UIDAI database to remove duplicate and nonexistent beneficiaries as well as a variety of additional sources. For example, Petroleum and Natural Gas (PAHAL) eliminated subsidies for inactive LPG connections as well as removing ineligible consumers from the program, Rural Development (MGNREGS) saved an estimated 10% in wages paid, and the Department of Fertilizers reduced fertilizer sales by 120.88 lakh metric tonnes.

Figure 4. Process improvement using Aadhaar

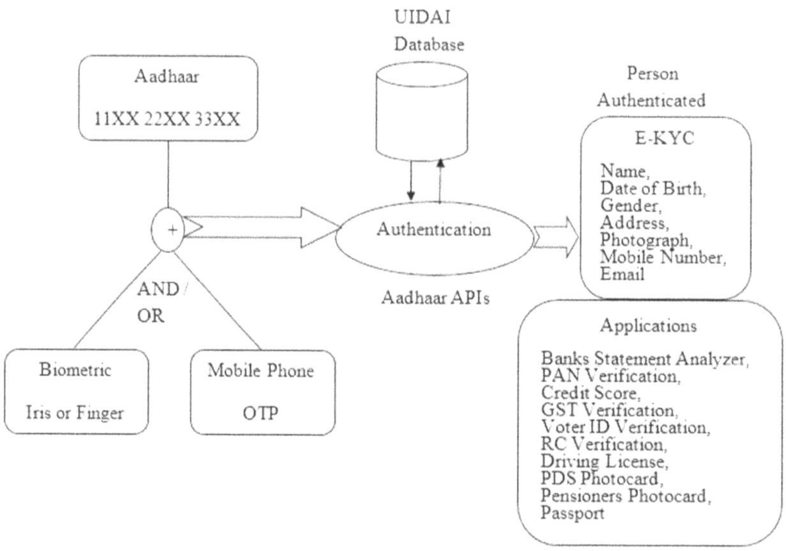

Legal Challenges: Corruption and Transparency

Any success in governmental programs must be judged in terms of corruption and transparency which represent long standing challenges for India. According to the 2018 Corruption Perceptions Index (Transparency International, 2018) India ranks 78th out of the 180 countries ranked on its perceived ability to control corruption. India's rank had averaged 75.67 from 1995 until 2018. Perceptions varied considerably over that period, reaching a record low of 35 in 1995 and an all-time high of 95 in 2011 (Trading Economics, 2019), but the generally unfavorable perception of corruption persists at a relatively high level. Aadhaar enabled services are playing a critical role in reducing corruption and increasing transparency.

Corruption in the public domain involves the abuse or misuse of governmental structures, as well as improper acts, with a negative impact on the public interest or public opinion (Gardiner, 2002). Improper acts can be understood as a governmental entity that fails to treat all equal participants equally. Such corruption involves a society or political unit that exhibits discriminating norms across time and place (Kurer, 2005) and the subversion of government by special interests (Perry, 2018). Corruption weakens the effectiveness of government performance, and thus weakens the public trust and even the inherent trustworthiness of a government (Lessig, 2013). Left unchecked, corruption ruthlessly infects all classes and castes within a national body, crippling institutions and damaging lives (Rotberg, 2019).

Aadhaar helps the government resist corruption by dramatically reducing the capacity of government employees to siphon off government assets through the creation of bogus subsidies, incentives, or through the unequal treatment of individuals. To the extent that a government employee or agency might be tempted to serve special interests, the Aadhaar system provides structural barriers.

In a similar way, governmental transparency reduces the potential and the extent of corruption. Transparency itself carries no inherently ethical value. Defined somewhat neutrally, this simply addresses the degree of detail and disclosure made available regarding specific steps, decisions and judgments made during any process (Aguinis, Ramani, Alabduljader, 2018). A lack of transparency can lead to errors, however, as well as an environment in which it becomes possible to hide fraudulent acts (Aguinis, et al, 2018).

In contrast, transparent practices involve the deliberate revelation of actions, policies, and practices without regard to their positive or negative consequences (Rawlins, 2008). Institutional transparency represents a pro-ethical condition that enables other ethical practices by accounting for the differences between data, the dynamic and subjective processes by which data becomes information and building a platform to determine what information can and should be legitimately disclosed (Turilli & Floridi, 2009). The government that provides all information that it is legally and explicitly bound to disclose increases public trust and creates fair and accountable public administration (Langunes & Pascangre, 2019).Governmental transparency thus supports a democratic equilibrium and stabilizes democratic rule (Hollyer, Rosendorff & Vreeland, 2018).

Transparency across the institutions of the Indian government has not been brought about solely by the adoption of Aadhaar, but the centrality of the technical platform cannot be underestimated. The transparent release of information cannot reach its potential without attention to the quality of that information (Langunes & Pascangre, 2019), so the accuracy and reliability of the Aadhaar identification system provides an important foundation for any efforts to provide transparency in benefit programs. Further, the digital processes remove virtually any reason for personal verifications, conversations, interpretations or decisions. With the entire administrative process moved from governmental offices into a fully automated digital platform, every aspect of decision-making becomes transparent.

Specific effects of Aadhaar toward reducing corruption and increasing transparency are shown in Figure 5. The secure identity protocols of Aadhaar, particularly when used in conjunction with the digital Jan Dhan banking accounts and an individual's mobile phone number, has reduced the capacity for fake or duplicate beneficiaries and the corrupt misappropriation of government funds (Duodu, 2018; Ghosh, 2017). This anticorruption trinity is so foundational it has earned its own acronym, JAM.

With the secure identification and banking transactions, the transfer of funds to wrong persons reduces the corrupt misuse of funds. Aadhaar enabled attendance systems with biometric markers have eliminated the corruption potential of fake employees on government lists (Khera, 2017). Use of Aadhaar has resulted in a frictionless payment system where beneficiaries are not required to follow up their payments by visiting concerned offices again and again.

Decreasing the potential for official corruption has increased the willingness of all stakeholder adoptions. Private users such as mobile phone companies, banks, utilities, and insurance companies, as well as government entities not engaging in direct benefits such as traffic police, land record agencies, and courts have willingly adopted the Aadhaar tools. This increase of open digital transactions across multiple aspects of daily life increases the general transparency of every aspect of society. Further, linking Aadhaar to such broadly used services as mobile phones, insurance policies, income tax, and gas connections, the move toward digitized transparency has penetrated rural and hard to reach places across the continent (Raj & Aithal, 2018). With initial successes, the drive toward transparency and against corruption grows ever stronger.

Financial Inclusion: The Transformative Outcome

Began as an effort to reduce corruption and reduce the leakage of government funds, Aadhaar has enabled the somewhat unrelated but enormous drive toward financial inclusion. The economic infrastructure of India had been a largely cash economy, especially in rural areas and among the poor. The lack of a banking infrastructure creates real hurdles to a range of financial tools and economic resources. Cash economies lack tools for secure, private accumulation of savings. The mechanisms for any but the smallest transactions become impossibly cumbersome. The possibility of credit transactions is greatly curtailed, whether to fund entrepreneurial efforts or to weather the storms—both literal and metaphorical—of life. Certainly, the logistics of cash transfers greatly curtail the effective distribution of whatever subsidies and welfare distributions the government might deem appropriate or necessary for national welfare.

Financial inclusion has been defined in multiple ways. In general, any move toward financial inclusion involves the affordable establishment and use of financial services (e.g. bank accounts, credit, insurance) by rural and poor residents of an economic system (Allen, Demigug-Kunt, Klapper & Peria, 2016; Diniz, Birochi & Pozzebon, 2012; Dixit & Ghosh 2013). Key elements include financial literacy

Figure 5. Use of Aadhaar in different ways to increase transparency and reduce corruption

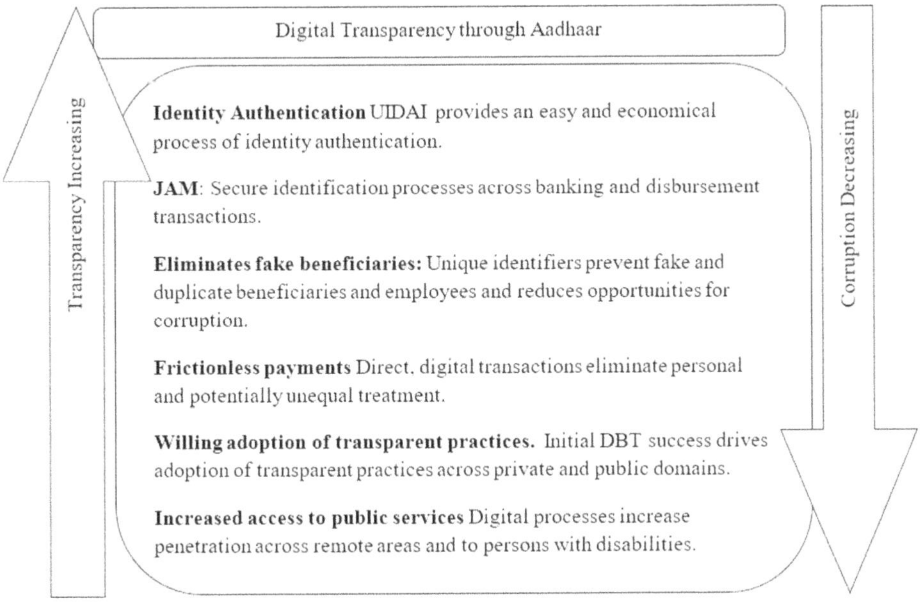

(Joshi, 2011), tools for risk management (Kelkar, 2010), access to financial resources (Demirgüç-Kunt, Klapper, Singer & Van Oudheusden, 2015; Toxopeus &Lensink, 2008)and financial advice (Mitton, 2008).

From a governmental perspective, financial inclusion serves as a robust method to eradicate poverty and meet economic development goals (Chibba, 2009; Demirgüç-Kunt, et, al., 2015; Diniz et al, 2012; Shah & Dubhashi, 2015). Significant advantages accrue to individuals, as well, including individuals' capability for the daily management of finances (Sarma & Pais, 2011), increased savings for future needs (Ghosh, 2017), and educational access (Demirgüç-Kunt, et. al., 2015).

The financial inclusion of a largely poor population that is lacking in financial literacy necessarily involves risk to service providers (Hannig & Jansen, 2010). The critical institutional stakeholders--smart card companies, mobile phone networks and banks—cannot successfully participate without the biometric authentication and security provided by Aadhaar (Allen et al, 2012; Diniz et al 2012; Sarma & Paies 2011; Shah & Dubhashi, 2015). Figure 6 shows the transformation of society to one of universal financial inclusion. The original point of Aadhaar was to reduce the potential for corrupt leakage of government benefits, but its existence has paved the last mile of connectivity that allows secure, universal access to the financial institutions that define financial inclusion. Government units and private financial service companies are further sheltered from risk by the greater integrity and accuracy of all transactions that allows a clearer picture of requirements and better planning of policies and strategy.

We conclude that on the whole, Aadhaar has offered immense benefits to the India. Concerns about the Aadhaar system are not misplaced; as with any biometric identification system, system errors can occur and data can be faked. Technical advances will continue to solve problems, however. For instance, fingerprint authentication, which has a high rate of failure during times of heavy usage, can ultimately be replaced with more robust facial recognition systems. This and other technological advances remain an ongoing goal.

We find convincing evidence, however, that despite the remaining potential for some leakage to fraudulent beneficiaries, the dramatic impact of financial inclusion far outweighs any remaining challenges. Aadhaar has made possible the digitized implementation of government services for all citizens, foundational to the overall Digital India initiative. Aadhaar supported Digital Benefit Transfers have removed intermediaries and connected the Indian government directly to the citizens. This has significantly reduced corruption, improved transparency, and creates a pathway for authentic financial inclusion across India.

Figure 6. Transformation of society to financial inclusion

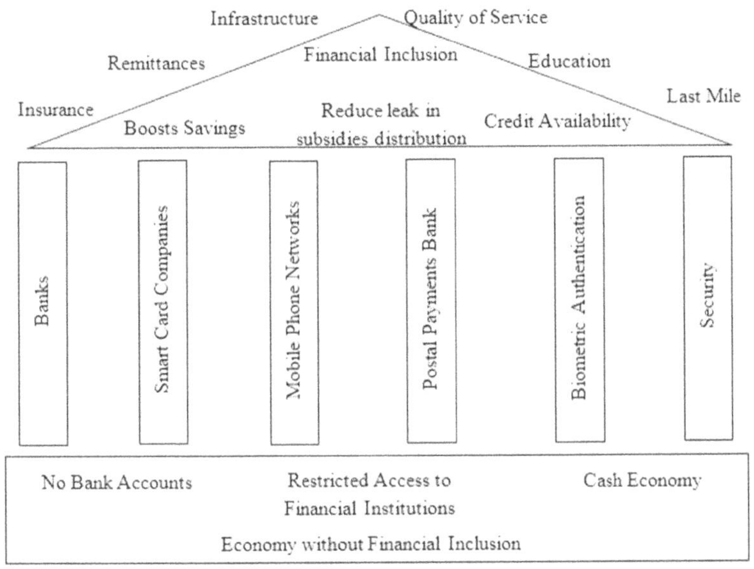

REFERENCES

Aguinis, H., Ramani, R. S., & Alabduljader, N. (2018). What you see is what you get? Enhancing methodological transparency in management research. *The Academy of Management Annals*, *12*(1), 83–110. doi:10.5465/annals.2016.0011

Allen, F., Demirguc-Kunt, A., Klapper, L., & Peria, M. S. M. (2016). The foundations of financial inclusion: Understanding ownership and use of formal accounts. *Journal of Financial Intermediation*, *27*, 1–30. doi:10.1016/j.jfi.2015.12.003

Chaudhuri, B., & König, L. (2018). The Aadhaar scheme: A cornerstone of a new citizenship regime in India? *Contemporary South Asia*, *26*(2), 127–142. doi:10.1080/09584935.2017.1369934

Chibba, M. (2009). Financial inclusion, poverty reduction and the millennium development goals. *European Journal of Development Research*, *21*(2), 213–230. doi:10.1057/ejdr.2008.17

DCAC. (n.d.) CDAC AUA-ASA Aadhaar based services. Retrieved from https://meity.gov.in/writereaddata/files/CDAC_AUA_ASA_Service.pdf

Demirgüç-Kunt, A., Klapper, L. F., Singer, D., & Van Oudheusden, P. (2015). The global find ex database 2014: Measuring financial inclusion around the world.

Diniz, E., Birochi, R., & Pozzebon, M. (2012). Triggers and barriers to financial inclusion: The use of ICT-based branchless banking in an Amazon county. *Electronic Commerce Research and Applications*, *11*(5), 484–494. doi:10.1016/j.elerap.2011.07.006

Direct Benefit Transfer, Government of India. (2019a). Estimated gains. Retrieved from https://dbtbharat.gov.in/page/frontcontentview/?id=ODM=

Direct Benefit Transfer, Government of India. (2019b). Success story. Retrieved from https://dbtbharat.gov.in/successstory

Dixit, R., & Ghosh, M. (2013). Financial inclusion for inclusive growth of India-A study of Indian states. [IJBMR]. *International Journal of Business Management & Research*, *3*(1), 147–156.

Duodu, E. E. (2018). Implementation of a National Identification System in Ghana: Lessons from the Indian Aadhaar System (Doctoral dissertation, University of Ghana).

Economic Times. (2019, Aug. 28) Is this Aadhaar of the Future? Facial biometric technology-based chip-enabled cards issued. Retrieved from https://economictimes.indiatimes.com/wealth/personal-finance-news/is-this-aadhaar-of-the-future-facial-biometric-technology-based-chip-enabled-cards-issued/articleshow/70875918.cms

Fund 'leakage' not as big as Rajiv Gandhi mentioned: PM (2009, Oct 11), *The Hindu*. Retrieved from https://www.thehindu.com/news/national/Fund-lsquoleakagersquo-not-as-big-as-Rajiv-Gandhi-mentioned-PM/article16886675.ece

Gardiner, J. (2002). Defining corruption. In A. Heidenheimer, & M. Johnston (Eds.), Political Corruption,(3rd ed., pp. 25-40). New York: Routledge.

Ghosh, S. (2017). Financial inclusion, biometric identification and mobile: Unlocking the JAM trinity. *International Journal of Development Issues*, *16*(2), 190–213. doi:10.1108/IJDI-02-2017-0012

Hannig, A., & Jansen, S. (2010). Financial inclusion and financial stability: Current policy issues.

Heeks, R., & Ospina, A. V. (2019). Conceptualising the link between information systems and resilience: A developing country field study. *Information Systems Journal*, *29*(1), 70–96. doi:10.1111/isj.12177

Hollyer, J. R., Rosendorff, B. P., & Vreeland, J. R. (2018). Transparency, protest and democratic stability. *British Journal of Political Science*, 1–27.

Joshi, D. P. (2011). Financial inclusion and financial literacy. Presented at BI OECD Seminar, Jakarta, Indonesia. Retrieved from https://www.oecd.org/finance/financial-education/48303408.pdf

Kelkar, V. (2010). Financial inclusion for inclusive growth. *ASCI Journal of Management*, *39*(1), 55–68.

Khera, R. (2017). Impact of Aadhaar in welfare programmes. *Available at SSRN 3045235*.

Kurer, O. (2005). Corruption: An alternative approach to its definition and measurement. *Political Studies*, *53*(1), 222–239. doi:10.1111/j.1467-9248.2005.00525.x

Lagunes, P., & Pocasangre, O. (2019). Dynamic transparency: An audit of Mexico's Freedom of Information Act. *Public Administration*, *97*(1), 162–176. doi:10.1111/padm.12553

Lessig, L. (2013). "Institutional corruption" defined. *The Journal of Law, Medicine & Ethics*, *41*(3), 553–555. doi:10.1111/jlme.12063 PMID:24088144

Ministry of Electronics & Information Technology. (n.d.a.). The Digital India programme is a flagship programme of the Government of India with a vision to transform India into a digitally empowered society and knowledge economy. Retrieved from https://digitalindia.gov.in/content/about-programme

Ministry of Electronics & Information Technology. (n.d.). How Digital India will be realized: Pillars of Digital India. Retrieved from https://digitalindia.gov.in/content/programme-pillars

Mitton, L. (2008). *Financial inclusion in the UK: Review of policy and practice*. York: Joseph Rowntree Foundation.

Mudliar, K., Parekh, H., & Bhavathankar, P. (2018, February). A comprehensive integration of national identity with blockchain technology. In *2018 International Conference on Communication information and Computing Technology (ICCICT)* (pp. 1-6). IEEE. 10.1109/ICCICT.2018.8325891

NSDL. (2016). Aadhaar authentication and e-KYC Services. Retrieved from https://www.egov-nsdl.co.in/e-kyc.html

Pati, R. K., Kumar, V., & Jain, N. (2015). Analysis of Aadhaar: A project management perspective. *IIM Kozhikode Society & Management Review*, *4*(2), 124–135. doi:10.1177/2277975215610687

Perry, P. J. (2018). *Political corruption and political geography*. New York: Routledge Revivals. doi:10.4324/9780429448072

Raj, K., & Aithal, P. S. (2018). Literature Review of Impact of Branding on Base of the Pyramid Markets with Special Reference to India. [IJAEML]. *International Journal of Applied Engineering and Management Letters*, *2*(1), 43–63.

Rawlins, B. R. (2008). Measuring the relationship between organizational transparency and employee trust. *The Public Relations Journal*, *2*(2), 1–21.

Rotberg, R. I. (2019). *The corruption cure: How citizens and leaders can combat graft*. Princeton, NJ: Princeton University Press.

Sahu, P. (2019, Mar. 21). DBT transfers increase 47 per cent, but little growth in saving. *Financial Express*. Retrieved from https://www.financialexpress.com/economy/dbt-transfers-increase-47-per-cent-but-little-growth-in-saving/1522994/

Sarma, M., & Pais, J. (2011). Financial inclusion and development. *Journal of International Development*, *23*(5), 613–628. doi:10.1002/jid.1698

Shah, P., & Dubhashi, M. (2015). Review Paper on Financial Inclusion-The Means of Inclusive Growth. *Chanakya International Journal of Business Research*, *1*(1), 37–48. doi:10.15410/cijbr/2015/v1i1/61403

Singh, R., & Jackson, S. J. (2017, May). From margins to seams: Imbrication, inclusion, and torque in the Aadhaar Identification Project. In *Proceedings of the 2017 CHI Conference on Human Factors in Computing Systems* (pp. 4776-4824). Denver, CO: ACM. 10.1145/3025453.3025910

Toxopeus, H. S., & Lensink, R. (2008). Remittances and financial inclusion in development. In Development Finance in the Global Economy (pp. 236-263). Palgrave Macmillan UK. doi:10.1057/9780230594074_10

Trading Economics. (2019). *India corruption rank*. Retrieved from https://tradingeconomics.com/india/corruption-rank

Transparency International. (2018). Corruption perceptions index 2018. Retrieved from https://www.transparency.org/cpi2018

Turilli, M., & Floridi, L. (2009). The ethics of information transparency. *Ethics and Information Technology*, *11*(2), 105–112. doi:10.100710676-009-9187-9

Unique Identification Authority of India. (2019). About UIDAI. Retrieved from https://uidai.gov.in/about-uidai.html

Varma, N., & Tyagi, R. K. (2017). Government of India prepares for big data analytics using aadhaar card unique identification system. In G. Richards (Ed.), *Big Data and Analytics Applications in Government* (pp. 115–130). Boca Raton, FL: Auerbach Publications. doi:10.4324/9781315153582-6

KEY TERMS AND DEFINITIONS

Aadhaar: It is 12-digit unique identification number issued to every citizen of India which will help in forming a digital identity.

Aadhaar API: It is an Application Programming Interface for enterprises for identity verification in products like Passport, VoterID, Driving License, PAN etc.

AeFDS: Aadhaar enabled Fertilizer Distribution System for farmers based on their land area, soil configuration, type of food grain, season at subsidized rates.

AePDS: Aadhaar enabled Public Distribution System based on biometric authentication for distribution of food and non-food items at subsidized rate for beneficiaries.

AePS: Aadhaar enabled Payment System enables for cashless transactions by using Aadhaar number and fingerprint for withdrawal and deposition of money.

API: Application Programming Interface in any defined inter-program interface for applications like web, atmospheric, analytical etc.

AYUSH: Indian Ministry for Ayurveda, Yoga and Naturopathy, Unani, Siddha and Homeopathy to develop and propagate this system of medicine and healthcare.

Cloud: A model for enabling users to unlimited access to resources like infrastructure, platform, software, database etc.

CSC: Common Service Centers established by Indian Government for eServices to rural and remote locations where computers and internet are not present.

DietY: Department of Electronics and Information Technology have under taken UIDAI and Aadhaar project to promote eGovernance for empowering citizens.

Digital Identity: It refers to the traits, attributes and preferences on which one may receive personalized services.

e-Kranti: It is one of the nine pillars of Digital India program for delivering government services electronically to citizens in transparent and efficient manner.

e-Governance: It is the application of information and communication technology for delivering government services, exchange of information and transactions.

e-KYC: Electronic Know Your Customer is a paperless process of a business verifying identity of a client for potential risks in business relationship.

GST: Goods and Services Tax is an indirect tax imposed in India which is comprehensive and has subsumed almost all other indirect taxes.

GUN: Government User Network connects Union, State, District and local level official sites websites and has feature to customized content displayed.

IBA: Indian Bank Association is a representative body for managing banking in India which includes all private, public and foreign banks operating in country.

Identity: It is an individual's condition of oneself, itself, not another and is transmitted in digital form for establishing trust.

ITES: Information Technology Enabled Services is defined as outsourcing of services that can be enabled through IT for finance, administration, human resource etc.

LPG: Liquefied Petroleum Gas is a flammable mixture of hydrocarbon gases used as a fuel for cooking utensils, vehicles and heating appliances.

MeghRaj Cloud: Is an initiative of Government of India which offers variety of service models like IaaS, PaaS, SaaS for optimal utilization of infrastructure.

MGNREGS: Mahatma Gandhi National Rural Employment Act which guarantees 100 days of wage-employment in a financial year.

microATM: These are handheld point of sale terminals to disperse cash in remote locations where core bank branches can't reach.

MSME: Micro Small and Medium Enterprises are classified in two categories i.e. manufacturing in plant & machinery and servicing in equipment.

NHTS: Nutrition and Health Tracking System is implemented for reducing Infant Mortality Rate, Maternal Mortality ratio and malnutrition.

NIC: National Informatics Centre is a premier organization for informatics services and information and communication technology applications.

NKN: National Knowledge Network is to interconnect all higher education institutions in India to facilitate knowledge sharing and collaborative research.

NOFN: National Optical Fibre Network is an initiative to establish broadband in rural areas by reaching all village panchayats.

NPCI: National Payments Corporation of India is an organization for operating retail payments and settlement systems in India.

NSAP: National Social Assistance Programme is a scheme that provides financial assistance to elderly, widows and disability persons in form of social pensions.

OTP: One Time Password is a dynamic password or one time pin valid for only one transaction on a computer system or digital device.

PAHAL: It is a consumers Direct Benefits Transfer of LPG (DNTL) scheme which requires mandatory Aadhaar number seeding for availing subsidy.

PAN: Permanent Account Number is a ten character alpha numeric number issued by Indian Income Tax department and serves as important proof of identification.

PMMVJ: Pradhan Mantri Matru Vandana Yojna is a maternity benefit program which provides conditional cash transfer to pregnant and lactating women.

RBI: Reserve Bank of Indiais India's central banking institution which controls supply of Indian rupee, regulate banks and provide financial services.

RC: A vehicle Registration Certificate is an official document providing proof of registration of vehicle on national vehicle register.

SIM: Subscriber Identification Moduleis an integrated circuit to securely store international mobile subscriber identity (IMSI) and its related information.

SMS: Short Messaging Systemis a text messaging service of most telephone, mobile and internet devices using standardized protocols.

SWAN: State Wide Area Network is a core infrastructure component of National eGovernance plan to create high speed connectivity for all state headquarters.

UIDAI: Unique Identification Authority of India is an authority to empower citizens of India with a unique identity and a platform to authenticate anytime, anywhere.

Voter ID: It is an identity document issued by Election Commission of India to citizens who have attained age of 18 years and can participate at different elections.

VSAT: Very Small Aperture Terminal is a satellite communication system which interfaces between computer and outside antenna with a transceiver.

APPENDIX

Cost savings to government by linking benefits to Aadhaar (up to March 2019)

S. No.	Scheme(Mandatory linkage with Aadhaar)	Scheme	Cost Savings (in Crores)
1	Crop loan waiver system software	State of Karnataka	₹5,500/-
2	Petroleum and Natural Gas	PAHAL	₹42,275/-
3	Food and Public distribution	PDS	₹29,708-
4	Rural Development	MGNREGS and NSAP	₹16,512/-
5	Social Justice and Empowerment	Scholarship Schemes	₹238/-
6	Minority Affairs	Scholarship Schemes	₹159/-
7	Direct Benefits Transfer through Aadhaar validation	Government of India	₹90,012/-

Source: dbtbharat.gov.in

Success stories of direct benefits transfers

S. No.	Scheme	Success Story
1	Pradhan Mantra Matru Vandana Yojana (PMMVY)	The scheme is 100% DBT Compliant with 99% of beneficiaries under the scheme enrolled using Aadhaar i.e. 4.75 millions. Issues resolved include beneficiaries receiving cash incentives on time. Discrepancy in figures of cash received by the State authorities and beneficiaries resolved. Pending funds since 2013-14 for many blocks released. No reporting of stipulated amount being received or beneficiaries not aware of payments being made.
2	State Health Society (Bihar)	A pilot project to digitize the health incentive payments to front line health workers like ASHAs, Anganwadi workers and beneficiaries. The objective is to increase transparency, timeliness and accuracy in process. It is reported that about 75% of time is saved by health workers in enquiry about payments which is utilized in field works now. Also delay in average time of receiving the payments has been reduced to 35%.
3	Chandigrah – Kerosene Free City	Chandigarh has become the first State/UTs to be kerosene free since 1st April, 2016. With the help of UID, Food and Supplies department has identified 35,000 families having LPG connections and still drawing subsidized kerosene oil. These names were removed and a subsidized LPG connection was given to remaining. This step made the city kerosene free with the help of newspapers, volunteers, pamphlets, radio jingles etc.
4	Disbursement of Pensions	The pilot project implemented in Krishna district of Andhra Pradesh. It got attraction from Government of India, Bill Gates Foundation, World Bank, Tanzanian Government and other States. The disbursement of pension ate beneficiary door step, increasing the habit of savings through bank account. Technology used is JAM Trinity i.e. Jan Dhan Yojana, Aadhaar Number and Mobile Number with Micro ATMs etc.
5	AePS (Aadhaar Enabled Payment System)	Payment system for MGNREGS workers to improve transparency and efficient funds transfer. It has resulted in timely payments to genuine wage workers. It is using Aadhaar based authentication so duplicate musters and other fraudulent practices are avoided. Mostly paperless procedure as bank accounts are open through eKYC and biometric attendance is recorded through finger printers and IRIS in Aadhaar database.
6	NHTS (Nutrition and Health Tracking System)	Women and Child Health is prioritize by targeting pregnant and lactating women and children below 1 year of age with malnutrition children below 5 years. Information for these women were taken from Anganwadi Centre (AWC). An unique id was generated for each beneficiary with services required. The initiative is Aadhaar based so benefits were transferred to concerned persons directly anywhere without any hindrance.
7	AePDS (Aadhaar Enabled Public Distribution System)	Aadhaar enabled Public Distribution System is an attempt to provide good quality food commodities to eligible beneficiaries.This system provides a monitoring option of commodities from warehouses to customers. Each shop is provided with an ePOS (Electronic Point of Sale) with biometric authentication of customers to prevent any corruption options. Cost of all these services is borne by government with zero investment from users.
8	AeFDS (Aadhaar Enabled Fertilizer Distribution System)	Aadhar Enabled Fertilizer Distribution System (AeFDS)is an attempt to monitor the supply chain and provide correct fertilizers to farmers. This is authenticated by biometrics of farmers so that fertilizers reaches to correct persons and at correct time. It holds land records and soil analysis report which helps in supplying required fertilizers for the farmers. This helps in getting entitled fertilizers anytime and anywhere.
9	Project Biometric-pur	This project was first implemented for ensuring last mile connectivity for residents of Balrampur district, Chhhatisgarh. This is a citizen centric project which prevents a lot of time and efforts of residents in getting benefits from Government. The project has altered system of financial services distribution at multiple levels. Official's efforts are also saved in disabusing cheques and monitoring for payment to right beneficiaries.
10	SAMAGRA Portal	A common integrated platform to facilitate population of Madhya Pradesh through a model of Governance.It was started with SPR (Samagra Population Register) to create online database for different types of beneficiaries with their requirements. This transformed the society to entitle based service delivery, single window, time bound implementation, real time monitoring, efficient resource utilization and direct benefit transfer.

Definition of transparency

S. No.	Reference	Definition of Transparency
1	Aguinis et al (2018)	It is degree of detail and disclosure about specific steps, decisions and judgment calls. Lack of transparency is research performance problem as it leads to errors, fraudulent acts and reproducibility. At each stage of the process efforts must be placed in increasing transparency.
2	Hollyer et al (2018)	It supports a democratic equilibrium and stabilizes democratic rule. It effectively resolves selection problems, increases satisfaction and inhibits challenges. It also reduces probability of collapse. It also reduces probability of collapse and irregular removal of leaders.
3	Rawlings (2008)	It is defined as information with three main elements truthful, substantial and useful. It is deliberately revealing the actions, policies and practices whether positive or negative. It is exactly opposite of secrecy and leads to openness in organization and society.
4	Turilli & Floridi (2009)	It is a pro-ethical condition for enabling other ethical practices. It takes into account dynamics of information production and difference between data and information. It provides an understanding of which information should be disclosed by an organization.
5	Langunes & Pacasangre (2019)	It increases a fair and accountable public administration. It provides quality information which is legal and explicitly bound to disclose. It is the disclosure of information about decisions and actions for the purpose of performance of any organization.

Definition of corruption

S. No.	Reference	Definition of Corruption
1	Gardiner (2017)	It leads to a series of problems linked in public domain referring 'to abuse', 'to misuse' or 'to do something improper'. It is also based on the impact in public interest and public opinion.
2	Kurer (2005)	It is defined as an impartiality principle where a state does not treat equally all those who deserve equally. It is prevalent in traditional societies and contemporary political ones with discriminating norms across time and place.
3	Lessig (2013)	It is a systemic and strategic influence that weakens effectiveness or performance which is legal. It may bring a change in regulation which is even at present ethical. This weakens public trust and inherent trust worthiness.
4	Perry (2018)	It leads to unhappiness in human society with impacts on geography and legal process. It leads to frustrating results with public immortality, official lawlessness and subversion of government by special interests.
5	Rotberg (2019)	It is a dangerous cancer of a national body which is all-encompassing and ruthless. It infects elites, classes, castes, cripples institutions, consumes communities and cuts deeply into people's lives.

Chapter 9
Constructing the Internet Panoptic-Fortification:
A Legal Study on China's Internet Regulatory Mechanism

Juan Du
https://orcid.org/0000-0003-1306-8437
Peking University, China & PKU-HKUST Shenzhen-Hong Kong Institution, Hong Kong

ABSTRACT

This chapter investigates China's Internet regulatory mechanism through the systematical analysis on Internet law in China. It argues that China has developed a hybrid Internet regulatory model, which values both external defense and internal control of in pursuit of the cybersecurity, and which combines hierarchical regulation with horizontal monitoring to address challenges brought by contemporary network society. Based on Michel Foucault's governmentality theory, the Internet panoptic-fortification model is developed to illuminate China's Internet regulatory mechanism. The model is featured by the centralized control, the establishment of Chinese sovereign cyberspace, the implementation of the network real-name system and the Internet-surfing record backup system, and the tight ideological control. This chapter suggests that China's Internet law has become a state instrument to promote the social discipline in the sovereign cyberspace, and the Internet regulatory mechanism serves for the national security and social stability in a broader context.

DOI: 10.4018/978-1-7998-1791-8.ch009

Copyright © 2020, IGI Global. Copying or distributing in print or electronic forms without written permission of IGI Global is prohibited.

INTRODUCTION

When the Internet was first introduced into China in the 1980s, it was understood as an advanced international technology, which could be used to promote modernization in China. As a result, not many restrictions were put in place. In 1994, China's information technology networks were officially connected to the international Internet, and began to extend to civilian and commercial uses. Since then, the Chinese authorities had started to formulate relevant regulations (Wang & Hu, 2016). In the early 21st century, the Internet had a broader and more profound influence on the Chinese society and the daily lives of citizens. The Chinese authorities' attitude towards the Internet also underwent subtle changes. While taking advantage of the Internet to accelerate the process of modernization and globalization, they also attempted to construct a relatively controllable network. In this sense, the Chinese authorities sought a delicate balance between open markets and a relatively closed political and social environment.

Such an Internet policy had been maintained and strengthened over many years. Meanwhile, facing the increasing criticism of western countries on China's strict control over the Internet, as well as the challenging idea that viewed the Internet censorship as barriers to trade in services under the WTO framework, the Chinese authorities sought political justification from the perspectives of national sovereignty and security (Lin, 2010; Wu, 2006; Yan, 2015). A series of measures have been taken to improve the legal system and to strengthen the institutional framework of Internet regulation. In this context, China has gradually developed its Internet regulatory mechanism based on the principle of cyberspace sovereignty.

In this process, law has become the major technique of Internet regulation in China. To better regulate the Internet by law, the Chinese authorities have issued a number of legislative documents to cover major aspects of Internet regulation. These documents provide a legitimate foundation for the use of multiple means to regulate the Internet. This chapter aims to investigate China's Internet regulatory mechanism from a legal perspective. Through comprehensive and systematical legislative document analysis, it seeks to answer the question: what is the Internet regulatory mechanism constructed by law in China? Furthermore, this chapter attempts to use Foucault's theory of governmentality to reach an in-depth understanding of China's situation, and to construct a theoretical model of the Internet regulatory mechanism in China.

BACKGROUND

The Rise of Internet Regulation

At the initial stage of the birth and development of the Internet (1957 – 1990s), the Internet was often considered as a separate space distinguished from the physical space, called 'cyberspace', with few regulations imposed (Palfrey, 2010). Based on the Internet's key features, technical communities tended to envision a network utopia that would eliminate traditional hierarchical governance structures and rules, and that would be merely regulated by 'rough consensus and running code' (Clark, 1992).

In the late 1990s and early 21st century, the Internet experienced commercialization and began to reach the global masses. At first, Internet regulation was proposed and implemented under the telecommunications regulatory framework, treated in the way similar to the telephone regulation. Yet with the development and popularization of the Internet, it was argued that the Internet service should be regarded as information service rather than merely as telecommunications service, and should undergo corresponding regulation (Ehrlich, 2014). In this sense, it suggested the justification of government's involvement, with some regulatory responses.

In view of this shift, scholars from social science communities began to take part in the discussion, bringing fresh insights to Internet regulation. Lawrence Lessig (1999) listed four interdependent constraints for Internet regulation, including the law, the norms of the Internet organizing committees and user communities, the market and the whole technological architecture of the Internet (summarized as 'code') (pp. 87–90). Yochai Benkler (2000) conceptualized regulation at three layers of Internet, including a physical infrastructure layer, a code or logical layer and a content layer. Lawrence Solum (2009) argued that regulation of the technical infrastructure of the Internet had implications for the regulation of applications and content, and further proposed the following modes for Internet regulation: (1) cyberspace and spontaneous ordering, (2) transnational institutions and international organizations, (3) code and Internet architecture, (4) national governments and law, and (5) market regulation and economics. Jan van Dijk (2012) recognized four actors in Internet regulation: governments, Internet communities (including both self-regulatory bodies and online communities of affinity), corporations and designers of architecture software and security systems; their control of Internet had been backed by new legislation (p. 143).

Stepping into the 2010s, the Internet has become part of real lives of billions of people globally. Under this circumstance, the complexity of Internet regulation is increasing dramatically. In this phase, the idea of the borderless Internet has been challenged by the multilateral approach that emphasizes state sovereignty (Cattaruzza et al., 2016). In this process, states and governments have played and would play the leading role (Drake, 2014).

Research on Internet Regulation in China

A collaborative research project, the OpenNet Initiative, studied the Internet filtering situation in 70 states covering every region of the world, and found that content regulation was norm in almost all states (Palfrey, 2010). However, some states, such as China, have called for stronger regulation, which had instituted the most intricate regime in the world 'at multiple levels of the network and covering content that spans a wide range of topic areas' (p. 8). Comprehensive mechanisms and measures have been explored and implemented to meet different regulatory demands. Indeed, China has developed a regulatory model that 'prioritizes security over liberty, emphasizes nationalism over freedom, and promotes state-centered multilateralism over multi-stakeholder partnership' (Hong, 2014, Abstract, para. 1).

In addition to the five models summarized by Solum (2009), Jiang Min (2010, 2013) presented the Chinese model as neo-authoritarianism model, as it 'modifies open Internet architecture, prioritizes national government control, distorts market mechanisms, and substantially limits individual freedoms online' (Jiang, 2013, Extended Abstract, para. 1). Jiang's research traced the history of Internet regulation in China, and analyzed the Chinese authorities' efforts to legitimate cyber policies in areas of economy, nationalism, ideology, culture and governance, which received mass compliance. Jiang's arguments identify key features of Internet regulation in China, and point to directions for further theoretical research. However, Jiang does not develop a model of the whole mechanism, as this chapter is committed to do.

Zheng Yongnian's study (2008/2014) explored interactions among the Internet, state and society in China. Starting from the relationship between science and democracy, Zheng pointed out that the Chinese authorities inevitably faced two conflicting requirements: promoting the economic development while maintaining the political control. Two corresponding mechanisms were established to support these two ends. The regulatory mechanism was developed mainly for administrative purposes, while the controlling mechanism was subject to political demands. However, Zheng's research does not focus too much on Internet regulation, so relevant discussion seems to be fragmentary, based on other priorities.

Liu Bing (2007) used economic theories to analyze China's Internet content regulatory mechanism, reaching the conclusion that top-down control, plus a 'third party' supervisory institution, would be the best alternative for Internet content regulation. Li Yonggang (2009) examined how the Chinese authorities applied traditional regulatory approaches successfully to cyberspace by interpreting the action logic of the central government, various departments and local governments.

Both studies recognize the leading role of governments in Internet regulation, and suggest that the participation of multiple stakeholders is the direction of Internet regulation in the future. This view is also supported by Greg Austin's study of the history of China's process of informationization and the policy values involved (2014).

Other relevant theoretical research has addressed specific topics or fields of discourse. For example, Henry Hu (2011) analyzed the crucial role of Internet service providers (*hereinafter referred to as* ISPs) in China's Internet regulation with an emphasis on the Great Firewall at the national level and ISP censorship at the local level. Bai Jing's legal study (2013) concluded that the joint liabilities of ISPs for Internet users' behaviors led to the more robust censorship conducted by ISPs, which facilitated government surveillance. However, the lack of theoretical analysis of China's Internet regulatory mechanism as a whole calls for research with a broader vision and a deeper understanding.

Introducing Governmentality to Internet Studies

This chapter introduces the governmentality theory as the basis of a deeper understanding of China's Internet regulatory mechanism. The term 'governmentality' was coined by Michel Foucault to characterize modern forms of power. From a Foucauldian perspective, governmentality is the way in which the state exercises its power to control the population as a whole, while also governing individuals by guiding, shaping and channeling their conduct. It aims not only to govern the society according to a perceived ideal, but also to cultivate each individual towards an ideal citizenship.

The governmentality theory has been used to investigate issues of health, education, environment, community and religion. Some studies have attempted to extend this conceptual framework to Internet research. For example, in a study of law in cyberspace, James Boyle introduced Foucault's suggestive insights concerning 'the subtle private, informal and material forms of coercion that are enforced through "surveillance" and "discipline"' to analyze the ways in which power was exercised on the Internet (Boyle, 1997; Wacker, 2003, p. 60). Mehta and Darier (1998) found the Foucauldian concept of governmentality helpful in understanding effects of the Internet on governments, social structures and individuals. Delmas (2007) presented multiple regimes of governmentality of the Internet at the international level.

Most governmentality studies focus on developed liberal democratic societies, and preclude considerations of governmentality in non-western and non-liberal settings. In fact, the Chinese authorities view the Internet from a fundamentally utilitarian perspective, in relation to their twin goals of economic development and social stability. This provides the premise for introducing the governmentality theory in the current research project. One relevant study addressed the governmentality of mass supervision in China. Built on Foucault's description of 'a decentralized network of power' (p. 10), Gorman (2012) explored the social interactions between the Chinese authorities and the civil society, through an investigation of the 'human flesh search'. From Gorman's perspective, Foucault's governmentality is useful to understand China's governance strategies and methods.

The panopticon is a metaphor that is frequently cited to illustrate the term 'governmentality'. The structure of the panopticon forces each prisoner to behave as if they were being watched at all times, thus maintaining the regular operation of the prison at minimum cost. Entering the digital age, the panopticon model has been widely used in Internet studies. Allmer (2010) classified studies on this topic into two categories. One set features the non-panoptic notion of Internet surveillance based on a value-neutral or positive conception, and understands Internet surveillance as a useful and effective management tool, and as a fair method and procedure for monitoring individuals online. For example, Zuboff (1988) used the architectural strategies of the panopticon as a metaphor to describe how information systems translated, recorded, and displayed human behavior. The other set of studies considered online surveillance to be negative and accompanied by coercion, repression, discipline, power and domination. Lyon (1994) viewed the panopticon as a powerful and compelling metaphor for understanding electronic surveillance. Mark Poster (1995) further proposed the term super-panopticon to refer to enhanced surveillance supported by databases.

So far, in terms of the panopticon, most Internet studies have been confined to the influence of databases, with little attention paid beyond. In addition to the disruptions brought on by technological innovation, China has institutionalized the panoptic mechanism to strengthen its surveillance and control over the Internet. This chapter attempts to develop the panopticon metaphor to model the Internet regulatory mechanism in the Chinese context.

CONCEPTUAL FRAMEWORK

Based on the literature review and preliminary research, a conceptual framework is offered to more clearly illustrate the Internet regulatory mechanism in China. The framework incorporates the economical and efficient design of the panopticon, while introducing improvements made to adapt to China's Internet regulatory ecosystem. Considering that the panopticon's features of closure and separation run contrary to the open feature of the Internet, another metaphor is sought to specify the conceptual framework more precisely.

In this chapter, panoptic-fortification is proposed to replace the panopticon as a model for China's Internet regulatory mechanism. In essence, the Internet panoptic-fortification is a fortification with an emphasis on the sovereign space, which suggests both function of defense towards the foreign space and function of control towards the sovereign space. Thus, the use of the fortification concept in this study is based on the principle of cyberspace sovereignty. Inside the fortification, a panoptic design is adopted to exert the control over the whole population and each individual. The term 'panoptic' means that seeing the whole at one view. In this sense, the panoptic design focuses on insight into everything from a focal point. Panopticon is a typical design that applies the panoptic concept to a prison. Yet, the panoptic design has a broader range of applications. In this study, combination of the panoptic design and the fortificated design contributes to an enhanced defensive and controlling mechanism.

The Internet panoptic-fortification model retains the essential characteristics of the panopticon. One significant innovation of the panopticon is the physical ordering of the cells in a ring surrounding a single focal point. Such a hub-and-spoke structure demands three basic components: the core, the existing boundary and unidirectional links from the core to units close to the boundary. These three components are also embodied in the design of the Internet panoptic-fortification model. A typical structure of this panoptic-fortification is constituted by a guard tower at the center and a specific territory within the boundary. Individuals and their actions are observed inside the boundary and recorded without their knowledge, which leads to their behaving as if under surveillance.

Yet the panoptic-fortification model is not completely enclosed like the panopticon itself. In normal situations, controlled gateways connect the territory under control and projection with the outside world. When an emergency occurs, these gateways can be shut down immediately for defense. Also, in the panopticon, prisoners are imprisoned in cells, in order to prevent collective action. However, in panoptic-fortification, there is no special requirement to keep individuals apart from each other. Control of the inner panoptic-fortification is achieved in subtle and hidden ways, appealing to methods such as observation, recording and training. Fortification is used to reinforce defense against the outside, while the main purpose of the panoptic design is to prevent any potential action within the fortification that might pose a threat to the cybersecurity. Consequently, the structure of the Internet panoptic-fortification guarantees enhanced cybersecurity.

Figure 1 is a simplified presentation of the basic conceptual framework of China's Internet regulatory mechanism. To some extent, China has constructed a solid Internet panoptic-fortification based on the priority of the centralized control, the insistence on the principle of cyberspace sovereignty, the establishment of the Internet access control mechanism, the implementation of the network real-name system and the Internet-surfing record backup system, as well as the tight ideological control. For one thing, the Internet regulatory mechanism is the application of the existing social control measures in the cyberspace, with the centralized power, the sovereignty principle and the ideological control still effective and even enhanced. For another, facing challenges brought by the booming network society, more technical and regulatory measures have been introduced to define the scope of the regulated population, as well as to regulate each individual.

In 1996, two years after China's official access to the Internet, the fundamental Internet access mode in China was confirmed by a series of law, including *Interim Provisions on the Management of International Networking of Computer Information Networks* (promulgated by the State Council on February 1, 1996 and revised on May 20, 1997), *Administrative Measures for the International Networking of the Chinanet* (promulgated by Ministry of Posts and Telecommunications on April 9, 1996), *Administrative Measures for International Networking Exchange Gateway Channel of Computer Information Network* (promulgated by Ministry of Posts and Telecommunications on April 9, 1996), and *Interim Provisions on Networking between the Private Network and the Public Network* (promulgated by Ministry of Posts and Telecommunications on July 24, 1996). It was then followed by the promotion of the network real-name system and the Internet-surfing record backup system step by step. In 2012, the issuance of *Decision of the Standing Committee of the National People's Congress on Strengthening Information Protection on Networks* fully affirmed the prior legislation and practices in this regard. By then, the basic framework of China's Internet regulatory mechanism had been established, with more tools and measures explored under this framework.

First, Internet regulation in China displays a typical hierarchical structure. Traditional political power holders perform a powerful central role in China's national and social affairs, and the Communist Party of China (*hereinafter referred to as* the CPC) exercises absolute authorities over government institutions as well as other organizations and entities. The existing distribution of political power is also reflected in the Internet regulatory mechanism, and those holding political powers constitute the essential core in this mechanism.

The Chinese authorities construct this centralized control with the support and assistance of ISPs. Relying on their economic and technological advantages, ISPs obtain a certain degree of control over the Internet in China (Li, 2009, p. 187). ISPs attempt to present themselves as independent, to attract more users and to create more value. At the same time, they have to cater to the authorities to maintain their current status and to seek further development. Fundamentally, both local and foreign-owned ISPs have to cooperate with the authorities to survive in China. In this sense, ISPs form an outer ring around the authorities.

Another key element of this design is the boundary used to define the regulated objects. As the literature reveals, China has followed a multilateral approach to regulate the Internet, based on a strong appeal to cyberspace sovereignty, namely,

Figure 1. Conceptual model of China's Internet regulatory mechanism

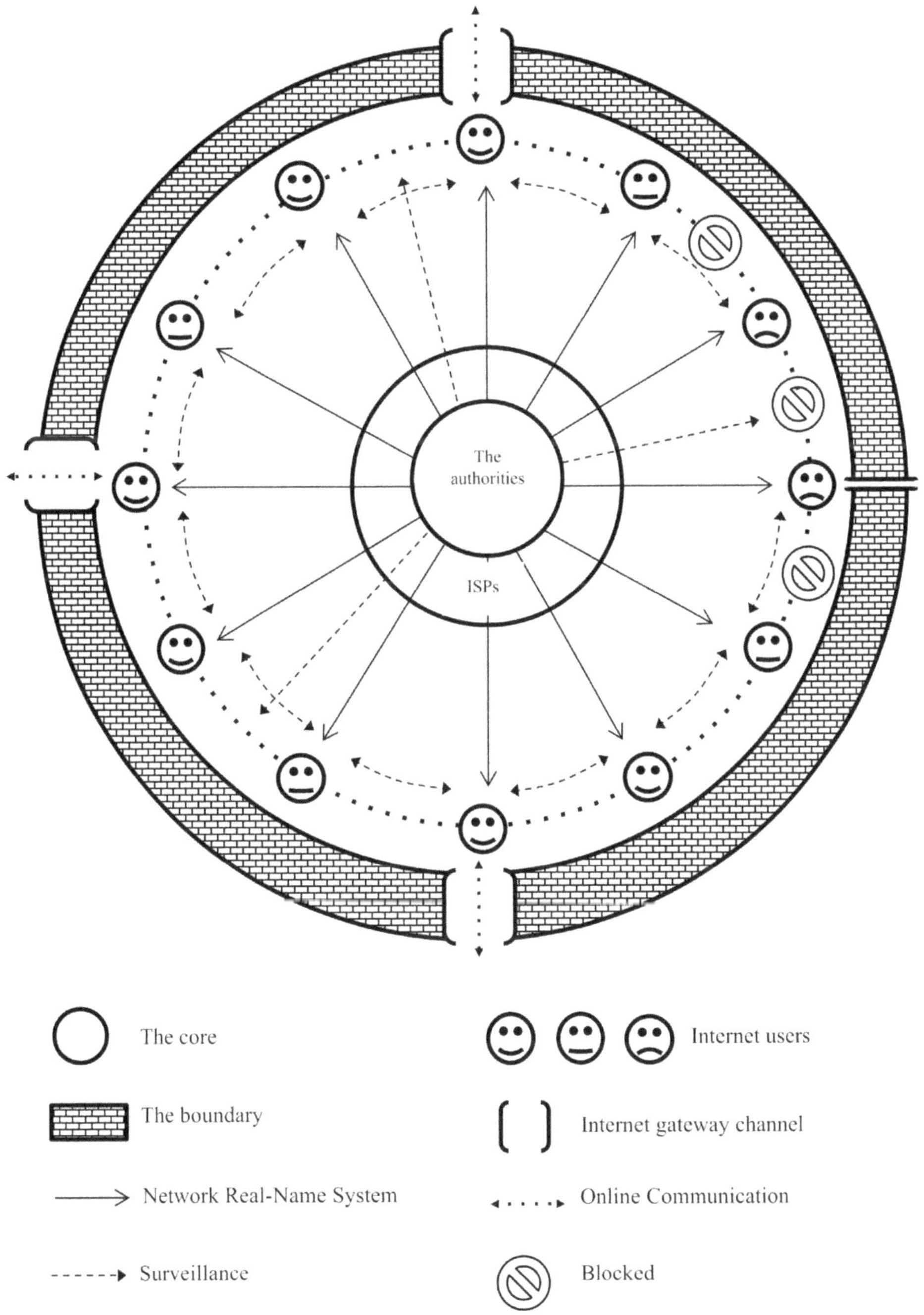

the claim that the Internet within Chinese territory is under the jurisdiction of China's sovereignty (State Council Information Office of China, 2010). Chinese law therefore can equally be applied to any Internet-related acts within Chinese territory or involving Chinese connecting factors. To guarantee sovereignty in cyberspace, the state has the substantial control over the physical infrastructure layer and the logic layer of the Internet within Chinese territory. On this basis, a hierarchical Internet access control system has been built within the political territory to offer necessary technical supports. This system allows connections between domestic networks and the Internet, yet such connections are subject to the hierarchical regulation, and the only designated gateways are controlled by the core. Thus, in this conceptual framework, the boundary signifies China's political territory and its Internet access control system.

Within this boundary, the network real-name system is designed to pierce the veils resulting from the anonymity of the Internet. The network real-name system is an institutional design in which the virtual identities of Internet users correspond to their real identities. Information tracking and recording technologies enable the localization of device access to the Internet. Thus, the so-called anonymous Internet actually leads to exposure rather than preserving privacy. Internet browsing data make it possible to identify and to locate each Internet user, thus facilitating the diffusion of power at the micro level. The ultimate aim of these systems is to integrate the huge online database with the all-encompassing surveillance network (Walton, 2001). In light of this, in cyberspace, man is supposed to be free, but everywhere he is in chains.

The original design of the panopticon demanded partitions between cells. The solitude it created sought to make the inmate 'a subject of information, never a subject in communication', to remove opportunities for coordination that could lead to a 'collective effect' (Foucault, 1975/1978, p. 200). Yet the Internet is a global system for information exchange and processing, featured by interconnected computer networks. It offers increasing opportunities for Internet users to observe and to communicate with one another. Thus, the panoptic-fortification model does not adopt the design of isolated cells. Instead, as long as the core does not feel threatened by potential consequences that might be brought by Internet user's online words and deeds, communication between the regulated would be allowed and even encouraged. This consent follows the utilitarian tradition by the implementation of multiple supervisions. It is proposed that not only surveillance from the core, but also monitoring from numerous networked individuals, has been conducted on the Internet.

The essence of governmentality lies in 'the centrality of the inspector's situation, combined with the well-known and most effectual contrivances for seeing without being seen' (Bentham, 1791, p. 23). The constant uncertainty as to whether one is actually being observed or not results in one's behaving as though one is being observed at all times. This deterrent effect has become particularly evident in the Internet era. On the one hand, the authorities and ISPs play a role similar to big brother on the strength of their existing political, economic and technical advantages. To avoid any action that might pose a threat to their interests, they have taken extremely comprehensive surveillance measures. Not only channels of communication but also the information itself is closely monitored to ensure it is within their tolerance. Once there is any indication of undesired action, the information would be blocked and the communication would then be interrupted at multiple levels when needed. Such online surveillance is further combined with offline measures. By exerting pressures from real lives, individual Internet users are trained to behave following idealized norms of conduct.

At the same time, the authorities also apply the mass supervision to the Internet regulatory mechanism. Mutual monitoring is encouraged among networked individual users to ensure their good behaviors. As a result, the more communication happens, the more information can be acquired, and the more effective monitoring is conducted. As Bentham believed, the more strictly we are watched, the better we behave. This increasing uncertainty can lead to self-discipline rather than collective action, thus contributing to the maximization of regulatory effects. Moreover, a series of measures have been taken to condition Internet users and to tighten the ideological restrictions placed on the Internet in China. In the following parts, details of the Internet panoptic-fortification model will be further explored and analyzed.

RESEARCH METHOD

Law has become the major means of Internet regulation in China, and China's Internet regulatory mechanism is supported by a comprehensive legal framework. The construction of the Chinese Internet regulatory mechanism is largely achieved through the formulation and implementation of relevant law. The approach of legal studies is therefore the most appropriate one with which to examine Internet regulation in China. By regulating the construction of infrastructure, Internet access, and Internet content, cyber law empowers the Chinese authorities with overall control of the Internet within Chinese territory (Hu, 2008, p. 319).

The purpose of this chapter is to examine the Internet regulatory mechanism in China, as well as the instruments and measures used. To achieve this goal, the study draws most of its support from legislative documentation. Law in China is presented in the form of statutes; these are publicly available with high reliability, thus constituting the basic resources for this research project. There are several kinds of sources of law in China, including formal sources such as Laws, Administrative

Regulations, Rules issued by Departments under the State Council *(hereinafter referred to as* Departmental Rules) and Judicial Interpretations, and informal sources such as Administrative Normative Documents. All kinds of sources of law are made in accordance with the statutory limits of authorities and procedures, with a hierarchy among different sources of law. To distinguish these specific sources of law, the title for each will be capitalized throughout the chapter when used in this technical sense. Performing legislative document analysis is to categorize, investigate, interpret and identify existing legislative documents. It is helpful to investigate both the macro-level structure and micro-level details of China's Internet regulatory mechanism.

Internet law in this study refers to valid nationwide legislative documents that were issued on or before December 31, 2016 concerning the Internet infrastructure, basic resources of the Internet, and the Internet content (in the broadest sense). Only legislative documents or provisions special for the Internet are included in this study, which means the current research project will exclude general Laws and Administrative Regulations that are equally applicable to both online and offline situations. After the comprehensive collection and the careful selection, 238 national legislative documents in relation to the Internet remained, all of which were numbered for coding. These legislative documents included 18 Laws, 10 Administrative Regulations, 47 Departmental Rules, 15 Judicial Interpretations, and 148 Administrative Normative Documents.

Facing numerous complicated legislative documents, legal coding is an effective solution to facilitate retrieving, sorting and reviewing the huge volume of legislative documents. Legal coding is the process used to create an index, and also a database, to extract keyword data systematically from legislative documents for further analysis. The result of legal coding is to create a database for further legislative document analysis. The specific qualities of legislative documents call for a high level of professional insight. Therefore, high-quality legal coding is built on an effectively designed framework and standardized conventions, and is conducted by highly trained coders using appropriate technology and multiple levels of quality control (Hall & Wright, 2008).

In light of this, this study developed a coding system to code relevant legislative documents systematically and effectively. The design of the coding framework took features of the Internet panoptic-fortification model fully into consideration. The coding framework contained ten sets of data: (1) basic properties, (2) common information, (3) the core, (4) the boundary, (5) unidirectional links from the core to the units within the boundary, (6) content regulation, (7) mass supervision, (8) self-regulation, (9) penalties, and (10) others. Both objective coding and subjective coding were conducted. It should be noted that, during the coding process, the codebook was continuously improved. Consequently, not only does the final legislative document database provide sufficient details for further research, but also the codebook framework itself offers an intuitive display of the Internet regulatory mechanism in China.

After coding these legal resources to appropriate positions in the database, they are interpreted and analyzed according to the issues identified, using both methods of quantitative content analysis and traditional legal analysis. The quantitative analysis uses statistics to indicate the general disposition of Internet law in China, while the legal analysis offers more normative insights for identifying and interpreting specific supporting tools and measures within this mechanism. Through a comprehensive legislative document analysis design, the study aims to understand both the overall structure and details of operation of China's Internet regulatory mechanism.

FINDINGS AND DICUSSION

General Situation of Internet Law in China

Development of Internet Law in China

As it is shown in Figure 2, in general, legislative activities concerning the Internet were quite frequent at every legislative level. The Internet-related legislation normally began with the formulation of Administrative Regulations, Departmental Rules and Administrative Normative Documents. On the basis of the practice of administrative legislation, Laws were then made or amended in accordance with the development needs at that time. The formulation of Laws was followed by the formulation supporting legislative instruments, such as Judicial Interpretations and administrative legislative documents, to implement these Laws.

The Internet-related legislation commenced in 1994, at the same year when the Chinese network officially accessed the Internet for the first time. Developing the Internet became a national policy issue, and the authorities began their attempt to regulate the Internet by law. During the period between 1994 and 1999, the main focus of the Internet law stayed on the physical infrastructure layer, with an emphasis on the network security.

The next ten years, from 2000 to 2009, were considered as 'the period of steady development of the Internet in China' (Wang & Hu, 2016, p. 129). During this period, the Standing Committee of the National People's Congress promulgated two important Internet Laws, as well as five general Laws with Internet-related provisions. In addition, 7 out of all 10 Administrative Regulations were issued, covering areas of basic telecommunications business, Internet access services and Internet content services. Mainly due to the formulation of Internet Laws and Regulations in this period, the number of Departmental Rules, Judicial Interpretations and Administrative

Figure2. Number of nationwide Internet law issued each year in China (by the end of 2016)

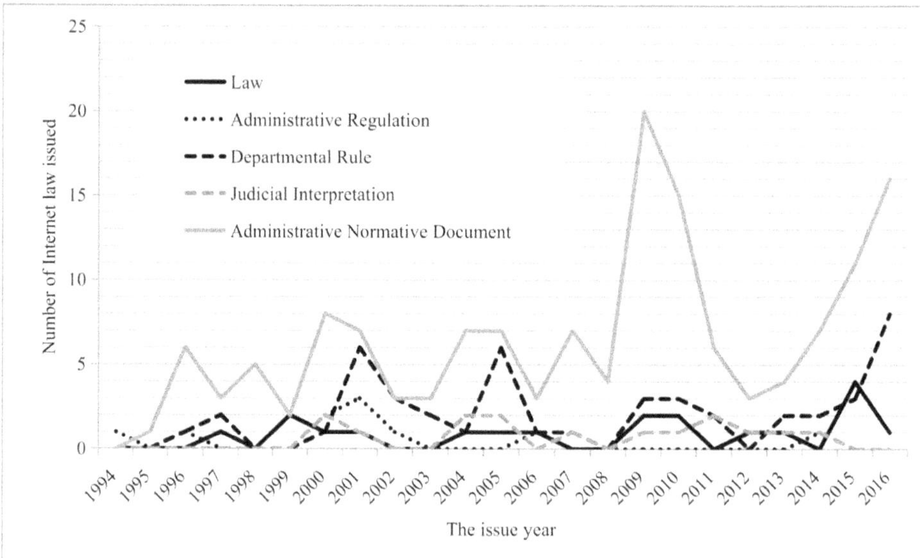

Normative Documents all climaxed in this period. It suggests that Internet legislation had become a major measure to regulate the Internet.

Since 2010, Internet-related legislative activities have been both active and frequent. On the one hand, the Xi-Li government continued basic Internet policies made by former leaderships; on the other hand, the new leaderships re-designed the Internet regulatory mechanism from the perspective of national security. This was also reflected in the Internet-related legislation. In five Laws issued after 2010, four concerned cybersecurity. In this context, a large number of Departmental Rules, Judicial Interpretations and Administrative Normative Documents were made to handle all kinds of emerging issues on the Internet. To some extent, China's Internet law is featured by its instrumentality, serving for the goal of cybersecurity. Such a comprehensive legislative mode will continue in the near future.

Distribution of Legal Sources and Legislators

As Figure 3 shows, legislative documents issued by administrative organs account for 82% of all legislative documents. While Laws and Administrative Regulations are made to oversee basic but important issues related to the Internet, Departmental Rules and Administrative Normative Documents have become major sources for Internet regulation. Meanwhile, Judicial Interpretations focus on the elaboration and application of Laws and Regulations, rather than on making new rules. In terms of the number of different sources of law, Figure 3 indicates that administrative authorities have played a significant role in the process of Internet regulation.

Actually, Internet-related legislation involves a variety of administrative authorities, which indicates the complexity of Internet regulation. Specifically, 20 departments under the State Council have been involved in the formulation of 47 Internet-related Departmental Rules. Comparably, as many as 50 authorities have participated in the formulation of 148 Administrative Normative Documents. It is worth mentioning that the Cyberspace Administration of China was reorganized and authorized to formulate and implement cyber policies in 2014. By the end of 2016, in just two years, it had made and issued two Departmental Rules and 13

Figure 3. Proportions of different sources of 238 nationwide Internet laws in China

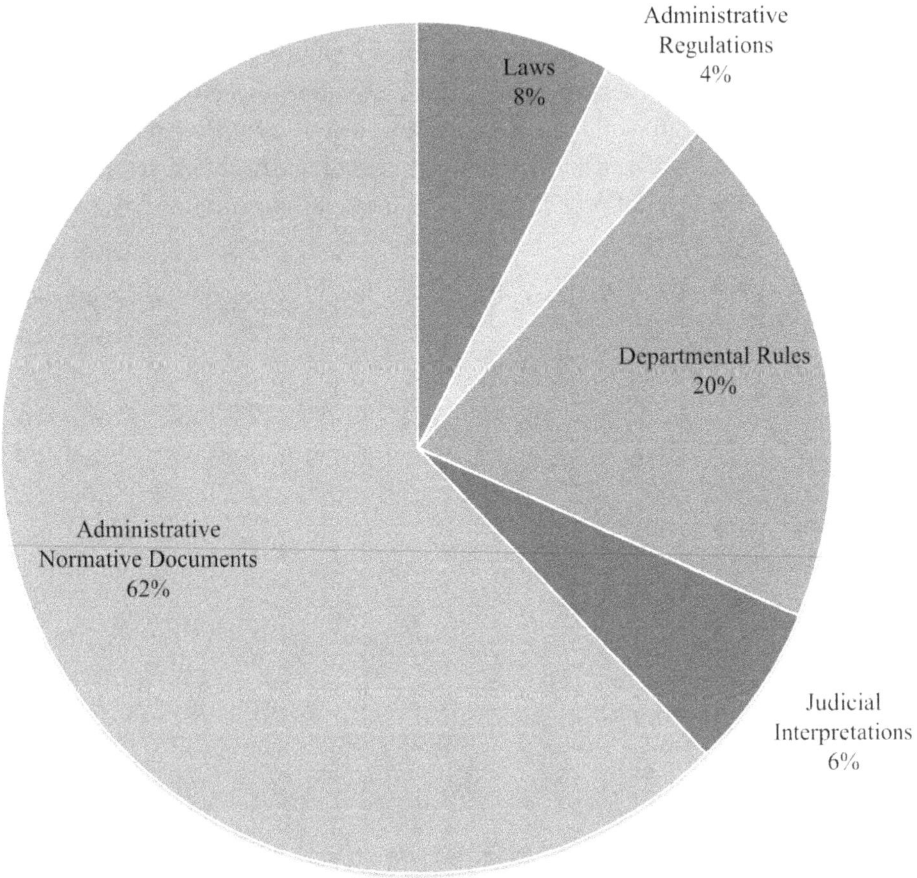

influential Administrative Normative Documents. The Cyberspace Administration of China has become a key regulator in the process of Internet regulation in China.

In addition to the diversity of legislators, joint legislation is another characteristic of Internet-related legislation in China. Figure 4 presents the number of Departmental Rules and Administrative Normative Documents made by multi-legislators. In most situations, two or three legislators are involved. But in individual cases, the number of legislators might reach seven for Departmental Rules and even 16 for Administrative Normative Documents. It suggests that the authorities tend to adopt the networked regulatory model to better handle ever-changing Internet issues.

Value Orientation of China's Internet Law

While the emergence and penetration of the Internet provide an unprecedented and unparalleled potential for changing the society, the process of Internet regulation inevitably involves all kinds of value demands from multiple stakeholders. Therefore, the formulation and implementation of Internet law should recognize these values, and should further recommend certain choices among these different or even competing values. In order to understand values and choice in China's Internet law, this study examine legislative purposes of all legislative documents in the prior coding process, with 55 legislative purposes recognized. These legislative purposes have subsequently been categorized into a framework constituted by different relationship levels, including the level of private rights and interests (*hereinafter referred to as*

Figure 4. Number of administrative legislative documents made by multi-legislators

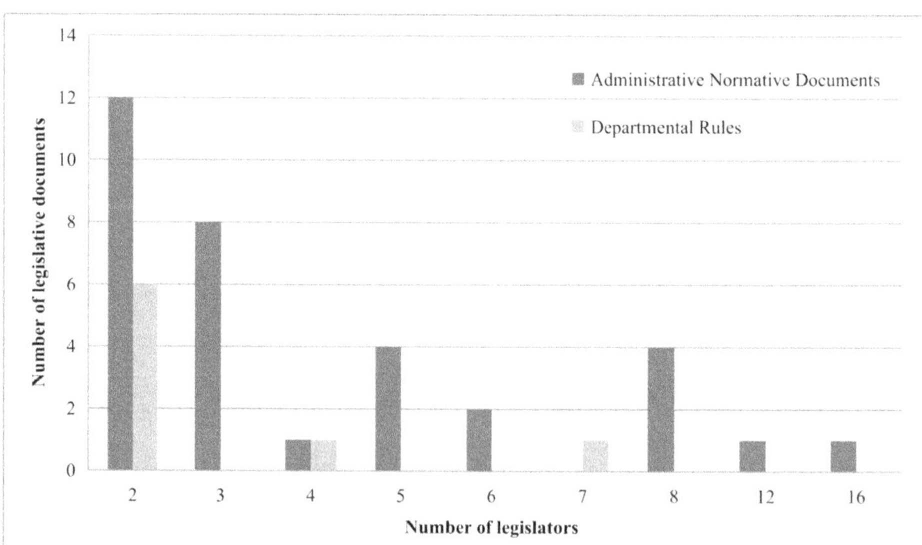

Level 1), the level of justice and administration (*hereinafter referred to as* Level 2), and the level of national stability and social development (*hereinafter referred to as* Level 3).

The results show that legislative purposes in Level 2 are mentioned the most (299 times), followed by those in Level 3 (189 times). Expressions for purposes in these two levels are quite diverse. Among them, 'to promote the development' in Level 3 appears the most (81 times); 'to enhance the regulation' and 'to regulate behaviors' in Level 2 are also dominant values (61 times and 60 times, respectively). This reflects the authorities' dual attitudes towards the Internet: promoting rapid economic development while maintaining political control. Meanwhile, although the purpose 'to protect lawful rights and interests' is frequently used in all kinds of sources of law (74 times), in general, purposes in Level 1 only appear for 82 times, fewer than one-half of those in the other two levels.

The results of value analysis show that China's Internet law presents a strong regulatory orientation. By developing a series of regulatory measures, it pursues to a comprehensive and efficient Internet regulatory model. To some extent, Internet law in China has become an instrument for the authorities to govern the cyberspace. The essence of choice among different values indicates an inclination between power of the authorities and individual rights and freedom. The expansion of power of the authorities in some sense means the withdrawal of individual rights and freedom. Traditional Chinese culture has a long history of advocating power of the authorities while ignoring or even debasing the pursuit of individual rights and freedom. Even though awareness of protecting individual rights and freedom has begun to increase since market economy system reforms, the traditional thought of great unity remains influential in practice (Wang, 2007, pp.227-230).

As Lü (2005) pointed out, contemporary China is undergoing social transformation. As a result, China neither solely positions power as its only standard – as traditional Chinese society did – nor positions rights and freedom as its only standard, as occurs in most fully modern societies. This is specifically manifested in the fact that, on the one hand, individual rights and freedom have been gradually recognized and protected by law; and on the other, that these rights and interests are subject to many restrictions, especially power of the authorities. Exercising the power to strengthen the regulation over individuals remains the main focus of legislative and administrative activities. Such a value orientation penetrates the entire process of Internet regulation as well.

Forming the Core

Traditional Political Authorities as the Core

As the research outcome summarized through legislative document analysis on regulators and their functions, Figure5 displays the framework of current central political institutions for Internet regulation. The legislative document analysis finds that, the CPC and the central government constitute the core of the Internet regulatory mechanism, where the CPC is the absolute leading core of Internet regulation.

The CPC as the Absolute Leading Core

The leadership of the CPC is said to be the most essential feature of socialism with Chinese characteristics. The CPC's leadership is based on its existing power in state governance and is embodied in aspects of political leadership, ideological leadership and organizational leadership. Firstly, as the most important aspect of the CPC's leadership, political leadership is reflected in their function to formulate relevant routes, principles and policies.

Secondly, ideological leadership is the significant premise and foundation of the CPC's leadership. To better regulate the Internet and to create a cyberspace that is compatible with Chinese socialist core value system, the Propaganda Department of the CPC Central Committee is in charge of the macro coordination and guidance of ideological work over the Internet, and then further strengthens its ideological control by taking over regulatory functions of press, publication and film from administrative organs. To some extent, the CPC's ideological control agrees with Foucault's exposition on power/knowledge.

Thirdly, organizational leadership is the means by which the CPC can achieve leadership. On the one hand, the CPC establishes relevant party organizations in the army, governmental organs, social organizations, enterprises and institutions, city communities and rural grassroots. Leaders in these organizations and institutions should be CPC members, thereby guaranteeing the CPC's leadership in all fields and at every level. On the other hand, a specialized agency, the Office of the Central Cyberspace Affairs Commission, has been set up under the Central Committee of the CPC to handle Internet-related issues. Actually, the Office of the Central Cyberspace Affairs Commission and the abovementioned Cyberspace Administration of China are the same agency with two brands, and are directly under the CPC Central Committee. In order to safeguard the security and interests of national cyberspace, the regulatory function of National Computer Network and Information Security Management Center has been transferred to the Office of the Central Cyberspace

Figure 5. Framework of traditional central authorities as Internet regulators in China (2018)

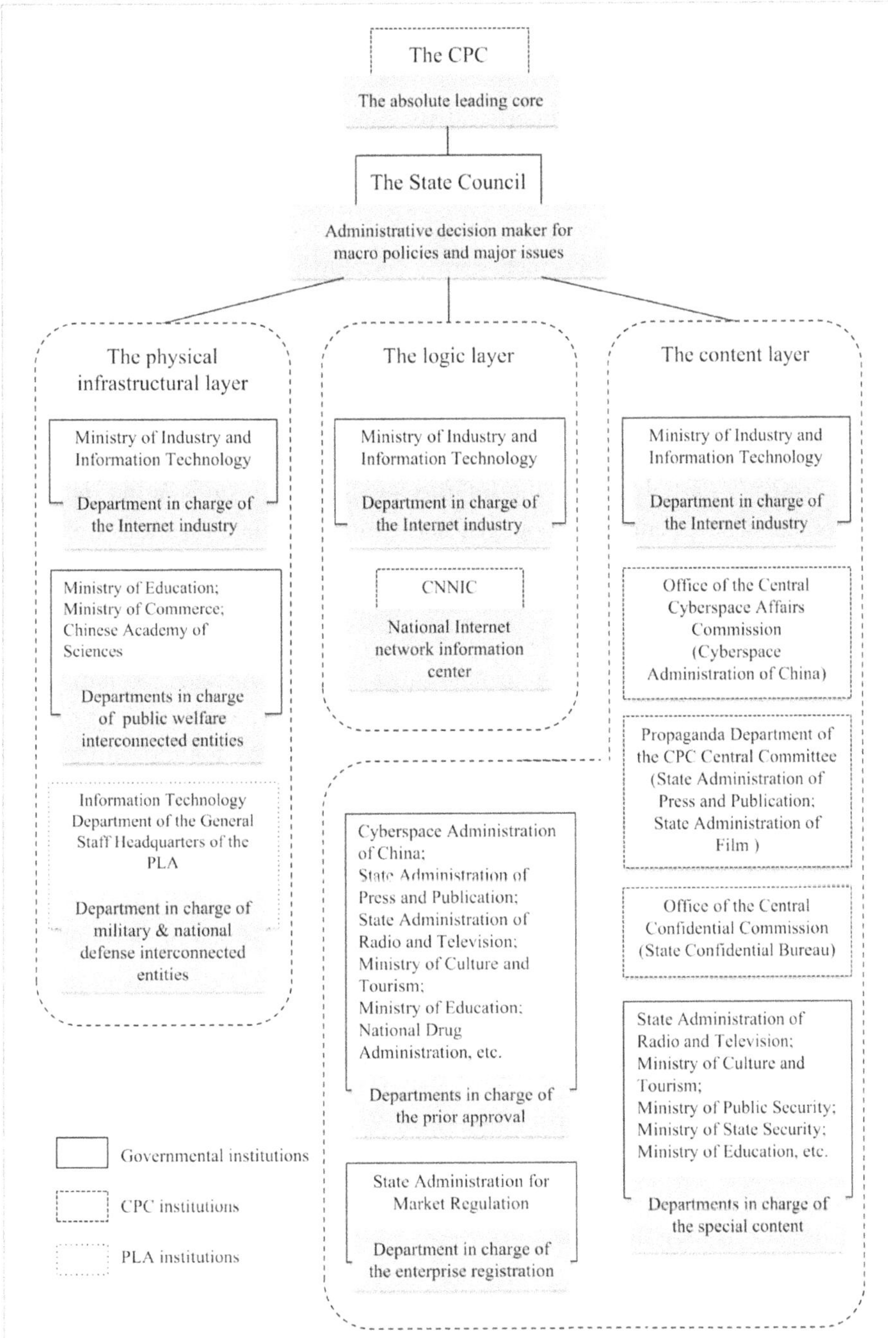

Affairs Commission. In this way, the CPC tightens its grip on critical power in the process of Internet regulation.

Administrative Authorities as Major Regulators

Led by the CPC, the State Council and its subordinate departments engage in the Internet-related administrative work. The State Council leads the national administration system. It is responsible for carrying out policies formulated by the CPC and Laws promulgated by the National People's Congress, and for dealing with major issues relevant to the Internet, such as establishing or authorizing relevant administrative bodies, approving important international telecommunications construction projects, and establishing new interconnected networks, etc.

Meanwhile, departments under the State Council are in charge of specific Internet-related affairs. According to statistics from legislative document analysis, by the end of the year 2016, there were at least 30 departments under the State Council that have directly participated in the Internet regulation. Besides, numerous other governmental departments have engaged in the Internet-related work as well. With the promotion of the Internet Plus policy, more governmental bodies are extending their traditional functions and authorities to the Internet, thus becoming involved in the process of Internet regulation.

The governmental bodies work around three layers of Internet regulation, i.e., the physical infrastructure layer, the logic layer and the content layer. The physical infrastructure layer focuses on the basic physical supports for the building and operation of the Internet, including but not limited to network construction, network interconnection and network access. The major regulator of the physical infrastructure layer of the Internet is the Ministry of Industry and Information Technology, who tends to view the Internet from a technical perspective and mainly uses technical and market means to achieve its regulation. It dominates the construction and development plan of the network infrastructure.

Specifically, the Ministry of Industry Information Technology is mainly in charge of overseeing for-profit networks, including the China Net, the Unicom Net, the China Mobile Net, the China Golden Bridge Network and others. In addition, the Ministry of Education and the Chinese Academy of Sciences are responsible for operating and regulating the China Education and Research Network and the China Science Technology Network. Meanwhile, the China International Economy Trade Internet was built in 2000 and is overseen by the Ministry of Commerce; yet, it is gradually being phased out. Other than these networks, the China Great Wall Network is used for military purposes and is under the control of the Information Technology Department of the General Staff Headquarters of the People's Liberation Army of China.

The logic layer focuses on critical codes and protocols that enable functions of physical infrastructure to be realized, in order to regulate the information transmission. The Ministry of Industry and Information Technology is also in charge of the logic layer of Internet regulation. It is responsible for the assignment, management and coordination of communication resources, including resources of communication network code number, domain name and IP address.

In terms of communication resources, the China Internet Network Information Center (*hereinafter referred to as* CNNIC) was authorized by law to manage national network fundamental resources (including the CN DNS, the Chinese DNS, and Internet addresses, etc.), and to provide relevant service. The CNNIC was established in 1997 as the national Internet network information center headed by the Chinese Academy of Sciences and guided by the Ministry of Industry and Information Technology, and is now an institution directly under the Office of the Central Cyberspace Affairs Commission. This shift indicates that it will play a greater role in both Internet regulation and Internet development.

The content layer focuses on various forms of information and its flow on the Internet. Compared to the physical infrastructure layer and the logic layer, regulators of the content layer are much more complicated. According to *the Work Program on the Coordination of Internet Website Administration* and other relevant legislative documents, regulators of the content layer can be further classified into (1) the department in charge of the Internet industry, (2) departments in charge of the special content, (3) departments in charge of the prior approval, and (4) the department in charge of the enterprise registration. A single authority might play several roles mentioned above.

The Ministry of Industry and Information Technology is the department in charge of the Internet industry, yet its power in the Internet content regulation is relatively limited. The main function for the Ministry of Industry and Information Technology in this regard is to regulate the Internet industry and Internet content services. This means that the Ministry of Industry and Information Technology does not regulate the Internet information directly. Instead, it cooperates with other departments to carry out Internet content regulation. This is because the Internet is not merely technically important, but also economically and politically significant, which attracts to the CPC and governmental agencies to strengthen the intervention. Consequently, the CPC and other governmental bodies also claim their legitimate powers to regulate the Internet based on national security and ideological control. In this situation, the Ministry of Industry and Information Technology has to share its power with the party's organs and other government bodies.

Under the uniform ideological leadership of the Propaganda Department of the CPC Central Committee, multiple departments take charge of the special content on the Internet within their departmental functions, including but are not limited to departments in charge of press and publishing, departments in charge of radio, film and television, departments in charge of culture, departments in charge of education, public security organs, national security organs, and departments in charge of the protection of state secrets, etc. These departments in charge of the special content shall examine the specific content within their respective functions, and shall provide examination opinions to the department in charge of the Internet industry for further action.

To better sort out relations among multiple authorities and further determine their divisions, the Cyberspace Administration of China was authorized by the State Council to take charge of Internet content regulation, and of supervision of law enforcement. As the general department in charge of Internet content regulation, the Cyberspace Administration of China is responsible for dealing with illegal or harmful information, and coordinating efforts to safeguard cybersecurity. This re-organization further consolidates the position of the Cyberspace Administration of China in the Internet regulatory mechanism.

There is a third category involving the administrative licensing function, i.e. departments in charge of the prior approval. The prior approval is an administrative procedure. It demands the applicants to go through administrative examination and approval to obtain necessary licenses required by Laws and Administrative Regulations before applying to the department in charge of the Internet industry for the Internet Content Provider (*hereinafter referred to as* ICP) license or before submitting documents to the department in charge of the Internet industry for the record. It focuses on regulating Internet content services. As the legislative document analysis reveals, departments in charge of the prior approval include departments in charge of the Internet content, departments in charge of press and publishing, departments in charge of education, departments in charge of drug, departments in charge of culture, and departments in charge of radio, film and television, etc. These departments should take charge of the examination and approval prior to the ICP application procedure, should regulate the Internet content services, and should provide annual examination opinions to the department in charge of the Internet industry.

Finally, based on administrative decisions made by the department in charge of the Internet industry, the department in charge of the enterprise registration handles the enterprise registration affairs for the for-profit ICPs. The State Administration for Market Regulation is the department in charge of the enterprise registration, and exercises functions of market regulation in a uniform manner.

The legislative document analysis also suggests that, in the process of Internet regulation, the authorities are encouraged to establish coordination and cooperation mechanisms in order to jointly address new issues and challenges brought about by the rapidly changing Internet, as well as to minimize conflicts of interests between departments and to improve regulatory efficiency.

Developing Technical Power Holders as the Sub-Core

Yet, the authorities are not always involved in trivial Internet-related matters; instead, they develop a number of ISPs – the emerging technical power – as the sub-core of the Internet panoptic-fortification model. ISPs include basic telecommunication business operators, Internet access service providers and Internet content service providers. The legislative document analysis finds that multiple measures and means have been taken by the authorities to regulate ISPs' behaviors, including the administrative licensing and filing systems, the daily supervision, penalties and rewards, and the blacklist system. Essentially, these measures are basic regulatory methods mentioned by Foucault, including recording, observation, normalizing judgment and disciplinary control. The comprehensive application of these measures is to ensure that ISPs are under the political control of the authorities.

The most critical measures taken by the authorities to control ISPs are the ubiquitous administrative licensing system and administrative filing system. The main function of the administrative licensing system is to concentrate the granting of industry access and behavioral qualifications in the hands of the authorities. Meanwhile, the administrative filing system is implemented as an important supplement to the administrative licensing system. Administrative filing refers to that citizens, legal persons or other entities submit documents regarding the conduct of specified activities to the administrative authorities for records. The main function of the administrative filing system rests in information collection and recording for further reference. It is helpful to conduct the real-time monitoring of ISPs.

Simply put, the authorities have an absolute control of the industry access for basic telecommunication business operators and Internet access service providers; this control further serves the establishment of the boundary in the Internet panoptic-fortification. Meanwhile, the authorities implement the administrative licensing system for for-profit Internet content service providers, and the administrative filing system for not-for-profit Internet content service providers, with the prior approval system and other licensing schemes effective in specified areas. Through the implementation of the administrative licensing system and administrative filing system, the authorities not only control the industry access and some behavioral qualifications, but also produce sufficient knowledge about ISPs, which in turn generates more power towards their better regulation. It can be argued that the combination of administrative licensing system and administrative filing system is the most effective tool the authorities have to control ISPs.

At the same time, the authorities carry out supervision in order to gain information about ISPs, and to produce corresponding knowledge for further judgments and decisions. There are several ways to obtain the knowledge, such as conducting annual reviews by ways of administrative licensing and filing. All types of ISPs are required to take the initiative to submit the annual report and other relevant information to the authorities for the annual review. Then, the authorities make decisions and provide comments on the review results within their respective functions and authorities. During this process, ISPs must pass all checks and reviews; otherwise they might fail to maintain their status and qualifications. In addition to the annual report, in individual cases, for example, when accidents happen, ISPs must report to the authorities for further handling or record according to Laws and Regulations.

Another common measure is to conduct inspections. An inspection can be either regular or irregular, and can be made via file review, on-the-spot inspection, cyber patrol, or spot check by telephone. Particularly, the following means can be taken to conduct inspections: asking the staff, consulting and copying relevant materials, retrieving and accessing electronic data, checking relevant facilities, making detections and identifications, and investigating relevant situations, etc. However, the inspection should not impede ISPs' normal productive and operative activities, and no fees should be charged. The whole inspection process should be recorded accurately and exhaustively, and the inspection results should usually be open to the public for mass supervision.

In addition, the monitoring platform offers a useful tool for the authorities to accomplish dynamic monitoring: using networks to govern networks has become a trend in Internet regulation. As the legislative documents reveal, in areas of domain name services, online taxi booking services, Internet publishing services, Internet mapping and geoinformation services, Internet cafe services and online transaction services, monitoring platforms have been built and put into operation. Relevant ISPs are required to access to the monitoring platforms to accept administrative supervision. Adopting technical means in Internet regulation is helpful for the improvement of databases and data quality, thus improving the foresight and effectiveness of supervision. This further facilitates information sharing and cooperation among multiple authorities towards achieving the networked regulation.

It is worth mentioning that the authorities have attempted to introduce the liaison system and to establish the working relationship with ISPs in the daily supervision. To be specific, both the authorities and ISPs must designate specified staff as contacts whose information should be updated in order to ensure the smooth flow of working channels. In some cases, a regular meeting system is established to strengthen communication between the authorities and ISPs, and to discuss and to solve outstanding problems in a direct way. The liaison system is beneficial for the authorities to strengthen the regulation of ISPs and to receive intelligence more quickly and directly.

When the information is collected, files and databases are established and updated correspondingly. These materials, together with other relevant information, are subject to various kinds of analysis. New knowledge is thereby generated for further actions. At the macro level, such knowledge constitutes the foundation for the authorities to exercise their power by making policies, planning, formulating administrative documents and developing criteria and catalogues. At the micro level, such knowledge enables the authorities to further evaluate and classify ISPs, and to take corresponding measures. From the Foucauldian perspective, these measures contain not only punishment stipulated by law, but also a mix of micro-penalties and rewards deployed by discipline.

On the one hand, the authorities motivate ISPs to act in accordance with their intentions in multiple, inter-related ways to achieve common goals. First, they encourage and support ISPs to engage in certain activities by providing preferential policies and facilitated measures. Second, the authorities guide ISPs' certain actions by ways of providing technical guidance, putting forward proposals of administrative guidance, strengthening training and education, and implementing relevant systems and measures. Third, the authorities conduct the ideological guidance to lead ISPs and others to conduct in the way the authorities prefer. Fourth, the authorities commend and reward those ISPs and their staff who have made great contributions to Internet regulation and industry development.

On the other hand, the authorities take multiple actions to deal with ISPs' illegal or irregular activities. Holding an interview is a measure taken by the authorities in the event of security risks, safety accidents or irregular acts. During the interview with the representative of a legal person and/or the principal officer of ISPs in accordance with legal authority and procedures, the authorities usually give a warning, point out problems and command ISPs to correct them. Meanwhile, backed by the coercive force of the state, the authorities can pursue corresponding legal liabilities from ISPs that break Laws, Regulations and Rules in forms of administrative penalties or criminal punishments.

Based on the administrative licensing and filing system, the daily supervision, and the corresponding rewards and penalties, the authorities gradually develop files of ISPs, which provide necessary knowledge for the authorities to strengthen the regulation of ISPs. The blacklist system is a typical measure in this regard. When an ISP engages in any serious illegal and/or irregular practices, the authorities will handle them and keep corresponding records; if necessary, the ISP will be blacklisted. Once placed on a warning list or blacklist, the ISP will be restricted or prohibited from participating in some activities for a certain period. In principle, such a record should not be removed from the blacklist even after the said period. Meanwhile, the blacklist is shared among the authorities. In order to prevent the resurgence of illegal websites and their hosts through alternative means, joint disciplinary action is recommended, which would restrict the blacklisted ISPs everywhere, regardless of the domain name resolution service, the Internet access service or the Internet content service. Essentially, the blacklist system is a comprehensive application of Foucauldian observation, recording, classification and discipline. By temporarily removing the disobedient ISPs from the normal operation of the Internet, it is expected to train these ISPs to behave in a normal and acceptable way.

Defining the Boundary

In the Internet panoptic-fortification model, there is a boundary around the core, which divides the cyberspace into the inside and the outside. This is significant because the inside comprises an independent space, thus defining the scope of regulation. Although the Internet has been designed in the form of network with the possibility of unlimited expansion, regulating the Internet is subject to realistic boundary constraints. In this chapter, this boundary is further defined by the political territory and supported by the technical barrier.

Political Territory

Political territory represents the natural boundary for Internet panoptic-fortification. China always adheres to the sovereignty principle, which emphasizes the state's independent role in dealing with both foreign and domestic affairs. The sovereignty principle is further extended to the cyberspace, and constitutes the foundation of the cyberspace sovereignty principle. Actually, the cyberspace sovereignty principle has been implemented in long-term practices in China, as Internet regulation has been considered to be a part of state regulation. The cyberspace sovereignty has also been expressly written into the *National Security Law* (promulgated by the Standing Committee of the National People's Congress on July 1, 2015) and the *Cybersecurity Law* (promulgated by the Standing Committee of the National People's Congress on November 7, 2016). The cyberspace sovereignty principle has been reflected in the physical infrastructure layer, the logic layer and the content layer.

First, the cyberspace sovereignty principle is reflected in the Internet infrastructure construction and operation. The state possesses the power to make overall plans for the construction layout and resource utilization for international networking. Strict licensing administration is implemented for the construction and operation of international telecommunication facilities. If a construction project involves foreign capital, it should be reported for multiple approvals according to Laws and Regulations. For enterprises that operate basic telecommunications business, state-owned shares should not be less than 51%. For enterprises that operate value-added telecommunications business, the proportion of foreign investment should not exceed 50%. Meanwhile, international communications gateway exchanges should be established and maintained by wholly state-owned telecommunications service providers, and are subject to unified regulation.

Moreover, the state claims its ownership of logic resources and participates in relevant international affairs in its own name. For example, the Ministry of Industry and Information Technology and its authorized institution represent the state to apply to international organizations for code number resources. These allocated code number resources are owned by the state. Based on the ownership, the state further assigns and charges for the use of the code number resources, which guarantees the state's effective control over scarce logic resources. Similarly, the state officially registers with the Internet Network Information Center and operates the top-level domain name CN. Under CN, a hierarchical structure is used to set up domain names at all levels. It is clear that the state both possesses and dominates important logic resources, which in turn consolidates its strong position in Internet regulation.

The cyberspace sovereignty principle is also reflected in the content layer of Internet regulation. According to the legislative document analysis, in the following categories, foreign investment is absolutely prohibited: Internet audio-visual programme services, Internet news information services, online publishing services, online games and Internet mapping services. All these categories directly concern ideological control or national security, thus excluding foreign capital interventions.

In fields like Internet audio-visual programme services, wholly state-owned enterprises or state-controlled enterprises are further required. However, as a trend, the state special management share system has been promoted and implemented in online publishing enterprises and some other cultural and media enterprises since 2015 (Jin, 2016; Wu, 2018). Special management share refers to a kind of classified shares, each share of which has veto voting power or special governance power (Ip, Bailey, & Gong, 2016). On the one hand, it has been gradually recognized that wholly state-owned or state-controlled systems might not be well-suited to the establishment of a modern enterprise system or the improvement of corporate governance structure; thus, shareholding system reform has been introduced to convert state-owned or state-controlled enterprises into shareholding corporations. But, on the other hand, the culture and media industries are closely related to ideological control. Facing diversified shareholders, the question of how to insist on the correct ideological direction becomes a great challenge. The introduction of the special management share system in the culture and media industries offers a possible solution for maintaining enterprise vitality while preserving ideological control.

Another measure for maintaining cyberspace sovereignty and cybersecurity is to demand that servers and storage devices in key areas be stored within the territory of China (not including Hong Kong, Macao and Taiwan). As stated by law, these key areas include but are not limited to online publishing services, Internet drug transaction services, online lending services, Internet mapping services, online taxi booking services, data centers and cloud computing service platforms for use by the Party and government institutions, as well as other critical information services. Unless otherwise provided by Laws or Regulations, key information and data collected and produced should not be allowed to provide overseas.

Activities involving foreign factors, such as introducing overseas TV dramas, overseas maps, imported online games and other overseas products, news information published by overseas news media and Internet sites, and legal effects of overseas electronic signature authentication certificates, are also closely monitored. When there is any illegal information from outside China, the authorities have the legitimate power to take technical and other necessary measures to interrupt the transmission. This is analogous to performing the function of gatekeepers of the panoptic-fortification in order to defend against foreign attacks.

Technical Barrier

To adhere to the cyberspace sovereignty principle, the state provides substantial technical support for building the panoptic-fortification. State technical support enables connections between domestic networks and the international network, yet such connections are conditional and subject to political control.

According to law, Internet access in China is regulated by level – that is, the level of interconnected entities, the level of access entities, and the user level. Figure 6 offers a simple illustration of the current Internet access regulatory system in China. Specifically, users' computers, computer information networks and other communication terminals must access the Internet through access networks. Access networks refer to the computer information networks that connect to the international network through interconnected networks. Access networks can be connected at multiple levels. Either the leased circuit or the public switched telecommunications network can be provided for entering the access network.

Next, these access networks should be connected to the Internet through interconnected networks. Interconnected networks are computer information networks that access the Internet directly. Access network entities must obtain international networking licenses or administrative approval before accessing interconnected networks for international networking. Meanwhile, computer information networks of enterprises and other computer information networks that are connected to international networks via the leased circuit should be for internal use only.

Finally, all computer information networks within the territory of China should use the international networking exchange gateway channel provided by the public

Figure 6. Model of Internet access regulatory system in China

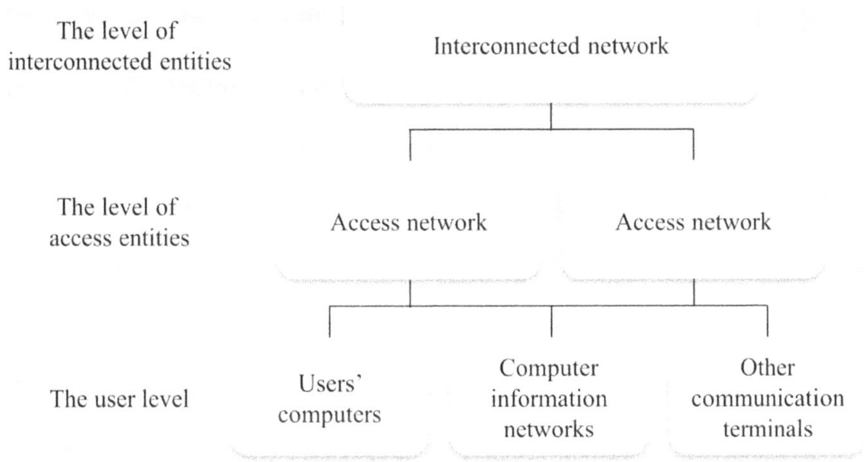

telecommunications network to access the Internet. No other information channels are allowed for international networking.

To better implement the Internet access administrative mechanism and further regulate the Internet access service market, the Ministry of Industry and Information Technology issued the *Notice on Cleaning up and Regulating the Internet Access Service Market* on January 17, 2017. It aims to regulate unauthorized Internet access services, including illegally providing international private leased circuit services or virtual private network services. Consequently, a large number of Internet users in China who once relied on these unauthorized Internet connection services to bypass the barrier have to remain inside the panoptic-fortification. However, foreign trade enterprises, transnational enterprises and other institutions and organizations are still able to apply for leased circuits to qualified basic telecommunications business operators, in order to use the Internet to connect with their home office and to operate the international business in a lawful manner (Liu & Sun, 2017; Sun & Shi, 2017).

The structure of Internet access in China reflects a strong hierarchy. By firmly controlling the international networking exchange gateway channel, the authorities actually control the only legitimate thoroughfare for accessing the Internet. On this basis, the authorities further demand ISPs to strengthen the management of networks and users. In this way, the authorities are able to obtain knowledge from Internet access at all levels comprehensively and dynamically, which helps them to exercise powers for daily regulation as well as for incident processing.

Establishing Unidirectional Links

The establishment of the boundary enables the core to confirm the fundamental jurisdiction. To regulate the booming Internet use in China, the core adopts comprehensive measures to exercise its power over the Internet. Among them, the network real-name system and the Internet-surfing record backup system are typical means for managing such a huge population and regulating each individual Internet user.

The Network Real-Name System

The network real-name system is a regulatory tool by which the virtual identities of Internet users could correspond to their real identities. Anonymity is one of the original features of the Internet. Regarding the Internet as a new kind of public sphere, anonymity first refers to freedom from identification, and then further refers to freedom from surveillance (Westin, 1967), Yet, the real-name system is designed to lift veils of anonymity in cyberspace.

In the current mechanism, ISPs are authorized to manage the personal information of Internet users directly. By requiring users to submit relevant information or make relevant agreements before using Internet services, ISPs take the initiative to obtain users' basic identity information and to turn this information into ISPs' knowledge, which in turns strengthens their power and facilitates more effective management. Meanwhile, ISPs have the responsibility to report relevant identity information to the authorities according to law or on demand. As a result, the authorities also share such knowledge to achieve regulation over the entire population as well as each individual user.

The currently valid legislative documents concerning the network real-name system can be traced to the year 1997. In *Interim Provisions on the Management of International Networking of Computer Information Networks* (promulgated by Ministry of Public Security on December 16, 1997, and revised on January 8, 2011), it is clearly stated that when applying for Internet access, users should submit a user record form. Meanwhile, the interconnected entities, Internet access service providers and other relevant institutions should register those who are authorized to publish information, as well as those who use BBS services.

Since then, legislative documents have been crafted in a planned and systematic way. At the initial stage, focus was placed on network access. Gradually, an increasing number of legislative documents have been promulgated to promote the network real-name system in the content layer. In addition to identity certificates, some legislative documents even require additional contact information. Later, several Internet Laws definitely require users to provide personal information when applying for telecommunications services and Internet services. Only when their real identities are provided and authenticated can Internet users register accounts and use Internet services.

'Compulsory to register with real identity, voluntary to use real identity online' is the basic principle of the network real-name system. Apparently, it allows Internet users to enjoy a certain degree of privacy. Yet in essence, it enables the authorities and ISPs to firmly obtain key information about personal identities. As the implementers of the network real-name system, ISPs should take reasonable and feasible measures to verify the authenticity of users' identity information, to properly preserve relevant information and to keep it updated. Meanwhile, when demanded by the authorities according to law, ISPs have the responsibility to provide relevant personal information for the regulatory purpose.

Furthermore, the state vigorously promotes the cyberspace trustworthy identity strategy. On the one hand, the state supports the research and development of secure and convenient electronic identity authentication technologies, which leaves little room for identity fraud. On the other hand, the state promotes mutual recognition among different electronic identity authentication technologies, which benefits the unified management of related information so as to better accomplish networked regulation.

The Internet-Surfing Record Backup System

While the network real-name system challenges Internet anonymity by investigating users' identities, surveillance conducted via the concomitant Internet-surfing record backup system destroys Internet anonymity completely.

The Internet-surfing record backup system requires ISPs to preserve the Internet-surfing records for a certain period as stipulated by law. According to law, Internet access service providers should record the following information of Internet users: user accounts, login and logout times, corresponding IP addresses, Internet addresses or domain names, and phone numbers. For Internet content service providers, beyond the abovementioned items, they should also record user logs, including users' online activities, the information content provided, publication date and time, sources (e.g., IP addresses and email addresses), and Internet addresses or domain names. These records and backups should be preserved, accurately and safely, for 60 days or more, and should bc provided on demand by the authorities according to law.

Based on daily real-time surveillance, ISPs further develop the hierarchical management system and the blacklist management system. The former attempts to classify users according to their credit ratings and daily behaviours, and to provide corresponding services and management. The latter emphasizes disciplinary functions and disposes users who violate laws or agreements. Both measures divide the user population into different categories, label these categories from good to bad, and take corresponding measures targeted at individual users. In this way, management efficiency has been greatly improved.

In general, the comprehensive implementation of the network real-name system and the Internet-surfing record backup system is an overall trend in China. In the Internet panoptic-fortification model, the network real-name system plays an important role in linking the core and each individual user within the boundary, and offers an institutional foundation for the implementation of other measures. On this basis, the Internet-surfing record backup system serves as a surveillance tool for the core to monitor the overall situation on the Internet as well as online behaviours of each individual Internet user.

The combination of these measures offers a considerable body of knowledge about who users are, where they are, and what they do. To some extent, the design of these systems follows the tradition of utilitarianism to establish an effective and efficient regulatory model, within which the regulated can be easily recognized and traced. In addition, the chilling effect it brings would probably result in the normalization of users' online behaviours and the enhancement of their self-discipline. In this sense, it coincides with Foucault's theory of governmentality, which is concerned with modern forms of institutional power aimed at achieving political ends, as well as with the use of that power to produce the ideal citizen for that form of society (Gorman, 2012).

Encouraging the Mass Supervision

In addition to tight censorship from both the authorities and ISPs, the whole society is encouraged to participate in Internet regulation to create a ubiquitous surveillance network. Mass supervision in the Internet regulatory mechanism is embodied in the bottom-up supervision aiming at the core, as well as in the peer monitoring among the masses.

Stipulate by law, both the authorities and ISPs have responsibilities to place themselves under mass supervision. Furthermore, they should announce channels for complaints and reports in a prominent manner, accept complaints and reports through the Internet, over telephone, and in other ways, and deal with accepted complaints and reports in a timely fashion within the specified time limits. The authorities also award those who have made significant contributions to reporting Internet-related illegal and irregular actions in order to encourage mass supervision, which indicates the authorities' intention to make each Internet user an informant.

Actually, the state mobilizes social forces to participate in Internet regulation. Nine of the collected legislative documents expressly mention mobilizing social forces. Social forces refer to citizens, legal persons and other organizations, including but not limited to Internet users, families, schools, communities, media and social organizations. In fact, each person is born into a network society insofar as family, affiliation and community exert a great influence over one's behaviours. These offline influences are further applied to Internet regulation, and play unique roles.

In the Internet panoptic-fortification model, surveillance is conducted everywhere at all times. Despite no compartments having been designed to isolate individual users as in the original panopticon model, in the strict and ubiquitous surveillance environment, Internet users tend to perform as though they are being observed. Surveillance in the Internet era is not only achieved by the centralized authorities and ISPs, but also by the masses in the immediate environment. Even when channels and opportunities are open to communication, users cannot be certain of the security and confidentiality of such communication. Are they talking to an informant? Can informants access the communication? Will the communication bring adverse consequences? In fact, the more they use the Internet to communicate, the more information they leave behind, and thus the more easily they risk substantial surveillance. Thus, the non-isolated design of the Internet panoptic-fortification model, an innovation that distinguishes the Internet panoptic-fortification from the traditional panopticon that is both closed and isolated, is still able to fully achieve the deterrent effect.

CONCLUSION

This chapter follows Foucault's theory of governmentality to develop the metaphor of the panopticon to propose a conceptual framework for China's Internet regulatory mechanism, namely Internet panoptic-fortification. The Internet panoptic-fortification is in essence a fortification that emphases sovereign power over certain space. By the establishment of the Internet access control mechanism and the performance of gatekeepers, information and communication from outside of mainland China are monitored and censored; only selective information distribution and communication between mainland China and overseas cyberspace is allowed. Meanwhile, when an emergency occurs, controlled gateway channels would be closed and communication within network would be interrupted at multiple levels according to Law for security reasons. Inside the fortification, the panoptic approach is followed to conduct the internal control, combining both hierarchical regulation and horizontal monitoring, with both online and offline surveillance conducted. By constant recording, observation and training, individual Internet users are trained to be self-disciplined and the whole population of Internet users tends to be satisfied with the status quo, which guarantee the steady operation of the Internet regulatory mechanism. Consequently, the panoptic design in the Internet fortification contributes to the economic and efficient regulation, as it maximizes the regulatory effects at the minimum cost of force.

This model reflects important aspects of Foucault's account of governmentality, incorporating both centralized power and diffuse micro-power. Contemporary Internet law in China not only defines powers, but also offers direction in their exercise. To some extent, China's Internet law has become an instrument of discipline, the key feature of the modern power. Through normalization, behaviors that deviate from the idealized norms of conduct are recognized for further processing, which encourages people to behave in normal, acceptable ways. The comprehensive application of management measures and the tools provided by law guarantees control over the whole population while promoting individual Internet user's self-discipline. In this sense, the regulatory effect of the Internet panoptic-fortification constructed by law is significant.

FUTURE RESEARCH DIRECTIONS

The Internet regulatory model generated in this chapter is remains normative and calls for more empirical research. Further research can be conducted to investigate the implementation of the existing Internet law in practices, and to obtain more empirical evidences to improve the theoretical framework of Internet regulatory mechanism in China. Another important issue to address concerns the principle of cyberspace sovereignty. For historical and political reasons, within the 'One Country Two Systems' policy, China's Internet regulatory mechanism is currently not applicable to Hong Kong, Macau and Taiwan. However, it has been suggested that the Chinese authorities have the ambition to extend their cyberspace sovereignty and regulatory practices to Hong Kong, which lies outside the boundary of the Internet panoptic-fortification (Tsui, 2015). Meanwhile, changes in the political situation of these regions might also impact the status quo of their separate Internet regulatory mechanisms. Whether and how the Chinese authorities extend control over cyberspace awaits future research. Furthermore, it is necessary to examine China's response to the global Internet governance practices, and to study how Chinese wisdoms are used to harmonize different Internet governance ideas and paths in the global context, which would be beneficial for both theoretical and practical purposes.

ACKNOWLEDGMENT

This chapter is based on the author's PhD thesis under the supervision of Professor LEE Alice Yuet Lin.

REFERENCES

Allmer, T. (2010). *Critical Internet surveillance studies and economic surveillance*. Retrieved from http://www.sns3.uti.at/wp-content/uploads/2010/10/The-Internet-Surveillance-Research-Paper-Series-4-Thomas-Allmer-Critical-Internet-Surveillance-Studies-and-Economic-Surveillance.pdf

Austin, G. (2014). *Cyber policy in China*. Cambridge: Polity Press.

Bai, J. (2013, August 12). *Cong 'hulianwang xinxi guwu huanli banfa (xiuding caoan)' kan zhongguo hulianwang guanzhi qushi [Research on the trend of Internet regulation in China from the revised draft of Administrative Measures for Internet Content Services]*. Retrieved from http://gbcode.rthk.org.hk/TuniS/rthk.hk/mediadigest/20130812_76_123013.html

Benkler, Y. (2000). From consumers to users: Shifting the deeper structures of regulation towards sustainable commons and user access. *Federal Communications Law Journal*, *52*(3), 561.

Bentham, J. (1791). *Panopticon or the inspection house*. London, UK: T. Payne.

Boyle, J. (1997). Foucault in cyberspace: Surveillance, sovereignty, and hard-wired censors. *Social Science Electronic Publishing*, *66*(1), 177–205.

Cattaruzza, A., Danet, D., Taillat, S., & Laudrain, A. (2016). Sovereignty in cyberspace: Balkanization or democratization. In *Proceedings of 2016 International Conference on Cyber Conflict (CyCon U.S.)*. Washington, DC: IEEE. 10.1109/CYCONUS.2016.7836628

Clark, D. D. (1992). *A cloudy crystal ball: Visions of the future*. Paper presented at the 24th Meeting of the Internet Engineering Task Force, Cambridge, UK.

Delmas, R. (2007). The Internet: New principles of political right, new social contract. In P. Goujon, S. Lavelle, P. Duquenoy, K. Kimppa, & V. Laurent (Eds.), *The information society: Innovation, legitimacy, ethics and democracy in honor of Professor Jacques Berleur s.j* (pp. 147–152). Boston, MA: Springer. doi:10.1007/978-0-387-72381-5_14

Drake, W. (2014). *The global Internet governance ecosystem*. Paper presented at European Summer School on Internet Governance. Meissen.

Ehrlich, E. (2014). *A brief history of Internet regulation*. Retrieved from http://www.progressivepolicy.org/wp-content/uploads/2014/03/2014.03-Ehrlich_A-Brief-History-of-Internet-Regulation.pdf

Foucault, M. (1978). *Discipline and punish: The birth of the prison* (A. Sheridan, Trans.). New York: Pantheon Books. (Original work published 1975)

Gorman, P. (2012). *Human flesh search: The governmentality of mass surveillance in China* (Unpublished master's thesis). Carleton University, Canada.

Hall, M. A., & Wright, R. F. (2008). Systematic content analysis of judicial opinions. *California Law Review*, *96*(1), 63–122.

Hong, S. (2014). *Beyond cyber-sovereignty: China's internet policy toward global internet governance (1994-2013)*. Paper presented at the International Communication Association 64th Annual Conference, Seattle, WA.

Hu, H. L. (2011). The political economy of governing ISPs in China: Perspectives of net neutrality and vertical integration. *The China Quarterly*, *207*, 523–540. doi:10.1017/S0305741011000634

Hu, Y. (2008). *The rising cacophony: Personal expression and public discussion in the Internet age*. Guilin: Guangxi Normal University Press.

Ip, K., Bailey, D., & Gong, G. (2016, April 5). *SARPPFT Clarifies New Online Publishing Regulations*. Retrieved from https://www.lexology.com/library/detail.aspx?g=a3572276-5cdd-46bc-8421-c9b0edb2a474

Jiang, M. (2010). Authoritarian informationalism: China's approach to Internet sovereignty. *SAIS Review (Paul H. Nitze School of Advanced International Studies)*, *30*(2), 71–89.

Jiang, M. (2013). *Road to neo-authoritarianism? A 25-year review of China's Internet policies*. Paper presented at the 2013 International Communication Association Annual Conference, London, UK.

Jin, X. (2016). Woguo chuanmei lingyu youxiao tuijin teshu guanligu zhidu de sikao [Reflections on the effective promotion of special management share system in China's media sector]. *China Development Observation*, *21*, 51–54.

Lessig, L. (1999). *Code and other laws of cyberspace*. New York: Basic Books.

Li, Y. (2009). *Our great firewall: Expression and governance in the era of the Internet*. Guilin: Guangxi Normal University Press.

Lin, Z. (2010). Lun hulianwang guanli he maoyi bilei [On Internet management and trade barriers]. *China Communication Trade*, *12*, 50–52.

Liu, B. (2007). *The theory research about research of Internet's contents in China* (Unpublished doctoral dissertation). Beijing University of Posts and Telecommunications, Beijing.

Liu, R., & Sun, B. (2017, January 24). *Gongxinbu huiying wangmin VPN deng shiyong wenti [MIIT responded to the VPN issue and other issues]*. Retrieved from http://finance.people.com.cn/n1/2017/0124/c1004-29047306.html

Lü, Y. (2005). Privacy and data privacy issues in contemporary China. *Ethics and Information Technology*, *7*(1), 7–15. doi:10.100710676-005-0456-y

Lyon, D. (1994). *The electronic eye: the rise of surveillance society*. Cambridge, UK: Polity Press.

Mehta, M. D., & Darier, E. (1998). Virtual control and disciplining on the Internet: Electronic governmentality in the new wired world. *The Information Society*, *14*(2), 107–116. doi:10.1080/019722498128917

Palfrey, J. G. (2010). Four Phases of Internet Regulation. *Social Research*, *77*(3). Retrieved from https://papers.ssrn.com/sol3/papers.cfm?abstract_id=1658191

Poster, M. (1995). *The second media age*. Cambridge, UK: Polity.

Solum, L. B. (2009). Models of Internet governance. In L. A. Bygrave, & J. Bing (Eds.), *Internet governance: Infrastructure and institutions* (pp. 48–91). Oxford, UK: Oxford University Press. doi:10.1093/acprof:oso/9780199561131.003.0003

State Council Information Office of China. (2010, June 8). *The Internet in China*. Retrieved from http://www.china.org.cn/government/whitepaper/node_7093508.htm

Sun, Q., & Shi, F. (2017, February 6). *Zhishengxia menfeng de VPN hequ hecong [Where will the remaining VPN go]*. Retrieved from http://www.bbtnews.com.cn/2017/0206/180250.shtml

Tsui, L. (2015). The coming colonization of Hong Kong cyberspace: Government responses to the use of new technologies by the umbrella movement. *Chinese Journal of Communication*, *8*(4), 1–9. doi:10.1080/17544750.2015.1058834

van Dijk, J. A. (2012). *The network society* (3rd ed.). London, UK: Sage.

Wacker, G. (2003). The Internet and censorship in China. In C. R. Hughes, & G. Wacker (Eds.), *China and the Internet: Politics of the digital leap forward* (pp. 58–82). London, UK: Routledge.

Walton, G. (2001). *China's Golden Shield: Corporations and the development of surveillance technology in China*. Canada: Rights & Democracy.

Wang, M., & Hu, Y. (2016). Zhongguo hulianwang zhili de lishi yanbian [The historical evolution of Internet governance in China]. *Modern Communication, 4*, 127–133.

Wang, X. (2007). *On the constitutional protection of the right of privacy*. Beijing, China: Social Sciences Academic Press.

Westin, A. F. (1967). *Privacy and freedom*. New York: Atheneum.

Wu, G. (2018). On nature of the state special management share. *Law Science Magazine, 39*(1), 47–53.

Wu, T. (2006). The world trade law of censorship and Internet filtering. *Chicago Journal of International Law, 7*(1), 263–287.

Yan, M. N. (2015). The impact of new media on freedom of expression in China and the regulatory responses. In P. Molnár (Ed.), *Free speech and censorship around the globe* (pp. 381–407). Budapest, Hungary: Central European University Press.

Zheng, Y. (2014). *Technological empowerment: The Internet, state, and society in China* (D. Qiu, Trans.). Beijing, China: The Oriental Press. (Original work published 2008)

Zuboff, S. (1988). *In the age of the smart machine: The future of work and power*. New York: Basic Books.

KEY TERMS AND DEFINITIONS

Cyber Patrol: Inspection on ISPs and their activities conducted by the law enforcement officials using search engines, online browsing and other technical means.

Governmentality: The way in which the state exercises its power to control the population as a whole, while also governing individuals by guiding, shaping and channelling their conduct.

Internet Plus: The in-depth integration of Internet innovation with various economic and social fields, in order to promote the technological advance, to improve efficiency, and to drive organizational change, thus to enhance the creativity and productivity of the real economy, and finally to generate a new form for economic and social development that recognizes the Internet as infrastructure and innovation element in a broader way.

Legal Coding: The process used to create an index, and also a database, to extract keyword data systematically from legislative documents for further analysis.

Panopticon: The model of prison, which was conceived by Jeremy Bentham, adopts a one-way, hub-and-spoke structure, with unidirectional links to its ends.

The Authorities: The central and state organs in charge of Internet-related affairs.

The Network Real-Name System: A regulatory tool by which the virtual identities of Internet users could correspond to their real identities.

Chapter 10
Social Media as Disruptive Technologies in an Era of Fake News:
Examining the Efficacy of Social Media in the Shaping of the Political Landscape in Africa

Osée Kamga
InSitu Services Linguistiques, Canada

ABSTRACT

Since the Arab Spring (2010-2012), there has been a growing interest in the transformative power of social media, with a number of studies looking at its power to mobilize hitherto silent majority of the people, its ability to spread information at a lightning speed or to shape government-citizen relationship. This chapter is part of that trend, and it focuses specifically on Sub-Saharan Africa. It borrows Christensen's concept of "disruptive technologies" and uses it as a framework to analyze the processes of social media appropriation in the political field in that part of the continent. The chapter articulates ways in which social media are transforming the political landscape in the region and wonders about the outcome of these processes in the backdrop of the emerging and spreading of fake news.

DOI: 10.4018/978-1-7998-1791-8.ch010

Copyright © 2020, IGI Global. Copying or distributing in print or electronic forms without written permission of IGI Global is prohibited.

INTRODUCTION

There is a consensus that social media played an essential role in the uprisings that started in December 2010, led to the overthrown of dictators in the Arab world and shook up many autocratic regimes in the world (Rezaei and Cohen, 2012). Since then, thanks to growing mobile penetration and improved connectivity, social media have gained a prominent place in the political arena in sub-Saharan Africa. Messages, documents, photos and videos shared on these platforms reach the world at the speed of light, thus making them an instrument of choice for political activism and mobilization. Everywhere on the continent, Africans, especially the younger generation, are using social media to push for change. As they facilitate citizens' involvement in political debate, as well as the public's push for more transparency in the political process, social media have been perceived as a threat by some governments (Dwyer and Molony, 2019). For instance, in March 2018, the Republic of Chad banned social media platforms including Facebook and Twitter (The ban was lifted in 16 months later). Adegoke (2017) rightfully notes that "social media has been so influential and consequential in the lives of young Africans over the last five years that some governments now target social media specifically for blockages around elections and political protests". The general assumption is that "the use of social media tools has high potential for purposes of bringing about political and social change throughout the continent as use thereof enhances opportunities for political participation and opens new spaces for active citizenship" (Bohler-Muller and van der Merwe, 2011: 1). In short, a number of scholars continue to portray the positivity of social media for effective governance on the continent.

There are, however, other scholars who have expressed some caution about the positive impact of social media on the continent. To these scholars, there are a number of problems associated with the use of social media, which may impact on the overall development of the continent. In short, to these scholars, social media on the continent has not been all that positive. For instance, Cox et al. (2019) have noted that while social media has contributed to "economic development and encouraged political engagement", it has "also led to a number of less desirable impacts". Part of these fewer desirable impacts has been attributed to the emergence and spreading of fake news, with serious consequences on people perceive and understand things. For instance, in a the heat of the 2018 presidential campaign in Cameroun, a video appeared on Facebook showing a group of soldiers savagely beating up a boy who appeared to be not older than 10 years, with the caption: "That's how our soldiers treat a boy just because he said Kamto president". Although, there were repression against supporters of Kamto, the leader of the main opposition party in the country, researching the video with just few mouse clicks, showed that not only was the video an old clip (recorded in 1995), but also that event took place, not in Cameroun but in

Conakry, the capital city of the Republic of Guinea. Yet, the discussions following the post were largely made of angry interventions, vilifying the Cameroonian government. This example illustrates the double standard observed in how Africans are using social media.

The objective of this chapter is therefore to examine the transformative power of social media in the political field in Sub-Saharan Africa within the framework of disruptive technologies. We consider social media as 'disruptive' in that it challenges and modifies the existing norms, institutional behaviours, and practices of society (Santra et al. 2019). We believe that social media holds the potential for liberating the political field from the grip of authoritarian regimes, which had been the hallmark of governance since independence from colonial rule in the early 1960s. In spite of this, how can that potential be translated into reality? Can social media change in a significant way how the political game plays out on the continent? What are some of the challenges facing the productive appropriation of social media in the political arena in the region? With these questions, our position is far from the demiurgic apprehension of technology, which characterizes techno-determinist approaches. In other words, we do not believe that a given technology by itself can generate the desired social, political or economic change. Instead, our position is that such changes proceed from a number of processes in which technology plays an important role. The study thus explores this further through the glass of political mobilization, transparency, and the electoral process.

Although a number of studies continue to be conducted on the impact of social media in Sub-Saharan Africa, none in our knowledge has been undertaken within the framework of disruptive technologies. Such framework is greatly useful to identify what habits are actually fading away due to social media and what new ones are being introduced and institutionalized. This is necessary since disruptive technologies supersede "an older process, product, or habit. It usually has superior attributes that are immediately obvious, at least to early adopters" (Smith, 2019). The framework helps to understand how profound in nature and in substance observable changes are. In a nutshell, are these changes "multi-dimensional, multi-level, qualitative, discontinuous, radical organizational change involving a paradigmatic shift" (Levy and Merry, 1986: 5), or simply incremental one on the existing dynamics? Using disruptive technologies, as the theoretical framework provides the study with a heuristic value in that it helps to shed an objective light, devoid of an optimistic or pessimistic leaning, on the interrelation between social media and political game in Sub-Saharan Africa.

On the methodological level, this work is simply documentary analysis (Bowen, 2009). We study a set of texts exploring the relationship between social media and politics in Africa in order to identify their disruptive value. Thus, the work is a review of the extant literature, as well as some primary documents obtained through internet search. In short, we used a desktop research approach, defined as "the process of accessing published secondary data" (Jackson, 1994: 21), and which includes all sources of information that do not involve a field survey. Through this approach, we draw on examples from various countries to examine and understand the role of social media in the current governance dispensation.

The chapter is organized as follows: first, we will review the extant literature on the concept of "disruptive technologies". In doing so, we will examine its etymology as an academic concept, explain what it entails and underline some its dominant characteristics with the view to show how these media meet the designation of disruptive technologies. Then we will look at the politico-media context prior to the advent of social media in sub-Saharan Africa. Thereafter, we will consider how the use social media represents a disruption in the political field in the region. The last section will discuss fake news as the main challenge facing an effective appropriation of social media. We conclude the chapter with considerations on the future prospects of social media in the political field in the region of sub-Saharan Africa.

Disruptive Technology: A Fruitful Concept

The concept 'disruptive technology' has now become a household word as part of the so-called 4th Industrial Revolution to understand the impact new technologies are having on society in general. There is a consensus in the literature that the concept was coined by Bower and Christensen in 1997 (Adler, 2002; Utterback and Acee, 2005). The concept has been handy in accounting for the profound transformations new technologies continue to have in the various areas of the socioeconomic and political life in the last two decades. For instance, Pierce (2004) uses it to account for how major war fighting innovations emerge and survive in United States military forces. Moodie (2016) exploits the term to review significant changes, which have occurred in the field of education, particularly how new technologies have affected university' students, shaped libraries, curriculum, pedagogy, lectures, assessment, and even research. Sanglier (2018), whose work focuses on the internal audit profession, borrows the concept to analyze how auditors are anticipating technological changes and their impact on the profession. The concept has been very fruitful in the medical field (Ekekwe & Islam, 2012; Balgrosky, 2014; Barlow, 2016). Coleman (2017) wrote about the changing paradigm taking place in the political arena in the United States, whereby technology is fostering a bottom up approach to civic engagement, the emerging of a "disruptive 'leaderful' era" which is "challenging traditional forms of authority, social norms and hierarchy to try to push through to a new social model." A monograph edited by Kloby (2012) focuses on the disruptive potential of the Web 2.0 in the public sector, as they foster democratic participation and engagement, coproduction between the government and the public in designing and delivering services, facilitate access and even improve transparency and accountability. In sum, as new technologies have been transforming every aspect of human life, the concept of disruptive technology, as an analytical concept has become appealing idea for examining this transformation.

The concept of disruptive technologies first emerged in the business field. Bower and Christensen (1995) coined the term to analyze how leading companies in an established market are often outpaced by emerging companies, which have anticipated the performance potential a new technology and bet on it. They described key characteristics of a disruptive technology, as "a different package of performance attributes—ones that, at least at the outset, are not valued by existing customers," (Bower and Christensen, 1995) and a rapid improvement rate of the performance attributes valued by existing customers (Bower & Christensen, 1995). Christensen (1997) further crystallized the concept in his book *The Innovator's Dilemma*, where he articulated the distinction between disruptive and sustaining technologies. For Christensen (1997), sustaining technologies improve product performance within an established market. He wrote, "they improve the performance of established products, along the dimensions of performance that mainstream customers in major markets have historically valued." (Christensen 1997, p. XV) As such their introduction aims at consolidating the existing pool of customers. Disruptive technologies, on the other hand, "bring to the market a very different value proposition than had been available previously." (Christensen 1997, p. XV). Such technologies therefore endow products with features aimed, not at the mainstream, but at "fringe (and generally new)" markets. (Christensen 1997, p. XV)

In this model, disruptive technologies represent for a company the potential of efficiency, expenses reduction, or new markets development. These are technologies that "enable the breaking of long-held business rules that inhibit organizations from making radical business changes." (Dixit & Kumar 2007, p. 127) In sum, and from the business perspective, a disruptive technology is one exploited by markets entrants, whose products or services initially appeal only to a fringe, but as their attributes improve, they gradually succeeded in overcoming mainstream's resistance. For Christensen (1997), dismissing the value of these technologies has time and again proven fatal for dominant corporations.

Unfortunately, despite its overwhelming acceptance in the academic lexicon, there seems to be some confusion over what the concept actually means, as well as serious criticisms about how Christensen perceived the idea (Danneels, 2004). This has come about as many scholars seek to use it to understand and explain emerging technologies and technological changes being witnessed in the word. Another issue which has led to the definitional quagmire is that a number of scholars are now using the notion 'disruptive innovation' with disruptive technology interchangeable, while others simply see the two as distinctive entities (Lepore, 2014). Indeed, this definitional hullaballoo has led Christensen (2015) to clarify what he meant by 'disruptive technology'.

As it is often the case, the overuse of the concept has led to what some consider a misuse. Christensen et al. (2015) put it this way, "the theory's core concepts have been widely misunderstood and its basic tenets frequently misapplied". He argues that much technological advancement labeled disruptive by analysts are rather "sustaining", since they represent not a revolution, but an incremental performance improvement in existing practices. However, such perspective implies that a concept has a standardized meaning beyond which its usage will be incorrect. Yet, the reality is that over time, an expanded use of a concept leads to the expansion of its meaning. We accept the view of Meek (1994, p. 266) that "there is nothing wrong with one discipline borrowing concepts from another discipline; this process has resulted in important theoretical innovations." But such borrowing should be done carefully, with the concept framed with precision, in a way that leaves no ambiguity as to its contextual meaning.

Christensen himself displays such attitude with regards to the concept of technology, which he defines as "the process by which an organization transforms labor, capital, materials, and information into product and services of greater value." (Christensen 1997, p. Xiii) The concept of technology assuredly caries various meaning (Ferré, 1995), and for Christensen (1997, p. Xiii), it "extends beyond engineering and manufacturing to encompass a range of marketing, investment, and managerial processes." Sharing this perspective, Burgelman et al. (2001, p. 2) conceive technology as "the theoretical and practical knowledge, skills and artifacts that can be used to develop products and services as well as their production and delivery systems." Thus, a concept can be redefined and reinvested with a new meaning to serve a particular purpose.

As indicated in the outset, the concept of disruptive technology in no longer confined to the field of business or solely ascribed to technical innovations. As noted in Ernst & Young's (2017) trends analysis, "disruption does not stem solely from technology or business innovations - it is also influenced by demographic shifts, globalization, macroeconomic trends and more. It is also evident that the effects of disruption are beginning to extend far beyond the business world". (12) Therefore, the concept of disruptive technology as used in this paper is essentially a framework which goes beyond technical object and encompasses any idea, initiative, approach or even method which introduces "a paradigm shift" (Levy and Merry, 1986), in a given field of the social activity. In this sense, the concept is parallel to that of 'transformational innovation' (Mulgan, 2007) or even 'breakthrough technologies' (Karlsson et al. 2013).

Thus, we consider the concept of disruptive technology as a basic framework for discussing any disruptive innovation. In this sense, approaches such as AGILE methods in project management which are especially based on prioritization, collaboration, human interaction, adaptability, as well as a continual user involvement in project development. (Dixit & Kumar 2007; Layton & Ostermiller, 2017) could legitimately be discussed under the framework of disruptive technology. Idem for systems thinking approaches (Deming, 1994; Seddon, 2008), based on the idea that "organizations should be managed as systems" (Wastell 2011: 95). In fact, it is within the framework of disruptive technologies that Bowman (2011: 6), focusing on the Zambian case, analyses how the changing ideologies, policies, expert knowledge, and technologies have transformed the agricultural sector in sub-Saharan Africa.

Social Media as Disruptive Technologies

We understand by social media websites and applications conceived to allow people to rapidly share content, whether texts, audio or video in real-time. Wikipedia, the free online encyclopedia defines them as "interactive computer-mediated technologies that facilitate the creation or sharing of information, ideas, career interests and other forms of expression via virtual communities and networks." Social media vary widely in form, content or purpose, which makes any attempt to classify them very challenging. Let's simply say that, among others, they include social networks which connect people, media sharing networks which serve to share photos, videos, and other media content, discussion forums which serve to share news and ideas, blogging and publishing platforms, as well as anonymous social networks which are designed to help people communicate anonymously (Kumar & Nanda, 2019). If major social media such as Facebook, Twitter, LinkedIn, Instagram, or YouTube are well known and are gaining popularity in Africa, some platforms are developed locally to serve a specific goal. This is, for example, the case with the Présimètre, which we will discuss a little later. It is also the case with the CongoBlog launched in the Democratic Republic of Congo by a young journalist from Kinshasa, the South African Zoopy considered one of the most popular networks on the continent in terms of visits, Afrigator which is the most important African directory on the Internet, or the legendary Ushahidi platform developed in Kenya. Because social media allows a personalized connection with other users' networks of influence, they represent a powerful tool for mobilization

One of the fundamental characteristics of disruptive technologies is that they tend to face some resistance when they are introduced, which resistance may be due to the fact that their values are not initially perceived or understood by the mainstream (Christensen, 1997; Ekekwe et al. 2012); or it may also be because they represent a threat to the existing order of things. (Christensen, 2002) In Sub-Saharan Africa, social media have faced and to a certain extent, continue to face censorship by the dominant political structures (Dwyer and Molony, 2019). In this respect, they do meet one of the criteria of disruptive technologies, which is that they generate resistance. Another characteristic of disruptive technologies rests in that their adoption rate grows rapidly after a slow beginning. "At first," note Bower & Christensen (1995), "disruptive technologies tend to be used and valued only in new markets or new applications; in fact, they generally make possible the emergence of new markets." However, thanks to their tested performance in these fringe markets where they built their appeal, and the slow reaction of unalarmed dominant corporations, they rapidly spread. Bower and Christensen (1995) described the process this way:

Once the companies have secured a foothold in the markets and improved the performance of their technologies, the established markets above them, served by high-cost suppliers, look appetizing. When they do attack, the entrant companies find the established players to be easy and unprepared opponents because the opponents have been looking up market themselves, discounting the threat from below.

The growth of social media in Africa has been exponential. For instance, in 2014, 100 million people were using Facebook each month across Africa. Two years later, the figure jumped to over 120 millions. At the end of 2018, the number of Facebook subscribers on the continent had surpassed 200 millions. Similar trends have been observed with other social media. As Amy Watson noted," social media sites are also becoming increasingly widespread in these smaller markets, with some African entertainers and influencers garnering millions of followers "(2019).

Disruptive technologies are also characterized by the fundamental nature of the transformation they introduce (Manyika et al. 2013;. Wastell 2011,) For Ekekwe et al. (2012:. 85), such technologies affect the "existing technological, production and/ or management processes with the tacit objective to change the existing behavior of both actors and users." As we shall see with the example of the political field, the depth of the changes introduced by social media in sub-Saharan Africa is irreducible.

The Media-Politics Relationship in Africa Prior to Social media

In order to understand why social media can be considered disruptive technologies in the political field in Sub-Saharan Africa, one must be aware of the media-political environment that preceded the emergence social media. Thus, we agree with the statement by Dwycr and Molony (2019) that "any credible research into social media should be permeated by an acute awareness of how the past informs the present." At the time of independence in the 1960s by the majority of African countries, developmental thinking was in full swing, with the idea that newly independent nations need to transition to a modern, industrial, capitalist economy to improve their quality of life and their standard of living (Paquot, 2002). Developmental doctrine held that the media, like all other national resources, should be put at the service of development and thus of state initiatives. According to this logic, the control of information wasn't only a legitimate right; it was a national political necessity (Rosenblum, 1979: 206).

In countries that adopted this doctrine, the media outlet was generally owned by the state. The public authorities, where appropriate, did everything possible to restrict the emergence and development of private newspapers, through state largesse by means of subsidies and access to state owned newspapers. In some cases, various tactics were used to intimidate independent media. These tactics included threats to journalists, raids on media premises, temporary and even definitive closures of premises, confiscation of property, not to mention unending trials and imprisonment. In Nigeria, for example, until 1990, most newspapers were government-owned, with the exception of a few private newspapers such as the *Nigerian Tribune*, *The Punch*, *Vanguard* or the Guardian, which were constantly subjected to harassment by the public authorities (Green and *Karolides*, 2014). In Cameroon, the government newspaper *Cameroon Tribune* was the absolute master of the written press until the advent of Pius Njawe's newspaper, *Le Messager* in 1979, which came under enormous state pressure. It should be noted that Njawe, before his death in 2010, had more than 120 arrests to his credit (Lewis, 2010). Other control mechanisms, including all forms of censorship, were also used to break up any media that showed any independence from the government. In short, authoritarian tendencies and a certain conception of the state as the ultimate agent of development combined to create a media environment dominated by the state. Needless to say that in such context, the common people had little, if any, say in the political process. The mission of the press at that time was simply to give a more didactic translation of the State's action, and if necessary, its constructive criticism (Perret, 2001: 158) but not to go beyond the limits authorized by the State. Such journalism committed to state propaganda quickly gave way to the cult of personality on the continent (Badibanga, 1979). It is this press system, far from the rigorous objective journalism, that dominated the African media landscape for the three decades following the independences, from the early 1960s to the early 1990s.

The early 1990s, however, marked a new era for the African press. It followed the end of the Cold War (1989) and the break-up of the Soviet Union (1991) and the emergence of good governance idea, which typically referred to political liberalization. Fukuyama (1992) has described this period as 'the end of history,' and argued that the ideological evolution of humanity had culminated in the triumph of liberal democracies. A wind of democracy blew across the planet. African leaders pressed both by freedom-loving populations and by international donor community, began to show an openness to political and media pluralism (source). Expressions long suppressed by the public authorities, were now experiencing certain liberation-This is not clear. I don't know what you mean by "expression" (Kamga, 2019). The first years of the 1990s thus marked the emergence of the private print media, although the audiovisual media remained state owned for a little longer (Tidiane et al. 1997). In short, the entire continent witnessed the establishment of thousands of new private media; newspapers and magazines randomly (de la Brosse, 1999: 102).

The democratic transition of the early 1990s thus marked the end of political monolithism in Africa. Alliances were quickly forged between the nascent opposition parties and private newspapers. For the latter, this was often a strategy for economic survival while for the former it was a matter of having a voice in the public arena. The problem with this though is the co-optation of many journalists (Kakdeu, 2015) and hence defeating the idea of the media as being the fourth estate of the state. Thus, as a result of this co-optation, many journalists have become virtually lobbyists and press officers than information professionals (Kakdeu: 2015). To many Africans, professional journalists are expected to get a message across, to carry out the same missions as those assigned to communication officers (Balima, 2006: 192).

As already stated, the spaces for expression that emerged in the early 1990s gave rise to the multiplicity of media outlets. Unfortunately, these outlets have quickly phagocytized by special interests, leaving the citizens somewhat muzzled and voiceless. In sum, whereas states media outlets such as TV and print were dedicated to state propaganda, private outlets which emerged in the early 1990s as part of the democratization process has ended up at the mercy of special interests. This is the context in which social media emerged in the 2000s and has become an effective way for citizens to participate in the affairs of their countries.

Social Media and Political Mobilization in Sub-Saharan Africa

In the context of the one-party system that characterized Sub-Saharan Africa during the first three decades following the independence, the abolition of the separation of powers and the control of the entire state apparatus were presented as the best way to achieve development (Gazibo, 2018). Ruling elites felt legitimized to suppress pluralism in the name of national interest, although the line between the state and the rulers quickly became blurred (source). The ensuing political climate became poisonous, dominated by fear and suspicion. The repressive apparatuses of the state, such as the army, the police, the court, the prison, etc., were at the rulers' disposal to crush political dissention. There were high abuses and all sorts of human right violations (Balencie and de La Grange, 2001). Therefore, not only political activism and contestation were risky business, but also there was no possibility for individuals to bypass the media system controlled by the State. Thus, there was a twofold difficulty. The first being the difficulty if not the impossibility of voicing one's opinion; and the second being the difficulty to establish the solidarity needed to mobilize a community around mutual ideas and projects. For instance, how to reach out to those sharing the same idea and mobilize them around a given project or a given action? How to organize an impactful demonstration without knowing who will be there? Even the newspapers which emerged at the liberation of the information sector in the early 1990s proved limited in scope, given that they were generally served special interests. As well, their inadequate resources limited their ability to enhance their circulations across their countries of operation and thus affected political mobilization.

The advent of social media introduced a new dynamic in political mobilization not only in developing countries but developed ones, as well. It is worth mentioning that the power of the Internet as a tool for mobilization was first displayed in the United States in 1999 at the Seattle World Trade Organization (WTO) protests. During this event, over 40 to 50 000 demonstrators took the street to protest against the WTO in what at the time looked like a spontaneous mobilization of people for demonstration. But as argued by Eagleton-Pierce (2001: p.331), "preparations had started months prior to the summit, with considerable mobilization conducted through the Internet" by a handful of non-governmental organizations. Twenty years later, the Internet has significantly evolved and provided the platform for new levels of political mobilization. It offers among other things platforms people are using to share information, opinions, experiences, and perspectives, with various forms of content, including texts, images, audio, and video. These platforms use technologies that allow the individual users to create virtual communities to communicate and interact, as well as a mobilizing tool, in what has been described as "Supersize Effects" (Earl and Kimport, 2011). This refers to the idea that social media "reduces the cost of protest (both time and money), increases the speed in which mobilization occurs (transmission of information and communication), and changes the scale on which mobilization takes place" (Tamarelli, et al. 2019).

In Africa, social media networks have grown exponentially over the years, with a significant impact in the way political activism and mobilization are being done. The Arab Spring and the use of social media has widely been discussed (source). Other events in Sub-Saharan Africa have also been discussed as evidence of the power of social media. For example, the 2014 popular uprising which ended to Blaise Compaoré's 27 years reign in Burkina Faso, as well as the ousting of the former Zimbabwean President Robert Mugabe, are but a few of how Africans are mobilizing against authoritarian regimes on the continent. Writing on Zimbabwe, for instance, Gilbert (2019) has suggested that, "it was on social media that Zimbabweans first found their voice to rise up against the 93-year-old strongman, with platforms like WhatsApp, Facebook, and Twitter proving to be vital in mobilizing and coordinating countrywide protests."

It is, however, necessary to recognize that the disruptive value of these media goes beyond these historical moments crystallized in time, and could be perceived in the way they transform the political arena and undermining old logics. Recent events (2018-2019) in Cameroon help illustrate this point. After the October 2018 presidential elections, the ruling regime had Maurice Kamto the leader of the main opposition party and his entire staff arrested for challenging the results proclaimed by the Cameroonian Constitutional Court in favor of the incumbent president. The detainees were liable to the death penalty if found guilty by a military court they were to stand trial. The strategy of political repression always tries to appear legitimate (Braud, 2006), but ultimately it aims at silencing opponents, at driving them out of the political life (Davenport, 2007) Although it was a strategy that had been tried and tested for decades in Cameroon, it came up against an unexpected phenomenon, online mobilization. Kamto supporters set in motion a multi-pronged mobilization on social media, with the aim to provide material support to the defendants and their families, legal support for their defense, as well as political and diplomatic support. As a result of this, his popularity soared both inside and outside the country. After 9 months, internal popular protests essentially organized through online, and diplomatic pressures forced the government to stop all proceedings against the accused and freed them from detention.

In this mobilization, the coordination of local supporters and Cameroonian Diaspora in the Western world must be emphasized. The Cameroonian Diaspora used all the levers at their disposal, including financial resources, influential relations, lobbying and protests in Western countries to put pressure on the Cameroonian government to abort the trials of the opposition leader. This mobilization proved to be a typical example of the intersection between the local and the global, where "international reach of social media allows localized campaigns to swiftly reach international audiences, and create opportunities for the development of transnational networks" (Dwyer and Molony 2019: 10).

Such online mobilizations create and reinforce transboundary and transcontinental solidarities whose goal is not a single event or a single project, but a permanent mobilization as a fully-fledged in the socio-political life of a country. It leads to the development of networks, which have become forces with which Sub-Saharan political system are contending and are expected to have greater impact on sociopolitical life. As suggested by some scholars, transformations in policies "are influenced by individual and organizational political protest." (Tamarelli et al. 2019)

Social Media and the Push for Transparency

The sixth General Assembly of the African Ombudsman and Mediation Association was held in Kigali in November 2019 under the theme: "The Role of the Ombudsman/

Mediators in Promoting Transparency and Accountable Governance in Africa". In line with the African Union dedication of the year 2018 as "winning the fight against corruption as sustainable path to Africa's transformation", participants stressed the need to hold political leaders accountable to political transparency. It is worth noting that transparency sustains "confidence in the legal environment, making regulations more secure and accessible, less influenced by special interests, and therefore more open to competition, trade and investment" (OECD 2010, p. 61). Interestingly, it can be said that the push for transparency has been carried out on social media in the form of civic journalism since the advent of social media.

In Africa, the intensification of this phenomenon has been seen as an "emergent force in anti-corruption efforts by professional journalists and citizens alike" (Schauseil 2019). As noted by Jamme (2011), "more transparent, user-generated content is breaking through, with websites holding leaders to account". The push for transparency and openness has also led many Sub-Saharan governments to join the Open Government initiative. Consequently, these governments have developed open data initiatives with the view of using created platforms to provide data to their citizens. For instance, in 2011, the Kenyan government launched the Kenya Open Data Initiative (KODI), an online platform meant to provide government information to citizens. The KODI provides data organized into 11 categories, namely Agriculture, education, environment, energy, finance, governance, government accounts, health, infrastructure, population and census, as well as water. Each of these categories is constantly fed with up-to-date relevant regional or sectorial datasets. For instance, the Governance category features data on complaints filed against public or private institutions and public officers, data on the effects of election crimes and offences in Kenya, on the number of officers trained in different institutions by the Commission on Administrative Justice since its beginning. It also provides data that show the effects of election crimes and offences in Kenya, data on the various factors contributing to election offences, data on the various types of election offences and their frequency in Kenya, on analysis of political rallies and issues observed by Commission on Administrative Justice, and much more. In the Water category, we find among other things, a dataset which profile the country's counties "according the level of service provided, including the percentages of local populations serviced by the provider, Sewerage coverage, and the unit cost of water" (Kenya Open Data, 2017 The KODI platform provides both official data from the government and its agencies and crowdsourced ones generated by the private sector and individual citizens.

Outlining the value of the KODI project in Kenya, Mungai and Van Belle point out that, among other advantages, it "empowers citizens to keep the government in check, which results in better utilization of funding (tax revenue and donor aid) and government resources" as well as more informed policy making process, and helps the general public "to make better decisions such as who to elect in public office." They also note how, thanks to the ready availability of data, the media are "slowly moving towards fact driven journalism" (Mungai & Van Belle 2018: 344). The transformative potential of the KODI project can be illustrated with the Ma3route initiative, put in place to provide "data on traffic patterns and accidents in Kenya, with the aim of improving the mobility experience of people in the major cities" (Mungai, 2008). As a crowdsourcing service, "Ma3Route uses information from the more than 500,000 users from its various online services to collect the data it needs for updates", notes the *Business Daily*. To understand better users' actual experiences, the platform generates a map of accidents in Nairobi, posting information that includes time, location, description and photo, which information is validated by an algorithm for their accuracy. Ultimately, these data offer public authorities the opportunity to make traffic policy accordingly and enforce them for public interest.

Following the presidential and legislative elections of November 2015, Burkina Faso committed to strengthen its governance in order to better meet the expectations of citizens though an open data initiative. The Présimètre emerged thereafter as an instrument to help meet that goal. The Présimètre is an online information sharing platform that tracks the implementation of the priority policies of the Burkinabe government in some key sectors of the economy; notably education, health, water hygiene and sanitation, food safety, environment, youth training, advancement of women, defense and security, and enables citizens to assess online the progress made, while promoting a direct dialogue between citizens and public authorities (Présimètre, 2016). Each one of these categories lists the number of commitments made by the authorities in power and tracks how many, if any, have been fulfilled. A chart indicates the percentage of commitments achieved, whereas a chronometer counts down the time left for the government to achieve its policy goals in a given sector. This citizen watch platform, a crowdsourced one which mobilizes advocacy groups and academics, as well as other professional associations, facilitates an ongoing dialogue between the government and its citizens.

The Présimètre is gradually introducing a culture of transparency in Burkina Faso. Within its framework, local and regional governments are organizing more and more communications events to generate public interest in public policies, to create an ongoing dialogue between public authorities and local population and shed light on government action. In September 2018, the EU Special Rapporteur on Human Rights nominated the Présimètre for its significant contribution to citizen control of public action in Burkina Faso. A recognition that follows its December 2017 Participation and Democracy Prize awarded by Transparency International and the Agence française de développement médias (Rédaction B24, 2018)

Social Media and the Electoral Process

One of the domains in which social media are making a significant 'disruption' is that of the electoral process. As already discussed, although the political spaces were liberalized in the early 1990s, citizens found it merely impossible to interact with public officials, as a result of the control of state-owned media and the co-optation of the private media. The emergence of social media platforms has, however, altered this, as they have created spaces for engagement and debate and helped prevent electoral fraud, for example. For instance, during the 2011 Nigerian presidential campaign, national and international press underscored the activism and mobilization of the youth, who used social media to organize debate and inquire about candidates' policies. Other social constituents, individual citizens, political parties, politicians, journalists, and civil society organizations leveraged social media to fully meet their electoral goals. As a result,

citizens not only had a voice but believed that they were heard. Incidents of violence and fraud were made known and quickly stopped as ordinary citizens were able to report them quickly, easily and with low cost. The high visibility acted as a deterrent to illegal activity such as vote rigging. The ability of the man in the street to participate by reporting and commenting on the election and related incidents increased interest and this is believed to have increased the percentage of eligible voters who did in fact vote. (Mungai, 2018)

This election set in motion a trend whereby social media became a constitutive part of the electoral process. The 2015 general elections which brought back Muhammadu Buhari to power intensified the trend, so much so that Sunday Dare, the media adviser to the head of Buhari's political party suggested in an interview, that social media served "as a watchdog in keeping the integrity of the process. Within minutes of votes being counted at a polling unit, the results were all over social media. (…) In a way, social media seized the day from the legacy media. You had almost everyone depending on social media for the breaking news" (Eddings, 2015).

Similar observations were made with regard to the 2015 presidential elections in Côte d'Ivoire.

Observing Election Day in a sampled polling station from the start to the end allowed the civil society coalition to collect reliable data on the process in real time. Observers, 50 percent of whom were women, transmitted their observations on the opening of the polling station, the turnout rate, the violence or peacefulness of the day, the reliability of the electoral officials and equipment, and finally on the results for the presidential candidates in each specific polling station. All these observations were transformed in coded data sent by SMS. (N'Gotta 2016)

The significance of these experiences is that they represent patent cases of disruptive technologies, as they illustrate how new technologies have produced a paradigm shift, not only in transparency and accountability in terms of government policies but in the political processes, as well. In Nigeria, the use of social media in the electoral process has been deeply transformational. It is worth noting that Levy and Merry define transformational changes as "multi-dimensional, multi-level, qualitative, discontinuous" (1986: 5). Changes in the Nigerian political environment appear to be precisely of this nature. For example, the process is not longer under the absolute control of the elites, and the public does not longer have to wait for official channels and traditional news outlets to access the results. In other words, social media have boosted mobilization and have introduced a level of transparency which gives the process more credibility.

Social Media and Fake News

In view of the experiences and emerging trends discussed above, it is clear that social media will continue to play an increasingly prominent role in the political life of sub-Saharan African countries, affecting both how the political game is played and how public affairs are conducted. The rise of social media has also led to the idea of fake news on the continent. Fake news has been defined as "a form of news consisting of deliberate disinformation or hoaxes spread via traditional news media (print and broadcast) or online social media" (Wikipedia). Fake news encompasses disinformation which is Information that is false and deliberately created to harm a person, social group, organization or country, misinformation or information that is false but not created with the intention of causing harm and mal-information which is information that is based on reality, used to inflict harm on a person, social group, organization or country. (UNESCO, 2018)

Milos Stanic (2019) notes that "the main aggregator of fake news traffic is social media. Where stories have gone viral, they have often done so in the news feeds of social media users." Often used to influence the political process, fake news has not spared the African continent. Under Muriel Edjo's pen, the online newspaper *Ecofin Hebdo* (2019) reported that on October 14 2018, after the Nigerian opposition leader Atiku Abubakar confirmed his candidacy for the 2019 presidential election, a fake Twitter account in his name published a message of thanks to the Nigerian Gay Men's Association for their support. In the post Mr Abubakar was allegedly pledging that once elected, he will get rid of the country's highly controversial anti-gay legislation enacted in 2014 by Goodluck Jonathan, a former Nigerian president.

The information was picked up by two Nigerian blogs and then made its way in two major Nigerian newspapers, *The Nation* and *The Vanguard*. However, it turned out that this false information was published to damage the candidate's image among the very influential Muslim and Christian leaders, who favored the anti-gay legislation. This incident is not merely an isolated example. The problem of fake news is so worrying that in the early 2019, Facebook opened its first fact-checking centre in sub-Saharan Africa to clean up its platform, which has become one of the main relays for disinformation on the continent (Ndong, 2019). Wasserman and Madrid-Morales conducted a survey in Kenya, Nigeria, and South Africa in 2018 as an attempt to measure the scope of fake news in those countries. They wanted "to measure the prevalence of disinformation, to learn who people believe is responsible for stopping fake news, and to understand the relationship between disinformation and media trust." (Wasserman and Madrid-Morales, 2018). Among other key findings are that:

- Respondents perceive that they were "exposed to "fake news" about politics on a fairly regular basis", encounter news stories about politics that they thought were completely made up, and only 1 to 3% say they have never come across fabricated news.
- They shared "fake news" with a much higher frequency than Americans do: 38% Kenyans, 28% Nigerians and 35% South Africans acknowledged having shared stories which turned out to be made up. In the US only 16% did so. One-in-five South Africans and one-in-four Kenyans and Nigerians said they had shared stories that they knew were made up.
- Those who believed they were exposed to "fake news" more regularly had lower levels of trust in the media.

Madrid-Morales, the co-author of the study indicated that "people in sub-Saharan Africa particularly distrust information on social media, such as Facebook, Twitter and WhatsApp because that's where they find 'fake news' most often" (University of Houston 2019) Therefore, the growing presence of misinformation on social media carries with it the danger of creating confusion and discrediting the validity of these media as catalysts for socio and political progress.

CONCLUSION

The impact of social media in the political arena is clearly transformational. We considered their impact on political mobilization and activism, on transparency in the conduct of public affairs, as well as on the electoral process. As we have seen with the example of political struggle in Cameroon, even though political engagement remains dangerous for civil society and opposition parties, an effective mobilization of social media could produce positive results by getting the public authorities to yield to popular pressure. The utilization of social media has generally started with those marginalized from the mainstream media structure, namely individuals, civil society groups or political opposition with little or no voice at all in the traditional media. They saw in social media a space of expression somewhat sheltered from harassment, intimidation, and other forms of violence from the political elites in power. Gradually, these elites realized the scope of these media and began to take an active interest in them. Thus, the political power structure initially dismissive and resistant to social media is now contending with them, using them as strategic communication tools for self-promotion and self-preservation, as means of surveillance and censorship, or enacting legislative or other coercive measures such as Internet shutdown to curtail their usage (Freedom House, 2019)

The fact that we highlighted ways in which social media are transforming the political field does not mean that we that we embrace a techno-deterministic with its fundamental assumption according to which technology by itself effects social or political changes. While recognizing the centrality of technologies, we believe that social transformations depend on the social trajectory technologies will take. And theses trajectories, in turn, proceed from social context and political decision. (Vinck, 1994; Kamga, 2017). In a sense, we recognize that "technology, human, and culture are all co-constructed, constituting and mediating each other in ways that open up new possibilities for thinking and acting" (Clark, 2009: 96), and the outcome of such co-construction could hardly be predetermined, as competing force are always at play, adding to the complexity of the process of appropriation.

The growing penetration of mobile telephony and the reduction of the cost of connectivity suggest that there is an even greater prospect for social media development in sub-Saharan Africa. Such prospect has moved major social media companies to expand their presence in the region, by adding local languages to facilitate access to their platform, offering lighter versions of their apps, with products such as Facebook Lite, Facebook Messenger Lite, Twitter Lite, Google Go, which use less data and therefore are more affordable to users with limited resources. Although the advent of social media in Sub-Saharan Africa represents for the common people real opportunities for challenging the existing dominant power structure and for mobilizing to effect sociopolitical changes, given other developing trends such fake news or censorship, caution needs to be exercised in predicting the qualitative natures of changes that will occur.

REFERENCES

Adegoke, Y. (2017). Why social media is the only media in Africa. Retrieved from https://www.weforum.org/agenda/2017/03/why-social-media-is-the-only-media-in-africa

Adner, R. (2002). When are technologies disruptive? A demand-based view of the emergence of competition. *Strategic Management Journal*, *23*(8), 667–688. doi:10.1002mj.246

Afful-Dadzie, E., & Afful-Dadzie, A. (2017). Open government data in Africa: A preference elicitation analysis of media practitioners. *Government Information Quarterly*, *34*(2), 244–255. doi:10.1016/j.giq.2017.02.005

Ayres, R. U. (1989). *Technological Transformation and Long Waves*. Laxenburg, Austria: International Institutes of Applied Systems Analysis; Retrieved from https://pdfs.semanticscholar.org/3f41/ab13d03434e08bf521061c9b9af8a07fb6d2.pdf

Balancie, J.-M., & de La Grange, A. (Eds.). (2001). *Mondes rebelles. Guerillas, Milices, groupes terroristes*. Paris, France: Éditions Michalon.

Bertot, J. C., Jaeger, P. T., & Grimes, J. M. (2010). Using ICTs to create a culture of transparency: E-government and social media as openness and anti-corruption tools for societies. *Government Information Quarterly*, *27*(3), 264–271. doi:10.1016/j.giq.2010.03.001

Bertot, J. C., Jaeger, P. T., & Grimes, J. M. (2012). Promoting transparency and accountability through ICTs, social media, and collaborative e-government. *Transforming Government: People, Process, and Policy*, *6*(1), 78–91. doi:10.1108/17506161211214831

Beyene, Z., & Zerai, A. (2014) The Role of ICTs in Governance, State-building, and Peacebuilding in Africa: The Case of Ethiopia, CGCS Occasional Paper Series # 2, Retrieved from https://global.asc.upenn.edu/app/uploads/2014/08/The_Role_of_ICTs_in_Governance__Statebuilding__and_Peacebuilding-The_Case_of_Ethiopia.pdf

Birdsall, N., & Fukuyama, F. (2011). *The Post-Washington Consensus: Development After the Crisis Bohler-Muller, Narmia and Van Der Merwe, Charl (2011), "The Potential Of Social Media To Influence Socio-Political Change On The African Continent", Policy Brief, NO 46*. Africa Institute of South Africa.

Bowen, G. A. (2009). Document Analysis as a Qualitative Research Method. *Qualitative Research Journal*, *9*(2), 27–40. doi:10.3316/QRJ0902027

Bower, J. L., & Christensen, C. M. (1995). 'Disruptive technologies: Catching the wave'. *Harvard Business Review*, 73, 43–53 https://hbr.org/1995/01/disruptive-technologies-catching-the-wave

Braud, P. (2006). Violences politiques. Les raisons d'une déraison, in R. Meyran (ed.), Les mécanismes de la Violence, Paris, Editions Sciences Humaines, pp. 57-65.

Cariolle, J. (2018). The digital revolution in Sub-Saharan Africa: What perspectives for employment? https://www.entreprenanteafrique.com/en/the-digital-revolution-in-sub-saharan-africa-what-perspectives-for-employment/

Christensen, C. M., Raynor, M., & McDonald, R. (2015). 'What is disruptive innovation?'. *Harvard Business Review*, *93*, 44–53.

Clark, S. L. (2009). Theories: Mediatization and Media Ecology. In K. Lundby (ed.), Mediatization Concept, changes, consequences, New York: Peter Lang, pp. 85-100.

Cox, K. W. M., Bellasio, J., Ward, A., Galai, K., Meranto, S., & Paoli, G. P. (2019). Social Media. In *Africa A Double-Edged Sword For Security And Development Research Report*. UNDP.

Danneels, E. (2004). Disruptive technology reconsidered: A critique and research agenda. *Journal of Product Innovation Management*, *21*(4), 246–258. doi:10.1111/j.0737-6782.2004.00076.x

Davenport, C. (2007). *State Repression And The Domestic Democratic Peace*. Cambridge: Cambridge University Press. doi:10.1017/CBO9780511510021

de la Brosse, R. (1999). Afrique subsaharienne en transition: Des journaux nécessairement engagés. *Les Cahiers du Journalisme*, *6*, 102–122.

du Venage, G. (2018). Social Media Shines a Light on Corruption in Africa. Retrieved from https://www.thenational.ae/business/technology/social-media-shines-a-light-on-corruption-in-africa-1.775929

Dwyer, M., & Molony, T. (2019). *Social Media and Politics in Africa. Democracy, Censorship and Security*. London: Zed Books.

Eagleton-Pierce, M. (2001). The Internet and the Seattle Protests. *Peace Review*, *13*(3), 331–337.

Earl, J., & Kimport, K. (2011). *Digitally Enabled Social Change: Activism in the Internet Age*. Cambridge: The MIT Press. doi:10.7551/mitpress/9780262015103.001.0001

Ernst & Young. (2017). *The upside of Disruption Megatrends shaping 2016 and beyond*. EYGM Limited.

Essoungou, A.-M. (2010). Les jeunes politisent les médias sociaux. Retrieved from https://www.un.org/africarenewal/fr/magazine/april-2010/les-jeunes-politisent-les-m%C3%A9dias-sociaux

Evans, G. L. (2017). Disruptive technology and the board: The tip of the iceberg. *Economics and Business Review*, *3*(1), 205–222. doi:10.18559/ebr.2017.1.11

Foreman, C. (2017). 10 Types of Social Media and How Each Can Benefit Your Business. Retrieved from https://blog.hootsuite.com/types-of-social-media/

Freedom House. (2019). Democracy in Retreat. *Freedom in the World 2019*. Retrieved from https://freedomhouse.org/report/freedom-world/freedom-world-2019/democracy-in-retreat

Gazibo, M. (2018). L'exercice Du Pouvoir. In *Afrique Postcoloniale, Introduction à la politique africaine* (pp. 89–116). Montréal, Canada: Presses De L'université de Montréal.

Gilbert, D. (2019). Zimbabwe Is Trying to Build a China Style Surveillance State. Retrieved from https://www.vice.com/en_ca/article/59n753/zimbabwe-is-trying-to-build-a-china-style-surveillance-state

Grindle, M. (2004). Good enough governance: Poverty reduction and reform in developing countries. *Governance: An International Journal of Policy, Administration, and Institutions*, *17*(4), 525–548. doi:10.1111/j.0952-1895.2004.00256.x

Grindle, M. (2007). Good enough governance revisited. *Development Policy Review*, *25*(5), 553–574. doi:10.1111/j.1467-7679.2007.00385.x

Hartley, K., Kuecker, G., & Woo, J. J. (2019). Practicing public policy in an age of disruption. *Policy Design and Practice*, *2*(2), 163–181. doi:10.1080/25741292.2019.1622276

Hasselbalch, J. (2014). Regulating disruptive innovations: The policy disruption of electronic cigarettes, Paper presented at Global Reordering: Towards the Next Generation of Scholarship conference in Brussels, November 18-20, 2014.

Intelligence, G. S. M. A. (2018). The Mobile Economy: Sub-Saharan Africa 2018. Retrieved from https://www.gsma.com/mobileeconomy/sub-saharan-africa/

Jamme, M. (2011). Africa's new generation is using social media to push for change. Retrieved from https://www.theguardian.com/global-development/poverty-matters/2011/jun/17/social-media-transforming-communication-africa

Kamga, O. (2017). Constructivisme social in Jean-Paul Lafrance, 100 notions sur la civilisation numérique, Paris, Les éditions de l'Immatériel, pp. 33-35.

Kamga, O. (2019). *Difficile émergence d'un journalisme objectif en Afrique* (Vol. 36, p. 1). Communication. [on ligne]

Krugman, P. (2007). Is there a Post-Washington consensus? Initiative for Policy Dialogue Working Paper Series.

Kumar, V., & Nanda, P. (2019). Social Media in Higher Education: A Framework for Continuous Engagement. [IJICTE]. *International Journal of Information and Communication Technology Education*, *15*(1), 109–120. doi:10.4018/IJICTE.2019010107

Levina, M. (2017). Disrupt or die: Mobile health and disruptive innovation as body politics. *Television and Media*, *18*(6), 548–564. doi:10.1177/1527476416680451

Manuel, T. A. (2003). Africa aid the Washington Consensus: Finding the 'Right Path. *Finance & Development*, (September): 18–20. Available at http://www.sarpn.org/documents/d0000654/Manuel_Sept2003.pdf

Maseh, E., & Katuu, S. (2017). The Kenyan Judiciary's Open Government Initiative: Prospects and challenges. *Journal of Science and Technology Policy Management*, *8*(1), 76–94. doi:10.1108/JSTPM-04-2016-0007

McKeon, T. R., & Gitomer, D. H. (2019). Social Media, Political Mobilization, and High-Stakes Testing. Retrieved from https://www.frontiersin.org/articles/10.3389/feduc.2019.00055/full

N'Gotta, S. (2016). YALI Voices: How Can We Inspire Young People to Use Technology for Promoting Transparency and Accountability in West Africa? Retrieved from https://yali.state.gov/yali-voices-how-can-we-inspire-young-people-to-use-technology-for-promoting-transparency-and-accountability-in-west-africa/

Naim, M. (1999). Fads and Fashion in Economic Reforms: Washington Consensus or Washington Confusion. Working Draft of a Paper Prepared for the IMF Conference on Second Generation Reforms, Washington, D.C. October 26. Available at http://www.imf.org/external/pubs/ft/seminar/1999/reforms/naim.htm

Ndong, N. (2019). Afrique: l'explosion des fake news, une vraie menacc pour la paix sociale. Retrieved from http://www.adiac-congo.com/content/afrique-lexplosion-des-fake-news-une-vraie-menace-pour-la-paix-sociale-96061

Ohemeng, F. L. K., & Ofosu-Adarkwa, K. (2015). One way traffic: The open data initiative project and the need for an effective demand side initiative in Ghana. *Government Information Quarterly*, *32*(1), 419–428. doi:10.1016/j.giq.2015.07.005

Patterson, J., Schulz, K., Vervoort, J., van der Hel, S., Widerberg, O., Adler, C., ... Barau, A. (2017). Exploring the governance and politics of transformations towards sustainability. *Environmental Innovation and Societal Transitions*, *24*, 1–16. doi:10.1016/j.eist.2016.09.001

Peters, B. G. (2017). What is so wicked about wicked problems? A conceptual analysis and a research program. *Policy and Society*, *36*(3), 385–396. doi:10.1080/14494035.2017.1361633

Peters, B. G., & Tarpey, M. (2019). Are wicked problems really so wicked? Perceptions of policy problems. *Policy and Society*, *38*(2), 218–236. doi:10.1080/14494035.2019.1626595

Rao, B., Angelov, B., & Nov, O. (2006). Fusion of disruptive technologies: Lessons from the skype case. *European Management Journal*, *24*(2-3), 174–188. doi:10.1016/j.emj.2006.03.007

Raynor, M. E. (2011b). Disruption theory as a predictor of innovation success/failure. *Strategy and Leadership*, *39*(4), 27–30. doi:10.1108/10878571111147378

Rezaei, F., & Cohen, R. A. (2012). The Role of Social Media in the Recent Political Shifts in the Middle East and North Africa, *OSR Journal of Humanities and Social Science (JHSS) 4*(6) (Nov. - Dec. 2012), pp. 1-10.

Santra, S., Mandal, T. S., & Das, P. (2019). Leveraging Disruptive Technology Innovations for Healthcare Delivery in Sub-Saharan Africa, ORF Issue Brief No. 298.

Schwab, K. (2016) *The Fourth Industrial Revolution*. Davos: World Economic Forum.

Shao, D. D., & Saxena, S. (2019). Barriers to open government data (OGD) initiative in Tanzania: Stakeholders' perspectives. *Growth and Change*, *50*(1), 470–485.

Shapshak, T. (2019). *Africa's Booming Tech Hubs Are "Backbone of Tech Ecosystem" Having Grown 40% This Year*. Retrieved from https://www.forbes.com/sites/tobyshapshak/2019/07/11/africas-booming-tech-hubs-are-backbone-of-tech-ecosystem-having-grown-40-this-year/#1ec713fd24c2

Smith, T. (2019). Disruptive Technology. Retrieved from https://www.investopedia.com/terms/d/disruptive-technology.asp

Sood, A., & Tellis, G. J. (2011). Demystifying disruption: New schema, model, and findings. *Marketing Science, 30*(2), 339–354. doi:10.1287/mksc.1100.0617

Stanic, M. (2019). Retrieved from https://whatsnewinpublishing.com/fake-or-not-decoding-the-authenticity-of-online-news, https://whatsnewinpublishing.com/fake-or-not-decoding-the-authenticity-of-online-news

Tamakloe, S. (2018) Ghana's mobile phone subscribers to hit 40m by 2020 – Report, JoyBusiness. Retrieved from https://www.myjoyonline.com/business/2018/march-19th/ghanas-mobile-phone-subscribers-to-hit-40m-by-2020-report.php

UNESCO. (2018). Journalism, fake news & disinformation: handbook for journalism education and training. Retrieved from https://en.unesco.org/fightfakenews

UNESCO Courier. (2019). Fake news: sound bites on a burning topic. Retrieved from https://en.unesco.org/courier/july-september-2017/fake-news-sound-bites-burning-topic

University of Houston. (2019). 'Fake news,' diminishing media trust and the role of social media. Retrieved from https://phys.org/news/2019-08-fake-news-diminishing-media-role.html

Utterback, J., & Acee, H. J. (2005). Disruptive technologies: An expanded view. *International Journal of Innovation Management, 9*(01), 1–17. doi:10.1142/S1363919605001162

Vinck, D. (1995). *Sociologie des sciences*, Paris, A. Colin, coll. « "U" / Sociologie ».

Wakabi, W., & Åke, G. (2015). Enhancing social accountability through ICT: Success factors and challenges. In *Proceedings of CeDEM, (International Conference for E-Democracy and Open Government),* Danube University, Krems, Austria, May 20-22.

Wasserman, H., & Madrid-Morales, D. (2018). Study sheds light on scourge of "fake" news in Africa. Retrieved from https://phys.org/news/2018-11-scourge-fake-news-africa.html

Watson, A. (2019). Media in Africa - Statistics & Facts. Retrieved from https://www.statista.com/topics/5032/media-in-africa/

Weeks, M. (2015). Is disruption theory wearing new clothes or just naked? Analyzing recent critiques of disruptive innovation theory. *Innovation: Organization & Management, 17*(4), 417–428. doi:10.1080/14479338.2015.1061896

Williamson, J. (1990). What Washington Means by Policy Reform. In J. Williamson (Ed.), *Latin American Adjustment: How Much Has Happened?* Washington, DC: Institute for International Economics.

Williamson, J. (1999). What Should the Bank Think About the Washington Consensus. Background Paper to the World Bank's *World Development Report 2000* (July).

Zanello, G., & Maassen, P. (2011). Strengthening citizen agency through ICT: An extrapolation for Eastern Africa. *Public Management Review*, *13*(3), 363–382. doi:10.1080/14719037.2011.553265

Chapter 11
Role of Social Media in Environmental Democracy

Manju Lata
https://orcid.org/0000-0001-6722-8171
Chaudhary Bansi Lal University, India

Anu Gupta
Guru Jambheshwar University of Science and Technology, India

ABSTRACT

Environmental democracy sets a standard for how decisions should be made. At its core, environmental democracy involves three mutually reinforcing rights that, while independently important, operate best in combination: the ability for people to freely access information on environmental quality and problems, to participate meaningfully in decision-making, and to seek enforcement of environmental laws or compensation for damages. There are three fundamental rights: Access to Information, Citizen Participation, and Access to Justice. Social media can certainly play a vital role in all three fundamental rights. This chapter identifies the role of social media in these three fundamental rights with respect to environmental democracy. The chapter introduces environmental democracy and associated challenges. It then builds a model based on social media to lead to successful environmental democracy campaigns.

DOI: 10.4018/978-1-7998-1791-8.ch011

Copyright © 2020, IGI Global. Copying or distributing in print or electronic forms without written permission of IGI Global is prohibited.

INTRODUCTION

The world is facing several fundamental challenges and reduction of natural resources & climate change are most important of them. The changing climate patterns are also leading to the food and water security issues across the Globe. Studies have forecasted an average global temperature increase by 1.4–5.8^{0}C by end of 21st century and this will lead to a reduction of agricultural harvest and freshwater resources (Misra, 2014). The Himalayan glaciers are on depletion and may disappear in the coming years. Furthermore, the rainfall could drop by 10% in Africa by 2050, which would cause the reduction of drain age by 17%. There has been a depletion of mainstream of freshwater resources and this has a reducing effect on the agricultural production universally, whereas the food demand via the population in increasing continuously (Turral et al., 2011). Some of the prominent climate change impacts on natural disasters are the growing deserts, floods and droughts. The prevention of Low-frequency, high-impact events such as earthquakes and tsunamis have become very difficult and there have been high osses of human life in the recent years. Table 1 has outlined the deadliest disasters of 21st century (https://ourworldindata.org/natural-disasters).

The World Meteorological Organization (WMO) report on the global climate have reported a 20% increase in the CO_2 growth rates during 2015-2019 as compared to the last five years ("WMO", 2019). The atmospheric concentrations of greenhouse gases (GHGs) have also increased significantly with the growing industrialisation in the past five decades. If the greenhouse gas emissions are continued similar to the past decade, global warming can reach to 1.5°C between 2030 and 2052 (IPCC 2018). However, each additional unit of warming will significantly increase the climate-related risks for all natural and human systems. Specifics of the risks certainly depends on the pace of climate change, geographic location, levels of socio-economic development, resilience and vulnerability, and also the adaptation and mitigation options followed (IPCC 2018; NASA 2019). Thus, the climate change and the reduction of natural resources need a bigger attention towards the sustainable development, as well as ensuring sustainable consumption and production patterns. There is a world-wide need to minimize the release of pollutants and introduction of circular economy. These challenges however cannot be met by any individual actor. In 1992 the Rio declaration was adopted and principle 10 stated that: "Environmental issues are best handled with participation of all concerned citizens, at the relevant level. At the national level, each individual shall have appropriate access to information concerning the environment that is held by public authorities, including information on hazardous materials and activities in their communities, and the opportunity to participate in decision-making processes. States shall facilitate and encourage public awareness and participation by making information widely available. Effective access to judicial

Table 1. Deadliest natural disasters (2000-2019)

Year	Death toll	Event	Location
2000	800	2000 Mozambique flood	Mozambique
2001	20,085	2001 Gujarat earthquake	India
2002	1,030	2002 Indian heat wave	India
2003	70,000	2003 European heat wave	France, Portugal, United Kingdom, Netherlands, Germany, Spain, Sweden, Italy, Luxemburg, Ireland
2004	227,898	2004 Indian Ocean earthquake and tsunami	Indonesia, Sri Lanka, India, Thailand, Somalia
2005	87,351	2005 Kashmir earthquake	Pakistan
2006	5,782	2006 Yogyakarta earthquake	Indonesia
2007	15,000	Cyclone Sidr	Bangladesh, India
2008	138,373	Cyclone Nargis	Myanmar
2009	1,115	2009 Sumatra earthquake	Indonesia
2010	160,000	2010 Haiti earthquake	Haiti
2011	15,897	2011 Tōhoku earthquake and tsunami	Japan
2012	1,901	Typhoon Bopha cyclone	Philippines
2013	6,340	Typhoon Haiyan cyclone	Philippines, Vietnam, China
2014	729	2014 Ludian earthquake	China
2015	8,964	2015 Nepal earthquake	Nepal
2016	676	2016 Ecuador earthquake	Ecuador
2017	3,059	Hurricane Maria cyclone	Puerto Rico, Dominica
2018	4,340	2018 Sulawesi earthquake and tsunami	Indonesia
2019	1,303	Cyclone Idai	Mozambique, Zimbabwe, Malawi

and administrative proceedings, including redress and remedy, shall be provided." ("UN Environment Program", 2016). This turn requires a wide-spread acceptance of the concept of environmental democracy. Endorsement of the environmental democracy through the effective commitment of civil society, including NGOs, native people, academia, stakeholders, complements and reinforces the government's ability to address these problems The modern concept of environmental democracy have been quoted and presented by many researchers and a summary of the same has been presented in Table 2.

ENVIRONMENTAL DEMOCRACY RIGHTS

Environmental democracy implicates three commonly reinforcing rights that exists when the public is able to freely access information around environmental concerns, participate in the decision-making related to environment, and demand enforcement of environmental laws or compensation for damage (Antypas, 2003). These three rights are also considered as procedural rights grouped into three areas: access to information, public participation and access to justice.

Access to Information: When implemented and well-designed, the right to access to information makes it essential that the organisations, companies and governments make the information freely and easily available. Most importantly, the information related to environmental impact assessments, the details of development project plans, and timely information on pollution discharges should be freely accessible to the public. This can lead to public participation and public can contribute more effectively in decision-making and can hold the governments and other agencies accountable for any actions against the environment. Particularly, the actions, which are not in agreement with the law. The formats and presentation for such information should also be designed in a manner that people can freely use this information without any constraints on account of literacy, readability, language, technology acceptance or others. However, a lot of effort is required from the Governments to ensure this availability of information. For example, the first-ever Pollutant Release and Transfer Register (PRTR) was developed by United States and this was called as the Toxics Release Inventory (TRI) in 1986. This initiative was a result of the continued pressure due to several environmental disasters, including a chemical release in 1985 from the Union Carbine plant in West Virginia (https://www.wri.org/our-work/project/access-initiative-tai/commissions). The TRI makes is mandatory to submit data on the quantity of toxic chemicals for the industrial facilities releasing such chemicals. After this initiative of United States in 1986, more than 50 countries have developed such PRTRs or at least implemented pilot programs (https://www.wri.org/our-work/project/access-initiative-tai/commissions). This kind of a mandatory public disclosure by the companies have reduced the incidences of toxic release in United States. However, as the environmental concerns keep on growing with the technological changes, there is always a scope for the continuous improvement. Similarly, the Govt of India had established the Bureau of Energy Efficiency (BEE) to assist in the development of policies and strategies to encourage self-regulation and market principles related to energy efficiency. The primary objective is to reduce the energy consumption in the Indian economy within the overall framework of the Energy Conservation Act, 2001.The Energy Conservation Building Code (ECBC) was developed by BEE and this was adopted in June 2017 to replace the earlier 2007 code.

Table 2. Definitions of environmental democracy

Definitions	References
"Each individual shall have appropriate access to information concerning the environment that is held by public authorities, including information on hazardous materials and activities in their communities, and the opportunity to participate in decision-making processes. States shall facilitate and encourage public awareness and participation by making information widely available. Effective access to judicial and administrative proceedings, including redress and remedy, shall be provided"	Shelton (1991)
"The introduction of environmental rights clearly has the potential to alter radically the established framework of decision making in favour of the environment. Such procedural rights for the environmental democracywould not only help to redress the current under-representation of environmental interests but would also provide a firmer guarantee of environmental decision making according to law – thereby redressing the pervasive 'implementation deficit' in environmental law and administration".	(Eckersley, 1996; Eckersley, 2000)
"It is by far the most impressive elaboration of principle 10 of the Rio Declaration, which stresses the need for citizen's participation in environmental issues. As such, it is the most ambitious venture in the area of environmental democracy so far undertaken under the auspices of the United Nations."	Kofi (2000)
"All persons have the right to a secure, healthy and ecologically sound environment", and that " all persons have the right to an environment adequate to meet equitably the needs of present generations and that does not impair the rights of future generations to meet equitably their needs."	Hayward (2000)
"It was the environmental movement in the North that first challenged the overarching claims to legitimacy by political systems based on representative democracy [...] During the 1970s and 1980s, thousands of young men and women protested against their democratically elected governments on the sitting of nuclear power stations. Simply because certain people had been elected by majority, they argued, was not enough to give them the untrammeled right to decide how the local environment could be used without the consent of the people who were worst affected by this decision. They essentially wanted a deepening of the democratic process."	Hay (2002); Parola, (2013)
"The activities backgrounds and interest of political representatives and decision makes are seen as far removed from the lives and perspectives of citizens. Although periodic elections act the mandate that representatives enjoy extends over a period during which time citizens have very little impact on decisions made in their name"	Graham (2003)
"Democratic deliberation cannot effectively progress without adequate environmental information, much of which is held by public and private authorities. Legal redress offers the opportunity to object to decisions and actions of public and private bodies that contravene environmental rights and law. Thus, environmental law acts as a legitimate constraint on the outcomes of democratic policy making. But given the right to participation, the content of environmental policy, standards and law itself becomes legitimate subject of democratic deliberation"	Graham (2003)
"It is not correct to identify hierarchical relations as the basis of the overall environmental problems, rather, one could suggest that reformation of social relations should go hand-in-hand with or perhaps even follow resolution of human nature relations". Secondly, anarchist solutions do not necessarily provide any good grounds for the resolution of either because "feudal and tribal societies both typically small scale – can be exploitative of both people and nature, or networks of small communities may not provide an effective mechanism to prevent environmental harm."	Wilkinson (2004)
"Environmental democracy is about government being transparent, accountable, and involving people in decisions that affect their environment"	Acharya (2008)
"New term 'environmental democracy', now taking hold, reflects increasing recognition that environmental issues must be addressed by all those affected by their outcome, not just by governments and industrial sectors. It captures the principle of equal rights for all those in the environment debate – including the public, community groups, advocates, industrial leaders, workers, governments, academics and health care professionals. For those whose daily lives reflect the quality of their environment, participation in environmental decision-making is as important as in education, health care, finance and government"	Hazen,(2010)
"A decentralised social organisation is more responsive to 'feedback mechanisms' and the people on the ground know more about the situation than those in control". On the other hand, there is "the problem of local communities attempting to free-ride and avoid ecological policies. When there is insufficient mutual adaptation and a lack of centrally guided co-ordination of environmental polices there is a danger that the vulnerable ecological equilibrium of society might be violated".	Parola, (2013)

Public Participation: The rights of public participation is very much important to improve the communication and information flow between the communities, government and other stake holders. This information exchange can lead to a greater support towards the decision making and help in decreasing the unintended consequences of poor decision making. The better decisions can also lead to a more equitable distribution of costs and benefits due to improved participation. People should be encouraged to participate in the decision making process and they should be informed well in time about the opportunities to participate. This can be done through the community workshops or other events like the town hall meetings. Every effort should be made that people are not discouraged to participate because of the cost burdens such as traveling to the capital city for participation. Also, they information related to the environmental impact analysis etc. should be made available to them well in time to have their meaningful participation. Public participation becomes less meaningful, when they are just informed about an upcoming decision and there is no opportunity to influence this decision (CEPAL, 2018).The best way to encourage the public participation is through the Environmental Impact Assessments (EIA), where many countries require public consultations before the development of projects having environmental impacts (Clark, 1994).

The European Community (EC) has set a Directive 85/337/EEC as the legal requirement for EIA of specific projects to complete the assessment of certain private and public projects (CEC, 1985). The formal public participation procedures of the European Economic Community (EEC) Directive became law in the United Kingdom (UK) in 1988 and this was implemented by a series of regulations where the projects require planning permissions as well as need to follow the other statutory controls (Barker, 2001). In India, the ministry of Environment, Forests and Climate Change (MoEFCC) has put a lot of efforts for implementation of the EIA in India. Water Act (1974), Indian Wildlife Protection Act (1972), Air (Prevention and Control of Pollution) Act (1981), Environment Protection Act (1986),Biological Diversity Act(2002) (Ghosh, 2013) are most important regulations being followed in India. The Central Pollution Control Board is the main responsible body for this. In Iraq, the Ministry of Environment of the federal government is looking after the Environmental compliance certificates and these certificates are issued on the basis of EIA report prepared by professional consultants and thoroughly reviewed by the ministry (Abaas, 2016). EIA appears to offer good opportunities to involve the public informally (Stephenson et al, 1994). The World Bank is also playing a very critical catalytic role in the development of EIA in developing countries. Although there are many reasons behind this, the World Bank can play a vital role in the implementation as the World Bank has offered loans to many developing country governments.

The European Bank for Reconstruction and Development (EBRD) is playing an important role to ensure the participation of Central and Eastern Europe Public in the EBRD's investment decision-making processes. This is confirmed by the following statement: "The Bank will ensure that project sponsors provide adequate information on the environmental impacts of projects to governments at all levels and to the general public, especially potentially affected parties, and that the comments and opinions expressed by these parties will be taken into account in the project-approval procedures of the Bank" (EBRD, 1993). Public Participation in the EIA process in 1993, Similarly the Hugarian Govt passed a Government Decree 86/1993 (VI.4) in 1993 to ensure the public participation on the assessment of the environmental impact of certain activities. The Ministry for Environment and Regional Policy in Hungary has the overall responsibility for the EIA process coordination. EIA Section, the Central Environmental Protection Fund and the Chief Inspectorate have been established to smoothen the process. Many other countries have also established the similar offices.

Access to Justice: As per this right, the general public should be able to exercise a right to seek justice, compensation or appealing to a project. This is particularly important when the pubic lacks information access and easy participation in the environment related concerns. All these accountability mechanisms should be very much independent and impartial. In ideal conditions, they should be able to enforce the mandatory and binding conditions. India's National Green Tribunal (NGT) is a very good examples of the regulatory mechanisms that provide access to justice related to the environmental concerns. This tribunal was established in 2010 by the Govt of India, recognising a large number of court cases regarding the environmental disputes. The tribunal has jurisdiction over all civil cases involving "substantial questions related to the environment," and has a mandate to attempt to conclude within six months of it filing.

International institutions like United Nations Development Programme has also recognised the environmental democracy as an essential tool to sustainable development, as it can improve information flow for environmental concerns (Gleditsch et al., 2002).The United Nations Environment Programme's (UNEP) Bali Guidelines for the Development of National Legislation on Access to Information, Public Participation and Access to Justice in Environmental Matters have also come-up with the Environmental Democracy Index (EDI). This index is being used as an international standard to benchmark the county specific laws. The Environmental Democracy Index (EDI) has been developed by The Access Initiative (TAI) and the World Resources Institute (WRI) and it is the first of its kind index designed specifically to measure the procedural rights in environmental context ("World Resources Institutc," n.d.).

The Environmental Democracy Index (EDI) is a comprehensive tool to strengthen the procedural rights. This has become very much essential considering the recent surge in laws on accessing the environmental information and their quality, scope or implementation. EDI has been designed to address the global environmental challenges on air and water pollution. This is capable to address the extractive industry impacts and biodiversity loss by establishing a centralized hub of legal analysis and implementation data on procedural rights. The implementation results will help establish both best practices and benchmarking standards (Worker et al., 2015). The unique design and contributions of EDI include:

- **Comprehensive Evaluation of Environmental Democracy:** EDI serves as an internationally accepted tool to measure the procedural rights in an environmental context. The index can evaluate, whether the Governments are enacting national laws to promote transparency, accountability, and continuous engagement of the citizens in environmental decision making.
- **International Benchmarking Standard:** EDI benchmarks the rights against an international standard established by UNEP.
- **Actionable Evidence:** The indicators specified by EDI are very much actionable in nature and it is supported by legal evidence and stories on the ground.
- **Assessment of Laws in Practice:** With a set of practice indicators, piloted in the 2014; EDI, provides a snapshot of laws being practiced in a country.
- **Up-to-date Scoring:** As a practice, EDI will be calculated every two years to ensure that the scores remain relevant and useful.

SOCIAL MEDIA AND ENVIRONMENTAL DEMOCRACY

Governments, Development Agencies, NGOs and other organizations across the Globe are working to reduce the global worries of environment degradation. This concern has led a lot of initiatives to spread environmental awareness among people to get them aware about the environment protection, global warming and other natural hazards. Environmental concerns have given rise to the Earth Stewardship practices, through which many organizations are committing to adopt the sustainable practices (UNESCO, 1997). Therefore, the civil society organisation and general public is playing a major role in global environmental control including collecting, disseminating, and analyzing information; providing input to plan setting and policy development processes; performing operational functions; assessing environmental conditions and monitoring compliance with environmental agreements; and advocating environmental justice (Gemmill et al., 2002). Media can certainly play a vital role in mobilizing the support from civil society for all of these objectives. It has been very well established that countries with a larger newspaper circulation and having largest number of social media sites have better responsive to environmental concerns, on average, despite controlling for the extent of environmental regulation (Dyck et al., 2002).

Facebook, WhatApp, WeChat, Linkedln, Skype, Google+, Instagram, Twitter, Snapchat, all these names have become very much popular in present day society. Each of these social networking sites have their own format own style own attraction and applications, and all of them are playing vital role in gaining trust of the people (Kumar & Pradhan, 2015). Correspondingly, they can do excellent work in the promotion and action on various issues of environment. From global warming, climate change to solid waste management, renewable energy news etc. can be easily taken-up by these media and the active participation by a large number of people can be ensured (Robelia et al., 2011). The number of users for the social media platforms are continuously increasing and this can be seen that Facebook itself has crossed the mark of 2.4 billion monthly active users in 2019 ("Most Popular Social Networks", 2019). This can certainly guarantee the user's accessibility of information on social media sites for the environmental outcomes.

Furthermore, public opinion pressure generated by active users is also essential to efforts by private sector organizations to use self-regulation to improve corporate control for the environment. Consequently, spread of environmental knowledge and awareness of environmental issues requires certain tools of communication, offline or online. Social media sites are gaining importance in increasing environmental concern and environmental responsible behaviours in public (Kratziget al., 2014). Social media permit users to generate and exchange of user generated contents on different themes and help in creating a continuous engagement (Kumar & Nanda, 2019; Kumar & Nanda, 2020). Social Media can play an important role in generating the user trust and hence it can have a larger implication for creating awareness on the environmental issues (Kumar & Pradhan, 2015). Concern for environment and awareness of environmental issues influence society and it leads to identify different ways to resolves these environmental crises by changing their behavioural actions. Research studies have examined positively that social media had its inception since 1978 through the use of e-mail for communication and information sharing (Shao, 2009). Emergence of social media transforms consumers to be active creators of information rather than mere receivers of information (Shao, 2009). Changes in technology, lifestyles and education mode have led to unprecedented growth in usage of networking sites.

Social media is a powerful tool of content creation, sharing ideas, disseminating and expressing knowledge, opinions (Ayodeji & Kumar, 2019). This is not limited to sharing and communication of information, but it has emerged as a platform of webcasting, gaming and blogging also. Social media provides space to users to participate in collaborative projects enabling them to create, add or edit web contents (Kumar & Sharma, 2016). Blogging on social sites provides information on recent events in informal way. Communities or groups interact with each other on this platform for information sharing. In short, social sites help individuals in socializing and expressing their views through the one-to-one, one-to-many and many-to-many communication modes. Social Media promotion of environment friendly behaviours need communication on environment related issues but it encounters with certain problem like lack of significant awareness. To spread awareness regarding environmental issues and to promote environmental friendly products, various communication tools are used. Traditionally, the media has played a significant role in this (https://aifs.gov.au/cfca/publications/role-mass-media-facilitating-community-education). But now a days, traditionally non-standard forms of communication are getting popular to address these issues. With the growth of internet services and applications, users become more prone to digital world. They are using web based applications for their personal as well as professional use and for entertainment also (Kumar & Ayodeji, 2020). Social media extensively influences users' attitudes, knowledge and perceptions. These practices can certainly be harnessed for usage towards the environmental concerns.

Social media embraces a group of online activities like blogging, chatting, gaming and instant messaging and even more of this (Boyd & Ellison, 2008). Different groups or communities are formed on social media platform. Environment friendly groups are actively harnessing the power of social media by using it to spread information and awareness on environment issues through environment protection fan pages, environment related posts, green blogging (http://www.treehuggers.com, http://www.greenthinkers.com) etc. Online videos, other electronic content and communication contributes to the efforts of groups in promoting environmental conservation and protection actions by users. Social media such as you tube, Facebook, Instagram and twitter may prove beneficial to access users' mind set and to influence their attitude and perceptions. Many users use social media to share real time videos or photos on variety of environmental issues such as illegal dumping, flowing of chemical spills in water ways; fires in forests and issues on endanger species. This results in awareness and arise attention among help groups and common people. Social media thus helps in inspiring environment activism with the help of messages such as quotations and videos, stories on responsible behaviours. Social media helps in providing momentum to spread awareness and knowledge on these issues. The ability for organizations to use the crowd, highly connected through social media, to support and spread environmental messages in a rapid, dynamic format. On the other hand, social media has propelled the rise of the independent activist. For instance, during the Deepwater Horizon Oil Spill, Gulf Coast residents used Facebook and Twitter as platforms to share their personal stories and provide independent or alternative new sources and media that was captured by their communities. Since people now look to their social media streams as primary sources of news and information, this type of independent vocalization can be both positive (encouraging alternative streams of information) and problematic when information isn't verified or trustworthy.

Hence, the social media content needs to be carefully designed for its effective use in the environmental democracy.

EXAMPLES AND SUCCESS STORIES

Environmental campaigns have the ability to provide individuals with the knowledge, skills and attitude required to reduce environmental impact. Social media have been used by environmental activists to conduct environmental awareness campaigns. Social Media for EnviroNmental Awareness (SMENA) model is a popular model for improving knowledge and thereby awareness of environmental issues by means of a social media campaign. The model consists of three phases of the campaign: (a) Strategy development phase, (b) planning phase and the (c) implementation phase (Tlebere, 2016). In the strategy development phase, the environmental goals and objectives are identified and prioritised towards the environmental categories. Whereas the preferences of learners with regards to social media are identified in the planning phase. Twitter and Facebook are considered as the most popular social media for the users. The implementation phase is responsible of the frequent information updates as recommended by Walther (2010). The SMENA mode has been designed to facilitate the design and implementation of an environmental awareness social media campaign and has been very much successful in this. The primay aim of the SMENA model is to improve public awareness on environmental issues. The model was implemented at a South African University and activities of the environmental awareness campaign were conducted on a social media website (SMENA website) and the popular social media sites Twitter and Facebook (Tlebere, 2016). The results have shown that environmental knowledge increased as a result of the campaign. However, this is just one example, there have been many other evidences, where social media has proved vital for creating awareness on the environmental issues. Some of the most popular and effective social media campaigns include:

J.J. Watt: #Hurricane Harvey Fundraiser

Hurricane Harvey was one of the costliest and high impact environmental disasters to hit the United States. The fundraising through crowd sourcing was created a history by J.J. Watt, when he succcssfully raised 37 million dollars through his campaign. He launched a fundraising campaign on YouCaring.com to start raising money across social media on August 26th, 2017 with an initial goal of $200,000. Watt raised an amazing $37,068,102, which was much more than his original goal. He was also named as Walter Payton NFL Man of the Year in early 2018 for his efforts for this humanitarian cause.

Patagonia: #Black Friday Donation

The outdoor clothing brand Patagonia has been a front runner for the environmental activism since the company was started in 1973. In 2016 on Black Friday, Patagonia announced that it would donate 100% of its sales to organizations that benefit the environment. The campaign got very much hit on social media and it spread like wildfire. This tweet received nearly 1,000% greater engagement rate than others on their profile. The initial projection of the was around $2 million in sales, however it was able to sell more than $10 million worth of products (https://www.patagonia.com/100-percent-for-the-planet.html). Social media was the prime actor and force behind the success of this campaign. The company Patagonia explained that the campaign allowed them to help hundreds of grassroots environmental organizations which are contributing to the Global environment through a number of different ways. There used Twitter, Facebook,LinkedIn to share the information on its campaigns. The company has also pledged to give 1% of all sales to non for profit environmental groups since 1985 on everyday basis.

NASA: #AdoptThePlanet

Earth Day is celebrated across the world on April 22, every year. This is day provides an opportunity to celebrate our planet and bring attention to the natural world. A number of events are organised on this day to celebrate, educate and aware the people. This day also provides a perfect opportunity to launch social media campaigns on environment. In 2017, NASA launched a campaign and invited people to "adopt" a portion of Earth's surface with their #AdoptThePlanetcampaign.. 64,000 individual pieces of earth are seen from the space and NASA invited people to adopt each of these pieces. NASA helped to educate millions of people around the world with their integrated website and social media campaign approach. (https://www.nasa.gov/feature/goddard/2017/nasa-celebrates-earth-day-by-letting-us-all-adopttheplanet).

World Wide Fund for Nature (WWF): #EndangeredEmoji

WWF is on a Global mission to build a sustainable future, where people live in harmony with the earth and nature. WWF is the leading independent conservation body of the world and is always involved in several big campaigns around the world. All of its campaigns are targeted to make the big impacts. One of the popular WWF social media campaign was called #EndangeredEmoji campaign. In this campaign, genius use of emoji on social media helped to raise awareness for endangered animals around the world (http://wwf.panda.org/wwf_news/?246970/wwf-turns-tweets-to-donations-withendangeredemoji-social-campaign). Under this campaign, people use animal emoji every day into the texts with friends and posts on social media sites like Twitter, Instagram, Blog, and YouTube. The campaign certainly makes a very good connect with the animal world.

GetUp! Action for Australia: #Great Barrier Reef

GetUp is an independent group of activists from Australia and more than 600,000 people have already joined the Great Barrier Reef Campaign by GetUp!. One of its biggest campaigns is a bid to protect the Great Barrier Reef. The Great Barrier Reef is the world's largest living organism. It is an extraordinary array of sealife living in an interconnected ecosystem, which is very much fragile in nature. A recent petition to the federal environment minister has attracted some 120,000 signatures, the petition is to halt all industrial development activity in the Great Barrier reef area. The campaign is very much democratic independent, seeks to educate, and inform. (https://www.getup.org.au/).

Fossil Free: #350.org

The Fossil Free campaign by 350.org is one of the biggest campaigns towards the usage of renewable energy. Following environmentalist Bill McKribben's mantra that 'if it's wrong to wreck the climate, it's wrong to profit from that wreckage, the Fossil Free campaign attempts to get public institutions, such as universities and churches, to stop using fossil fuels. With supporters encouraged to set up their own individual campaigns, the impact of this campaign is very high. Also, by working with local community groups, 350.org aims to hold corporations and world leaders accountable to the realities of science and the principles of social justice. The 350 in the name stands for 350 ppm (parts per million) of carbon dioxide, which has been identified as the safe upper limit to avoid a climate tipping point. As of 2019, the current level has reached 415 ppm (https://campaigns.350.org/).

Greenpeace and TckTckTck: #Oxfam International, World Wildlife Fund

Global Campaign for Climate Action (GCCA) is a global alliance formed with the participation of thc non-governmental organizations, trade unions, and faith groups. They had collaborated to influence the world leaders attending the COP 15 conference in Copenhagen in 2009. The public face of this campaign is "TckTckTck". The billboard campaign featured the likes of Barack Obama and Angela Merkel as imagined in 2020. The TckTckTck campaign was created by the Global Humanitarian

Forum and strategic communications partner HavasWorldwide/Euro RSCG. (http://www.ghf-ge.org/tcktcktck.php).

Connect4Climate: #Electrification, #decentralisation and #digitalisation #renewables

Connect4Climate is a global partnership program under the communication for environment revolutionizes Multi-Donor Trust Fund of the World Bank Group. The objective of the programme is to broaden the climate literacy on a worldwide level and to promote the concrete action against climate change. It has a focus on the implementation of renewable energy and the reduction of industrial waste. Connect4Climate get hold of a large number of students with its iChange competition. It uses a blog and other social media sites like Twitter, Instagram, and etc(https://www.connect4climate.org/).

Liberate Tate: #Free Art from Oil

Liberate Tate is an art collective exploring the role of creative intervention in social change. The group aims to "free art from oil" with a primary focus on the art museum Tate ending its corporate sponsorship with BP. Anti-oil activists Liberate Tate gained note-worthy popularity for their attempts to stop the art gallery receiving funding from petroleum company BP. Their acts of creative disobedience have included a naked man being covered in oil and carting a 1.5 tonne wind turbine blade into the gallery's main hall (http://ecflive.fairsay.com/liberate-tate-winning-campaigns-with-creative-intervention/). They used Twitter, Pinterest, Google+ and Instagram for creating awareness and sharing the information.

CONCLUSION

With high level of industrialization and lot of developments in science and technology, environmental challenges are increasing across the Globe. Participation of the general public as well as other organisations of the civil society is very much important to take-up these issues along with Government and development agencies. Social media has high implications for communication at different levels in the society, correspondingly it can also play a vital role in creating awareness on the environmental issues. Social media has emerged as an effective tool for public to participate in the dialogue and influence the environment related decisions taken by governments and corporate, in favour of the society. People have got more connected with the local environmental challenges and are able to take-up these to the global community. There have been a lot of success stories, where social media has contributed enormously to the environmental challenges and it has not only remained restricted to awareness campaigns. Most importantly, it has emerged as a democratic tool to bring people at the same level and work for the cause of environment. Still it is going to become an essential marketing and communication tool for Govt., private, public and non-governmental organisations, organisations and general public across the world to promote environmental democracy.

REFERENCES

Abaas, Z. R. (2016). *"The Role Of Environmental Impact Assessment Tool in Achieving Sustainable Urban Development and Its Challenges in Iraq", Mesop. environ. j., 2016* (pp. 138–148). Special Issue A.

Acharya, A. (2008). Democracy in Burma: Does Anyone Really Care? In Asia Rising: Who Is Leading? pp. 149-153.

Antypas, A. (2003). A New Age for Environmental Democracy: The Aarhus Convention in Hungary. *Environmental Liability*, *11*(6), 199–208.

Ayodeji, O. G., & Kumar, V. (2019). Social media analytics: A tool for the success of online retail industry, *Int. J. Services Operations and Informatics*, *10*(1), 79–95. doi:10.1504/IJSOI.2019.100630

Barker, A., & Wood, C. (2001). Environmental assessment in the European Union: Perspectives, past, present and strategic. *European Planning Studies*, *9*(2), 243–254. doi:10.1080/713666468

Boyd, D., & Ellison, N. (2008). Social Network Sites: Definition History, and Scholarship. *Journal of Computer-Mediated Communication*, *13*(1), 210–230. doi:10.1111/j.1083-6101.2007.00393.x

CEPAL, N. (2018). Access to Information, Participation and Justice in Environmental Matters in Latin America and the Caribbean: Towards Achievement of the 2030 Agenda for Sustainable Development. pp. 1-144.

Clark, B. D. (1994). Improving Public Participation In Environmental Impact Assessment, Built Environment (1978-), pp. 294-308.

Commission of the European Communities (CEC). (1985) European Communities Directive 85/337/EEC on the Assessment of Certain Public and Private Projects on the Environment. Brussels, Belgium: Commission of the European Communities. Available at https://eur-lex.europa.eu/legal-content/EN/TXT/PDF/?uri=CELEX:52003DC0334&from=EN

Dosemagen, S. (2016). Social Media and Saving the Environment: Clicktivism or Real Change. *Huffington Post*. Available at https://www.huffpost.com/entry/social-media-and-saving-t_b_9100362

Dyck, A., & Zingales, L. (2002). The Corporate Governance Role of the Media, August, 2002, p. 5. Available at http://faculty.chicagobooth.edu/finance/papers/corporate%20governance.pdf

Eckersley, R. (1996). Greening Liberal Democracy: The Rights Discourse Revisited. In B. Doherty, & M. de Geus (Eds.), *Democracy and Green Political Thought* (p. 216). doi:10.4324/9780203449554_chapter_11

Eckersley, R. (2000). Deliberative Democracy, Ecological Representation and Risk: Towards a Democracy of the Affected. In M. Saward (Ed.), *Democratic Innovation: Deliberation, Representation and Association* (p. 230).

European Bank for Reconstruction and Development. (EBRD, 1993). Public participation - The EBRD approach, The Environ mental Bulletin of EBRD, Winter. Available at https://www.ebrd.com/publications/annual-report-1993-english.pdf

Gemmill, B., & Bamidele-Izu, A. (2002). The role of NGOs and civil society in global environmental governance, Global environmental governance: Options and opportunities, pp. 77-100.

Ghosh, S. (2013). Demystifying the Environmental Clearance Process in India. *NUJS L. Rev.*, *6*, 433.

Glasson, J., & Therivel, R. (2013). *Introduction to Environmental Impact Assessment* (pp. 1–490). Routledge.

Gleditsch, N. P., & Sverdrup, B. O. (2002). Democracy and the Environmental, Human security and the environment: International comparisons, p. 45.

Graham, S. (2003). *Deliberative Democracy and the Environment* (pp. 53–108). London, UK.

Hay. (2002). This environmental thought was defined "Hobbesian deeply despairing and anti-democratic", p. 174.

Hayward, T. (2000). Constitutional environmental rights: A case for political analysis. *Political Studies*, *48*(3), 558–572. doi:10.1111/1467-9248.t01-1-00275

Hazen, S. (2010). Environmental Democracy, UNEP. Retrieved from http://www.unep.org/ourplanet/imgversn/86/hazen.html

Intergovernmental Panel on Climate Change (IPCC). (2018). Global Warming of 1.5 ºC. Retrieved from http://report.ipcc.ch/sr15/pdf/sr15_spm_final.pdf

Jenkins, H. (2010). *Convergence Culture: Where old and new media collide*. New York: New York University Press.

Kofi, A. (2000). Foreword. In UNECE, The Aarhus Convention: An Implementation Guide, p. v.

Kratzig, S., & Warren-Kretzschmar, B. (2014). Using interactive web tools in Environmental Planning to improve communication about Sustainable Development. *Sustainability*, *6*(1), 236–250. doi:10.3390u6010236

Kumar, V., & Ayodeji, O. G. (2020). Web Analytics for Knowledge Creation: A Systematic Review of Tools, Techniques and Practices [IJCBPL]. *International Journal of Cyber Behavior, Psychology and Learning*, *10*(1), 1–14. doi:10.4018/IJCBPL.2020010101

Kumar, V., & Nanda, P. (2019). Social Media in Higher Education: A Framework for Continuous Engagement. [IJICTE]. *International Journal of Information and Communication Technology Education*, *15*(1), 109–120. doi:10.4018/IJICTE.2019010107

Kumar, V., & Nanda, P. (2020). Social Media as a Tool in Higher Education: A Pedagogical Perspective. In *Handbook of Research on Diverse Teaching Strategies for the Technology-Rich Classroom* (pp. 239–253). IGI Global. doi:10.4018/978-1-7998-0238-9.ch016

Kumar, V., & Pradhan, P. (2015). Trust Management Issues in Social-Media Marketing [IJOM]. *International Journal of Online Marketing*, *5*(3), 47–64. doi:10.4018/IJOM.2015070104

Kumar, V., & Sharma, D. (2016). CreatingCollaborativeandConvenientLearningEnvironmentUsingCloud-Based Moodle LMS. *International Journal of Web-Based Learning and Teaching Technologies*, *11*(1), 35–49. doi:10.4018/IJWLTT.2016010103

Mallick, R., & Bajpai, S. P. (2019). Impact of Social Media on Environmental Awareness. In *Environmental Awareness and the Role of Social Media* (pp. 140–149). IGI Global. doi:10.4018/978-1-5225-5291-8.ch007

Misra, A. K. (2014). Climate Change and Challenges of Water and Food Security. *International Journal of Sustainable Built Environment, 3*(1), 153–165. doi:10.1016/j.ijsbe.2014.04.006

Morel, A., Friedman, R., Tulloch, D. J., & Caldecott, B. (2016). Stranded Assets in Palm Oil Production: A Case Study of Indonesia. Sustainable Finance Programme, SSEE, University of Oxford, Working Paper, pp. 1-83.

NASA. (2019). Retrieved from https://climate.nasa.gov/vital-signs/carbon-dioxide/

Parola, G. (2009). Towards Environmental Democracy (Doctoral dissertation), pp. 1-94.

Parola, G. (2013). *Environmental Democracy at the Global Level: Rights and Duties for a New Citizenship*. Walter de Gruyter. doi:10.2478/9788376560144

Robelia, B. A., Greenhow, C., & Burton, L. (2011). Environmental learning in online social networks: Adopting environmentally responsible behaviours. *Environmental Education Research, 17*(4), 553–575. doi:10.1080/13504622.2011.565118

Shao, G. (2009). Understanding the Appeal of User-Generated Media: A Uses and Gratification Perspective. *Internet Research, 19*(1), 7–25. doi:10.1108/10662240910927795

Shelton, D. (1991). Human rights, environmental rights, and the right to environment, *Stan. J. Int'l L., 28*, 103.

Statista. Most Popular Social Networking Worldwide as of October 2019 Ranked by Number of Active Users. (2019, October). Retrieved from https://www.statista.com/statistics/272014/global-social-networks-ranked-by-number-of-users//

Stephenson, D. N. A., & Brooke, C. (1994). Public Participation in EIA: A Review of the Experience in Europe and the UK. Aberdeen: CEMP. Available at https://www.jstor.org/stable/23287802

Tlebere, T., Scholtz, B., & Calitz, A. P. (2016). Using social media to improve environmental awareness in higher education institutions. In *Information Technology in Environmental Engineering* (pp. 101–111). Cham, Switzerland: Springer. doi:10.1007/978-3-319-25153-0_9

Turral, H., Burke, J., & Faurès, J. M. (2011). *Climate Change, Water, And Food Security (No. 36), Food and Agriculture Organization of the United Nations* (pp. 1–200). FAO.

UN Environment Program. NNEP implementing Principle 10 of the Rio Declaration. (2016, August 16). Retrieved from https://www.unenvironment.org/news-and-stories/story/unep-implementing-principle-10-rio-declaration

UNESCO. (1997). United Nations Educational, Scientific and Cultural Organization educating for A Sustainable future.

Walther, D. (2010). Critical success factors of social media marketing campaigns for consumer goods knowledge management. Retrieved from http://daenu.net/joomla/index.php?option1/4com_docman&task1/4doc_download&gid1/440

Wilkinson, I., & Welch, C. (2004). The political embeddedness of international business networks. *International Marketing Review*, *21*(2), 216–231. doi:10.1108/02651330410531411

Worker, J., & De Silva, L. (2015). The Environmental Democracy Index. Technical Note. Washington, DC: World Resources Institute, 3. pp. 1-56.

World Resources Institute. The Assess initiative. No Date. Retrieved from https://www.wri.org/our-work/project/access-initiative-tai/commissions

Chapter 12
Role of IT and Social Media in Democratic Change:
Paraphernalia Around Information Technology and Social Media

Anuradha Tiwari
https://orcid.org/0000-0002-9726-0698
GD Goenka University, India

Tarakeshwar Gupta
https://orcid.org/0000-0002-2110-3282
GD Goenka University, India

ABSTRACT

In the last decade or so there have been plenty of innovations pertaining to information technology and social media that has taken place. This has brought in a tremendous amount of change in the society and the quality of life. The chapter explores the various aspect of change that has happened due to information technology and social media in a democratic setup. The chapter highlights how social change has occurred due to innovation in information technology and social media. This chapter explores how information technology and social media have supported the various elements of social change which have improved social wellbeing and quality of life such as education, healthcare, personal safety, transport, predictive tool, and the economics around social change.

DOI: 10.4018/978-1-7998-1791-8.ch012

Copyright © 2020, IGI Global. Copying or distributing in print or electronic forms without written permission of IGI Global is prohibited.

INTRODUCTION

Innovation is generating, accepting, and implementing fresh thoughts, procedures, goods or services. (Thompson's, 1965). Innovation in information technology includes using technology in new ways to build a more effective organization and enhance alignment between technology projects and company objectives. Innovation in Information Technology can happen in many forms such as – developing new applications that open new markets, to convert various business processes to automated IT functions to reduce operating costs, to create systems which enhance better manageability. The need for innovation, flexibility, and adaptability has led to important modifications in the demands of the information system, especially those hosting infrastructures for information technology. (Volonino, Robinson and Watson, 1992). The fast development of information technology has created s system which is similar to that of the nervous system in human beings. Technology is changing society by altering the environment we are adapting to. This shift is generally in the material setting, customs and social institutions are often modified by the adjustment we make to the modifications (Ogburn, 1947).

Any technological change that is sufficiently large will result in some other social change. (Cohen, 1968). Social change is the modification of social structure processes, defined by modifications in cultural symbols, behavioural laws, social organisations or value systems. (Wilterdink, & Form, 2014). A significant volume of analytical and empirically studies on information technology and social change has been conducted which a strong linkage between them. (Kling, 2000).

In democracies, information technology has created new opportunities for the citizens and this has boosted the economy in a positive way but along with it has also brought threats such as fraud or information technology security risks, invasion of privacy and criminal conduct, technical issues such as viruses, and social and psychological issues such as depression and addiction. (Sjöberg, & Fromm, 2001). Information technology has dramatically increased over the past few years and so has the information security risks (Kumar & Bhardwaj, 2018). Information security infringement have a higher degree of economic impact. (Nofer, et. al., 2014). It has been noted that a broad area research on the development of the state-of-the-art technical resources to monitor and protect vital information resources has been done, and it is imperative to highlight that though technology has evolved around it but it may not be enough to protect and safeguard the same. (Siponen et al., 2008).

Another very important aspect about a properly functioning democracy is that it provides access to information. (Harrison and Sayogo, 2014). Hence any threat or risk of such information or data would lead to an attempt to disrupt the democratic functioning. It becomes very imperative to have data privacy policies and security in place to keep a check.

DRIVERS OF SOCIAL CHANGE

In 2017, former Rwandan health minister urged that the true measure of democracy is not elections, but education, health, and security of people. Though numerous studies have been conducted over the years to see if there is a link between democracy and healthcare, and largely these studies support that there is a strong effect of democracy on better health, such as by Franco et al., (2004) and Bollyky et. al., (2019). Democracy has an independent positive association with health that persists after adjustment to the wealth of the country, it's inequality level, and public sector size. (Franco et al., 2004). Studies depict that democracy is for better health for the population. In countries where democratic transition happened by 3%, the life expectancy of HIV/AIDS patients increased to 15%. In 2016, the four disease for which it has been observed that democratic setup matters are cardiovascular disease, tuberculosis, transport injuries, and other non-communicable disease; in low and middle income nations, 25.3% of total deaths and injuries occurred to people younger than 70 years of age. Results indicate that an one point rise in democratic practice decreased deaths by 2%. (Bollyky et. al., 2019). Hence, democracy is always for the well being of its people. This induces a tremendous amount of positive change in society as citizens prefer that the state creates policies and looks after its citizens in the best possible way.

Primary and higher education play a very important role in a democracy. Primary education brings in certain remuneration such as building citizenship skills and respectful challenges to authority and it also enhances the growing middle class. Higher education offers students the opportunity to obtain the most marketable skills by obtaining university degrees. (Sanborn & Thyne, 2014). This also can be seen as the epicentre of social change in a democratic setup. For any society that values democracy, quality education is a top priority as the basis of democracy is the symbiotic relationship between quality education and robust democratic society. (Dewey, 1963; Greene, 1986; Meier, 2000; Parker, 2006; Tocqueville, 1862). The relationship between education and democracy has been discussed for over a hundred years now; hence education from elementary schools to higher education in universities are vital institutions to people and a strong componenet of a democratic society, who are encouraged to become enduring learners and to progress in their professional lives, and to societies. This in turn depends on universities to drive modernization and development, and democracies enable such individual endeavours. A comparison of countries drifting towards democracy particularly in Eastern Europe, display that there is a high degree of correlation between democracy and education. Also, higher educational rates within a given population increase participation in support of democratic setup as more citizens choose to engage in the political space. (Glaeser, Ponzetto, & Shleifer, 2007). Democracy is not considered to be a relevant system of government in countries where level of education is low. In other words, we can say education is not considered meaningful in non-democratic societies. (Fortunato & Panizza, 2015). Hence from the above studies, a connotation can be drawn that education drives trained human capital which in turn drives the economy in a democratic setup in a progressive manner.

Human security has gradually shifted much of its focus on the individual, and the state has become the safety guarantor of security primarily in democracies. Hence, from time to time laws are amended and new laws are passed to make the citizens feel secure and to ensure them that their rights are protected. The willingness of authoritarian and democratic states to guarantee the safety of their citizens varies considerably. The lack of effective accountability in authoritarian mechanisms in authoritarian states means that legitimate challenges to human security can be silenced or ignored to ensure the regime's stability. However, the stability factor in semi-authoritarian regimes is less clear. (O'Brien, 2015). Democracy has its own drivers of social change. Citizens in democratic regime expect to be protected and their rights guarded. This expectation induces a social change in democracy which is not to be seen in non-democratic countries as the expectation from the regime is not there. Hence, there is a strong correlation between personal security and democracy.

Transportation policies and planning decisions around it have a strong relation with economy of a country because it creates a direct impact on employment, productivity, profits, tax revenues, and wealth accumulation. (Litman, 2017). Transport infrastructure investment promotes private capital accumulation and also assists in the construction of other public infrastructure and both of these eventually support economic growth. This economic development then promotes increased resource allocation towards the creation of public transport infrastructure, propagating a process of public investment, private investment, and economic growth. (Tong, Yu, & Roberts, 2014). This in turn drives the economy of a country which induces a major social change in a democratic setup. Hence, healthcare, education, personal security and transportation are important elements of a democratic setup and these elements have a direct or indirect relation to induce a strong social change. A number of researchers have also indicated these drivers of social change in their research and a summary of the review has been presented in the Table 1.

INFORMATION TECHNOLOGY AND SOCIAL CHANGE

Information technology is the main driver of economic growth and quality of life in the new age global economy. Innovation stands on digital technologies and business models which in turn can propel economic and social benefits from information technology if used in an intelligent manner. Government must prioritize

Table 1. Drivers of social change

Drivers	Source
Healthcare	Liaw, 2002
	Franco, Álvarez-Dardet, & Ruiz, 2004
	Lester & Hobbs, 2007
	Atkinson & Castro, 2008
	Thakur, Hsu, & Fontenot, 2012
	Schoen; Osborn; Squires; Doty; Rasmussen; Pierson; & Applebaum, 2012
	Lindberg, Nilsson, Zotterman, Söderberg, & Skär, 2013
	Bollyky, Templin, Cohen, Schoder, Dieleman, & Wigley, 2019
Education	Vygotsky, 1980
	Roschelle, Pea, Hoadley, Gordin, & Means, 2000
	Piaget, 2001
	Linn, Clark, & Slotta, 2003
	Gleaser, Ponzetto, & Shleifer, 2007
	Lange, Requejo, Flynn, Rizzo, Valero-Cuevas, Baker, & Winstein, 2010
	Lee, 2012
	Doyle, Garrett, & Currie, 2014
	Fortunato & Panizza, 2015
	Ezawa, 2016
Security	Sung; Marci; Pentlang, 2005
	Banks, Harms, Sarvestani, & Bastianini, 2009
	Patel; Park; Bonato; Chan; & Rodgers, 2012
	Nofer, Hinz, Muntermann, & Roßnagel, 2014
	Karusala & Kumar, 2017
Transportation	Atkinson, & Castro, 2008
	Digital Britain, 2009
	Boulton, 2010
	Pratt, Sarmiento, Montes, Ogilvie, Marcus, Perez, & Lancet, 2012
	Porter, Linse, & Barsaz, 2015
	Litman, 2017
	Speranza, 2018

how companies adopt information technology to exploit them for their growth. A sustainable digital economy will depend on rapidly changing governance frameworks that enable societies to anticipate and shape the impact of emerging technologies and responding rapidly to changing circumstances. (Baller, Dutta, & Lanvin, 2016). Some of the areas where information technology is used abundantly are such as education and training, healthcare, personal safety and transport.

Information Technology in Education and Training

Information technology enables the interests, needs, and strengths and weaknesses of the student to drive the learning process, facilitating rather than dictating the teacher. Information technology has a global impact on nursing schools and academic organizations are adapting their teaching environments to guarantee that the use of mobile devices increases patient care without harming the connection between patient and nurse. (Doyle, et al., 2013). For higher education in universities and colleges, AR (Augmented Reality) is a effective technology which assists in teaching. AR (Augmented Reality) is used to teach subjects such as astronomy, chemistry, physics, biology, mathematics, and geometry. (Lee, 2012). Collaborative learning is based on constructivism and theories of social learning which is structured on the fact that learning occurs when learners communicate *(Sharma & Kumar, 2017).* Research shows that networked learning using information and communication technology can help to develop higher-level abilities such as scientific inquiry and critical thinking. (Roschelle et al., 2000; Linn et al., 2003). Information and communication technologies play a pivotal role in enhancement of higher education institutions and acts as a channel of innovation, quality, and excellence in this sector. (Pavel, Fruth, & Neacsu, 2015). Literacy is being re-defined by the presence of technology in our schools and our society (Smyth, 2011). Countries like Australia, Canada, and US have strengthened their education framework by incorporating Information and Communication Technology to their educational curriculum. This incorporation of ICT to the new educational framework is to prepare the youth of the country for acquiring skills which will lead them to work and life in the information age era and may also lead to new knowledge management models in the organisations (Mittal & Kumar, 2019). Another massive development in education the MOOC (Massive Open Online Course). Based on the type of activities provided to students, MOOCs of any kind can help develop digital literacy skills. (Stewart, 2013). Most importainly, the integration of ICT in education also offers cost reduction for the educational institutes in a number of scenarios *(Nayar & Kumar, 2018)*

Information Technology in Healthcare

Some of the benefits that information technology is directly providing are – reducing the cost of healthcare, enhancing access to data on healthcare, improving healthcare quality, and improved access to healthcare. (Groves et al., 2016). The future of healthcare lies in better management of information than better doctors or better medicines. Telemedicine provides patients with access to medical professionals even if they are separated from them geographically. An application by Cisco called HealthPresence, uses the network as a platform for patients and physicians to communicate securely via high-definition audio and video connections. It also enables physicians to acquire vital signs and diagnostic data from their patients using unique networked medical devices. To extract benefit of this service, patients visit a Cisco HealthPresence pod staffed by a caregiver who helps with the technology and ensures that the pod is clean. (Atkinson & Castro, 2008). Innovation is guided by strategic implementation of information technology. (Thakur et al., 2012). Innovation studies have shown that the healthcare industry's success and survival rely on the efficiency and effectiveness of information technology. (Liaw, 2002). In the United States, it has been noticed that there has been a significant amount of increase in the number of health information seekers. For instance, 79.04% of American adults have used the internet to search health-related information for themselves, and 57.04% have used the internet to search someone else's health-related information. Advances in information technology and databases have assisted healthcare managers and professionals to set the groundwork for basic modifications within the organization of healthcare. It has also enabled physicians to interact with patients and staff members readily and rapidly. Also, has boosted awareness of healthcare among customers through internet healthcare forums and information technology. (Thakur, Hsu, & Fontenot, 2012). A global study in some democratic countries on primary care physicians in Australia, Canada, France, Germany, Netherland, New Zealand, Norway, Switzerland, United Kingdom, and the United States have discovered advancement in the use of health information technology in healthcare procedures. (Schoen; Osborn; Squires; Doty; Rasmussen; Pierson; & Applebaum, 2012). Countries such as Canada and United States have lately adopted domestic policies to encourage the dissemination and use of health information technology. (Schoen et al., 2012). According to World Health Organization, eHealth is used for the transmission of digital data in healthcare, including information stored and electronically collected to promote healthcare, both locally and remotely. E-Health involves patient to healthcare service providers or peer-to-peer communication between patients or healthcare practitioners. (Lindberg et al., 2013).

The development of healthcare information technology systems will allow healthcare professionals to collect a broad variety of information such as population, clinic, medication, etc,, which are specific to patient and will help to develop integrated, affordable digital health records. (Lester and Hobbs, 2007). Electronic health information technology systems have the ability to provide primary care physicians with instruments in multidisciplinary teams to handle patient care and operate. (Schoen; Osborn; Squires; Doty; Rasmussen; Pierson; & Applebaum, 2012).

Information Technology in Personal Security

Personal safety has come a long way; the first electro mechanical alarm system was invented in the 1850s by Edwin Holmes, when a door or window was opened, a spring was released, an electrical circuit was closed and the alarm was sounded. Now, information technology has allowed the implementation of sensor-enabled alarms which makes homes safer than ever. Remote monitoring of prospective hazardous sources improves individual safety and can make life much easier and more comfortable; for instance, check whether the stove or the coffee machine is turned off and if required can be turned off remotely. Personal security can be enhanced by combining essential information measures with household device surveillance and control. Innovative solutions for acknowledging home emergencies can be accomplished by combining surveillance of the vital parameters of the individual residing at home and overseeing the circumstances of home appliances. (Patel; Park; Bonato; Chan; & Rodgers, 2012). Several continuing studies focus on clinically evaluating wearable devices that have been created as part of significant study initiatives. For example, LiveNet, a system created at the MIT Media Laboratory that measures 3-D acceleration, ECG, EMG and galvanic skin behaviour, is being evaluated to monitor Parkinson's symptoms and detect epileptic seizures. (Sung; Marci; Pentlang, 2005). Numerous systems have been created for tracking personal safety of individuals, such as detecting falls and relaying alarm messages to a caregiver or emergency response staff. Commercially available systems such as "The Life Alert Classic" by Life Alert Emergency Response Inc. (http://www.lifealertmedical.com/classic.html) and the "AlertOne medical alert system" devices created for tracking of personal safety. (http://www.alert-1.com/). These devices are emergency response devices generally composed of a pendant or a watch consisting of a push button. By pressing the button an alarm message can be transmitted wirelessly to operators in a distant call centre. A large number of women used smartphones to hold strangers responsible for their behaviour and even when they are alone to stimulate their social network; a lot of women also felt that such technology gives them a sense of security. (Karusala & Kumar, 2017). Another important element in personal safety is the development of SmartBrick; a low cost structural health observing device developed by Banks, Harms, Sarvestani, & Bastianini, (2009). This system has the capability to collect data such as tilt, water level, etc., pertaining to a bridge or segment of a roadway and can be accessed through SMS, email, etc., by motorists who have subscribed to the service.

Information Technology in Transportation

One of the most important contribution of information technology in the last decade or so has been the GPS-enabled navigation system and with voice prompts which further assists people with visual impairments. Global megatrends in information and communication technologies and transportation appear to have significant effects directly on physical activity and by potentiating intervention strategies. (Pratt, Sarmiento, Montes, Ogilvie, Marcus, Perez, & Lancet, 2012). Information technology enables the transportation sector to be more effective by enhancing capacity. For instance, airlines use information technology to better plan flights and increase the use of seats, enabling them to fly fewer flights, save fuel and money. The end outcome is reduced airline tariffs and reduced energy consumption. (Atkinson, & Castro, 2008). Digital technologies are often used to improve the efficiency and effectiveness of mainstream public services such as educational institutes, healthcare, transport, etc. (Boulton, 2010). Instance of such digital technologies include internet access through broadband, intelligent mobile phones and personal computers. Various levels of access to digital infrastructure, techniques, expertise and abilities needed to use digital systems have resulted in concepts of 'digital divide' with gender, age, earnings, ethnicity, place being identified as important variables in identification of 'haves' and 'have nots' in the digital space. (Digital Britain, 2009; Boulton, 2010). The traditional barrier seems to be narrowing down between freight and passenger transportation. This has been possible as mobile applications have been made accessible on smartphones and tablets through digital distribution platform. (Speranza, 2018). According to Porter, Linse, & Barsaz, (2015), there are significant trends in human transport that will alter the way we travel such as – *Independent vehicles:* Hands and feet free driving will be a reality with independent vehicles. *Electric vehicles:* Number of electric vehicles such as public buses and short vehicles will increase. It will be more economical and environment friendly. *Internet connectivity vehicles:* Vehicles with internet connectivity will be available on roads and will have all data pertaining to traffic and driving readily available for use.

SOCIAL MEDIA AND SOCIAL CHANGE

According to Cambridge dictionary, social media means "Websites and computer programs that enable individuals to use a computer or mobile phone to interact and share data on the internet". In 1979, Duke University's Tom Truscott and Jim Ellis developed the Usenet, a global discussion system that enabled internet users to post messages on public platform. The social media age began approximately 20 years ago, when Bruce and Susan Abelson established an early social networking site called "Open Diary" which leaguered together online diary writers into one society. The increasing availability of high-speed internet access added to the concept's popularity, creating social networking sites such as MySpace (2003) and Facebook (2004). In turn, this invented the word, "Social Media" and led to its prominence today. Social media is a set of internet-based applications built on Web 2.0 taking into account it's ideological and technological foundations and enable user-generated content to be created and exchanged. (Kaplan and Haenlein, 2010). Some forms of social media are blogs, content communities, social networking sites, virtual game worlds, virtual social worlds. *Blogs* – Earliest form of social media. A special kind of website which shows in reverse chronological order date-stamped entries. (OECD, 2007). *Content communities* – A term denoted to media content sharing communities. People from different countries on this platform share content such as pictures, powerpoint presentations, videos, etc. *Social networking sites* – Applications that allow users to connect with each other through profiles that consist personal data by inviting friends and peers to access their profile and send emails and instant messages. Several businesses use social networking sites to help build brand communities. (Muniz & O'Guinn, 2001). *Virtual game worlds* – Virtual worlds are platform in which users can appear in the form of personalized avatars and interact with each other as they would in real life. Some examples are World of Warcraft, EverQuest, etc. *Virtual social worlds* – Virtual social world users appear in the form of avatars and interact in a virtual environment of three dimensions; however, there are no rules in this realm restricting the range of possible interactions, except for basic physical laws such as gravity. (Haenlein & Kaplan, 2009; Kaplan & Haenlein, 2009a, 2009b).

The popularity of social media has led the emergence of a new concept "Social Commerce" and customer creation through social relations over the internet. Consumers in their groups and communities use social media to share their expertise, date and experience with other colleagues. These advances make customers part of a value-creating process for the company by providing online social support. Study shows that there is information and emotional support in their social support. This clearly shows that with the propulsion of social media the e-commerce industry is drifting towards the concept of social commerce. Hence, it becomes very important to identify the emerging changes in social behaviour which has forced this change. (Hajli, 2014a). Though social media has numerous uses and its use is increasing many folds in various areas. Some very important sectors where social media is being used are education, healthcare, politics, and it is also used as a predicting tool.

Social Media in Education

For many teachers, the enhanced existence of social media in higher education environment is crucial for universities to connect with these learners (Kumar and Nanda, 2019a). Universities now use social networking sites as alternative places for learners to adapt to their university lifestyle via internet interaction with colleagues and teachers. (Yu et al., 2010). Hence, shared community spaces and intergroup communications are a huge component which excites young individuals and should therefore help to motivate them to learn. (Mason and Rennie, 2007). The objective of use of social media from an education perspective should be active co-producers of information rather than passive consumers of content; also learning should be participatory social method that supports private life objectives and needs. (Lee and McLoughlin, 2010). However, because of this a difference of opinion arises between those who think that social media can be used to enhance the institution of higher education and those who think that social media can disrupt in the current scheme of things because of ethical and social challenges (Kumar & Nanda, 2019b). Numerous teachers are of the opinion that universities can accommodate these changes which eventually will benefit them; they have started talking about the need to create innovative pedagogies that use these resources to promote the decision and independence. (Kumar & Nanda, 2020; Kumar & Bhardwaj, 2020). However, studies on social media in education indicates that incorporating social media into learning and teaching settings can produce fresh types of investigation, communication, cooperation, identity work or have beneficial cognitive, social and emotional effects. The usage of social media encourages learners to engage in and develop in-depth learning through communication, critical thinking, and cooperation; also, the importance of social media integration in higher education is based on the theories of socio-cultural learning. (Liburd & Christensen, 2013). It has been ovserved that more than 40% of the professors allocated learners to read or view social media as part of their course tasks, and 20% of learners were allocated to comment or post on social media sites. In total, 80% of professors are using social media in teaching some parts of the course. (Moran, Seaman, & Tinti-Kane, 2011). Empirical studies have demonstrated the following instructional advantages in the use of social media techniques – (A) Improved communication between learners and instructors. (B) Students are exposed to technology and skill enhancement which makes them a better employable resource. (C) The official learning management system is backed up by a substitute platform. (D) Express resource contribution and sharing. (E) Students have access to instruction materials post sessions, (Legaree, 2015). University learners engage on a regular basis in social media operations, there is an increasing concern about the probable adverse effects of social media on the social well-being of learners. The adverse impact of non-academic social media use on scholarly performance has been empirically proven. The research also recognized video games as the main determinant of bad academic results. (Oye et al., 2012 and Ravizza et al., 2014). Oye et al. (2012) and Ravizza et al. (2014).

Social Media in Healthcare

Use of social media by the nurses has increased to influence the connection between healthcare professionals and patients, leading to more equal communication between patient and healthcare professionals, enhanced physician switching, harmonious interactions, and suboptimal interaction between patient and healthcare professionals. (Smailhodzic, Hooijsma, Boonstra, & Langley, 2016). Some of the tangible benefits of use of social media in healthcare according to a study conducted by Panahi, Watson, & Partridge, (2016) are – reaching out and connecting with peer group, knowledge sharing, getting involved in continued medical knowledge attainment, sharing of recognized clinical best practices, and also personal branding. Healthcare organizations gradually are getting well adapted with the use of social media. Increasing numbers of hospitals, medical experts, and health officials have started using Facebook, YouTube, and Twitter to reach out to prospective customers. According to a research conducted by the Journal of Medical Internet Research, almost 95% of U.S. hospitals are on Facebook, whereas only 50% have a Twitter account. (Griffis, Kilaru, Werner, Asch, Hershey, Hill, 2014). New concepts such as eHealth, Health 2.0 etc. have come in place which has the foundation of social media. E-Health is a broad concept and goes beyond the usage of just computer and keyboard for operational and navigational skills. Health 2.0 refers to applications that gives all kinds of interactive techniques that help individuals to interact about their health with colleagues and healthcare professionals; for instance, through forums or e-consults; self-monitoring of their health through patient portals; and even treatment over the internet through web-based cognitive behavioural therapy. (Van De Belt, Engelen, Berben, & Schoonhoven, 2010). In United States, a total of 61% adults browse online and around 39% use Facebook to lookout for health related information. Social media adoption levels differ in Europe; around 45% of Norwegian and Swedish hospitals use LinkedIn and 22% of Norwegian hospitals use facebook for health communication. Recent UK statistics revealed that Facebook is the fourth most common source of health information. (Moorhead, Hazlett, Harrison, Carroll, Irwin, & Hoving, 2013); however, it is important to point out here that in some non-democratic regimes social networking platforms such as facebook is not allowed. According to a study by Radovic, Gmelin, Stein, & Miller, (2017), there seems to be a connection between depressed adolescents and soaring use of social media. In such a scenario, it is important for the healthcare professionals to understand what kind of use of social media is happening by an adolescent who is depressed, as it may have helpful and unhelpful use. Hence, it is important to engage with adolescents with depression about the use of social media to enhance good use and avoid some of the unfavourable effects.

Social Media as Predictive Tool

In recent times, the geometric rise of digital data (online newspapers, blogs, social networks, etc.,) has made it possible from a distinct view to tackle the predictability of financial markets; for instance, big data, terabits of data on economic transactions can be combined to similar quantity of online news to explore the decision making process. Therefore, internet has altered the way investors receive data and how investors can act on it. (Barber and Odean, 2001; Moeal et al., 2014). An examination of online reviews on features of some electronic goods such as digital camera, audio-video player, etc, which was categorized as "reviewer – related features", "review subjectivity features" and "review readability features", had adequate information which could be analyzed to predicting of sales of products (Ghose, and Ipeirotis, 2011). Several studies have investigated the effect of customer reviews on product sales. (Archak et al., 2011; Hu et al., 2013). These online reviews primarily contain numerical ratings and textual content which adds value to the information. Predicting stock prices is a very difficult job because there are many variables that affect the stock prices. However, Nguyen & Shirai (2015), devised a technique (Sentiment analysis) to predict the stock market prices with an accuracy of 60% through the reviews obtained on social media. The research took the sentiments associated with the online reviews into account and proposed a method (Aspect method) for the prediction. A number of analytics applications have been presented by Ayodeji & Kumar (2019) and Kumar & Ayodeji (2020).

Social Media and Dimensions of Time

According to Christian Fuchs (2014), corporate social media happens to have a link with all the five dimensions of time in capitalist society or in a democracy. Hence, this link is bringing in a social change from the economic perspective such as –

- Social media plays an important part in economic, political, and cultural acceleration.
- The advent of crowdsourcing, playing labour and presumption applies to leisure time the working day. This complete production of surplus value is complemented by comparative manufacturing of surplus value, in which at the same moment more advertising and more targeted advertising are displayed using personalized advertising and financial monitoring.

- Social media is an expression of the fact that the employee and the factory have become social and spread throughout society.
- Targeted online advertising attempts to make consumers eat more commodities by providing them with customized advertisements.
- Based on fictitious capital investments, corporate social media hopes that targeted advertising will result elevated future profits. However, the real success rate of targeted advertising is purchasing more commodities from customers is unknown making social media extremely susceptible to financial crisis.

Use of corporate social media is the link between use and exchange value. Therefore, social media serves user needs and profit interests; also, serves as a communication and production means. (Fisher, 2012). Apparently, the new media consumer sees himself as a social and creative entity; (Allmer, 2015), but is treated as an item that serves the capital interests of platform owners.

Karl Marx's labour theory of value, which takes the role of time in capitalism into account as to how time plays a very crucial role in today's context of social media. Facebook continually tracks interests and behaviour with respect to usage, browsing, demographic information, content generated by users, social relations etc. These are user-specific, affective, social, financial, political, cultural information about users. The more time a user who is also a potential customer spends on Facebook; more information about the user is produced which serves as commodity to advertising clients. Hence, time plays a fundamental part in social media for corporations. (Fuchs, 2013).

DISCUSSION

Healthcare, education, personal security, and transportation are important drivers of social change. It is very interesting to see how these drivers flourish and grow and much importance is given to each of them in a democratic setup. Healthcare is related to well being of citizens and has a great potential to drive social change. Any factor that brings in well being of the citizens has the aptitude to change the society in a positive way as it lowers mortality rate and enhances quality of life which is of sheer importance to citizens in a democratic setup. On the other hand, education has its root in growth of an individual and collectively it also enhances the growth of a nation. It has been observed in nascent democracies that education has changed the lives of individuals which in turn has changed the course of a particular house and subsequently the nation. For example, a poor farmer from a democratic setup which has provided education to his children has paved new opportunities for his children.

As they grow up they can choose other careers which are a part of the knowledge economy such as lawyer, doctor, accountant etc. Hence, such stories are common in democracies where education has changed the course of the family. This only proves that education is a strong driver of social change.

A citizen should feel safe in his or her country irrespective of any regime. This is the least a regime can provide to the citizens of its country. Such feeling only exists in democratic setup where a citizen feels safe pertaining to its personal security which in turn gives him the confidence to pursue or function in a way he or she wants to function. This feeling of personal security cannot be ignored as this feeling is a strong driver pertaining to social change. Unfortunately, this feeling is curbed in non-democratic regimes. Transportation or mobility has a direct relation to productivity and economy; economy is one of the strongest drivers of social change. One of the most important aspects of economic growth is transportation. There is a lot of emphasis on transportation logistics and supply chain economics to provide support to industrial activities and distribution of goods and materials. Transportation grows in democratic regimes as public and private players both play a crucial role and contributes towards the growth of economy. These attributes of transportation has the ability to bring in a social change, much in a positive way.

These elements have a direct relation to an individual's life and a citizen happens to use them almost on a daily basis. It is imbibed in their daily routine and hence a habit is formed. This in turn induces a change in society. This change happened over a period of time and is the social change we are talking about. It would be interesting to observe how information technology and social media have brought in the social change that we see today through these drivers of social change. Information and information technology is intertwined in the democracy that we see today. Access to data and information is the right of any citizen in a democracy; it is also very important to highlight that this has been observed in democracies as this is controlled in a non-democratic setup which eventually never reaches to citizen. This information and access to data is the new power for the citizens as it gives them the opportunity to make a better choice and voice their opinion based on information and data.

CONCLUSION

It is imperative that technology has in impact on society more so with information technology. In the last decade or so, information technology and social media together has brought in many changes in the society primarily from a higher education, healthcare, personal safety and transportation perspective which has impacted the society. It has not only improved the quality of living but also it has ventured into spaces where there were gaps in management of technology and improved the management of information which in turn has lead to better quality of life to the human kind. Social media has brought in a dynamic change in the way we do things. Also, it has opened new avenues. As we proceed ahead in 2019, a great deal of innovation or emerging trends in information technology would be seen in the following segments; Artificial intelligence, 5G proliferation, Quantum computing, Blockchain evolution, and Drones. (Sakovich, 2019).

REFERENCES

Allmer, T. (2015). *Critical Theory and Social Media: Between Emancipation and Commodification*. London, UK: Routledge. doi:10.4324/9781315750491

Archak, N., Ghose, A., & Ipeirotis, P. G. (2011). Deriving the Pricing Power of Product Features by Mining Consumer Reviews. *Management Science*, *57*(8), 1485–1509. doi:10.1287/mnsc.1110.1370

Arthur, W. B. (1989). Competing Technologies, Increasing Returns, and Lock-In by Historical Events. *Economic Journal (London)*, *99*(394), 116–131. doi:10.2307/2234208

Atkinson, R. D., & Castro, D. (2008). Digital quality of life: Understanding the personal and social benefits of the information technology revolution. *Available at SSRN 1278185*.

Ayodeji, O. G., & Kumar, V. (2019). 'Social media analytics: A tool for the success of online retail industry', *Int. J. Services Operations and Informatics*, *10*(1), 79–95. doi:10.1504/IJSOI.2019.100630

Baller, S., Dutta, S., & Lanvin, B. (2016). *Global information technology report 2016*. Geneva, Switzerland: Ouranos.

Banks, B., Harms, T., Sarvestani, S. S., & Bastianini, F. (2009, March). A low-cost wireless system for autonomous generation of road safety alerts. In Sensors and Smart Structures Technologies for Civil, Mechanical, and Aerospace Systems 2009 (Vol. 7292, p. 72920E). International Society for Optics and Photonics. doi:10.1117/12.817851

Barber, B., & Odean, T. (2001). The internet and the investor. *The Journal of Economic Perspectives*, *15*(1), 41–54. doi:10.1257/jep.15.1.41

Bhamra, T., Lilley, D., & Tang, T. (2011). Design for sustainable behaviour: Using products to change consumer behaviour. *The Design Journal*, *14*(4), 427–445. doi:10.2752/175630611X13091688930453

Bollyky, T. J., Templin, T., Cohen, M., Schoder, D., Dieleman, J. L., & Wigley, S. (2019). The relationships between democratic experience, adult health, and cause-specific mortality in 170 countries between 1980 and 2016: An observational analysis. *Lancet*, *393*(10181), 1628–1640. doi:10.1016/S0140-6736(19)30235-1 PMID:30878225

Boulton, G. (2010). Digital Scotland. Report by Royal Society of Edinburgh. Retrieved from http://www.royalsoced.org.uk/enquiries/Digital_Scotland/Digital%20 Scotland%20(med%20res).pdf

Britain, D. (2009). Final Report to department for culture, media and sport and department for business innovation and skills. ISBN: 9780101765022.

Cohen, J. E. (1968). Alternate derivations of a species-abundance relation. *American Naturalist*, *102*(924), 165–172. doi:10.1086/282533

Dewey, J. (1938/1963). *Experience and Education*. New York: Simon & Schuster.

Dirican, C. (2015). The impacts of robotics, artificial intelligence on business and economics. *Procedia: Social and Behavioral Sciences*, *195*, 564–573. doi:10.1016/j.sbspro.2015.06.134

Dixon, H. (1997). Controversy: The Source and Measurement of Technical Change- Editorial Note. *Economic Journal (London)*, *107*(September), 1518–1519. doi:10.1111/j.1468-0297.1997.tb00062.x

Dodgson, M., & Rothwell, R. (Eds.). (1995). *The Handbook of Industrial Innovation*. London, UK: Edward Elgar. doi:10.4337/9781781954201

Doyle, G. J., Garrett, B., & Currie, L. M. (2014). Integrating mobile devices into nursing curricula: Opportunities for implementation using Rogers' Diffusion of Innovation model. *Nurse Education Today*, *34*(5), 775–782. doi:10.1016/j.nedt.2013.10.021 PMID:24268745

Edwards, P. (1994). From "impact" to social process: Computers in society and culture. In eds. S. Jasanoff, G. E. Markle, & J. C. Peterson (Eds.), Handbook of Science and Technology Studies, Chap. 12. Beverly Hills, CA: Sage.

Edwards, P. (1998). Y2K: Millennial reflections on computers as infrastructure. *History and Technology*, *15*, 7–29.

Ellul, J. (1964). *The Technological Society*. New York: Knopf.

Ezawa, K. (2016, January). Virtual & Augmented Reality. In Investment Themes in 2016. In Citi Global Perspectives & Solution. Citigroup Inc. Retrieved from https://www.citivelocity.com/citigps/ReportSeries.action?recordId=45

Fisher, E. (2012). How Less Alienation Creates More Exploitation? Audience Labour on Social Network Sites. *TripleC*, *10*(2), 171–183. doi:10.31269/triplec.v10i2.392

Fortunato, P., & Panizza, U. (2015). Democracy, education and the quality of government. *Journal of Economic Growth*, *20*(4), 333–363. doi:10.100710887-015-9120-5

Franco, Á., Álvarez-Dardet, C., & Ruiz, M. T. (2004). Effect of democracy on health: Ecological study. *BMJ (Clinical Research Ed.)*, *329*(7480), 1421–1423. doi:10.1136/bmj.329.7480.1421 PMID:15604165

Fuchs, C. (2013). Digital prosumption labour on social media in the context of the capitalist regime of time. *Time & Society*, *23*(1), 97–123. doi:10.1177/0961463X13502117

Fuchs, C. (2014). Digital prosumption labour on social media in the context of the capitalist regime of time. *Time & Society*, *23*(1), 97–123. doi:10.1177/0961463X13502117

Gao, F., Luo, T., & Zhang, K. (2012). Tweeting for learning: A critical analysis of research on microblogging in education published in 2008-2011. *British Journal of Educational Technology*, *43*(5), 783–801. doi:10.1111/j.1467-8535.2012.01357.x

Gao, Luo and Zhang, 2012; Greenhow, Burton and Robelia, 2011; Greenhow and Robelia, 2009a, 2009b; Pimmer, Linxen and Grohbiel, 2012; Ranieri, Manca and Fini, 2012.

Ghose, A., & Ipeirotis, P. G. (2011). Estimating the Helpfulness and Economic Impact of Product Reviews: Mining Text and Reviewer Characteristics. *IEEE Transactions on Knowledge and Data Engineering*, *23*(10), 1498–1512. doi:10.1109/TKDE.2010.188

Glaeser, E. L., Ponzetto, G. A. M., & Shleifer, A. (2007). Why Does Democracy Need Education? *Journal of Economic Growth*, *12*(2), 77–99. doi:10.100710887-007-9015-1

Greene, M. (1986). In Search of Critical Pedagogy. *Harvard Educational Review*, *56*(4), 427–441. doi:10.17763/haer.56.4.010756lh36u16213

Greenhow, C., Burton, L., & Robelia, B. (2011). Help from my "Friends:" Social capital in the social network sites of low-income high school students. *Journal of Educational Computing Research*, *45*(2), 223–245. doi:10.2190/EC.45.2.f

Greenhow, C., & Robelia, E. (2009a). Old communication, new literacies: Social network sites as social learning resources. *Journal of Computer-Mediated Communication*, *14*(4), 1130–1161. doi:10.1111/j.1083-6101.2009.01484.x

Greenhow, C., & Robelia, E. (2009b). Informal learning and identity formation in online social networks. *Learning, Media, and Technology*, *34*(2), 119–140. doi:10.1080/17439880902923580

Griffis, H. M., Kilaru, A. S., Werner, R. M., Asch, D. A., Hershey, J. C., Hill, S., ... Merchant, R. M. (2014). Use of social media across US hospitals: Descriptive analysis of adoption and utilization. *Journal of Medical Internet Research*, *16*(11), e264. doi:10.2196/jmir.3758 PMID:25431831

Groves, P., Kayyali, B., Knott, D., & Kuiken, S. V. (2016). The 'big data' revolution in healthcare: Accelerating value and innovation.

Haenlein, M., & Kaplan, A. M. (2009). Flagship brand stores within virtual worlds: The impact of virtual store exposure on real life brand attitudes and purchase intent. *Recherche et Applications en Marketing*, *24*(3).

Haenssgen, M. J., & Ariana, P. (2017). The social implications of technology diffusion: Uncovering the unintended consequences of people's health-related mobile phone use in Rural India and China. *World Development*, *94*, 286–304. doi:10.1016/j.worlddev.2017.01.014

Hajli, N. (2014a). The role of social support on relationship quality and social commerce. *Technological Forecasting and Social Change*, *87*, 17–27. doi:10.1016/j.techfore.2014.05.012

Harrison, T., & Sayogo, D. (2014). Transparency, participation and accountability practices in open government: A comparative study. *Government Information Quarterly*, *31*(4), 513–525. doi:10.1016/j.giq.2014.08.002

Hongo, J. (2015, April 16, 1:14 pm JST). Robotic Customer Service? In This Japanese Store, That's the Point. The Wall Street Journal News Paper, Japan Real Time. http://blogs.wsj.com/japanrealtime/2015/04/16/toshiba-humanoid-robot-to-debut-in-tokyo-departmentstore/?mod=WSJAsia_hpp_LEFTTopStories (Access Date: 19.04.2015). http://www.lifealertmedical.com/classic.html http://www.alert-1.com/ http://memex.lib.indiana.edu/ siwkshop/SocInfo1.html (As seen on 15th June, 2019) https://www.britannica.com/topic/social-change (As seen on 12th June, 2019) https://www.sam-solutions.com/blog/top-five-information-tech/nology-trends-to-watch-in-2019 (As seen on 12th June, 2019)

Hu, N., Koh, N. S., & Reddy, S. K. (2013). 'Ratings Lead You to the Product, Reviews Help you Clinch It? The Mediating Role of Online Review Sentiments on Product Sales. *Decision Support Systems*, *57*(1), 42–53.

Jiang, R., Kleer, R., & Piller, F. T. (2017). Predicting the future of additive manufacturing: A Delphi study on economic and societal implications of 3D printing for 2030. *Technological Forecasting and Social Change*, *117*, 84–97. doi:10.1016/j.techfore.2017.01.006

Kaplan, A. M., & Haenlein, M. (2009a). Consumer use and business potential of virtual worlds: The case of Second Life. *The International Journal on Media Management*, *11*(3).

Kaplan, A. M., & Haenlein, M. (2009b). Consumers, companies, and virtual social worlds: A qualitative analysis of Second Life. *Advances in Consumer Research. Association for Consumer Research (U. S.)*, *36*(1), 873–874.

Kaplan, A. M., & Haenlein, M. (2010). Users of the world, unite! The challenges and opportunities of Social Media. *Business Horizons*, *53*(1), 59–68. doi:10.1016/j.bushor.2009.09.003

Karusala, N., & Kumar, N. (2017, May). Women's Safety in Public Spaces: Examining the Efficacy of Panic Buttons in New Delhi. In *Proceedings of the 2017 CHI Conference on Human Factors in Computing Systems* (pp. 3340-3351). ACM. 10.1145/3025453.3025532

Kling, R. (2000). Learning about information technologies and social change: The contribution of social informatics. *The Information Society*, *16*(3), 217–232. doi:10.1080/01972240050133661

Kumar, V., & Ayodeji, O. G. (2020). Web Analytics for Knowledge Creation: A Systematic Review of Tools, Techniques and Practices [IJCBPL]. *International Journal of Cyber Behavior, Psychology and Learning*, *10*(1), 1–14. doi:10.4018/IJCBPL.2020010101

Kumar, V., & Bhardwaj, A. (2018). Identity Management Systems: A Comparative Analysis. *International Journal of Strategic Decision Sciences*, *9*(1), 63–78. doi:10.4018/IJSDS.2018010105

Kumar, V., & Bhardwaj, A. (2020). Role of Cloud Computing in School Education. In *Handbook of Research on Diverse Teaching Strategies for the Technology-Rich Classroom* (pp. 98–108). IGI Global.

Kumar, V., & Nanda, P. (2019a). Social Media to Social Media Analytics: Ethical Challenges. [IJT]. *International Journal of Technoethics*, *10*(2), 57–70. doi:10.4018/IJT.2019070104

Kumar, V., & Nanda, P. (2019b). Social Media in Higher Education: A Framework for Continuous Engagement. [IJICTE]. *International Journal of Information and Communication Technology Education*, *15*(1), 109–120.

Kumar, V., & Nanda, P. (2020). Social Media as a Tool in Higher Education: A Pedagogical Perspective. In *Handbook of Research on Diverse Teaching Strategies for the Technology-Rich Classroom* (pp. 239–253). IGI Global. doi:10.4018/978-1-7998-0238-9.ch016

Lange, B. S., Requejo, P., Flynn, S. M., Rizzo, A. A., Valero-Cuevas, F. J., Baker, L., & Winstein, C. (2010). The potential of virtual reality and gaming to assist successful aging with disability. *Physical Medicine and Rehabilitation Clinics of North America*, *21*(2), 339–356. doi:10.1016/j.pmr.2009.12.007 PMID:20494281

Lee, K. (2012). Augmented reality in education and training. *TechTrends*, *56*(2), 13–21. doi:10.100711528-012-0559-3

Lee, M., & McLoughlin, C. (2015). *Web 2.0-based e-learning*. Hershey, PA: IGI Global.

Legaree, B. A. (2015). Considering the changing face of social media in higher education. *FEMS Microbiology Letters, 362*(16), 1e3.

Lester, H., & Hobbs, F. D. R. (2007). Major policy changes for primary care: Potential lessons for the US New Model of family medicine from the quality and outcomes framework in the United Kingdom. *FAMILY MEDICINE-KANSAS CITY*, *39*(2), 96. PMID:17273951

Leu, D. J., Zawilinski, L., Forzani, E., & Timbrell, N. (2014). Best practices in teaching the new literacies of online research and comprehension. *Best practices in literacy instruction*, 343-364.

Liaw, S. S. (2002). Understanding user perceptions of world-wide web environments. *Journal of Computer Assisted Learning, 18*(2), 137–148. doi:10.1046/j.0266-4909.2001.00221.x

Liburd, J. J., & Christensen, I. M. F. (2013). Using web 2.0 in higher tourism education. *Journal of Hospitality, Leisure, Sport, & Tourism Education, 12*(1).

Lilley, D. (2009). 'Design for sustainable behaviour: Strategies and perceptions'. *Design Studies, 30*(6), 704–720. doi:10.1016/j.destud.2009.05.001

Lindberg, B., Nilsson, C., Zotterman, D., Söderberg, S., & Skär, L. (2013). Using information and communication technology in home care for communication between patients, family members, and healthcare professionals: A systematic review. *International Journal of Telemedicine and Applications*, 2013. PMID:23690763

Linn, M. C., Clark, D., & Slotta, J. D. (2003). WISE design for knowledge integration. *Science Education, 87*(4), 517–538. doi:10.1002ce.10086

Litman, T. (2017). *Evaluating transportation economic development impacts*. Victoria Transport Policy Institute.

Markus, M. L., & Robey, D. (1988). Information technology and organizational change: Causal structure in theory and research. *Management Science, 34*(5), 583–598. doi:10.1287/mnsc.34.5.583

Mason, R., & Rennie, F. (2007). Using web 2.0 for learning in the community. *The Internet and Higher Education, 10*(3), 196–203. doi:10.1016/j.iheduc.2007.06.003

Meier, D. (2000). *Educating a Democracy. Boston Review*. Champaign, IL: University of Illinois Press.

Mittal, S., & Kumar, V. (2019). Study of knowledge management models and their relevance in organisations, *Int. J. Knowledge Management Studies, 10*(3), 322–335. doi:10.1504/IJKMS.2019.101491

Moat, H. S., Preis, T., Olivola, C., Liu, C., & Chater, N. (2014). Using Big Data to predict collective behavior in the real world. *Behavioral and Brain Sciences, 37*(1), 92–93. doi:10.1017/S0140525X13001817 PMID:24572233

Moorhead, S. A., Hazlett, D. E., Harrison, L., Carroll, J. K., Irwin, A., & Hoving, C. (2013). A new dimension of health care: Systematic review of the uses, benefits, and limitations of social media for health communication. *Journal of Medical Internet Research, 15*(4). doi:10.2196/jmir.1933 PMID:23615206

Moran, M., Seaman, J., & Tinti-Kane, H. (2011). *Teaching, Learning, and Sharing: How Today's Higher Education Faculty Use Social Media*. Babson Survey Research Group.

Nayar, K. B., & Kumar, V. (2018). Cost benefit Analysis of Cloud Computing in Education. [IJBIS]. *International Journal of Business Information Systems*, *27*(2), 205–221. doi:10.1504/IJBIS.2018.089112

Nelson, R. R., & Winter, S. G. (1982). *An Evolutionary Theory of Economic Change*. Cambridge: Belknap Press/Harvard University Press.

Nguyen, T. H., & Shirai, K. (2015, July). Topic modeling based sentiment analysis on social media for stock market prediction. In *Proceedings of the 53rd Annual Meeting of the Association for Computational Linguistics and the 7th International Joint Conference on Natural Language Processing (*Volume 1*: Long Papers)* (pp. 1354-1364). 10.3115/v1/P15-1131

Nofer, M., Hinz, O., Muntermann, J., & Roßnagel, H. (2014). The economic impact of privacy violations and security breaches. *Business & Information Systems Engineering*, *6*(6), 339–348. doi:10.100712599-014-0351-3

Norman, D. A., & Verganti, R. (2014). Incremental and radical innovation: Design research vs. technology and meaning change. *Design Issues*, *30*(1), 78–96. doi:10.1162/DESI_a_00250

O'Brien, T. (2015). Human (in) security and democracy in Central America. *Democracy and Security*, *11*(1), 44–59. doi:10.1080/17419166.2015.1006396

OECD. (2007). *Participative web and user-created content: Web 2.0, wikis, and social networking*. Paris, France: Organisation for Economic Co-operation and Development.

Ogburn, W. F. (1947). How Technology Changes Society. *The Annals of the American Academy of Political and Social Science*, *249*(1), 81–88. doi:10.1177/000271624724900111

Oye, N. D., Adam, M. H., & Nor Zairah, A. R. (2012). Model of perceived influence of academic performance using social networking. *International Journal of Computers and Technology, 2*(2).

Panahi, S., Watson, J., & Partridge, H. (2016). Social media and physicians: Exploring the benefits and challenges. *Health Informatics Journal*, *22*(2), 99–112. doi:10.1177/1460458214540907 PMID:25038200

Parker, W. (2006). Public Discourses in Schools: Purposes, Problems, Possibilities. *Educational Researcher*, *35*(8), 11–18. doi:10.3102/0013189X035008011

Patel, S., Park, H., Bonato, P., Chan, L., & Rodgers, M. (2012). A review of wearable sensors and systems with application in rehabilitation. *Journal of Neuroengineering and Rehabilitation*, *9*(1), 21. doi:10.1186/1743-0003-9-21 PMID:22520559

Piaget, J. (2001). *The Psychology of Intelligence*. London, UK: Routledge.

Pimmer, C., Linxen, S., & Gröhbiel, U. (2012). Facebook as a learning tool? A case study on the appropriation of social network sites from mobile phones in developing countries. *British Journal of Educational Technology*, *43*(5), 726–738. doi:10.1111/j.1467-8535.2012.01351.x

Porter, B., Linse, M., & Barasz, Z. (2015). Six transportation trends that will change how we move. *Forbes, January*.

Pratt, M., Sarmiento, O. L., Montes, F., Ogilvie, D., Marcus, B. H., Perez, L. G., & Brownson, R. C.Lancet Physical Activity Series Working Group. (2012). The implications of megatrends in information and communication technology and transportation for changes in global physical activity. *Lancet*, *380*(9838), 282–293. doi:10.1016/S0140-6736(12)60736-3 PMID:22818940

Radovic, A., Gmelin, T., Stein, B. D., & Miller, E. (2017). Depressed adolescents' positive and negative use of social media. *Journal of Adolescence*, *55*, 5–15. doi:10.1016/j.adolescence.2016.12.002 PMID:27997851

Ranieri, M., Manca, S., & Fini, A. (2012). Why (and how) do teachers engage in social networks? An exploratory study of professional use of Facebook and its implications for lifelong learning. *British Journal of Educational Technology*, *43*(5), 754–769. doi:10.1111/j.1467-8535.2012.01356.x

Ravizza, S. M., Hambrick, D. Z., & Fenn, K. M. (2014). Non-academic internet use in the classroom is negatively related to classroom learning regardless of intellectual ability. *Computers & Education, 78,* 109e114.

Roschelle, J. M., Pea, R. D., Hoadley, C. M., Gordin, D. N., & Means, B. M. (2000). Changing how and what children learn in school with computer-based technologies. *The Future of Children*, *10*(2), 76–101. doi:10.2307/1602690 PMID:11255710

Ruttan, V. W. (1997). Induced Innovation, Evolutionary Theory and Path Dependence: Sources of Technical Change. *Economic Journal (London)*, *107*(444), 1520–1529. doi:10.1111/j.1468-0297.1997.tb00063.x

Sanborn, H., & Thyne, C. L. (2014). Learning democracy: Education and the fall of authoritarian regimes. *British Journal of Political Science*, *44*(4), 773–797. doi:10.1017/S0007123413000082

Sathre, R., & Gustavsson, L. (2007). Effects of energy and carbon taxes on building material competitiveness. *Energy and Building*, *39*(4), 488–494. doi:10.1016/j.enbuild.2006.09.005

Sathre, R., & Gustavsson, L. (2009). Using wood products to mitigate climate change: External costs and structural change. *Applied Energy*, *86*(2), 251–257. doi:10.1016/j.apenergy.2008.04.007

Schoen, C., Osborn, R., Squires, D., Doty, M., Rasmussen, P., Pierson, R., & Applebaum, S. (2012). A survey of primary care doctors in ten countries shows progress in use of health information technology, less in other areas. *Health Affairs*, *31*(12), 2805–2816. doi:10.1377/hlthaff.2012.0884 PMID:23154997

Sharma, D., & Kumar, V. (2017). A Framework for Collaborative and Convenient Learning on Cloud Computing Platforms. [IJWLTT]. *International Journal of Web-Based Learning and Teaching Technologies*, *12*(2), 1–20. doi:10.4018/IJWLTT.2017040101

Sherwin, C., & Bhamra, T. (1998). Ecodesign innovation: Present concepts, current practice and future directions for design and the environment. Design History Society Conference 1998. Huddersfield, UK, University of Huddersfield, September 1998.

Siponen, M., Wilson, R., & Baskerville, R. (2008). Power and practice in information systems security research, In *2008 Proceedings of the International Conference on Information Systems (ICIS), 26.*

Sjöberg, L., & Fromm, J. (2001). Information technology risks as seen by the public. *Risk Analysis*, *21*(3), 427–442. doi:10.1111/0272-4332.213123 PMID:11572424

Smailhodzic, E., Hooijsma, W., Boonstra, A., & Langley, D. J. (2016). Social media use in healthcare: A systematic review of effects on patients and on their relationship with healthcare professionals. *BMC Health Services Research*, *16*(1), 442. doi:10.118612913-016-1691-0 PMID:27562728

Smyth, T. S. (2011). The new literacy: Technology in the classroom. Retrieved from http://files.eric.ed.gov/fulltext/ED534255.pdf

Speranza, M. G. (2018). Trends in transportation and logistics. *European Journal of Operational Research*, *264*(3), 830–836. doi:10.1016/j.ejor.2016.08.032

Stewart, B. (2013). Education for a Digital Age? | the theoryblog. Retrieved from http://theory.cribchronicles.com/2013/01/09/education-for-a-digital-age/

Sung, M., Marci, C., & Pentland, A. (2005). Wearable feedback systems for rehabilitation. *Journal of Neuroengineering and Rehabilitation*, *2*(1), 17. doi:10.1186/1743-0003-2-17 PMID:15987514

Swedish Energy Agency. Energy in Sweden. (2005). Retrieved from http://www.energimyndigheten.se/

Thakur, R., Hsu, S. H., & Fontenot, G. (2012). Innovation in healthcare: Issues and future trends. *Journal of Business Research*, *65*(4), 562–569. doi:10.1016/j.jbusres.2011.02.022

Tocqueville, A. (1862). *Democracy in America and Two Essays on America*. London, UK: Longman, Green, Longman, and Roberts.

Tong, T., Yu, E., & Roberts, R. K. (2014). Dynamics of transport infrastructure, exports and economic growth in the United States. In *Journal of the Transportation Research Forum* (Vol. 53, No. 1424-2016-117851, pp. 65-81). 10.5399/osu/jtrf.53.1.4204

Van De Belt, T. H., Engelen, L. J., Berben, S. A., & Schoonhoven, L. (2010). Definition of Health 2.0 and Medicine 2.0: A systematic review. *Journal of Medical Internet Research*, *12*(2). doi:10.2196/jmir.1350 PMID:20542857

Volonino, L., Robinson, S., & Watson, H. J. (1992). EIS and organizational change, In T. Jelassi, M. R. Klein, & W. M. Mayon-White (Eds.), *IFIP Transactions A (Computer Science and Technology)* (pp. 309-321). Amsterdam, The Netherlands: North-Holland. 10.1016/B978-0-444-89673-5.50028-8

Vygotsky, L. S. (1980). *Mind in society: The development of higher psychological processes*. Harvard University Press. doi:10.2307/j.ctvjf9vz4

Wilterdink, N., & Form, W. (2014). Social change. *Encyclopædia Britannica Online*. Retrieved from http://www. britannica. com/topic/social-change

Yu, A., Tian, S., Vogel, D., & Kwok, R. (2010). Embedded social learning in online social networking. In *ICIS 2010 Proceedings*. Retrieved from http://aisel.aisnet.org/icis2010_submissions/100

Compilation of References

Abaas, Z. R. (2016). *"The Role Of Environmental Impact Assessment Tool in Achieving Sustainable Urban Development and Its Challenges in Iraq", Mesop. environ. j., 2016* (pp. 138–148). Special Issue A.

Abdullah, R. (2005). Taking the E-train: The development of the Internet in Egypt. *Global Media and Communication*, *1*(2), 149–165. doi:10.1177/1742766505054630

Acharya, A. (2008). Democracy in Burma: Does Anyone Really Care? In Asia Rising: Who Is Leading? pp. 149-153.

Adegoke, Y. (2017). Why social media is the only media in Africa. Retrieved from https://www.weforum.org/agenda/2017/03/why-social-media-is-the-only-media-in-africa

Adler, R. P., & Goggin, J. (2005). What do we mean by "civic engagement"? *Journal of Transformative Education*, *3*(3), 236–253. doi:10.1177/1541344605276792

Adner, R. (2002). When are technologies disruptive? A demand-based view of the emergence of competition. *Strategic Management Journal*, *23*(8), 667–688. doi:10.1002mj.246

Adolph, M. (2017). The identity of mediatization: Theorizing a dynamic field. In O. Driessens, G. Bolin, A. Hepp, & S. Hjarvard (Eds.), *Dynamics of mediatization: Institutional change and everyday transformations in a digital age* (pp. 11–33). London, UK: Palgrave. doi:10.1007/978-3-319-62983-4_2

Afful-Dadzie, E., & Afful-Dadzie, A. (2017). Open government data in Africa: A preference elicitation analysis of media practitioners. *Government Information Quarterly*, *34*(2), 244–255. doi:10.1016/j.giq.2017.02.005

Aguinis, H., Ramani, R. S., & Alabduljader, N. (2018). What you see is what you get? Enhancing methodological transparency in management research. *The Academy of Management Annals*, *12*(1), 83–110. doi:10.5465/annals.2016.0011

Ahmed, S., Jaidka, K., & Cho, J. (2016). The 2014 Indian elections on Twitter: A comparison of campaign strategies of political parties. *Telematics and Informatics*, *33*(4), 1071–1087. doi:10.1016/j.tele.2016.03.002

Alessi, C. (2012, March 12). Can China change? Interviewee: Minxin Pei, Director, Keck Center for International and Strategic Studies, Claremont McKenna College. Retrieved March 14, 2014 from http://www.cfr.org/china/can-china-change/p27688

Alexa. (2011) *Top Sites in Egypt*. Retrieved from http://www.alexa.com/topsites/ countries; 2/EG

Allen, F., Demirguc-Kunt, A., Klapper, L., & Peria, M. S. M. (2016). The foundations of financial inclusion: Understanding ownership and use of formal accounts. *Journal of Financial Intermediation*, *27*, 1–30. doi:10.1016/j.jfi.2015.12.003

Allmer, T. (2010). *Critical Internet surveillance studies and economic surveillance*. Retrieved from http://www.sns3.uti.at/wp-content/uploads/2010/10/The-Internet-Surveillance-Research-Paper-Series-4-Thomas-Allmer-Critical-Internet-Surveillance-Studies-and-Economic-Surveillance.pdf

Allmer, T. (2015). *Critical Theory and Social Media: Between Emancipation and Commodification*. London, UK: Routledge. doi:10.4324/9781315750491

Allport, G. W. (1979). *The Nature of Prejudice (25th Anniv)*. Reading, MA: Addison-Wesley.

Alterman, J. (1998). *New media, new politics?: From satellite television to the Internet in the Arab world*. Washington: Washington Institute for Near East Policy.

Altheide, D. L., & Snow, R. P. (1979). *Media Logic*. Beverly Hills, CA: Sage.

Amin, H. (2003). *The Arabic Satellite TV Media: Accomplishments and challenges. Unpublished research carried by Pan Arab Research Centre (PARC) for the Egyptian Company for Satellites*. Cairo: Nilesat.

Analiz reklamnykh kampaniy kandidatov v mery Moskvy v razlichnykh media [The analysis of advertising campaigns of Moscow's mayoral candidates in different media] (2013, September 23). *Advertology*. Retrieved from http://www.advertology.ru/article117613.htm

Anderson, J., & Eickelman, D. (2008) *New Media and New Publics in the Arab World*. Paper presented at *Nouveaux medias dans le monde arab: Colloque organisé par le GREMMO* (Groupe de recherches et d'études sur la Méditerranée et le Moyen-Orient). Université Lyon, France. Retrieved from http://faculty.cua.edu/anderson /photo.htm

Anderson, B. (2006). *Imagined Communities*. London, UK: Verso.

Andrejevic, M. (2013). Whither-ing critique. *Communication and Critical/Cultural Studies*, *10*(2-3), 222–228. doi:10.1080/14791420.2013.812592

Antypas, A. (2003). A New Age for Environmental Democracy: The Aarhus Convention in Hungary. *Environmental Liability*, *11*(6), 199–208.

Aouragh, M. (2012). Social Media, Mediation and the Arab Revolutions. *TripleC*, *10*(2), 518–536. doi:10.31269/triplec.v10i2.416

Archak, N., Ghose, A., & Ipeirotis, P. G. (2011). Deriving the Pricing Power of Product Features by Mining Consumer Reviews. *Management Science*, *57*(8), 1485–1509. doi:10.1287/mnsc.1110.1370

Ardic, N. (2012). Understanding the "Arab Spring": Justice, Dignity, Religion, and International Politics in *Afro Eurasian Studies*, 1(1), 8-52.

Armbrust, W. (2007). New Media and Old Agendas: The Internet in the Middle East and Middle Eastern Studies. *International Journal of Middle East Studies*, *39*(4), 531–533. doi:10.1017/S0020743807071048

Arter, D. (1999). *Scandinavian politics today*. Manchester, UK: Manchester University Press.

Arthur, W. B. (1989). Competing Technologies, Increasing Returns, and Lock-In by Historical Events. *Economic Journal (London)*, *99*(394), 116–131. doi:10.2307/2234208

Arvidsson, A., & Colleoni, E. (2012). Value in informational capitalism and on the internet. *The Information Society: An International Journal*, *28*(3), 135–150. doi:10.1080/01972243.2012.669449

Asp, K. (1986). *Mäktiga massmedier: Studier om politisk opinionsbildning (Powerful Mass Media: Studies of Political Opinion Shaping)*. Stockholm, Sweden: Akademilitteratur.

Asp, K. (2014). News media logic in a New Institutional Perspective. *Journalism Studies*, *15*(3), 256–270. doi:10.1080/1461670X.2014.889456

Atkinson, R. D., & Castro, D. (2008). Digital quality of life: Understanding the personal and social benefits of the information technology revolution. *Available at SSRN 1278185*.

Austin, G. (2014). *Cyber policy in China*. Cambridge: Polity Press.

Ayodeji, O. G., & Kumar, V. (2019). Social media analytics: A tool for the success of online retail industry, *Int. J. Services Operations and Informatics*, *10*(1), 79–95. doi:10.1504/IJSOI.2019.100630

Ayres, R. U. (1989). *Technological Transformation and Long Waves*. Laxenburg, Austria: International Institutes of Applied Systems Analysis; Retrieved from https://pdfs.semanticscholar.org/3f41/ab13d03434e08bf521061c9b9af8a07fb6d2.pdf

Badran, M. (2011). Is ICT Empowering Women in Egypt? An empirical study. Retrieved from http://mak.ac.ug

Bai, J. (2013, August 12). *Cong 'hulianwang xinxi guwu huanli banfa (xiuding caoan)' kan zhongguo hulianwang guanzhi qushi [Research on the trend of Internet regulation in China from the revised draft of Administrative Measures for Internet Content Services]*. Retrieved from http://gbcode.rthk.org.hk/TuniS/rthk.hk/mediadigest/20130812_76_123013.html

Bail, C. A., Argyle, L. P., Brown, T. W., Bumpus, J. P., Chen, H., Hunzaker, M. B. F., ... Volfovsky, A. (2018). Exposure to opposing views on social media can increase political polarization. *Proceedings of the National Academy of Sciences of the United States of America*, *115*(37), 9216–9221. doi:10.1073/pnas.1804840115 PMID:30154168

Bakir, V. (2010). *Sousveillance, Media and Strategic Political Communication. Iraq, USA, UK*. New York: Continuum.

Bakkar, A. (2008) Who Says What on the Arabic Internet? Notes About Content of Arabic Internet Messages, In the *Journal of Website Promotion*, (3)1-2, 2-13.

Balancie, J.-M., & de La Grange, A. (Eds.). (2001). *Mondes rebelles. Guerillas, Milices, groupes terroristes*. Paris, France: Éditions Michalon.

Baller, S., Dutta, S., & Lanvin, B. (2016). *Global information technology report 2016*. Geneva, Switzerland: Ouranos.

Banks, B., Harms, T., Sarvestani, S. S., & Bastianini, F. (2009, March). A low-cost wireless system for autonomous generation of road safety alerts. In Sensors and Smart Structures Technologies for Civil, Mechanical, and Aerospace Systems 2009 (Vol. 7292, p. 72920E). International Society for Optics and Photonics. doi:10.1117/12.817851

Banning, M. E. (2016). Shared entanglements – Web 2.0, info-liberalism & digital sharing. *Information Communication and Society*, *19*(4), 489–503. doi:10.1080/1369118X.2015.1061573

Barberá, P., Jost, J. T., Nagler, J., Tucker, J. A., & Bonneau, R. (2015). Tweeting from left to right is online political communication more than an echo chamber? *Psychological Science*, *26*(10), 531–1542. doi:10.1177/0956797615594620 PMID:26297377

Barberá, P., Vaccari, C., & Valeriani, A. (2017). Social Media, Personalisation of News Reporting, and Media Systems' Polarisation in Europe. In M. Barisione, & A. Michailidou (Eds.), *Social Media and European Politics. Rethinking Power and Legitimacy in the Digital Era* (pp. 25–52). London, UK: Palgrave MacMillan. doi:10.1057/978-1-137-59890-5_2

Barber, B. R. (2003). *Strong Democracy: Participatory Politics fora New Age (Twentieth)*. Berkeley, CA: University of California Press.

Barber, B., & Odean, T. (2001). The internet and the investor. *The Journal of Economic Perspectives*, *15*(1), 41–54. doi:10.1257/jep.15.1.41

Barker, A., & Wood, C. (2001). Environmental assessment in the European Union: Perspectives, past, present and strategic. *European Planning Studies*, *9*(2), 243–254. doi:10.1080/713666468

Barnhart, J. E. (1969). Democracy as Responsibility. *The Journal of Value Inquiry*, *3*(4), 281–290. doi:10.1007/BF00139978

Barry, E. (2012, July 31). Russia charges anticorruption activist in plan to steal timber. *The New York Times*. Retrieved from http://www.nytimes.com/2012/08/01/world/europe/aleksei-navalny-charged-with-embezzlement.html?_r=0

Barry, E. (2013, January 12). Russian lawmakers aim at foreign cars, films and schooling in patriotic purge. *The New York Times*. Retrieved from http://www.nytimes.com/2013/01/13/world/europe/ russian-lawmakers-move-to-purge-foreign-influences.html? pagewanted=all

Bastrykin Vzyalsya za Navalnogo i Belykh [Bastrykin gets down to Navalny and Belykh] (2012, July 7). [Video file]. Retrieved from http://www.youtube.com/watch?v=H3u7BKl6oKU

Baudrillard, J. (1988). *Jean Baudrillard, Selected Writings*. Stanford, CA: Stanford University Press.

Baumeister, R. F. (1997). The Self and Society: Changes, Problems, and Opportunities. In *Self and Identity: Fundamental Issues* (pp. 191–217). Oxford, UK: Oxford University Press.

Bechmann, A. (2012). Towards Cross-Platform Value Creation. *Information Communication and Society*, *15*(6), 888–908. doi:10.1080/1369118X.2012.680483

Beck, U. (1995). *Att uppfinna det politiska; Bidrag till en teori om reflexiv modernisering (To Invent Politics. Contribution to a Theory of Reflexive Modernization)*. Göteborg: Daidalos.

Beer, D. (2009). Power through the algorithm? Participatory web cultures and the technological unconscious. *New Media & Society*, *11*(6), 985–1002. doi:10.1177/1461444809336551

Bekheit, E. S. (2005). *Al Sahafa wal Internet* [Newspapers and the Internet]. Cairo, Egypt: Al Arabi.

Bell, D. (2014). What Is Liberalism? *Political Theory*, *42*(6), 682–715. doi:10.1177/0090591714535103

Benkler, Y. (2000). From consumers to users: Shifting the deeper structures of regulation towards sustainable commons and user access. *Federal Communications Law Journal*, *52*(3), 561.

Benkler, Y. (2006). *The Wealth of Networks: How Social Production Transforms Markets and Freedom*. New Haven, CT: Yale University Press.

Benson, R., Blach-Orsten, M., Powers, M., Willig, I., & Zambrano, S. V. (2012). Media systems online and off: Comparing the form of news in the United States, Denmark, and France. *Journal of Communication*, *62*(1), 21–38. doi:10.1111/j.1460-2466.2011.01625.x

Bentham, J. (1791). *Panopticon or the inspection house*. London, UK: T. Payne.

Berardi, F. (2009). The Soul at Work: From Alienation to Autonomy. Translated by F. Cadel and G. Mecchia, with preface by J. E. Smith. Los Angeles, CA: Semiotext(e).

Berger, P. L., & Luckmann, T. (1966). *The Social Construction of Reality*. London, UK: Penguin Books.

Berry, D. (2014). *Critical Theory and the Digital*. New York, NY: Bloomsbury Academic.

Bershidsky, L. (2013, August 26). What Alexei Navalny learned from Obama. *Bloomberg View*. Retrieved from http://www.bloombergview.com/articles/2013-08-26/what-alexei-navalny-learned-from-obama

Bertot, J. C., Jaeger, P. T., & Grimes, J. M. (2010). Using ICTs to create a culture of transparency: E-government and social media as openness and anti-corruption tools for societies. *Government Information Quarterly*, *27*(3), 264–271. doi:10.1016/j.giq.2010.03.001

Bertot, J. C., Jaeger, P. T., & Grimes, J. M. (2012). Promoting transparency and accountability through ICTs, social media, and collaborative e-government. *Transforming Government: People, Process, and Policy*, *6*(1), 78–91. doi:10.1108/17506161211214831

Beyene, Z., & Zerai, A. (2014) The Role of ICTs in Governance, State-building, and Peacebuilding in Africa: The Case of Ethiopia, CGCS Occasional Paper Series # 2, Retrieved from https://global.asc.upenn.edu/app/uploads/2014/08/The_Role_of_ICTs_in_Governance__Statebuilding__and_Peacebuilding-The_Case_of_Ethiopia.pdf

Bezanson, K., & Luxton, M. (2006). *Social Reproduction: Feminist Political Economy Challenges Neoliberalism*. Montreal, Canada: McGill Queen's University Press.

Bhamra, T., Lilley, D., & Tang, T. (2011). Design for sustainable behaviour: Using products to change consumer behaviour. *The Design Journal*, *14*(4), 427–445. doi:10.2752/175630611X13091688930453

Biao, T. (2012). Rights defence (*weiquan*), microblogs (Weibo), and the surrounding gaze (*weiguan*). *China Perspectives, 2012*(3), 29-41.

Bimber, B. (1998). The Internet and political mobilization: Research note on the 1996 election season. *Social Science Computer Review*, *16*(4), 391–401. doi:10.1177/089443939801600404

Birdsall, N., & Fukuyama, F. (2011). *The Post-Washington Consensus: Development After the Crisis Bohler-Muller, Narmia and Van Der Merwe, Charl (2011), "The Potential Of Social Media To Influence Socio-Political Change On The African Continent", Policy Brief, NO 46.* Africa Institute of South Africa.

Blanchard, B., Holden, M., & Wu, V. (2017, June 30). China says Sino-British Joint Declaration on Hong Kong no longer has meaning.Retrieved on July 29, 2019 from Reuters.com.

Blankenship, C. (2019). President, Wrestler, Spectacle: An Examination of Donald Trump's Firing Tweets and The Celebrity Appresident as Response to Trump's Media Landscape. *The Journal of Communication Inquiry*. doi:10.1177/0196859919833785

Bloch, E. (1986). *The principle of hope*. Cambridge, MA: The MIT Press.

Bloomberg News. (2018, September 11). Trade war with U.S. likely to cost China 700,000 jobs plus millions more if things get worse. *Bloomberg News*, Retrieved on July 27, 2019 from https://business.financialpost.com/news/economy/the-trade-war-will-likely-cost-china-700000-jobs-jpmorgan-says

Blumler, J., & Gurevitch, M. (1995). *The Crisis of Public Communication*. New York: Routledge.

Bodrunova, S. S. (2013). Fragmentation and polarization of the public sphere in the 2000s: Evidence from Italy and Russia. Global Media Journal German Edition, 3(1), 1–35.

Bollyky, T. J., Templin, T., Cohen, M., Schoder, D., Dieleman, J. L., & Wigley, S. (2019). The relationships between democratic experience, adult health, and cause-specific mortality in 170 countries between 1980 and 2016: An observational analysis. *Lancet*, *393*(10181), 1628–1640. doi:10.1016/S0140-6736(19)30235-1 PMID:30878225

Bondes, M., & Schucher, G. (2014). Derailed emotions: The transformation of claims and targets during the Wenzhou online incident. *Information Communication and Society*, *17*(1), 45–65. do i:10.1080/1369118X.2013.853819

Boote, J. (1998). Towards a comprehensive taxonomy and model of consumer complaining behavior. *Journal of Consumer Satisfaction, Dissatisfaction & Complaining Behavior*, *11*, 140–151.

Boulton, G. (2010). Digital Scotland. Report by Royal Society of Edinburgh. Retrieved from http://www.royalsoced.org.uk/enquiries/Digital_Scotland/Digital%20Scotland%20(med%20res).pdf

Bowen, G. A. (2009). Document Analysis as a Qualitative Research Method. *Qualitative Research Journal*, *9*(2), 27–40. doi:10.3316/QRJ0902027

Bower, J. L., & Christensen, C. M. (1995). 'Disruptive technologies: Catching the wave'. *Harvard Business Review*, 73, 43–53 https://hbr.org/1995/01/disruptive-technologies-catching-the-wave

Boyd, D. (2010). "Social network sites as networked publics: Affordances, dynamics, and implications." In N. Papacharissi (Ed.), *Networked Self: Identity, Community, and Culture on Social Network Sites* (pp. 39-58). New York, NY: Routledge.

Boyd, D. (2011). Social Network Sites as Network Publics. Affordances, Dynamics and Implications. In Z. Papacharissi (Ed.), *A Networked Self* (pp. 39-59). New York: Routledge.

Boyd, D., & Ellison, N. (2008). Social Network Sites: Definition History, and Scholarship. *Journal of Computer-Mediated Communication*, *13*(1), 210–230. doi:10.1111/j.1083-6101.2007.00393.x

Boyle, J. (1997). Foucault in cyberspace: Surveillance, sovereignty, and hard-wired censors. *Social Science Electronic Publishing*, *66*(1), 177–205.

Braud, P. (2006). Violences politiques. Les raisons d'une déraison, in R. Meyran (ed.), Les mécanismes de la Violence, Paris, Editions Sciences Humaines, pp. 57-65.

Brennan, C. (2014a, May 23). Yandex offices searched during investigation into Navalny backers. *The Moscow Times.* Retrieved from http://www.themoscowtimes.com/article/500749.html

Brennan, C. (2014b, May 26). Navalny's popularity takes a dive, poll says. *The Moscow Times.* Retrieved from http://www.themoscowtimes.com/news/article/navalnys-popularity-takes-a-dive-poll-says/500899.html

Briggs, A., & Burke, P. (2005). *A Social History of Media From Gutenberg to the Internet.* Cambridge, MA: Polity Press.

Britain, D. (2009). Final Report to department for culture, media and sport and department for business innovation and skills. ISBN: 9780101765022.

Briziarelli, M. (2014). The Ideological Reproduction: (Social) Working and Laboring in Digital Landscapes. *TripleC*, *12*(2), 1–21. doi:10.31269/triplec.v12i2.537

Briziarelli, M., & Karikari, E. (2016). Mediating Social Media's Ambivalences in the Context of Informational Capitalism. *International Journal of Civic Engagement and Social Change*, *3*(1), 1–22. doi:10.4018/IJCESC.2016010101

Brown, R. (2010). *Prejudice: Its Social Psychology (Second)*. West Sussex, UK: Wiley-Blackwell.

Bush, R. (2014, September 2). *China's Decision on Universal Suffrage in Hong Kong*. Washington, DC: Brookings Institute.

Caiani, M., & Kröll, P. (2015). The transnationalization of the extreme right and the use of the Internet. *International Journal of Comparative and Applied Criminal Justice*, *39*(4), 331–351. doi:10.1080/01924036.2014.973050

Caiani, M., & Parenti, L. (2013). *European and American extreme right groups and the Internet*. London, UK: Routledge.

Calamur, K. (2017, October 26). China's Xi Jinping Era. *The Atlantic*, Retrieved on July 29, 2019 from https://www.theatlantic.com/international/archive/2017/2010/china-xi/544035/

Calderaro, A. (2018). *Social media and politics*. Cardiff University. doi:10.4135/9781526416513.n46

Campbell, V. (2004). *Information Age Journalism. Journalism in an International Context*. New York: Arnold.

Cariolle, J. (2018). The digital revolution in Sub-Saharan Africa: What perspectives for employment? https://www.entreprenanteafrique.com/en/the-digital-revolution-in-sub-saharan-africa-what-perspectives-for-employment/

Carothers, T., & O'Donohue, A. (2019, October 1). How to Understand the Global Spread of Political Polarization. Retrieved from https://carnegieendowment.org/2019/10/01/how-to-understand-global-spread-of-political-polarization-pub-79893

Carpentier, N. (2014). 'Fuck the clowns from Grease!!' Fantasies of participation and agency in YouTube comments on a Cypriot Problem documentary. *Information Communication and Society*, *17*(8), 1001–1016. doi:10.1080/1369118X.2013.875582

Cassin, R. (2014, April 22). Navalny convicted of Twitter libel, could be jailed [Web log post]. Retrieved from http://www.fcpablog.com/blog/2014/4/22/navalny-convicted-of-twitter-libel-could-be-jailed.html# Central Electoral Committee (2012). *Elections*. Retrieved from http://cvk2012.org/

Castells, M. (2007). Communication, power and counter-power in the network society. *International Journal of Communication*, *1*, 238–266.

Castells, M. (2008). The New Public Sphere: Global Civil Society, Communication Networks, and Global Governance. *The Annals of the American Academy of Political and Social Science*, *616*(1), 78–93. doi:10.1177/0002716207311877

Castells, M. (2009). *Communication power*. Oxford, UK: Oxford University Press.

Cattaruzza, A., Danet, D., Taillat, S., & Laudrain, A. (2016). Sovereignty in cyberspace: Balkanization or democratization. In *Proceedings of 2016 International Conference on Cyber Conflict (CyCon U.S.)*. Washington, DC: IEEE. 10.1109/CYCONUS.2016.7836628

Center for Preventive Action. (2019, January 14). The top conflicts to watch in 2019: South China Sea. *Council on Foreign Relations*, Retrieved from https://www.cfr.org/blog/top-conflicts-watch-2019-south-china-sea

CEPAL, N. (2018). Access to Information, Participation and Justice in Environmental Matters in Latin America and the Caribbean: Towards Achievement of the 2030 Agenda for Sustainable Development. pp. 1-144.

Chadwick, A. (2013). *The Hybrid Media System. Politics and Power*. Oxford, UK: Oxford University Press. doi:10.1093/acprof:oso/9780199759477.001.0001

Chadwick, A. (2017). *The hybrid media system: Politics and power*. Oxford, UK: Oxford University Press. doi:10.1093/oso/9780190696726.001.0001

Chan, K., Kwan, W., & Thomsen, C. (2019). EM outlook: Look beyond trade tensions for sustainable growth trends. *Capital Ideas*, Retrieved on July 27, 2019 from https://www.thecapitalideas.com/articles/outlook/emerging-markets-outlook

Chan, L. (2019, April 24). Hong Kong's 'Occupy Central' activists handed prison terms. *Al Jazeera News*, Retrieved on July 29, 2019 from https://www.aljazeera.com/news/2019/2004/hong-kong-occupy-central-activists-handed-prison-sentences-190424013728788.html

Chan, M., Wu, X., Hao, Y., Xi, R., & Jin, T. (2012, July). Microblogging, online expression, and political efficacy among young Chinese citizens: The moderating role of information and entertainment needs in the use of Weibo. *Cyberpsychology, Behavior, and Social Networking*, *15*(7), 345–349. doi:10.1089/cyber.2012.0109 PMID:22780993

Channel News Asia . (2019, July 22). Masked men assault protesters, commuters in Hong Kong MTR station. *Channel News Asia*, Retrieved from https://www.channelnewsasia.com/news/asia/hong-kong-yuen-long-mtr-station-protesters-masked-men-white-11741840

Chao, R. (2014). How much influence did social media have on India's election? Retrieved August 25, 2019 http://techpresident.com/news/wegov/25062/India-election-social-media-influence

Charitsis, V., Yngfalk, A. F., & Skålén, P. (2018). "Made to Run": Biopolitical Marketing and the Making of the Self-Quantified Runner. *Marketing Theory*. Published online. Accessed September 24, 2018. doi:10.1177/1470593118799794

Chaudhuri, B., & König, L. (2018). The Aadhaar scheme: A cornerstone of a new citizenship regime in India? *Contemporary South Asia*, *26*(2), 127–142. doi:10.1080/09584935.2017.1369934

Chen, J.-T., & She, J. (2012, June 18-21). *An analysis of verifications in microblogging social networks -- Sina Weibo.* Paper presented at 2012 32nd International Conference on the Distributed Computing Systems Workshops (ICDCSW), Macau, China.

Chen, S.-Y., Zhang, H.-M., Lin, M., & Lv, S.-H. (2011, December). *Comparison of microblogging service between Sina Weibo and Twitter.* Paper presented at the Computer Science and Network Technology (ICCSNT), Harbin, China.

Chen, W.-H. (2014). Taking stock, moving forward: The Internet, social networks and civic engagement in Chinese societies. *Information Communication and Society, 17*(1), 1–6. doi:10.1080/1369118X.2013.857425

Chibba, M. (2009). Financial inclusion, poverty reduction and the millennium development goals. *European Journal of Development Research, 21*(2), 213–230. doi:10.1057/ejdr.2008.17

China Internet Network Information Center. (CINIC) (2013, January). *Statistical report on Internet Development in China.* Retrieved May 1, 2014 from http://www1.cnnic.cn/IDR/ReportDownloads/201302/P020130221391269963814.pdf

China Internet Network Information Center. (CINIC). (2012, December 31). *Basic data.* Retrieved September 17, 2014 from http://www1.cnnic.cn/IDR/BasicData/

China Internet Network Information Center. (CINIC). (2014, January). *Statistical report on Internet Development in China.* Retrieved on September 17, 2014 from http://www1.cnnic.cn/IDR/ReportDownloads/201404/U020140417607531610855.pdf

China Internet Watch. (2012, November 23). Penetration rate of Weibo and SNS in China. Retrieved December 8, 2012 from http://www.chinainternetwatch.com/1830/penetration-rate-of-weibo-and-sns-in-china/#ixzz2EZfmyDNn

Chinese Internet Network Information Center (CNNIC). (2018, January). *Statistical Report on Internet Development in China (The 41 Survey Report).* Beijing, China: Chinese Internet Network Information Center (CNNIC).

Christensen, C. M., Raynor, M., & McDonald, R. (2015). 'What is disruptive innovation?'. *Harvard Business Review, 93*, 44–53.

Clark, B. D. (1994). Improving Public Participation In Environmental Impact Assessment, Built Environment (1978-), pp. 294-308.

Clark, D. D. (1992). *A cloudy crystal ball: Visions of the future.* Paper presented at the 24th Meeting of the Internet Engineering Task Force, Cambridge, UK.

Clark, S. L. (2009). Theories: Mediatization and Media Ecology. In K. Lundby (ed.), Mediatization Concept, changes, consequences, New York: Peter Lang, pp. 85-100.

Clarke, K., & Kocak, K. (Forthcoming). Launching Revolution: Social and the Egyptian Uprising's First Movers. *British Journal of Political Science.*

Clover, C., & Weaver, C. (2013, July 18). Russian opposition leader Alexei Navalny jailed for five years. *The Financial Times*. Retrieved from http://www.ft.com/intl/cms/s/0/ 82cc107e-ef71-11e2-8229-00144feabdc0.html#slide0

Coconuts Hong Kong & AFP. (2019, July 7). Tens of thousands rally as Hongkongers take anti-extradition protest to streets of Kowloon. *Coconuts Hong Kong*, Retrieved on July 29, 2019 from https://coconuts.co/hongkong/news/tens-of-thousands-rally-as-hongkongers-take-anti-extradition-protest-to-streets-of-kowloon/

Cohen, C., Kahne, J., Bowyer, B., Middaugh, E., & Rogowski, J. (2012). *Participatory politics: New media and youth political action*. Oakland, CA: Mills College School of Education.

Cohen, J. E. (1968). Alternate derivations of a species-abundance relation. *American Naturalist*, *102*(924), 165–172. doi:10.1086/282533

Cohen, N. (2008). The valorization of surveillance: Towards a political economy of Facebook. *Democratic Communiqué*, *22*(1), 5–22.

Commission of the European Communities (CEC). (1985) European Communities Directive 85/337/EEC on the Assessment of Certain Public and Private Projects on the Environment. Brussels, Belgium: Commission of the European Communities. Available at https://eur-lex.europa.eu/legal-content/EN/TXT/PDF/?uri=CELEX:52003DC0334&from=EN

Contarello, A. (2003). Body to Body: Copresence in Communication. In L. Fortunati, K. Katz, & R. Riccini (Eds.), *Mediating the Human Body. Technology, Communication, and Fashion*. Mahwah, NJ: Lawrence Erlbaum Associates.

Corner, J. (2018). *'Mediatization': Media theory's word of the decade. Media Theory*, May 21. Available at http://mediatheoryjournal.org/john-corner-mediatization/

Couldry, N. (2010). *Why voice matters: Culture and politics after neoliberalism*. London, UK: Sage.

Couldry, N., & Hepp, A. (2013). Conceptualizing Mediatization: Contexts, Traditions, Arguments. *Communication Theory*, *23*(3), 191–202. doi:10.1111/comt.12019

Council of Europe. (2019). *Study on the use* of *internet in electoral campaigns*. Retrieved from https://rm.coe.int/study-use-of-internet-in-electoral-campaigns/1680776163(accessed on 10th August, 2019)

Cox, K. W. M., Bellasio, J., Ward, A., Galai, K., Meranto, S., & Paoli, G. P. (2019). Social Media. In *Africa A Double-Edged Sword For Security And Development Research Report*. UNDP.

Crawford, K. (2009). Following you: Disciplines of listening in social media. *Continuum*, *23*(4), 525–535. doi:10.1080/10304310903003270

Dahlgren, P. (1996). Media Logic in Cyberspace: Repositioning Journalism and its Publics. *Javnost - the Public, 3*(1996), 59-72.

Dahlgren, P. (2006). Doing citizenship: The cultural origins of civic agency in the public sphere. *European Journal of Cultural Studies*, *9*(3), 267–286. doi:10.1177/1367549406066073

Dahlgren, P. (2009). *Media and Political Engagement. Citizens, Communication, and Democracy*. New York: Cambridge University Press.

Danneels, E. (2004). Disruptive technology reconsidered: A critique and research agenda. *Journal of Product Innovation Management*, *21*(4), 246–258. doi:10.1111/j.0737-6782.2004.00076.x

Dannye po Auditori [Audience data] (2013). *TNS-Global*. Retrieved from http://www.tns-global.ru/services/media/ media-audience/radio/radio-index/information/

Davenport, C. (2007). *State Repression And The Domestic Democratic Peace*. Cambridge: Cambridge University Press. doi:10.1017/CBO9780511510021

DCAC. (n.d.) CDAC AUA-ASA Aadhaar based services. Retrieved from https://meity.gov.in/writereaddata/files/CDAC_AUA_ASA_Service.pdf

De Huszar, G. B. (1945). *Practical application of democracy*. New York, NY: Harper. doi:10.2307/2263272

de la Brosse, R. (1999). Afrique subsaharienne en transition: Des journaux nécessairement engagés. *Les Cahiers du Journalisme*, *6*, 102–122.

de Saint Simon, H. (1964). *Social organization, the science of man and other writings*. New York, NY: Harper & Row.

Dean, J. (2009). *Democracy and other neoliberal fantasies: Communicative capitalism and left politics*. Durham, NC: Duke University Press. doi:10.1215/9780822390923

Dean, J. (2010). Affective networks. *Media Tropes*, *2*(2), 19–44.

Dean, J. (2014). Communicative Capitalism: This Is What Democracy Looks like. In J. S. Hanan, & M. Hayward (Eds.), *Communication and the Economy: History, Value, and Agency* (pp. 147–164). New York, NY: Peter Lang.

Deibert, R. (1997). *Parchment, Printing, and Hypermedia: Communication in World Order Transformation*. New York, NY: Columbia University Press.

Deleuze, G., & Guattari, F. (1987). *A Thousand Plateaus* (B. Masummi, Trans.). Minneapolis, MN: Minnesota University Press.

Delmas, R. (2007). The Internet: New principles of political right, new social contract. In P. Goujon, S. Lavelle, P. Duquenoy, K. Kimppa, & V. Laurent (Eds.), *The information society: Innovation, legitimacy, ethics and democracy in honor of Professor Jacques Berleur s.j* (pp. 147–152). Boston, MA: Springer. doi:10.1007/978-0-387-72381-5_14

DeLong, M., & Martinson, B. (2012). *Color and design*. London, UK: Berg.

Demirgüç-Kunt, A., Klapper, L. F., Singer, D., & Van Oudheusden, P. (2015). The global find ex database 2014: Measuring financial inclusion around the world.

Dent, H. (2018, June 4). Social unrest in China. *Economy & Markets*, Retrieved on July 28, 2019 from https://economyandmarkets.com/economy/demographic-trends/socialunrestinchina/

Deuze, M. (2007). Toward an ethics of the sociable web: A conversation between Trebor Scholz and Mark Deuze. Retrieved from http://mailman.thing.net/pipermail/idc/2007-July/002652.html

Deuze, M. (2003). The web and its journalisms: Considering the consequences of different types of news media online. *New Media & Society*, *5*(2), 203–230. doi:10.1177/1461444803005002004

Deuze, M. (2008). Understanding journalism as a network: How it changes, and how it remains the same. *Westminster Papers in Communication and Culture*, *5*(2), 4–23. doi:10.16997/wpcc.61

Dewey, J. (1938/1963). *Experience and Education*. New York: Simon & Schuster.

De-Wit, L., Brick, C., & van der Linden, S. (2019, January 16). Are Social Media Driving Political Polarization? Retrieved from https://greatergood.berkeley.edu/article/item/is_social_media_driving_political_polarization

Dibos, A. (2002). Democracy as Responsibility, Meaning, and Hope: Introductory Reflections on a Democratic Project in Education. *Journal of Thought*, *37*(1), 11–24.

DiFranzo, D., & Gloria-Garcia, K. (2017). Filter bubbles and fake news. *XRDS: Crossroads. The ACM Magazine for Students*, *23*(3), 32–35. doi:10.1145/3055153

Diniz, E., Birochi, R., & Pozzebon, M. (2012). Triggers and barriers to financial inclusion: The use of ICT-based branchless banking in an Amazon county. *Electronic Commerce Research and Applications*, *11*(5), 484–494. doi:10.1016/j.elerap.2011.07.006

Direct Benefit Transfer, Government of India. (2019a). Estimated gains. Retrieved from https://dbtbharat.gov.in/page/frontcontentview/?id=ODM=

Direct Benefit Transfer, Government of India. (2019b). Success story. Retrieved from https://dbtbharat.gov.in/successstory

Dirican, C. (2015). The impacts of robotics, artificial intelligence on business and economics. *Procedia: Social and Behavioral Sciences*, *195*, 564–573. doi:10.1016/j.sbspro.2015.06.134

Dixit, R., & Ghosh, M. (2013). Financial inclusion for inclusive growth of India-A study of Indian states. [IJBMR]. *International Journal of Business Management & Research*, *3*(1), 147–156.

Dixon, H. (1997). Controversy: The Source and Measurement of Technical Change- Editorial Note. *Economic Journal (London)*, *107*(September), 1518–1519. doi:10.1111/j.1468-0297.1997.tb00062.x

Djupe, P. A., & Peterson, D. (2002). The impact of negative campaigning: Evidence from the 1998 Senatorial primaries. *Political Research Quarterly*, *55*(4), 845–860. doi:10.1177/106591290205500406

Dodgson, M., & Rothwell, R. (Eds.). (1995). *The Handbook of Industrial Innovation*. London, UK: Edward Elgar. doi:10.4337/9781781954201

Dosemagen, S. (2016). Social Media and Saving the Environment: Clicktivism or Real Change. *Huffington Post*. Available at https://www.huffpost.com/entry/social-media-and-saving-t_b_9100362

Doyle, G. J., Garrett, B., & Currie, L. M. (2014). Integrating mobile devices into nursing curricula: Opportunities for implementation using Rogers' Diffusion of Innovation model. *Nurse Education Today*, *34*(5), 775–782. doi:10.1016/j.nedt.2013.10.021 PMID:24268745

Dragomir, M., & Thompson, M. (Eds.). (2011). *Mapping digital media: Russia*. London, UK: Open Society Foundation.

Drake, W. (2014). *The global Internet governance ecosystem*. Paper presented at European Summer School on Internet Governance. Meissen.

du Venage, G. (2018). Social Media Shines a Light on Corruption in Africa. Retrieved from https://www.thenational.ae/business/technology/social-media-shines-a-light-on-corruption-in-africa-1.775929

Duodu, E. E. (2018). Implementation of a National Identification System in Ghana: Lessons from the Indian Aadhaar System (Doctoral dissertation, University of Ghana).

Dutton, W. (2008). The Fifth Estate Emerging Through the Network of Networks, *Prometheus*, (27), 1, 1-15. Retrieved from http://ssrn.com/abstract=1167502.

Dwyer, M., & Molony, T. (2019). *Social Media and Politics in Africa. Democracy, Censorship and Security*. London: Zed Books.

Dyck, A., & Zingales, L. (2002). The Corporate Governance Role of the Media, August, 2002, p. 5. Available at http://faculty.chicagobooth.edu/finance/papers/corporate%20governance.pdf

Dyer-Witheford, N. (2015). *Cyber-Proletariat: Global Labour in the Digital Vortex*. London, UK: Pluto Press. doi:10.2307/j.ctt183p1zg

Eagleton-Pierce, M. (2001). The Internet and the Seattle Protests. *Peace Review*, *13*(3), 331–337.

Eagleton, T. (1976). *Marxism and Literary Criticism*. Berkeley, CA: University of California Press.

Eagleton, T. (2007). *Ideology: An Introduction* (2nd ed.). New York, NY: Verso.

Earl, J., & Kimport, K. (2011). *Digitally Enabled Social Change: Activism in the Internet Age*. Cambridge: The MIT Press. doi:10.7551/mitpress/9780262015103.001.0001

Eckersley, R. (1996). Greening Liberal Democracy: The Rights Discourse Revisited. In B. Doherty, & M. de Geus (Eds.), *Democracy and Green Political Thought* (p. 216). doi:10.4324/9780203449554_chapter_11

Eckersley, R. (2000). Deliberative Democracy, Ecological Representation and Risk: Towards a Democracy of the Affected. In M. Saward (Ed.), *Democratic Innovation: Deliberation, Representation and Association* (p. 230).

Economic Times. (2019). *How the mobile phone is shaping to be BJPs most important weapon in elections.* Retrieved from https://economictimes.indiatimes.com/news/politics-and-nation/how-the-mobile-phone-is-shaping-to-be-bjps-most-important-weapon-in-elections/articleshow/65508743.cms

Economic Times. (2019). *Social Media Engineering- How Congress BJPs war room are trying to woo voters in Karnataka.* Retrieved from https://economictimes.indiatimes.com/news/politics-and-nation/social-media-engineering-how-congress-bjps-war-room-are-trying-to-woo-voters-in-karnataka/articleshow/63445558.cms

Economic Times. (2019, Aug. 28) Is this Aadhaar of the Future? Facial biometric technology-based chip-enabled cards issued. Retrieved from https://economictimes.indiatimes.com/wealth/personal-finance-news/is-this-aadhaar-of-the-future-facial-biometric-technology-based-chip-enabled-cards-issued/articleshow/70875918.cms

Economy, E. C. (2018, June 29). The Great Firewall of China: Xi Jinping's internet shutdown. *The Guardian*, Retrieved on July 28, 2019 from https://www.theguardian.com/news/2018/jun/2029/the-great-firewall-of-china-xi-jinpings-internet-shutdown

Edwards, P. (1994). From "impact" to social process: Computers in society and culture. In eds. S. Jasanoff, G. E. Markle, & J. C. Peterson (Eds.), Handbook of Science and Technology Studies, Chap. 12. Beverly Hills, CA: Sage.

Edwards, P. (1998). Y2K: Millennial reflections on computers as infrastructure. *History and Technology*, *15*, 7–29.

Ehrlich, E. (2014). *A brief history of Internet regulation*. Retrieved from http://www.progressivepolicy.org/wp-content/uploads/2014/03/2014.03-Ehrlich_A-Brief-History-of-Internet-Regulation.pdf

El Gody, A. (2000). *Egyptian based model for the uses and limitations of online journalism applications.* (Master's thesis), American University in Cairo.

El Gody, A. (2003). Egypt. In R. Stanbridge (Ed.), African Media and ICT4D: A Baseline Study on the State of Media Reporting on ICT and Information Society Issues in Africa. London, UK: Economic Commission for Africa.

El Gody, A. (2009). Development of Media Industry in Egypt, in The International Media Handbook (28th ed.), Hamburg, Germany: hans- bredow- Institut.

El Gody, A. (2005). Arab media: Did it cover the same war. In S. A. Nohrstedt, & R. Ottosen (Eds.), *Journalism in Global Age*. Sweden: Nordicom.

El Gody, A. (2007). New Media New Censorship. In P. Seib (Ed.), *New Media and the New Middle East*. New York: Palgrave.

El Gody, A. (2008). *US Image in Arab Blogsphere. Paper submitted to the International Communication Association (ICA).* Conference Chicago.

El Gody, A. (2012). *Journalism in a Network: Role of ICTs inside Egyptian newsrooms. Örebro.* Örebro University Press.

El Gody, A. (2016). Network Journalism and the Egyptian Revolution. In M. Ben Mousa, & A. Doui (Eds.), *Mediated Identities and New Journalism in the Arab World : Mapping the 'Arab Spring'*. London, UK: McMillan. doi:10.1057/978-1-137-58141-9_10

El Khazen, J. (2007). *Censorship and State Control in the Arab World*, Paper presented to the Arab Media Forum Dubai, United Arab Emirates

El Sherif, A. (2015). *Egypt's Salafists At A Crossroads.* Massachusetts: Carnegie Endowment for International Peace.

El Zalaky, I. (2008) *Egyptian Bloggers: Practices and Challenges*, Paper presented to the Conference on New Media and The Press Freedom Dimension. UNESCO Headquarters, Paris, February 15-16.

Elias, N. (1998). The Social Constraint towards Self-Constraint. In S. Mennell, & J. Goudsblom (Eds.), *Norbert Elias. On Civilization, Power, and Knowledge.* Chicago, IL: The University of Chicago Press. (Original work published 1939)

Ellison, N., & Boyd, D. (2007). Social Network Sites: Definition, History and Scholarship. *Computer-Mediated Communication, 13*(1). Retrieved from http://onlinelibrary.wiley.com/doi/10.1111/j.1083-6101.2007.00393.x/full

Ellul, J. (1964). *The Technological Society.* New York: Knopf.

eMarketer.com. (2018, November 8). Weibo Now Used by Nearly 25% of Population in China. *eMarketer.com*, Retrieved on July 28, 2019 from https://content-na2011.emarketer.com/weibo-now-used-by-nearly-2025-of-population-in-china

Entman, R., & Usher, N. (2018). Framing in a Fractured Democracy: Impacts of Digital Technology on Ideology, Power and Cascading Network Activation. *Journal of Communication, 68*(2), 298–308. doi:10.1093/joc/jqx019

Ernst & Young. (2017). *The upside of Disruption Megatrends shaping 2016 and beyond.* EYGM Limited.

Essoungou, A.-M. (2010). Les jeunes politisent les médias sociaux. Retrieved from https://www.un.org/africarenewal/fr/magazine/april-2010/les-jeunes-politisent-les-m%C3%A9dias-sociaux

Etling, B., Alexanyan, K., Kelly, J., Faris, R., Palfrey, J., & Gasser, U. (2010). *Public discourse in the Russian blogosphere: Mapping RuNet politics and mobilization.* Cambridge, MA: Berkman Center for Internet & Society, Harvard University.

Etling, B., Faris, R., & Palfrey, J. (2010). Political change in the digital age: The fragility and promise of online organizing. *SAIS Review (Paul H. Nitze School of Advanced International Studies)*, *30*(2), 37–49.

European Bank for Reconstruction and Development. (EBRD, 1993). Public participation - The EBRD approach, The Environ mental Bulletin of EBRD, Winter. Available at https://www.ebrd.com/publications/annual-report-1993-english.pdf

European Parliamentary Blog. (2019). *The role played by social media in political participation and electoral campaigns.* Retrieved from https://epthinktank.eu/2014/02/12/the-role-played-by-social-media-in-political-participation-and-electoral-campaigns/ (European Parliamentary Blog)

Evans, G. L. (2017). Disruptive technology and the board: The tip of the iceberg. *Economics and Business Review*, *3*(1), 205–222. doi:10.18559/ebr.2017.1.11

Ezawa, K. (2016, January). Virtual & Augmented Reality. In Investment Themes in 2016. In Citi Global Perspectives & Solution. Citigroup Inc. Retrieved from https://www.citivelocity.com/citigps/ReportSeries.action?recordId=45

Fahmi, S. W. (2009). Blogger's Street Movement and the Right to the City. (Re)claiming Cairo's real and virtual "spaces of freedom". *Environment and Urbanization*, *21*(1), 89–107. doi:10.1177/0956247809103006

Fahmy, N. (2010). *Revealing the "Agenda-Cutting" through Egyptian Blogs: An Empirical Study.* Paper presented to Online Journalism Symposium, Austin, TX.

Faris, D. (2015). *Dissent and Revolution in a Digital Age: Social Media, Blogging and Activism in Egypt.* New York: IB Tauris.

Federalny Zakon Rossiyskoy Federatsii ot 8 Iunya 2012 g. N 65-FZ g. Moskva [Federal law of Russian Federation, 2012, June 8, N 65-FZ, Moscow] (2012, June 9). *Rossiyskaya Gazeta.* Retrieved from http://www.rg.ru/2012/06/09/mitingi-dok.html

Federici, S. (2012). *Revolution at Point Zero: Housework, Reproduction, and Feminist Struggle.* Oakland, CA: PM Press.

First we take Sakharov Avenue. The capital sees its biggest demonstration yet against the Kremlin. (2011, December 31). *The Economist.* Retrieved from http://www.economist.com/node/21542205

Fisher, E. (2012). How less alienation creates more exploitation? Audience labor on social network sites. *TripleC*, *10*(2), 171–183. doi:10.31269/triplec.v10i2.392

Foreman, C. (2017). 10 Types of Social Media and How Each Can Benefit Your Business. Retrieved from https://blog.hootsuite.com/types-of-social-media/

Fortunati, L. (2005). Is Body-to-Body Communication Still the Prototype? *The Information Society*, *21*(1), 53–61. doi:10.1080/01972240590895919

Fortunato, P., & Panizza, U. (2015). Democracy, education and the quality of government. *Journal of Economic Growth*, *20*(4), 333–363. doi:10.100710887-015-9120-5

Foucault, M. (1978). *Discipline and punish: The birth of the prison* (A. Sheridan, Trans.). New York: Pantheon Books. (Original work published 1975)

Foucault, M. (1978). The History of Sexuality: Vol. I. *An Introduction*. New York, NY: Pantheon Books.

Foucault, M. (1995). *Discipline and Punish*. New York, NY: Vintage Books.

Fourier, C. (1971). *Design for Utopia: Selected Writings. Studies in the Libertarian and Utopian Tradition*. New York, NY: Schocken.

Franco, Á., Álvarez-Dardet, C., & Ruiz, M. T. (2004). Effect of democracy on health: Ecological study. *BMJ (Clinical Research Ed.)*, *329*(7480), 1421–1423. doi:10.1136/bmj.329.7480.1421 PMID:15604165

Fraser, N. (1990). Rethinking the public sphere: A contribution to the critique of actually existing democracy. *Social Text*, *25*(26), 56–80. doi:10.2307/466240

Frayer, J. M. (2018, March 11). Analysis: Xi Jinping returns China to era of one-man rule. *CNBC News*, Retrieved on July 29, 2019 from https://www.nbcnews.com/news/world/analysis-xi-jinping-retuns-china-era-one-man-rule-n851531

Freechild Organization. (2019). *Youth and Politics*. Retrieved from https://freechild.org/youth-and-politics/(accessed on 5th August, 2019)

Freedom House. (2019). Democracy in Retreat. *Freedom in the World 2019*. Retrieved from https://freedomhouse.org/report/freedom-world/freedom-world-2019/democracy-in-retreat

Freedomhouse. (2013). 'Egypt, Freedom in the World 2010' Retrieved from http://www.freedomhouse.org/template.cfm?page=251&year=2010

Freeman, M., & Gambarato, R. R. (Eds.). (2018). *The Routledge companion to transmedia studies*. New York, NY: Routledge. doi:10.4324/9781351054904

Froio, C., & Gattinara, P. C. (2015). Neo-fascist mobilization in contemporary Italy. Ideology and repertoire of action of CasaPound Italia. *Journal of Deradicalization*, *15*(2), 86–118.

Fuchs, C. (2014). Social media and the public sphere. *Triple C (Cognition, Communication, Co-Operation)*, *12*(1), 57-101.

Fuchs, C. (2016). Critical Theory of Communication: New Readings of Lukács, Adorno, Marcuse, Honneth and Habermas in the Age of the Internet. London, UK: University of Westminster Press

Fuchs, C. (2010). Labor in Informational Capitalism and on the Internet. *The Information Society: An International Journal*, *26*(3), 179–196. doi:10.1080/01972241003712215

Fuchs, C. (2012). With or without Marx? With or without Capitalism? A rejoinder to Adam Arvidsson and Eleanor Colleoni. *TripleC*, *10*(2), 1–12. doi:10.31269/triplec.v10i2.434

Fuchs, C. (2013). Digital prosumption labour on social media in the context of the capitalist regime of time. *Time & Society*, *23*(1), 97–123. doi:10.1177/0961463X13502117

Fuchs, C. (2014). *Social Media. A Critical Introduction*. London, UK: Sage. doi:10.4135/9781446270066

Fuchs, C. (2015). *Culture and Economy in the Age of Social Media*. Abingdon, UK: Routledge Publishing. doi:10.4324/9781315733517

Fuchs, C. (2017). *Social Media: A Critical Introduction* (2nd ed.). Thousand Oaks, CA: Sage.

Fuchs, C. (2018). Propaganda 2.0: Herman and Chomsky's Propaganda Model in the Age of the Internet, Big Data and Social Media. In J. Pedro-Carañana, D. Broudy, & J. Klaehn (Eds.), *The Propaganda Model Today: Filtering Perception and Awareness* (pp. 71–92). London, UK: University of Westminster Press. doi:10.16997/book27.f

Fuchs, C. (2018b). *Digital Demagogue: Authoritarian Capitalism in the Age of Trump and Twitter*. London, UK: Pluto. doi:10.2307/j.ctt21215dw

Fuchs, C., & Mosco, V. (Eds.). (2016). *Marx in the Age of Digital Capitalism*. Leiden, The Netherlands: Brill Publishers. doi:10.1163/9789004291393

Fuchs, C., & Sevignani, S. (2013). What is digital labor? What is digital work? What's their difference? And why do these questions matter for understanding social media? *TripleC*, *11*(2), 237–293. doi:10.31269/triplec.v11i2.461

Fund 'leakage' not as big as Rajiv Gandhi mentioned: PM (2009, Oct 11), *The Hindu*. Retrieved from https://www.thehindu.com/news/national/Fund-lsquoleakagersquo-not-as-big-as-Rajiv-Gandhi-mentioned-PM/article16886675.ece

Galloway, A. (2004). *Protocol: How Control Exists After Decentralization*. Cambridge, MA: The MIT Press. doi:10.7551/mitpress/5658.001.0001

Gambarato, R. R. (2012). Signs, systems and complexity of transmedia storytelling. *Estudos em Comunicação*, *12*, 69–83.

Gambarato, R. R. (2013). Transmedia project design: Theoretical and analytical considerations. *Baltic Screen Media Review*, *1*(1), 80–100. doi:10.1515/bsmr-2015-0006

Gambarato, R. R. (2014). Transmedia storytelling in analysis: The case of final punishment. *Journal of Print and Media Technology Research*, *3*(2), 95–106.

Gambarato, R. R. (2018). Russia: Interactive documentary, slow journalism and the transmediality of Grozny: Nine Cities. In M. Freeman, & W. Proctor (Eds.), *Global convergence cultures: Transmedia earth* (pp. 206–226). New York, NY: Routledge. doi:10.4324/9781315188478-13

Gambarato, R. R., & Alzamora, G. (Eds.). (2018). *Exploring transmedia journalism in the digital age*. Hershey, PA: IGI Global. doi:10.4018/978-1-5225-3781-6

Gambarato, R. R., & Lapina-Kratasyuk, E. (2016). Transmedia storytelling panorama in the Russian media landscape. *Russian Journal of Communication*, *8*(1), 1–16. doi:10.1080/19409419.2015.1121789

Gans, H. (2003). *Democracy and the news*. Oxford, UK: Oxford University Press.

Gao, Luo and Zhang, 2012; Greenhow, Burton and Robelia, 2011; Greenhow and Robelia, 2009a, 2009b; Pimmer, Linxen and Grohbiel, 2012; Ranieri, Manca and Fini, 2012.

Gao, F., Luo, T., & Zhang, K. (2012). Tweeting for learning: A critical analysis of research on microblogging in education published in 2008-2011. *British Journal of Educational Technology*, *43*(5), 783–801. doi:10.1111/j.1467-8535.2012.01357.x

Gardiner, J. (2002). Defining corruption. In A. Heidenheimer, & M. Johnston (Eds.), Political Corruption,(3rd ed., pp. 25-40). New York: Routledge.

Garrett, K. (2006, April). Protest in an information society: A Review of literature on social movements and new ICTs. *Information Communication and Society*, *9*(2), 202–224. doi:10.1080/13691180600630773

Garrison, B. (2005). 'Online newspapers', in M. B. Salwen, B. Garrison, & P. D. Driscoll (Eds.), Online News and the Public, New Jersey: Lawrence Erlbaum Associates.

Gazibo, M. (2018). L'exercice Du Pouvoir. In *Afrique Postcoloniale, Introduction à la politique africaine* (pp. 89–116). Montréal, Canada: Presses De L'université de Montréal.

Gemmill, B., & Bamidele-Izu, A. (2002). The role of NGOs and civil society in global environmental governance, Global environmental governance: Options and opportunities, pp. 77-100.

Gendron, B. (1977). *Technology and the human condition*. New York, NY: St. Martin's Press.

Gergen, K. J. (2002). The challenge of absent presence. In J. E. Katz, & M. Aakhus (Eds.), *Perpetual Contact. Mobile Communication, Private Talk, Public Performance* (pp. 227–241). Cambridge: Cambridge University Press. doi:10.1017/CBO9780511489471.018

Gessen, M. (2012, October 22). For fair elections. *The New York Times*. Retrieved from http://latitude.blogs.nytimes.com/2012/10/22/russian-opposition-stages-alternative-election/?_php=true&_type=blogs&_r=0

Ghareeb, E. (2000). 'New media and the information revolution in the Arab world: An assessment.' *Middle East Journal, 54*(3), 395-418. Retrieved from http://www.jstor.org /stable/ 4329508

Ghose, A., & Ipeirotis, P. G. (2011). Estimating the Helpfulness and Economic Impact of Product Reviews: Mining Text and Reviewer Characteristics. *IEEE Transactions on Knowledge and Data Engineering*, *23*(10), 1498–1512. doi:10.1109/TKDE.2010.188

Ghosh, S. (2013). Demystifying the Environmental Clearance Process in India. *NUJS L. Rev.*, *6*, 433.

Ghosh, S. (2017). Financial inclusion, biometric identification and mobile: Unlocking the JAM trinity. *International Journal of Development Issues*, *16*(2), 190–213. doi:10.1108/IJDI-02-2017-0012

Giddens, A. (1984). *The Constitution of Society - Outline of the Theory of Structuration.* Cambridge, UK: Polity Press.

Giddens, A. (1991). *Modernity and Self-Identity: Self and Society in the Late Modern Age.* Cambridge, UK: Polity Press.

Giglietto, F., & Selva, D. (2014). Second screen and participation: A content analysis on a full season dataset of Tweets. *Journal of Communication*, *64*(2), 260–277. doi:10.1111/jcom.12085

Gil de Zúñiga, H., Veenstra, A., Vraga, E., & Shah, D. (2010). Digital democracy: Reimagining pathways to political participation. *Journal of Information Technology & Politics*, *7*(1), 36–51. doi:10.1080/19331680903316742

Gilbert, D. (2019). Zimbabwe Is Trying to Build a China Style Surveillance State. Retrieved from https://www.vice.com/en_ca/article/59n753/zimbabwe-is-trying-to-build-a-china-style-surveillance-state

Glaeser, E. L., Ponzetto, G. A. M., & Shleifer, A. (2007). Why Does Democracy Need Education? *Journal of Economic Growth*, *12*(2), 77–99. doi:10.100710887-007-9015-1

Glasson, J., & Therivel, R. (2013). *Introduction to Environmental Impact Assessment* (pp. 1–490). Routledge.

Gleditsch, N. P., & Sverdrup, B. O. (2002). Democracy and the Environmental, Human security and the environment: International comparisons, p. 45.

Globalstats, S. (2019) *Social Media Stats in India.* Retrieved from https://gs.statcounter.com/social-media-stats/all/india (accessed on 3rd November, 2019)

Goffman, E. (1959). *The Presentation of Self in Everyday Life.* New York, NY: Doubleday.

Goffman, E. (1967). *Interaction Ritual.* New York, NY: Anchor Books.

Gorman, P. (2012). *Human flesh search: The governmentality of mass surveillance in China* (Unpublished master's thesis). Carleton University, Canada.

Government of the Russian Federation. (1993). The constitution of the Russian Federation. Retrieved from http://www.constitution.ru/en/10003000-01.htm

Graham-Harrison, E. (2007, April 3). China's inevitable rise risks conflict: Kissinger. *Reuters.com*, Retrieved on July 27, 2019 from https://www.reuters.com/article/us-china-kissinger-idUSPEK30303020070403

Graham, S. (2003). *Deliberative Democracy and the Environment* (pp. 53–108). London, UK.

Greene, M. (1986). In Search of Critical Pedagogy. *Harvard Educational Review*, *56*(4), 427–441. doi:10.17763/haer.56.4.010756lh36u16213

Greenhow, C., Burton, L., & Robelia, B. (2011). Help from my "Friends:" Social capital in the social network sites of low-income high school students. *Journal of Educational Computing Research*, *45*(2), 223–245. doi:10.2190/EC.45.2.f

Greenhow, C., & Robelia, E. (2009a). Old communication, new literacies: Social network sites as social learning resources. *Journal of Computer-Mediated Communication*, *14*(4), 1130–1161. doi:10.1111/j.1083-6101.2009.01484.x

Greenhow, C., & Robelia, E. (2009b). Informal learning and identity formation in online social networks. *Learning, Media, and Technology*, *34*(2), 119–140. doi:10.1080/17439880902923580

Gregg, M. (2011). *Work's Intimacy*. Cambridge, MA: Polity Press.

Gregory, E. J. (2018, August 20). Why China's zombified 'civil society' is a cautionary tale for the West. *National Interest*, Retrieved on July 28, 2019 from https://nationalinterest.org/feature/why-china%E2012%2080%2099s-zombified-civil-society-cautionary-tale-west-29312

Griffis, H. M., Kilaru, A. S., Werner, R. M., Asch, D. A., Hershey, J. C., Hill, S., ... Merchant, R. M. (2014). Use of social media across US hospitals: Descriptive analysis of adoption and utilization. *Journal of Medical Internet Research*, *16*(11), e264. doi:10.2196/jmir.3758 PMID:25431831

Grindle, M. (2004). Good enough governance: Poverty reduction and reform in developing countries. *Governance: An International Journal of Policy, Administration, and Institutions*, *17*(4), 525–548. doi:10.1111/j.0952-1895.2004.00256.x

Grindle, M. (2007). Good enough governance revisited. *Development Policy Review*, *25*(5), 553–574. doi:10.1111/j.1467-7679.2007.00385.x

Groves, P., Kayyali, B., Knott, D., & Kuiken, S. V. (2016). The 'big data' revolution in healthcare: Accelerating value and innovation.

Guess, A., Lyons, B., Montgomery, J. M., Nyham, B., & Reifler, J. (2019). *Fake news, Facebook ads, and misperceptions: Assessing information quality in the 2018 U.S. midterm election campaign*. Retrieved from http://www.dartmouth.edu/~nyhan/fake-news-2018.pdf

Guess, A., Nyhan, B., & Reifler, J. (2018). *Selective Exposure to Misinformation: Evidence from the consumption of fake news during the 2016 U.S. presidential campaign*. Retrieved from http://www.dartmouth.edu/~nyhan/fake-news-2016.pdf

Gurevitch, M., Coleman, S., & Blumler, J. G. (2009). Political communication—Old and new media relationships. *The Annals of the American Academy of Political and Social Science*, *625*(1), 164–181. doi:10.1177/0002716209339345

Habermas, J. (1984). Theory of communicative action (T. McCarthy, Trans.). Boston, MA: Beacon Press.

Habermas, J. (1984). Theory of Communicative Action: Vol. 1. *Reason and the Rationalization of Society*. Boston, MA: Beacon Press.

Habermas, J. (1989). *The structural transformation of the public sphere: An inquiry into a category of bourgeois society*. Cambridge, MA: MIT Press.

Habermas, J. (1991). *The structural transformation of the public sphere: An inquiry into category of bourgeois society*. Cambridge, MA: The MIT Press.

Habermas, J. (2006, November 6). Political communication in media society: Does democracy still enjoy an epistemic dimension? The impact of normative theory on empirical research. *Communication Theory*, *16*(4), 411–426. doi:10.1111/j.1468-2885.2006.00280.x

Haenlein, M., & Kaplan, A. M. (2009). Flagship brand stores within virtual worlds: The impact of virtual store exposure on real life brand attitudes and purchase intent. *Recherche et Applications en Marketing*, *24*(3).

Haenssgen, M. J., & Ariana, P. (2017). The social implications of technology diffusion: Uncovering the unintended consequences of people's health-related mobile phone use in Rural India and China. *World Development*, *94*, 286–304. doi:10.1016/j.worlddev.2017.01.014

Hafez, K. (2006). 'Arab Satellite Broadcasting: Democracy without Political Parties', *Transnational Broadcasting Studies* 15, 2006, Retrieved from www.tbsj ournal.com/Archives/Fall05/Hafez.html

Hajli, N. (2014a). The role of social support on relationship quality and social commerce. *Technological Forecasting and Social Change*, *87*, 17–27. doi:10.1016/j.techfore.2014.05.012

Hallin, D., & Manchini, P. (2004). *Comparing Media Systems*. Cambridge, MA: Cambridge University Press. doi:10.1017/CBO9780511790867

Hall, M. A., & Wright, R. F. (2008). Systematic content analysis of judicial opinions. *California Law Review*, *96*(1), 63–122.

Hamdy, N. (2009). Arab Citizen Journalism in Action: Challenging Main- stream Media, Authorities and Media Laws. *Westminster Paper in Communication and Culture*, *6*(1), 92–112. doi:10.16997/wpcc.110

Hamdy, N. (2010, Fall/Winter). Arab media adopt citizen journalism to change the dynamics of conflict coverage. *Global Media Journal Arabian Edition*, *1*(1), 3–15.

Hannig, A., & Jansen, S. (2010). Financial inclusion and financial stability: Current policy issues.

Haraway, D. (1991). A Cyborg Manifesto: Science, Technology, and Socialist-Feminism in the Late Twentieth Century. In *Simians, Cyborgs and Women: The Reinvention of Nature* (pp. 149–181). New York, NY: Routledge.

Hardt, M., & Negri, A. (2000). *Empire*. Cambridge, MA: Harvard.

Hardt, M., & Negri, A. (2004). *Multitude: War and Democracy in the Age of Empire*. London, UK: Penguin Books.

Hardt, M., & Negri, A. (2009). *Commonwealth*. Cambridge, MA: Harvard. doi:10.2307/j.ctvjsf48h

Harris, L., & Harrigan, P. (2015). Social Media in Politics: The Ultimate Voter Engagement Tool or Simply an Echo Chamber? *Journal of Political Marketing*, *14*(3), 251–283. doi:10.1080/15377857.2012.693059

Harrison, J., & Wessels, B. (2009). *Mediating Europe: New media, mass communications and the European public sphere*. New York: Berghahn Books.

Harrison, T., & Sayogo, D. (2014). Transparency, participation and accountability practices in open government: A comparative study. *Government Information Quarterly*, *31*(4), 513–525. doi:10.1016/j.giq.2014.08.002

Harter, S. (1997). The Personal Self in Social Context: Barriers to Authenticity. In R. D. Ashmore, & L. Jussim (Eds.), *Self and Identity: Fundamental Issues* (pp. 81–105). Oxford, UK: Oxford University Press.

Hartley, K., Kuecker, G., & Woo, J. J. (2019). Practicing public policy in an age of disruption. *Policy Design and Practice*, *2*(2), 163–181. doi:10.1080/25741292.2019.1622276

Hasselbalch, J. (2014). Regulating disruptive innovations: The policy disruption of electronic cigarettes, Paper presented at Global Reordering: Towards the Next Generation of Scholarship conference in Brussels, November 18-20, 2014.

Hassid, J. (2012). Safety valve or pressure cooker? Blogs in Chinese political life. *Journal of Communication*, *62*(2), 217–230. doi:10.1111/j.1460-2466.2012.01634.x

Hay. (2002). This environmental thought was defined "Hobbesian deeply despairing and anti-democratic", p. 174.

Hayward, T. (2000). Constitutional environmental rights: A case for political analysis. *Political Studies*, *48*(3), 558–572. doi:10.1111/1467-9248.t01-1-00275

Hazen, S. (2010). Environmental Democracy, UNEP. Retrieved from http://www.unep.org/ourplanet/imgversn/86/hazen.html

He, L. (2019, July 15). China's economic growth slumps to lowest in 27 years as the trade war hits. *CNN*, Retrieved on July 27, 2019 from https://www.cnn.com/2019/2007/2015/economy/china-gdp-growth/index.html

Heeks, R., & Ospina, A. V. (2019). Conceptualising the link between information systems and resilience: A developing country field study. *Information Systems Journal*, *29*(1), 70–96. doi:10.1111/isj.12177

Heidegger, M. (1962). *Being and Time*. Oxford, UK: Blackwell.

Heng, X.-N. (2016, July 14). Capitalism with Chinese Characteristics: From socialism to capitalism. *The Epoch Times*, Retrieved on July 28, 2019 from https://www.theatlantic.com/technology/archive/2017/2001/trolling-by-distraction/514589/

Hermes, J. (2006). Hidden Debates: Rethinking the Relationship Between Popular Culture and The Public Sphere. *Javnost - The Public, 13*(4), 27-44.

Hincks, J. (2018, March 13). Your complete guide to Russia's presidential election. *Time*. Retrieved from https://time.com/5196905/russia-presidential-election-2018-candidates/

Hindustan Times. (2019). *BJP way ahead of competition on social media in 2014, says Stanford University*. Retrieved from https://www.hindustantimes.com/india-news/bjp-way-ahead-of-competition-on-social-media-in-2014-says-stanford-university-study/story-6Uq81HOwstzCwgCmiSyMWI.html(accessed on 25th July, 2019)

Hjarvard, S. (2008). The Mediatization of Religion: A Theory of the Media as Agents of Religious Change. In *Northern Lights 2008, Yearbook of Film & Media Studies* (p. 7). Bristol: Intellect Press. doi:10.1386/nl.6.1.9_1

Hofheinz, A. (2005). The Internet in the Arab world: Playground for political liberalisation. *International Political Sociology*, *3*, 78–96.

Hollyer, J. R., Rosendorff, B. P., & Vreeland, J. R. (2018). Transparency, protest and democratic stability. *British Journal of Political Science*, 1–27.

Hong Kong Free Press. (2019, June 13). Hong Kong's anti-extradition law protests were "riots", Beijing claims. *Hong Kong Free Press*, Retrieved on July 29, 2019 from https://www.hongkongfp.com/2019/2006/2013/hong-kongs-anti-extradition-law-protests-riots-beijing-claims/

Hong, S. (2014). *Beyond cyber-sovereignty: China's internet policy toward global internet governance (1994-2013)*. Paper presented at the International Communication Association 64th Annual Conference, Seattle, WA.

Hongo, J. (2015, April 16, 1:14 pm JST). Robotic Customer Service? In This Japanese Store, That's the Point. The Wall Street Journal News Paper, Japan Real Time. http://blogs.wsj.com/japanrealtime/2015/04/16/toshiba-humanoid-robot-to-debut-in-tokyo-departmentstore/?mod=WSJAsia_hpp_LEFTTopStories (Access Date: 19.04.2015). http://www.lifealertmedical.com/classic.html http://www.alert-1.com/ http://memex.lib.indiana.edu/siwkshop/SocInfo1.html (As seen on 15th June, 2019) https://www.britannica.com/topic/social-change (As seen on 12th June, 2019) https://www.sam-solutions.com/blog/top-five-information-tech/nology-trends-to-watch-in-2019 (As seen on 12th June, 2019)

Horkheimer, M., & Adorno, T. (1974). *The Dialectics of enlightenment*. London, UK: Verso.

Hsieh, Y.-L. P., & Li, M. H. (2014). Online political participation, civic talk, and media multiplexity: How Taiwanese citizens express political opinions on the Web. *Information Communication and Society*, *17*(1), 26–44. doi:10.1080/1369118X.2013.833278

Huang, E. (2018, July 27). China tried to crush #MeToo, but it's making a comeback. *QUARTZ*, Retrieved on July 28, 2019 from https://qz.com/1265510/china-tried-to-crush-metoo-but-its-making-a-comeback/

Huang, R.-G., & Sun, X.-Y. (2014, January). Weibo network, information diffusion and implications for collective action in China. *Information Communication and Society*, *17*(1), 86–104. doi:10.1080/1369118X.2013.853817

Hudson, H. (2006). *From Rural Village to Global Village: Telecommunications for Development in the Information Age*. London, UK: Routledge.

Hu, H. L. (2011). The political economy of governing ISPs in China: Perspectives of net neutrality and vertical integration. *The China Quarterly*, *207*, 523–540. doi:10.1017/S0305741011000634

Hu, N., Koh, N. S., & Reddy, S. K. (2013). 'Ratings Lead You to the Product, Reviews Help you Clinch It? The Mediating Role of Online Review Sentiments on Product Sales. *Decision Support Systems*, *57*(1), 42–53.

Hung, C.-F. (2010, October). The politics of China's *wei-quan* movement in the Internet Age. *International Journal of China Studies*, *1*(2), 331–349.

Huws, U. (2003). *The making of a cybertariat: Virtual work in a real world.* New York, NY: Monthly Review Press.

Huws, U. (2014). *Labor in the Global Digital Economy*. New York, NY: Monthly Review Press.

Hu, Y. (2008). *The rising cacophony: Personal expression and public discussion in the Internet age*. Guilin: Guangxi Normal University Press.

Indina, T. (2014). Moscow mayoral elections & another Navalny effect. Retrieved from http://www.newmediacenter.ru/2014/01/22/moscow-mayor-elections-another-navalny-effect/

Information and Decision Support Centre. (2010b). *Profiling Social Media in Egypt* (in Arabic) Retrieved from www.idsc.gov.eg

Inspired by "The Wire" (2013, September 7). *The Economist*. Retrieved from http://www.economist.com/news/europe/21585043-charismatic-dissident-runs-american-style-campaign-inspired-wire

Intelligence, G. S. M. A. (2018). The Mobile Economy: Sub-Saharan Africa 2018. Retrieved from https://www.gsma.com/mobileeconomy/sub-saharan-africa/

Intergovernmental Panel on Climate Change (IPCC). (2018). Global Warming of 1.5 °C. Retrieved from http://report.ipcc.ch/sr15/pdf/sr15_spm_final.pdf

Ip, K., Bailey, D., & Gong, G. (2016, April 5). *SARPPFT Clarifies New Online Publishing Regulations*. Retrieved from https://www.lexology.com/library/detail.aspx?g=a3572276-5cdd-46bc-8421-c9b0edb2a474

Iqbal, M. (2019, February 27). WeChat Revenue and Usage Statistics (2019). *Business of Apps*, Retrieved on July 28, 2019 from https://www.businessofapps.com/data/wechat-statistics/

Ito, J. (2004). *Weblogs and emergent democracy.* Retrieved from http://joi.ito .com/static/emergentdemocracy.html

Iyengar, R. (2014, September 3). 6 questions you might have about Hong Kong's Umbrella Revolution. *Time*, Retrieved on July 29, 2019 from https://time.com/3471366/hong-kong-umbrella-revolution-occupy-central-democracy-explainer-3471366-questions/

Jacobs, N. (1992). *Mass media in modern society*. New Brunswick, NJ: Transaction Publishers.

James, W. (1927). *The principles of psychology*. New York, NY: Dover.

Jamieson, K. H. (2018). *Cyberwar: How Russian Hackers and Trolls Helped Elect a President – What We Don't, Can't, and Do Know*. New York, NY: Oxford University Press.

Jamme, M. (2011). Africa's new generation is using social media to push for change. Retrieved from https://www.theguardian.com/global-development/poverty-matters/2011/jun/17/social-media-transforming-communication-africa

Jansson, A. (2013). Mediatization and social space: Reconstructing mediatization for the transmedia age. *Communication Theory*, *23*(3), 279–296. doi:10.1111/comt.12015

Jaramillo, M., & Wright, G. D. (2015). Participatory Democracy and Effective Policy: Is There a Link? Evidence from Rural Peru. *World Development*, *66*, 280–292. doi:10.1016/j.worlddev.2014.08.011

Jenkins, H. (2003, January 15). Transmedia storytelling. *Technology Review*. Retrieved from http://www.technologyreview.com/news/401760/transmedia-storytelling/

Jenkins, H. (2008, November 13). Obama: The candidate for all platforms [Web log post]. Retrieved from http://henryjenkins.org/2008/11/whew_i_am_still_trying.html

Jenkins, H. (2010, April 27). Hollywood goes "transmedia" [Web log post]. Retrieved from http://henryjenkins.org/2010/04/hollywood_goes_transmedia.html

Jenkins, H. (2019, May 30). Participatory politics in the age of crisis: Henry Jenkins & Nico Carpentier (part I) [Web log post]. Retrieved from http://henryjenkins.org/blog/2019/5/30/participatory-politics-in-an-age-of-crisis-henry-jenkins-amp-nico-carpentier-part-i

Jenkins, H. (2006). *Convergence culture: Where old and new media collide*. New York, NY: New York University Press.

Jenkins, H. (2010). *Convergence Culture: Where old and new media collide*. New York: New York University Press.

Jenkins, H., Ford, S., & Green, J. (2013). *Spreadable media: Creating value and meaning in networked culture*. New York, NY: NYU Press.

Jensen, M. J. (2017). Social media and political campaigning: Changing terms of engagement? *The International Journal of Press/Politics*, *22*(1), 23–42. doi:10.1177/1940161216673196

Jiang, M. (2013). *Road to neo-authoritarianism? A 25-year review of China's Internet policies*. Paper presented at the 2013 International Communication Association Annual Conference, London, UK.

Jiang, M. (2010). Authoritarian informationalism: China's approach to Internet sovereignty. *SAIS Review (Paul H. Nitze School of Advanced International Studies), 30*(2), 71–89.

Jiang, R., Kleer, R., & Piller, F. T. (2017). Predicting the future of additive manufacturing: A Delphi study on economic and societal implications of 3D printing for 2030. *Technological Forecasting and Social Change, 117*, 84–97. doi:10.1016/j.techfore.2017.01.006

Jin, X. (2016). Woguo chuanmei lingyu youxiao tuijin teshu guanligu zhidu de sikao [Reflections on the effective promotion of special management share system in China's media sector]. *China Development Observation, 21*, 51–54.

Jones, R. H., Chik, A., & Hafner, C. A. (Eds.). (2015). *Discourse and digital practices: Doing discourse in the digital age*. London, UK: Routledge. doi:10.4324/9781315726465

Joshi, D. P. (2011). Financial inclusion and financial literacy. Presented at BI OECD Seminar, Jakarta, Indonesia. Retrieved from https://www.oecd.org/finance/financial-education/48303408.pdf

Joyce, S. (2018). *Transmedia Storytelling and the Apocalypse*. Basingstoke, UK: Palgrave MacMillan. doi:10.1007/978-3-319-93952-0

Jutel, O. (2018). American populism, Glenn Beck and affective media production. *International Journal of Cultural Studies, 21*(4), 375–392. doi:10.1177/1367877916688273

Kahne, J., Middaugh, E., & Allen, D. (2015). Youth, new media, and the rise of participatory politics. *From voice to influence: Understanding citizenship in a digital age, 35.*

Kahne, J., & Bowyer, B. (2019). Can media literacy education increase digital engagement in politics? *Learning, Media, and Technology, 44*(2), 211–224. doi:10.1080/17439884.2019.1601108

Kak Moskva vibirala mera [How Moscow chose the mayor] (2013, September 9). *Vedomosti*. Retrieved from http://www.vedomosti.ru/special/map/moscow-map-2013?utm_source=vedomosti&utm_medium=widget&utm_campaign=vedomosti&utm_content=link

Kamel, S., & Hussein, M. (2002). The emergence of e-commerce in a developing nation Case of Egypt, *Benchmarking: An International- Journal, 9*(2).

Kamga, O. (2017). Constructivisme social in Jean-Paul Lafrance, 100 notions sur la civilisation numérique, Paris, Les éditions de l'Immatériel, pp. 33-35.

Kamga, O. (2019). *Difficile émergence d'un journalisme objectif en Afrique* (Vol. 36, p. 1). Communication. [on ligne]

Kang, H., & McAllister, M. (2011). Selling you and your clicks: Examining the audience commodification of Google. *TripleC, 9*(2), 141–153. doi:10.31269/triplec.v9i2.255

Kaplan, A. M., & Haenlein, M. (2009a). Consumer use and business potential of virtual worlds: The case of Second Life. *The International Journal on Media Management, 11*(3).

Kaplan, A. M., & Haenlein, M. (2009b). Consumers, companies, and virtual social worlds: A qualitative analysis of Second Life. *Advances in Consumer Research. Association for Consumer Research (U. S.)*, *36*(1), 873–874.

Kaplan, A., & Haenlein, M. (2010). Users of the world, unite! The challenges and opportunities of Social Media. *Business Horizons*, *53*(1), 59–68. doi:10.1016/j.bushor.2009.09.003

Karusala, N., & Kumar, N. (2017, May). Women's Safety in Public Spaces: Examining the Efficacy of Panic Buttons in New Delhi. In *Proceedings of the 2017 CHI Conference on Human Factors in Computing Systems* (pp. 3340-3351). ACM. 10.1145/3025453.3025532

Kaur, M., & Verma, R. (2018). Social media: An emerging tool for political participation. In Media Influence: Breakthroughs in Research and Practice (pp. 1-8). IGI Global.

Keating, A., & Melis, G. (2017). Social media and youth political engagement: Preaching to the converted or providing a new voice for youth? *British Journal of Politics and International Relations*, *19*(4), 877–894. doi:10.1177/1369148117718461

Kelkar, V. (2010). Financial inclusion for inclusive growth. *ASCI Journal of Management*, *39*(1), 55–68.

Kelly-Meyrick, R. (2017, July 10). Social unrest in China: A threat to regime legitimacy and the economy? *Global Risk Insights*, Retrieved on July 27, 2019 from https://globalriskinsights.com/2017/2007/social-unrest-china-threat-regime-legitimacy-economy/

Kenski, K., & Stroud, N. J. (2006). Connections between Internet use and political efficacy, knowledge, and participation. *Journal of Broadcasting & Electronic Media*, *50*(2), 173–192. doi:10.120715506878jobem5002_1

Kent Jennings, M., & Zeitner, V. (2003). Internet use and civic engagement: A longitudinal analysis. *Public Opinion Quarterly*, *67*(3), 311–334. doi:10.1086/376947

Khera, R. (2017). Impact of Aadhaar in welfare programmes. *Available at SSRN 3045235*.

Khvostunova, O. (2013, December 6). A brief history of Russian media. *The Interpreter*. Retrieved from http://www.interpretermag.com/a-brief-history-of-the-russian-media/

Kim, J., Kim, J., & Kim, A. H. (2013, December 20). The communication adaptiveness and power dynamics of the state, the market, and civil society in the information age: The case of Korea. *Information Communication and Society*, *17*(8), 956–973. doi:10.1080/1369118X.2013.869241

King, G., Pan, J., & Roberts, M. E. (2013). How censorship in China allows government criticism but silences collective expression. *The American Political Science Review*, *107*(2), 326–343. doi:10.1017/S0003055413000014

Kleiner, D. (2010). *The Telekommunist Manifesto*. Amsterdam, The Netherlands: Institute of Network Cultures.

Klinger, U., & Svensson, J. (2015). The Emergence of Network Media Logic in Political Communication. A Theoretical Approach. *New Media & Society*, *17*(8), 1241–1257. doi:10.1177/1461444814522952

Klinger, U., & Svensson, J. (2016). Network Media Logic. Some Conceptual Clarification. In A. Bruns, G. Enli, E. Skogerbö, A. Larsson, & C. Christensen (Eds.), *Routledge Companion to Social Media and Politics* (pp. 23–38). London, UK: Routledge.

Kling, R. (2000). Learning about information technologies and social change: The contribution of social informatics. *The Information Society*, *16*(3), 217–232. doi:10.1080/01972240050133661

Knoche, M. (2015). The Media Industry's Structural Transformation in Capitalism and the Role of the State: Media Economics in the Age of Digital Communications. *TripleC*, *14*(1), 18–47. doi:10.31269/triplec.v14i1.730

Koc-Michalska, K., Lilleker, D. G., & Vedel, T. (2016). Civic political engagement and social change in the new digital age.

Kofi, A. (2000). Foreword. In UNECE, The Aarhus Convention: An Implementation Guide, p. v.

Kosinetz, R. (2011). *Netnografi*. Lund: Studentlitteratur.

Kovalyova, A., & Smith, A. (2013, September 6). Protests ahead of Moscow vote as Putin critic Navalny surges in polls. *NBC News*. Retrieved from http://www.nbcnews.com/news/other/protests-ahead-moscow-vote-putin-critic-navalny-surges-polls-f8C11089526

Kratzig, S., & Warren-Kretzschmar, B. (2014). Using interactive web tools in Environmental Planning to improve communication about Sustainable Development. *Sustainability*, *6*(1), 236–250. doi:10.3390u6010236

Kravtsova, Y. (2013, August 22). Navalny's campaign relies on innovation. *The Moscow Times*. Retrieved from http://www.themoscowtimes.com/news/article/navalnys-campaign-relies-on-innovation/484899.html

Krotz, F. (2008). Media Connectivity: Concepts, Conditions, and Consequences. In A. Hepp, F. Krotz, & S. Moores (Eds.), *Connectivity, Networks and Flows: Conceptualizing Contemporary*. New York, NY: Hampton Press.

Krugman, P. (2007). Is there a Post-Washington consensus? Initiative for Policy Dialogue Working Paper Series.

Krutov, M. (2013, June 4). Politolog Dmitry Oreshkin: Sobyanin poka populyaren [Political expert Dmitry Oreshkin: Sobyanin is popular yet]. *Radio Svoboda*. Retrieved from http://www.svoboda.org/content/article/25006532.html

Kumar, V., & Ayodeji, O. G. (2020). Web Analytics for Knowledge Creation: A Systematic Review of Tools, Techniques and Practices [IJCBPL]. *International Journal of Cyber Behavior, Psychology and Learning*, *10*(1), 1–14. doi:10.4018/IJCBPL.2020010101

Kumar, V., & Bhardwaj, A. (2018). Identity Management Systems: A Comparative Analysis. *International Journal of Strategic Decision Sciences*, *9*(1), 63–78. doi:10.4018/IJSDS.2018010105

Kumar, V., & Bhardwaj, A. (2020). Role of Cloud Computing in School Education. In *Handbook of Research on Diverse Teaching Strategies for the Technology-Rich Classroom* (pp. 98–108). IGI Global.

Kumar, V., & Nanda, P. (2019 b). Social Media to Social Media Analytics: Ethical Challenges. [IJT]. *International Journal of Technoethics*, *10*(2), 57–70. doi:10.4018/IJT.2019070104

Kumar, V., & Nanda, P. (2019a). Social Media in Higher Education: A Framework for Continuous Engagement. [IJICTE]. *International Journal of Information and Communication Technology Education*, *15*(1), 109–120. doi:10.4018/IJICTE.2019010107

Kumar, V., & Nanda, P. (2020). Social Media as a Tool in Higher Education: A Pedagogical Perspective. In *Handbook of Research on Diverse Teaching Strategies for the Technology-Rich Classroom* (pp. 239–253). IGI Global. doi:10.4018/978-1-7998-0238-9.ch016

Kumar, V., & Pradhan, P. (2015). Trust Management Issues in Social-Media Marketing [IJOM]. *International Journal of Online Marketing*, *5*(3), 47–64. doi:10.4018/IJOM.2015070104

Kumar, V., & Sharma, D. (2016). CreatingCollaborativeandConvenientLearningEnvironment UsingCloud-Based Moodle LMS. *International Journal of Web-Based Learning and Teaching Technologies*, *11*(1), 35–49. doi:10.4018/IJWLTT.2016010103

Kuo, L. (2018, April 16). China's Weibo reverses ban on 'homosexual' content after outcry. *The Guardian*, Retrieved on July 28, 2019 from https://www.theguardian.com/world/2018/apr/2016/china-weibo-bans-homosexual-content-protest

Kurer, O. (2005). Corruption: An alternative approach to its definition and measurement. *Political Studies*, *53*(1), 222–239. doi:10.1111/j.1467-9248.2005.00525.x

Kvasha, S. (2013, April 4). Eastern Europe's largest social network VKontakte refuses to pay for copyrighted music. *Russia Beyond the Headlines*. Retrieved from http://rbth.asia/society/2013/04/04/eastern_ europes_largest_social_network_vkontakte_refuses_to_pay_for_c_45849.html

Laer, J. V., & Aelst, P. V. (2010). Internet and social movement action repertoires. *Information Communication and Society*, *13*(8), 1146–1171. doi:10.1080/13691181003628307

Lagunes, P., & Pocasangre, O. (2019). Dynamic transparency: An audit of Mexico's Freedom of Information Act. *Public Administration*, *97*(1), 162–176. doi:10.1111/padm.12553

Laine, T. (2019, November 1). Thumb-Boat Diplomacy Could Undo U.S. Foreign Policy. Retrieved from https://foreignpolicy.com/2019/11/01/trump-policymakers-twitter-promote-policy-condemn-adversaries/

Lange, B. S., Requejo, P., Flynn, S. M., Rizzo, A. A., Valero-Cuevas, F. J., Baker, L., & Winstein, C. (2010). The potential of virtual reality and gaming to assist successful aging with disability. *Physical Medicine and Rehabilitation Clinics of North America*, *21*(2), 339–356. doi:10.1016/j.pmr.2009.12.007 PMID:20494281

Lang, K., & Lang, G. E. (2009). Mass Society, Mass Culture, and Mass Communication: The Meanings of Mass. *International Journal of Communication*, *3*(20), 998–1024.

Larsson, A. O. (2017). Going viral? Comparing parties on social media during the 2014 Swedish election. *Convergence*, *23*(2), 117–131. doi:10.1177/1354856515577891

Larsson, A. O., & Svensson, J. (2014). Politicians online – Identifying current research opportunities. *First Monday*, *19*(4). doi:10.5210/fm.v19i4.4897

Lau, R. R., & Pomper, G. M. (2001). Negative campaigning by US Senate candidates. *Party Politics*, *7*(1), 69–87. doi:10.1177/1354068801007001004

Lazzarato, M. (2006). *The Machine*. European Institute for Progressive Cultural Politics. October. Retrieved from http://eipcp.net/transversal/1106/lazzarato/en

Lazzarato, M. (1996). *Immaterial labor. In radical thought in Italy: A potential politics*. Minneapolis, MN: University of Minnesota Press.

Lazzarato, M. (2009). Neoliberalism in Action: Inequality. *Insecurity and the Reconstruction of the Social*, *26*(6), 109–133. doi:10.1177/0263276409350283

Lee, K. Y. (2011, March 9). China's growing might and the consequences. *Forbes*, Retrieved September 15, 2014 from http://www.forbes.com/forbes/2011/0328/billionaires-11-current-events-lee-kuan-yew-china-consequences.html

Lee, K. (2012). Augmented reality in education and training. *TechTrends*, *56*(2), 13–21. doi:10.100711528-012-0559-3

Lee, M. (2011). Google ads and the blindspot debate. *Media Culture & Society*, *33*(3), 433–447. doi:10.1177/0163443710394902

Lee, M., & McLoughlin, C. (2015). *Web 2.0-based e-learning*. Hershey, PA: IGI Global.

Lee, P. S. N., So, C. Y. K., Lee, F., Leung, L., & Chan, M. (2018). Social media and political partisanship – A subaltern public sphere's role in democracy. *Telematics and Informatics*, *35*(7), 1949–1975. doi:10.1016/j.tele.2018.06.007

Lee, S. J., & Melissen, J. (Eds.). (2011). *Public diplomacy and soft power in East Asia* (1st ed.). New York: Palgrave Macmillan. doi:10.1057/9780230118447

Legaree, B. A. (2015). Considering the changing face of social media in higher education. *FEMS Microbiology Letters, 362*(16), 1e3.

Lessig, L. (1999). *Code and other laws of cyberspace*. New York: Basic Books.

Lessig, L. (2013). "Institutional corruption" defined. *The Journal of Law, Medicine & Ethics*, *41*(3), 553–555. doi:10.1111/jlme.12063 PMID:24088144

Lester, H., & Hobbs, F. D. R. (2007). Major policy changes for primary care: Potential lessons for the US New Model of family medicine from the quality and outcomes framework in the United Kingdom. *FAMILY MEDICINE-KANSAS CITY*, *39*(2), 96. PMID:17273951

Leu, D. J., Zawilinski, L., Forzani, E., & Timbrell, N. (2014). Best practices in teaching the new literacies of online research and comprehension. *Best practices in literacy instruction*, 343-364.

Levina, M. (2017). Disrupt or die: Mobile health and disruptive innovation as body politics. *Television and Media*, *18*(6), 548–564. doi:10.1177/1527476416680451

Levin, B. (1970). *The pendulum years: Britain in the Sixties*. London, UK: Jonathan Cape.

Levine, S. (1997, December 8). Hong Kong's return to China. *Encyclopædia Britannica*, Retrieved on July 29, 2019 from https://www.britannica.com/topic/reversion-to-Chinese-sovereignty-1020544

Liaw, S. S. (2002). Understanding user perceptions of world-wide web environments. *Journal of Computer Assisted Learning*, *18*(2), 137–148. doi:10.1046/j.0266-4909.2001.00221.x

Liburd, J. J., & Christensen, I. M. F. (2013). Using web 2.0 in higher tourism education. *Journal of Hospitality, Leisure, Sport, & Tourism Education, 12*(1).

Li, J., & Rao, H. R. (2010). Twitter as a rapid response news service: An exploration in the context of the 2008 China earthquake. [EJISDC]. *The Electronic Journal on Information Systems in Developing Countries*, *42*(4), 1–22. doi:10.1002/j.1681-4835.2010.tb00300.x

Lilley, D. (2009). 'Design for sustainable behaviour: Strategies and perceptions'. *Design Studies*, *30*(6), 704–720. doi:10.1016/j.destud.2009.05.001

Li, M. (Ed.). (2009). *Soft power: China's emerging strategy in international politics*. Lanham: Rowman & Littlefield Publishers.

Lindberg, B., Nilsson, C., Zotterman, D., Söderberg, S., & Skär, L. (2013). Using information and communication technology in home care for communication between patients, family members, and healthcare professionals: A systematic review. *International Journal of Telemedicine and Applications*, 2013. PMID:23690763

Linn, M. C., Clark, D., & Slotta, J. D. (2003). WISE design for knowledge integration. *Science Education*, *87*(4), 517–538. doi:10.1002ce.10086

Lin, Z. (2010). Lun hulianwang guanli he maoyi bilei [On Internet management and trade barriers]. *China Communication Trade*, *12*, 50–52.

Lipman, M. (2013, September 6). Alexey Navalny's miraculous, doomed campaign. *The New Yorker*. Retrieved from http://www.newyorker.com/online/blogs/newsdesk/2013/09/aleksey-navalnys-miraculous-doomed-campaign.html

Litman, T. (2017). *Evaluating transportation economic development impacts*. Victoria Transport Policy Institute.

Liu, B. (2007). *The theory research about research of Internet's contents in China* (Unpublished doctoral dissertation). Beijing University of Posts and Telecommunications, Beijing.

Liu, R., & Sun, B. (2017, January 24). *Gongxinbu huiying wangmin VPN deng shiyong wenti [MIIT responded to the VPN issue and other issues]*. Retrieved from http://finance.people.com.cn/n1/2017/0124/c1004-29047306.html

Liu, R.-S. (2013, October). A survey of China's new media development in 3rd season 2013 (English). *China Media Report Overseas*, *9*(4), 95–99.

Livemint. (2019) *How smart viral content helped BJP Trump Congress on social media*. Retrieved from https://www.livemint.com/politics/news/how-smart-viral-content-helped-bjp-trump-congress-on-social-media-1559663323348.html(accessed on 12th July, 2019)

Livingstone, S. (2008). Taking risky opportunities in youthful content creation: Teenagers use of social network sites for intimacy, privacy and self-expression. *New Media & Society*, *10*(3), 393–411. doi:10.1177/1461444808089415

Livingstone, S. (2009). On the mediation of everything. ICA Presidential address 2008. *Journal of Communication*, *59*(1), 1–18. doi:10.1111/j.1460-2466.2008.01401.x

Li, Y. (2009). *Our great firewall: Expression and governance in the era of the Internet*. Guilin: Guangxi Normal University Press.

Loader, B. D., Vromen, A., & Xenos, M. A. (2014). The networked young citizen: social media, political participation and civic engagement.

Long, G. (2007). *Transmedia storytelling: Business, aesthetics and production at the Jim Henson Company*. (Unpublished master's thesis), Massachusetts Institute of Technology, Cambridge, MA.

Lowrey, W. (2017). The Emergence and Development of News Fact-Checking Sites. Institutional logics and population ecology. *Journalism Studies*, *18*(3), 376–394. doi:10.1080/1461670X.2015.1052537

Lund, A. (2014). Playing, Gaming, Working and laboring: Framing the concepts and relations. *TripleC*, *12*(2), 735–801. doi:10.31269/triplec.v12i2.536

Lundby, K. (2014). *Mediatization of politics: Transforming democracies and reshaping politics*. Berlin, Germany: De Gruyter Mounton.

Luo, X., & Zhang, J. (2013). How do consumer buzz and traffic in social media marketing predict the value of the firm? *Journal of Management Information Systems*, *30*(2), 213–238. doi:10.2753/MIS0742-1222300208

Lü, Y. (2005). Privacy and data privacy issues in contemporary China. *Ethics and Information Technology*, *7*(1), 7–15. doi:10.100710676-005-0456-y

Lyon, D. (1994). *The electronic eye: the rise of surveillance society*. Cambridge, UK: Polity Press.

Magistad, M. K. (2012, August 9). How Weibo is changing China. *YaleGlobal Online*, Retrieved on July 28, 2019 from https://yaleglobal.yale.edu/content/how-weibo-changing-china

Mallick, R., & Bajpai, S. P. (2019). Impact of Social Media on Environmental Awareness. In *Environmental Awareness and the Role of Social Media* (pp. 140–149). IGI Global. doi:10.4018/978-1-5225-5291-8.ch007

Maly, I. (2019). New Right Metapolitics and the Algorithmic Activism of Schild & Vrienden. *Social Media + Society,* 1-15. doi/ doi:10.1177/2056305119856700

Manuel, T. A. (2003). Africa aid the Washington Consensus: Finding the 'Right Path. *Finance & Development*, (September): 18–20. Available at http://www.sarpn.org/documents/d0000654/Manuel_Sept2003.pdf

Manzerolle, V., & Kjosen, A. (2015). Digital Media and Capital's Logic of Acceleration. In C. Fuchs, & V. Mosco (Eds.), Marx in the Age of Digital Capitalism (151-179). Boston, MA: Brill.

Markus, M. L., & Robey, D. (1988). Information technology and organizational change: Causal structure in theory and research. *Management Science*, *34*(5), 583–598. doi:10.1287/mnsc.34.5.583

Marx, K. (1978). Capital: Volume Two. (D. Fernbach, Trans.) London, UK: Penguin Books, Harmondsworth, in association with New Left Review.

Marx, K. (1867). Capital: A critique of political economy.: Vol. 1. *(B. Fowkes, Trans.)* London, UK: Penguin Classics.

Marx, K., & Engels, F. (2001). *The German ideology Part One*. New York, NY: International.

Maseh, E., & Katuu, S. (2017). The Kenyan Judiciary's Open Government Initiative: Prospects and challenges. *Journal of Science and Technology Policy Management*, *8*(1), 76–94. doi:10.1108/JSTPM-04-2016-0007

Mason, E. (2013, June). Shaking up the anaconda: The new face of censorship in China. *Index on Censorship*, *10*(2), 43–45. doi:10.1177/0306422013491869

Mason, R., & Rennie, F. (2007). Using web 2.0 for learning in the community. *The Internet and Higher Education*, *10*(3), 196–203. doi:10.1016/j.iheduc.2007.06.003

Mathiason, J. (2013, June 20). *Information and communication technologies and e-participation for the empowerment of people and e-governance.* Paper presented at the Expert Group Meeting on E-Participation: Empowering People through Information Communication Technologies (ICTs), Geneva, The Switzerlands.

Maulana, I. (2016). Social Media as Public Political Instrument. In M. Adria, & Y. Mao (Eds.), *Handbook of Research on Citizen Engagement and Public Participation in the Era of New Media*. Hershey, PA: IGI Global; doi:10.4018/978-1-5225-1081-9.ch013

Maulana, I. (2018a). Mutual Understanding in the Age of Vulnerable Truth. In B. L. Cook (Ed.), *Handbook of Research on Examining Global Peacemaking in the Digital Age*. Hershey, PA: IGI Global. doi:10.4018/978-1-5225-3032-9.ch005

Maulana, I. (2018b). Spontaneous Taking and Posting Selfie: Reclaiming the Lost Trust. In S. Hai-Jew (Ed.), *Selfies as a Mode of Social Media and Work Space Research* (pp. 28–50). Hershey, PA: IGI Global; doi:10.4018/978-1-5225-3373-3.ch002

McAdams, D. P. (1997). The Case for Unity in the (Post)Modern Self: A Modest Proposal. In *Self and Identity: Fundamental Issues* (pp. 46–78). Oxford, UK: Oxford University Press.

McGuigan, J. (2014). *Raymond Williams on Culture & Society: Essential Writings*. Thousand Oaks, CA: Sage. doi:10.4135/9781473914766

McKeon, T. R., & Gitomer, D. H. (2019). Social Media, Political Mobilization, and High-Stakes Testing. Retrieved from https://www.frontiersin.org/articles/10.3389/feduc.2019.00055/full

McStay, A. (2011). Profiling phorm: An autopoietic approach to the audience-as-commodity. *Surveillance & Society*, *8*(3), 310–322. doi:10.24908s.v8i3.4166

Medierådet. (2010). *Unga & Medier 2010. Fakta om barns och ungas användning och upplevelser av medier* (Youth & Media 2010. Facts about children's and youths' use and perceptions of media). Stockholm, Sweden: Kulturdepartementet. http://www.medieradet.se/upload/Rapporter_pdf/Ungar%20och%20medier%202010.pdf

Mehta, M. D., & Darier, E. (1998). Virtual control and disciplining on the Internet: Electronic governmentality in the new wired world. *The Information Society*, *14*(2), 107–116. doi:10.1080/019722498128917

Meier, D. (2000). *Educating a Democracy. Boston Review*. Champaign, IL: University of Illinois Press.

Meng, Q., & Li, M. (2001, September). *New economy and ICT development in China*. Helsinki, Finland: UNU World Institute for Development Economics Research. Retrieved September 15, 2014 from http://www.econstor.eu/bitstream/10419/53080/1/335220010.pdf

Merleau-Ponty, M. (2005). *Phenomenology of Perception*. London, UK: Routledge Classics.

Miller, C. (2019, October 26). Crossing Divides: How a social network could save democracy from deadlock. Retrieved from https://www.bbc.com/news/technology-50127713

Ministry of Communication and Information Technology. Egypt. (2013). Quarterly Statistics Retrieved from www.mcit.gov.eg

Ministry of Communication and Information Technology. Egypt. (2019). Quarterly Statistics Retrieved from www.mcit.gov.eg

Ministry of Electronics & Information Technology. (n.d.). How Digital India will be realized: Pillars of Digital India. Retrieved from https://digitalindia.gov.in/content/programme-pillars

Ministry of Electronics & Information Technology. (n.d.a.). The Digital India programme is a flagship programme of the Government of India with a vision to transform India into a digitally empowered society and knowledge economy. Retrieved from https://digitalindia.gov.in/content/about-programme

Ministry of Statistics and Programme Implementation (MOSPI). (2019). *Youth in India.* Retrieved from http://mospi.nic.in/sites/default/files/publication_reports/Youth_in_India-2017.pdf(GOI Report)

Misra, A. K. (2014). Climate Change and Challenges of Water and Food Security. *International Journal of Sustainable Built Environment*, *3*(1), 153–165. doi:10.1016/j.ijsbe.2014.04.006

Mittal, S., & Kumar, V. (2019). Study of knowledge management models and their relevance in organisations, *Int. J. Knowledge Management Studies*, *10*(3), 322–335. doi:10.1504/IJKMS.2019.101491

Mitton, L. (2008). *Financial inclusion in the UK: Review of policy and practice*. York: Joseph Rowntree Foundation.

Moat, H. S., Preis, T., Olivola, C., Liu, C., & Chater, N. (2014). Using Big Data to predict collective behavior in the real world. *Behavioral and Brain Sciences*, *37*(1), 92–93. doi:10.1017/S0140525X13001817 PMID:24572233

Mohd, A. (2009). *The public sphere and media politics in Malaysia*. Newcastle, UK: Cambridge Scholars.

Mollen, A., & Wilson, H. (2010). Engagement, telepresence and interactivity in online consumer experience: Reconciling scholastic and managerial perspectives. *Journal of Business Research*, *63*(9-10), 919–925. doi:10.1016/j.jbusres.2009.05.014

Moneycontrol.com. (2019) *Influence of social media during elections might have been exaggerated.* Retrieved from https://www.moneycontrol.com/news/politics/influence-of-social-media-during-elections-might-have-been-exaggerated-study-4090561.html(accessed on 25th July, 2019)

Moorhead, S. A., Hazlett, D. E., Harrison, L., Carroll, J. K., Irwin, A., & Hoving, C. (2013). A new dimension of health care: Systematic review of the uses, benefits, and limitations of social media for health communication. *Journal of Medical Internet Research*, *15*(4). doi:10.2196/jmir.1933 PMID:23615206

Moran, M., Seaman, J., & Tinti-Kane, H. (2011). *Teaching, Learning, and Sharing: How Today's Higher Education Faculty Use Social Media*. Babson Survey Research Group.

Morel, A., Friedman, R., Tulloch, D. J., & Caldecott, B. (2016). Stranded Assets in Palm Oil Production: A Case Study of Indonesia. Sustainable Finance Programme, SSEE, University of Oxford, Working Paper, pp. 1-83.

Morozov, E. (2011). *The Net Delusion: How Not to Liberate the World.* London, UK: Penguin Books.

Mosco, V. (2005). *The digital sublime - myth, power, and cyberspace*. Cambridge, MA: The MIT Press.

Mou, Y., Atkin, D., Fu, H., Lin, C. A., & Lau, T. Y. (2013). The influence of online forum and SNS use on online political discussion in China: Assessing "Spirals of Trust." *Telematics and Informatics*, *30*(4), 359–369. doi:10.1016/j.tele.2013.04.002

Mou, Y., Fu, H., & Atkin, D. (2011). Predicting political discussion in a censored virtual environment. *Political Communication*, *28*(3), 341–356. doi:10.1080/10584609.2011.572466

Moy, P., Xenos, M. A., & Hess, V. K. (2005). Communication and Citizenship: Mapping the Political Effects of Infotainment. *Mass Communication & Society*, *8*(2), 111–131. doi:10.120715327825mcs0802_3

Mudliar, K., Parekh, H., & Bhavathankar, P. (2018, February). A comprehensive integration of national identity with blockchain technology. In *2018 International Conference on Communication information and Computing Technology (ICCICT)* (pp. 1-6). IEEE. 10.1109/ICCICT.2018.8325891

Murphy, E. (2010). The Arab State and (Absent). *Civility in New Communicative Spaces Third World Quarterly*, *32*(5), 959–980. doi:10.1080/01436597.2011.578972

Murray, M. (2016). *Clinton maintains ad spending advantage over Trump*. NBC, October 4. Available at http://www.nbcnews.com/politics/2016-election/clinton-maintains-ad-spending-advantage-over-trump-n659331?cid=smtw

Murray, J. (1997). *Hamlet on the Holodeck: The future of narrative in cyberspace*. Cambridge, MA: MIT Press.

Musgrave, S., & Nussbaum, M. (2018, April 4). *Trump thrives in areas that lack traditional news outlets Relentless use of social media and partisan outlets helped him swamp Clinton and exceed Romney's performance in places lacking trusted local news media*. Retrieved from https://www.politico.com/story/2018/04/08/news-subscriptions-decline-donald-trump-voters-505605

N'Gotta, S. (2016). YALI Voices: How Can We Inspire Young People to Use Technology for Promoting Transparency and Accountability in West Africa? Retrieved from https://yali.state.gov/yali-voices-how-can-we-inspire-young-people-to-use-technology-for-promoting-transparency-and-accountability-in-west-africa/

Naim, M. (1999). Fads and Fashion in Economic Reforms: Washington Consensus or Washington Confusion. Working Draft of a Paper Prepared for the IMF Conference on Second Generation Reforms, Washington, D.C. October 26. Available at http://www.imf.org/external/pubs/ft/seminar/1999/reforms/naim.htm

NASA. (2019). Retrieved from https://climate.nasa.gov/vital-signs/carbon-dioxide/

Navalny, A. (2013). Alexey Navalny: Kandidat v mery Moskvy 2013: Otchet o predvybornoy kampanii [Alexey Navalny: Candidate for Moscow mayor 2013]. Campaign Report.

Navalny, A. (2014). Navalny. Retrieved from https://navalny.com/

Navalny, A. (2015). Chto takoe sistema Zhnets i pochemu ona prekrasna [What Zhnets system is and why it is beautiful]. Retrieved from https://navalny.com/p/4343/

Navalny, A. (n.d.). Navalny [Web log]. Retrieved from http://navalny.livejournal.com/

Navalny, A. [Alexey Navalny] (2017, March 2). Don't call him "Dimon." [Video file]. Retrieved from https://www.youtube.com/watch?v=qrwlk7_GF9g

Nayar, K. B., & Kumar, V. (2018). Cost benefit Analysis of Cloud Computing in Education. [IJBIS]. *International Journal of Business Information Systems*, *27*(2), 205–221. doi:10.1504/IJBIS.2018.089112

Ndong, N. (2019). Afrique: l'explosion des fake news, une vraie menace pour la paix sociale. Retrieved from http://www.adiac-congo.com/content/afrique-lexplosion-des-fake-news-une-vraie-menace-pour-la-paix-sociale-96061

Negt, O., & Kluge, A. (1993). *Bourgeois and proletarian public sphere*. Minneapolis, MN: University of Minnesota Press.

Nelson, R. R., & Winter, S. G. (1982). *An Evolutionary Theory of Economic Change*. Cambridge: Belknap Press/Harvard University Press.

Nguyen, T. H., & Shirai, K. (2015, July). Topic modeling based sentiment analysis on social media for stock market prediction. In *Proceedings of the 53rd Annual Meeting of the Association for Computational Linguistics and the 7th International Joint Conference on Natural Language Processing (*Volume 1*: Long Papers)* (pp. 1354-1364). 10.3115/v1/P15-1131

Nixon, B. (2011). Dialectical method and the critical political economy of culture. *TripleC*, *10*(2), 439–456. doi:10.31269/triplec.v10i2.371

Nofer, M., Hinz, O., Muntermann, J., & Roßnagel, H. (2014). The economic impact of privacy violations and security breaches. *Business & Information Systems Engineering*, *6*(6), 339–348. doi:10.100712599-014-0351-3

Nordicom. (2019). *Mediebarometern 2018*. Göteborg: Nordicom.

Norman, D. A., & Verganti, R. (2014). Incremental and radical innovation: Design research vs. technology and meaning change. *Design Issues*, *30*(1), 78–96. doi:10.1162/DESI_a_00250

North, D. (1990). *Institutions, Institutional Change and Economic Performance*. Cambridge, MA: Cambridge University Press. doi:10.1017/CBO9780511808678

NSDL. (2016). Aadhaar authentication and e-KYC Services. Retrieved from https://www.egov-nsdl.co.in/e-kyc.html

O'Brien, T. (2015). Human (in) security and democracy in Central America. *Democracy and Security*, *11*(1), 44–59. doi:10.1080/17419166.2015.1006396

O'Neill, M. (2017, June 17). 1.5 million Mainland migrants change Hong Kong. *ejinsights on the pulse*, Retrieved on July 29, 2019 from http://www.ejinsight.com/20170619-20170611-20170615-million-mainland-migrants-change-hong-kong/

O'Reilly, T. (2005). *What is Web 2.0.* Design Patterns and Business Models for the Next Generation of Software; Retrieved from oreilly.com/web2/archive/what-is-web-20.html

OECD. (2007). *Participative web and user-created content: Web 2.0, wikis, and social networking.* Paris, France: Organisation for Economic Co-operation and Development.

Ogburn, W. F. (1947). How Technology Changes Society. *The Annals of the American Academy of Political and Social Science*, *249*(1), 81–88. doi:10.1177/000271624724900111

Ohemeng, F. L. K., & Ofosu-Adarkwa, K. (2015). One way traffic: The open data initiative project and the need for an effective demand side initiative in Ghana. *Government Information Quarterly*, *32*(1), 419–428. doi:10.1016/j.giq.2015.07.005

Ortiz-Ospina, E. (2019, September 18). The rise of social media. Retrieved from https://ourworldindata.org/rise-of-social-media

Oswald, K. (2009). Mass Media and the Transformation of American Politics. *Marquette Law Review*, *77*(2), 385–414.

Otstavka Sobyanina i dosrochnie vibory mera: prichiny i posledstviya [Sobyanin's resignation and snap elections: causes and consequences] (2013, June 6). *RIA Novosti*. Retrieved from http://web-balancer-main.rian.ru/politics/20130604/941316905.html

Owen, D. (2018). The New Media's Role in Politics, In BBVA Open Mind, *The Age of Perplexity: Rethinking the World We Knew.*

Owen, R. (1995). *A new view of society and other writings*. New York, NY: Penguin.

Oye, N. D., Adam, M. H., & Nor Zairah, A. R. (2012). Model of perceived influence of academic performance using social networking. *International Journal of Computers and Technology, 2*(2).

Palfrey, J. G. (2010). Four Phases of Internet Regulation. *Social Research*, *77*(3). Retrieved from https://papers.ssrn.com/sol3/papers.cfm?abstract_id=1658191

Palmer, A., & Koenig-Lewis, N. (2009). An experiential, social network-based approach to direct marketing. *Direct Marketing: An International Journal*, *3*(3), 162–176. doi:10.1108/17505930910985116

Panahi, S., Watson, J., & Partridge, H. (2016). Social media and physicians: Exploring the benefits and challenges. *Health Informatics Journal*, *22*(2), 99–112. doi:10.1177/1460458214540907 PMID:25038200

Panibratov, A. (2012). *Russian multinationals: From regional supremacy to global lead.* London, UK: Routledge.

Pao, J. (2019, July 14). Anti-extradition Hong Kong protesters march in Shatin. *Asia Times*, Retrieved on July 29, 2019 from https://www.asiatimes.com/2019/2007/article/anti-extradition-hong-kong-protesters-march-in-shatin/

Papacharissi, Z., & Rubin, A. M. (2000). Predictors of Internet use. *Journal of Broadcasting & Electronic Media*, *44*(2), 175–196. doi:10.120715506878jobem4402_2

Parker, R. B. (2014). Two Visions of Democracy. In A. E. Cudd, & S. J. Scholz (Eds.), *Philosophical Perspectives on Democracy in the 21st Century* (pp. 75–86). Heidelberg, Germany: Springer. doi:10.1007/978-3-319-02312-0_6

Parker, W. (2006). Public Discourses in Schools: Purposes, Problems, Possibilities. *Educational Researcher*, *35*(8), 11–18. doi:10.3102/0013189X035008011

Parkinson, H. J. (2016, November 14). Click and elect: how fake news helped Donald Trump win a real election. Retrieved from https://www.theguardian.com/commentisfree/2016/nov/14/fake-news-donald-trump-election-alt-right-social-media-tech-companies

Parola, G. (2009). Towards Environmental Democracy (Doctoral dissertation), pp. 1-94.

Parola, G. (2013). *Environmental Democracy at the Global Level: Rights and Duties for a New Citizenship*. Walter de Gruyter. doi:10.2478/9788376560144

Paruthi, M., & Kaur, H. (2017). Scale development and validation for measuring online engagement. *Journal of Internet Commerce*, *16*(2), 127–147. doi:10.1080/15332861.2017.1299497

Patel, S., Park, H., Bonato, P., Chan, L., & Rodgers, M. (2012). A review of wearable sensors and systems with application in rehabilitation. *Journal of Neuroengineering and Rehabilitation*, *9*(1), 21. doi:10.1186/1743-0003-9-21 PMID:22520559

Pati, R. K., Kumar, V., & Jain, N. (2015). Analysis of Aadhaar: A project management perspective. *IIM Kozhikode Society & Management Review*, *4*(2), 124–135. doi:10.1177/2277975215610687

Patterson, J., Schulz, K., Vervoort, J., van der Hel, S., Widerberg, O., Adler, C., ... Barau, A. (2017). Exploring the governance and politics of transformations towards sustainability. *Environmental Innovation and Societal Transitions*, *24*, 1–16. doi:10.1016/j.eist.2016.09.001

Pavlik, J. (2001). *Journalism and New Media*. New York: Columbia University Press. doi:10.7312/pavl11482

Pedro-Carañana, J., Broudy, D., & Klaehn, J. (2018). *The Propaganda Model Today: Filtering Perception and Awareness*. London, UK: University of Westminster Press. doi:10.16997/book27

Perry, P. J. (2018). *Political corruption and political geography*. New York: Routledge Revivals. doi:10.4324/9780429448072

Peter, T. (2019, July 22). Why Hong Kong's angry and disillusioned youth are making their voices heard. *South China Morning Post*, Retrieved on July 29, 2019 from https://www.scmp.com/magazines/post-magazine/long-reads/article/3019591/why-hong-kongs-angry-and-disillusioned-youth-are

Peters, B. (2009). And lead us not into thinking the new is new: A bibliographic case for new media history. *New Media & Society*, *11*(1&2), 13–30. doi:10.1177/1461444808099572

Peters, B. G. (2017). What is so wicked about wicked problems? A conceptual analysis and a research program. *Policy and Society*, *36*(3), 385–396. doi:10.1080/14494035.2017.1361633

Peters, B. G., & Tarpey, M. (2019). Are wicked problems really so wicked? Perceptions of policy problems. *Policy and Society*, *38*(2), 218–236. doi:10.1080/14494035.2019.1626595

Peters, J. (1999). *Speaking into the air: A history of the idea of communication*. Chicago, IL: University of Chicago Press. doi:10.7208/chicago/9780226922638.001.0001

Piaget, J. (2001). *The Psychology of Intelligence*. London, UK: Routledge.

Pierandrei, E. (2007). 'Impact of covering New Media in Journalism: A New Tool to Foster Information in Egypt', (Master's thesis), The American University in Cairo.

Pimmer, C., Linxen, S., & Gröhbiel, U. (2012). Facebook as a learning tool? A case study on the appropriation of social network sites from mobile phones in developing countries. *British Journal of Educational Technology*, *43*(5), 726–738. doi:10.1111/j.1467-8535.2012.01351.x

Pintak, L. (2010). Arab media and Al Jazeera Effect. In *T. McPhail (Ed.), Global Communication: Theories, Stakeholders, and Trends*. Wiley-Blackwell.

Politics, H. (2019). *Youth political engagement era social media*. Retrieved from http://harvardpolitics.com/hprgument-posts/youth-political-engagement-era-social-media/

Pool, I. D. S. (1983). Technologies of freedom. Cambridge, MA: Harvard University Press.

Porter, B., Linse, M., & Barasz, Z. (2015). Six transportation trends that will change how we move. *Forbes, January*.

Poster, M. (1995). *The second media age*. Cambridge, UK: Polity.

Post, R. (2005). Democracy and Equality. *Law, Culture, and the Humanities*, *1*(2), 142–153. doi:10.1191/1743872105lw013oa

Pradhan, P., & Kumar, V. (2016). Trust Management Models for Digital Identities. [IJVCSN]. *International Journal of Virtual Communities and Social Networking*, *8*(4), 1–24. doi:10.4018/IJVCSN.2016100101

Pratt, M., Sarmiento, O. L., Montes, F., Ogilvie, D., Marcus, B. H., Perez, L. G., & Brownson, R. C.Lancet Physical Activity Series Working Group. (2012). The implications of megatrends in information and communication technology and transportation for changes in global physical activity. *Lancet*, *380*(9838), 282–293. doi:10.1016/S0140-6736(12)60736-3 PMID:22818940

Prentice, A. (2014, April 29). Putin foes fear Internet crackdown as 'blogger law' sails through. *Reuters*. Retrieved from http://www.reuters.com/article/2014/04/29/us-russia-internet-idUSBREA3S0QF20140429

Pri Luzhkove takogo ne bylo: moskvichi pokazali rekordno nizkuyu yavku ["With Luzhkov was not like this" Muscovites showed a record low turnout] (2013, September 9). *RBC*. Retrieved from http://top.rbc.ru/politics/09/09/2013/875417.shtml

Putin says opposition white stripes look like condoms (2011, December 15). *Gazeta.ru*. Retrieved from http://en.gazeta.ru/bears/2011/12/15/f_3928598.shtml

Quartz. (2019). *How India's youth feel about elections 2019.* Retrieved from https://qz.com/india/1583361/how-indias-youth-feel-about-elections-2019/(accessed on 9th August, 2019)

Quartz. (2019). *Modi's Twitter strategy of following common Indians worked.* Retrieved from https://qz.com/india/1630274/modis-twitter-strategy-of-following-common-indians-worked/ (accessed on 28th July, 2019)

Quinn, S., & Walters, T. (2004). Al-Jazeera: Ripples in a stagnant media pool. In R. Berenger (Ed.), *Global Media go to War.* Cairo, Egypt: American University in Cairo Press.

Radovic, A., Gmelin, T., Stein, B. D., & Miller, E. (2017). Depressed adolescents' positive and negative use of social media. *Journal of Adolescence*, *55*, 5–15. doi:10.1016/j.adolescence.2016.12.002 PMID:27997851

Radsch, C. (2008). 'The Evolution of Egypt's Blogosphere'. Paper presented at the annual meeting of the Middle East Studies Association MESA.

Radsch, C. (2016). *Cyberactivism and citizen journalism in Egypt: Digital dissidence and political change*. Washington, DC: Palgrave Macmillan. doi:10.1057/978-1-137-48069-9

Ragab. (2007). 'Egyptian Press: What do we Miss?' *Al Akhbar newspaper*, p. 8.

Raj, K., & Aithal, P. S. (2018). Literature Review of Impact of Branding on Base of the Pyramid Markets with Special Reference to India. [IJAEML]. *International Journal of Applied Engineering and Management Letters*, *2*(1), 43–63.

Ramzy, A. (2011a, February 17). Wired Up. *Time*, Retrieved March 1, 2014 from http://content.time.com/time/magazine/article/0,9171,2048171,00.html

Ramzy, A. (2011b, February 21). State stamps out small "Jasmine" Protests in China. *Time*, retrieved on March 1, 2014 from http://content.time.com/time/world/article/0,8599,2052860,00.html

Ranieri, M., Manca, S., & Fini, A. (2012). Why (and how) do teachers engage in social networks? An exploratory study of professional use of Facebook and its implications for lifelong learning. *British Journal of Educational Technology*, *43*(5), 754–769. doi:10.1111/j.1467-8535.2012.01356.x

Rao, B., Angelov, B., & Nov, O. (2006). Fusion of disruptive technologies: Lessons from the skype case. *European Management Journal*, *24*(2-3), 174–188. doi:10.1016/j.emj.2006.03.007

Ravizza, S. M., Hambrick, D. Z., & Fenn, K. M. (2014). Non-academic internet use in the classroom is negatively related to classroom learning regardless of intellectual ability. *Computers & Education, 78,* 109e114.

Rawlins, B. R. (2008). Measuring the relationship between organizational transparency and employee trust. *The Public Relations Journal*, *2*(2), 1–21.

Rawls, J. (2005). *Political Liberalism, Expanded Edition*. New York, NY: Columbia University Press.

Raynor, M. E. (2011b). Disruption theory as a predictor of innovation success/failure. *Strategy and Leadership*, *39*(4), 27–30. doi:10.1108/10878571111147378

Report, T. (2019). *Political Advertising for India.* Retrieved from https://transparencyreport.google.com/political-ads/region/IN?hl=en(accessed on 12th August, 2019)

Rey, P. J. (2012). Alienation, exploitation, and social media. *The American Behavioral Scientist*, *56*(4), 399–420. doi:10.1177/0002764211429367

Rezaei, F., & Cohen, R. A. (2012). The Role of Social Media in the Recent Political Shifts in the Middle East and North Africa, *OSR Journal of Humanities and Social Science (JHSS) 4*(6) (Nov. - Dec. 2012), pp. 1-10.

Rheingold, H. (1993). *The Virtual Community: Homesteading on the Electronic Frontier*. Reading, MA: Addison-Wesley.

Ritzer, G. (2015). Prosumer Capitalism. *The Sociological Quarterly*, *56*(3), 413–445. doi:10.1111/tsq.12105

Robelia, B. A., Greenhow, C., & Burton, L. (2011). Environmental learning in online social networks: Adopting environmentally responsible behaviours. *Environmental Education Research*, *17*(4), 553–575. doi:10.1080/13504622.2011.565118

Robinson, L., Schulz, J., Dunn, H. S. Aguiar, P., Artopoulos, A., Baldwin, J., ... & Straubhaar, J. D. (2016). Communication and Information Technologies Annual. Emerald.

Roschelle, J. M., Pea, R. D., Hoadley, C. M., Gordin, D. N., & Means, B. M. (2000). Changing how and what children learn in school with computer-based technologies. *The Future of Children*, *10*(2), 76–101. doi:10.2307/1602690 PMID:11255710

Rosenblatt, J. P. (2011). *Milton's selected poetry and prose: authoritative texts, biblical sources, criticism.* New York, NY: W.W. Norton & Co.

RosPil. (2014). Retrieved from http://rospil.info/

Rotberg, R. I. (2019). *The corruption cure: How citizens and leaders can combat graft.* Princeton, NJ: Princeton University Press.

Roth, A. (2012, April 30). Russia's regional governors to be directly elected. *The Telegraph*. Retrieved from http://www.telegraph.co.uk/sponsored/rbth/politics/9236729/Russia-regional-governors.html

Rozanov, D. (2014, May 12). Winds of change leave Russia's opposition out in the cold. *Russia Beyond the Headlines*. Retrieved from http://m.rbth.com/politics/2014/05/12/winds_of_change_leave_russias_opposition_out_in_the_cold_36525.html

Rugh, W. A. (1987). *The Arab Press: News Media and Political Process in the Arab World*. Syracuse, NY: Syracuse University Press.

Russialize. (2011, December 10). Bolotnaya Square protest: Today we saw a civil society that is capable of great things [Web log post]. Retrieved from http://russialize.tumblr.com/post/14014318702/bolotnaya

Russian Federal State Statistics Service. (2011). Vserossiyskaya perepis naseleniya 2010 [2010 National Population Census]. Retrieved from http://www.gks.ru/free_doc/new_site/perepis2010/croc/perepis_itogi1612.htm

Russmann, U. (2017, May). *Going Negative on Facebook*: Paper presented at the 67th Annual Conference of the International Communication Association (ICA), San Diego, CA.

Rutigliano, W. (2008). 'Covering the Unknown City: Citizen Journalism and Marginalized Communities', (Doctoral Dissertation), University of Texas, Austin.

Ruttan, V. W. (1997). Induced Innovation, Evolutionary Theory and Path Dependence: Sources of Technical Change. *Economic Journal (London)*, *107*(444), 1520–1529. doi:10.1111/j.1468-0297.1997.tb00063.x

Safiullah, M., Pathak, P., Singh, S., & Anshul, A. (2017). Social media as an upcoming tool for political marketing effectiveness. *Asia Pacific Management Review*, *22*(1), 10–15. doi:10.1016/j.apmrv.2016.10.007

Sahu, P. (2019, Mar. 21). DBT transfers increase 47 per cent, but little growth in saving. *Financial Express*. Retrieved from https://www.financialexpress.com/economy/dbt-transfers-increase-47-per-cent-but-little-growth-in-saving/1522994/

Salama, S. (2009). *Al Sahafa Fauf Safeeh Sakhen* [Journalism over Hot Tin Roof]. Cairo, Egypt: Dar Al Ain.

Sanborn, H., & Thyne, C. L. (2014). Learning democracy: Education and the fall of authoritarian regimes. *British Journal of Political Science*, *44*(4), 773–797. doi:10.1017/S0007123413000082

Sandoval, G. (2009, March 24). China bans YouTube, Chinese officials confirm that they are blocking the Web's largest video site but haven't disclosed the reason. *The Wall Street Journal*, Retrieved April 30, 2014 from http://www.cnet.com/news/wsj-china-bans-youtube/

Santra, S., Mandal, T. S., & Das, P. (2019). Leveraging Disruptive Technology Innovations for Healthcare Delivery in Sub-Saharan Africa, ORF Issue Brief No. 298.

Sarker, M. M., & Islam, M. S. (2017). Social Capital and Political Participation: A Case Study from Rural Bangladesh. *European Review Of Applied Sociology*, *10*(15), 54–64. doi:10.1515/eras-2017-0009

Sarma, M., & Pais, J. (2011). Financial inclusion and development. *Journal of International Development*, *23*(5), 613–628. doi:10.1002/jid.1698

Sathre, R., & Gustavsson, L. (2007). Effects of energy and carbon taxes on building material competitiveness. *Energy and Building*, *39*(4), 488–494. doi:10.1016/j.enbuild.2006.09.005

Sathre, R., & Gustavsson, L. (2009). Using wood products to mitigate climate change: External costs and structural change. *Applied Energy*, *86*(2), 251–257. doi:10.1016/j.apenergy.2008.04.007

Schliefer, A. (2005). 'The Impact of Arab Satellite Television on the Prospects for Democracy in the Arab World', *Transnational Broadcast Studies. Dar Al Kutub*, *1*(2), 309–315.

Schoen, C., Osborn, R., Squires, D., Doty, M., Rasmussen, P., Pierson, R., & Applebaum, S. (2012). A survey of primary care doctors in ten countries shows progress in use of health information technology, less in other areas. *Health Affairs*, *31*(12), 2805–2816. doi:10.1377/hlthaff.2012.0884 PMID:23154997

Scholz, T. (2011). Facebook as Playground and Factory. In D. E. Wittkower (Ed.), Facebook and Philosophy, 241–252. Chicago, IL: Open Court.

Schwab, K. (2016) *The Fourth Industrial Revolution*. Davos: World Economic Forum.

Scott, W. R. (2014). *Institutions and Organizations: Ideas, Interests, and Identities* (4th ed.). Thousand Oaks, CA: Sage.

Sen, A. (2009). *The Idea of Justice*. Cambridge, MA: Harvard University Press. doi:10.2307/j.ctvjnrv7n

Shah, P., & Dubhashi, M. (2015). Review Paper on Financial Inclusion The Means of Inclusive Growth. *Chanakya International Journal of Business Research*, *1*(1), 37–48. doi:10.15410/cijbr/2015/v1i1/61403

Shah, V., Nojin Kwak, R., & Lance Holbert, D. (2001). Connecting" and" disconnecting" with civic life: Patterns of Internet use and the production of social capital. *Political Communication*, *18*(2), 141–162. doi:10.1080/105846001750322952

Shambaugh, D. L. (2013). *China goes global: The partial power*. Oxford, UK: Oxford University Press.

Shao, D. D., & Saxena, S. (2019). Barriers to open government data (OGD) initiative in Tanzania: Stakeholders' perspectives. *Growth and Change*, *50*(1), 470–485.

Shao, G. (2009). Understanding the Appeal of User-Generated Media: A Uses and Gratification Perspective. *Internet Research*, *19*(1), 7–25. doi:10.1108/10662240910927795

Shapshak, T. (2019). *Africa's Booming Tech Hubs Are "Backbone of Tech Ecosystem" Having Grown 40% This Year*. Retrieved from https://www.forbes.com/sites/tobyshapshak/2019/07/11/africas-booming-tech-hubs-are-backbone-of-tech-ecosystem-having-grown-40-this-year/#1ee713fd24c2

Sharma, D., & Kumar, V. (2017). A Framework for Collaborative and Convenient Learning on Cloud Computing Platforms. [IJWLTT]. *International Journal of Web-Based Learning and Teaching Technologies*, *12*(2), 1–20. doi:10.4018/IJWLTT.2017040101

Shelton, D. (1991). Human rights, environmental rights, and the right to environment, *Stan. J. Int'l L.*, *28*, 103.

Shen, X. (2019, June 12). Chinese users are beating the censors to talk about Hong Kong. *Abacus*, Retrieved on August 20, 2019 from https://www.abacusnews.com/digital-life/chinese-users-are-beating-censors-talk-about-hong-kong/article/3014159

Sherwin, C., & Bhamra, T. (1998). Ecodesign innovation: Present concepts, current practice and future directions for design and the environment. Design History Society Conference 1998. Huddersfield, UK, University of Huddersfield, September 1998.

Shirky, C. (2009). *Here Comes Everybody. How Change Happen when People Come Together*. London, UK: Penguin Books.

Shirky, C. (2011, January/February). The political power of social media: Technology, the public sphere, and political change. *Foreign Affairs*, 1–12.

Simon, J. P. (2011). *The ICT landscape in BRICS countries: Brazil, India, China*. Seville, Spain: European Commission Joint Research Centre, Institute for Prospective Technological Studies.

Singer, B. D. (1973). Mass society, mass media and the transformation of minority identity. *The British Journal of Sociology*, *24*(2), 140–150. doi:10.2307/588374

Singh, R., & Jackson, S. J. (2017, May). From margins to seams: Imbrication, inclusion, and torque in the Aadhaar Identification Project. In *Proceedings of the 2017 CHI Conference on Human Factors in Computing Systems* (pp. 4776-4824). Denver, CO: ACM. 10.1145/3025453.3025910

Siponen, M., Wilson, R., & Baskerville, R. (2008). Power and practice in information systems security research, In *2008 Proceedings of the International Conference on Information Systems (ICIS), 26.*

Sjöberg, L., & Fromm, J. (2001). Information technology risks as seen by the public. *Risk Analysis*, *21*(3), 427–442. doi:10.1111/0272-4332.213123 PMID:11572424

Slater, M. D. (2007). Reinforcing Spirals: The Mutual Influence of Media Selectivity and Media Effects and Their Impact on Individual Behavior and Social Identity. *Communication Theory*, *17*(3), 281–303. doi:10.1111/j.1468-2885.2007.00296.x

Smailhodzic, E., Hooijsma, W., Boonstra, A., & Langley, D. J. (2016). Social media use in healthcare: A systematic review of effects on patients and on their relationship with healthcare professionals. *BMC Health Services Research*, *16*(1), 442. doi:10.118612913-016-1691-0 PMID:27562728

Smirnova, E., & Surnacheva, E. (2012, February 2). Na chto potrachen «Koshelyok Romanovoy» – dengi 24 dekabrya [What «Romanova's Wallet» was spent for – the money of December 24th]. *Slon.* Retrieved from http://slon.ru/russia/ kuda_potrachen_koshelek_ romanovoy_dengi_24_ dekabrya-736878.xhtml

Smith, T. (2019). Disruptive Technology. Retrieved from https://www.investopedia.com/terms/d/ disruptive-technology.asp

Smyth, T. S. (2011). The new literacy: Technology in the classroom. Retrieved from http://files. eric.ed.gov/fulltext/ED534255.pdf

Smythe, D. (1981). *Dependency road: Communication, Capitalism, Consciousness, and Canada.* Santa Barbara, CA: Praegar Publishing.

Social Media Today. (2019) *How much time do people spend on social media.* Retrieved from https://www.socialmediatoday.com/marketing/how-much-time-do-people-spend-social-media-infographic(accessed on 6th August, 2019)

Solum, L. B. (2009). Models of Internet governance. In L. A. Bygrave, & J. Bing (Eds.), *Internet governance: Infrastructure and institutions* (pp. 48–91). Oxford, UK: Oxford University Press. doi:10.1093/acprof:oso/9780199561131.003.0003

Sood, A., & Tellis, G. J. (2011). Demystifying disruption: New schema, model, and findings. *Marketing Science*, *30*(2), 339–354. doi:10.1287/mksc.1100.0617

Sopova, A. (2017, November 3). How independent Russian newsrooms keep reporting. *Nieman Report.* Retrieved from https://niemanreports.org/articles/how-independent-russian-newsrooms-keep-reporting/

Soy, S. K. (1997). *The Case Study as a Research Method.* Retrieved on July 26, 2017 from https:// www.ischool.utexas.edu/~ssoy/usesusers/l391d1b.htm

Speranza, M. G. (2018). Trends in transportation and logistics. *European Journal of Operational Research*, *264*(3), 830–836. doi:10.1016/j.ejor.2016.08.032

Splichal, S. (2012). *Transnationalization of the public sphere and the fate of the public* (1st ed.). New York: Hampton Press.

Srnicek, N. (2017). *Platform Capitalism.* Cambridge, UK: Polity Publishing.

Stalder, F., & Sützl, W. (2011). Ethics of sharing. *International Review of Information Ethics*, *15*, 2–3. Retrieved from http://www.i-r-i-e.net/inhalt/015/015_full.pdf

Stanford. (2019). *India's #TwitterElection 2014.* Retrieved from http://snap.stanford.edu/class/ cs224w-2014/projects2014/cs224w-24-final.pdf

Stanic, M. (2019). Retrieved from https://whatsnewinpublishing.com/fake-or-not-decoding-the-authenticity-of-online-news, https://whatsnewinpublishing.com/fake-or-not-decoding-the-authenticity-of-online-news

State Council Information Office of China. (2010, June 8). *The Internet in China*. Retrieved from http://www.china.org.cn/government/whitepaper/node_7093508.htm

Statista. Most Popular Social Networking Worldwide as of October 2019 Ranked by Number of Active Users. (2019, October). Retrieved from https://www.statista.com/statistics/272014/global-social-networks-ranked-by-number-of-users//

Stephenson, D. N. A., & Brooke, C. (1994). Public Participation in EIA: A Review of the Experience in Europe and the UK. Aberdeen: CEMP. Available at https://www.jstor.org/stable/23287802

Stewart, B. (2013). Education for a Digital Age? | the theoryblog. Retrieved from http://theory.cribchronicles.com/2013/01/09/education-for-a-digital-age/

StricklerE. (2012). *10 questions*. Retrieved from http://transmediadesign.wordpress.com/assigments/ 10-questions/

Strömbäck, J., & Esser, F. (2014). Mediatization of politics: Transforming democracies and reshaping politics. In K. Lundby (Ed.), *Mediatization of Communication* (pp. 374–404). Berlin, Germany: De Gruyter Mounton.

Suh, H., Yee, J., & Chang, D. (2013). Type of trust and political participation in five countries: Results of social quality survey.

Suleymanov, S. (2013, August 28). How the Moscow mayoral candidates are winning the Internet. *The Interpreter*. Retrieved from http://www.interpretermag.com/how-the-moscow-mayoral-candidates-are-winning-the-internet/

Sullivan, J. (2012, September). A tale of two microblogs in China. *Media Culture & Society*, *34*(6), 773–783. doi:10.1177/0163443712448951

Sullivan, J. (2014, February). China's Weibo: Is faster different? *New Media & Society*, *16*(1), 24–37. doi:10.1177/1461444812472966

Sun, Q., & Shi, F. (2017, February 6). *Zhishengxia menfeng de VPN hequ hecong [Where will the remaining VPN go]*. Retrieved from http://www.bbtnews.com.cn/2017/0206/180250.shtml

Sung, M., Marci, C., & Pentland, A. (2005). Wearable feedback systems for rehabilitation. *Journal of Neuroengineering and Rehabilitation*, *2*(1), 17. doi:10.1186/1743-0003-2-17 PMID:15987514

Sunstein, C. (2018). *Republic: Divided Democracy in the Age of Social Media*. Princeton, NJ: Princeton University Press.

Sunstein, C. R. (2007). *Republic.com 2.0*. Princeton, NJ: Princeton University Press.

Svensson, J. (2011). The Expressive Turn of Citizenship in Digital Late Modernity. *JeDEM eJournal of eDemocracy, 3*(1), 42-56.

Svensson, J. (2014b). Participation as a Pin. Political Discussions in an Online Swedish LGBT Community. In A. Ionas (Ed.), *Proceedings of the 14th European Conference on eGovernment ECEG 2014* (pp. 235-241). Reading: Academic Conferences and Publishing International Ltd.

Svensson, J. (2015). Participation as a Pastime Political Discussion in a Queer Community Online. *Javnost-The public, 22*(3), 283-297.

Svensson, J. (2013). Power, Identity and Feelings in Digital Late Modernity. The Rationality of Reflexive Emption Displays Online. In T. Benski, & E. Fischer (Eds.), *Internet and Emotions* (pp. 17–32). London, UK: Routledge.

Svensson, J. (2014a). Amplification and Virtual Back-Patting. The Rationalities of Social Media Uses in the Nina Larsson Web-Campaign. In A. M. G. Solo (Ed.), *Political Campaigning in the Information Age* (pp. 59–65). Hershey, PA: IGI Global. doi:10.4018/978-1-4666-6062-5.ch003

Svensson, J., & Larsson, A. O. (2016). Interacting with Whom? Swedish Parliamentarians on Twitter during the 2014 Elections. *International Journal of E-Politics, 7*(1), 1–15. doi:10.4018/IJEP.2016010101

Swamy, R. (2014). Did social media really impact the Indian elections? Retrieved August 25, 2019 http://gadgets.ndtv.com/social-networking/features/did-social-media-really-impact-the-indian-elections-527425

Swedish Energy Agency. Energy in Sweden. (2005). Retrieved from http://www.energimyndigheten.se/

Tamakloe, S. (2018) Ghana's mobile phone subscribers to hit 40m by 2020 – Report, JoyBusiness. Retrieved from https://www.myjoyonline.com/business/2018/march-19th/ghanas-mobile-phone-subscribers-to-hit-40m-by-2020-report.php

Tang, L., & Sampson, H. (2012, July). The interaction between mass media and the internet in non-democratic states: The case of China. *Media Culture & Society, 34*(5), 457–471. doi:10.1177/0163443711436358

Tapsell, R. (2019, March 22). The polarisation paradox in Indonesia's 2019 elections. Retrieved from https://www.newmandala.org/the-polarisation-paradox-in-indonesias-2019-elections/

Tay, J., & Turner, G. (2010). Not the Apocalypse: Television Futures in the Digital Age. *International Journal of Digital Television, 1*(1), 31–50. doi:10.1386/jdtv.1.1.31/1

Taylor, A. (2014, March 13). We treat him like he's mad, but Vladimir Putin's popularity has just hit a 3-year high. *The Washington Post*. Retrieved from http://www.washingtonpost.com/blogs/ worldviews/wp/2014/03/13/we-treat-him-like-hes-mad-but-vladimir-putins-popularity-has-just-hit-a-3-year-high/

Taylor, D. (2004). Beyond learning theory. In E. Hargreaves, & A. Varchevker (Eds.), *In Pursuit of Psychic Change: The Betty Joseph Workshop* (pp. 136–149). New York, NY: Brunner-Routledge.

Terranova, T. (2004). *Network culture: Politics for the information age*. London, UK: Pluto Press.

Tétrault-Farber, G. (2014, May 13). Public's desire to protest hits record low. *The Moscow Times*. Retrieved from http://www.themoscowtimes.com/news/article/publics-desire-to-protest-hits-record-low/500066.html

Thakur, R., Hsu, S. H., & Fontenot, G. (2012). Innovation in healthcare: Issues and future trends. *Journal of Business Research*, *65*(4), 562–569. doi:10.1016/j.jbusres.2011.02.022

The Economist. (2012, January 28). Unrest in China, A dangerous year, Economic conditions and social media are making protests more common in China—at a delicate time for the country's rulers. *The Economist*, Retrieved May 1, 2014 from http://www.economist.com/node/21543477

The Economist. (2014, January18). From Weibo to WeChat. *The Economist,* Retrieved November 17, 2014 from http://www.economist.com/news/china/21594296-after-crackdown-microblogs-sensitive-online-discussion-has-shifted-weibo-wechat

The Economist. (2018a, March 1). How the West got China wrong. *The Economist*, Retrieved on July 28, 2019 from https://www.economist.com/leaders/2018/2003/2001/how-the-west-got-china-wrong

The Economist. (2018b, June 2). Perfected in China, a threat in the West. *The Economist*, p. 11.

The Moscow Times. (2017, July 17). Anti-corruption protests didn't make Navalny more popular – Poll. Retrieved from https://www.themoscowtimes.com/2017/07/17/navalny-protests-didnt-make-him-popular-poll-a58404

The platform of Alexey Navalny. (n.d.). Retrieved from http://five.navalny.ru/medicine.html

The Wire. (2019). *BJP Modi political funding money*. Retrieved from https://thewire.in/politics/bjp-modi-political-funding-money(accessed on 11th August, 2019)

Thorburn, E. D. (2016). Networked Social Reproduction: Crises in the Integrated Circuit. *TripleC*, *14*(2), 380–396. doi:10.31269/triplec.v14i2.708

Thorburn, E. D. (2017). Social Reproduction in the Live Stream. *TripleC*, *15*(2), 423–440. doi:10.31269/triplec.v15i2.774

Thornton, P. H., Ocasio, W., & Lounsbury, M. (2012). *The Institutional Logics Perspective. A New Approach to Culture, Structure and Process*. Oxford, UK: Oxford University Press. doi:10.1093/acprof:oso/9780199601936.001.0001

Tlebere, T., Scholtz, B., & Calitz, A. P. (2016). Using social media to improve environmental awareness in higher education institutions. In *Information Technology in Environmental Engineering* (pp. 101–111). Cham, Switzerland: Springer. doi:10.1007/978-3-319-25153-0_9

Tocqueville, A. (1862). *Democracy in America and Two Essays on America*. London, UK: Longman, Green, Longman, and Roberts.

Tong, T., Yu, E., & Roberts, R. K. (2014). Dynamics of transport infrastructure, exports and economic growth in the United States. In *Journal of the Transportation Research Forum* (Vol. 53, No. 1424-2016-117851, pp. 65-81). 10.5399/osu/jtrf.53.1.4204

Tong, J. G., & Zuo, L. D. (2014). Weibo communication and government legitimacy in China: A computer-assisted analysis of Weibo messages on two 'mass incidents.'. *Information Communication and Society*, *17*(1), 66–85. doi:10.1080/1369118X.2013.839730

Toxopeus, H. S., & Lensink, R. (2008). Remittances and financial inclusion in development. In Development Finance in the Global Economy (pp. 236-263). Palgrave Macmillan UK. doi:10.1057/9780230594074_10

Trading Economics. (2019). *India corruption rank*. Retrieved from https://tradingeconomics.com/india/corruption-rank

Transparency International. (2018). Corruption perceptions index 2018. Retrieved from https://www.transparency.org/cpi2018

Trudolyubov, M. (2013, September 6). An election in Russia (well, almost). *The New York Times*. Retrieved from http://www.nytimes.com/2013/09/07/opinion/an-election-in-russia-well-almost.html?_r=2&

Tsui, L. (2015). The coming colonization of Hong Kong cyberspace: Government responses to the use of new technologies by the umbrella movement. *Chinese Journal of Communication*, *8*(4), 1–9. doi:10.1080/17544750.2015.1058834

Tufekci, Z. (2017). *Twitter and Tear Gas: The Power and Fragility of Networked Protest*. New Haven: Yale University Press.

Turilli, M., & Floridi, L. (2009). The ethics of information transparency. *Ethics and Information Technology*, *11*(2), 105–112. doi:10.100710676-009-9187-9

Turner, J. (2019). Death By A Thousand Hyperlinks: The Commodification of Communication and Mediated Ideologies. In C. Battista, & M. Sande (Eds.), *Critical Theory and the Humanities in the Age of the Alt-Right* (pp. 173–192). London, UK: Palgrave Macmillan. doi:10.1007/978-3-030-18753-8_10

Turral, H., Burke, J., & Faurès, J. M. (2011). *Climate Change, Water, And Food Security (No. 36), Food and Agriculture Organization of the United Nations* (pp. 1–200). FAO.

Tuten, T. L., & Solomon, M. R. (2013). Social media marketing. Boston, MA: Pearson.

Twitter. (2014). *What are @replies and mentions?*

Ulrich, B. (2009). Historicizing Arab Blogs: Reflections on the Transmission of Ideas and Information in Middle Eastern History. *Arab Media & Society,* 8. Retrieved from http://www.arabmediasociety.com/?article=711

UN Environment Program. NNEP implementing Principle 10 of the Rio Declaration. (2016, August 16). Retrieved from https://www.unenvironment.org/news-and-stories/story/unep-implementing-principle-10-rio-declaration

UNESCO Courier. (2019). Fake news: sound bites on a burning topic. Retrieved from https://en.unesco.org/courier/july-september-2017/fake-news-sound-bites-burning-topic

UNESCO. (1997). United Nations Educational, Scientific and Cultural Organization educating for A Sustainable future.

UNESCO. (2018). Journalism, fake news & disinformation: handbook for journalism education and training. Retrieved from https://en.unesco.org/fightfakenews

Unique Identification Authority of India. (2019). About UIDAI. Retrieved from https://uidai.gov.in/about-uidai.html

University of Houston. (2019). 'Fake news,' diminishing media trust and the role of social media. Retrieved from https://phys.org/news/2019-08-fake-news-diminishing-media-role.html

Utterback, J., & Acee, H. J. (2005). Disruptive technologies: An expanded view. *International Journal of Innovation Management*, *9*(01), 1–17. doi:10.1142/S1363919605001162

Van De Belt, T. H., Engelen, L. J., Berben, S. A., & Schoonhoven, L. (2010). Definition of Health 2.0 and Medicine 2.0: A systematic review. *Journal of Medical Internet Research*, *12*(2). doi:10.2196/jmir.1350 PMID:20542857

Van Dijck, J. (2013). *The Culture of Connectivity. A Critical History of Social Media*. Oxford, UK: Oxford University Press. doi:10.1093/acprof:oso/9780199970773.001.0001

Van Dijck, J., & Poell, T. (2013). Understanding social media logic. *Media and Communication*, *1*(1), 2–14. doi:10.17645/mac.v1i1.70

van Dijk, J. A. (2012). *The network society* (3rd ed.). London, UK: Sage.

Varis, P., & Hou, M. (2019). Digital approaches in linguistic ethnography. In K. Tusting (Ed.), *The Routledge handbook of linguistic ethnography*. Abingdon, UK: Routledge. doi:10.4324/9781315675824-17

Varma, N., & Tyagi, R. K. (2017). Government of India prepares for big data analytics using aadhaar card unique identification system. In G. Richards (Ed.), *Big Data and Analytics Applications in Government* (pp. 115–130). Boca Raton, FL: Auerbach Publications. doi:10.4324/9781315153582-6

Vasilyeva, N., & Isachenkov, V. (2013, July 19). Russian opposition leader freed in surprise move. *Associated Press*. Retrieved from http://bigstory.ap.org/article/prosecutors-ask-free-russian-opposition-leader

Vaynerchuck, G. (2011). *The Thank You Economy*. New York, NY: HarperBusiness.

Verba, S., & Nie, N. H. (1987). *Participation in America: Political democracy and social equality*. University of Chicago Press.

Vinck, D. (1995). *Sociologie des sciences*, Paris, A. Colin, coll. « "U" / Sociologie ».

Volonino, L., Robinson, S., & Watson, H. J. (1992). EIS and organizational change, In T. Jelassi, M. R. Klein, & W. M. Mayon-White (Eds.), *IFIP Transactions A (Computer Science and Technology)* (pp. 309-321). Amsterdam, The Netherlands: North-Holland. 10.1016/B978-0-444-89673-5.50028-8

Vremya Prishlo! Vooruzhaysya! [The time has come! Take up arms!] (2013, September 1). [Video file]. Retrieved from http://www.youtube.com/watch?v=DM6xm5JB_dQ

Vygotsky, L. S. (1980). *Mind in society: The development of higher psychological processes.* Harvard University Press. doi:10.2307/j.ctvjf9vz4

Wacker, G. (2003). The Internet and censorship in China. In C. R. Hughes, & G. Wacker (Eds.), *China and the Internet: Politics of the digital leap forward* (pp. 58–82). London, UK: Routledge.

Waddell, K. (2017, January 27). 'Look, a Bird!' Trolling by Distraction. *The Atlantic*, Retrieved on July 28, 2019 from https://www.theatlantic.com/technology/archive/2017/2001/trolling-by-distraction/514589/

Wakabi, W., & Åke, G. (2015). Enhancing social accountability through ICT: Success factors and challenges. In *Proceedings of CeDEM, (International Conference for E-Democracy and Open Government),* Danube University, Krems, Austria, May 20-22.

Wallis, C. (2011). New media practices in China: Youth patterns, processes, and politics. *International Journal of Communication*, *5*, 406–436.

Wall, S. (2007). Democracy and Equality. *The Philosophical Quarterly*, *57*(228), 416–428. doi:10.1111/j.1467-9213.2007.495.x

Walther, D. (2010). Critical success factors of social media marketing campaigns for consumer goods knowledge management. Retrieved from http://daenu.net/joomla/index.php?option1/4com_docman&task1/4doc_download&gid1/440

Walton, G. (2001). *China's Golden Shield: Corporations and the development of surveillance technology in China*. Canada: Rights & Democracy.

Wang, M., & Hu, Y. (2016). Zhongguo hulianwang zhili de lishi yanbian [The historical evolution of Internet governance in China]. *Modern Communication*, *4*, 127–133.

Wang, Q., Fink, E. L., & Cai, D. A. (2008). Loneliness, gender, and parasocial interaction: A uses and gratifications approach. *Communication Quarterly*, *56*(1), 87–109. doi:10.1080/01463370701839057

Wang, X. (2007). *On the constitutional protection of the right of privacy*. Beijing, China: Social Sciences Academic Press.

Wasserman, H., & Madrid-Morales, D. (2018). Study sheds light on scourge of "fake" news in Africa. Retrieved from https://phys.org/news/2018-11-scourge-fake-news-africa.html

Watson, A. (2019). Media in Africa - Statistics & Facts. Retrieved from https://www.statista.com/topics/5032/media-in-africa/

We Are Social. (2018). Global Digital Report 2018. *We_Are_Social*, Retrieved on July 28, 2019 from https://digitalreport.wearesocial.com/download

Weaver, C., & Clover, C. (2013, June 4). Moscow mayor surprises Russian opposition by calling election. *The Financial Times*. Retrieved from http://www.ft.com/cms/s/0/ 000a3534-cd2b-11e2-90e8-00144feab7de.html#axzz2xTcSGsmo

Weeks, M. (2015). Is disruption theory wearing new clothes or just naked? Analyzing recent critiques of disruptive innovation theory. *Innovation: Organization & Management*, *17*(4), 417–428. doi:10.1080/14479338.2015.1061896

Weiner, M. (1971). Political participation: Crisis of the political process. Crises and Sequences in political development, 159-204.

Westin, A. F. (1967). *Privacy and freedom*. New York: Atheneum.

Wilkinson, I., & Welch, C. (2004). The political embeddedness of international business networks. *International Marketing Review*, *21*(2), 216–231. doi:10.1108/02651330410531411

Williams, B. A., & Delli Carpini, M. X. (2011). *After Broadcast News*. New York, NY: Cambridge University Press. doi:10.1017/CBO9780511846366

Williamson, J. (1999). What Should the Bank Think About the Washington Consensus. Background Paper to the World Bank's *World Development Report 2000* (July).

Williamson, J. (1990). What Washington Means by Policy Reform. In J. Williamson (Ed.), *Latin American Adjustment: How Much Has Happened?* Washington, DC: Institute for International Economics.

Wilterdink, N., & Form, W. (2014). Social change. *Encyclopædia Britannica Online*. Retrieved from http://www. britannica. com/topic/social-change

Wirtz, J., & Mattila, A. S. (2004). Consumer responses to compensation, speed of recovery and apology after a service failure. *International Journal of Service Industry Management*, *15*(2), 150–166. doi:10.1108/09564230410532484

Wittel, A. (2016). Digital Marx: Toward a Political Economy of Distributed Media. In C. Fuchs, & V. Mosco (Eds.), *Marx in the Age of Digital Capitalism* (pp. 68–105). Leiden, The Netherlands: Brill Publishers. doi:10.1163/9789004291393_004

Wojcieszak, M. (2009). "Carrying online participation offline"—Mobilization by radical online groups and politically dissimilar offline ties. *Journal of Communication*, *59*(3), 564–586. doi:10.1111/j.1460-2466.2009.01436.x

Worker, J., & De Silva, L. (2015). The Environmental Democracy Index. Technical Note. Washington, DC: World Resources Institute, 3. pp. 1-56.

World Resources Institute. The Assess initiative. No Date. Retrieved from https://www.wri.org/our-work/project/access-initiative-tai/commissions

Wu, G. (2018). On nature of the state special management share. *Law Science Magazine*, *39*(1), 47–53.

Wu, T. (2006). The world trade law of censorship and Internet filtering. *Chicago Journal of International Law*, *7*(1), 263–287.

Yale World Fellows. (n.d.). *Alexey Navalny: Biography*. Retrieved from http://worldfellows.yale.edu/alexey-navalny

Yandex. (2013). *Development of the Internet in Russia's regions*. Retrieved from http://download.yandex.ru/company/ya_russian_regions_report_2013.pdf

Yang, G. (2003a). The Internet and civil society in China: A preliminary assessment. *Journal of Contemporary China*, *12*(36), 453–475. doi:10.1080/10670560305471

Yang, G. (2003b). The Internet and the rise of a transnational Chinese cultural sphere. *Media Culture & Society*, *25*(4), 469–490. doi:10.1177/01634437030254003

Yan, M. N. (2015). The impact of new media on freedom of expression in China and the regulatory responses. In P. Molnár (Ed.), *Free speech and censorship around the globe* (pp. 381–407). Budapest, Hungary: Central European University Press.

Yao, Y. (2014, November). *A new normal, but with robust growth: China's growth prospects in the next 10 years.* Paper presented at the Think Tank 20: Growth, Convergence and Income Distribution: The Road from the Brisbane G-20 Summit, Washington, DC.

Yeung, R. L. K. (2008, April). *Digital democracy: How the American and Hong Kong civil societies use new media to change politics.* Washington, DC: The Brookings Institution.

Yoffa, J. (2014, March 28). Putin's new war on "traitors". *The New Yorker*. Retrieved from http://www.newyorker.com/online/blogs/newsdesk/2014/03/putin-new-hunt-for-internal-enemies.html

Yu, A., Tian, S., Vogel, D., & Kwok, R. (2010). Embedded social learning in online social networking. In *ICIS 2010 Proceedings*. Retrieved from http://aisel.aisnet.org/icis2010_submissions/100

Yves Rocher withdraws accusations against Navalny on eve of hearing (2014, April 22). *The Moscow Times*. Retrieved from http://www.themoscowtimes.com/news/article/yves-rocher-withdraws-accusations-against-navalny-on-eve-of-hearing/498738.html

Zanello, G., & Maassen, P. (2011). Strengthening citizen agency through ICT: An extrapolation for Eastern Africa. *Public Management Review*, *13*(3), 363–382. doi:10.1080/14719037.2011.553265

Zheng, Y. (2014). *Technological empowerment: The Internet, state, and society in China* (D. Qiu, Trans.). Beijing, China: The Oriental Press. (Original work published 2008)

Zhou, V. (2019, June 14). An actress "liked" a video of Hong Kong protests, and regrets it. *inkstone*, Retrieved on July 29, 2019 from https://www.inkstonenews.com/politics/hong-kong-actress-charmaine-sheh-denies-supporting-anti-extradition-protests/article/3014491

Zhu, T., Phipps, D., Pridgen, A., Crandall, J. R., & Wallach, D. S. (2013). *The velocity of censorship: High fidelity detection of microblog post deletions*. Ithaca, NY: Cornell University Library.

Zhyzhylkin, G. (2018). IT infrastruktura shtabov Navalnogo i sbor podpisey: Zhnets-2018 [IT infrastructure of Navalny's campaign offices and the signature collection: Zhnets-2018]. *Habr*. Retrieved from https://habr.com/ru/company/fbk/blog/347320/

Zotova, N., & Feldman, E. (2011, December 16). December 5 and 6, Moscow. *Novaya Gazeta*. Retrieved from http://en.novayagazeta.ru/politics/50111.html

Zou, L. (2013, October). The social effect system of Weibo public opinion (English). *China Media Report Overseas*, *9*(4), 53–57.

Zuboff, S. (1988). *In the age of the smart machine: The future of work and power*. New York: Basic Books.

Zuboff, S. (2015). Big Other: Surveillance Capitalism and the Prospects of an Information Civilization. *Journal of Information Technology*, *30*(1), 75–89. doi:10.1057/jit.2015.5

About the Contributors

Vikas Kumar received MSc in Electronics from Kurukshetra University, Haryana, India. This was followed by M Sc in Computer Science and further PhD from the same university. His PhD work was in collaboration with CEERI, Pilani and he has worked in a number of ISRO sponsored projects. He is a life member of Indian Science Congress Association, Computer Society of India, IETE, ICEIE, IPA, VEDA, IVS, and Magnetic Society of India. Dr. Kumar has designed and conducted number of training programs for the corporate sector and is a trainer for a number of Govt of India departments. Along with eight books, he has more than 100 research papers to his credit in various national and international conferences and journals. He was the Editor of International Quarterly Refereed Journal "Asia-Pacific Business Review" during June 2007-June 2009. He is a regular reviewer for a number of International Journals and on panel of examiners on a number of Govt. Universities for UG / PG and doctoral programmes. Dr. Kumar is serving as a Professor at the Chaudhary Bansi Lal University, Bhiwani, India and is a visiting Professor at the Indian Institute of Management, Indore and University of Northern Iowa, USA. The specific areas of his interest include Business Intelligence, Research Methodology, Social Media Analytics, Decision Support Systems.

Geetika Malhotra is presently working as Assistant Professor in Department of Social Work, Chaudhary Bansi Lal University, India. She earned her doctorate from Kurukshetra University, India on the topic of "Child Labour in Informal Sector: A Study of Child Rag Pickers in Delhi". Earlier, she did her Masters in Social Work from the Panjab University, India and has been a Gold Medallist in this course. She has participated in SWACHH SHAKTI 2017 programme and received a certificate from Prime Minister of India. She also served as project coordinator of "UTTHAN", a collaborated project of Delhi University and Lion International Club, India. She also served as research assistant, University of North Texas, America. She has authored a number of books and research papers in reputed journals, national and international conferences. Her areas of interest include child labour, women and child development, community health, domestic violence against women and self-help groups.

* * *

Aashish Bhardwaj is working as Head of Department (Computer Science & Engineering) at Guru Tegh Bahadur Institute of Technolgy, New Delhi. He is a life member of Indian National Science Congress Association, Indian Society for Technical Education, Institute of Electronics & Telecommunication Engineers and Computer Society of India. He has published research papers in IGI Global Journal (IJSSMET, IJSDS), Inderscience Journal (IJCC), IIJCS, IJRECE, IJCMS etc. He has published papers in International conferences like IPMC-2006 at Quaid-i-Azam University, Islamabad, IEEE Conference ICCIT-2011 at Dhaka, M4D2012 at New Delhi, Indian Science Congress 93rd at Hyderabad and 101st at Jammu. He is an IBM Certified Deployment Professional Tivoli Directory Server V6.1, Rational Functional Tester for Java, DB2 9 Fundamentals and Rational Application Developer foe WebSphere Software 6.0.

Dale Cyphert, Ph.D. (Speech Communication), Pennsylvania State University; M.A. (Rhetoric), University of California at Davis; B.A. (Speech Communication), San Diego State University. Specializing in cross-cultural rhetorical theory, Cyphert's current research explores communication competence in business organizations, methods of improving team communication behaviors, and the intersection of rhetorical theory and complexity science. Cyphert currently directs the MBA program at the University of Northern Iowa.

Juan Du received her Ph.D. from Hong Kong Baptist University in 2018. She is currently a post-doctoral researcher in the Peking University Shenzhen Graduate School and the PKU-HKUST Shenzhen-Hong Kong Institution.

Joseph L. Flores is a Ph.D. Candidate at the University of New Mexico studying the role of digital media from a political economic perspective with a focus on its effects on political communication, populism and propaganda.

Renira Rampazzo Gambarato is Associate Professor in Media and Communication Studies at Jönköping University, in Sweden. She is co-editor of the recent books Exploring Transmedia Journalism in the Digital Age (2018) and The Routledge Companion to Transmedia Studies (2018).

Ahmed El Gody, Assistant Professor, media and communication studies Orebro University, Sweden. He is the author of African Media and ICTs published in (2008) by United Nations Economic Commission in Africa and Journalism in a Network published by Orebro University press (2012). El Gody authored several academic articles and book chapters in areas of newsroom operation, media liberation and democratization process in the Middle East, social media, Arab spring and empowerment of societies and lately in migration and integration policies in the EU.

Anu Gupta received B.Tech in Chemical Engineering from Punjab Technical University, Jalandhar, India and then M Tech in Polymers from the Panjab University, Chandigarh, India. She has worked in the area of sustainable composite materials for her doctoral thesis at Indira Gandhi National Open University, New Delhi, India. She has been a recipient of the prestigious NFP (Govt of Netherlands) and DAAD (Germany Govt) fellowships. She has got Early Carrer Award in International Chemical Congress of Pacific Basin Societies (Pacifichem 2015), Honolulu, USA in 2015 by the American Chemical Society. Shea has been working on a research project sponosored by the department of Science & Technology, Govt of India under the Fast Track Young Scientist Scheme. She has also received grants from CSIR (India), Author Aid (UK), Education Strategy Center (Ethiopia), Society for Education and Research Development (India), Sandia Laboratories (USA) and the Indian National Science Academy. Dr. Gupta has been an active member of the International Union of Pure and Applied Chemistry, Indian Society For Technical Education, Society For Education & Research Development, Electrochemical Society (USA) and the International Association of Engineers. She has a number of research papers to her credit in the journals and has been serving on the editorial board of numerous international journals. Presently, Dr. Anu Gupta is working as Assistant Professor in Department of Environmental Science and Engg. at Guru Jambheswar University of Science and Technology, Hisar, Haryana, India.

Gaurav Gupta is an Assistant Professor at the School of Business Studies at the Sharda University, India. He earned his Master's and is pursuing his PhD at the Punjabi University Patiala. His research interests are in the areas of Brand Management and Indian culture. He is also a recipient of Erasmus+ and IIM-Bangalore Scholarship.

Tarakeshwar Gupta is a Research Scholar at School of Management of G. D. Goenka University (India). He had done Masters in Business Administration from Pondicherry University (India). He has also done a course on Strategic Management from Indian Institute of Management Calcutta (IIM Calcutta). He is also a Six Sigma Green Belt Certified. He has conducted communication and employability skills enhancement programs at Jaipuria Management Institute (Noida – India). He has also acquired around 8 years of work experience in the Corporate sector; primarily in operations and training & development. His current research interests include training & development, organization behaviour, business communication and strategic management.

Yowei Kang (Ph.D.) is Assistant Professor at Degree Program of Oceanic Cultural Creative Design Industry, National Taiwan Ocean University, Taiwan. His research interests focus on new media design, digital game research, visual communication, and experiential rhetoric. Some of his works have been published in International Journal of Strategic Communication, and Journal of Intercultural Communication Studies.

Ikbal Maulana is a researcher in Indonesian Institute of Sciences (LIPI). His research interests include sociology of knowledge, sociology of technology, philosophy of technology and media studies. Recently, he focuses his research on the impact of social media on politics, social transformation, as well as individual transformation from the perspective of philosophy of technology and sociology of technology.

Sergey Medvedev is a PhD candidate and Fiosraigh scholar at Technological University Dublin, Ireland. He is the author of many peer-reviewed articles, book chapters and conference papers on different aspects of political campaigning. Sergey is also an active member of the UK Political Studies Association and International Communication Association. Sergey's primary research centers on political dynamics between populist conservative movements and governing elites in the Western and Russian contexts.

Priyam Mendiratta is associated with School of Business Studies, Sharda University, in the area of Finance and Accounts. She completed her Masters in Commerce from University of Delhi in 2016. She is currently a CFA level 3 candidate.

Mandakini Paruthi, PhD, is an Assistant Professor (Marketing) at School of Management Studies, Chaitanya Bharathi Institute of Technology, Gandipet, Hyderabad, India. Her work-to-date, which has centred on online engagement, consumer brand engagement, Indian culture is published in journals like Journal of Internet Commerce, Telematics and Informatics, International Journal of Indian Culture and Business Management. Her areas of interest are consumer engagement, social media-based brand communities and volatile consumer behavior.

Jakob Svensson is full professor in Media and Communication Studies at Malmö University, School of Arts & Communication (K3). He obtained his PhD from Lund University 2008 under the supervision of professor Peter Dahlgren and was promoted associate professor at Karlstad University in 2014. He is currently leading the research project Behind the Algorithm, funded by the Swedish Research Council, focusing on people, cultures and logics behind our online experiences. Professor Svensson has worked extensively on social media and political communication as well as the use of mobile phones among marginalized groups in the Global South.

Anuradha R. Tiwary is presently working as Associate professor of Economics in the School of Humanities & Social Sciences (SOHSS) in G. D. Goenka University, Gurgoan, India. Prior to G. D. Goenka University, she was associated with G. D. Goenka World Institute, Lancaster University, UK (GDGWI). Anuradha received a BCom in Commerce from Jiwaji University, India and her MBA and MA (Economics) from DAVV Indore, India. She has more than 17 years experience in teaching and research. Her research interest includes gender studies, social entrepreneurship.

Kenneth C. C. Yang is a Professor at the Department of Communication. His research focuses on new media and advertising, consumer behavior in East Asia, impacts of new media in Asia. Dr. Yang is also interested in applying computational data processing to study communication phenomena and have published or presented papers on media framing, representations, gamer research, LGBT issues, national securities, among others.

Index

A

C

D

E

Purchase Print, E-Book, or Print + E-Book

IGI Global's reference books can now be purchased from three unique pricing formats: Print Only, E-Book Only, or Print + E-Book.
Shipping fees may apply.
www.igi-global.com

Recommended Reference Books

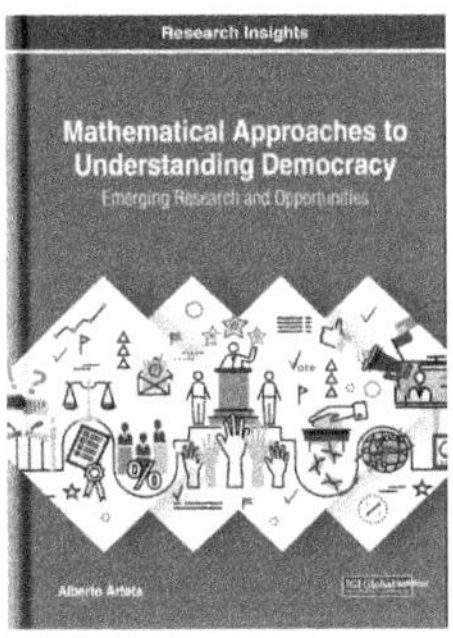

ISBN: 978-1-5225-7558-0
© 2019; 148 pp.
List Price: $165

ISBN: 978-1-5225-6918-3
© 2019; 740 pp.
List Price: $495

ISBN: 978-1-5225-7591-7
© 2019; 441 pp.
List Price: $215

ISBN: 978-1-5225-8160-4
© 2019; 450 pp.
List Price: $295

ISBN: 978-1-5225-8909-9
© 2019; 469 pp.
List Price: $330

ISBN: 978-1-5225-7429-3
© 2019; 453 pp.
List Price: $265

Looking for free content, product updates, news, and special offers?
Join IGI Global's mailing list today and start enjoying exclusive perks sent only to IGI Global members.
Add your name to the list at **www.igi-global.com/newsletters.**

Publisher of Peer-Reviewed, Timely, and Innovative Academic Research

IGI Global
DISSEMINATOR OF KNOWLEDGE

www.igi-global.com Sign up at www.igi-global.com/newsletters facebook.com/igiglobal twitter.com/igiglobal

Ensure Quality Research is Introduced to the Academic Community

Become an IGI Global Reviewer for Authored Book Projects

The overall success of an authored book project is dependent on quality and timely reviews.

In this competitive age of scholarly publishing, constructive and timely feedback significantly expedites the turnaround time of manuscripts from submission to acceptance, allowing the publication and discovery of forward-thinking research at a much more expeditious rate. Several IGI Global authored book projects are currently seeking highly-qualified experts in the field to fill vacancies on their respective editorial review boards:

Applications and Inquiries may be sent to:
development@igi-global.com

Applicants must have a doctorate (or an equivalent degree) as well as publishing and reviewing experience. Reviewers are asked to complete the open-ended evaluation questions with as much detail as possible in a timely, collegial, and constructive manner. All reviewers' tenures run for one-year terms on the editorial review boards and are expected to complete at least three reviews per term. Upon successful completion of this term, reviewers can be considered for an additional term.

If you have a colleague that may be interested in this opportunity, we encourage you to share this information with them.

IGI Global Proudly Partners With eContent Pro International

Receive a 25% Discount on all Editorial Services

Editorial Services

IGI Global expects all final manuscripts submitted for publication to be in their final form. This means they must be reviewed, revised, and professionally copy edited prior to their final submission. Not only does this support with accelerating the publication process, but it also ensures that the highest quality scholarly work can be disseminated.

English Language Copy Editing

Let eContent Pro International's expert copy editors perform edits on your manuscript to resolve spelling, punctuaion, grammar, syntax, flow, formatting issues and more.

Scientific and Scholarly Editing

Allow colleagues in your research area to examine the content of your manuscript and provide you with valuable feedback and suggestions before submission.

Figure, Table, Chart & Equation Conversions

Do you have poor quality figures? Do you need visual elements in your manuscript created or converted? A design expert can help!

Translation

Need your documjent translated into English? eContent Pro International's expert translators are fluent in English and more than 40 different languages.

Hear What Your Colleagues are Saying About Editorial Services Supported by IGI Global

"The service was very fast, very thorough, and very helpful in ensuring our chapter meets the criteria and requirements of the book's editors. I was quite impressed and happy with your service."

– Prof. Tom Brinthaupt, Middle Tennessee State University, USA

"I found the work actually spectacular. The editing, formatting, and other checks were very thorough. The turnaround time was great as well. I will definitely use eContent Pro in the future."

– Nickanor Amwata, Lecturer, University of Kurdistan Hawler, Iraq

"I was impressed that it was done timely, and wherever the content was not clear for the reader, the paper was improved with better readability for the audience."

– Prof. James Chilembwe, Mzuzu University, Malawi

Email: customerservice@econtentpro.com

www.igi-global.com/editorial-service-partners

IGI Global
DISSEMINATOR OF KNOWLEDGE
www.igi-global.com

Celebrating Over 30 Years of Scholarly Knowledge Creation & Dissemination

InfoSci®-Books

A Database of Over 5,300+ Reference Books Containing Over 100,000+ Chapters Focusing on Emerging Research

InfoSci®-Books Database

The **InfoSci®-Books** database is a collection of over 5,300+ IGI Global single and multi-volume reference books, handbooks of research, and encyclopedias, encompassing groundbreaking research from prominent experts worldwide that span over 350+ topics in 11 core subject areas including business, computer science, education, science and engineering, social sciences and more.

Open Access Fee Waiver (Offset Model) Initiative

For any library that invests in IGI Global's InfoSci-Journals and/ or InfoSci-Books databases, IGI Global will match the library's investment with a fund of equal value to go toward **subsidizing the OA article processing charges (APCs) for their students, faculty, and staff** at that institution when their work is submitted and accepted under OA into an IGI Global journal.*

INFOSCI® PLATFORM FEATURES

- No DRM
- No Set-Up or Maintenance Fees
- A Guarantee of No More Than a 5% Annual Increase
- Full-Text HTML and PDF Viewing Options
- Downloadable MARC Records
- Unlimited Simultaneous Access
- COUNTER 5 Compliant Reports
- Formatted Citations With Ability to Export to RefWorks and EasyBib
- No Embargo of Content (Research is Available Months in Advance of the Print Release)

**The fund will be offered on an annual basis and expire at the end of the subscription period. The fund would renew as the subscription is renewed for each year thereafter. The open access fees will be waived after the student, faculty, or staff's paper has been vetted and accepted into an IGI Global journal and the fund can only be used toward publishing OA in an IGI Global journal. Libraries in developing countries will have the match on their investment doubled.*

To Learn More or To Purchase This Database:
www.igi-global.com/infosci-books
eresources@igi-global.com • Toll Free: 1-866-342-6657 ext. 100 • Phone: 717-533-8845 x100

IGI Global
DISSEMINATOR OF KNOWLEDGE
www.igi-global.com

IGI Global
DISSEMINATOR OF KNOWLEDGE
www.igi-global.com

Publisher of Peer-Reviewed, Timely, and Innovative Academic Research Since 1988

IGI Global's Transformative Open Access (OA) Model:
How to Turn Your University Library's Database Acquisitions Into a Source of OA Funding

In response to the OA movement and well in advance of Plan S, IGI Global, early last year, unveiled their OA Fee Waiver (Offset Model) Initiative.

Under this initiative, librarians who invest in IGI Global's InfoSci-Books (5,300+ reference books) and/or InfoSci-Journals (185+ scholarly journals) databases will be able to subsidize their patron's OA article processing charges (APC) when their work is submitted and accepted (after the peer review process) into an IGI Global journal.*

How Does it Work?

1. When a library subscribes or perpetually purchases IGI Global's InfoSci-Databases including InfoSci-Books (5,300+ e-books), InfoSci-Journals (185+ e-journals), and/or their discipline/subject-focused subsets, IGI Global will match the library's investment with a fund of equal value to go toward subsidizing the OA article processing charges (APCs) for their patrons.

   Researchers: Be sure to recommend the InfoSci-Books and InfoSci-Journals to take advantage of this initiative.

2. When a student, faculty, or staff member submits a paper and it is accepted (following the peer review) into one of IGI Global's 185+ scholarly journals, the author will have the option to have their paper published under a traditional publishing model or as OA.
3. When the author chooses to have their paper published under OA, IGI Global will notify them of the OA Fee Waiver (Offset Model) Initiative. If the author decides they would like to take advantage of this initiative, IGI Global will deduct the US$ 1,500 APC from the created fund.
4. This fund will be offered on an annual basis and will renew as the subscription is renewed for each year thereafter. IGI Global will manage the fund and award the APC waivers unless the librarian has a preference as to how the funds should be managed.

Hear From the Experts on This Initiative:

"I'm very happy to have been able to make one of my recent research contributions, 'Visualizing the Social Media Conversations of a National Information Technology Professional Association' featured in the *International Journal of Human Capital and Information Technology Professionals*, freely available along with having access to the valuable resources found within IGI Global's InfoSci-Journals database."

– **Prof. Stuart Palmer**,
Deakin University, Australia

For More Information, Visit: www.igi-global.com/publish/contributor-resources/open-access or contact IGI Global's Database Team at eresources@igi-global.com

ARE YOU READY TO PUBLISH YOUR RESEARCH?

IGI Global
DISSEMINATOR OF KNOWLEDGE

IGI Global offers book authorship and editorship opportunities across 11 subject areas, including business, computer science, education, science and engineering, social sciences, and more!

Benefits of Publishing with IGI Global:

- Free, one-on-one editorial and promotional support.
- Expedited publishing timelines that can take your book from start to finish in less than one (1) year.
- Choose from a variety of formats including: Edited and Authored References, Handbooks of Research, Encyclopedias, and Research Insights.
- Utilize IGI Global's eEditorial Discovery® submission system in support of conducting the submission and blind review process.
- IGI Global maintains a strict adherence to ethical practices due in part to our full membership with the Committee on Publication Ethics (COPE).
- Indexing potential in prestigious indices such as Scopus®, Web of Science™, PsycINFO®, and ERIC – Education Resources Information Center.
- Ability to connect your ORCID iD to your IGI Global publications.
- Earn royalties on your publication as well as receive complimentary copies and exclusive discounts.

Get Started Today by Contacting the Acquisitions Department at:

acquisition@igi-global.com

www.igi-global.com/infosci-ondemand

InfoSci®-OnDemand

Continuously updated with new material on a weekly basis, InfoSci®-OnDemand offers the ability to search through thousands of quality full-text research papers. Users can narrow each search by identifying key topic areas of interest, then display a complete listing of relevant papers, and purchase materials specific to their research needs.

Comprehensive Service

- Over 125,000+ journal articles, book chapters, and case studies.
- All content is downloadable in PDF and HTML format and can be stored locally for future use.

No Subscription Fees

- One time fee of $37.50 per PDF download.

Instant Access

- Receive a download link immediately after order completion!

"It really provides an excellent entry into the research literature of the field. It presents a manageable number of highly relevant sources on topics of interest to a wide range of researchers. The sources are scholarly, but also accessible to 'practitioners'."

- Lisa Stimatz, MLS, University of North Carolina at Chapel Hill, USA

"It is an excellent and well designed database which will facilitate research, publication, and teaching. It is a very useful tool to have."

- George Ditsa, PhD, University of Wollongong, Australia

"I have accessed the database and find it to be a valuable tool to the IT/IS community. I found valuable articles meeting my search criteria 95% of the time."

- Prof. Lynda Louis, Xavier University of Louisiana, USA

Recommended for use by researchers who wish to immediately download PDFs of individual chapters or articles.

www.igi-global.com/e-resources/infosci-ondemand

IGI Global
DISSEMINATOR OF KNOWLEDGE
www.igi-global.com

www.ingramcontent.com/pod-product-compliance
Lightning Source LLC
LaVergne TN
LVHW080607300926
849162LV00005B/1071